Multinational Drug Companies: Issues in Drug Discovery and Development

Other Books By Bert Spilker

Guide to Clinical Studies and Developing Protocols (Raven Press, 1984)

Guide To Clinical Interpretation of Data (Raven Press, 1986)

Guide to Planning and Managing Multiple Clinical Studies (Raven Press, 1987)

Presentation of Clinical Data (with John Schoenfelder, Raven Press, 1989)

Multinational Drug Companies: Issues in Drug Discovery and Development

Bert Spilker, Ph.D., M.D.

Department Head, Project Coordination, Burroughs Wellcome Co.
Research Triangle Park, North Carolina
Adjunct Professor of Pharmacology and Clinical Assistant Professor of Medicine
University of North Carolina Medical School
Clinical Professor of Pharmacy, University of North Carolina School of Pharmacy
Chapel Hill, North Carolina

Raven Press New York

Raven Press, 1185 Avenue of the Americas, New York, New York 10036

Made in the United States of America

Library of Congress Cataloging-in-Publication Data

Spilker, Bert.
Multinational drug companies.

Bibliography: p.
Includes index.
1. Pharmaceutical industry. 2. Pharmaceutical industry—Technological innovations. 3. Drugs—Research—Management. 4. International business enterprises. I. Title. [DNLM: 1. Drug Industry. 2. Drug Screening. 3. Research. 4. Technology, Pharmaceutical. QV 736 S756m]
HD9665.5.S68 1989 338.8′87 88-42830
ISBN 0-88167-463-X

The material contained in this volume was submitted as previously unpublished material, except in the instances in which credit has been given to the source from which some of the illustrative material was derived.

Great care has been taken to maintain the accuracy of the information contained in the volume. However, neither Raven Press nor the editors can be held responsible for errors or for any consequences arising from the use of the information contained herein.

To everyone in the drug industry who helps discover, develop, produce, and market new drugs of medical value.

About The Author

Bert Spilker, Ph.D., M.D. is Department Head, Project Coordination at Burroughs Wellcome Co. and holds faculty appointments at the University of North Carolina in the Schools of Medicine (Departments of Medicine and Pharmacology) and of Pharmacy. Dr. Spilker has 16 years experience in the pharmaceutical industry, having worked for Pfizer Ltd. (United Kingdom), Philips-Duphar B.V. (The Netherlands), Sterling Drug Inc. (Rensselaer, New York), and the Burroughs Wellcome Co. He has experience with a private consulting company in the Washington, DC area and has additional experience in the private practice of general medicine.

Bert Spilker received his Ph.D. in Pharmacology from the State University of New York, Downstate Medical Center, and did post-doctoral research at the University of California Medical School in San Francisco. He received his M.D. from the University of Miami Ph.D. to M.D. Program and did a residency in internal medicine at Brown University Medical School. Bert Spilker is the author of over 60 publications plus several books in a wide area both of pharmacology and clinical medicine.

Dr. Spilker is married and has two children.

Foreword

This is a valuable book for anyone, within or without the pharmaceutical industry, who would like to understand the complexities involved in discovering and developing new drugs—what *Newsweek* magazine has called the "enchanted substances" that prolong and improve the quality of life.

This is the first time, as far as I know, in which all of the many elements of pharmaceutical research and development are discussed in one book—medical, scientific, production, marketing, financial, legislative, and public affairs. The result is a unique overview of the various factors that must be considered in the quest to develop new and more effective medicines.

The book is *not* a dry and technical treatise, although the technical aspects of drug discovery and development are fully covered. Rather, it is written in an interesting manner that reflects the author's wide knowledge of literature, philosophy, history, and management. It nicely mixes the practical and the theoretical.

The book clearly shows that, while pharmaceutical companies are similar in many ways to other businesses, they are also unique. A research-based pharmaceutical company is in the innovation business, involved in the long, expensive, highly risky, and highly regulated activity of finding new ways to cure and treat age-old diseases, like cancer, and new plagues, like AIDS. It is a business literally of life and death—in which we all have a stake.

This book, by a physician/pharmacologist who has spent more than 16 years in research and development with four different drug companies, provides a real insight into the critical pharmaceutic R&D process.

Gerald J. Mossinghoff, President
Pharmaceutical Manufacturers Association

Preface

People who want to identify possible solutions to problems in drug discovery and development, to learn about current standards, and to improve their efficiency have a difficult task in finding published sources of help. Those who desire to understand the processes and issues involved in multinational drug discovery and development also have a hard time finding useful references. This book provides information that addresses those needs. The specific approaches this book uses to achieve these goals and the specific audiences targeted are described more fully at the start of Chapter 1.

The book focuses on five broad topics, each dealt with in a separate section of the book. The first section covers the central issue of discovering and developing drugs. Processes are discussed along with means of enhancing the success of these activities. Section two focuses on the corporate level and describes organizational, personnel, and future-oriented issues. It also identifies many ways in which companies differ from each other. The third section concentrates on research and development. Research and development activities are discussed from various perspectives. The discussions focus on organization, management, personnel, productivity, and efficiency issues. The fourth section presents more detailed descriptions of many technical functions and departments, including information management, toxicology, clinical, marketing, and production. Lastly, the fifth section discusses interactions and relationships between drug companies and external groups or organizations such as government agencies, academic institutions, trade associations, the press, and the public. It is hoped that this book will be useful to both experienced managers and other individuals who wish to learn more about the drug industry.

Bert Spilker

Acknowledgments

It is a great pleasure to thank Mr. Doug Henderson-James, Dr. John Kelsey, and Dr. John Schoenfelder who reviewed the manuscript and made many valuable suggestions.

The author appreciates helpful discussions with the following people, most of whom also reviewed portions of this book. Mr. Glenn Andrews, Mr. J.M. Arnold, Ms. Kathy S. Bartlett, Mr. Michael T. Burke, Dr. Donald Clive, Ms. Karen Collins, Mr. Jerry D. Crandall, Dr. Joann Data, Mr. N. Ranthi Dev, Dr. Gertrude B. Elion, Ms. Janyth Fredrickson, Dr. Charles W. Gorodetsky, Mr. Robin K. Henning, Dr. David W. Henry, Dr. Steven Jacobs, Mr. Tim Kvanvig, Mr. Al MacKinnon, Dr. Warren McAllister, Dr. Lloyd G. Millstein, Mr. David A. Moyer, Dr. Donald H. Namm, Dr. Lawrence A. Nielsen, Dr. Joel E. Sutton, Dr. Roy Swaringen, Dr. George Szczech, Dr. Hugh Tilson, Ms. Ildiko Trombitas, Mr. Glenn K. Weingarth, Dr. Thomas L. Wenger, and Mr. J.R. Whitehead.

There are a number of individuals who have had a great effect on helping to formulate the author's views over the last decade and it is a pleasure to acknowledge their contributions. They are Drs. Allen Cato, Gilles Cloutier, Pedro Cuatrecasas, Howard J. Schaeffer, and S. Winston Singleton.

Excellent editorial help of Mr. Allen Jones, assistance with literature searches by Mr. Rolly Simpson, and illustrations by Ms. Jacqueline Jenks are appreciated. A very special thanks is due Mrs. Joyce B. Carpunky, who cheerfully typed each of the drafts and revisions as this book took shape.

The views expressed in this book are solely those of the author and do not reflect opinions or practices of any specific company, unless clearly indicated.

Contents

List of Tables

Section I

Section II

Section III

Section IV

Section V

List of Figures

Section I

Section II

Section III

Section IV

Section V

List of Abbreviations and Terms

AIDS	Acquired Immune Deficiency Syndrome.
FDA	Food and Drug Administration. Regulatory agency in the United States that must approve new drugs for marketing. Oversees many postmarketing practices of the pharmaceutical industry.
GCP	Good Clinical Practices. Unofficial term used to include proposed United States regulations governing conduct of sponsors and investigators during clinical studies. Also refers to approved United States regulations governing IRBs, INDs, and informed consents.
GLP	Good Laboratory Practices. United States regulations governing quality assurance procedures in toxicology facilities and other preclinical laboratories. Approved in 1978.
GMP	Good Manufacturing Practices. United States regulations governing quality assurance procedures in drug manufacturing. Approved in 1963.
HMO	Health Maintenance Organization. A prepaid health group.
IND	Investigational New Drug Application. FDA regulatory document allowing clinical studies to proceed on an investigational drug or investigational use of an approved market drug.
IRB	Institutional Review Board. An ethics committee that must approve protocols for human studies at the institution where they are to be done.
NCE	New Chemical Entity. A novel chemical compound that may be tested as a drug.
NDA	New Drug Application. An application to the FDA for approval of a new drug in the United States.
OTC	Over-the-counter drugs. Drugs sold without a prescription.
Phase I	Initial clinical studies in normal volunteers and sometimes patients to test a drug's safety.

Phase II	Clinical studies in patients to test if the drug has the desired efficacy.
Phase III	Clinical studies in patients to gain additional safety, efficacy, and other information prior to marketing.
Phase IV	Clinical studies conducted after a drug is marketed. Includes postmarketing surveillance studies.
PLA	Product License Application. A regulatory application for any NCE outside the United States or for a biological drug in the United States.
PPO	Preferred Provider Organization. A prepaid health group.
QA	Quality Assurance. Process of validating individual steps in a toxicology study, manufacturing process, or other area.
QC	Quality Control. Process of validating the final step in manufacturing or another area.
R and D	Research and development.
USP	United States Pharmacopeia.
WHO	World Health Organization.

Section I

Drug Discovery and Development

1 / *The Big Picture*

To survive and succeed in a hot market, a company must be willing to change everything about itself except its basic beliefs . . . Give the individual full consideration, spend a lot of time making customers happy, go the last mile to do a thing right. Thomas J. Watson, Jr., former chief executive of IBM. From *Fortune* (August 31, 1987).

THE CRUCIAL ISSUE FACING DRUG COMPANIES TODAY

For research-based drug companies the most critical issue today is maintaining a flow of new, innovative drugs that insure the company's growth and even survival. Most drug companies are fully committed to this challenge, because the alternative of having a dry period without new products is unattractive and its consequences clear. To meet the challenge, companies are adopting strategies of developing their drugs on a global basis utilizing state-of-the-art technologies and attempting to improve their efficiency of drug discovery and development. Companies primarily obtain their new drugs from in-house research discoveries, licensing from other companies or groups, and joint ventures with other companies. This book describes the state-of-the-art standards that exist in many aspects of drug discovery and development.

Another response to the challenge of preventing dry periods without new products is to conduct a detailed analysis of the entire research and development process and seek ways of improving current systems, organizational structures, and approaches. These internal evaluations used to occur approximately once in a five- to ten-year period and often involved an outside consulting firm. At the present time, this process tends to occur on a more frequent or even on a continual basis. This book provides specific techniques to help managers judge a company's strengths and weaknesses and many detailed methods used to analyze a drug company or its research and development activities are presented.

The world of drug discovery and development is rapidly changing, and there is a need for companies to take a broad view to develop useful strategies and take advantage of opportunities. The information explosion in the published literature provides details of technical aspects of drug discovery and development on a daily basis. The press, trade associations, and numerous other sources provide information about the drug industry as a whole (or selected parts) to the public and to health professionals. There are no sources, however, that provide a broad view of the issues of drug discovery and development from a specific company's perspective. That is the intention of this book.

ORIENTATION AND APPROACH OF THIS BOOK

This book examines many issues unique to discovering and developing drugs. Although its primary focus is on research and development, this book includes consideration of overall corporate issues as well as specific issues relating to marketing, production, financial, legislation, public affairs, and other areas.

Purpose of the Book

This book has two major objectives—to present both specific and general information on issues faced within a company during drug discovery and development. The specific information is intended to help both experienced and inexperienced individuals in the drug industry perform their own work more effectively and better understand other areas with which they interact.

The general information is intended to help individuals either within or outside the drug industry achieve a better understanding and awareness of the operations and issues faced by the entire company or by a specific part of that company. A discussion of various means of addressing issues and problems is also presented. Both specific and general standards used in drug discovery and development are mentioned and discussed.

Approaches Used in This Book

Most issues are not covered in great depth for two reasons. First, the book would expand to many times its present length, and second, almost every situation that arises regarding drug discovery and development differs in some aspects from those that have been previously experienced. One advantage of the broad approach of this book is that it allows the reader to view a wide range of drug discovery and development issues from a single perspective. Both practical and theoretical information is presented as a guide to both understand and improve the inner workings of a drug company. The specific approach used in this book is to present and discuss a mixture of concepts, problems, state-of-the-art procedures, and considerations that may influence decisions. Numerous examples, tips, approaches, suggestions, options, and opinions are offered to help the reader select those pieces of information of greatest value.

Intended Audiences

Many senior and junior positions in a pharmaceutical company's hierarchy are held by executives who have little formal scientific training. The fundamental ways in which the drug industry differs from other industries (e.g., long time required to develop drugs, uncertainty of a drug's future, impossibility of making many decisions on a quantitative basis, the necessity of making decisions with incomplete information) are not fully understood by many of them. Some of these individuals, however, often must make decisions involving research or development issues. This book is intended to provide knowledge and indicate considerations that those individuals require to make informed decisions. It presents a broad overview of the drug development process using a common sense approach to help these nonscientists, as well as other nonscientists in a drug company, gain a better understanding of many scientific and nonscientific issues.

This book is also directed to scientists and clinicians directly involved in drug discovery and development. These people may be located in industry, government, or academia; or they may function as independent consultants or contractors. Most of these individuals work in one discipline and do not deal with the broad spectrum of issues found in drug discovery and development. By placing most of the issues that they deal with in a broader perspective, this book will allow them to see how their work fits into the overall process.

The issues discussed are also addressed to professionals and health care workers in government agencies, trade associations, academic centers, hospitals, and other places who interact with the drug industry. Many interactions are described in this book in separate chapters devoted to government agencies, trade associations, and academic institutions. This book should help these individuals who are not employed in the drug industry better understand the nature and complexity of many issues faced during drug discovery and development.

The chapters of this book are self-contained and may be read in any order. Entire books have been written on the subjects of many of the individual chapters. The information in this book is based on the author's experiences at four drug companies, the literature, and communications with individuals employed at many companies; it is not a reflection of any single company.

OVERALL PERSPECTIVE OF DRUG COMPANIES

Uniqueness of the Drug Industry

It is critically important for senior executives to have a detailed understanding of their industry. This helps them reach more informed and sometimes better decisions about many important issues, policies, and questions that frequently arise. Yet, one often reads speeches of a drug company's chief executive or senior company officers who may be top lawyers, financiers, or marketing experts, but do not understand the basic concepts and processes of how drugs are discovered and developed. The various factors that influence drug discovery and development may also not be well understood. Although most companies may be operated and managed as if they make "widgets," a drug company must not.

Major factors that differentiate drug companies from other companies are listed below. Some of these factors are only a matter of degree (1) the long period of time required to develop and market a newly discovered drug, (2) the high degree of financial risk and uncertainty of a drug's future, even after it is launched, (3) the large number of highly restrictive regulations that govern all aspects of a drug's development, production, and marketing, (4) the inability to predict when the next important drug discovery will occur, and (5) the large number of variables and factors that are involved in biological experiments, technical development, and especially clinical studies. This last point means that a large number of interpretations are possible in many situations. Each of these critical aspects requires an understanding of the drug discovery and development process. It is also important to understand the factors that relate to creating and maintaining an appropriate environment in which drug discovery may occur.

The drug industry shares some characteristics with many other industries, including other high technology industries.

1. A rapidly changing environment in which products are sold. Many of these changes are highly unpredictable, both in the nature and rate of change.

2. Competition in many areas including product discovery, development, and marketing.

Many aspects of the corporate environment in which these activities take place are nuances of the corporate culture. Corporate culture shapes the strategies used by a company to develop drugs and is discussed in several other chapters of this book. This culture-strategy interaction is also discussed by Shrivastava and Guth (1985).

Attributes of Drug Companies

Many individuals, especially those who have limited time to devote to an issue or question, want to understand "the big picture." In some circles this cliche is as common as "the bottom line" (i.e., the overall impression or amount). The big picture obtained after looking at a drug company includes consideration of its (1) core and other businesses, (2) overall size, (3) current and planned activities, (4) profitability, (5) approaches to drug discovery and development, and (6) current portfolio of marketed and investigational drugs.

Core and Other Businesses

Is the company strictly a pharmaceutical company, a health care company, or a company engaged in a wide variety of businesses? If the latter, how does the drug business fit into the company's overall mission?

Overall Size

This aspect may be described in terms of sales per year, numbers of workers, assets, or other factors. Size does not necessarily correlate with profit or number of drugs marketed. This topic is described more in Chapter 5.

Current and Planned Activities

This aspect primarily relates to whether the company is research based or generic, is development oriented (i.e., licenses-in most or all of its drugs), or is a biotechnology company. This topic is described throughout this book.

Profitability

The relative profitability of a drug company may be based on a comparison with other drug companies, or a between-industry comparison with other companies of the same size. A few means of illustrating a company's profitability are illustrated in Chapter 15 and establishing drug prices in Chapter 21.

Approaches to Drug Discovery and Development

Companies vary from those that utilize highly formal approaches to drug development to those that emphasize flexibility. This aspect is described throughout this book. Organizational structures are primarily described in Chapters 5 and 10.

Current Portfolio of Marketed and Investigational Drugs

The portfolio of marketed drugs may include both multisource (i.e., drugs susceptible to generic competition), patent protected, or otherwise protected (e.g., with exclusivity under the Orphan Drug Act) drugs. Drugs under development (i.e., investigational drugs) are assessed by the medical and commercial value of the company's portfolio of potential new products (see Chapter 15).

Drug Costs and Profits

A significant part of the "big picture" relates to profits. Food and Drug Administration (FDA) regulations and guidelines since 1962 have required many more premarketing studies to be conducted than previously. Good Laboratory Practices (GLP) and Good Manufacturing Practices (GMP) regulations have also increased costs of bringing a new drug to market. Regulations, however, are only one of many factors that have resulted in higher prices charged for drugs. Other factors include the steadily mounting costs for laboratory equipment, clinical studies, staff salaries, and other components of drug discovery and development. As a result of increased health care expenditures during the 1960s and 1970s, the government reacted. It has taken various steps (e.g., encouraging generic competition, passing maximum allowable cost regulations, providing bonuses to pharmacists who dispense generic drugs) to force drug prices down. Food and clothing prices, however, have been kept artificially high by government price support programs for agriculture and tariffs and import quotas on foreign textiles.

The major reason why drug companies are willing to invest hundreds of millions in high-risk research is that the rates of return for the few commercially successful drugs are also high. If the rates of return are markedly diminished, as is already occurring in some countries, drug companies will be much less willing in the future to invest their money in research. Economic analyses clearly show that if regulations diminish profits for drug companies on their few successful drugs below a certain minimum, the companies will reduce investments they are willing to make in research. Without sufficient research, drug discovery will slow and this will decrease the rate at which new drugs will reach the market.

Competition within the Drug Industry

An additional piece of the "big picture" is the risk from competition. Competition within the drug industry exists on several levels. These include (1) being first to enter new therapeutic markets, (2) price and other types of competition (e.g., perceived benefits) on similar products within a single therapeutic market, and (3) manufacturing generic versions of the same drug. The evidence that supports the view that there is significant competition in the drug industry includes (1) price flexibility on specific products; (2) instability of market share over a period of a few years; (3) high rate of corporate mergers, buyouts, and bankruptcies; and (4) licensing arrangements. The drug industry has the second highest rate of market share instability of all industries in the United States (Schnee and Caglarcan, 1978).

Perspectives of Different Groups about New Drugs

When drug discovery and development issues are being presented and discussed, numerous perspectives could be used. These include those of various groups both within and outside the drug industry. Representative groups within the industry would include people in marketing, production, science, medical, and technical development functions. Representative groups outside the industry include patients, physicians, and regulatory agencies. Most of this book presents the perspectives of those within the industry. Nonetheless, it is useful to briefly review the perspective of some groups from both within and outside the industry.

Perspectives about New Drugs by Groups within the Drug Industry

Perspectives of drug company employees about new drugs are somewhat influenced by their background and discipline within their company. Informed and knowledgable people view drugs in terms of a combination of medical, scientific, and commercial parameters. Others focus more on one of these (or other) aspects of a new drug.

Many groups within and outside the drug industry often ascribe a logic to a drug's discovery or its development that is actually a convenient teleological explanation. Events usually seem more clear in hindsight when numerous activities are rearranged in people's minds, rough edges are smoothed out, and loose threads (e.g., false leads and approaches) are conveniently forgotten or ignored. As a result, the story of many drug's discovery and development appears logical and orderly, whereas many false turns, accidents, mistakes, and luck were involved. Lucky errors may have directed the drug along the right path to its success. Many drug discoveries have occurred and paths of development correctly followed despite some people's attempts to proceed in a different direction. There are some noteworthy exceptions to this somewhat cynical view, that illustrate a logical and stepwise approach to drug discovery and development.

People in each company often talk about new upcoming drugs much as company stocks are described. The perceived value of a drug to a company often has precipitous changes based on casual or formal comments from the FDA, investigators, or company scientists. These changes are often more related to emotional reactions to the drug's characteristics, uninformed judgments, or other reactions that do not reflect the drug's true value. The perceived value of a drug to stockbrokers and to stockholders in terms of eventual profit also rises and falls precipitously based on news, which may or may not be accurate or relevant to the drug's true value.

Perspectives about New Drugs by Groups Outside the Drug Industry

The perspective about new drugs under development in groups outside the drug industry varies widely depending on the drug and the specific audience. A number of generalizations, however, can be made because different groups have differing frames of reference for looking at new drugs.

1. *Patients* Patients view new drugs in terms of hopes for improvement of symptoms, underlying disease, or risk factors. Cost of new therapy may also be a major consideration. More sophisticated patients will have at least some awareness of risks and the benefit to risk ratio present with the new therapy.
2. *Regulatory authorities* Regulatory authorities view new drugs from the nation's health perspective in terms of potential health problems resulting from adverse reactions as well as potential benefits. Regulatory agencies often focus on worst-case scenarios.
3. *Competitors* Competitors within the drug industry view a new drug as a minor to major threat to their own marketed drugs and/or new investigational drugs. In some cases a company's own development strategies will be markedly influenced by competitors, and in other cases the potential competitors will be ignored.

Some perspectives of consumer advocates, trade associations, physicians, academicians, legislators, and other groups are discussed in the last section of this book.

SYNOPSIS OF DRUG DISCOVERY AND DEVELOPMENT

Drug Discovery

When asked for a definition of Hinduism one religious scholar said "It's simple, anyone who says he is a Hindu is one." The reason for this statement is that Hinduism has not rejected or cast out beliefs of the past but has continued to build on them and to add new beliefs. Likewise, the processes of drug discovery are multifaceted and new ways of finding drugs are continually being added without discarding methods of the past. Thus, some people view drug discovery primarily in terms of the new methods of biotechnology, whereas others emphasize the importance of computer-assisted methods of drug discovery. Neither of these relatively new approaches is the major means of discovering novel drugs, nor are the oldest methods of random screening or haphazard trial and error that have been used for over 100 years.

The major methods of discovering new drugs today are those used during the past 50 years. The most important method is the trial and error empirical approach. Novel compounds called analogues are made that are similar to marketed or known drugs. Other compounds are also made that are distantly related or totally unrelated to marketed or known drugs. These compounds are hypothesized to have biological activity and are then tested by empirical methods using relevant animal models. Some animal models are related to human disease. If the compound is found to have biological activity of interest it is called a chemical lead or a *lead compound*. If the lead is highly active it will stimulate chemists to make many new compounds that are chemically related to the lead compound. Eventually, a compound is hopefully found that has sufficient positive qualities and few negative qualities compared to existing therapy to justify additional animal studies. It is usually hoped that this compound will become a drug. *This marks the end of the drug discovery period and the start of drug development.* The compound is now considered as a *candidate compound* for drug development.

The processes of drug discovery are not straightforward. There is a certain amount of disorder in the system. Too much order and control are usually considered detrimental, although there should be a sound rationale underlying the activities conducted.

Many factors must be considered by scientists when choosing specific compounds to make and test. These issues as well as other methods of discovering drugs are discussed in Chapter 2. The one final method of drug discovery that must be mentioned is serendipity or accident. Mark Twain once aptly said that the greatest inventor of all was accident.

Drug Development

Drug development is a highly complex process involving thousands of different activities. For the most part these activities are not described in this book, but may be found in references (see Bibliography). Figures 18.1 and 18.2 in the book *Guide to Planning and Managing Multiple Clinical Studies* (Spilker, 1987c) illustrates how many of these activities are interconnected. As opposed to drug discovery, where a certain degree and type of disorder is encouraged, drug development has order, organization, and discipline as goals. Too much disorder can be highly detrimental to the process of bringing a drug to market.

After a candidate compound to be studied further as a potential drug is identified, we enter the world of drug development. Early activities of drug development involve an in-depth analysis of the candidate compound's profile in additional animal studies. This period usually lasts from six to 18 months. If both the positive and negative attributes are acceptable, it means that the compound has a benefit to risk ratio adequate to pursue development. At that point the candidate compound is elevated to become a *project compound*, which means that it will be tested in humans if it can pass other preclinical requirements. Project compounds are developed by a project team whose members represent different departments within the company.

The project compound progresses through technical development, toxicology, metabolism, and other animal studies until it receives a green light to be tested in humans. At the time of initial testing in humans a project compound becomes a *project drug*. There are three phases of clinical studies (see terminology page) that a drug passes through before it receives regulatory approval and may be sold as a *marketed drug*. In a few situations (e.g., drug for a life-threatening disease without adequate treatment, drug for a rare disease) Phase III may be omitted.

The attrition rate from stage to stage is usually high. It is estimated that 10,000 compounds are synthesized for every 10 that reach the stage of human testing. Of these 10 compounds only one eventually reaches the market. The success rate of new compounds and projects is discussed further in Chapter 16.

Terms used to describe the various stages a drug passes through (lead compound, candidate compound, project compound, project drug, marketed drug) are presented to clarify the various stages of discovery and development. These terms are not all in current use throughout the industry.

Drug development involves a feedback loop to help future drug discoveries. Information on a project compound in preclinical studies may indicate a beneficial attribute or toxicological effect that may be hopefully accentuated in the former case or eliminated in the latter case. This information helps chemists design new (and hopefully better) compounds to make and test for their activity. A feedback loop also exists between the clinic and laboratory. Human data enables chemists to design and make better compounds that may eventually be tested as new drugs.

Influence of Regulations on Drug Discovery and Development

Advances in science and changes in government regulations are the two most important factors to influence the discovery and development of drugs since the Second World War. Specific advances in science will not be discussed here, except to note that many breakthroughs in basic science have eventually led to discoveries of important new drugs.

Many regulations have affected drug development but two of the most important are the 1938 Food, Drug, and Cosmetic Act, which mandated that drugs must be safe, and the 1962 Kefauver-Harris amendments to the 1938 Act. The latter amendments raised the standards for approval of new drugs, especially in terms of their efficacy. This has provided benefits to many patients who buy and take drugs. Because of these amendments, certain ineffective and partially effective drugs were removed from the market. On the other hand, there is a price paid for these gains: (1) fewer drugs are brought to market each year, (2) the time after a company submits a New Drug Application (NDA) to the FDA until its approval has grown significantly longer, (3) the higher standards have raised the costs of drug development, (4) the FDA has decreased the physician's ability (according to some) to choose a drug to prescribe for patients as freely as in the past, and (5) a drug lag developed (i.e., there was a greater delay for introducing most drugs in the United States than in certain European countries).

Golden Rules of Drug Development

Although the golden rules (i.e., important principles) of drug development are well known, most (if not all) drug companies are continually violating these principles. There are some exceptions to each of these principles, but if generally adhered to they will often save both years of unnecessary or inefficient work and large amounts of resources. Each of these 18 principles is described in detail elsewhere in this book or in the *Guide to Clinical Studies* trilogy (Spilker, 1984, 1986b, 1987c).

The overriding principle of *drug development* is that activities may be planned, coordinated, and to some degree controlled using appropriate systems and methods—after the specific compound to be developed has been identified. The processes of *drug discovery*, however, are much less susceptible to planning or control. Attempts to control drug discovery often stifle and destroy the creative process. The following principles apply to drug development.

1. Focus development activities in a relatively limited number of therapeutic areas. There are few companies, if any, that can adequately develop drugs in all

therapeutic areas. By focusing efforts, companies can develop areas of strength that help drug development, as well as drug discovery and drug marketing activities.

2. Formulate an overall concept and strategy of how each drug, indication, and formulation will be developed. Seek input from Marketing to help formulate various strategies. Establish minimal criteria that a drug must achieve to continue its development. Detailed strategies must be developed in several functional areas (e.g., marketing, research and development) and at several levels (e.g., individual sections and departments). Insure that an appropriate balance of effort is spent between developing, reviewing, and revising plans with efforts spent on carrying out the plans. See Chapter 2 and *Guide to Planning and Managing Multiple Clinical Studies* (Spilker, 1987c, Chapters 2 and 3).

3. Create an international development plan that minimizes duplication and stresses efficiency. Determine the appropriate balance between a *lean plan* that will generate the absolute minimal amount of data required for regulatory approval and a *fat plan* that goes far beyond what is required. See Chapter 19 and *Guide to Planning and Managing Multiple Clinical Studies* (Spilker, 1987c, Chapter 13).

4. Avoid tangents that depart from the chosen path of development, except when (a) the tangent is to become the new path (i.e., a new strategy is adopted) or (b) the tangent is carefully reviewed before it is implemented and is considered worthy of pursuit. The tangent is then incorporated into the existing strategy. See Chapter 4 and *Guide to Planning and Managing Multiple Clinical Studies* (Spilker, 1987c, Chapter 3).

5. Hire the best people possible for all positions in a company even at the most junior level. Appropriately train and orient staff in both methods and ethos of the company. Do not appoint academic scientists or government administrators to head a drug company's research and development division, unless they are highly experienced in drug discovery and development. See Chapters 7 and 12.

6. Assign personnel and other resources according to both the value and the importance of each indication and formulation being developed. Scientific, medical, and commercial values must be considered, although each are not of equal importance. Consideration must also be given to other drugs in the portfolio. See Chapters 14 through 16. A balance must be achieved between placing almost all resources on a few projects and spreading resources thinly across many projects.

7. Do whatever is necessary to encourage openness, honesty, cooperation, teamwork, and shared goals between functions (e.g., research and development, marketing, production). Achievement of these goals depends on trust, accurate communications, and the creation of a positive working environment. Disseminate appropriate information both upwards and downwards throughout the company. Stress the concept of sharing information and avoiding surprises whenever possible. See Sections II and III of this book.

8. Adhere to the highest standards of ethics in scientific, medical, marketing, and other activities. This behavior will provide numerous benefits to the company in terms of regulatory reviews and ability to respond to questions, criticisms, and accusations from external sources, besides providing a strong motivating factor to staff.

9. Create and use systems and standard operating procedures that assist the development processes. Do not allow systems to become bureaucracies, restrain development, or compromise efficiency. Each chapter in this book discusses aspects of this theme. Utilize computer systems that are either identical or compatible between each major site of a company developing drugs.

10. Develop a portfolio of investigational drugs that balances high- and low-risk projects, and include drugs that will be developed in both a long-term and short-term time period. Attempt to have some projects that have a chance of becoming breakthrough drugs.

11. Reevaluate each project and the overall portfolio on a relatively frequent periodic basis. Reviews must be objective. Reviewers must not be misled by a strong desire of some or many people for a drug to be effective and safe with the actual demonstration of a sufficient amount of hard data of appropriate magnitude that it actually is effective and safe. Insure that all appropriate managers and workers understand current priorities of the research and development division as well as the priorities of their specified department, insofar as the two differ.

12. Identify the rate-limiting steps of each drug's development. Insure that appropriate and adequate resources and attention are focused on these areas.

13. Develop a clear licensing policy and strategy that allows all product, technology, and other opportunities (e.g., acquisitions) to be rapidly reviewed and assessed for possible benefit to the company. This includes both licensing-in and licensing-out opportunities. Establish alliances with other companies (e.g., joint ventures) that enhance drug development activities. See Chapter 26.

14. Attempt to create and maintain a cooperative relationship with the FDA and other regulatory authorities. Regulatory guidelines must be viewed as guidelines and not requirements. In discussions with regulatory authorities it is necessary to differentiate between real demands or requirements, imagined demands, suggestions, and hearsay. See Chapter 25.

15. Prepare logical and straightforward regulatory submissions. Lead the regulatory reviewer step-by-step through each aspect of the application. Do not make reviewers work hard to understand the content of the application and the company's logic in proceeding in a specific direction. Be up-front with any problems in the application and do not attempt to hide bad data. When it is reasonable to perform multiple analyses of data, conduct most, if not all. Include complete analyses of the most relevant ones (one) and summaries of less important ones in regulatory applications. Indicate the reasons why a particular analysis is preferred (if that is the case). See Chapter 25.

16. Protect and extend the drug's indications and formulations after initial marketing. Protection may include conducting additional clinical studies, synthesizing additional compounds, or conducting postmarketing studies. Extension of a product's available formulations, approved indications, and current packaging usually enhances appropriate medical uses of a drug and improves its commercial returns.

17. Attempt to learn everything of importance about a drug, even what may be considered as bad news. It is vital for a company to know as much important and relevant information as possible about their drugs. This enables them to deal most effectively with questions, criticisms, and accusations.

18. Insure that activities to implement and carry out each of these principles follow an appropriate pace. If any of these principles is pushed too rapidly then the quality of the results will suffer, problems will arise, mistakes will be made, and waste occur. If the pace of development is too slow, then valuable patent life will be lost and competitive drugs may overtake one's own drug. The balance desired should involve conducting appropriate activities simultaneously at a rapid pace that may be followed in an efficient manner. The pace should not be so rapid or pressures applied that

encourage professionals to cut corners or make unwarrented assumptions about a drug's efficacy or safety.

Other important principles could be included in this list. Their omission does not signify that their importance is any less than the 18 included, especially in specific situations. Each individual department or function involved in drug development could also create their own list of general or more specific golden rules.

Decisions that influence a drug's development should be based on logical, practical, and other rational considerations that consider the company's past, present, and future. It is hoped that progressively fewer decisions are based on emotions, whims, political considerations, or for other personal reasons.

Implementing These Golden Rules

Merely understanding and believing in the golden rules described is not sufficient to have them realized. It is also necessary to have a competent group of managers who are able to put these rules into practice. There is a final step required beyond understanding, acceptance, and having competent staff. That step is the collective will, and desire to have these principles followed and become the ethos of drug development.

The attitudes most conducive to efficient drug development must be present throughout the organization, not only in the research and development division where these principles are most important. It may be possible for a company to develop drugs efficiently if there are one or two senior research and development managers who do not share the attitudes described or who do not believe in the golden rules. But, if more than a small number of senior managers or if senior managers in critical positions do not share these beliefs, the entire development process will be adversely affected. A company operating with one or more albatrosses about its collective neck must shed them or risk the undesirable consequences of inefficient drug development.

The correct attitude toward developing drugs involves a positive view that may be expressed as "We will do whatever is necessary to insure that we meet realistic plans and targets." This attitude requires a commitment of staff to:

1. Identify the most pertinent issues and problems to address. Discuss these issues and problems appropriately before initiating action.
2. Make active decisions and not allow decisions to be made by avoiding issues.
3. Cooperate as fully as possible with all relevant individuals who are members of a drug development team.

Attitudes toward drug development are described more fully in Chapter 7.

METAPHORS OF DRUG DISCOVERY AND DEVELOPMENT

Because the processes of drug discovery and development are so complex there are often times when it is useful to describe them using metaphors or analogies. These metaphors are described because they are an easy way to conceptualize many of the processes of drug discovery or development. There is no single metaphor or

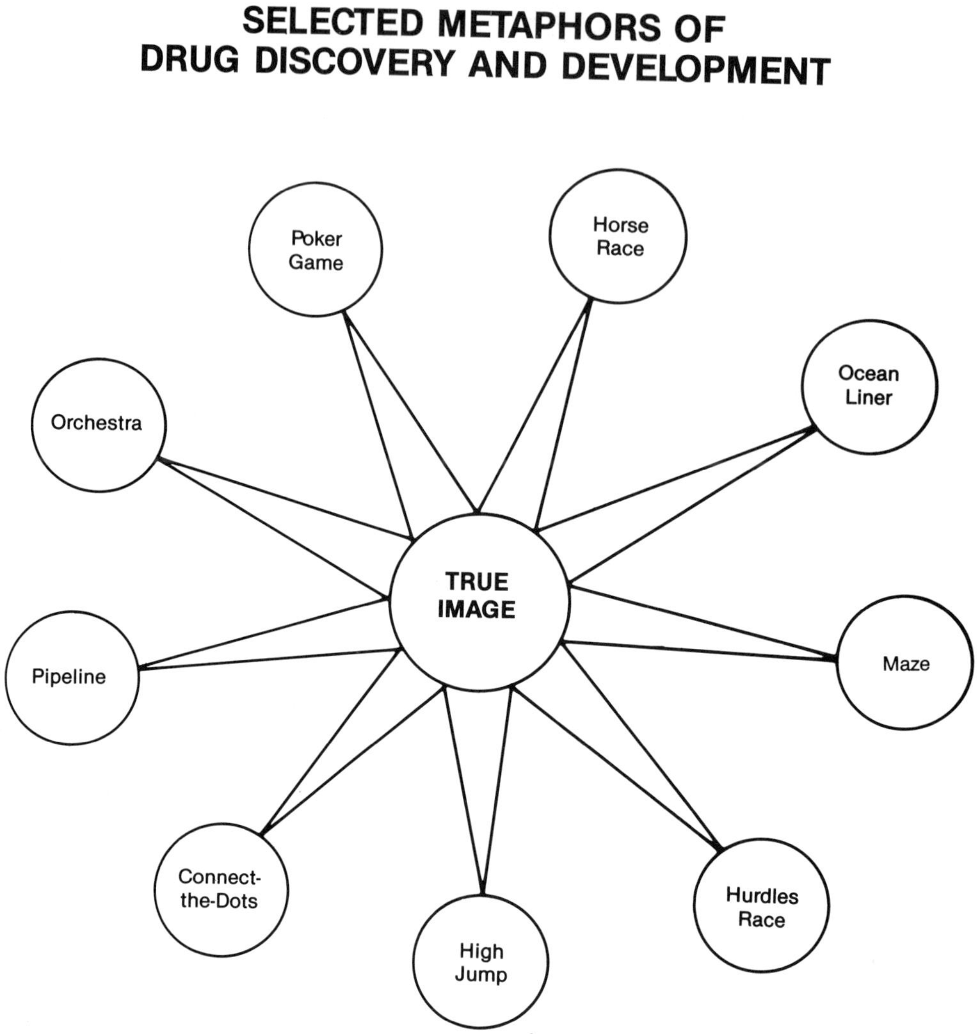

Fig. 1.1. Selected metaphors of drug discovery and development. The true image for a particular drug is a combination of some or all of these metaphors.

analogy that is entirely appropriate or best and many have been used (Fig. 1.1). The metaphors described are (1) pipeline, (2) horse race, (3) poker game, (4) orchestra, (5) hurdles race, (6) ocean liner, (7) connect-the-dots, (8) maze, and (9) high jump.

The pipeline metaphor refers to both discovery and development, the maze refers to only discovery, the orchestra and connect-the-dots only to development, and the others may refer to either discovery or development. Managers often have one or two that they particularly favor. In some situations one metaphor may stand out and capture its essence.

Pipeline of Drug Discovery, Development, and Marketing

The overall picture of drug discovery and development has sometimes been described as a pipeline with three main parts: drug discovery, drug development, and drug marketing (Fig. 1.2). Drug discovery originates with ideas and new chemicals and includes biological testing in various animal models. Eventually, one or more chemicals emerge as a significant lead (i.e., an important compound to evaluate further and to use as a model to make other related compounds). These leads advance through many stages of preclinical biological testing, and if they do not falter they are evaluated in humans. Clinical evaluation, toxicology, and preclinical studies continue up to the point of the regulatory submission of a New Drug Application (NDA). A myriad of interactions, feedback loops, and other activities continue throughout this process. Thus, drug development should be viewed as a dynamic system that has various bulges of activities and bottlenecks, and not as a rigid pipeline.

As a simple exercise, try to imagine the development activities of a single drug (i.e., a single project) as it travels through the pipeline. The first stage is the discovery of the compound that will proceed through the pipeline. This may take any number of years, because there is no way to predict when (or if) a discovery will be made. The usual range would be from 1 to 12 years for most drugs. Once the compound is identified, activities are initially begun in some preclinical science departments to evaluate the compound's profile and safety in detail. Eventually, more departments become involved (e.g., chemical scaleup, formulations, statistics, regulatory affairs) as the compound progresses along the pipeline. Some departments remain active throughout a project's life, while others may be active for only a limited period. This major pipeline is really composed of many smaller pipelines or subpipelines, within a single department or single function. A few of these are shown in Fig. 1.3. The typical time period required to take a drug through the pipeline after it has been identified and chosen for development is 8 to 12 years (Table 1.1).

The single project described may be major in terms of resources required and it may stretch the capacity of the company's resources as it travels along the pipeline. When a major project is being developed, the pipeline is sometimes viewed like a snake that has swallowed a large ball. A "visible" bulge passes progressively through its body. The resolution of temporary bottlenecks (i.e., areas that have insufficient personnel or other resources and have created a large backlog of work) often may be expedited with temporary staff or novel solutions.

In practice, the overall pipeline within a company involves more than a single drug, because many projects are pursued simultaneously. Imagine a long snake that has swallowed not one project, but 40 or more. Some are small and others far greater in magnitude. In addition to adding new projects to the system, other projects are expanding, and still others are being terminated. New regulations also have a marked influence on many of the activities within this pipeline by influencing which areas of the snake must expand or change.

To address many of these issues, a company must monitor what is occurring at each part of the pipeline (i.e., within various departments) and insure that each department is prepared for the projects that are heading toward it. Sometimes it is necessary to add more staff because of markedly increased work loads. But, there are many other solutions that may also be tried in attempting to maintain the balance among the work load of groups active in drug development. These solutions include reassigning personnel, hiring temporary staff, contracting work to outside groups, and delaying some projects. Other factors to consider include building new facilities, purchasing new equipment, and licensing drugs in (or out). As a result of this dynamic

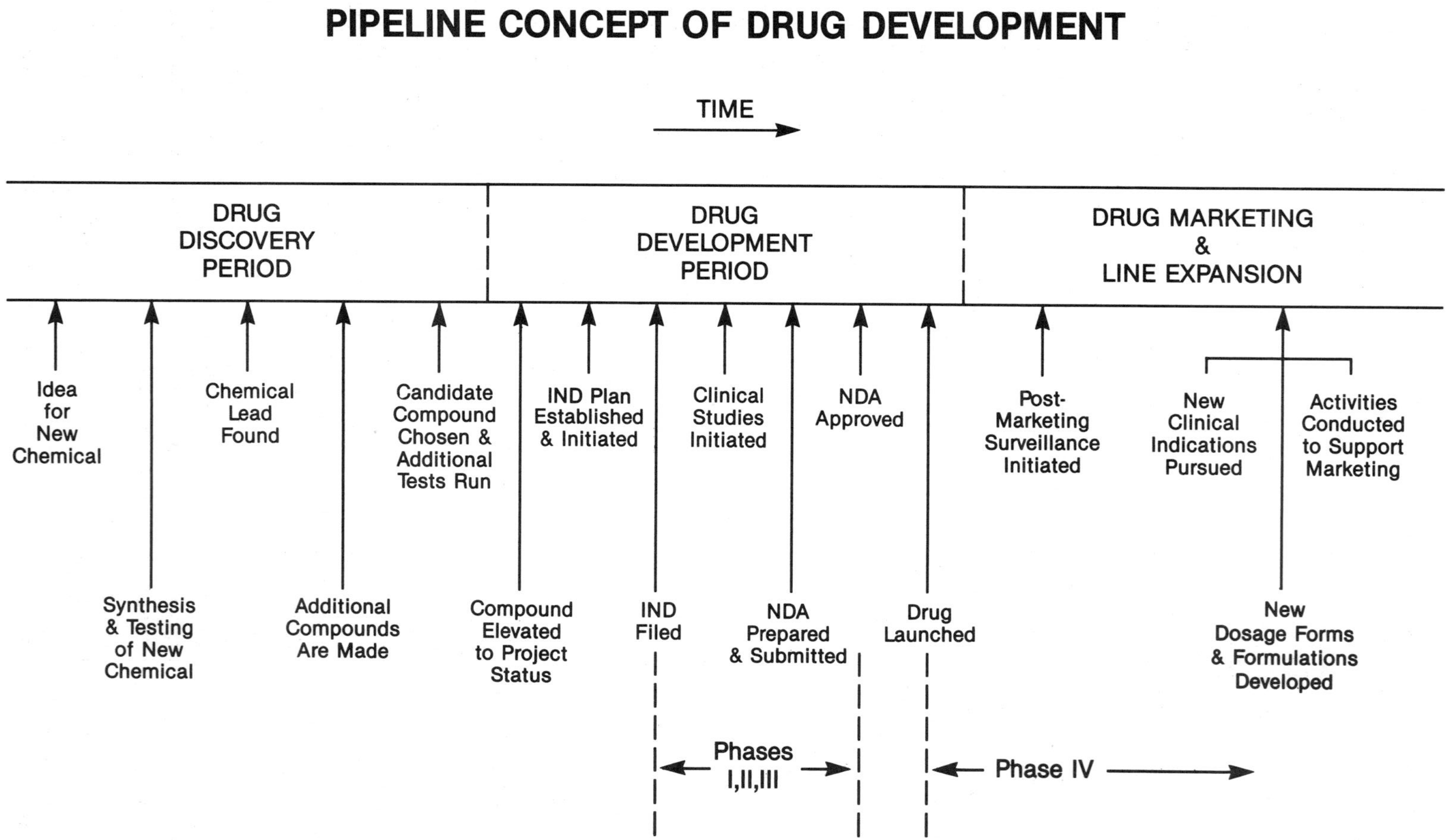

Fig. 1.2. Pipeline concept of drug development. This figure illustrates general categories of activities that take place during the three main periods of drug discovery, drug development, and drug marketing, shown within the pipeline. IND, Investigational New Drug Application; NDA, New Drug Application.

Table 1.1 Typical periods of time required to develop new drugs

Stage of development	Usual range of time required (years)	Approximate mean time (years)
1. Project formation to IND[a] filing	0.5 to 2.5	1.5
2. Phase I clinical studies	0.5 to 1.5	1.0
3. Phase II clinical studies	1.0 to 5.0	2.5
4. Phase III clinical studies and preparation of NDA[a]	1.0 to 5.0	2.5
5. FDA[a] review of NDA	1.0 to 5.0	2.5
Total	4.0 to 19.0	10.0

[a] FDA, Food and Drug Administration; IND, Investigational New Drug Application; NDA, New Drug Application.

environment the balance between research and development activities in the pipeline must be periodically, if not continually, observed and readjusted.

The third stage of the pipeline occurs after a drug is launched on the market. It includes development of new formulations, routes of administration, dosage forms, and new indications. These activities are often critical in the ability of a company to improve the drug's market share and viable life.

Horse Race

Some companies occasionally put a lot of their resources on one of their horses entered in a commercially minor race. The company works hard to win that race while allowing its horses, competing in more important races, to finish back in the pack. It is clearly better from a commercial viewpoint to come in second or even third in an important horse race than to win a minor race. The difficult part for companies to know is whether each of the races they enter is an important race or not. Many seemingly important races turn into minor ones after the horses are halfway around the track.

For example, interferon had so much media and scientific hype in the late 1970s that it appeared to be an incredibly important race. As a result, many companies invested enormous resources, despite the fact that most of the ultimate clinical uses of the drug were purely speculative. Little hard data were available and no clinical uses were documented. As the data were received and a sound judgment made, it became apparent that the true market size was minuscule compared to original expectations. The two major companies in this area continued to invest enormous resources, and apparently did not markedly scale back their efforts. The opposite situation can also occur. A commonly accepted minor race turns into a major one (e.g., the development of antiulcer drugs).

Poker Game

The poker game describes drug research as a game where numerous competitors are at the same table. The table usually refers to a specific disease or therapeutic area. A certain investment is required to enter and to play the game. Before each card is taken, players must either ante up more money or withdraw from the game.

SELECTED TYPES OF SUBPIPELINES IN DRUG DEVELOPMENT

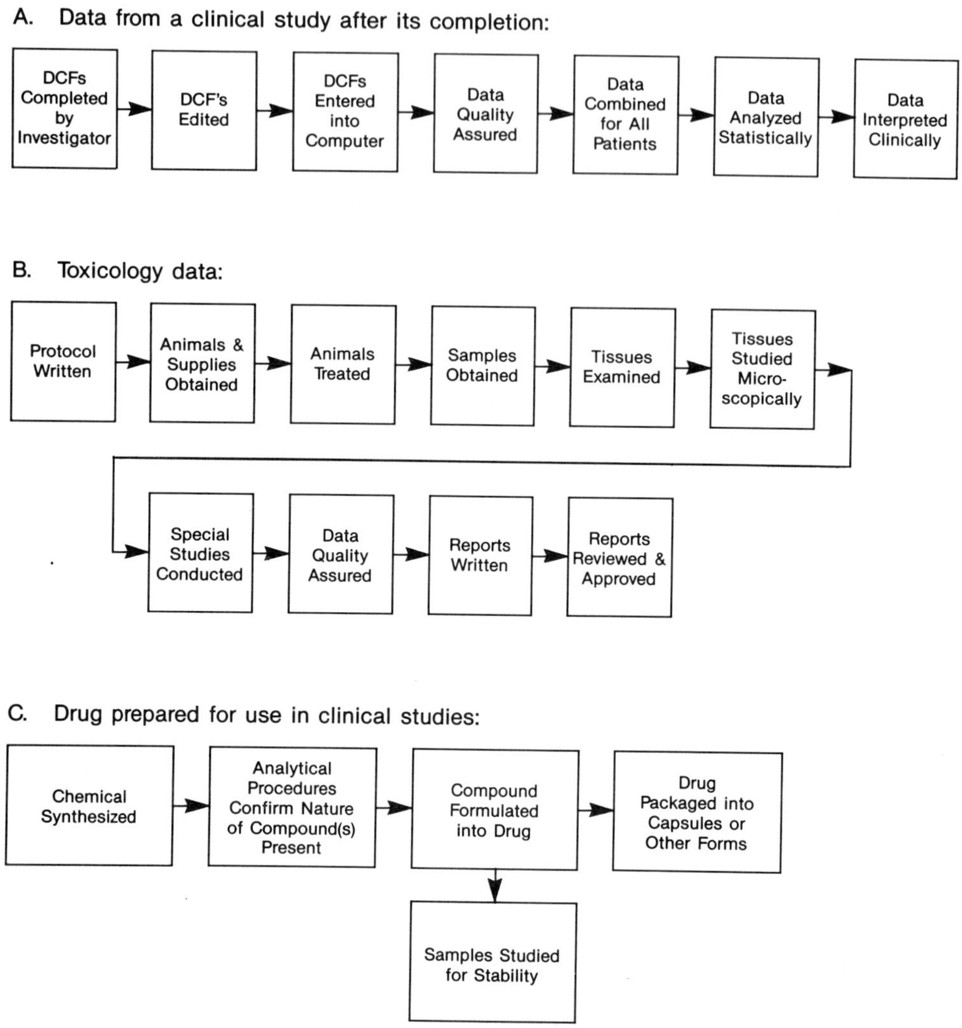

Fig. 1.3. Selected types of subpipelines in drug development. Five representative subpipelines are presented that occur during drug development. Each is usually modified for the development of specific drugs. In panel B, many steps are performed in the United States according to GLP (Good Laboratory Practices) regulations. In panel E, samples refer to blood, urine, or other biological samples. DCF, data collection form.

As in stud poker, a few cards of each player are on the table for all to see, but what is not seen is usually of critical importance. Decisions on whether to fold or to continue playing are based on how one's own cards are evaluated and on guesses of what cards are held by the other players. If the game is in a new therapeutic area, it is possible for beginners to win and players usually continue until one or more do win. Nonetheless, most games are won by the professionals. The stakes in a game

D. Drug packaged for clinical studies:

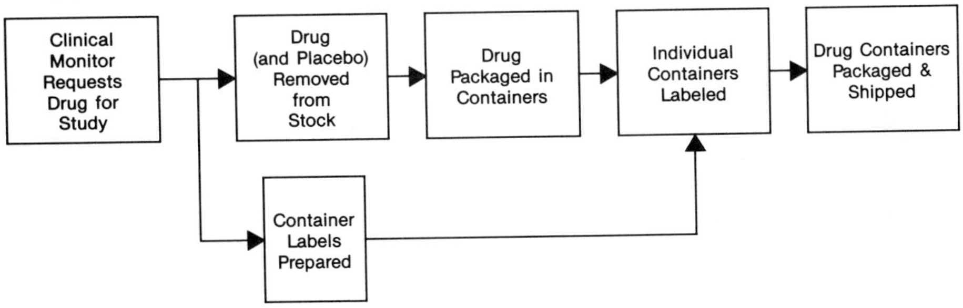

E. Drug levels measured in animal or human samples:

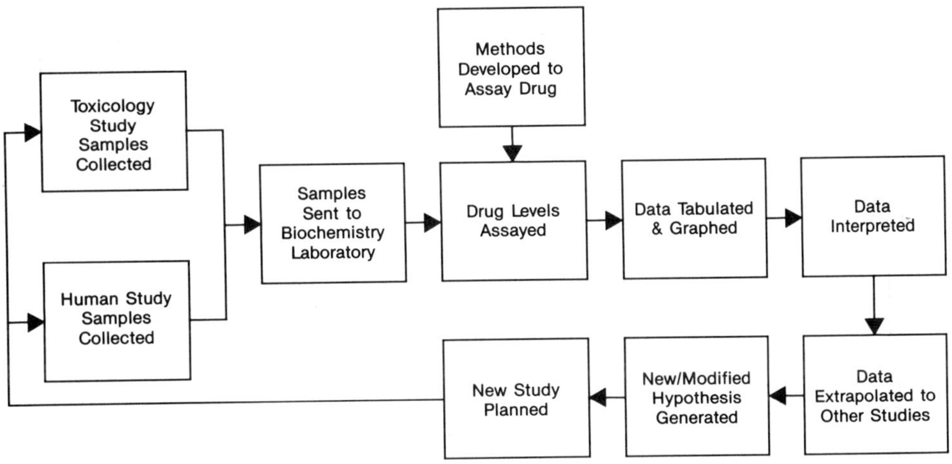

Fig. 1.3. Continued

may be small or high depending on how each player sees the commercial importance of what is in the pot. If the game is to see who can first develop a new drug that is available to several players (e.g., interferons, interleukins, tissue plasminogen activator), then most players will quickly drop out of the game or develop a new game plan. Some players will be using more of their chips in that game, whereas others may be using them at another table. The strategy of two or more players may be to combine their hands and play their best cards (i.e., a joint venture). Another strategy is to start a new game in a new therapeutic or disease area where no one else or few others are involved. Each company is involved in a different number and choice of games, all of which are being played simultaneously.

Orchestra

Each major function in a drug company working on drug development may be viewed as one of the sections of an orchestra. Preclinical groups may be viewed as the string section, marketing as the brass section, technical development as the woodwinds, and so forth. Within each orchestra section are individual instruments (i.e., departments) and there are individual musicians (i.e., professionals) who play them. Unless the entire group plays together and in harmony the piece will not sound correct. The better the musicians in the orchestra, the faster they will learn the score and create a better sound.

The conductor is usually the head of research and development, and the musical score he follows is the drug development plan. Sometimes, the musical score must be rearranged to sound better or to suit the musicians playing it. Sometimes, the tempo may have to be adjusted. There are a small group of music teachers (i.e., regulators) who are listening to the practices and dress rehearsal. These teachers must approve the performance before it is played for the audience of physicians and patients on opening night (i.e., product launch). If the performance gets rave reviews from the critics, then it will usually have a long and commercially successful run. Of course, performances by other orchestras may draw the crowds away, and problems with the quality of the performance may always arise that can close the show.

Hurdles Race

Developing a drug may be imagined as a race with a series of both high and low hurdles that the drug must jump over while racing around the track. Each company in this race occupies one or more lanes. Each lane is occupied by a separate indication or dosage form for the drug to compete in. Drugs may start in one lane and transfer to another lane or run in multiple lanes at the same time. It is important to prevent the drug's development from going off on tangents, such as off the track. Most tangents are along paths that never return to the main track nor reach the finish line of the race.

Ocean Liner

Large drug companies, as well as the individual events of drug development, have been described as a huge ocean liner steering a course through calm or stormy seas. This metaphor is mainly used to describe the situation that occurs when the captain decides to turn the boat sharply (or gradually) in a different direction. It takes both time and distance for any effect on the boat's course to occur and to be seen. The captain's command must be relayed to the people controlling the steering wheel and then sheer inertia takes the boat many miles further before any difference in direction is noted. Most drug development projects start out as small motorboats darting in and out amongst larger boats, but over time they generally increase in size and slow in their ability to rapidly maneuver toward their goal.

Maze

The image of a maze probably originated because there are usually many choices of paths to follow in drug discovery. Many of these paths lead to dead ends, and it is rarely certain that the goal of discovering a new drug will be achieved. This

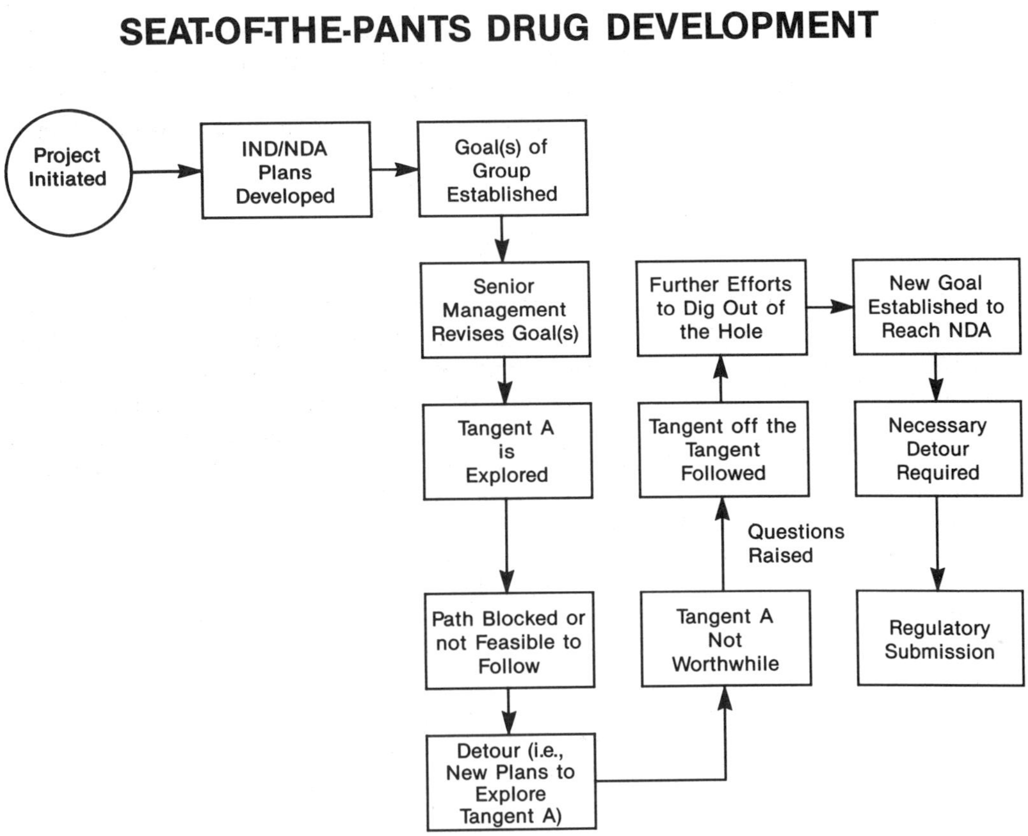

Fig. 1.4. "Seat-of-the-pants" drug development. An example of a haphazard approach to developing drugs.

metaphor should not be used to describe drug development because it would imply that drug development is either haphazard, lost, or nonfocused (Fig. 1.4).

Connect-the-Dots, Lottery, and Other Metaphors

A simple metaphor of drug development often used as a slur by some managers who are outside the complexity of research and development activities is connect-the-dots. This simplistic image is an attempt by nonscientific people to provide a frame of reference for themselves to tie together many activities that they know occur, but do not understand. This book attempts to demystify many of those activities and also to indicate why this metaphor is not correct.

The lottery image has nothing to recommend it, except that there is usually a certain amount of luck involved in discovering a new drug. But, in almost all cases there is much more to discovery than just luck. The concept of drug development being a lottery is totally inaccurate.

Two metaphors were used by Weisblat and Stucki (1974) to describe the differences between two types of research and development organizations. They described the traditional discipline-oriented approach to drug discovery and development as resembling a relay team where the baton is passed from one solo performer to another. The therapeutic area team approach used at The Upjohn Company was described as being similar to a football team where the ball is moved forward under a quarterback's direction.

High Jump

One final metaphor of drug development is that of the high jump. Safety and efficacy standards for treating a particular disease are established when a novel drug is introduced for a previously untreatable disease. All new drugs to be discovered and developed in the future must meet or surpass those levels to be acceptable to regulatory authorities and to physicians. As more effective and safe treatments become available, the standards are progressively raised (by the drugs themselves). Drugs that would have been approved a short period before can no longer get over the regulatory bar (standards) required for approval.

Do you the reader think of drug discovery or development in terms of metaphors? It would be interesting for some people to learn if scientists usually use different metaphors than nonscientists, if Americans use different metaphors than Europeans, managers different than workers, or actually how many people even think about drug discovery or development in this way. This information would indicate whether the basic concept of drug discovery or development is viewed in generally similar or different terms. A company might decide to promote one particular metaphor as a means of encouraging their employees to utilize the same concept about their activities.

FUNCTIONS OF DRUGS

When Sir Walter Raleigh was facing the headman's ax in his final moments, he reportedly said, "It's a sharp medicine, but it cures all ills." Many people believe that drugs are intended to "cure all ills," but relatively few drugs actually cure a disease. Most have other functions. They are briefly described because during the drug discovery process, scientists are consciously seeking to find a compound with specific properties or functions. During clinical development one or more of these functions are specifically studied. The various uses or functions of drugs can be arbitrarily divided into six categories.

1. *Prevention* Some drugs are used prophylactically to prevent disease. Drugs such as vaccines or fluoride may be given to normal individuals to prevent the initial occurrence of a disease (e.g., polio, smallpox, dental carries) or may be given to patients at high risk of contracting a certain disease or problem to reduce the chance of its occurrence. Another form of disease prevention is sometimes called suppression (see category 4).

2. *Cure* The ideal form of treatment occurs when drugs are used to cure a disease (e.g., antibiotics are used to cure certain bacterial infections, antihelminthics are used to cure certain worm infections). A cure represents a complete eradication of the disease.

3. *Treatment* Drugs are often used to alleviate symptoms for patients who have many chronic diseases. These drugs do not cure a disease and usually do not affect the underlying pathophysiology (e.g., antiasthmatics, antianginals). But, the drugs improve the patient's signs and/or symptoms and lead to clinical improvement. Drugs that reduce the risk of disease progression illustrate a type of treatment.

4. *Suppression* Drugs are often used to suppress the signs and/or symptoms of a disease and prevent them from occurring, or to prevent the disease process from progressing. Suppression is often a continuation of maintenance therapy after the acute episode or problem has improved. Suppression is a type of prevention, but is used in patients who have a disease as opposed to normals who want to prevent getting a disease.

5. *Diagnosis* Some drugs are used to help physicians establish the diagnosis of a patient's disease or problem (e.g., radiocontrast dyes). It would be desirable if there were many drugs available for this purpose, but relatively few such drugs exists.

Drugs are sometimes used for a short time as a therapeutic trial to help prove a diagnosis. It is assumed that if a patient improves after a therapeutic trial with a drug that the diagnosis is proven. If the patient does not improve, the conclusion is reached that the diagnosis is incorrect. This practice is considered to be an undesirable way of practicing medicine in many situations (e.g., to use antibiotics without obtaining cultures), because physicians should assiduously attempt to diagnose medical problems before initiating treatment.

6. *Enhancement of health* People desire the best state of health possible. Many try and achieve this state through drugs (e.g., vitamins, minerals) as well as through other means (e.g., diet, exercise). These drugs cannot be said to be replacing a deficiency and may only offer a psychological sense of well-being.

Many drugs fit into two or more of these categories. Such drugs may be used for either one or two functions at the same time. One example of this latter situation is illustrated with the Fab antibody fragment of digoxin. This drug (Digibind) simultaneously diagnoses and treats life-threatening digoxin toxicity by binding molecules of digoxin in the blood making them unavailable for binding at their site of action on cells in the body. If the patient has toxicity resulting from a digoxin overdose, then he or she will usually be helped with the drug. If the patient does not have a digoxin-induced toxicity, then the drug will be ineffective. Some drugs that usually fit in one category may also be used for other purposes. One example is when antibiotics are used prophylactically in high-risk patients to prevent development of a bacterial infection, as well as therapeutically in others to cure many specific infections.

2 / *The Nature of Drug Discovery and Development*

The discovery of adrenaline came about through a mistaken impression. A certain Dr. Oliver had developed a gadget which he thought measured the diameter of that artery at the wrist which is used for feeling the pulse. He measured the diameter of this artery in his son under a variety of conditions. One of the conditions involved the injection of an extract of calves' adrenal glands. He thought he detected that this injection decreased the size of the artery. We now know that the effect of adrenaline on the diameter of a large artery would be undetectable. Dr. Oliver rushed off to let the world know of his discovery. The world, as represented by Professor Schafer, a renowned physiologist, was disbelieving. But Dr. Oliver's enthusiasm eventually persuaded the professor to inject some of the extract into a dog whose blood pressure was being measured. To his amazement the blood pressure rose in an extraordinary fashion. Adrenaline had been discovered.

It is possible to point out many other instances where an effective discovery came at the end of a line of reasoning which was certainly not correct at every stage. It is like walking over a rocky beach. One way is to move slowly and cautiously; making sure that at each step you are firmly balanced on the rock on which you are standing before you take another step. The other way is to move swiftly over the rocks pausing so briefly on each that a precise balance at every step is no longer required. When you have got somewhere interesting, that is the time to look back and pick out the surest way of getting there again. Sometimes it is very much easier to see the surest route to a place only after you have arrived. You may have to be at the top of a mountain to find the easiest way up. Edward de Bono, English physician and writer. From *The Use of Lateral Thinking.*

SOURCES OF NEW DRUGS

What Is Meant by "Sources?"

From a company's perspective there are several different usages of the term "sources of new drugs." They include (1) the source of the intellectual idea that led to the drug's discovery, (2) the source of the material that is the drug, (3) the business source from which the company obtained the drug, and (4) the type of institution in which the drug was discovered.

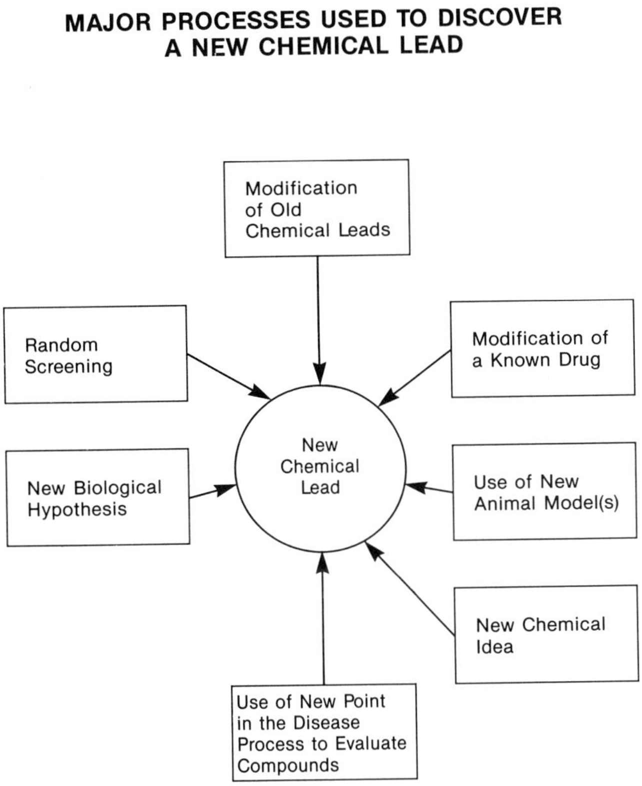

Fig. 2.1. Major processes used to discover a new chemical lead.

The first usage refers to the discovery of the drug. Did the idea and the drug itself solely result from the company's research or was it originally discovered in another company or at an academic institution, government facility, or other place? If the drug was synthesized, what was the source of the idea that led to the compound? Was it a close analogue or metabolite of a known compound, a prodrug (i.e., a chemical that is converted inside the body into the active drug), or did the idea come from another direction? Figure 2.1 shows a number of processes or sources used to discover a chemical with an interesting biological activity (i.e., a chemical lead). The second usage refers to whether the molecule's origins came from a natural source (i.e., plant, mineral, or animal), or whether it was artificially synthesized.

The third group of sources refers to business sources. These include licensing arrangements, joint ventures, in-house research, purchases, or other types of business arrangements. The fourth type of source refers to the nature of the institution that developed the idea. Marketed drugs may come from drug companies, private entrepreneurs, academicians, government laboratories, or other types of businesses. Nonetheless, approximately 90 percent of new drugs come from the drug industry (Schwartzman, 1976). This subject is reviewed by Kahn et al. (1982, p. 109, 110).

Sources of Ideas for New Drugs

There is no limit to the intellectual sources of ideas for new drugs. Four common sources are shown in Fig. 2.2. Ideas may also result from problems (e.g., adverse

MAJOR SOURCES OF A NEW DRUG

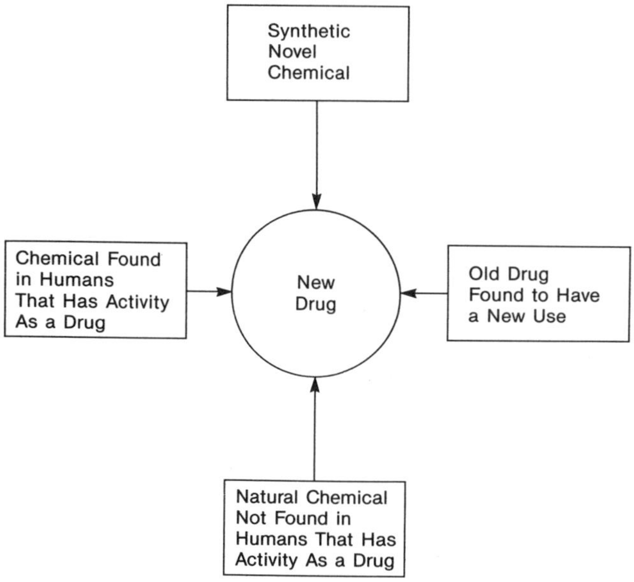

Fig. 2.2. Major sources of a new drug.

reactions) with existing drugs. Adverse reactions for one use of a drug may serve as a new indication for the same drug. For example, a drug that is found to cause constipation as an adverse reaction (e.g., morphine) may be used as an active antidiarrheal. A drug that causes sedation (e.g., certain antihistamines) may be used as a sleep-promoting agent. Adverse reactions also stimulate companies to search for chemically related compounds that have more potent actions of the desired type. A well-known example of this situation relates to the sulfonamide antibacterial drugs. It was noticed that "sulfa" drugs lowered blood sugar and caused diuresis (excessive urination) as adverse reactions. Many new compounds were synthesized over many years in an attempt to exploit these adverse reactions. Eventually, the oral antidiabetic drugs (sulfonylureas) were discovered. Thiazide diuretics are also a descendent of many years of molecular modifications, searching for a sulfonamide diuretic.

Benefits observed with some drugs have provided the impetus to companies to try to improve on this activity and develop a new therapeutic agent. In some cases the original benefit is either a weak effect or is not observed in all patients. Therefore, there is need to improve the magnitude of the effect. For example, 6-mercaptopurine (6MP) is an antileukemic drug. It was found by Dr. Robert Schwartz at Tufts Medical Center in Boston to influence the immune response. Dr. Schwartz convinced Dr. G. Hitchings and Dr. G. Elion at the Burroughs Wellcome Co. that it was important to search for other immunosuppressive compounds that might have less toxicity. They screened numerous compounds in the laboratory and found that azathioprine (Imuran) was highly active and had a much better therapeutic index in mice. During this time Dr. Roy Calne in London read Dr. Schwartz's paper on 6MP and tested it in dogs who had received kidney transplants. He found that the drug had some

Table 2.1. Selected drugs that are prepared from natural plants

Names of drugs	Plant source	Therapeutic use
A. General classes of drugs		
1. Digitalis glycosides (e.g., digoxin, digitoxin)	Foxglove	Cardiac stimulant
2. Opium alkaloids (e.g., morphine, codeine)	Opium poppy	Analgesics (pain killers)
3. Belladonna alkaloids (e.g., atropine, scopolamine)	Belladonna, stramonium	Parasympathomimetic blocking drugs
4. Catharanthus alkaloids (e.g., vincristine, vinblastine)	Madagascar periwinkle	Anticancer agents
B. Specific drugs		
1. Quinidine	Bark of Cinchona tree	Antiarrhythmic
2. Quinine	Bark of Cinchona tree	Antimalarial
3. Cocaine	Cocoa plant	Local anesthetic
4. Curare	South American plants	Skeletal muscle relaxant
5. Reserpine	Root of plant—Rauwolfia serpentina	Antipsychotic
6. Pilocarpine	Leaf of Pilocarpus microphyllus	Antiglaucoma agent
7. Colchicine	Autumn crocus	Antigout

activity in preventing the body's rejection of the kidney. He came to the United States to do a fellowship and on his way to Boston stopped by the laboratories of Burroughs Wellcome Co. just outside New York City. In discussions about a better drug than 6MP, Drs. Hitchings and Elion gave Dr. Calne azathioprine to test as an immunosupressive drug. He did. This drug had better activity than 6MP and eventually opened up the whole field of renal transplantation.

Sources of Materials for New Drugs

Drugs Found in Natural Plants

Plants have been a source of drugs for many millennia, and some of the most important drugs still come from plants (Table 2.1). Additional information on this topic is plentiful (e.g., Balandrin et al., 1985; Steiner, 1986). Nonetheless, proportionally fewer and fewer drugs are derived from plants, and the science of pharmacognosy is less frequently taught in pharmacy schools. There are some strong believers who think that there are many effective drugs in Chinese, African, and other societies' folk medicine that are unknown or underutilized in western countries. On the other hand, several drug companies have screened many thousands of folk remedies (seeking active drugs) with limited success.

Drugs Found in Animals and Humans

Drugs have been obtained from human and animal glands for several decades (e.g., insulin, vitamin B_{12}, adrenaline, thyroid hormone, growth hormone). The advent of

Table 2.2 Selected examples of clinical serendipity

Drug(s)	Original use(s) or intended use(s)	Uses discovered serendipitously in clinical practice[a]
Chlorpromazine	Antimotion sickness	Antipsychotic
Tricyclics	Major tranquilizers	Antidepressants
Meprobamate	Muscle relaxant	Tranquilizer
Iproniazid	Antituberculous agent	Antidepressant
Procaine	Local anesthetic	Antiarrhythmic
Amantadine	Antiviral	Parkinson's disease
Propranolol	Antiarrhythmic	Antimigraine
	Antianginal	Prevention of myocardial reinfarction
Allopurinol	Adjunct in cancer chemotherapy[b]	Antigout
Corticosteroids	Adrenal steroid replacement	Anti-inflammatory

[a] While most of these drugs' uses were found purely by serendipity, a few also involved hypothesis testing (e.g., allopurinol for gout, propranolol for prevention of myocardial reinfarction).
[b] Allopurinol was originally used in conjunction with 6-mercaptopurine (6MP) to prevent its oxidation and therefore potentiate 6MP's anticancer effect.

biotechnology brought a virtual explosion in the type and number of biologicals that are being developed as drugs (e.g., tissue plasminogen activator, interferons, various growth factors, factor 8, and numerous others). The last section of this chapter has a more detailed discussion on biotechnology.

Drugs Originally Used in Animals

There are many examples where drugs used in humans were subsequently tested and eventually marketed for use in animals. There are few examples, however, of the opposite situation where drugs used in animals were eventually used in humans. One example of this situation occurred with permethrin. Permethrin is applied as an ear tag to cattle and helps keep flies away. This is important because certain types of flies interfere with normal grazing of these animals. This drug has been found to kill lice and to treat scabies in humans.

Old Drugs Developed for New Uses

The discovery that an already marketed drug could be useful for treating a new disease is usually made in the clinic. This discovery may have been logically conceived prior to evaluation or it may result from serendipity. A number of examples are given in Table 2.2.

Who Discovers Drugs?

A drug's discovery is rarely the sudden achievement of one person's sole idea. Many people's ideas and brainpower invariably contribute to the discovery. Because of human nature and many people's desire to simplify the truth, one person usually receives credit for the discovery of a newly synthesized compound with important biological activity. This individual is often a chemist, although other people may provide intellectual input into the compound's design. With some well-known drugs, however, other individuals (e.g., pharmacologists, research managers) have been given credit for a drug's discovery. In some situations this is clearly an example of power and glory going to the powerful. On the other hand, these people are often critically important as promoters of a drug. Many drugs would never reach the market if they were not pushed and promoted within a company, because of the strong competition that usually exists for attention and resources.

When is a Drug Discovered?

The discovery of a drug may be defined as occurring at the time when a new biological or clinical use of a compound or drug is identified. With this broad definition, uses of a drug are discovered at numerous times and by numerous processes during its life from initial synthesis to end of marketing. Major points in this period are mentioned.

1. An idea for a new drug stimulates a chemist to synthesize a compound that is found to have the hypothesized activity.
2. A biologist (e.g., pharmacologist) provides feedback of information to a chemist that leads to synthesis of a new compound that eventually becomes a drug.
3. Biological activity of an unanticipated type is discovered during preclinical testing. This use is eventually developed as an indication (or as *the* indication) for the drug.
4. A novel clinical activity of a drug is discovered serendipitously during investigational studies in humans. This use becomes a major, or possibly the only, use of the drug (e.g., the antihypertensive effect of propranolol was discovered during antianginal studies in humans).
5. A theory is tested in humans for a new use of an investigational drug and found to be correct.
6. Processes described in items 4 or 5 above may occur for a drug that is already marketed.

Table 2.2 lists some examples where marketed drugs were found to have new activities that became their major use.

CHOOSING THERAPEUTIC AREAS TO RESEARCH

Description and Definitions of Therapeutic Areas

One of the most sensitive and important issues in research-based drug companies concerns the decision of which therapeutic areas to explore in a search for new drugs. Although this issue may superficially appear to have a simple answer (e.g., those areas of greatest medical and commercial need), it is actually a complex issue at many companies, with many tensions and pressures from both within and outside the research groups. Identifying new therapeutic areas to explore is an infrequent but important decision at most companies.

A therapeutic area is defined as a major area of medicine in which drugs are presently or could potentially be used. These areas include basic specialties of internal medicine (e.g., cardiology, gastroenterology, rheumatology, nephrology) plus psychiatry, neurology, anesthesiology, and numerous other fields of medicine. These categories may be viewed as a *primary level.* Specific diseases, syndromes, or conditions within each of those medical areas represent a *secondary level* of the therapeutic areas.

A *tertiary level* relating to therapeutic areas may be defined as the approaches and methods followed to discover new drugs within each of the secondary areas (i.e., diseases) being researched. More specifically, this tertiary level refers to the number of different places in biochemical pathways, pharmacological systems, physiological processes, and/or pathological stages of a disease that are being explored (often simultaneously) in looking for a new drug. Decisions about therapeutic areas to explore are made on at least the three different levels described. These may be summarized as (1) broad therapeutic areas, (2) specific diseases, and (3) approaches to be used. More decisions relate to the latter two levels than to the first.

Who Has Input and Who Decides about Therapeutic Areas to Explore?

Within the research and development group the major individuals who have input into decisions about therapeutic areas to explore (primary level) are the (1) director of research and development, (2) head of research, (3) department heads of relevant preclinical departments (e.g., organic chemistry, pharmacology, biochemistry, molecular biology), and (4) senior scientists within the relevant preclinical departments. The actual decision may be made at one or more of these administrative levels and usually depends primarily on whether the proposal contains good ideas scientifically. In addition, the decision makers will usually consider company objectives, marketing goals, and the company's comfort zone. If the decision is not made by the director of research and development, then each of the relevant individuals must usually review decisions made with those people above them in the research and development hierarchy. Depending on the training and personality of the company's president and chief executive officer, he may also desire to review and approve these decisions.

Decisions on secondary areas to explore and the tertiary level of approaches are usually made at lower levels in the organization. Research scientists often propose the tertiary level approaches they believe offer the best opportunities for discovering a new drug.

The above discussion assumes that a company has a single site at which research to discover drugs is conducted. This is often untrue because multinational companies usually have two or more research centers. In those instances, each site may explore and also develop different therapeutic areas or another means of dividing their research activities may be used.

Marketing Input into Choosing Therapeutic Areas to Explore

Outside the research and development environment there are a number of groups (primarily in marketing) that often seek to influence the areas in which research is conducted. Marketing personnel are usually primarily interested in the second level of therapeutic areas (i.e., specific diseases). Research scientists are generally aware of which medical areas have unmet therapeutic needs and usually understand whether there is or is not commercial value for such potential drugs. It is often important to identify therapeutic areas that a company does not wish to explore.

Commercial information from marketing personnel provides valuable input to research scientists in assisting them to make decisions about the first two levels. One of the difficulties with accepting a marketing assessment of which therapeutic or disease areas to research is that a group attempting to find a drug for disease X may uncover a drug for disease Y or Z. Drugs for diseases Y or Z may be much less attractive to marketing than a drug for disease X. Also, the commercial value of a drug depends to a large degree on how closely its activity profile compares with that of an ideal or best available drug for the specific disease. The answer to that question cannot be known until the drug has been in clinical studies for a number of years. A "slight" change in efficacy or safety often determines whether a drug is a large money-maker or an "also ran" that never repays its cost of development. Finally, drugs developed for one disease are sometimes found to be useful for others. In addition to this happening for a number of common drugs, many and possibly most drugs used to treat rare diseases (i.e., orphan drugs) are found in this manner.

How Many Different Therapeutic Areas Should be Explored Simultaneously?

This question stimulates endless debate between those who wish to explore a small area intensively and those who believe that spreading research resources thinly over a broad area increases the chances of success (i.e., discovering a drug). There are no simple answers to this debate.

The decision of how broadly to explore each therapeutic area being researched is usually made by the director of research and development in conjunction with the head of research. Other individuals may also be involved in this decision. The personalities, philosophies, and interests of the individuals involved will determine the decisions reached. One aspect of their philosophy would involve their general concept of research. If they have an image analogous to looking for a few diamonds lying on the surface of a large endless landscape, they might tend to deploy their staff over a broad area. If their image is analogous to looking for a diamond amidst tons of coal and rubble in a deep mine, they may choose to focus activities on a smaller number of areas to search more intensively. One of these basic approaches is usually followed at a drug company, although it probably makes sense for most companies to use both approaches, but in different therapeutic areas.

To illustrate possible approaches to the three levels of therapeutic areas, basic combinations are listed below. The therapeutic areas and diseases being researched may represent any of the combinations found in Table 2.3.

It is unlikely that any company's research group approaches this issue as systematically as described here, but their philosophy will tend to lead them toward using a few of these eight general directions. The actual situation followed at many research-based drug companies is that within some therapeutic areas many diseases are pursued and within other therapeutic areas few diseases are pursued.

Table 2.3. Basic combinations of approaches to the three levels of therapeutic areas

	Number of general therapeutic areas (Primary level)	Number of diseases within each therapeutic area (Secondary level)	Number of approaches used to study each disease (Tertiary level)
1.	Few	Few	Few
2.	Few	Many	Few
3.	Few	Many	Many
4.	Few	Few	Many
5.	Many	Few	Few
6.	Many	Many	Few
7.	Many	Many	Many
8.	Many	Few	Many

What Are the Criteria to Use in Determining Which Therapeutic Areas to Explore?

There are numerous broad or general criteria, as well as many specific criteria that should be considered in determining which general therapeutic areas to explore. Once these criteria are used, the decision about each of the potential therapeutic areas to explore should be more straightforward. Broad criteria include:

1. Medical value in terms of therapeutic need in each of the areas being considered (e.g., Fig. 2.3).
2. Commercial value of each market area in terms of both present and anticipated future size.
3. Skills of the scientific staff presently employed and those available to be hired or consulted.
4. Interests of the scientific staff and managers.
5. Other drugs (both marketed and investigational) in the area from the same company.
6. Availability of suitable animal models to predict efficacy in humans.
7. Traditions of the company in emphasizing certain therapeutic areas.

A more specific criterion is the presence of worthwhile chemical leads or novel scientific ideas for developing drugs.

Choosing the Number of New Compounds of One Type to Develop

There may be sound medical reasons (e.g., greater convenience and compliance, improved tolerance, efficacy for patients unhelped by others) to develop several drugs of one therapeutic or chemical class such as beta-blockers or nonsteroidal anti-inflammatory drugs. But, after 10 or 15 drugs of the same type are marketed, it is difficult to justify development of additional ones. Some research and marketing directors believe that most markets can only support two to four drugs of any one type. Incentives to develop additional drugs of the same type generally decrease as regulatory agencies become more resistant to approving newer versions where many similar drugs exit. This trend is already occurring in North America where many nonsteroidal anti-inflammatory drugs, beta-receptor antagonists, and other examples

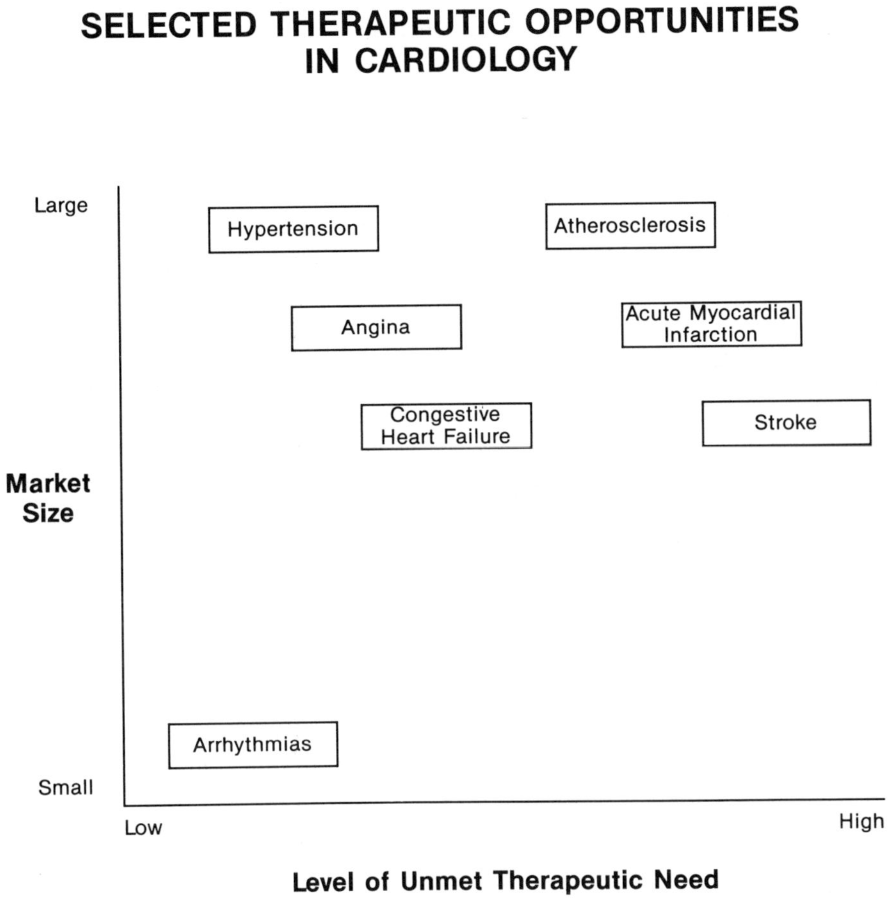

Fig. 2.3. Selected therapeutic opportunities in cardiology for new drug development.

exist. Another factor that will diminish "me-too" drugs is the fact that hospitals, Health Maintenance Organizations (HMOs), provinces with national health, and other medical provider organizations that have formularies are becoming resistant to including new drugs that have no demonstrated benefits over existing therapy. Such benefits may, however, be defined in terms of quality of life, cost-effectiveness, compliance, and other categories in addition to just efficacy and safety.

Competition of Drug Discovery Ideas for Resources

Within most drug discovery groups of research-based drug companies literally hundreds if not thousands of novel ideas surface each year. Many of these require resources in terms of staff effort and time to evaluate their feasibility or quality. Because of commitments to ongoing projects, only a small number of these ideas can be evaluated, and usually only a tiny number are fully evaluated. One critical question is which ideas are evaluated and to what degree? In an ideal world the ideas with the greatest scientific merit would be the ones evaluated. But, in this imperfect world, there are two other major factors that impact on the decision.

First, it is often impossible to determine the true scientific value of an idea until after the idea is actually tested. Some of the most outlandish ideas are found to be correct after the experiments have been done, and other ideas that seem both true and valuable are shown to be false. Therefore, there is a degree of guesswork at an early stage in ranking ideas according to their ultimate value.

Second, there is the issue of company politics. Everyone knows (or should know) that the value of an idea equals its intrinsic value times the position of the idea's proponent to the third power. Therefore, if someone wants to have their idea receive a more sympathetic hearing from management, they might wish to seek a superior in the company to sponsor their idea. Alternatively, they might turn the idea over to a superior in the hope that that will enhance its chance of being approved for evaluation. If a committee is to evaluate the idea it might be advisable for the idea's proponent to meet each of the members in advance to review and lobby for the idea before it is actually proposed. Many ideas are turned down because they were never properly understood by the group that discussed them. This situation could often be avoided by having the idea's sponsor conduct preliminary discussions with committee members. This is especially important when the idea's sponsor is not present at the major meeting where the idea's ultimate fate is determined.

Pertinent questions for a company to assess are whether the best ideas are being proposed or are they being suppressed? Do scientists believe their ideas are being given a fair hearing? Also, is there a formal system to air new ideas of drug discovery? For example, a written document could be presented every half year in which new ideas could be presented. In addition, a scientific forum could be held periodically where ideas would be presented and critiqued. Ultimately, ideas that require major resources must be evaluated by senior research managers and those that require little time or resources may be reviewed by scientists who would perform the experiments.

A few other suggestions for scientists or others who wish to have their research (or other) ideas adopted are to (1) attempt to integrate the proposed idea into existing work or into a part of the company (as opposed to proposing a totally new group or department be formed), (2) identify each of the steps that will be necessary to propose the idea, (3) plan each of those steps in a logical sequence, (4) initiate the process, but do not rush any of the individual steps, (5) show how others will benefit from the proposal, (6) include a clear rationale in the proposal, (7) conduct a few preliminary tests to demonstrate the likely value of the concept, (8) support the concept with published information, and (9) include other scientists in the proposal.

Initiating Activities in a New Therapeutic Area of Research

After a decision is reached to conduct research in a new therapeutic area (primary level) it may be quite convenient and straightforward to reassign scientists to the new therapeutic area within their own discipline (e.g., biochemistry). If the new area of research requires the same general skills and methods, then reassigning personnel is usually possible. The ability to reassign people successfully to a new therapeutic area depends on the individuals, their interests, and how well their knowledge and experience enable them to make the transition. If a totally new therapeutic area is to be explored, then many scientists would balk at being reassigned from an area in which they are trained, experienced, and are building their career. This is generally the case for pharmacologists and physiologists who are asked to take on totally new types of methodologies and approaches. On the other hand, many biochemists and chemists would not have to alter their technical skills and approaches in switching from one therapeutic field to another, and it is much easier to make a switch in those disciplines.

Because of limitations in moving personnel in many biological sciences it is often necessary to hire a number of new scientific staff when a decision is made to enter a new therapeutic area. When a relatively large group of five or more professional staff are needed within a single discipline, it is usually desirable to hire initially a single experienced individual to head the group. That person is then given the task of hiring the additional staff needed. This approach helps assure that the group assembled will work well together and have skills that are appropriate to deal with their newly assigned tasks.

Should Drug Companies be Engaged in Basic Research?

Many scientists talk about basic and applied research as if they were easily separated categories. The fact is that many definitions are used for each term, and sometimes there is a great deal of overlap between the two terms. Numerous scientists deny that any meaningful distinction can be made. For example, Bartholini (1983, p. 143), wrote "Basic and applied research, by my approach, are unified; the same investigator has to screen—which is a fundamental part of pharmacological research—and has to investigate biological mechanisms." The mechanisms referred to are usually considered as part of basic research and screening is considered as applied research. Nonetheless, these views depend on whom one speaks to. The author believes there are different types of research conducted within a drug company and that they may be visualized as a spectrum that includes both basic and applied research. One such spectrum is shown in Fig. 2.13. Toward the basic research end of the spectrum the connection to drug discovery or development becomes progressively weaker. Research-based drug companies must be engaged in both basic and applied types of research. One major issue is to decide how much of each activity should be conducted, although certain research has both applied and basic characteristics.

Some people use the term basic research to apply to speculative, fundamental, nondirected, nontargeted, or exploratory research that is curiosity-driven and without any clearly identifiable usefulness. This type of research is most often conducted in academic institutions. Using this definition, many research-based drug companies desire to conduct a limited amount of basic research. This is often justified by the belief that this type of work is far removed from drug discovery. It is accepted that basic research has the potential for leading to a major breakthrough in scientific understanding, which *may* be able to be converted into (1) a new animal test model, (2) a new chemical series, or (3) a new approach to discovering drugs. One of these three tools *may* eventually in turn lead to discovery of a breakthrough drug. For example, if a little-studied or previously unknown enzyme is found to be important for a specific disease (scientific breakthrough), then animal tests can be established to look for compounds that act as inhibitors, stimulators, or mimics of the enzyme. If an active lead compound is found, it would encourage chemists to make many analogues.

In the scenario described it is clear that a scientific breakthrough is not adequate on its own to discover a new drug. It is for this reason (and others) that many research-based companies rely on scientific breakthroughs achieved in the academic community, rather than trying to compete with the small staff that the company could assign to exploratory research. All research-based drug companies carefully read important scientific journals looking for information that could trigger a new approach to discover worthwhile and important drugs. Some research directors claim that *exploratory research* (i.e., toward the basic research end of the spectrum) conducted within the drug company is the "seed corn" of future drug discoveries for their company. But, a little reflection will reveal several weaknesses of this rationale (e.g., the small staff size of a single company is competing with much larger numbers of academicians, the connection between a successful scientific breakthrough and discovery of a drug that exploits the breakthrough may never be made, many major scientific discoveries are available to be exploited for drug discoveries by anyone who reads the literature).

Comroe and Dripps (1976) describe six types of basic research.

1. Basic research unrelated to the solution of a clinical problem (e.g., Landsteiner's discovery of human blood groups, found as he was investigating an immunological problem).
2. Basic research related to the solution of a clinical problem (e.g., Landsteiner's discovery that a virus caused poliomyelitis in monkeys).
3. Studies not concerned with basic biolgoical, chemical, or physical mechanisms (e.g., purely descriptive studies of a new disease, clinical observations that did not initially require research such as the observation that inhalation of ether causes anesthesia).
4. Review and critical analysis of published work and synthesis of new concepts without new data.
5. Developmental work to create, improve, or perfect apparatus or a technique for research use.
6. Developmental work to create, improve, or perfect apparatus or a technique for use in diagnosis or care of patients.

Research Programs

Research programs may be defined in many ways. One typical definition is that it is a research project that involves two or more scientists from two or more departments. Programs may be coordinated and led by formally appointed leaders or managed through informal reporting and communication lines. If the appointed leader coordinates activities in two or more departments, then this is an example of the matrix approach. The coordinator may also be responsible for the scientific and technical direction of the program as well as for conduct of the research within his or her discipline.

Each research program may be initiated informally or only after a written proposal for the new program has been prepared and adopted. This proposal could include minimum criteria for a new candidate drug to achieve. Progress on each program may be monitored through reports and periodic reviews. Criteria for a new compound to achieve before it is advanced toward human studies may be theoretical (i.e., ideal), realistic, or may represent the minimal acceptable criteria.

METHODS OF DRUG DISCOVERY

Scientists seek to identify a sensitive locus (target for a drug to act at) that has importance in a biological system (e.g., an important enzyme, a receptor, a physiological system) and then to look for compounds that affect this locus.

Which Comes First—the Biological Mechanism of Action or the New Chemical Compound?

A biological mechanism of action is an explanation of how a compound or drug elicits a biological (or clinical) activity. Biological mechanisms exist at many levels, such as subcellular, cellular, tissue, organ, entire animal or human organism, and population of animal or human organisms. Therefore, a drug does not have a single mechanism of action. The term, often refers to a biochemical description at the subcellular or cellular level, or to a physiological description at the tissue or organ level.

The answer to the question of which comes first is—either or both. Some compounds or drugs are found empirically to have a biological activity, and a search is then mounted to determine their mechanism of action. In other situations, biological mechanisms are used as targets in animal test models (e.g., enzyme stimulation, receptor inhibition, ion movements, biochemical changes). Newly made chemicals are evaluated in these tests for their activity. In those cases, knowledge of a compound's mechanism precedes the discovery of a chemical compound that has an acceptable profile. A test may be established to measure a compound's ability to stimulate a particular enzyme, which is believed to be responsible for eliciting a physiological effect that leads to clinical improvement. The mechanisms of action of most drugs are unknown. Even when a biological mechanism is known at one level, activities at other biological levels are often not known with certainty and must be investigated after an active compound is found. The usual situation involves a variety of theories and hypotheses about each of the multiple mechanisms for a single drug, and different amounts of evidence that exist in support of each.

Establishing Criteria for a Compound's Performance During the Discovery Period

Three major types of criteria may be established for a compound to meet during the discovery period; ideal, realistic/desirable, and minimally acceptable. A company may have some or all research programs or projects that use one (or more) of these criteria. It should be clear to both scientists and managers whether the criteria are of the first, second, or third type. The criteria would describe the nature and magnitude of activities, potencies, toxicities, and other relevant compound characteristics. These should be reviewed by all departments participating in the discovery phase of the particular program or project. This approach would insure that successful compounds would be advanced by consensus, and also that compounds that did not achieve at least minimal criteria would not be advanced. An example of ideal criteria is given in Table 3.2. The pros and cons of using realistic versus ideal versus minimal criteria are not discussed.

In addition to these three types of prospective criteria for a compound to meet, it is also important to determine which criteria are *musts* and which are *shoulds*. The latter criteria are desirable, but not essential. In some circumstances a range of activity may be used in describing a criterion.

There is some overlap between criteria used for a compound's performance during the discovery and development periods. Criteria for a drug's development are discussed later in this chpater. If a new indication is identified at any stage during the discovery or development period, the relevant criteria may be entirely or partially established retrospectively, instead of prospectively, as described.

Basic Approaches and Methods of Drug Discovery

A specific chemist who is synthesizing novel compounds to be evaluated as drugs and the biologists testing those compounds may or may not have a systematic and logical approach to their work. Even if their approach is not totally systematic, they usually do have a sound underlying concept or rationale. It is possible that their hypothesis is totally flawed, but their approach may still be sound and logical. This latter situation is known as being on a wild goose chase, because there is almost no chance of success. The general approaches of drug discovery utilize *empirical* (i.e., trial and error), *rational* (i.e., totally planned), *random* (i.e., testing any compounds), and *serendipitous* (i.e., pure chance) methods. These four approaches are described throughout this section. Some of the methods used to discover drugs focus on the following:

Animal Models of Human Diseases

It is desirable when an animal model that yields valid data is available to use for testing compounds. Extrapolations of data obtained in *in vivo* animal tests to human patients is usually better than extrapolating *in vitro* data. Unfortunately, data obtained in most animal models are often poorly extrapolatable to human patients. Table 2.4 lists ways that *in vivo* pharmacological data obtained in animals may be extrapolated to humans or animals.

Most drugs elicit many pharmacological and biochemical effects. In many situations it is uncertain which specific properties of a drug play an essential role in providing clinical benefits. This information is important if scientists are to design and develop the most appropriate animal models to test new compounds. Issues relating to animal models are described in more detail later in this chapter.

Biological Mechanisms of Human Diseases

It may be desired to find new compounds that act similarly to a particular known drug. A specific biological mechanism may be identified that is responsible for a

Table 2.4. Uses of extrapolating in vivo *pharmacological data from animals*

A. To understand and explain the following (in animals):
   1. Effects at a physiological, biochemical, or molecular level
   2. Effects of other *in vivo* pharmacological tests
   3. Effects of *in vitro* pharmacological tests
   4. Results in toxicology tests
   5. Results in the same test under different experimental conditions (e.g., different dosages, routes of administration, test parameters, dosing regimen)
B. To understand and explain the following (in humans):
   1. Efficacy in one or more diseases
   2. Toxicity
   3. Absorption
   4. Duration of action

desired therapeutic effect. In other cases, however, the biological mechanism of a known drug may be uncertain. For example, a known antidepressant may interact with an important chemical transmitter in the brain (e.g., dopamine, norepinephrine, serotonin). Even though it is uncertain that this mechanism is the basis for the drug's action, it is hypothesized to be important. Thus, new compounds are tested to determine if they possess the same effect. If they do, then consideration of advancing them toward clinical studies is made.

Hypothetical Systems to Evaluate Compound Activity

A specific biochemical reaction in a metabolic pathway or an enzyme's activity may be hypothesized to be important in a particular disease. Even though no drugs may currently exist that act specifically on the biochemical reaction or enzyme, new chemicals are made that are directed at one of these two targets. Preclinical studies are conducted to test for the desired activity.

Targeting Compounds to Interact with Receptors

A receptor may be thought of as whatever the drug attaches to in order to cause its effect. The chemist wants to know how the receptor "sees" the potential drug molecule and where the key points are for the drug to attach to on the receptor (e.g., enzyme, cell). In this manner, when a chemist makes a small compound that is a piece of an enzyme, hormone, or other large chemical, he hopes that it will preserve the activity of the much larger molecule. This has occurred in many situations (e.g., with enkephalins).

Evaluation of Metabolites

Metabolic aspects of drugs may also serve as a source of ideas for drug discovery. Most drugs, like food, are chemically changed or metabolized inside our bodies. Although this process primarily occurs in the liver, it also takes place in the kidneys, lungs, and other organs. Although drugs are usually converted to less toxic and less effective compounds, a number of metabolites are actually more toxic or more active

METABOLIC DEGRADATION LEADING TO USEFUL NOVEL AGENTS

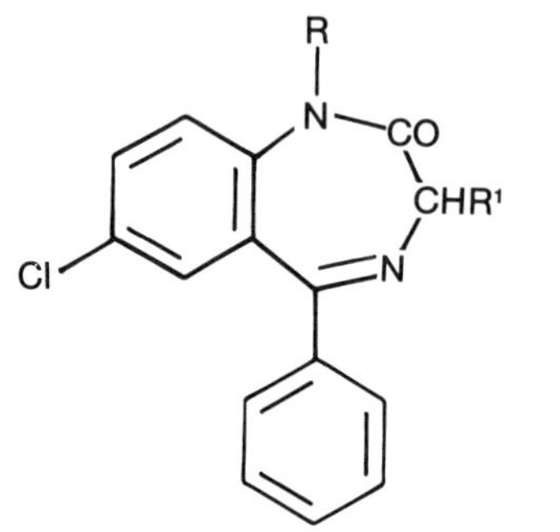

	R	R'
Diazepam	CH_3	H
↓	↓	↓
Nordiazepam	H	H
↓	↓	↓
Oxazepam	H	OH

Fig. 2.4. Metabolic degradation of diazepam leads to nordiazepam, which in turn is converted to oxazepam, each of which are useful drugs.

than the parent drug. Some metabolites may have unexpected activities. It is these unexpected activities that may make the metabolite a model for further chemical manipulation. The metabolite thus serves as a chemical lead that stimulates the chemist to synthesize new compounds.

A metabolite may have more desirable properties than the parent drug. In such situations the metabolite may also be developed as a drug (e.g., desmethylimipramine is a metabolite of imipramine and both are marketed for treatment of depression). Alternatively, the metabolite may replace the parent drug in medical therapy (e.g., acetaminophen is a metabolite of phenacetin) or the parent drug may be viewed as a prodrug that delivers the more active metabolite to the body (e.g., the prodrug 6-mercaptopurine is converted to the active metabolite 6-mercaptopurine ribonucleotide, the prodrug acyclovir is converted to the active metabolite acyclovir triphosphate). Some metabolites possess sufficient biological activity to be used as drugs. An example of this is shown in Fig. 2.4. Diazepam is metabolized to nordiazepam, which in turn is metabolized to oxazepam. Each of these metabolites was developed and marketed as a separate drug.

Using a Combination of Approaches

Two or more of the above approaches may be combined, either in the same test for a new drug, or as part of multiple biological (e.g., pharmacological) tests performed to evaluate a single drug. This topic is described in greater detail in Chapter 17 of *Guide to Clinical Interpretation of Data* (Spilker, 1986b).

Improving the Biological Profile of an Active Compound

Once a compound is found with a desired biological activity, others are made to try to optimize the beneficial activities while eliminating as many of the potentially toxic effects as possible (i.e., the chemists attempt to accentuate the positive and eliminate the negative). Although there is no relationship between the difficulty of making compounds and their biological activity, many chemists believe one of Nature's laws dictates that the most difficult compounds to make are the most active and interesting ones biologically. Another point of view is that the first compound made in a series is often the best.

One approach to designing chemicals is to create a hybrid compound that is based on two (or more) different structures that are each known to have activity. For example, if two drugs used to treat a disease act by different mechanisms, it may be possible to "marry" those two chemical structures into one molecule. It might also be possible to marry the *active* parts of those two molecules and achieve a drug that works by both mechanisms. This approach is usually unsuccessful, but there are enough successes to make it an attractive proposition to try in numerous situations.

Looking for Chemical Analogues When a New Activity is Found for a Marketed Drug

What happens when a marketed drug is found to have activity in a different disease than the one for which it is sold? Assume that the new disease was previously either untreatable or poorly treatable. Assume further that there are no adequate and widely accepted animal models that can predict activity in the new disease. What usually happens in this situation is as follows: the company whose drug this is, as well as some (or many) academicians will attempt to discern the drug's mechanism of action, i.e., how and why did the drug elicit a beneficial response in the new disease. The chances of success are small, because the actual molecular mechanism of action of most drugs is unknown. Nonetheless, theories and hypotheses are proposed to explain the activity of all drugs. There are often many theories to explain how a single drug works. Preclinical and clinical evidence is put forth in the medical literature to support or challenge each hypothesis.

If a particular hypothesis becomes widely accepted, and sometimes even if it does not, companies will establish biological tests to search for the same biological activity in other compounds. The assumption is that because the active drug has a specific biological effect, which is hypothesized to be responsible for its clinical activity, other compounds that have the same biological activity will have the same clinical effect. This scientific approach to drug discovery can be described as looking for analogues of the active drug. It was also previously described as the biological mechanism approach, but in this situation the connection between the mechanism and the clinical effect is often highly uncertain.

Companies are motivated to begin this search when an active drug has significant drawbacks. Therefore, close chemical analogues are often sought that may be more potent, less toxic, have a greater therapeutic index, or have some other desired characteristic. Once an analogue is found with the desired characteristic(s), that analogue is developed further and, if appropriate, it is studied in humans. If this analogue also possesses clinical activity and especially if the desired characteristics are found in humans (e.g., greater potency, less toxicity) it tends to strongly support, and to a degree validate, the model(s) that demonstrated better activity or less toxicity than the original drug.

Figure 2.5 illustrates a number of successful molecular manipulations that have been made in this way. Some of these required many compounds and years of effort before the improved drug was identified. The characteristics of the original drug that were improved are indicated in the figure.

Choosing the Specific Compounds to Synthesize

Figure 2.6 illustrates a sample of the enormously large number of different chemical substituents that can be placed on a simple or complex skeletal backbone. Realizing that the total number of possible changes is really the multiple of all possible changes at each point in the molecule (i.e., W possible changes at point 1, times X possible changes at point 2, times Y possible changes at point 3, times Z possible changes at point 4, etc.), it is clear that the number of different chemicals that could be synthesized based on a single, even simple, chemical structure could easily run into the hundreds of millions or billions. The basic structure shown in Fig. 2.6 is a natural product of the anthracycline group. Members of this chemical family are used as antitumor agents and antibiotics. Activities of related compounds vary by several orders of magnitude. In this particular example, substituents have been made at every possible position on the molecule.

The staggering numbers of possible compounds emphasize the need for scientific judgment in choosing which ones to synthesize. Fortunately, chemists usually have bits of information that help guide their choices so that they are not usually blindly choosing compounds to make. For example, they may know that adding certain types of chemical groups to the basic structure will raise or lower the compound's acidity or alkalinity, make the compound more (or less) soluble in water, mimic other compounds with known activity, enable the compound to resist metabolic breakdown in the body, assist in the compound's absorption, allow (or block) the compound's ability to penetrate the brain, or possess any one of numerous other physical, chemical, or biological properties. Certain parts of a chemical molecule are found to be more important than others for modifying a drug's activity or toxicity. All of this information is used when a chemist decides which compounds to synthesize.

Several chemical and physical properties can be predicted in advance by analyzing structure-activity relationships or through using sophisticated computer modeling and electronic techniques. Nonetheless, it is virtually always necessary to make each compound to determine accurately whether the theory is in fact correct. Many surprises do arise.

When two or more chemists are given the task of modifying the same drug or

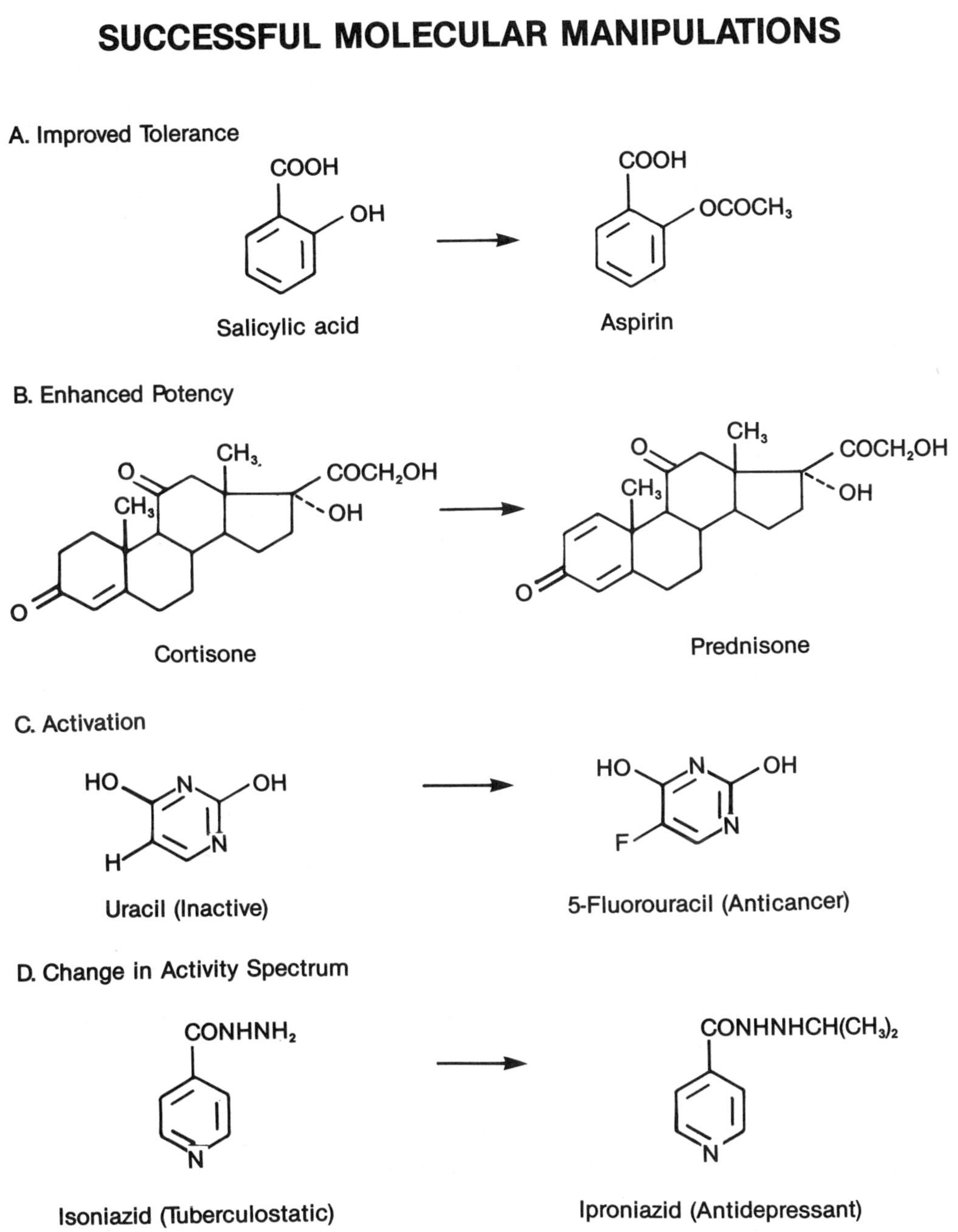

Fig. 2.5. Successful molecular manipulations leading to useful drugs. From Pletscher (1983) with permission of Raven Press.

POSSIBLE CHEMICAL MODIFICATIONS TO A CHEMICAL STRUCTURE

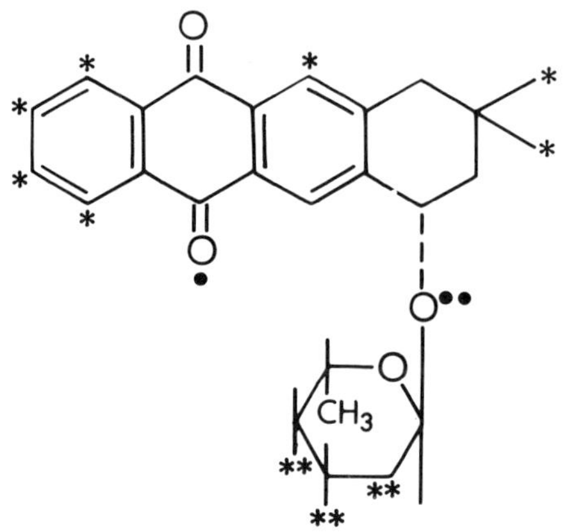

Site on Chemical	Representative Chemical Substituents to Add
*	H, OH, OCH_3, Cl, Br, I, F, NO_2 CN, OR, CH_2CH_3, $CH_2CH_2CH_3$, CF_3, CH_3, CH=CHR, $COCH_3$, $COCH_2OH$, $CO(CH_2)_nCH_3$, $CO(CH_2)_nOH$
**	H, NH_2, OH, Cl, Br, I, F, CF_3, $NHCOCH_3$, 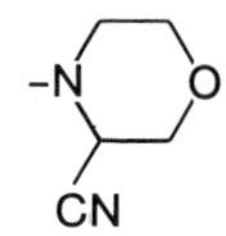 -N O CN
•	NH
• •	S, CH_2

R=Any of various other chemical groups

Fig. 2.6. Selected chemical groups that could be placed on a chemical backbone. The letter *R* stands for any chemical group.

basic molecule, they are apt to approach the problem in different directions. Alternatively, they may proceed in the same direction, but synthesize different specific compounds. Given the almost limitless number of possible variations to try, this is not surprising. On the other hand certain chemical substituents seem to capture the attention of chemists as useful pieces to attach to a basic chemical backbone. Some chemists excel at designing new compounds to make, whereas others are more skillful in solving technical problems that occur in actually making new compounds.

Structure-Activity Relationships

A minor chemical change on a molecule sometimes leads to major changes in biological activity, while at other times a major chemical change has little or no affect on biological activity. The relationship between chemical structures and a biological activity that the chemicals elicit is called a structure-activity relationship (SAR). If minor chemical changes lead to major differences in pharmacological activity, it usually means that a lot of chemical work is necessary to fully characterize the SAR.

Figure 2.7 illustrates a series of structure-activity relationships for a hypothetical series of compounds. The vertical axis of biological activity refers to any pharmacological or other biological endpoint measured. The horizontal axis illustrates a property of the chemical compounds in the particular series being evaluated. Figure 2.7 panel A illustrates 10 compounds from any chemical series where the structures differ only in length of one particular chain of atoms. Six of many possible SARs

STRUCTURE-ACTIVITY RELATIONSHIPS

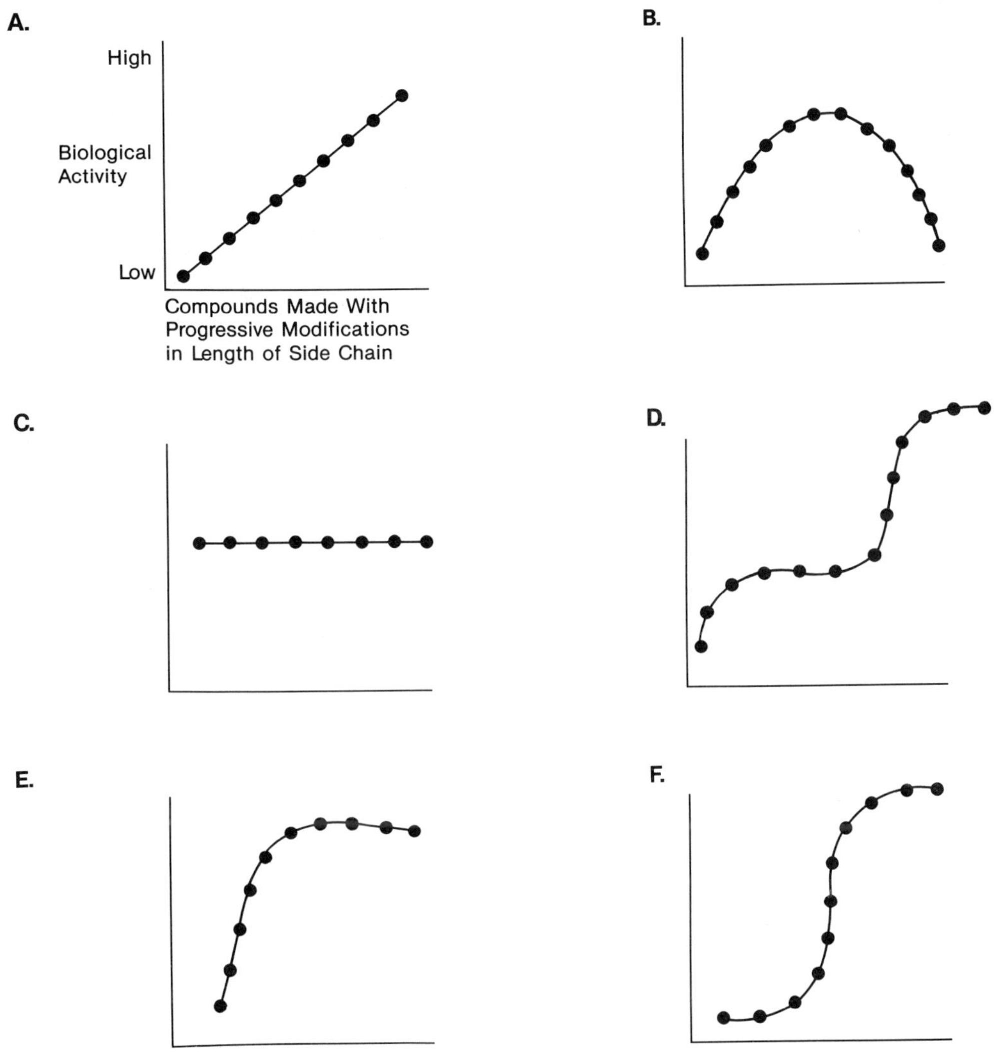

Fig. 2.7. Types of alterations in biological activity that may be observed in a series of closely related compounds with a single chemical modification. Each dot represents a single successive change (e.g., increasing the length of a side chain on the molecule).

are illustrated in panels A to F. Figure 2.8 illustrates an SAR pattern when the situation illustrated in Fig. 2.7, panel A, is modified so that changes are now occurring at different places on the chemical molecule. Individual chemicals are illustrated as dots in Figs. 2.7 and 2.8. SARs usually demonstrate more discontinuity than shown in either Figs. 2.7 or 2.8.

Many other chemical parameters beside chain length could be evaluated for their

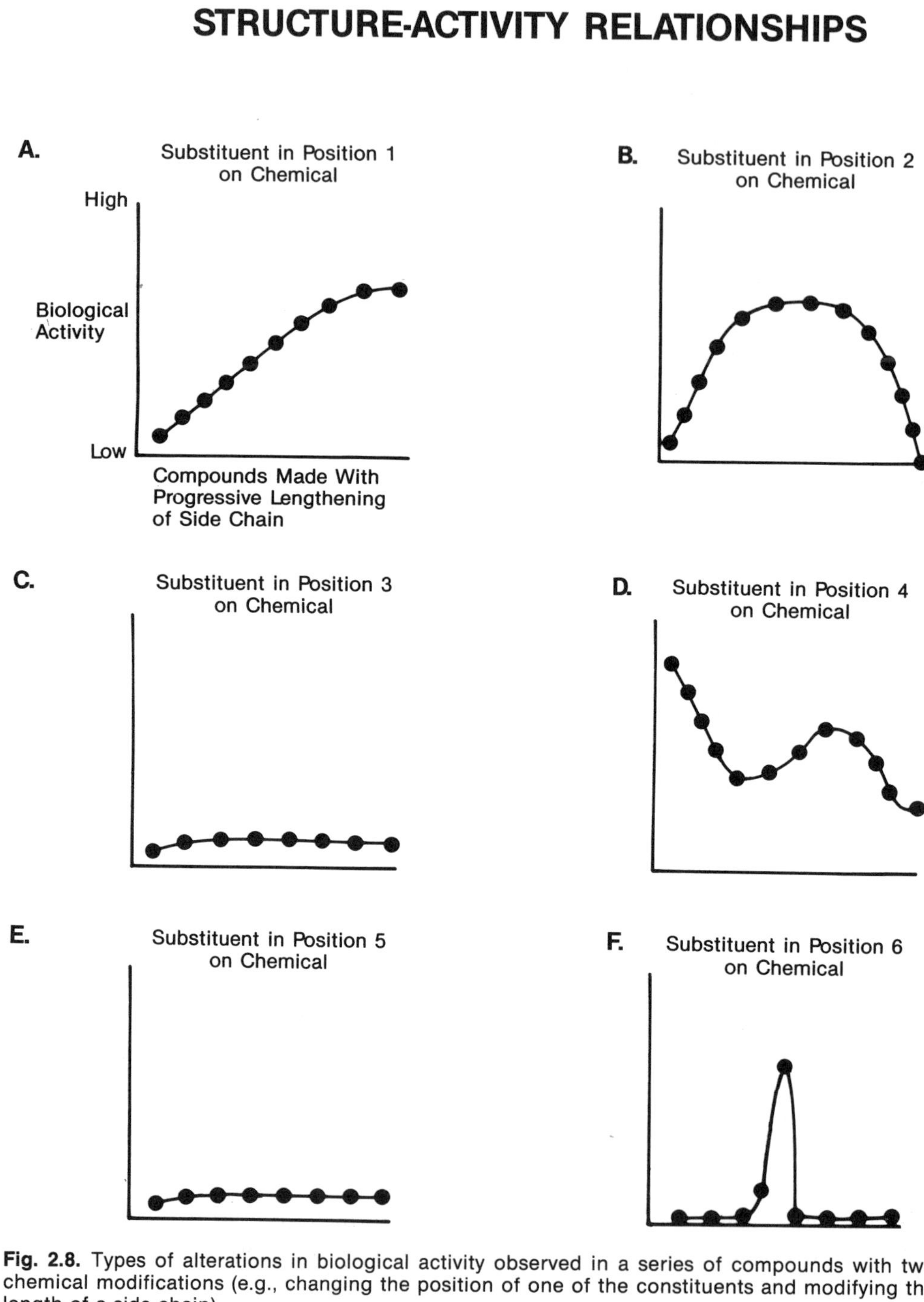

Fig. 2.8. Types of alterations in biological activity observed in a series of compounds with two chemical modifications (e.g., changing the position of one of the constituents and modifying the length of a side chain).

STRUCTURE-ACTIVITY RELATIONSHIPS

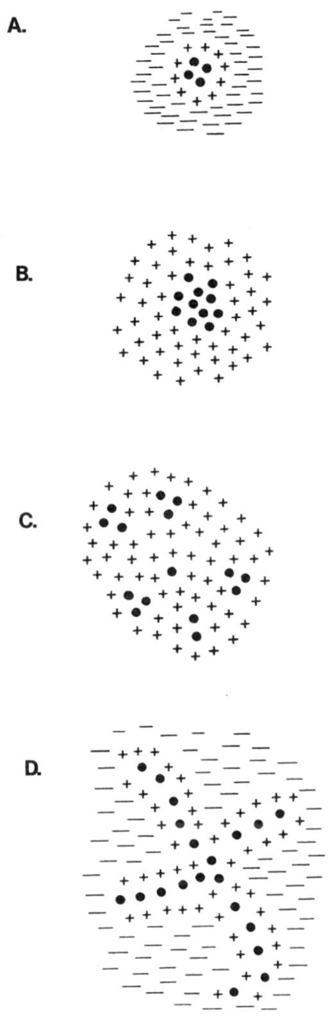

Fig. 2.9. Scope of biological activity in compounds with modified structures. Each circle and plus or minus symbol represents the overall biological activity of a single chemical in a related series. Panel A illustrates high activity in four closely related compounds, (•), lesser activity (i.e., fair to good) (+) in a group resembling them, and no activity (−) in all other variations made. Patent protection is relatively easy for this group. Panel B illustrates a situation where a wide variety of compounds are active though the best activity resides in a single group of closely related compounds. Panel C shows excellent activity in several groups of compounds with different structures. It will generally be more difficult to patent these compounds unless all groups are known. Panel D represents a series of highly active compounds that once defined may be patented. The compound in the center represents the index compound. Those further away have progressively more modifications.

influence on a specific biological activity. These parameters include basicity, acidity, lipophilicity, size of molecule, shape of molecule, and ability of the molecule to bind or dissociate. Chemists often do not change only one parameter at a time. Actual SARs are more complex when multiple parameters differ between chemically related compounds, which makes the interpretation of SARs more difficult.

When a patent application is submitted for a chemically related group of compounds, it is desirable to have identified the most active compounds. Figure 2.9 illustrates four of many possible situations that refer to this issue. Each symbol represents the overall biological activity of a different chemical. This figure is drawn in two dimensions, but is a schematic of a three-dimensional axis where three of the most important chemical parameters influencing biological activity are plotted. Panel

A illustrates the best patentable situation from a chemical perspective because there is a clear delineation between active and inactive compounds. Panels B and C provide a good patentable situation to make a broad claim, but it is important to know where inactive compounds begin. Panel D illustrates a situation where it would be difficult to make a good patent claim unless one had made all of the compounds where activity resided. Otherwise, competitors could make and patent related compounds with the likelihood of detecting good biological activity. An example of this situation is illustrated later in this chapter for antihistamines (see "Examples of Success Stories").

Basic Questions to Ask about New Compounds

There are numerous pertinent questions that chemists (and biologists) often ask about new compounds.

1. How reproducible are the biological data obtained?
2. What is the physiological significance of the specific biological activity measured in animals?
3. What is the projected clinical significance of the biological effects measured in animals? Some biologists may not have already asked and answered this question.
4. If predicted biological effects are not observed, how can that information be interpreted and used to best advantage?
5. Is there a correlation between observed biological effects and the structures of the chemicals made (i.e., is there a structure-activity relationship)? This is a crucial issue in the drug discovery process.

The information in this chapter hopefully points out that drug discovery is not a process of someone suddenly shouting "eureka." Instead, it is a gradual step-by-step improvement in activity and decrease of toxicity, involving the commitment of many people. Progress often seems to be a question of three steps forward and two steps backward. Eventually it is hoped that a compound with an acceptable biological profile will be found that may be developed into a drug.

Identifying Backup Candidates

A backup candidate is a compound that may replace the drug currently being developed (or one that is on the market) if it encounters serious problems (e.g., toxicity, lack of effect) and work must be terminated (or the drug must be withdrawn from the market). Backup compounds should have one or more clinically important advantages over the initial drug, which could be used by marketing people to position and sell the drug.

It is almost always important for a company to search for one or more backup compounds for several reasons:

1. The first drug may fail for reasons that might not cause the backup compound to fail.
2. The backup may have desirable characteristics not found in the first and could thus be marketed as an improvement—or a second generation drug.

3. The backup might have a better patent life than the original drug.
4. The backup could compete with the first drug and possibly enlarge the total market, or at the minimum make it difficult for other competitors to enter the market.
5. The backup could be licensed to another company.

Examples of Success Stories

Smith Kline & French Laboratories developed burimamide for duodenal ulcers, but terminated its development because of insufficient potency and a relative lack of oral activity. They then developed a backup compound metiamide, but this drug was terminated because of some cases of agranulocytosis. They developed a third compound, cimetidine (Tagamet), which was launched and became the most commercially successful drug in the world for a number of years. The chemical differences between these three drugs and their predecessors are shown in Fig. 2.10. Other companies started developing antihistamine type-2 drugs and found that similar chemical structures still retained biological activity (Fig. 2.11), but allowed new patents to be obtained. Whereas Smith Kline & French Laboratories used an imidazole ring structure, which they considered important for activity, other companies found that different chemical ring systems could also be used.

A similar case can be described for the beta-receptor blocking drugs of ICI Holdings Ltd. (Imperial Chemical Industries). Their first drug, dichloroisoproterenol, was followed by pronethalol and finally by propranolol (Fig. 2.12). The chemical differences between the drugs in each series described is not great, but the medical and commercial differences between them is astronomical.

SELECTED RESEARCH ISSUES PRESENTED IN GREATER DEPTH

Molecular Modeling Tools to Help Design Better Drugs

Molecular modeling techniques utilize computers to help design chemical structures of compounds that should be able to bind to their target (i.e., receptor). Sometimes these tools are also able to predict whether the compound will bind or attach to the target, and how well it will bind. A great deal of knowledge about the structure of enzyme is needed to use this sophisticated approach, and in most therapeutic areas this approach cannot currently be used because of a lack of this knowledge. It has been stated informally that these techniques were used to aid in the drug design process for certain angiotensin-converting enzyme inhibitors. The situation regarding molecular modeling is changing rapidly and a future hope is that predictions of biological events may be made based on changes in a compound's molecular structure.

Molecular modeling techniques involve determining X-ray structures of an enzyme and using computer graphics to convert this to a molecular image. This process stimulates chemists to design or modify a molecule by adding side chains or altering the constituents in a theoretical way. A computer is then used to predict how those changes will affect the compound's physical and chemical properties. The compound may then be synthesized and its binding to receptors measured in different systems

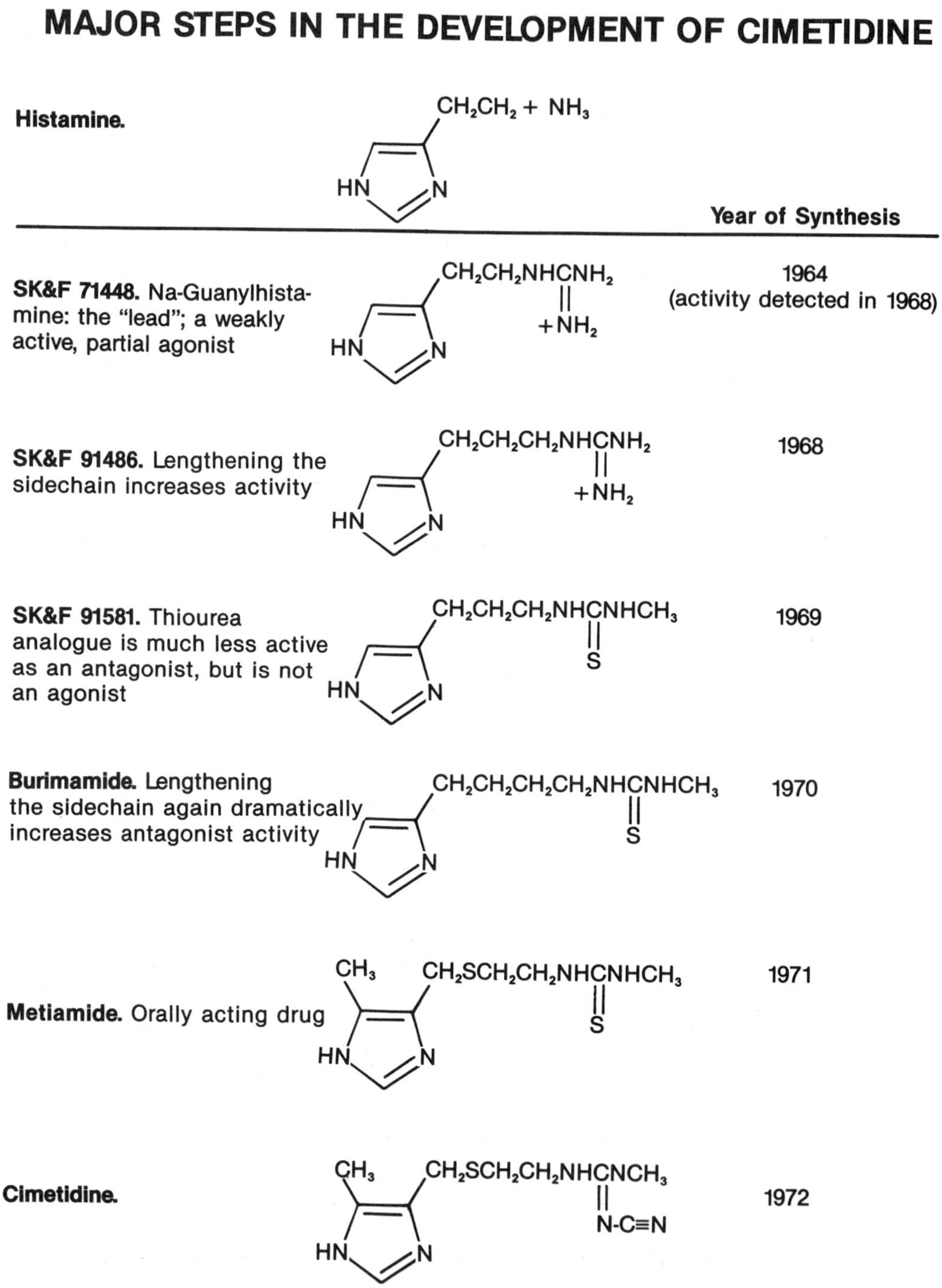

Fig. 2.10. Progressive improvements in histamine type-2 receptor antagonists. Compounds were all made by Smith Kline & French Laboratories and were modeled after histamine. Data obtained primarily from Duncan and Parsons (1980). The year of cimetidine's original synthesis was kindly supplied by Dr. Anthony Flind of Smith Kline & French Laboratories (United Kingdom).

HISTAMINE RECEPTOR TYPE 2 ANTAGONISTS

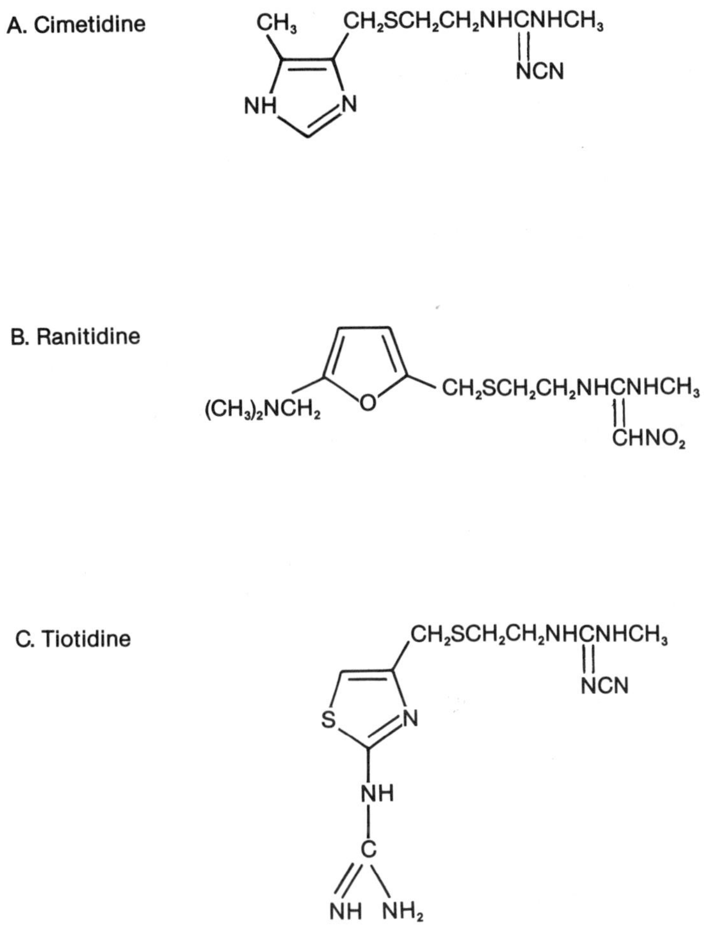

Fig. 2.11. Histamine receptor type-2 antagonists developed after cimetidine, which were able to be patented. Ranitidine is made by Glaxo Inc. and tiotidine by ICI Holdings.

to evaluate the accuracy of the original predictions. Even accurate predictions do not guarantee positive results in humans, because the wrong target may have been chosen or the actual target may be a combination of several enzymes or it may consist of other structures. It is usually not possible to determine the influence of a particular enzyme in affecting the course of a particular disease. These considerations indicate why imagination, creativity, and a certain degree of luck are necessary to achieve major advances in discovering drugs.

Is Drug Discovery a Rational Process?

Well, partly. It is currently fashionable to claim that drug discovery is evolving, or according to some, has evolved to a rational state. This latter statement is untrue

BETA RECEPTOR ANTAGONISTS

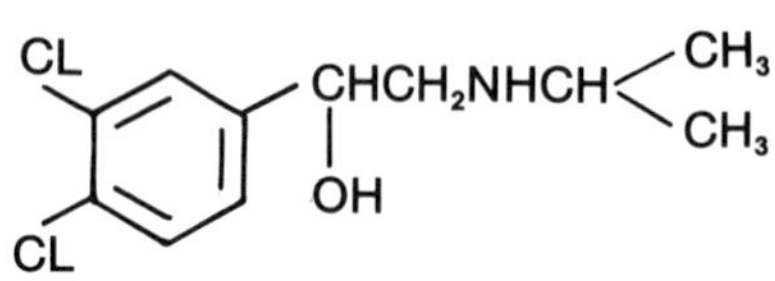

Dichloroisoproterenol

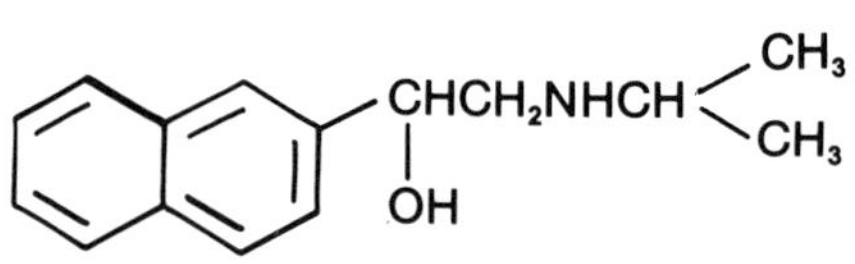

Pronethalol

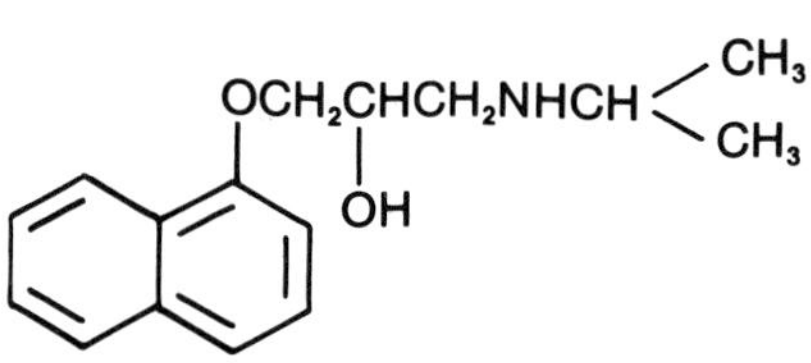

Propranolol

Fig. 2.12. Progressive improvements in the early development of beta-receptor antagonists.

and the former possibility ("is evolving") is partly true. Even when important biological activity is uncovered as a result of rational concepts, it is still the old empirical trial and error approach that is used to evaluate additional compounds and to select the best compound to test in humans.

The more pertinent issue is really how can drug discovery become a more rational process? The answer to this question must depend on development of newer technologies and experimental tools. With currently available methods the possibilities of utilizing a rational approach to discover new drugs are quite limited. Rational concepts may provide a starting point, but on their own they cannot lead to discovery of a satisfactory new drug. In addition to the process of trial and error, serendipity is still an important element in discovering a new drug or a new use for a marketed drug.

The way a research question is posed is essential to how experiments are designed and conducted. For example, if one asks "Why do platelets sometimes stick to the wall of patient's diseased arteries?" it will lead scientists in a different direction when designing experiments than if one asks "Why do platelets not stick to the walls of healthy people's arteries?" This point is to indicate that creative scientists may approach a standard problem in a nonstandard way and attain a solution that has eluded others. Many aspects of such novel approaches are described in the book *The Use of Lateral Thinking* (de Bono, 1967) and in his other books.

Gradient from Targeted to Exploratory Research

Almost all research in drug companies may be called targeted because with few exceptions, research may be associated with a particular disease or medical problem. Nonetheless, there is a gradient of research from that which is oriented toward discovering a new drug to that which is exploratory and far from the paths of traditional drug discovery (Fig. 2.13). In the more targeted discovery areas are those experiments and studies where new or known compounds are being screened for a biological activity, or improved animal testing methods are being developed. Research into a specific activity attempting to find a target that can be used to discover drugs is an intermediate stage, as are studies evaluating a hypothesis that if proven, could be used as a basis for drug discovery. Toward the more exploratory end of this spectrum are studies evaluating a hypothesis that will not directly relate to drug discovery. The connection of this type of exploratory research to new drug discovery

SPECTRUM OF RESEARCH ACTIVITIES IN A DRUG COMPANY

- Purely targeted "applied research"
- Work conducted solely for drug discovery or development
- Screening or evaluating compounds as potential drugs
- Developing improved biological or analytical methodologies to test compounds
- Evaluating potential targets to use for future screening and/or evaluation of compounds
- Evaluating hypotheses that probably will help in drug discovery activities
- Conducting research or evaluating a hypothesis that probably will not help in drug discovery activities
- Research without connections to drug discovery or development
- Purely exploratory "basic research"

Fig. 2.13. Spectrum of research activities in a drug company ranging from purely targeted to purely exploratory.

is usually remote and is generally viewed as having more long-term potential benefits to a company.

There is a widespread belief both inside and outside drug companies that most new breakthrough drugs will come from more exploratory types of research. The truth of this view is debatable, because there are also examples of major breakthrough drugs coming from evaluating hypotheses much closer to the targeted end of the spectrum (e.g., inhibition of histamine receptors in the stomach to decrease gastric acid and improve the clinical status of patients with peptic ulcers). This topic is often discussed using the terms basic research and applied research discussed earlier in this chapter.

Is There a Long-Term Future for the Empirical Approach to Drug Discovery?

There is no doubt that the empirical approach will always play a major role in discovering new drugs. The empirical approach, as differentiated from the rational, random, and serendipitous approaches to drug discovery, involves taking a theory or a chemical lead compound and going back and forth between the chemist and biologist in a feedback loop to explore and develop means of improving the compound's beneficial effects and decreasing the toxic effects. This is primarily done by making new compounds to test.

Many, if not most, chemicals that are part of our body are presently either unknown or poorly characterized. After the chemical identity and biological function of additional compounds become known, they are likely to provide a model for chemists to use when synthesizing mimics and antagonists. Biologists in various disciplines (e.g., pharmacology, biochemistry, virology) will develop new screens to test these compounds for appropriate activities. This empirical approach to drug discovery is the major approach currently used to discover new drugs at research-based drug companies.

Empirical testing will always remain an important cornerstone in drug discovery for a number of reasons. First, new scientific breakthroughs in many areas will indicate (1) certain chemical series that should be explored, (2) new biological processes to exploit, (3) new metabolic routes to influence, (4) new viruses to attack, and so forth in attempts to discover new drugs. It is naive to think that human knowledge will ever be so thorough that humans can *a priori* derive the most appropriate molecule from computer-generated information and that this molecule will turn out to be the best compound of a series to develop as a drug. Second, new chemicals are constantly being synthesized for a specific test of a particular type of biological activity. It is certain that companies will always desire to maximize their potential for drug discovery from each compound made. This means empirically testing it in a number of other test systems where there is a reasonable chance that it could demonstrate activity. This latter approach would therefore be an empirical and not a random test of the drug.

Use of Animal Models in Drug Discovery and Development

Purposes and Types of Animal Models

Animal models are used to evaluate compounds for potential efficacy and safety in humans. In some therapeutic areas models generally have great predictability for efficacy in humans (e.g., anti-infectives), whereas the predictability in other therapeutic areas is weak (e.g., compounds affecting the central nervous system). The predictability for safety also varies. In addition to providing data that may be extrapolated to humans, animal models help scientists investigate the etiology, progression, and prevention of the disease process. Animal models may use normal cells, tissues, organs, or entire organisms. Some animal models evaluate one time point in the progression of a disease (e.g., many *in vitro* tests in which a tissue is removed at a specific time after the animal is pretreated or affected in a desired manner). Other models mimic the entire progression of the disease (e.g., Japanese quail model of atherosclerosis which progresses to a fatal myocardial infarction in 60 to 80 percent of the animals at approximately nine months).

Animal models used to evaluate drugs may be described as belonging to one of three categories.

1. *Spontaneous models* An animal model has a natural or spontaneously developed characteristic of interest to study or evaluate (e.g., Syrian hamsters with spontaneous congestive heart failure).
2. *Experimental models* An animal model has an experimentally induced change to create characteristics of interest to study or evaluate (e.g., anesthetized dogs treated with propranolol to create heart failure).
3. *Normal models* An animal model is a normal counterpart of the disease state in humans (e.g., normal papillary muscles are used to measure contractions of heart tissue).

Few animal models, if any, are exact duplicates of human disease. Scientists usually attempt to create models that are as close as possible to the clinical situation. There are many reasons for the inability to create exact models, including incomplete knowledge of most diseases, the highly complex nature of many diseases, and technical difficulties in creating complex models. Animal models must be compared with the human situation in regard to the lesion or condition that is created and the predictability of the data that the model yields. It is clearly the latter consideration that is of primary importance, because a pathologically lesioned animal that exactly mimics human disease but provides spurious or inconsistent results is of little predictive value. Reasons for poorly predictive models of this type may relate to differences in absorption, distribution, metabolism, or excretion between species.

Although most animal tests are imperfect models of human disease, some models mimic human disease more closely than others. For example, spontaneously hypertensive rats are a better model of hypertension than merely injecting a normotensive animal acutely with a drug to raise its blood pressure. Animals that are normotensive yield relatively poor data about antihypertensive effects of drugs compared with data obtained in hypertensive animals. It is preferable to select compounds for initial testing in humans based on the most predictive models available.

Establishing and Validating a New Animal Model

It is important to develop a list of both required and desired characteristics for a new model. Required characteristics should include both aspects that must be present and those that must be absent.

Characteristics that are often required of new animal models are the ability to (1) yield predictive data for humans, (2) obtain statistically treatable data, (3) conduct a certain number of tests that can be performed each day, week, or month, (4) demonstrate activity of treatments that work in humans with an acceptable rate of false positive and negative responses, (5) utilize a given (i.e., minimum) amount of compound per test, and (6) cost no more than a specified amount per test. Desirable characteristics include the ability to obtain (1) objective data that may be tested statistically, (2) a dose-response relationship, (3) a preliminary estimate of toxicity, (4) reproducible results from experiment to experiment, (5) an indication of the duration of effect, (6) data that are relevant to study both cause and treatment of a specific disease, (7) a similarity of symptoms in the model and humans, and (8) underlying pathology, physiology, and biochemistry that are similar in animals and humans. The model should be able to be reproduced by other investigators. Required characteristics for some models would only be desirable characteristics for other models (and vice versa).

There are several ways in which a new animal model can be validated. These potentially include utilizing techniques from all biological disciplines, including histology, pathology, physiology, pharmacology, biochemistry, immunology, virology, and microbiology. In most cases, utilizing techniques of multiple disciplines will more firmly establish the model as valid. Within each discipline, numerous techniques may be applied. The use of multiple techniques will generally yield more convincing data than a single test and will help validate the model. One specific method to validate animal models as predictors of human efficacy data is to evaluate a series of different drugs in an animal test and to compare the relative potencies with data derived in human studies.

In some diseases such as Alzheimer it is virtually impossible to validate animal models until at least one drug is clearly shown to be active. If an animal test showed that specific drug to be active, but all others to be inactive, then that result would be an important step toward validation of the model.

Developing a Battery of Animal Models and Tests to Evaluate Compounds

There are no perfect animal models that provide all of the data required to determine if a given compound will be effective in humans. In addition to providing efficacy data, animal models must be used to derive safety and other types of data. Thus, a wide variety of animal models must be used. The pros and cons for each must be understood to interpret the data in a meaningful way.

In developing multiple tests, it is possible to use them in different ways, depending on the purpose(s) of the models and the nature of the scientific or therapeutic area being studied. Figure 2.14 illustrates five common patterns. In this figure each box represents a separate test and may yield different types of data. Each test may also be conducted with techniques of multiple scientific disciplines. Boxes may represent different animal models or the same model with different conditions or objectives (e.g., to obtain effects of a single dose or a dose-response relationship). Panel A illustrates a simple sequential ordering of models, whereas panel B illustrates a

REPRESENTATIVE TYPES OF BATTERIES OF ANIMAL TESTS

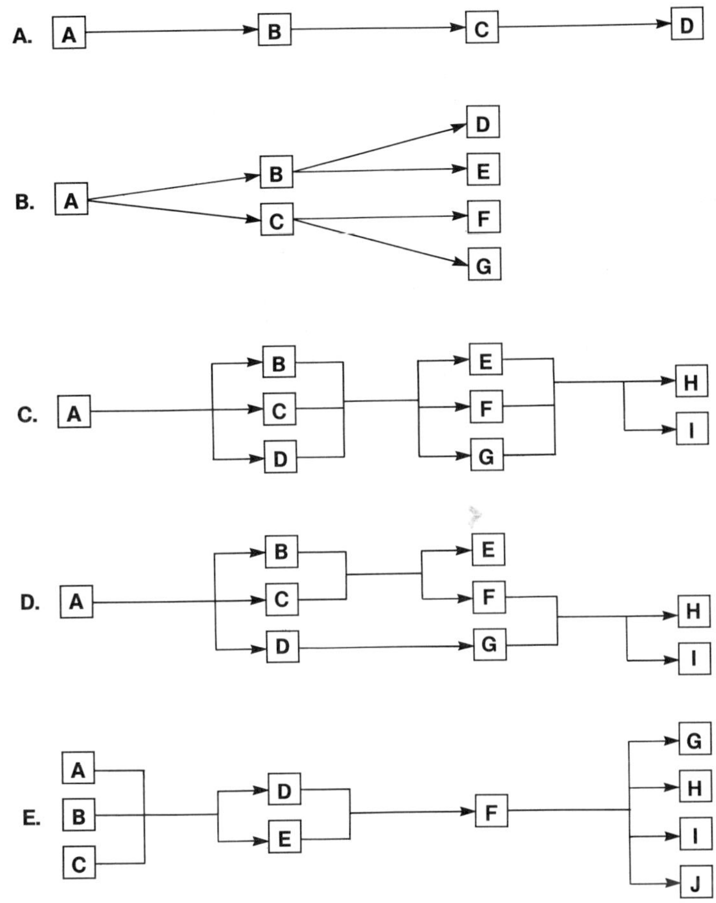

Fig. 2.14. Hypothetical formats for organizing multiple animal models and tests to screen for and study drug activity. Each letter represents a separate model or test.

pyramid type of ordering. Panels C, D, and E illustrate more complex patterns, and are the more usual systems used by pharmacology departments in the drug industry. Each system is used to screen and/or evaluate properties of drugs in a given therapeutic area or with a specific targeted objective.

When multiple animal models are used, there is a tendency in some therapeutic areas to initially use more broad screens and to progress to those that evaluate more specific biological questions (e.g., evaluating antibacterials). In other therapeutic areas or for other reasons, specific biological activity is screened for initially (e.g., when a specific biochemical activity is desired). Some animal models are highly selective for determining activity of compounds that act via a single specific mechanism, and others will show activity for compounds acting via any one of many mechanisms.

APPROACHES TO DRUG DEVELOPMENT

Nature of Drug Development

Drug development is the second major function of research and development groups. Drug discovery is the first function. Development is defined differently in different situations. It may specifically refer to technical aspects of chemical scaleup, analytical analysis of material, and pharmaceutical development of a dosage form and formulation. Alternatively, or in addition, the term development may refer to the entire process of taking a newly discovered compound through regulatory approval and to the point of marketing (Fig. 2.15). This broad definition is used in this book. Many aspects of drug development are described in other chapters (e.g., technical development, clinical studies, matrix concepts). A few additional points are presented below.

The importance of adhering to high standards in the conduct, analysis, and interpretation of all preclinical and clinical studies must be stressed. Poorly planned or conceived studies will often raise questions that will be difficult to explain. Such studies are shortsighted, as it may take many months or years plus valuable resources to sort out the details and explain problems that did not have to arise in the first place. In addition, the data they generate will generally delay important regulatory submissions.

How Does a Company Decide Which Compounds to Develop as Drugs?

The simplest answer to this question, and also one that has a lot of truth, is that written or unwritten criteria are established (or should be established) for all research efforts directed at discovering a new drug. When a chemical compound is found that meets these criteria, then it is (usually) developed as a drug. The compound continues to be developed until events demonstrate that some of the criteria (primarily of safety and efficacy) cannot be met and that a medically and commercially viable drug is no longer likely or possible to achieve.

Because research programs in one therapeutic area may lead to a compound that has activity in another area, carefully developed criteria are not always present when a new direction in a drug's development is debated. Considerations include determining how the compound fits into the company's strategies and portfolio for current and future drug development. This includes evaluation of old product line-extensions, entrance into new product lines, perceived medical need, perceived commercial gains, plus the patent situation on the new compound.

In addition to the company's basic strategies, there are issues about resources necessary to test and develop a new drug. Will it be relatively straightforward to evaluate the drug's efficacy, as with a diuretic or neuromuscular blocking agent, or will it be much more complex and expensive, as with an antipsychotic. Is the path to regulatory approval different than with an "average" drug? For instance, chemical classes of drugs with toxicity known to be greater than that of others in the same therapeutic class are not looked on favorably by regulatory authorities. In addition, each regulatory agency may require different types and degrees of proof of efficacy.

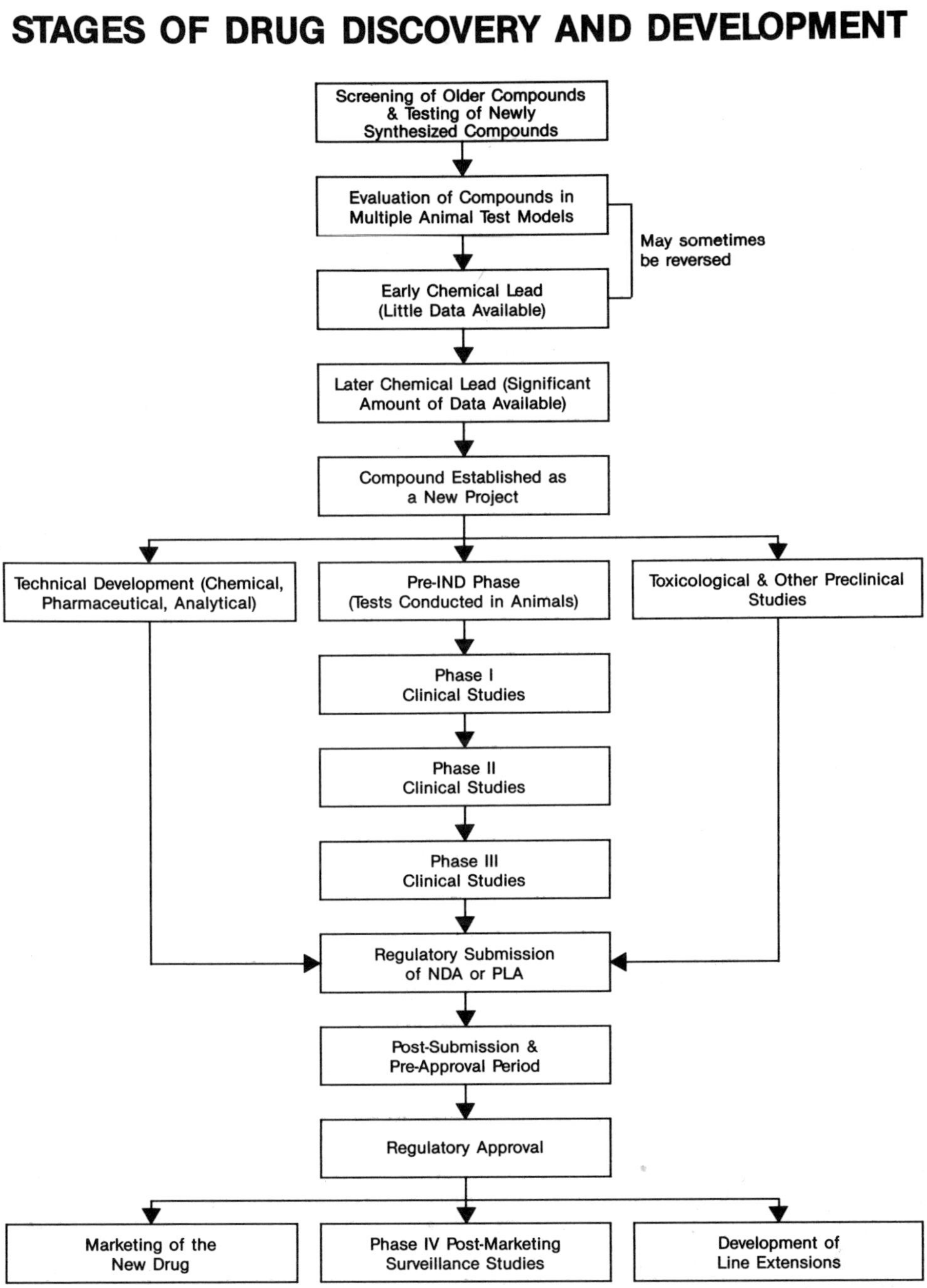

Fig. 2.15. Stages of drug discovery and development. Various feedback loops exist in this diagram, especially during the initial stages of drug discovery.

Table 2.5. Research and development criteria to evaluate a new compound for potential development as a drug[a]

1.	Likelihood of technical success
2.	Estimated time to develop the drug to NDA[b]
3.	Time to reach a go-no go decision[c]
4.	Anticipated technical development problems (e.g., stability of the product)
5.	Availability in desired dosage forms
6.	Presence of skills to develop the drug
7.	Degree of medical need for the type of drug
8.	Medical advantages of the drug compared with alternative therapies
9.	Actual or potential restrictions on the drug's use
10.	Cost to develop in comparison to anticipated third year sales or profits. May be calculated in terms of time to pay back the investment
11.	Number of potential indications
12.	Any known limitations or problems not covered above

[a] A number of additional criteria are described in the text.
[b] NDA, New Drug Application.
[c] This point usually occurs during Phase II.

This will tend to make a drug's development far more complex and costly for one country than for another.

Depending on the answers to these (and other) questions and criteria (Table 2.5), the company may decide to go all out, to go ahead with a limited program, to develop the drug only for certain countries, to license the drug to another company, or to take a different course of action.

Master Development Plan

Some companies prepare a comprehensive plan for a drug's development at the outset of the project formation. This usually occurs from one to two years before the drug is evaluated in humans for totally new drugs and approximately six months to one year for drugs that have already been evaluated in patients in other countries. The same times generally apply for drugs licensed-in from other companies. This master plan is put together by the project leader or manager and becomes a "bible" for many companies to follow. This document may be organized in any way a company desires or the format may be left to the author's discretion.

One approach is to present the plan in three separate parts. The first part includes preclinical activities from project initiation until early Phase II studies. This contains the background information nominating the compound for project status and discusses the pharmacology and toxicology programs. Alternatively, the compound may be proposed for project status in a prior document that focuses on the scientific, medical, and marketing rationales. A clinical feasibility section is included either in this part or as a separate document. Tables 1.1 to 1.3 in *Guide to Planning and Managing Multiple Clinical Studies* (Spilker, 1987c) illustrate three examples of table of contents of a clinical feasibility report.

Part Two covers the period from initial regulatory submission (e.g., Investigational New Drug Application [IND]) to the end of Phase II. This part contains the plan for metabolic studies, toxicology, regulatory affairs, chemical scaleup, supply sourcing, formulation, and clinical plan. The development of a product profile is considered, as are target dates for any end-of-Phase II meeting within the company or at the Food and Drug Administration (FDA). This part of the master plan may not be able to be written as soon as the first part, but should be completed prior to the initial regulatory submission. The clinical development plan may include consideration of alternative paths, depending on results of pilot studies. For example, if one study shows the drug to be effective and also toxic, plans may be developed to study lower doses. If the drug is found ineffective and safe, plans may be proposed to study different patient populations with the same disease who may be more sensitive to the drug, or to initiate new pilot studies in different diseases.

A go-no go decision point occurs in the development of many drugs toward the end of Phase II. At that point a sufficient amount of clinical efficacy and safety data are available to evaluate and the likelihood of the drug's going to a New Drug Application (NDA) is assessed. If this probability is relatively high, it provides the impetus to commit company resources necessary for large scale Phase III studies. There are certainly a few instances when such funds and an all-out development effort are appropriate to initiate before proof of efficacy is obtained. But, this decision should be made with full cognizance of the financial risks involved, as well as the awareness of which other drug development activities may be slowed or not pursued at all.

Part Three covers the period from mid-Phase II to registration filings. This part often contains a draft of the package insert, dosage forms to be developed, other aspects of technical development, details of manufacturing including location, data processing, registration plans, support functions, required clinical studies by country, specialized studies, and discussion of which expert opinions are required. Input on this section is required from all clinical and technical groups. This part may not be possible to write in detail until after the drug has entered or even completed Phase II studies.

Determining the Appropriate Scope of a Drug Development Plan

A preclinical and clinical program of appropriate and well-designed studies may be planned to address all appropriate issues. A company may attempt to do this by developing a plan that emphasizes any desired approach varying from a *lean* one that eliminates all studies that are not absolutely essential to a *fat* approach that includes all possible considerations and studies. If the approach chosen is too lean and incomplete, it may not achieve regulatory approval in some or all of the target countries. A plan that is far in excess of what is regulatorily necessary would not only take extra years to complete, but would generate excessive data that would require additional time for processing, analysis, and interpretation.

How may a company know that it has an appropriate balance between these extremes? In many cases the answer is difficult. But, there are some principles to follow. First, determine if it would be reasonable to conduct any of the clinical studies after the drug is marketed. Second, determine what would be lost if each study on the list were deleted. Which studies are mandatory to conduct? Third, review the size of each study with a statistician. Could any be abbreviated? Fourth, discuss the clinical plan in detail with the FDA and/or other regulatory authorities. Additional steps might be (1) to evaluate the number and nature of studies conducted on recently approved drugs of the same type, (2) to discuss the issue with knowledgeable consultants, or (3) to develop alternative stepwise plans.

The master plan must distinguish between studies that are nice or desirable to conduct and those that are necessary to conduct. This principle applies to clinical, toxicological, metabolic, pharmacokinetic, and other categories of studies. The distinction between these two types of studies often changes during a drug's development. Even though the master plan represents the blueprint of a drug's development, the plans must frequently be reassessed and necessary changes made.

Establishing Criteria for a Drug's Performance during Its Development

Compounds that have achieved the criteria established during the drug discovery period are advanced into drug development. Even if clear criteria have not been established preclinically during the discovery period, it is important to set criteria during drug development. This is primarily to know when the drug's development should be terminated.

Criteria established at an early stage of development to judge each drug's future performance should include medical, technical, and commercial considerations. If the drug falls below or otherwise fails to meet these standards, then its termination should be considered. This does not mean that a company would not develop one or more orphan drugs where there is little hope of ever repaying their development costs. However, it does mean that appropriate standards should be established for orphan drugs, just as for other drugs. Thus, the company's management would agree to accept lower minimal medical and/or commercial standards for some drugs. If medical and/or commercial criteria are established, a project's termination would be expedited if the drug's characteristics demonstrated that the minimally acceptable criteria could not be met.

The criteria used to determine whether a drug passes the go-no go decision point in Phase II may be set to a particularly high or low standard. This is often desirable from a marketing viewpoint. For example, the marketing group may believe they do not want to sell a drug unless it is sensational medically, or they may believe that it is desirable to have the drug available for sale, even if it is not as effective or safe as the medical staff and managers hope it will be.

An important new drug with great medical value is of limited commercial benefit to a company if actual sales are small or modest. But this type of drug often provides numerous other benefits to a company (e.g., enhanced reputation, improved access to physicians by sales representatives). The company's overall reactions to this type of drug as well as others depends to a large degree on their original expectations. These expectations relate in many ways to the criteria established for the drug's development.

Transfer of a Project from Preclinical to Clinical Development and from Clinical Development to Marketing and Production

The project team that oversees development activities during preclinical and clinical periods is usually similar, although representatives are usually added during the

Table 2.6. Activities performed on marketed drugs in research departments[a]

A. Any research department
   1. Additional evaluation of the drug's mechanism of action
   2. Training of sales representatives
   3. Support marketing, medical, legal, production, and other departments with information
   4. Participate in writing and reviewing promotional materials
   5. Participate in writing and reviewing technical materials for compendia (e.g., *United States Pharmacopeia*)
   6. Answer telephone calls and written requests for relevant information

B. Organic chemistry
   1. Synthesis of additional compounds for patent protection of marketed drugs. Important structural relatives of marketed drugs must be made to protect drugs from the inevitable intense research conducted in the same chemical areas by competitors as well as to seek successor drugs

C. Medicinal biochemistry
   1. Measure drug concentrations in samples obtained in clinical studies that are evaluating new indications
   2. Conduct biochemical or metabolic studies to evaluate the basis for adverse reactions
   3. Monitor drug concentrations in life-threatening situations
   4. Refine and report on assay methodologies that may be used by outside laboratories
   5. Participate in interlaboratory validation of methods
   6. Expand data base in specific patient populations, (e.g., neonates)
   7. Conduct studies to help develop new formulations

D. Pharmacology
   1. Investigation of drug–drug interactions that are reported in the literature or to the company
   2. Investigation of a newly found therapeutic indication

E. Toxicology
   1. Carcinogenicity or other toxicological studies dictated by clinical effects observed before or after marketing
   2. Limited toxicology on new formulations

F. Other departments
   1. Assay of clinical samples of patients participating in clinical studies, especially in pursuit of added indications
   2. Assay of samples from nonstudy patients treated with the drug
   3. Assistance to outside laboratories in setting up assays
   4. Pharmacokinetic studies in special patient groups (e.g., dialysis patients)
   5. Computer assistance for analysis of assay data collected by other labs
   6. Resistance studies

[a] Defined as preclinical departments not primarily concerned with technical development.

clinical period from departments that become more involved in development activities (e.g., data processing, statistics). Representatives of some preclinical departments (e.g., organic chemistry, pharmacology) may be dropped from the team. The leadership of the project often changes from a scientist to a clinician when the project compound enters Phase I or at some time during this period. Some companies have a bridge department manage a project during the transition from preclinical to clinical activities. This step should not be necessary, and the author believes that such a department would complicate rather than expedite efficient transfer and continuity.

Marketing representatives may form their own team or group during Phase III, but they often take over the management of the project after the drug is marketed. Production departments usually form an independent group to manage manufacturing issues. Even after drugs are marketed there still are many activities conducted in research departments (Table 2.6), medical departments (Table 2.7) and in technical development and regulatory affairs departments (Table 2.8).

The term "technology transfer" is purposely avoided in this book. It is currently

Table 2.7. Activities performed on marketed drugs in medical departments[a]

A. Developing new indications:
   1. Develop plans for new indications for marketed products
   2. Conduct clinical studies relative to new indications
   3. Process and analyze data collected into statistical and clinical reports
   4. Prepare regulatory submissions for new indications

B. Developing new product formulations and changes in product labeling:
   1. Improve product delivery systems or dosing of marketed products
   2. Conduct clinical studies
   3. Conduct postmarketing surveillance studies

C. Providing assistance to marketing:
   1. Conduct clinical studies requested for marketing purposes
   2. Answer telephone calls and written requests for information from physicians, pharmacists, health care personnel, and sales representatives
   3. Answer telephone calls about medical emergencies and adverse experiences; generate written correspondence relative to the documentation of these
   4. Approve advertisements; occasionally assist in the preparation of such advertisements with advertising agency personnel
   5. Approve marketing copy for other purposes, particularly sales promotion
   6. Aid marketing personnel in recommending/producing product plans and analyses of marketing data (such as IMS[b] data)
   7. Address pertinent issues relative to marketed products, such as adverse reactions reports and formulation problems. Plan and conduct clinical studies as appropriate to avert potential problems
   8. Assist in handling product complaints
   9. Participate in training of sales representatives at the company or at outside meetings
   10. Participate in meetings or symposia sponsored by marketing
   11. Monitor the published literature for relevant materials for promotional activity
   12. Provide drug to physicians for special needs, such as the conduct of clinical studies, at the recommendation of sales representatives
   13. Handle requests for compounds for use by clinical or research laboratories
   14. Participate in writing compendia for marketed products and their updates
   15. Assist in preparation of display materials, as well as manning exhibit booths at major medical meetings at the request of marketing
   16. Recommend and approach investigators for a speakers program
   17. Prepare annual reports or other documents for submission to regulatory agencies
   18. Aid in preparation of materials for submission to state formularies, including occasional travel to present data at meetings of state formularies
   19. Help plan and implement postmarketing studies
   20. Aid the marketing divisions of subsidiary companies in other countries

D. Providing assistance in legal activities:
   1. Review and analyze case documents
   2. Meet with attorneys and provide affidavits
   3. Give depositions or courtroom testimony

[a] Most of these activities may be coordinated loosely between individuals involved or they may be handled more formally between departments or between entire divisions. Payment in terms of internal company credit may be utilized, if desired, with several different mechanisms.

[b] IMS, Intercontinental Medical Statistics.

in vogue and widely used by many people in science as well as business. Nonetheless, this term often has a number of connotations that the author considers inappropriate. These include the implication that the initial group may not or does not adequately understand the implications of their work for the group that will continue the drug's development, or that the initial group is unable to transfer the project effectively to the next group without a third party to facilitate the transfer. This latter issue is promulgated by individuals and companies who promote themselves as experts at technology transfer.

It is the author's belief that most preclinical scientists who are engaged in either

Table 2.8. Activities performed on marketed drugs in technical development and regulatory affairs' departments

A. Library and information services[a]
   1. Monitor published literature for product papers
   2. Index published product papers
   3. Perform ad hoc searches on published product literature
   4. Prepare bibliographies for the FDA[b] and/or other regulatory agencies
B. Pharmaceutical research and development laboratories
   1. Provide technical support for production
   2. Improve various processes
   3. Develop improved formulations or additional dosage forms
   4. Conduct stability studies
   5. Evaluate new packaging components and prepare submissions
   6. Prepare drug materials for clinical studies
   7. Validate equipment and processes
   8. Prepare documents on formulation/manufacturing procedures/stability data for annual reports to FDA
   9. Evaluate new equipment
   10. Evaluate materials from alternate suppliers
   11. Participate in establishing release guidelines and revised specifications for marketed products
C. Chemical development laboratories
   1. Provide technical support for chemical production (e.g., troubleshoot problem batches or process steps, optimization/fine-tuning of processes, reuse or recover waste)
   2. Search for and develop improved synthetic route
   3. Transfer the synthesis to the United States of a foreign-synthesized product
   4. Provide regulatory affairs with documents supporting manufacturing changes
   5. Develop alternate source of key raw materials or intermediates
D. Analytical development laboratories
   1. Maintain and update development standards and analytical standards for reports to FDA
   2. Convert development standards to analytical standards where applicable
   3. Validate the file modifications to assays and other tests procedures with the FDA
   4. Validate and file modifications to analytical procedures found necessary as the result of improved formulations
   5. Validate and file modifications to the testing methods for raw materials, intermediates, and bulk drug
   6. Prepare USP[b] style monographs for drug and dosage forms
   7. Troubleshoot products to minimize back orders
E. Drug regulatory affairs department
   1. Submit annual reports to the FDA on each product, describing serious adverse reactions and ongoing clinical studies
   2. Compile, submit, and track all submissions on marketed drugs to the FDA for new indications, formulations, new routes of synthesis, labeling changes, manufacturing control supplements
   3. Provide support for state formulary activities
   4. Submit adverse reactions reports to the FDA and other regulatory agencies as required by law
   5. Assist the legal department in relevant activities including recalls and liability actions
   6. Maintain official records on all marketed drugs

[a] This group is usually situated organizationally in research and development, but is considered a company resource.
[b] FDA, Food and Drug Administration; USP, *United States Pharmacopeia*.

the search for new drug or the evaluation of compound activity understand both the clinical and marketing relevance of their work. Also, these scientists can effectively transfer the project to clinical staff at the appropriate time. Likewise, most clinical scientists understand the commercial value of the drugs they are developing and are also able to effectively transfer their project to both marketing and production individuals or groups at the appropriate time.

Should Drug A, Which is Being Studied in Disease W, Also be Tested in Diseases X, Y, or Z?

It is assumed that drug A is available in the appropriate dosage form(s) to treat patients with these diseases and that the drug's formulation is appropriate in terms of stability, bioavailability, and other technical considerations. Questions to ask include:

1. What clinical evidence already exists that drug A is also effective in patients with these other diseases? How strong (i.e., convincing) is this evidence?
2. What animal data already exists that drug A will be effective in patients with these other diseases? How strong is this evidence?
3. What clinical and animal data suggest that drug A will *not* be effective in patients with these other diseases? How strong is this evidence?
4. What is the medical need for a new drug to treat patients with other diseases?
5. What is the potential commercial value for a new drug to treat patients with other diseases?
6. What is the status of the original work on drug A to treat the disease for which the drug was originally developed?
7. Does treating one or more additional diseases represent a tangent or part of the anticipated development plan? See Fig. 8.4 on models of drug development, and the discussion on tangents in Chapter 4.
8. How will studies on other diseases affect resources allocated to the original project goals and the dates of achieving the original milestones?
9. What is the opinion of the marketing function on pursuing these other indications?
10. How easy or difficult will it be to obtain regulatory approval for the proposed indications?
11. How expensive will it be in terms of money, time, and resources to complete a regulatory submission for each disease?

Situations Where Evidence of Efficacy Is Weak

In many situations the animal and clinical evidence will be weak that drug A will be active in diseases X, Y, and Z. In those situations it is important to evaluate the hypotheses about how the drug works and also what causes the disease and how the disease process may be affected to help patients. These hypotheses may be speculative for a drug but known with a high degree of certainty for the disease (or vice versa). In this situation it often makes sense to conduct a pilot study to evaluate a drug's activity. But, if the mechanism of both the drug and the disease are speculative, and there is no evidence that the drug will have activity in treating patients with the disease, it should be strongly questioned whether the company's interests are best served by conducting a pilot study. It is hoped that the company will have more worthwhile hypotheses to test with a higher likelihood of success.

Patent Issues and Strategies

Many drug companies develop their own particular habits or strategies of dealing with patents. Company strategies must be periodically reevaluated or else they become merely habits. All assumptions and conclusions of the past should be periodically reexamined and challenged when appropriate.

Some drug companies prefer to file many patent applications relatively early on in the life of a potentially new and important compound. This provides early protection of the compound(s) of interest while they "fine tune" the chemical direction they decide to pursue. It is somewhat like a shotgun or broad approach to protection, and tends to be substantially more expensive than the opposite one of filing a minimal number of applications, especially when patent filings are made in multiple countries.

Other companies carefully examine their nonpatented compounds that have shown biological activity and prepare relatively few patent applications to protect their rights to the compounds of particular interest. These companies may either file early to insure protection or hold back to increase the total life of a patent.

Many companies file patents first in the United Kingdom because that procedure allows them an additional year in which to file in the United States and still achieve complete protection. It is not clear why some companies file initially in the United States on a compound that will take many years to develop, because that approach potentially loses a year of patent life. The most valuable (i.e., profitable) years of patent life are usually those at the end of the patent period, because minimal advertising and promotion are needed to sell what is probably an established drug. It is usually at that point as well that the financial return on the drug is maximal.

The natural tendency of scientists and even companies when they have made a major discovery is to apply for a patent to protect their invention. But, they know that their protection will be greater if they can synthesize related compounds (even of biologicals obtained from viable sources) and describe the biological activities as well. This is done as the lead compound progresses through testing and development as a drug. At the same time chemists are exploring other chemically related areas to better define activities and to better delineate and support the patent coverage. It is ironic that a company's own patents serve as "prior art" (after one year in the United States, two years in Canada, and immediately upon publication in most of the world) and may serve to block a company from patenting additional new compounds that are related to those in an earlier patent. Only if the inventor can overcome the rejection by the Patent Office on the basis of obviousness will it be possible to patent the new compounds. The obviousness issue may be challenged by a company if the new compound has unexpectedly high activity, a new activity, or improved physical properties.

Patents are awarded to the inventor of a drug who is the first to file a patent application. This occurs in all countries of the world with a single significant exception, the United States. In the United States it is the first person to make the invention who is eventually awarded a patent, even if that person was *not* the first person to file a patent application for the drug. A challenge must be made to institute formal proceedings to determine who has the priority of invention. These proceedings are known as an interference. The person considered to be the inventor of the drug is the one who first conceived the invention and demonstrated it in practice, not the one who made the chemical first. Laboratory notebooks are important document sources that are often used to demonstrate the dates on which a specific compound was conceived, synthesized, and tested. In some situations defining the concept is rather difficult, such as with totally new scientific ideas or discoveries that evolve over a period of time before they become fully appreciated, formulated, and identified.

How Is Drug Labeling Developed?

Drug companies often develop a standard worldwide labeling for a drug. This helps preserve consistency from country to country, because regulatory authorities and local medical and regulatory directors of the company both usually desire to make various modifications. The most important point for a company to insist on is that various aspects of drug labeling (e.g., contraindications, maximum dose per day or course, minimum age allowable, approved indications) must remain uniform throughout the world. To prevent safety warnings from being diluted, the precise wording of various key sentences should be as uniform as possible in every country in which the drug is registered.

Different approaches to the labeling issue are followed by drug companies. One approach is to develop a prototype of the label that the company expects to eventually have approved. Many companies initially write and approve the label at the outset of a project, even before the compound has usually been given to humans. As additional data are collected the labeling becomes more and more refined, until the NDA is eventually submitted and approved. One of the motivations for using this approach is to establish minimally acceptable criteria, for moving the drug forward in development. If the drug does not meet these criteria, the project is terminated.

An alternative approach is to wait until the NDA is nearly completed by the sponsor. At that time a specific person or group is requested to prepare the first draft of the labeling. This is then revised and included in the regulatory submission. Drafts of the labeling are often based on existing labeling for other drugs. The FDA utilizes class labeling for certain groups of drugs, which means that many sections of the labeling are identical for all drugs of the group. Additional details about labeling were recently published (Millstein, 1987).

Because drug companies and regulatory agencies want to be cautious about a drug's labeling, almost all adverse reactions observed with a drug tend to be listed. This occurs even if the association between the drug and adverse reaction is weak. No incidence figures of adverse reactions are routinely given in labeling or standard references used by most physicians. Prescribing physicians cannot usually get an adequate perspective from the drug's labeling of which adverse reactions are most important or most frequent for their patients.

ROLES OF BIOTECHNOLOGY IN DRUG DISCOVERY AND DEVELOPMENT

Different Perspectives and Uses of Biotechnology

A general definition of biotechnology is that it is the use of living cells to produce commercial products and processes. Various groups that have widely differing perspectives use biotechnology. Some of these groups are as follows.

1. Companies that research new drugs with biotechnology techniques.
2. Companies that manufacture new drugs with biotechnology techniques.
3. Physicians who transplant genes into patients with genetic deficiencies. This is primarily a future use of biotechnology.

Table 2.9. Selected techniques of biotechnology

1.	Recombinant DNA and expression cloning
2.	Human gene mapping
3.	Large fragment DNA separation
4.	Gene amplification
5.	Automated DNA sequencing
6.	Microprotein sequencing
7.	Human hybridoma formation
8.	Mammalian cell cultures
9.	Receptor isolation and identification
10.	Protein structure analysis

4. Hospitals that use diagnostic kits that utilize biotechnology principles in their development and effects.

5. Patients who use drugs manufactured with biotechnology methods.

6. Companies that release organisms into the environment for agricultural purposes.

Finally, it is worth mentioning that some products such as beer and wine have been made for millennia using biotechnology methods. Other industries that have also utilized biotechnology processes for a long time include paper making and tanning.

The modern era of biotechnology began with the identification of the structure of DNA. Major developments included the ability to (1) cut pieces of DNA out of a chromosome, (2) modify the DNA, (3) splice DNA back into cells, and (4) to implant these cells in other species (e.g., transgenic mice, replacement therapy in animals). Modified DNA is usually implanted, however, in cells of the same species. Genes are pieces of DNA that code for a specific product, which is a protein. Genes also contain information that regulates the formation of proteins.

Tools Used in Biotechnology

The recent revolution in biotechnology results from the development of methods to purposefully create new life forms to produce commercial products. This is the principle difference between modern biotechnology and more traditional forms. The three primary types of tools used in modern biotechnology are:

1. Recombinant DNA techniques (i.e., genetic engineering). This is the manipulation of hereditary material (i.e., DNA) by molecular and cellular methods.

2. Production of monoclonal antibodies by *in vitro* cultured hybridoma cell lines that have therapeutic or diagnostic uses (e.g., vaccination, antibiotic therapy).

3. Mass cell culture. Large numbers of cells are used to produce a specific product.

These and other techniques are listed in Table 2.9.

Applying the Tools of Biotechnology

The basic recombinant DNA method involves isolating the gene for a protein of interest (e.g., insulin, human growth hormone). The gene is then put into a cell or bacteria that will express (i.e., make) the protein in great quantity. The cell or bac-

Table 2.10. Sources of production of selected biological drugs

Selected types of biological products	Produced in/by (among other sources)
Vaccines (e.g., polio, rabies, measles) Many vaccines are antigens	Animal cells
Antibodies (e.g., immunoglobulins, antitetanus serum)	Animals
Lymphokines (e.g., interferon, interleukins)	White blood cells
Blood products (e.g., factor 8, factor 9)	Human blood, endothelial tissues
Monoclonal antibodies	Lymphocytes, myelomas, hybridoma cell lines
Enzymes (i.e., proteins)	Fermentation
Antibiotics (e.g., penicillin)	Fermentation
Synthetic peptides (e.g., enkephalins)	Synthetic chemistry

teria is acting as a factory to make the protein of interest. This technique, with numerous variations, is used to make a variety of proteins that have commercial importance. The DNA used may come originally from human cells.

Biotechnology and genetic engineering techniques are generally applied to developing natural or modified human proteins as drugs (e.g., interferon, tissue plasminogen activator, urokinase). This has stimulated a search for potential drugs among the many natural human proteins. Many proteins are currently being investigated in a wide variety of diseases (e.g., superoxide dismutase, interleukins, tumor necrosis factor, epidermal growth factor). There are also many proteins "looking for a disease." Although some of these proteins may become important new drugs, there is a great deal of hype in the medical and popular media about the importance of the "revolution" these drugs are initiating.

In addition to acting as a factory to make drugs (proteins), cells may be used for a specific task (e.g., to digest and inactivate toxins). A future use is hopefully to introduce a gene into the body to make an enzyme that is congenitally absent. For example, children with Lesch-Nyhan Syndrome are born without the enzyme hypoxanthine guanine phosphoribosyltransferase and a buildup of uric acid occurs, which leads to mental retardation and a syndrome that includes self-mutilation. Cells could theoretically be removed from these children's bone marrow, receive the genetically engineered gene from normal cells that make the enzyme, and the cells could then be reintroduced into the child's bone marrow to function normally. If this is done at an early age, then mental retardation and other disease-related symptoms should be avoided. Another target for enzyme replacement is in children who are deficient in adenosine deaminase.

Range of Biological Products

The types of biological drugs vary from pure biologicals produced in animals or animal cells to synthetic compounds produced by chemists in laboratories (Table 2.10).

Biotechnology as a Business

Approximately 100 biotechnology companies in the United States today are working on pharmaceutical products. Most of these companies are operating at a loss and many have been and are being acquired by larger more traditional-oriented drug companies. Other biotechnology companies are going bankrupt. Many biotechnology companies are entering into joint ventures with larger drug companies or are licensing their products to the larger companies. These business arrangements are necessary because the smaller companies are inexperienced in drug development, have insufficient resources, and do not have an adequate sales force to promote the company's products.

Current and Future Issues in Biotechnology

There are some significant differences between biologicals and common synthetic drugs. Contaminants from the host, virus, or bacteria may get through the manufacturing process and be present in the final product. These could have deleterious consequences for patients and must be eliminated with process controls. It is much more difficult to insure the quality of the final biological product with present physicochemical control methods than for most synthetic drugs. Other differences are included in the list below. Some of the actual and potential problems and issues of biotechnology include the following.

1. Ethical issues abound because new life forms are being created or modified. This is particularly true for potential future uses of gene replacement therapy.
2. Patent protection is a largely unknown area. Strong patents are vital for the successful commercialization of drugs, but there are many ill-defined areas. For example, is a protein expressed by yeast the same as the "same" protein expressed by *Escherichia coli* bacteria?
3. Financial costs of production are usually quite high, and a genetically engineered product will not be able to compete successfully with most synthetic chemical drugs that have the same clinical activity.
4. There is a need for improved delivery systems to make most potentially available proteins as practical as drugs. Proteins cannot usually be absorbed orally without being digested (broken down into smaller pieces) in the stomach and intestines and also because their molecular weight is too high. This implies that parenteral absorption, usually by intravenous injection, will be necessary to give these drugs to patients. This is often impractical.
5. Proteins create antigenic responses. This issue is presently of unknown clinical significance, although it is known that interferon does induce antigen formation in some patients.
6. Metabolism of proteins may pose problems in some patients or under certain conditions.
7. Social issues abound regarding many aspects of biotechnology. For example, if information about people's potential for disease can be measured, may these data be kept from insurance companies? If not, then the data have potential for great misuse and issues of privacy must be considered.
8. When a company desires to manufacture a biological product at a new facility, more extensive validations must be done than for other drugs. In addition, clinical validation studies (i.e., comparability studies) may be required. It is also necessary to confirm that the same product is being made from batch to batch grown at a single site.

9. The dosages of vials may be expressed in terms of bioassay units or in terms of protein weight. Numerous issues of standardization arise in this regard.

10. Some regulatory agencies focus on the processes used for manufacturing, whereas others emphasize the characteristics of the products. There is a gradual growth in what is demanded of the product's specifications.

11. It is essential to maintain a close dialogue with regulatory agencies about their reactions to various manufacturing changes. If the changes are considered to be routine they usually only require a demonstration that technical specifications of the product remain unchanged. If the change is not considered routine, new clinical studies may be required to demonstrate comparability of the new and original biological products. The following changes may or may not be considered routine for biologicals: (1) moving the purification site to a new building, (2) moving the cell culture to a new scaleup tank, (3) contracting out the filling of vials with product, and (4) contracting out the cell culture production to a company that is provided with part of the original sample.

Many of the above problems result from the fact that many biological products are proteins and not from the process that produced it (i.e., biotechnology). It is usually no more difficult to purify or do quality control on a protein produced by biotechnology than one extracted from natural sources. In fact, it is often easier to obtain biotechnology-derived proteins. For example, natural human growth hormone is given to young children deficient in this hormone to stimulate their growth. This polypeptide hormone came from human cadavers for many years, but is now prepared more easily by recombinant DNA techniques. Moreover, this recombinant growth hormone is free of a deleterious agent that caused severe problems (Jakob-Creutzfeldt disease) in some children who took the natural product.

3 / *How Do Scientists and Clinicians Evaluate and Interpret Data*

Men love to wonder, and that is the seed of science. Ralph Waldo Emerson (1803–1882), American essayist and poet. From *Society and Solitude,* 1870.

He who understands nothing but chemistry does not truly understand chemistry either. Georg Lichtenberg, 18th century philosopher.

The aim of science is to seek the simplest explanation of complex facts. We are apt to fall into the error of thinking that the facts are simple because simplicity is the goal of our quest. The guiding motto in the life of every natural philosopher should be, 'Seek simplicity and distrust it.' Alfred North Whitehead. From *Concept of Nature*.

BACKGROUND INFORMATION ABOUT DRUGS AND DISEASES

This chapter provides some background on drugs and diseases. It also provides an orientation for nonscientists to better understand how scientists and clinicians think and utilize information.

What Is a Drug?

No single definition of a drug is universally accepted. Instead, there are many definitions ranging from narrow and restricted ones to those that are extremely broad. The definition favored by the author in the general context of this book is: A drug is a chemical substance that affects living tissue and is used to achieve a desired biological effect in a living organism. Some aspects of this definition are a little vague or may be debated (e.g., when are foods considered drugs, what drugs are present in foods). Nonetheless, this general definition allows for great latitude in discussing drug development and uses.

A prodrug is defined as a substance that is converted inside the body into an active drug, usually by metabolic processes in the liver or blood. A prodrug may be inactive on its own or it may have the same biological profile as the active drug. Some people (including the author) believe that a chemical compound should first be referred to as a drug when it is initially given to humans (i.e., in Phase I studies). Others prefer to make this distinction when the compound is first shown to be active in patients, which occurs in Phase II studies.

Drugs Work at Multiple Levels

A drug works at a *clinical level* in addition to affecting organs and cells. A drug improves a patient's symptoms and thereby enables the patient to feel better on a *physical level*. This leads to an improved sense of well-being on a *psychological level*. This in turn enables the patient to have improved interactions with others on a *social level*. The drug acts to improve the patient's symptoms by affecting one or more processes on a *physiological level* (i.e., affecting organs such as the heart or stomach, tissues, or organ systems such as cardiovascular or gastrointestinal). It does this in turn through actions at a *tissue level* and *cellular level*, that result from biochemical effects within and/or outside cells. Some scientific studies of how a drug works investigate *subcellular* and *molecular levels*. For certain drugs, such as those with abuse potential, there is also a *population level* at which a drug acts. This level involves interactions among groups of people. Figure 3.1 illustrates these levels.

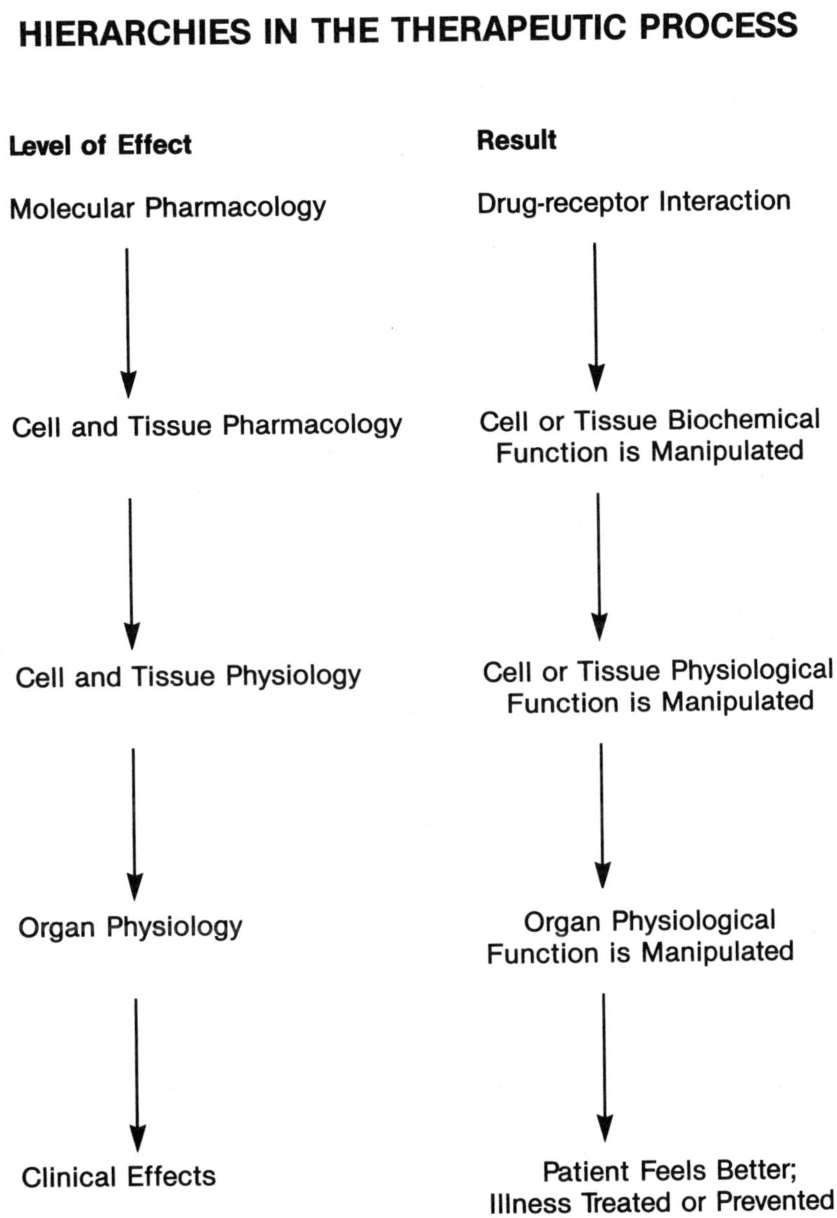

Fig. 3.1. Hierarchies (i.e., different levels) in the therapeutic process. From Grahame-Smith and Aronson (1984) with permission of Oxford University Press.

Drugs may and do affect all of these levels so that there is really no single *pharmacological level*. On the other hand, pharmacological studies are usually conducted in animals at the cellular, tissue, and physiological levels, whereas in humans, pharmacological studies are often conducted at the level of organ systems and the whole organism.

Scientific understanding of how most drugs act is full of gaps. Sometimes these gaps are filled by hypotheses or ideas of how the drug could work. Evidence is then gathered to support or refute the hypothesis. In some situations, multiple hypotheses are proposed to explain a single action of a drug. Many scientific ideas may be viewed and explained simply as turning biologically active materials (e.g., enzymes) on or off. Other drugs work by blocking certain receptors or antagonizing certain chemicals.

Sometimes it is not the facts of how a drug behaves at each level that is an issue, but how the effects at one level lead to effects at another level (Fig. 3.1). Those bridges are as important to understand as how a drug is acting at each specific level. An example is given in Fig. 3.2 that illustrates how cardiac glycosides work at multiple levels. Digitalis, digoxin, and ouabain are widely used drugs of this class.

Where Does One Look for a New Drug?

There is a well-known story that captures the essence of the answer to this question. An adult man was down on all fours late at night, obviously looking for something under a street lamp. Another man walked up and told the first man that he would be happy to help, but where did the man lose the object? The first man answered "Oh, about 20 yards away." "Then why look here," the other asked. "Because, this is where the light is," the first man replied.

In pharmaceutical research, companies are focusing most of their efforts in areas where the light is, not in many of the dark areas, where they believe many important drugs are. This is unfortunate, but researchers are generally limited to looking for new drugs where biological tests exist to evaluate compounds. Also, the data from those tests must be sufficiently predictive of human activity to justify spending the large sums of money necessary to develop a drug to the point where activity in humans can be assessed. In many situations, such as looking for new drugs for schizophrenia or Alzheimer's disease, we know that we would like to look in different areas using better glasses. Another way of expressing this concept is that we would like to have better tests to aid our search for new drugs. But, those improved glasses (animal test models) do not yet exist in many disease areas.

What Are Medical Facts?

Are medical facts absolute and true for all time, or are they relative and dependent on the scientific, social, and political environment in which they are established? The answer is that all medical facts are relative and may be eventually replaced by more accepted or stronger facts. Most people understand that when facts are shown to be wrong, they are usually replaced by others. No one can say that we have the correct facts in any area of medicine. Most currently accepted medical facts will be replaced by others, and they in turn will eventually be replaced, and so on. The general modes of perception of the most influential scientists and clinicians are the bases of what establish facts.

How Much Do We Really Know?

Many people have the perspective that medicine has made so much progress over the last century that we are getting to know most of what there is to know. The fallacy of this view can be commented on by describing an analogy.

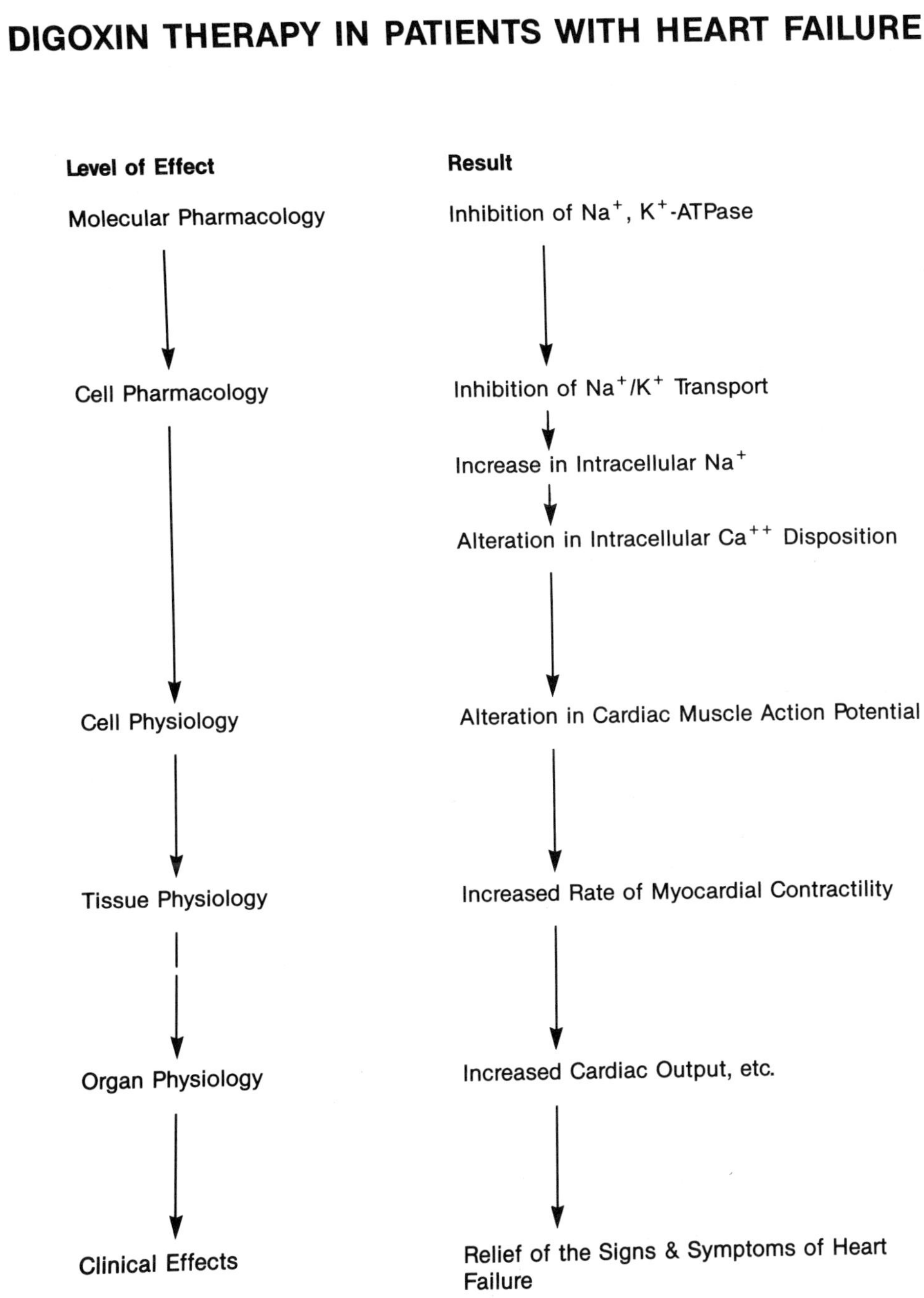

Fig. 3.2. Hierarchies in the actions of cardiac glycosides. From Grahame-Smith and Aronson (1984) with permission of Oxford University Press.

Understanding the workings of a single cell has been described as analogous to viewing the island of Manhattan from above. Scientists are said to be in a helicopter high over the island. A few centuries ago, scientists were so far above the island that they did not know of its existence. As scientific and technical abilities improved, especially through invention of the microscope, the island (i.e., cell) was discovered.

Over the last 200 or so years our helicopter has moved steadily closer to the island and now we are able to identify not only Central Park (which was an early observation), but a number of specific buildings. We can often determine which buildings are bigger than others. Traffic patterns can also be observed and we can identify where most of the outdoor activities are occurring. The buildings, traffic, parks, and bodies of water we observe are analogous to the structural details of a cell that can now be identified with electron and scanning microscopes.

The interesting questions, however, are what the many managers are doing in each of the buildings and also what motivates them to make the decisions they reach. Trying to answer these questions based on the gross details of the buildings and vehicles we observe on the streets below is impossible. We do not know the identity of most managers, let alone their actual activities. Nonetheless we make many hypotheses and develop theories. Inside our bodies and cells it is estimated that there are approximately 50,000 proteins, only one-tenth of which have been discovered. There is clearly a long way to go.

Why Do New Diseases Occur?

Diseases are usually a fixed concept in our minds that are all-or-none entities, even though we know we may get a mild or severe case of any disease. We may remember diseases that our parents or grandparents had and in some cases, think how lucky we are to be vaccinated and therefore protected against them. In other cases, we know that we too may get the same disease as our parents. If so, there may or may not be effective treatments available.

Diseases are not fixed entities but have their own natural history and characteristics that evolve over time. A disease may change in such aspects as severity, aftereffects, frequency, types of symptoms, or degree of mortality. These changes may occur because people who get the disease change or because the cause of the disease changes. People may become better protected against the disease because of immunological resistance or improved nutritional status. Resistance may be acquired genetically over a long period of time or may be acquired artificially, as with vaccines. Some characteristics of a disease change because of altered environmental factors that affect health, such as sanitation, crowding, nutrition, and personal hygiene. Also, as humans get to know more about each disease, ways of eradicating some diseases are found, as was done with the once dreaded disease smallpox. The development of vaccines have allowed us to think in terms of eventually eradicating a number of other diseases as well (e.g., measles). Finally, a disease may change over decades, centuries, or millenia because of genetic changes within the viruses or bacteria that cause the disease (e.g., syphilis).

Trying to control or even effectively treat a number of diseases is a difficult battle when the cause of the disease is rapidly changing. A good example is the common influenza virus disease or "flu." This disease changes every couple of years as a new strain emerges and requires development of a new vaccine to prevent effectively the disease in those innoculated.

New diseases emerge for numerous reasons including mutations in the genetic makeup of viruses, bacteria, or other disease-causing agents. New diseases may emerge in a country because people, animals, or plants may carry diseases from one place to another. Diseases may move (or return to) a place where people have little natural resistance. In such a situation the disease may not only spread rapidly but may occur in a more severe form than in the original population. An example of this reportedly occurred when syphilis was brought to Europe from either the New World or from Africa in the 15th century (Gottfried, 1983, p. 158,159). Interestingly, the Italians called syphilis the "French Pox" and the French called it the "Italian Pox." English called it the "Spanish Pox," Poles called it the "German Pox," and Russians called it the "Polish Pox" (Gottfried, 1983).

New cultural practices, environmental factors, or almost any type of change may cause diseases to alter their natural history. Two examples within the last century are (1) increases in people smoking cigarettes has caused an enormous increase in lung cancer, and (2) the high saturated fat diet in certain Western countries has led to increases in atherosclerosis and subsequently to an increased number of myocardial infarctions. Some diseases that were once limited to animal populations are now human diseases as well. The crossing of a disease from animals to humans may occur through close contact, eating part of the animal, or for unknown reasons. Some diseases may be transmitted from animals to humans (e.g., rabies, yellow fever, some types of food poisoning, malaria), whereas others are not (e.g., feline leukemia). Other diseases are presumed to be transmitted both from animals to humans and vice versa (e.g., brucellosis) or are not transmitted from humans to animals (e.g., common cold).

What Is the Natural History of a Disease?

The changing natural history of disease can be readily appreciated from the changing mortality statistics for tuberculosis. In New York City the death rate from tuberculous was 700 per 10,000 people in 1812. After some sanitation measures had been introduced, the rate fell to 400 per 10,000 about 1880. It further decreased to 180 (per 10,000 inhabitants) by 1910, and just before the age of antibiotic treatment of tuberculosis in 1945, the rate had decreased to 48 (per 10,000 inhabitants). Reasons for the changing nature of a disease over time vary from disease to disease. Sometimes, as with tuberculosis, the major reasons are primarily under human control (e.g., nutrition, sanitation). With other diseases the reasons for the changes are either unknown or are related to inherent changes in the cause(s) of disease (e.g., the viruses or bacteria) that are not under direct human control.

This chapter illustrates the dynamic nature of the medical environment in which drugs act. Changes in existing disease, emergence of new diseases (e.g., Acquired Immune Deficiency Syndrome [AIDS]), recognition of already existing diseases (e.g., Legionnaires' disease), and development of resistance or tolerance to drugs are all factors that impact directly on the quest for new drugs and the development of existing compounds and drugs.

SCIENTIFIC LOGIC AND INTERPRETATIONS

Choosing a Puzzle to Work On

Scientists are often driven by the challenge of solving puzzles. A creative scientist who solves a research problem uses many types of simple and complex concepts and often puts the pieces of a puzzle together in a novel way. Alternatively, a scientist may discover a new piece of a puzzle that eluded previous workers. The choice of a suitable problem to explore is an extremely important part of scientific research. Great scientists chose great problems to work on.

Many great scientific discoveries are made by people who are working in a field in which they were not trained. These people often view problems in a different way than those who are experts in the field. As a result, they approach problems differently and sometimes are able to solve them. For example, Dalton was a meteorologist who was studying the absorption of gases by water and the absorption of water by the atmosphere. To better understand the physical processes involved, he desired to learn the sizes and weights of the atomic particles involved in his mixtures. To condense a long story, Dalton invented the atomic theory of chemistry while trying to solve what was for him originally a meteorological problem.

What Does a Scientist See?

After a major scientific discovery has been made, the world is different! What people see is different. A lag period often exists between the discovery and the new way of seeing the world. There was a lag period before people saw what Copernicus discovered, that the earth revolves around the sun and not the other way around. Likewise, after Charles Darwin wrote *The Origin of the Species*, it took more than a generation for most people to see man as a descendent of animals and not as an almost instant creation of the Divine. In science, the Frenchman Lavoisier saw *oxygen*, whereas the Englishman Priestly saw "*dephlogisticated air*." Lavoisier also saw *compounds* in the material Priestly called *earth*. These concepts represented real differences in how the world was perceived and were not merely semantic arguments. Many more examples of this phenomenon could be described. They show that major scientific advances change the way in which scientists and many others view the world.

A widespread belief in the world of both medicine and science views the clinical investigator or scientific experimenter as a detached observer of patients or scientific experiments. The concept of the totally independent observer, however, is a fiction. The observer is always part of the experiment or study and influences it, sometimes in subtle ways. The very act of measuring something often affects or changes what is being measured. This is a major reason for adding control groups to many investigations, in the belief that both (or all) groups will be similarly affected. Except for using clairvoyance or revelation, the major hope of arriving at or approaching an important scientific truth is to eliminate as many biases as possible and to design good experiments.

Most people have preconceived ideas about what relationship or outcome should be observed in a study or experiment. When the outcome is unexpected, some scientists or clinicians stretch or mold the data in a way that best fits the expected pattern. Other scientists interpret the data more objectively, find flimsy explanations, or decide that no useful interpretation is possible. Racial, ethnic, religious, national, geographical region, and occupational factors often play a large role in the expectations that individuals have about anticipated outcomes. Scientists are trained to minimize the impact of these factors on their judgments in reaching an interpretation of experimental data.

Some scientists and clinicians do not actually conduct experiments in which they test carefully constructed hypotheses about how a drug acts in animals or patients. Rather, they choose a drug to evaluate in a given test system under specified conditions to observe what results will be obtained. They may make many independent observations and collect a great deal of data, but the scientific weight of such observations is often weak. This is especially true if the studies are not carefully controlled. Many experiments are usually required to have enough weight and credibility to constitute scientific or medical proof.

Holding Contradictory Beliefs or Ideas

Creative and intelligent scientists (and nonscientists) often have beliefs and principles that appear to be contradictory. This may occur because people's views are vague, mixed up in their minds, or for other reasons. On the other hand, this may be a highly positive situation where intellectual flexibility allows people to hold contradictory beliefs. Apparent contradictions often result from scientific evidence that supports two or more conflicting theories or models. F. Scott Fitzgerald once wrote that "the test of a first-rate intelligence is the ability to hold two opposed ideas in the mind at the same time, and still retain the ability to function." In most situations one set of principles will eventually be found to be correct.

Traps and Pitfalls in Thinking

Some of the more common pitfalls that trap nonscientists as well as naive scientists are:

1. Too much confidence is placed in early trends or results. Most scientists and clinicians have experienced numerous situations where the first several experiments yielded a positive response, only to be followed by others that failed to demonstrate the same effect. The opposite situation also occurs where negative studies are followed by positive ones. Scientists with wisdom therefore express the view that initial results are encouraging or promising, but that additional studies must be conducted to confirm the results. Scientists with less experience are highly enthusiastic when their first few studies are positive. They may use the preliminary results to bolster their biases and become even less objective.

2. There is a tendency for many individuals to explain away unexpected results that do not confirm or support the views which are anticipated. One or more reasons may almost always be found that could have caused the undesired result. The undesired data are then often dismissed from the sample and if the experiment is published, the existence of these data may never be known to the readers. This practice,

which may occur more commonly in animal and other preclinical studies than in clinical studies, is extremely uncommon in clinical studies sponsored by a drug company. This is because all data from sponsored studies on new drugs that are included in regulatory submissions are subject to regulatory review and audit.

3. Expectations of being able to reproduce studies or experiments are extremely high. Even if a scientist or clinician is replicating his or her own work, there are various reasons why results often differ the second time around. This leads to the view that it is extremely important to obtain a second study that confirms the results of a first. Also, data that have been independently observed or confirmed in a second laboratory or clinic are much more convincing than studies reported from a single institution.

4. People overestimate or do not consider the "power" of a study. This is a statistical term that relates to the chance that a positive effect will be observed in an investigation if such an effect truly exists. This is critically important because it means that one may determine ahead of time that a particular study or experiment has little or almost no chance of finding a certain result *even if that result exists and is true*! This pitfall is often manifested through enrolling an insufficient number of patients in a clinical study. This is an extremely common problem among academic clinicians, many of whom conduct studies where the chance of finding a positive response is unacceptably low. They may conduct such studies because they have insufficient funds to conduct studies in an appropriate number of patients or because they are unaware of the concept of power and are relying on the fact that many prior studies were also conducted in a comparable number of patients.

Why Scientists Often Require Conclusive Proof before Reaching a Conclusion and Making Decisions

Nonscientists are sometimes upset and frustrated when scientists seem incapable of reaching conclusions without all possible information. One reason for scientific caution relates to the outcomes that often result when people reach rapid decisions. Every adult has had numerous experiences where their beliefs or conclusions had to be reversed or modified when additional information was obtained. Scientists are trained to withhold judgment until sufficient data are present. The real issue is to know how much data are necessary to reach a conclusion and not to delay decisions past a reasonable point. Scientists usually demand far more information than is demanded by nonscientists before reaching a conclusion.

Post Hoc Ergo Propter Hoc Issues

One of the best known issues that results from making rapid decisions is the *post hoc ergo propter hoc* problem. This refers to a cause and effect situation where it is concluded that if event B follows event A, then event B is caused by event A. This is generally more strongly believed when event B consistently follows event A. Although David Hume, an 18th century English philosopher, conclusively showed the fallacy of this type of thinking, it still survives and thrives today in many people's thinking. It is also related to the reasoning underlying many beliefs of primitive peoples. A few practical examples illustrate this issue. Although these examples may seem simple and lead people to smile, it is often extremely difficult to determine whether the relationship between two scientific or medical events (e.g., giving a drug and measuring a response) is truly one of cause and effect.

Case 1

Certain green plants turn a light shade of green and then yellow during prolonged rain storms. Does this mean that an excessive amount of water causes the plants to turn yellow? No, careful studies have demonstrated that it is the lack of sunshine during the rain that affects these plants and causes them to turn yellow (i.e., less green).

Case 2

A man drinking a well-known and widely used soft drink has a heart attack. Does this mean that the soft drink caused the man's heart attack? Probably not, but the details would have to be examined. The carbonation or caffeine may have contributed to the problem in this particular person, or possibly he drank it improperly, choked, and in the excitement that ensued, experienced a heart attack. Nonetheless, it would not be reasonable to conclude that drinking a certain brand of soda is likely to cause a heart attack.

Case 3

Primitive tribes have developed many customs because it once (or more than once) happened that one event followed another. They therefore associated the events and believe that to have a desired outcome (e.g., rain, good crops, medical improvement) the initial event should be repeated. Therefore, they use an old ritual and utilize the medicines, dances, or chants that previously preceded the desired outcome. If that outcome does not occur, they create excuses for the exceptions, such as claiming that the gods were angry.

EXTRAPOLATIONS OF DATA AND INTERPRETATIONS

When scientists conduct experiments they seek to learn something from the specific results that will enable them to generalize the conclusion to another situation. The process of generalizing to a different situation is referred to as extrapolation. Data from scientific experiments or clinical studies are interpreted and these interpretations may be generalized (i.e., extrapolated). Drug companies base many important decisions on extrapolations. Basic types of extrapolations in research and development are divided in three arbitrary categories: (1) animal to animal, (2) animal to human, and (3) human to human.

Another classification of extrapolations is based on scientific discipline (e.g., pharmacology, biochemistry, toxicology, clinical medicine). In this classification, interpretations of data are extrapolated from the subcellular level to the cellular level and then to the tissue level and so on to the organ, organism, and society levels (Figs. 3.1 and 3.2). Data interpretations are also extrapolated in the other direction (i.e., from society toward the subcellular level). These extrapolations may be viewed as bridges in a hierarchical interpretation from one level to another. Clearly, most extrapolations do not involve all of these levels. Most involve a small number and may begin anywhere along the chain and move in either or both directions.

Examples of extrapolations include generalizing from effects observed with (1) one species to another, (2) a high dose of a drug to a low dose, (3) acute treatment to chronic treatment, (4) *in vitro* to *in vivo* situations, or (5) from one type of patient to another. All extrapolations of data involve some degree of judgment, especially when they are made across more than one of these five dimensions. It is much more difficult to extrapolate accurately across two or more of these dimensions.

A special case of extrapolation across three dimensions involves determining teratogenic (birth defect) risks. Data are often obtained in animals treated with extremely high doses of a drug. Results of these studies are not only extrapolated to a different species, humans (the first dimension), but are also extrapolated to humans who are receiving relatively small doses of the drug (second dimension) given over a prolonged period rather than a short time (third dimension).

Purposes of Extrapolations

One of the major purposes of extrapolating an interpretation of data is to develop a new hypothesis or model that may be tested in a future experiment or clinical study. Another important purpose is to better treat patients with drugs. Extrapolations may also lead to further experiments or tests that allow new treatments to be confirmed under different conditions and/or in different types of patients.

Extrapolations from Animals to Animals

An interpretation being extrapolated usually relates to the safety, efficacy, or pharmacokinetic profile of a compound or drug. Choosing the correct dose or dosage range to study in different animal tests involves extrapolation. This is necessary when data are extrapolated between *in vitro* and *in vivo* tests, or between two *in vitro* (or *in vivo*) tests. Extrapolations often involve two or more animal species, such as in toxicology or pharmacology studies. Experiments or clinical studies are often conducted to evaluate whether the extrapolations made are correct. If data demonstrate that an extrapolation is incorrect, then specific factors are evaluated to determine, whenever possible, the underlying reason(s) for results observed.

Extrapolations from Animals to Humans

The most important extrapolation made during drug development is the belief that data obtained in animal models suggests that a drug will have benefits in treating patients with a specific disease or condition. A new compound may be tested in humans because it has an important biological action (such as stimulating or inhibiting an enzyme) that is not directly associated with a specific disease. It is possible that no particular activity was observed with the compound in any animal tests indicative of a specific human disease in which to test the drug. In some of these cases it may still be thought worth evaluating the compound in one or a number of human diseases. The extrapolation made in this situation is that a drug with the characteristics observed may have a beneficial effect in one of several diseases.

Conflicting conclusions often exist between the safety profile of a drug tested in various species. It is usually impossible to predict in advance which species will best predict human results. Sometimes the reasons for differences between species are known or hypothesized. For example, species A may metabolize a drug to a toxic product, whereas species B does not. This in turn may result from the presence of an enzyme in species A that is not present, present to a lesser degree, or present in a different form in species B.

Other extrapolations are based on the assumption that adverse reactions or lesions observed in toxicological studies conducted in animals also will be observed in humans; alternatively, the risk of these adverse reactions in humans is unacceptable and that human testing must stop. This usually occurs when problems are severe enough that no company, physician, or regulatory authority wishes to test whether the drug will in fact cause the same toxicity in humans. This is one of the most common reasons why clinical studies (and all other work on a new drug) are stopped. There may be one or many reasons why the problem observed in animals is unlikely to occur in humans, but risk to benefit considerations for patients usually suggest that termination of the drug's development is advisable or necessary.

If an adverse reaction is found in animals and the drug is already marketed, then a search will be made to determine the incidence of the problem in humans. If the incidence is acceptably low or if no cases have been reported, then there will probably not be a strong reason to remove the drug from the market. One issue would relate to the question of what would be an "acceptably low" incidence. If the drug caused cancer and was being used for a non-life-threatening disease, then no incidence rate in humans would be acceptably low. Even if no human cases of cancer were found or reported in humans associated with the drug, sales of most drugs would stop, because the risks would be considered unacceptable. But, if the drug caused an adverse reaction that was reversible when the drug was stopped and many patients were benefiting from treatment with the drug, then it probably would be in most patients' interests to continue treatment, even if the problem were moderate or severe. The subgroups of patients who are at high risk of having the problem should be identified if possible. If this could be done, then special warnings would be given in the drug labeling and possibly through direct letters or even advertisements to physicians.

Establishing New Animal Models to Test Drugs and Establishing Criteria of an Ideal Drug

Animal models should be evaluated to see how predictive they are for human effects. When developing a new animal model, it is necessary to determine how close it comes to an ideal model. As an example, the characteristics of an ideal method for evaluating drugs on pruritus (itch) are presented in Table 3.1.

In addition to having criteria for an ideal model to test compounds or drugs, it is usually desirable to know the properties of an ideal drug of the therapeutic class of interest. These properties allow one to construct tests and models to test compounds

Table 3.1. Characteristics of an ideal clinical method for evaluating topical antipruritics[a]

1. Rapid onset of experimentally induced pruritus: Pruritus should begin within a few minutes after administering the pruritic stimulus.This eliminates the need of requiring volunteers to wait for extended periods before the clinical trial begins or to return for testing at a specified time
2. Moderate intensity: If the pruritus is too intense it might not allow the drugs being tested to demonstrate efficacy. If intensity is too weak, there might be an abnormally high placebo effect
3. Adequate duration: The duration produced must be long enough to allow the drugs being tested to demonstrate activity. The pruritus must disappear within a relatively short period of time to minimize the volunteers' discomfort. A duration of approximately 20 minutes is considered desirable if the presence of an antipruritic effect with rapid onset of activity is being evaluated. A longer duration would be required if the duration of a drug's antipruritic effect was being studied
4. The pruritus produced is analogous to that observed in clinical conditions: The experimental method should produce an insult to the skin that mimics at least some symptomatic aspects of cutaneous disease
5. The pruritic effect must be reproducible within and between volunteers
6. The methodology should be simple to perform with readily available equipment, should not require excessive time for the volunteer or investigator, and should be relatively inexpensive to conduct
7. The methodology must be validated by testing standard topical antipruritic drugs versus placebo in a double-blind study
8. No false-positives should be obtained with drugs that are not antipruritics
9. The methodology must be suitable for use in double-blind studies and should be amenable for drug evaluation and further clinical research
10. The data obtained must be quantifiable for statistical analysis

[a] From Spilker (1987b) with permission of S. Karger.

for these attributes. An example of requirements for an ideal drug to treat epilepsy is shown in Table 3.2. These criteria may readily be used to judge new methods or new drugs.

The characteristics of an ideal drug should not only list positive attributes that are present, but should include negative attributes that must be absent. In addition to characteristics that pertain specifically to the therapeutic field, there are other characteristics of the drug's activity that relate to virtually all drugs (e.g., onset of action, duration of action, cumulative effects, reversibility). Additional characteristics of technical development (e.g., stability at room temperature, compressibility into tablets, availability in multiple dosage forms) may be specified if desired. The test drug may be readily compared in a table with standard drugs and other investigational drugs in terms of ideal characteristics.

Table 3.2. Characteristics of an ideal antiepileptic drug for treating partial seizures[a]

1. Broad spectrum of activity: maximal electroshock, amygdala kindling, cortical kindling, and focal epilepsy models in various species
2. Lack of tolerance: test in 14-day maximal electroshock model
3. Selective pharmacological effect: devoid of effects on other organ systems
4. Long duration of action: half-life approximately 24 hours in humans and 8 to 12 hours in rodents
5. Water solubility: rapid and uniform dissolution in gastric juice
6. Lipophilicity: un-ionized form should penetrate the blood brain barrier easily and distribute preferentially in the central nervous system
7. Lack of drug interactions: low affinity to protein and lack of hepatic enzyme induction (P-450 microsomes)
8. Correlation should be high between blood level and antiepileptic activity

[a] From Cloutier et al. (1983) with permission.

Extrapolations from Humans to Humans

The general types of extrapolations of data made in clinical studies and treatment include extrapolations from:

1. One or a few patients to many patients.
2. Many patients (i.e., a patient population) to a particular patient.
3. One physician's experience to another physician, who has different training, facilities, and so on.
4. One treatment setting to another (e.g., rural versus urban, primary versus tertiary care).
5. One historical time period to another (e.g., interpretations of patient care for a particular disease in the 1950s to the 1980s).
6. One level of organization to another (e.g., biochemical to physiological, single patient to population). This topic was discussed earlier.

Each of these general types of extrapolations may be influenced by many specific factors. These factors and extrapolations are described in more detail in Chapter 23 of *Guide to Clinical Interpretation of Data* (Spilker, 1986b).

Forming a Concept of a Drug's Risks and Benefits

Patients as well as physicians should form a concept of a drug's risk in a specific situation so that it may be compared with the concept of a drug's benefit. This comparison is the well-known risk-to-benefit ratio and involves an extrapolation of previous data to a current clinical situation. Most patients do not know how to form an assessment of a drug's risk or benefit and drug companies may help educate physicians and indirectly patients through advertisements, brochures, and other educational tools, in addition to package inserts and the medical literature.

Major dimensions or spectrums along which both risk and benefit may be judged include:

1. *Knowledge of the risks and benefits* Unless a physician or patient is aware of each of the important risks and benefits, an informed risk-to-benefit comparison may not be made.
2. *Magnitude of the risks and benefits* The degree or magnitude of risks in terms of severity should be assessed. Some adverse reactions are mild, while others are life-threatening. Benefits may also be expressed along a similar but opposite scale.
3. *Probability of the risks and benefits occurring* This dimension requires that the incidence of an adverse reaction's occurrence be generally known in the clinical situation. This may only be able to be expressed as unlikely, possible, probably, or certain. Benefits may be similarly expressed.
4. *Means to decrease risks and improve the chance of benefits occurring* In some situations patients may diminish a risk by adhering to a specified behavior. For example, there is a risk of heart problems occurring if a beta-receptor antagonist is suddenly discontinued by a patient. This risk may be minimized, if not eliminated, if a patient remains compliant with his or her drug schedule. Various ancillary behaviors may almost always be followed to improve the chances of benefits occurring

(e.g., take the drug as directed, do not drink alcohol, lose a few pounds of weight, reduce salt intake, do not take other specific drugs).

5. *Risks and benefits of alternative drug or nondrug therapy* Comparison of risks should be made between each alternative therapy. The same type of comparison should be made for benefits. This is essentially stating that benefit-to-risk ratios should be compared between treatments But, the easiest means of doing this is to compare all risks separately from all benefits.

6. *Risk or benefits that may occur by not taking the drug* There is usually an option for patients not to take any drug or to follow any prescribed therapy for a problem. The risks of adhering to the no-treatment option should be compared with those of taking the drug. The same comparison should be made for benefits of the drug versus those of no treatment.

An important factor relating to the no-treatment option is that some people prefer to accept larger risks if the risk is not under their control than a smaller risk in which they must make a positive decision to take an action. This was reportedly the reason why some mothers chose not to vaccinate their babies against pertussis.

4 / *Stimulating the Innovative Process and Increasing the Efficiency of Drug Development*

The first intimations of a new idea may be too nebulous to be captured and arranged for logical presentation. There is a natural inclination to pounce on such an idea and drag it out into full consciousness by giving it a definite form and shape. Before the idea has had a chance to grow in a haphazard (and original) fashion, it is organized and given shape. But the shape is one that has been chosen for the idea, not the one it might have grown into on its own. The free flight of the idea is curtailed, and it is as firmly fixed as a butterfly to the collector's board. Pouncing on an idea as soon as it appears kills the idea. Too early and too enthusiastic logical attention either freezes the idea or forces it into the old molds. Concentration on an idea isolates it from its surroundings and arrests its growth. The glare of attention inhibits the fertile semiconscious processes that go to develop an idea. Edward de Bono, English physician and writer. From *The Use of Lateral Thinking*.

Those who cannot remember the past are condemned to repeat it. George Santayana.

INTRODUCTION

The magic formula to stimulate innovation and creativity in drug discovery is as elusive as the fountain of youth. Given that no universal formula is currently known, is it possible to write a useful chapter on this topic? I believe the answer is yes. As one scans the history of creative endeavors, one notices certain periods (e.g., the Renaissance) and certain places (e.g., Florence, Italy) where creativity flourished. The question then arises as to whether there are certain aspects of an environment in which creativity is more likely to occur. If so, then it would be important to create and nurture this environment for scientists who are trying to discover novel drugs. One model of where innovation fits into the process of drug discovery and development is shown in Fig. 4.1.

HAVING THE RIGHT PEOPLE AND GROUPS

Introduction to Personnel Issues

Stimulating innovation at a drug company involves numerous personnel issues. The nature of the training and experience of certain scientists contributes to their innate characteristics and makes the scientists more innovative. When a reasonable state of harmony does not exist both within the scientist and within the company, the chance of discovering an important new drug is diminished. This discussion assumes that the hypothetical company described has sufficient resources in terms of facilities, equipment, and money for efficient drug development. Personnel issues include whether there is a sufficient degree of (1) inherent intellectual curiosity and creativity within the professional staff, (2) interest and involvement of the staff in their current work, (3) technical skills and abilities of the staff, and (4) cooperation between different groups.

Management must hire the best scientists they can find and then trust them to

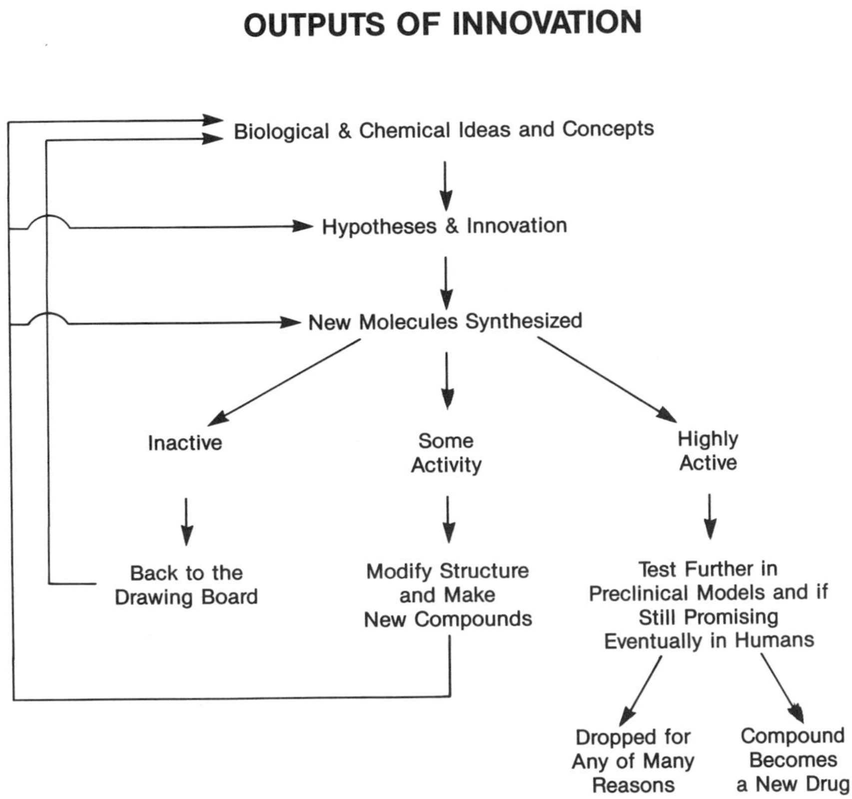

Fig. 4.1. Outputs of innovation and processes followed to improve on a chemical's activity.

conduct their research appropriately. The old rule of respecting and listening to the staff's ideas is important. This requires a somewhat loose approach to management in which managers are willing to tolerate ambiguity in some results and often suspend judgment about others. These points are extremely important because judgment, unfortunately, often acts to kill creativity. It is usually difficult for managers to suspend judgment, however, because passing judgment is what most managers have been specifically trained to do, and the temptation to pass judgment on research results is great. Strong egos of both scientists and managers are often a road block to creativity and drug discovery. The emphasis for both scientists and managers who wish to discover drugs must be to focus on the questions posed and not on the answers given. Being able to pose the correct questions will assist in deriving useful answers that will sometimes lead to a new drug discovery.

The Core Team for Drug Discovery

The core group involved in drug discovery usually consists of a chemist and biologist. They must work closely together in trying to discover novel and useful drugs. To achieve this goal, however, it is necessary that they have a certain degree of autonomy. They must also have the support and trust of their supervisors. The best climate for innovation comes from their establishing an effective relationship based on openness, respect, cooperation, and corporate responsibility. A certain degree of conflict and confrontation in some relationships may have a positive influence on their productivity.

Types of Consultants Who Interact with Drug Companies in the Research and Development Area

Consultants come in many shapes and sizes. In fact the only definition that seems to cover the field is that anyone who calls himself a consultant, is one. Consultants are people who provide services to others. Their services may be in the form of advice, evaluations, analyses, tangible work, or of another nature. Common types of consultants to the drug industry include:

1. Full-time university faculty who assist drug companies on either an ad hoc or periodic basis. They often listen or participate in company presentations and then offer opinions relating to the major issues or questions raised. Alternatively, they may be asked to make presentations or respond to problems. Many academic institutions have adopted policies that govern the amount of time a faculty member may consult and also the disclosure required of faculty members to the university (Zinder and Winn, 1984).
2. Full-time consulting companies assist drug companies, usually on a contract by contract basis, to place or conduct clinical studies, monitor studies, analyze biological samples, process data, analyze data, write medical or statistical reports, and prepare regulatory submissions. They may also assist companies by conducting audits of a small part of a department all the way to evaluating the overall corporation. These companies may be clinically, statistically, toxicologically, financially, management, or otherwise oriented.
3. Free-lance consultants assist companies in innumerable ways. These may be ex-company employees who are trying to develop a business of their own. It is often in a company's best interest to utilize the talents and experiences of these consultants in what can be an especially rewarding relationship.
4. Various other types of part-time and full-time consultants exist.

Management Consultant Companies

Some managers rely heavily on various types of consultants (e.g., academicians, management consultants) in charting the proper course to discover new drugs. Individual experts, consultants, and management firms may encourage the company's management to pursue activities in therapeutic areas or types of research that are incorrect for the company. Most management consultant companies lack adequate knowledge about the drug industry, drug development, and usually the particular company they are advising. Ironically, the consulting companies with some experience in advising the drug industry are often the most dangerous to their clients. These management consultant companies tout their drug industry experience. But, their often slick presentations belie their superficial approaches and lack of true understanding about research and development in the drug industry.

Cautions about Hiring Consultants

Numerous cautions must be considered before a consultant is hired. The situation described is where an in-depth analysis of a group or organization is required. If the most senior individual who hires a consultant(s) desires to maintain the status quo, then that is essentially what most consultants will recommend at the conclusion of their study. This occurs despite the fact that consultants are usually instructed to approach issues independently and without preconceived ideas. If consultants perceive that the person or group who hired them really wants to shake things up or provide an objective and impartial view, then there is a high likelihood that their report will reflect that approach. Careful instructions to consultants at the outset of their work are necessary if it is desired to avoid this problem.

Some consultants are hired as a personal favor to an executive in the company. Many of these consultants have a net negative effect because they require significant time of professional staff to educate them about current issues or problems. These consultants rarely make a real contribution toward reaching a solution or suggesting a desirable route to follow. Moreover, they may make suggestions of little value that "must" be followed because their personal contact in the company either gives the consultant unqualified support or does not wish to "insult" his friend or contact.

It is useful to have people who are (theoretically at least) using the services of consultants rate their usefulness on a periodic basis. That would help insure that the company was benefitting from the relationship. The details of contractual arrangements should also be periodically evaluated. It is usually better to hire consultants on an hourly, daily, or even weekly fee basis than to provide them an annual retainer for services to be given as needed. In addition to saving money, this suggestion avoids having consultants present in a company when they are not needed (or desired).

Choosing Consultants

In choosing between potential consultants it is important not only to critique carefully their presentation or proposal, but to evaluate their flexibility as well. A consultant's approach to various hypothetical problems that are raised "spontaneously" in a meeting may be used as a test of his or her potential usefulness. In addition, several references should be obtained and carefully checked to assess how well the consultants performed in previous assignments. It is essential to determine how well they understood their assignment, how efficient they were in conducting their work, and how closely their output matched their original plans. The impact and degree of interference the consultants had on daily operations of the company should be evaluated, as well as the quality of their experience in the drug industry.

Many otherwise excellent consultants bring inappropriate advice and approaches from other industries to problems they are asked to address in drug companies. Consultants without sufficient experience in the drug company may drain significant senior staff time away from important company business in order to educate the consultant about the drug industry. This may lead to highly educated consultants who are unable to provide useful advice to the company.

It is usually undesirable to use actual or potential investigators as consultants for a company. This practice introduces strong biases into their views on drug development strategies, approaches, and other issues. This conflict of interest does not seem to concern many companies who adhere to the practice of using consultants as investigators. Despite the author's objections to this practice, in most situations there do not appear to be problems. Nonetheless, it is desirable not to use investigators as consultants (or vice versa) whenever possible.

Task Forces

A task force is a group of people from different functional areas who are brought together and asked to address a specific issue or issues and to prepare a report. A task force may participate in any or all of the following activities: (1) gather information, (2) analyze information, (3) make recommendations, (4) participate in the decision-making process, and (5) reach a decision on the topic they are addressing. Almost any issue relating to drug discovery or development could be dealt with by a task force. Other functions may also be assigned to a task force (e.g., to help implement a new series of procedures). After the group completes its assignment it is generally disbanded.

Task forces can serve valuable functions by addressing specific issues that are not well suited to existing departments or groups, or where existing groups do not have adequate time to address the issue. Task forces often serve as internal consultants for a company, although outside consultants may also join or serve as advisors to the team.

Pitfalls and Potential Problems of Task Forces

There are a variety of issues relating to the use of task forces that should be considered before a decision is made to use such groups. One of the most important issues is that the appropriate professional level of people should be appointed to the task force. If the people appointed are too senior in the company, then they will not be using their time productively. If the members are at too junior a level, then they will either be unable to satisfactorily achieve the group's objectives, or possibly unable to convince others of the validity of their conclusions. In addition, the people appointed to "solve" a particular problem should have had at least some experience with that problem prior to the formation of the task force.

Another point is that people should not be taken away on a full-time basis from their regular job to participate on a task force. There are several problems with doing this. The most important ones are that a task force made up of full-time members will have a major concern about what they will be doing when the work of their task force is completed. Their major priority will generally not be to examine their assignment objectively but to make recommendations that provide future positions for themselves. This outcome will occur regardless of how relevant the proposed positions may be for the company's benefit and health. It is ironic that once this principle is perceived by senior managers, it will diminish the credibility of their report and make it unlikely that their recommendations will be accepted. One exception is for situations where the recommendations also meet the needs and/or desires of the manager(s) who appointed them.

A major problem that may affect any task force is the "swelled head syndrome." This refers to the fact that many people, especially at a junior level, who are placed on an important task force attribute this appointment to a recognition of their exceptional skills and talents. They believe that they have been anointed for an important future position in the company. If this public recognition fails to materialize (despite the fact that all individuals may have been told specifically that it would not happen), then some are likely to become disillusioned and even bitter when their "Cinderella" weekend is over. Their work may suffer and they will seek a transfer within the company or look for other employment. Being appointed to a task force may therefore be counterproductive for some people's career. This is especially true when junior level staff are appointed to a relatively important task force. The best workers at a certain level are often the ones chosen for task forces. It is ironic that it is these people who often develop "swelled heads" and become unhappy and less productive in their old positions after the task force is disbanded.

Special Deployment Teams

Special deployment teams are usually small groups of individuals who are trained in a specific scientific or technical area (e.g., chemistry, pharmacology, medical report writing, medical monitoring) and can be assigned to help solve personnel shortages for a temporary period. The team is usually composed of junior- and senior-level professionals with experience in the area they are to work in temporarily. This means that a special deployment team for chemistry projects consists of chemists and remains in the chemistry department, and a team conducting medical monitoring is based in the medical department. A group of medical report writers, however, could free-lance from their homes if they had a sample report to use as a model or template and the data and references necessary to write the report.

After the deployment group has helped solve a personnel shortage, it may be difficult to terminate their role, because they could easily become "indispensable" to the people they were assigned to help. To avoid this problem, it is best, for the length of their assignment to be fixed and to terminate it on a certain date. Alternatively, their assignment could terminate after a certain function or activity is completed. Renewals to continue their work for another fixed time or until another specified function is completed could be negotiated. This would generally depend on the priorities of competing activities.

CREATING THE RIGHT MILIEU

The milieu in which scientists work may be modified to help stimulate the innovative process. Some of the factors that affect this milieu include (1) scientific freedom to pursue ideas of personal interest, (2) ability of company scientists to interact with other scientists within and outside the company, and (3) an accepting view of scientists' opinions by their managers. Management policies and behavior clearly play an essential role in creating and maintaining a suitable environment in which creativity and drug discovery activities can flourish.

The nature and degree of cooperation between departments depends to a large degree on the personalities of the department heads and their desire to work together. If their relationships are not positive, it becomes difficult for their scientists to work together effectively. Solutions include creating guidelines (standard operating procedures), reorganizing departments, or transferring noncooperative people.

A stimulating environment will be fostered by inviting outside speakers into the company to talk about scientific issues, by encouraging staff to accept adjunct faculty appointments at nearby universities, by conducting internal workshops on topical issues, and by inviting important outside scientists to participate as consultants in relevant company affairs. Conducting off-site retreats, symposia, and business meetings that are possibly limited to company scientists are other means of creating a stimulating environment. Speakers at various company meetings could also come from other drug companies in addition to academia, government, and nondrug companies.

Even if an ideal milieu could be created at a drug company, it will change over time. A positive environment, like marriage and many other things in life, must be continually worked at by all concerned. This approach will help insure that the environment remains the way both management and scientists desire.

MINIMIZING NONPRODUCTIVE TANGENTS

Recognizing Tangents

Tangents are changes in the major direction or orientation of a project in terms of pursuing a new indication, new dosage form, new route of administration, or new patient population. It is best to recognize tangents when they are initially proposed. This is not always possible, and tangents are sometimes initially observed as a *fait accompli* or as an ongoing activity. The tangent is usually recognized because the proposed or actual activities do not adhere to the originally agreed-on plans and direction. Tangents vary greatly in the magnitude of time, effort, and resources expended and may use resources earmarked for the project's primary activities. Many types of possible tangents exist (Figs. 4.2 and 4.3).

After the proposed or actual tangent is recognized, it is important to evaluate whether that tangent represents an improvement over the original plan or an unwanted direction. Some tangents may lead the project in more productive directions, but the majority are nonproductive. Groups who advocate going off on tangents often seem to have new ideas and "better" approaches to propose each time they present a report to a reviewing committee. Some people on such groups may have difficulty sticking to a plan that takes several years to complete. It is often more "fun" for them to try or explore new activities. These are people and groups that managers must keep under close observation.

Most tangents may be described as being positive or negative. Although it may appear that this may only be determined in hindsight, the value of pursuing a tangent may usually be determined in advance. Tangents are offshoots of the drug's approved development plan. The group's intention may be to return to the original plan after the tangent is explored or to pursue both the original plan and tangent simultaneously. If the tangent is reviewed and approved by relevant senior managers or management committees, then the tangent is positive. For example, a few different types of can-

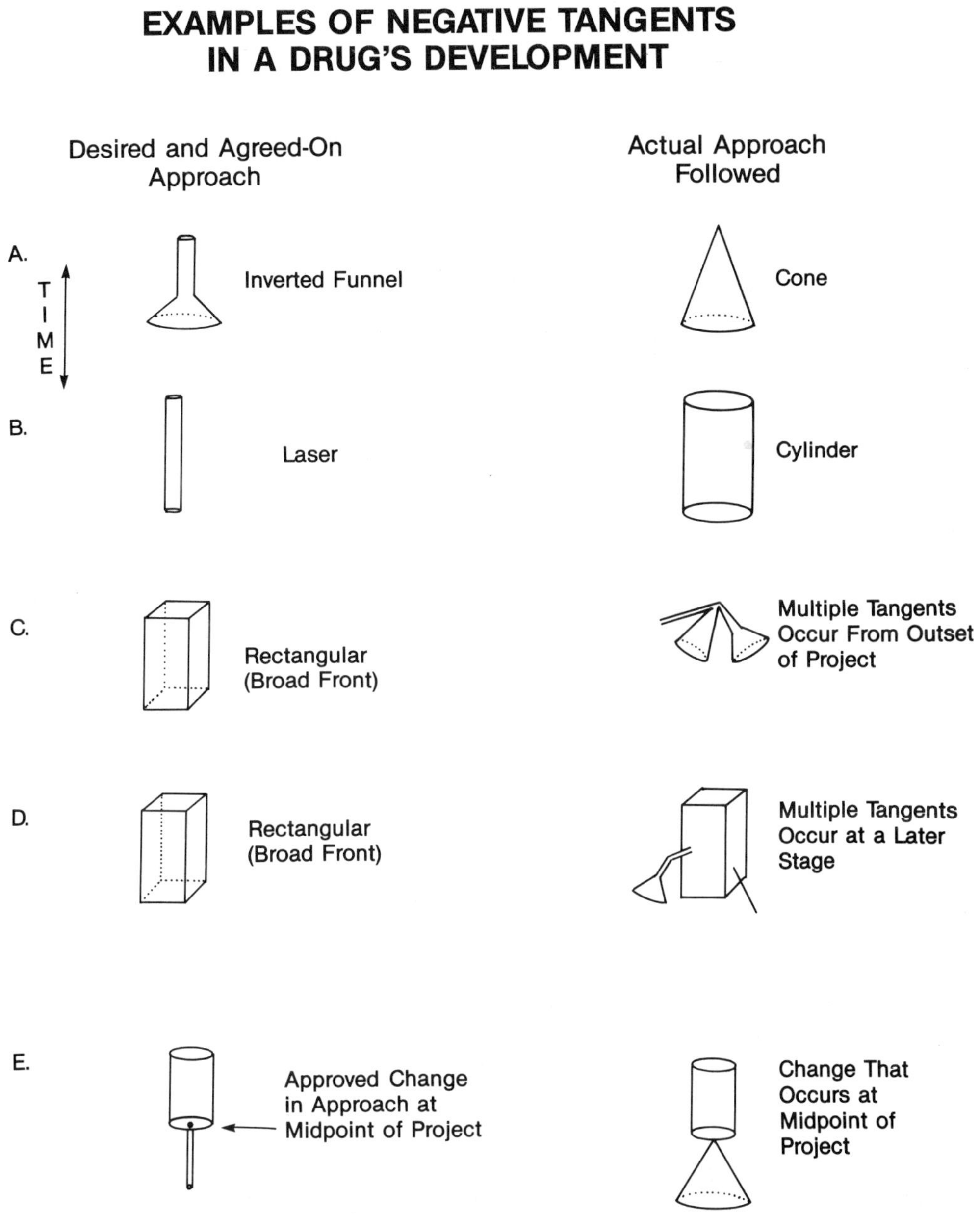

Fig. 4.2. Examples of negative tangents in a drug's development. (See Chap. 8 and Fig. 8.4 for a description of the basic approaches.)

cers may be evaluated with an anticancer drug during Phase II studies. A request to evaluate the drug in several new types of cancers in other Phase II pilot studies would be a tangent. If this request is appropriately reviewed and approved, it would represent a positive tangent or a modification of the development plan, regardless of whether the results turn out to be positive.

Many early clinical explorations in different therapeutic directions could be viewed

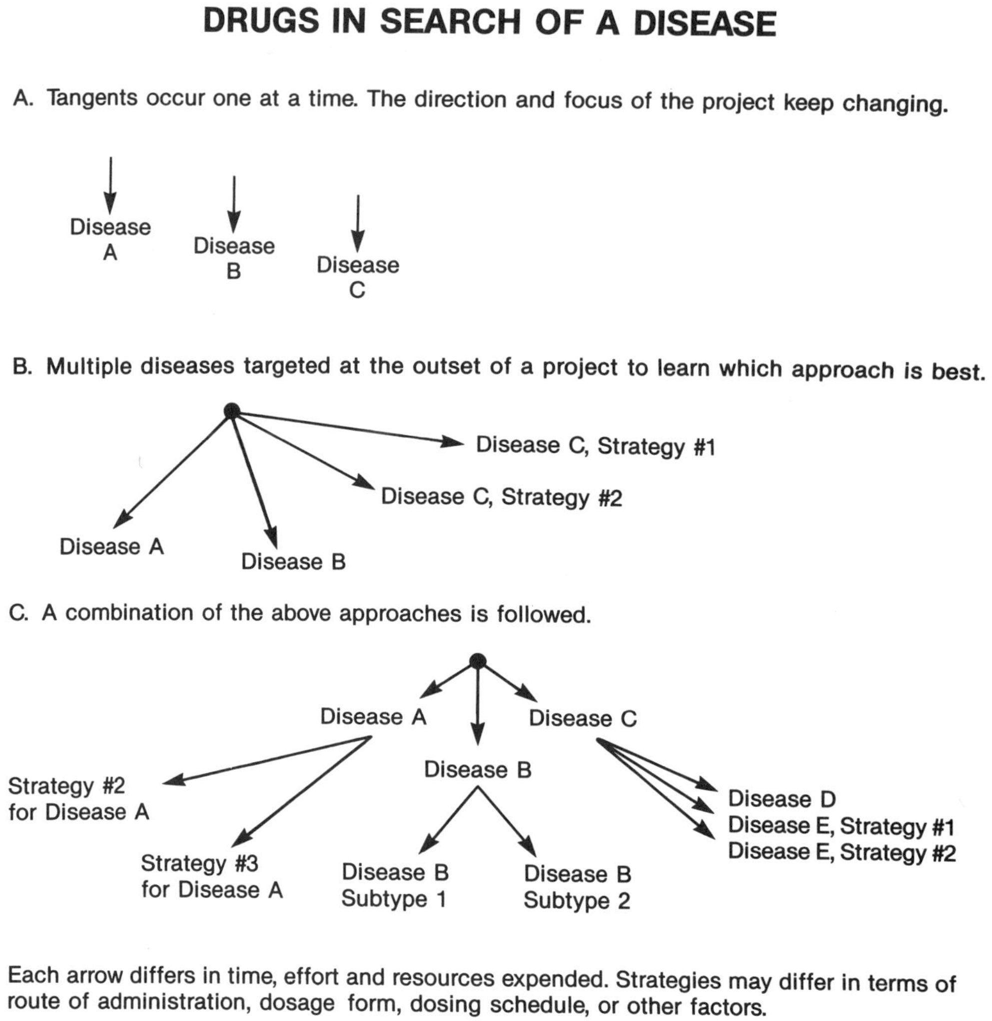

Fig. 4.3. Drugs in search of a disease. Each arrow differs in the amount of time, effort, and resources expended. Strategies may differ in terms of route of administration, dosage form, dosing schedule, or other factors.

as positive tangents if they were agreed to as part of the original development plan. If these explorations were not approved then they would be undesirable tangents. One of the most wasteful and negative types of tangents is where new directions or activities are conducted in a haphazard way. These efforts either dilute or replace efforts on the main approach and waste company resources. Moreover, such tangents can create innumerable problems for a drug company. These include clinical problems raised and the need to explain to regulatory agencies exactly what was done and why.

Issues Relating to Tangents

The major goals and issues relating to tangents that a review committee (or manager) should consider are:

1. To determine whether the idea or suggestion proposed is in fact a tangent to the agreed-on and approved project plans. For example, if the original clinical plan only covers Phases I and II, then plans for Phase III would not represent a tangent, because this represents a completion and not a change of plans.
2. To evaluate whether the tangent is of scientific, medical, or commercial interest. This implies that various groups should review the value of the proposed change.
3. To evaluate how the tangent would affect current and future activities on the main project in terms of staff, other resources, time, priority, and other factors. This area, that is often superficially brushed aside, is of great importance to a company.
4. To compare scientific, medical, and commercial values of a tangent with those of the major effort.
5. To evaluate the impact that a tangent will have on staff motivation, morale, and other nontangible factors. Is the proposal a seriously considered one or does the group frequently propose tangents and seem to desire things to work on that are more fun.
6. To evaluate how the tangent will impact on other projects. This is primarily assessed in terms of competition for resources.
7. To evaluate the overall priority of the tangent compared with those of the major approach and other drugs under development.

Minimizing Nonproductive Tangents

Some of the ways to minimize nonproductive tangents are to:

1. Encourage all professionals to verbalize their opinions when new proposals are presented and discussed.
2. Utilize independent people to review controversial proposals. These people may be within or outside the company.
3. Develop an appropriate combination of formal and informal systems to handle new proposals.
4. Appoint groups to review all proposals and projects periodically.
5. Appoint groups to review and coordinate activities being conducted at multiple sites.
6. Encourage all relevant groups and committees to ascertain whether their present activities and plans are being directed toward their goals.
7. Encourage all relevant groups and committees to ascertain whether their own proposed activities will take them more rapidly or more directly toward their goals.
8. Aim for consistent drug labeling between countries. Avoid conflicting information.
9. Utilize the fewest number of dosage shapes, tablet colors, and dosage forms consistent with sound business principles relating to marketing and regulatory responses.

Myths about Innovation, Drug Discovery, and Drug Development

The field of research is laden with myths about innovation and discovery. A number of general myths of innovation within research and development are listed in

Table 4.1. Selected myths of innovation[a]

1. Complete technical specifications and a thoroughly researched market plan are invariant first steps to success
2. Substantial strategic/technological plans greatly increase the odds of a "no surprises" outcome
3. Big teams are necessary to rapidly blitz a project, especially a complex one
4. Time for reflection and thought built into the development process is essential to creative results
5. Big projects are inherently different from small projects and must be managed differently
6. Strong functions such as marketing, production, and finance (and, consequently, functional organizations) are imperative if the would-be innovators are to get a fair hearing
7. Product line/product family compatibility is the key to economic success
8. Customers tell you only about yesterday's needs
9. Technology push is the cornerstone of business success
10. Strive to optimize technical forecasting with 100,000-bubble PERT[b] charts and other methods, because perfectionism pays off

[a] From Peters (1983a,b) with permission of the Stanford Alumni Association.
[b] PERT, program evaluation and review technique.

Table 4.1. Commonly perpetrated myths are one major reason why it is often dangerous to a company for scientific amateurs to become involved in decision making on technical issues.

In the world of drug discovery and development, many myths exist about various issues. Some of these represent wishful thinking by knowledgeable experts and others emanate from news stories put together by reporters to create a good story. Most are based on a certain amount of truth. A few myths are listed. Each of these has numerous variations and overlaps with others to some degree.

Myths of drug discovery

1. Empirical screening of compounds is being phased out as a means of discovering new drugs.
2. Rational drug discovery will be the major method used to discover drugs in the very near future.
3. Biotechnology methods are the most important tools for drug discovery.
4. Molecular designing of drugs on computers will enable drugs to be designed to reach almost any desired target.

Myths of drug development

1. The time planned to develop a drug can be accurately determined at the outset of a project.
2. The master plan for drug development can be followed without major alteration for most drugs.
3. A "quick and dirty" clinical study is usually adequate to determine whether a drug has activity in patients with a new disease.

STIMULATING INNOVATION

The Path of Innovation

The course of innovation is highly irregular and cannot be planned. Much of it appears to outsiders as sloppy and disorganized, and in many cases they are correct.

Major breakthroughs in technological discoveries often come from unexpected sources (e.g., Kodachrome film was invented by musicians). Does this mean that managers should encourage chaos or wild and wooly off-the-wall ideas? Certainly not. What it does mean is that managers should concentrate on hiring the most innovative, imaginative, and creative people they can find, providing them with a stimulating environment and a challenging problem, and then letting them have some flexibility to explore ways of solving the problem. Managers should neither control every step taken by scientists, nor allow them carte blanche.

Nonetheless, scientists should be held accountable for demonstrating that they are making some progress on their project. If more than two or three years are spent on a problem without achieving significant results, it is important to assess whether the talents and money expended might be better spent on another project of interest. There are clearly more worthwhile topics to study than there are creative scientists to carry out the research.

Stimulating Creativity

The motivational state of an individual often has a direct effect on his or her creativity. Young adults in science are often motivated by intrinsic factors and desire to accomplish something for its own sake, more than for an external goal that will be achieved. The environment that promotes this approach should not have (1) close supervision of all aspects of the work, (2) narrow choice in how to approach the problem, and (3) strong external evaluation and performance systems. Incentives play a role, in some individuals, but this is generally a minor role. Non-monetary rewards have been reported (Griggs and Manring, 1986) to have little impact on a scientist's effectiveness.

Targeting Research

Each company wants its researchers to discover drugs in specific therapeutic areas. This may be viewed as exploring the land surface for new leads in some therapeutic areas and not in others. Each therapeutic area could be viewed as a separate province with both urban and rural areas. The urban areas are where drug discoveries have been made or prior synthetic activities have pretty well combed the land surface looking for important leads. The rural areas are those relatively open and yet unexplored areas. The skill or trick (depending on one's viewpoint) is knowing (or guessing) where to look. Just as oil wells that are drilled usually come up empty, most compounds made either come up "empty" in terms of biological activity or they come up "full" in terms of serious toxicity problems.

The discovery of a potentially new drug may lead the company into a new therapeutic area that it does not wish to pursue. In that situation, the company may change its attitude about the therapeutic area, or the compound/drug may be licensed to another company. The decision about which path to follow is much easier to make if the company has identified its therapeutic comfort zone ahead of time.

Innovation flourishes in an environment of general scientific freedom. But, too much scientific freedom in terms of undermanagement can lead to serious problems of declining innovation. Some scientists are apt to dabble in various areas without an adequate focus to their search for new drugs, and some may completely lose their orientation toward new drug discovery. It is usually the department head and/or head of research who decide how much research effort and other resources to place on each disease and therapeutic area. Scientists, however, should have a strong voice in the approaches chosen to explore targeted diseases.

Many, if not most, drug companies tolerate some scientists working in nonconventional ways or on their own "pet" ideas for part of their time. Almost all companies, however, insist that scientists help with at least some screening of compounds when it is appropriate, and that their efforts are consistent with the objectives, goals, and strategies of the company.

Retreats and Off-Site Meetings

Retreats and other types of off-site meetings generally stimulate individuals' motivation, especially if the meeting is carefully planned. Meetings may encompass one or more departments, sections, or project teams. Managers from one or more functions or countries may be involved.

The retreat setting is often an ideal time and situation in which to deal with difficult issues. Issues and problems often seem more approachable for discussion when people have had a good meal, participated in vigorous sport competition, or have relaxed in a different environment. Openness of communication is often fostered along with a desire to resolve differences. If informality is desired, it may be encouraged by holding the meeting at a resort or under less formal conditions. If there is a serious problem to discuss, then spouses should generally not be invited. If social concerns are paramount and an informal atmosphere desired, then invitations to spouses should be considered.

Brainstorming

Brainstorming sessions, whether at formal meetings or over drinks at a bar, may be focused through a few simple and well-known techniques. These include provoking discussion and responses focused around a number of key questions or propositions.

1. What if . . .? This phrase is often followed by an event that is extremely negative, positive, or unlikely.
2. I wish . . .? People's strongest desires for a company. This may also be expressed as: If I had the power to do anything in this company, I would . . . Participants may each be asked to complete this phrase.
3. Why not . . .? This question is intended to initiate responses and discussion about new ideas or approaches.
4. If . . . then . . . This approach may be used to work out contingency plans or to insure that all relevant possibilities are considered (e.g., in a contract).

In discussing new concepts or interpreting data at brainstorming sessions, the interpretations reached must be accurate. If not, then incorrect conclusions will be drawn. For example, it was reported on English radio during a World War II air raid over England that the German bombs were all dropped at random. The next morning there were banner headlines in the German newspapers stating that the city of Random was completely destroyed.

Intellectual Turbulence

Bringing people with different backgrounds and experiences together in an environment where they can freely interact may lead to creative outputs. This situation may be achieved by physically placing certain departments in close proximity to each other within the company, having special spaces for socializing conveniently (and comfortably) placed in strategic areas, and arranging for meetings or other gatherings where personal interactions are likely to occur. These interactions should be planned to bring various groups together, including scientists with scientists, nonscientists with scientists, and marketing people with production people.

This approach is not easy to achieve if research and development is divided from the rest of a company and a separate research institute is established. It is one of the reasons why many research scientists in industry do not want to be separated from other scientists and nonscientists. Group meetings and social gatherings that precede or follow a talk or other event are particularly appropriate times for such interactions to occur. Any company that holds professional meetings without adequate time for social interaction (e.g., at long breaks) is missing an important opportunity for productive discussions and creativity. If time constraints become an issue at a particular meeting (as they often do), it is probably better to decrease the time for scientific presentations than to decrease the time allocated for breaks.

DEVELOPING OPERATING PROCEDURES

Having the right people and the right environment are the two most important aspects of creating the best situation in which a company may optimize its chances to discover and develop drugs. A lesser but also important aspect is to have operating procedures in place that facilitate rather than hinder the work of scientists, clinicians, and others who are discovering and developing drugs. Systems relate both to the bureaucracy that must be adhered to in any institution and to the facilities and equipment present to accomplish the work. Poor systems and facilities can easily lead to frustration and anger.

Examples of some of the pertinent questions that managers should ask about their systems and operating procedures are listed:

1. Are there 25 people in a company who must approve every request for an external grant?
2. Is there an excessive number of formal systems and standard operating procedures that are not really needed (or used)?
3. Are senior executives thinking and planning for the company's future health, or are they dealing with mundane issues created by systems that are either inefficient or do not work?
4. Is too much of a scientist's time and attention given to paperwork and are too many highly polished plans and reports generated rather than doing the work itself?

Many managers believe that all of the beautiful plans a company may generate on early stage drugs do not equal a single marketed drug that is generating revenue.

This reflects the philosophy that a drug-in-hand is worth the expectation of several that are currently at an early stage of development. Operating procedures used to bring a drug to market must be designed to expedite each drug's development.

Office automation is an area where great improvements in efficiency have been achieved over the last few decades. The number of new types of equipment and methods for speeding work output is truly staggering. The impact that this has had on improving business productivity, profitability, and competitive advantage is described in *The Information Edge* (Meyer and Boone, 1987).

Auditing Research, Development, and Manufacturing Activities (Quality Assurance and Quality Control Activities)

All drug companies audit many of their ongoing activities. The extent of these internal audits varies widely from informal checks to highly formalized systems developed to evaluate specific activities. The research and development areas that are audited include some that are mandated by Good Manufacturing Practices (GMP), and Good Laboratory Practices (GLP). Specific areas audited include manufacturing of drugs used in clinical studies, conduct of toxicology studies, and metabolism studies. Manufacturing audits (e.g., quality assurance and quality control) include a description of all analytical tests and procedures used to control chemical synthesis and drug manufacture. Also, each procedure and test used must be validated. Validation is the proof that each test actually does what it is supposed to do. This is further discussed in Chapter 22. Fig. 22.1 illustrates various approaches to the issue of conducting quality assurance and quality control investigations.

Quality assurance in toxicology studies are governed by GLP regulations. The people who conduct the quality assurance are different than those who conduct the toxicology study and do not report to the same supervisor. This is to prevent conflict-of-interest problems from arising. The most common pattern of conducting toxicology quality assurance is illustrated in panel A or panel E of Fig. 22.1 with the quality assurance steps shown in panel A. The final output is usually considered as a written final report of a toxicology study.

Clinical Audits Conducted by a Drug Company

Good Clinical Practices (GCP) guidelines have not yet officially been issued by the FDA in final form and the term GCP has no official definition. It is used in this book to include five regulations covering the following subjects. The first three are final approved United States regulations, whereas the last two are proposed.

1. Notice of Claimed Investigational Exemption for a New Drug (IND)
2. Institutional Review Boards (IRBs)
3. Informed Consents
4. Obligations of Sponsors
5. Obligations of Investigators

The FDA takes no official position on whether drug companies should conduct clinical audits of their own activities. IRBs and clinical monitors conduct quality assurance activities. Theoretically, there should not be any reason why a separate clinical audit is necessary. On the other hand, one or two individuals working for a sponsor could provide a valuable service to monitors and/or investigators by reviewing files and records that would be checked during an FDA inspection to insure that the files are accurate and complete.

A more thorough evaluation or audit of monitors' activities could be conducted; but this raises the possibility that the auditor would be viewed as a policeman and not as a helper. Some companies choose random clinical studies to audit, whereas other companies routinely audit all or only pivotal studies (i.e., generally the most well-controlled studies). The appropriate decision for a company regarding this issue is dependent on its traditions and culture as well as the nature of any problems that may exist. The author believes that clinical auditors should not be the same individuals who conduct GMP or GLP audits of data. GMP or GLP auditors do not report to the same managers as the people in the groups being audited, and the auditors are also generally perceived in an adversarial role. This situation does not necessarily apply for GCP auditors. Companies that utilize GCP auditors have a wide variety of approaches to consider and this is a rapidly changing field.

Examples of quality assurance in clinical studies involve literally hundreds of separate checks that often must be made. These are described in *The Guide to Clinical Studies* trilogy (Spilker, 1984, 1986b, 1987c), especially in the two chapters on monitoring. A few examples include (1) comparing unexpected laboratory results observed in data collection forms with actual laboratory slips, (2) comparing numbers in tables of reports with summary statements elsewhere in reports, (3) determining whether patients were treated according to the protocol, and so on. Quality assurance evaluations are also made of data entered into computers to evaluate the accuracy of several steps in the processing.

Communications between Functions

As drug companies grow in size, their various functions (e.g., marketing, research and development, production) usually grow further apart. Companies must put mechanisms in place to keep different functions close enough together in terms of their operations so that they work effectively and consider themselves as part of the same overall group. Common mechanisms to achieve this goal include forming committees, project teams, and task forces, plus holding joint retreats, seminars, and staff meetings. The difficulty that individuals have in crossing boundaries between departments or functions is usually greater in large companies. The best antidote to this problem is to promote managers who want to cooperate and be productive rather than those who want to promote their own views and build empires.

Adjusting Barriers between Departments: Are Walls Open, Flexible, Fixed, or Controlled?

Every so often there is a flurry of articles or books stating that the functional and emotional walls between departments and groups should be broken down (and sometimes the physical walls as well) and that people should interact more and work as a single large group. At other times, there is a flurry of articles or books emphasizing that people often work most efficiently and productively when they have the security of knowing the limits of their position and knowing that their area of work will not be invaded or encroached upon by others. It is sometimes difficult to determine the optimal balance between these two approaches when establishing the optimal work environment.

Clearly, some individuals and disciplines generally function better when they are operating in a more open, flexible environment, and others function better in a more fixed and controlled environment. The financial, production, and legal groups of a drug company tend (of necessity) to be more of the latter kind, while the marketing and research and development groups may be either. The particular style that suits a company at one point in its history may be less appropriate at another point. For example, during crisis periods it is not desirable for each person to be "doing their own thing," although this style may be more tolerated at other times. Also, the personalities of the chief executive officer, marketing head, and research and development director greatly influence the style of their group or company.

What should a company do about walls between groups? One approach is to think of them as movable. At appropriate times they should be higher and at other times they may be lowered. The trick is not to decide how high or low they should be, but to resolve how the decision will be reached of when to raise or lower them. More importantly, who will coordinate the different groups' attitudes and activities so that one department head is not raising his barriers to cross-group interactions at a time when another department head is lowering his.

INCREASING EFFICIENCY OF RESEARCH AND DEVELOPMENT

Research may be efficiently conducted in extremely small or large companies, in companies that have centralized or decentralized managements, and in companies with any organizational structure. On the other hand, research efficiency is often increased when there is (1) a positive attitude toward research and scientists from managers, (2) a sufficient number of peers for expert input and meaningful discussions, (3) adequate facilities and equipment, (4) adequate support staff and technical help, plus (5) various other factors that allow scientists to do their work effectively. A number of issues on increasing efficiency are discussed below; others are covered in Chapter 16 on productivity.

Exploring a Few or Many Therapeutic Areas

Some research directors believe that many scientists working on a few programs have a better chance of discovering a drug than having few scientists work on many programs. This is a controversial area. The former group of research and development heads place many resources on few projects. They believe that they are thereby able to achieve a critical mass and an adequate level of scientific expertise on each project. The appropriate number of these groups will depend on the size of the organization. Also, some research programs require much more scientific input and involvement than others. People who follow the opposite approach of placing few resources on many programs believe that a small number of dedicated, creative, and enthusiastic scientists unencumbered by bureaucratic restraints may make breakthroughs and discoveries as easily (or more easily) than larger groups.

When the size of research groups becomes too large their productivity often decreases. Large groups usually develop a vertical hierarchical structure. A relatively flat or horizontal structure is viewed by many senior managers as a means of increasing efficiency. A horizontal structure implies that there are fewer hierarchical levels in the organization and more people report to each manager. Each manager is closer to the most senior and junior people in a horizontal structure than in one where many hierarchical levels exist.

Improving Communications between Scientists

Scientists in different departments or sites of a research organization often are working on related research projects and could benefit from experiences and knowledge of others. Before dialogue can occur it is essential for them to know who has similar research interests. There is no single method that is best to facilitate these interactions, whether within a department, between departments, or across oceans.

One approach to this issue is to circulate a written synopsis of each scientist's research interests and active projects. Alternatively, this information could be entered in a computer, as a sort of bulletin board. One question that immediately arises is determining how much information is appropriate to circulate. The more information that is circulated about each scientist, the more precisely topics may be described. But, the information's security becomes a major concern and also, if "too much" information is gathered, then fewer people will utilize it. If too little information is circulated, it may have less usefulness. A few lines about current research topics may be sufficient to allow scientists to identify whom they wish to contact.

Any system that is established, especially if utilizing computers, should be user friendly. This will allow scientists to operate the system themselves. To whatever degree a system like this operates it will provide benefits to the users who may collaborate on projects or help each other with scientific lessons about what approaches or techniques work in specific situations.

Providing Feedback to Scientists

Providing feedback to scientists from peers at staff conferences and in small group sessions are effective methods and forums for discussing and improving the quality of scientific ideas. Many scientists seek and obtain feedback from their peers without any prompting. Scientists who are more reticent about seeking feedback or are antagonistic to criticism should be encouraged by their managers to place themselves in situations where feedback will occur. Managers may foster this interchange through staff meetings where scientists receive feedback on their presentations. Staff conferences include both intra- and interdepartmental meetings. Scientists receive feedback at many other forums, including (1) scientific meetings of all types, (2) during casual or formal discussions with colleagues, and (3) through submitting articles for publication. Consultants may also be asked to evaluate the quality of a

Table 4.2. Advantages in waiting until a generally complete profile is obtained about a chemical series before a lead compound is chosen for testing in humans, plus counterarguments

Advantage	Counterargument
1. There is a better chance that the optimal compound in a series has been found	1. The best compound in a series is often one of the first made (Vane, 1967). If standards are set too high, potentially valuable drugs may never be tested in humans
2. Less money is spent on drug development by being more certain about the potential of the compound that is advanced	2. It may take longer to get to this point than by deciding with less information. Time is usually more valuable than money in drug development
3. More specific biological data will be obtained on the specific compound of interest	3. Same as 2

scientist's or department's research and to provide input that may lead to its being improved.

When Should a Compound Advance toward Testing in Humans?

In deciding when a compound is ready to proceed to human testing, there are no rigid rules. This is a matter involving judgment, plus an assessment of the company's needs. Arguments can be made both for and against developing a complete preclinical profile prior to advancing a compound (Table 4.2) or going rapidly (Table 4.3) toward clinical tests.

When Should a Research Program be Terminated?

One of the most important decisions research managers make is which therapeutic, disease, or drug areas to terminate. In some ways this is more important than determining which areas or programs to initiate. Many research programs and projects appear to develop a life of their own after they are created, and it is often difficult to know how and when it is best to terminate them. The topic of terminating de-

Table 4.3. Advantages in taking early chemical leads rapidly into humans for testing, plus counterarguments

Advantage	Counterargument
1. More rapid feedback is obtained about a drug's efficacy and the value of developing a drug further and pursuing backup candidates is assessed	1. Information obtained may only relate to the compound tested and may not be extrapolatable to others in the series
2. Possible problems with safety that could provide information about the entire series will be uncovered.	2. A less toxic compound might be uncovered through additional synthetic work that would be a more rapid and less expensive way to learn the information
3. The entire series may be expanded in the laboratory to find the best backup candidate, while human work is underway	3. This is a costly approach and resources might be better applied to other projects while additional preclinical activities are carried out

velopment projects is discussed in Chapter 29 of *Guide to Planning and Managing Multiple Clinical Studies* (Spilker, 1987c).

The decision to terminate work on a particular research program may be made at any one of several levels, depending on the type and magnitude of the work that is to be terminated, as well as the particular company. Specific approaches to evaluating a disease may often be terminated by a scientist, work on a specific disease may usually be terminated by a department head, and work on a therapeutic area may be terminated by the head of research. Each of these decisions should generally be discussed and reviewed by management, and by others if relevant. It is sometimes desirable to allow experienced scientists to use their intuition in reaching a decision to terminate work. It is also important to have a consensus of both managers and scientists on the appropriateness of terminating a research program or development project.

Another approach to terminating research programs is to adopt the philosophy that all programs are to be terminated every one, two, or three years unless a strong rationale can be advanced for their continuation. This approach recognizes that many research programs seems to take on a life of their own and acquire resources and momentum that are difficult to move in a different direction, let alone terminate. Requiring all research programs to periodically be reassessed and compete for resources in an objective manner would prevent the pitfall of continued momentum. Reassessment must be carefully conducted to prevent people from (1) spending an excessive amount of time justifying their program rather than doing the work, (2) competing for resources in a negative atmosphere, and (3) demoralizing the losers. If handled appropriately, it should serve to improve the efficiency of research.

A fascinating anecdote about temporarily suspending drug development while safety questions are addressed concerns lovastatin, Merck & Co.'s new cholesterol-lowering drug. After it was reported that a competitor (Sankyo Co. Ltd.) had stopped clinical studies on their drug, reportedly because of cancerous tumors in dogs, Merck & Co. also stopped tests on their chemically related drug and initiated more toxicology studies. Sankyo Co. Ltd. reportedly later said that the rumors were false and that they merely were replacing their drug with a newer, more effective one (Byrne, 1987). According to the article in *Business Week*, Merck & Co. lost almost four years of their drug development (and patent protection) from September 1980 to May 1984 when large-scale clinical studies were resumed. One moral of this episode is that the truth of important rumors must be established before allowing them to greatly influence development of a valuable drug. This may be done via regulatory agencies and possibly in other ways.

Extracting Lessons from a Drug's History

Lessons and experience are what one has remaining when a drug fails. It is essential to learn from one's mistakes, because, as Santayana said, "Those who cannot remember the past are condemned to repeat it." Although lessons should be learned as they occur, it is sometimes necessary to conduct a systematic evaluation of some drugs' histories to extract lessons. The lessons learned may then be widely disseminated within the company.

The history of a drug's development to the time of marketing can be conveniently divided into four parts, although other divisions of activities could be used. The four are:

1. *Discovery*. How the compound was discovered.
2. *Preclinical evaluation*. How the compound was tested in animals.
3. *Clinical evaluation*. How the compound was tested in humans.
4. *Technical development*. How the compound was made into a drug.

Postmarketing experiences may also be examined for valuable lessons with those drugs that have been marketed. Additional categories could be created that focus on marketing, production, or other aspects of drug development.

Once an acceptable group of categories is chosen, it is necessary to choose the drugs to be examined. This examination exercise may be conducted because of general interest about a group of drugs and thus there would be no specific issue to evaluate. On the other hand, the exercise itself may have been suggested to specifically address a particular question or issue (e.g., have unsuccessful drugs been terminated more rapidly in the last three years than in a three-year period that occurred 12 years ago). In choosing drugs to evaluate, it is essential to pick those with the highest likelihood of providing worthwhile lessons that may be extrapolated to other situations. This does not mean to avoid types of drugs that are not currently being studied, but to avoid drugs where experiences gained were generally unique to that drug and are not likely to be repeated. Choose a variety of drugs to examine, not based on their therapeutic area, but on the plans followed for their development (e.g., laser, broad front, cone). Evaluate both successful and unsuccessful drugs, especially if the unsuccessful drugs could have been developed successfully by other companies and the failure was not because of inherent problems in the molecule.

Develop a plan to identify the lessons utilizing all available sources. This may require some formal planning, but it could also be done rather casually and informally. Should certain people be interviewed? The most important part of this activity is determining how the lessons learned from the exercise will assist future development of other drugs. This requires identifying how the lessons may be applied to drug discovery and/or development activities, plus attaining management support for any recommendations that result from this exercise. Recommendations may be in the form of changes in the (1) organization, (2) responsibilities of individuals or groups within the organization, (3) sign-off procedures, (4) use of check lists at appropriate places and times, or (5) any of the various other means of preventing similar problems from occurring again.

APPROACHES TO DIFFICULT DECISIONS

Everyone has their own style of making difficult decisions, and many methods are used at drug companies. A few of these techniques are briefly described. The assumption is made that all relevant information is available to assist in the decision-making process. The assumption is also made that the appropriate people are the ones who will deliberate about the decision. It is understood that these assumptions are often incorrect because the most appropriate people are not always the ones dealing with an issue, and not all information on any issue can ever be known.

Some of the formal methods and tools used to make decisions include decision trees, algorithms, and flow diagrams. These methods have the advantage of being able to illustrate and present the problem, relevant information, and alternatives in a clear manner. These techniques often expedite communications and allow one to identify where more information is needed, plus help in reaching a decision. The disadvantages are that not all decisions are amenable to these techniques, not everyone is comfortable with using them, and a rapid decision must sometimes be made before these tools could be used. These techniques utilize an extremely logical approach, although that in itself does not necessarily imply that they will lead to a correct answer. Many questions that do not lend themselves to black or white (i.e., yes or no) responses can not be addressed in this way. These techniques should be learned by all people who make frequent or important decisions for those situations where these methods will be useful. These methods also help organize one's way of thinking about an issue.

Commonly used methods to arrive at difficult decisions are to initially (1) discuss issues with others, (2) think about the issue, (3) review the issue, (4) weigh the pros and cons of alternative solutions, (5) consider if any of the alternatives could have negative outcomes, and finally (6) as an individual (or group) reach a decision. The decision should be tentative, when possible, to allow time for reflection, new information, and other opinions to be heard. Critiquing one's own decisions is often done using the devil's advocate approach. Finally, the technique of lateral thinking is sometimes appropriate to use (de Bono, 1967).

Determining Whether a Drug Should be Withdrawn from the Market?

Situations unfortunately arise when this question must be addressed. This discussion assumes that the question is posed within a drug company and that no regulatory agency has mandated that the drug must be withdrawn.

One of the most important considerations is that input is required from a variety of sources. These include legal, regulatory, commercial, medical, and possibly others. If a regulatory authority has not mandated a drug's withdrawal then the decision may be primarily legal, such as when Bendectin was withdrawn by Parke-Davis. This drug was unfairly persecuted and convicted in the press, which indirectly forced its removal from the market (Sheffield and Batagol, 1985).

The decision to withdraw a drug may be primarily made on commercial grounds. This happens with many products each year that are not commercially viable. At a certain point it becomes uneconomic for a company to produce a drug, and it is usually withdrawn from sale. Some of these drugs may not be readily or adequately replaced, and physicians may demand the drug's reintroduction. A few case histories of this phenomenon were recently described (Weintraub and Northington, 1986).

If It Ain't Broke, Don't Fix It

There are senior managers at all drug companies who are frequently heard to use this or a similar phrase. In many cases it represents sound advice. On the other hand, this phrase is also a trap because it may lead some people to become complacent about the status of various issues and not actively seek means of improving a company's performance and efficiency. Strategies and approaches that have led to past successes must continually be reappraised and updated if they will be used to achieve future successes.

When managers use the argument that there's no reason to change habits or rules, it is important to identify the reason for the statement. Are they seeking a reason to avoid facing either a problem or a change that would likely be beneficial (e.g., they are a passive individual) or are they providing sound advice?

Section II

Corporate Organization and Management Issues

5 / *Organizing at the Corporate Level*

A staff of four hundred represents the critical number in a firm taken over. It is the number which separates the personal boss from the high-level manager. A man (person) may run a firm of four hundred or fewer people extremely well, but that is the maximum he can run personally, knowing all their names, without too much delegated authority. If you expand that firm to, say, 1,100, (contd.) *you may destroy him: Instead of all being people he knows by name, they become pegs on a board; instead of just doing and deciding he has to do a lot of explaining and educating; instead of checking up on everything himself, he has to institute a system and establish procedures. All this demands skills quite different from those he built his success on, and ones which he may well lack.* Antony Jay. From *Management and Machiavelli.*

VIEWING AN OVERALL CORPORATE ORGANIZATION

Various Perspectives of a Company's Structure

Before discussing models that are frequently used to organize a drug company, it is important to identify how a company is viewed by managers who must establish and operate the organization. Two basic ways of viewing a company as an outside observer are in terms of either (1) current organizational structures and reporting relationships that have grown up over the years or (2) activities that are carried out by groups that make up the company. The former view takes cognizance of the contradictions and conflicts, plus other warts and blemishes in the way a company is structured and operates. Titles and even arbitrarily imposed reporting relationships are viewed as relevant and important. The other viewpoint is functionally oriented and sees a company in terms of flow charts. Relevant groups are considered in terms of their activities, procedures, and interactions. According to this functional view, a company should be organized to facilitate these activities and relationships.

A company may also be viewed from the outside as an allocation of resources from senior managers to more junior managers and then to even more junior managers and finally to the staff who use those resources. Resources are primarily staff and money, but also include information and other categories. Each level in a company has different needs and wants in terms of resources required to fulfill their function. When an organization is structured to facilitate communications amongst and between its employees and managers, it is better able to allocate its resources.

Finally, a company may also be viewed from the perspective of an insider in terms of one's own discipline and department. This view stresses the relationship between one's area and the overall organization in terms of structure and function. On this more personal level, employees may perceive benefits and drawbacks of their positions relative to the way that the company is organized. They may also assess the structure insofar as it facilitates or hinders various work activities, and facilitates or hinders progress in drug development. Other criteria used from an insider's personal perspective may be expressed in terms of company culture, image, traditions, personnel, political issues, and the way in which work actually is accomplished.

These different views present a challenge. How may a single organizational structure and set of operating procedures be established to fit all of the dissimilar and conflicting aspects of the perspectives described while maintaining balance and cooperation in developing drugs and running a company?

Issues to Address in Deciding How to Organize a Company or a Subunit

The two most important issues to focus on in deciding how to organize a company (or another group) in the drug industry are (1) personnel - specific individuals present who will be involved (or could be involved) in the organization and (2) functions that must be accomplished through the organization. Either of these considerations (or a blend of both) could be the major influence on the particular organizational structure that is established.

A company may be people oriented and want to use that factor as the basis for their organizational structure, but the company may not have a sufficient number of suitable staff around whom to structure their company, division, or department. In that situation, the most senior position should be filled first and that individual would then help recruit and hire the rest of the staff. For example, Glaxo Inc. hired Dr. Pedro Cuatrecasas to establish a research group in the United States. He then began to hire senior managers, and the research organization rapidly took shape. If a company believes that structure itself is more important to define than to identify the people who will fill each slot, then relevant individuals may proceed to organize their company on paper. The most appropriate people to fill each position are considered and chosen after the agreed-on organizational structure is in place. One of the justifications for this latter approach is that people come and go, but a company's structure should have a greater permanence. This is especially true for larger companies.

When building an organization based on function, it is especially important that the logic underlying the new structure make sense to employees. The logic used should mimic present routes of work that are efficient whenever it is realistic to do so. If work patterns and procedures are to change because of a new or modified structure, a great deal of education may be needed to convince people that the new organizational structure will improve efficiency.

Building a large organizational structure solely around people or around work functions is generally inappropriate. An organizational structure based on an ideal or theoretical set of functions is sterile, because it does not consider specific people present in the company who will be asked to fill most if not all positions. Building a structure solely around people may lead to serious problems when an important person leaves the company or changes positions within the company. This is a dilemma that is faced by many companies and there is no easy answer except to aim for a system that best fits the company.

When a company's organizational structure is to be modified, it is important that the changes made are in concert with other parts of the organization that are intended to remain stable. It is clearly necessary to plan carefully the integration of established and newly modified (or added) areas.

MODELS OF A COMPANY'S OVERALL ORGANIZATION

It is said by some theoretical business school academicians that all businesses are organized according to one of three basic models. These models are to organize (1)

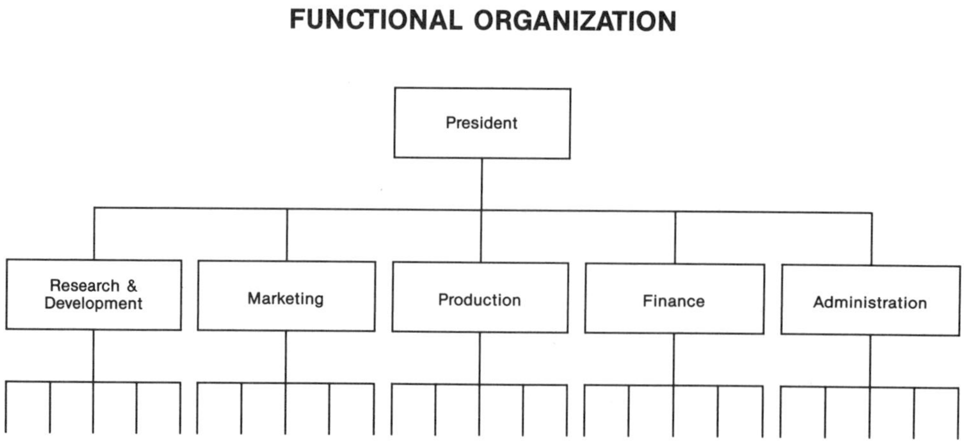

Fig. 5.1. Functional model of an organization.

by function, (2) by division or product (profit center), or (3) using a matrix approach. These three models are illustrated in Figs. 5.1 to 5.3.

Functional Model

The functional model (Fig. 5.1) is the structure present in most drug companies. The departments in each function report to a central person (e.g., department head), who governs the group's activities. The major advantages of organizing a company according to the functional model is that individuals deal most often with people who have similar backgrounds and training. The major disadvantages are that there tends to be little communication with groups in other functional areas, and fewer people have an overall or broad corporate view.

Product-Oriented Model

Figure 5.2 illustrates a product-oriented (i.e., division-oriented) organization. The prototype company that used the divisional approach is General Motors. Each car division was at one time organized like a stand-alone business and had its own marketing, research and development, and other functions. Some drug companies have organized themselves around self-contained business units such as consumer products, diagnostics, hospital supplies, and ethical drugs. In theory, at least, each of these business units could be almost totally independent. A major advantage of this approach is to encourage the General Manager of each division to be as successful as possible. The major disadvantage is a duplication of many functions that otherwise would be centralized. One variation on this theme is for only one of the functions in Fig. 5.1 to organize itself using this model.

Matrix Model

Figure 5.3 illustrates a matrix structure. The matrix approach recognizes the importance of both functional and product-oriented models. None of the business man-

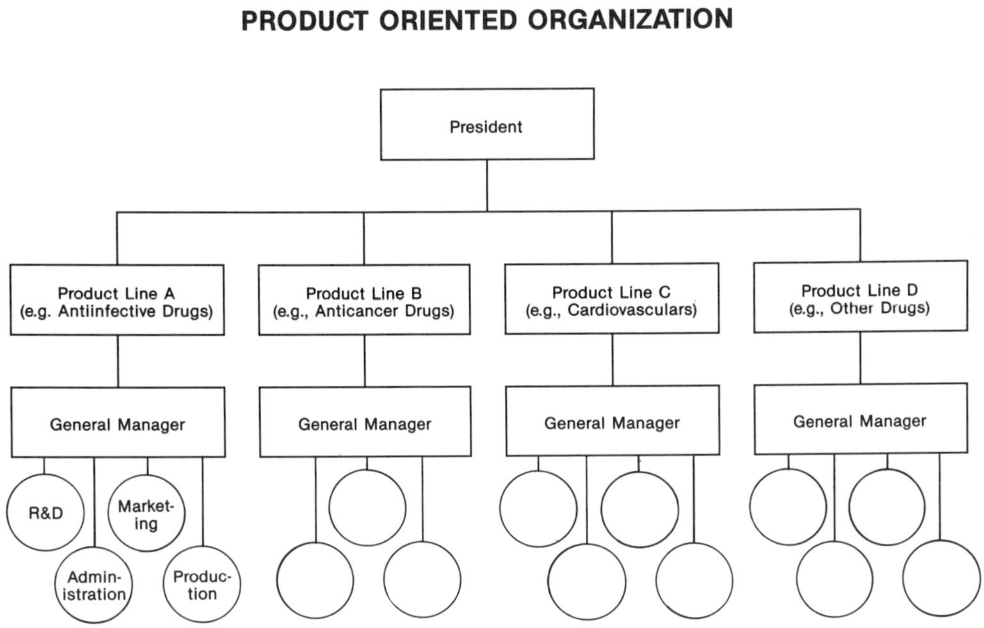

Fig. 5.2. Product-oriented model of an organization.

agers control the resources they need, but must negotiate with line managers to get resources. Businesses may therefore compete among themselves for resources. Separate teams are established to run each business. This model has advantages over the divisional model in Fig. 5.2 because there is less duplication, waste, and inefficiency. Resources are shared between businesses in the matrix model. The matrix model recognizes business interdependence and in theory offers greater flexibility than the other models.

Advantages of a matrix organization are that it is client oriented, promotes teamwork, minimizes intergroup conflict, is more responsive to change, provides greater visibility for lower level employees, and offers multiple career paths. Major disadvantages of a matrix organization are that it (1) dilutes authority of line function managers, (2) requires greater interpersonal skills on the part of numerous managers to succeed, (3) requires cooperation of line function managers, and (4) leads to a greater erosion of detailed technical skills.

An organization's matrix should not solely be viewed in two dimensions as shown in Figs. 5.3 to 5.5. It is really necessary to think along 3 axes. The major axes for a multinational drug company are (1) business areas, (2) function or discipline, and (3) geographical location. A particular company may be balanced or dominated by one or more of these dimensions. For example, the over-the-counter (OTC) business may be dominant (dimension one), the marketing function may be dominant (dimension two), or the United States operation may be dominant (dimension three).

Although the model in Fig. 5.3 illustrates integration of an entire company, it is possible for one group of a functional model (Fig. 5.1) to use some methods of this matrix model; however, the head of the functional group who uses a matrix cannot give as much autonomy to a matrix group as in the pure matrix model shown in Fig.

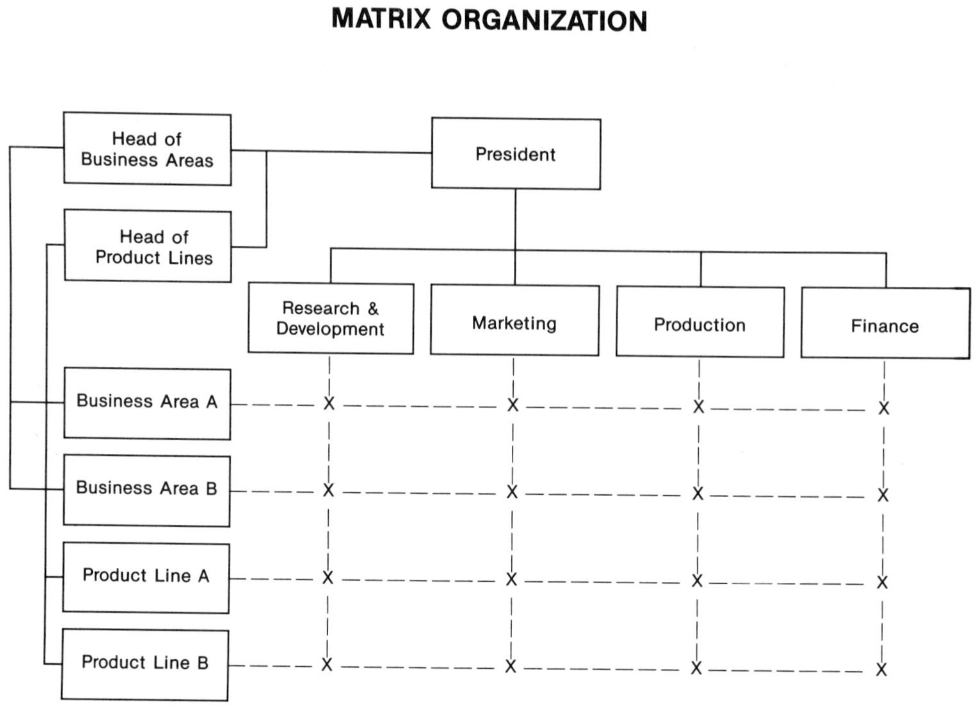

Fig. 5.3. Matrix model of an organization. The "*X*"s are coordination relationships. The business areas and product lines shown could be replaced by projects, each led by a project manager who would report to a single head of projects.

5.3 where all functional groups are involved. In the matrix model it is possible to organize a company around types or groups of products (e.g., diagnostics, OTCs) or customers (e.g., hospitals, Health Maintenance Organizations [HMOs], private doctors).

Other Models

In addition to the traditional models shown in Figs. 5.1 to 5.3, there are numerous hybrid type organizations that are possible (e.g., Figs. 5.4 and 5.5).

Of the many approaches that describe how to organize a company, the author prefers that of Futterman (1985). She boils the discussion down to three key issues or dimensions which, once addressed, give shape to a structure that will best meet a company's needs. These key issues are to identify where the company places itself along three scales:

1. *Scope of business activities*: From undiversified or narrow (e.g., a drug company that makes and sells only prescription drugs) to fully diversified (e.g., a company that makes and sells medical supplies, chemicals, veterinary products, OTC drugs, and prescription drugs).
2. *Domain of the company's business*: From stable to changing. Research-based

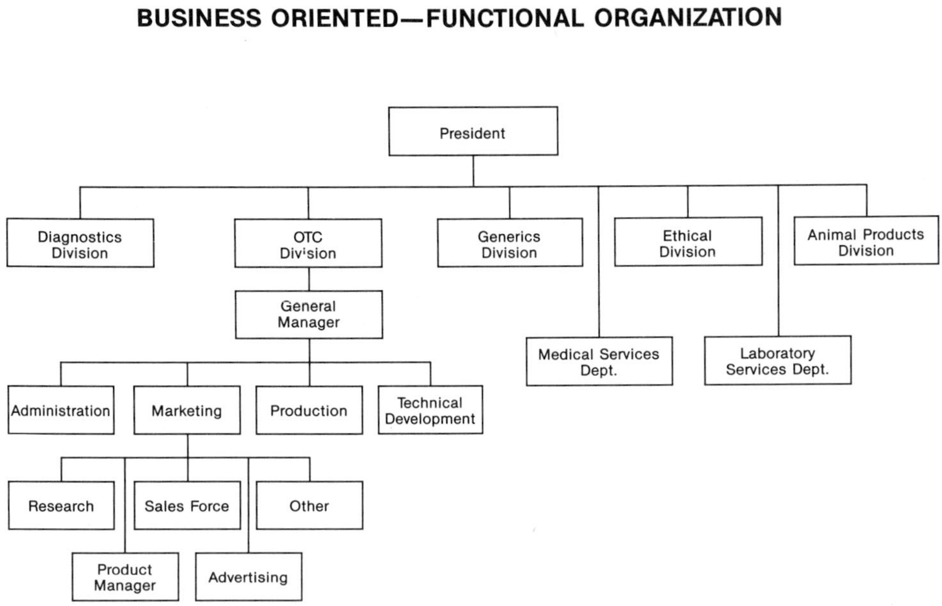

Fig. 5.4. Business- and function-oriented model of an organization. OTC, over-the-counter drugs.

drug companies are engaged in a changing market. Some of their other businesses may be more stable.

3. *Search for growth opportunities*: From purely internal (i.e., within the company's businesses) to external (i.e., to seek other opportunities, usually acquisition of new products, companies, or licensed products).

Based on a company's responses to these fundamental choices, which include considerations of current businesses and future plans, Futterman proposes eight organizational models (Figs. 5.6 and 5.7). She describes these as an indication of important organizational issues to consider rather than as a blueprint to follow. Utilizing this approach would lead a company toward developing a hybrid organizational structure in terms of the previously described models.

Placing Departments and Groups in the Correct Position in the Organizational Model Chosen

Many factors influence how a company places numerous groups and departments in the organizational chart. Placement usually depends primarily on personalities of managers involved and their relative power. Logic usually comes in a poor second in this decision-making exercise. Different companies place departments such as licensing, patents, and regulatory affairs in totally different functional areas. Service groups such as the library, computer support, and graphics services are examples of technical groups that are administratively located in widely different functional areas of different companies.

BUSINESS ORIENTED—MATRIX ORGANIZATION

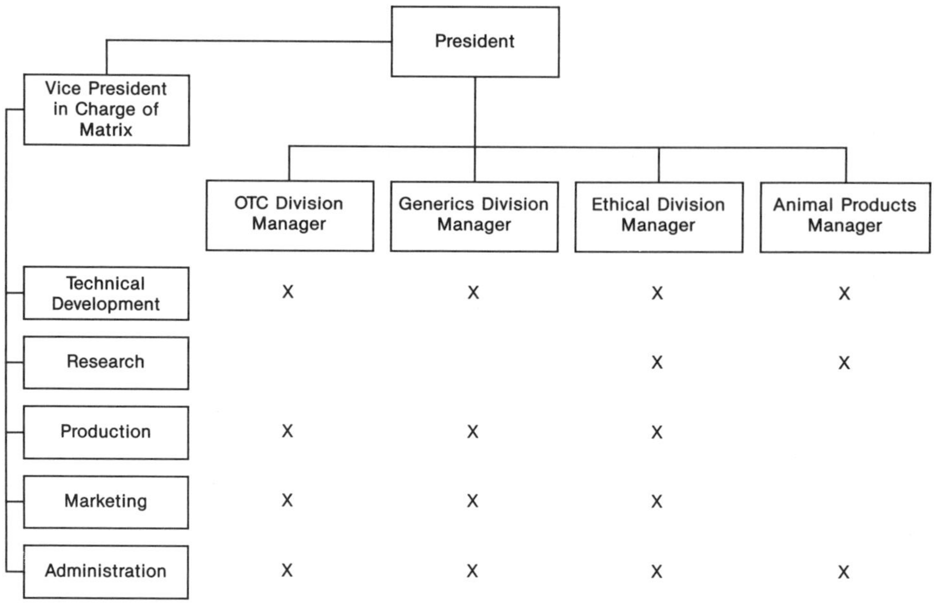

X=Contracts are negotiated with each of the groups on the left for services and support.

Fig. 5.5. Business- and matrix-oriented model of an organization. The "*X*s" are coordination relationships.

CORPORATE ORGANIZATIONAL ISSUES

Hierarchical Versus Flat Management

Some drug companies of approximately equal size have many more managerial levels than others. Those with many levels may be said to be hierarchically oriented, whereas those with relatively few levels are often said to have a broad or flat management. This latter type of company utilizes greater delegation of responsibility, has easier access to superiors, and usually has more flexibility than a more vertically structured company. Too many hierachical levels tend to choke a company in forms, procedures, and sign-offs, and usually results in decreased efficiency. The numerous advantages of a broad management and organization are only achieved if authority is delegated downward. If this is not done then too many people compete for their bosses' attention to make decisions, sign forms, and so on. Another requirement is a cadre of senior managers who want this approach to work and can manage relatively large numbers of other managers (e.g., 10 to 20) reporting to them.

Types of Subsidiaries of Drug Companies

Multinational drug companies often have several different types of subsidiaries around the world. Each subsidiary includes groups that are active in one or more of the following activities:

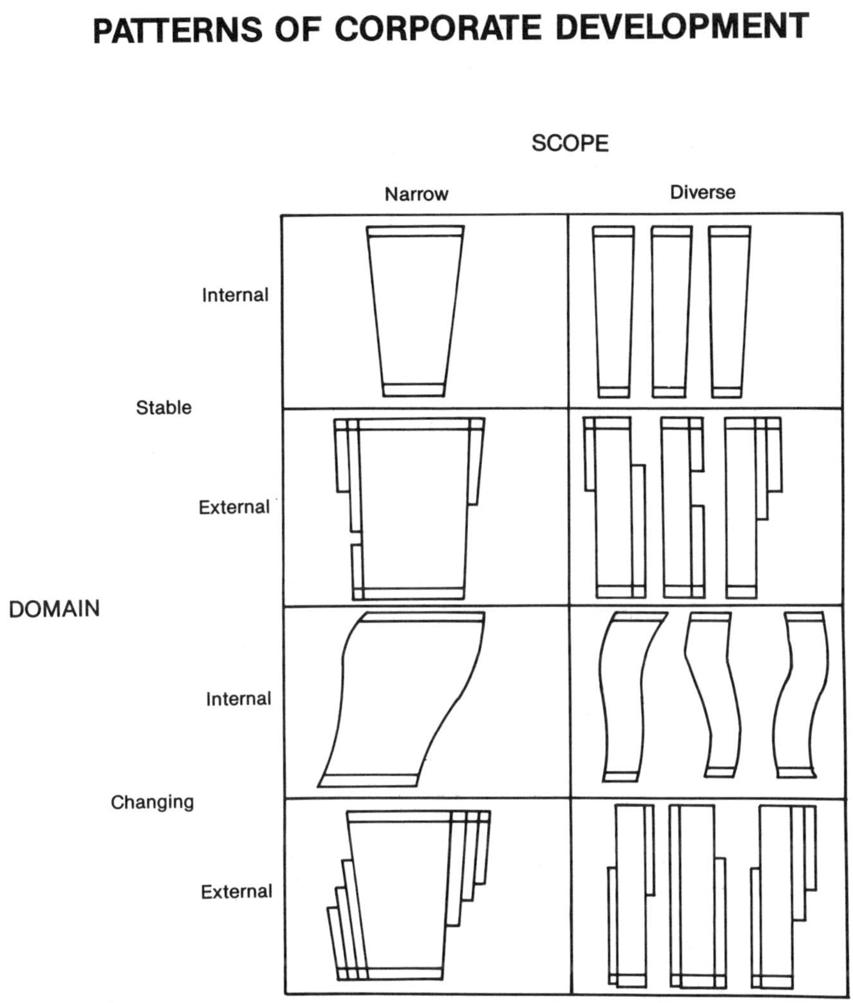

Fig. 5.6. Patterns of corporate development. From Futterman (1985) with permission of Warren, Gorham & Lamont, Inc. The parameters are defined and described in the text.

1. Conduct research and development.
2. Market drugs.
3. Manufacture drugs.
4. Conduct limited technical development activities for local use only.
5. Conduct clinical studies.
6. Conduct highly focused research.
7. Obtain regulatory approval of specific drugs.
8. Obtain drug-related information for the central company.

These groups may be autonomous and totally independent, or they may lie anywhere along the "independence spectrum" from total autonomy to total dependence on central headquarters. Multinational drug companies usually adopt a strategy of either marketing their drugs in almost all countries or limiting their activities to specific countries or regions.

ORGANIZATIONAL PROCESSES THAT SUPPORT IDENTIFIED DEVELOPMENT PATTERNS

Domain		Search	Scope: Narrow	Scope: Diverse
Domain	Stable	Internal	• Integrated operations • Decentralized • Middle management initiative Model I	• Autonomous operations • Decentralized • Middle management initiative Model III
		External	• Integrated operations • Decentralized • Top management initiative Model II	• Autonomous operations • Decentralized • Top management initiative Model IV
	Changing	Internal	• Integrated operations • Centralized • Middle management initiative Model V	• Autonomous operations • Centralized • Middle management initiative Model VII
		External	• Integrated operations • Centralized • Top management initiative Model VI	• Autonomous operations • Centralized • Top management initiative Model VIII

Fig. 5.7. Organizational processes that support development patterns in Fig. 5.6. From Futterman (1985) with permission of Warren, Gorham & Lamont, Inc.

Specific countries chosen for research and development, manufacturing, or other facilities are selected for different reasons. These include:

1. Country A may have a strong science tradition.
2. Country B may have a local company that was recently acquired.
3. Country C may have favorable tax laws or incentives.
4. Country D may have a suitable labor market.
5. Country E may have a government requiring many on-site activities of the company (i.e., political pressures may be exerted on the company). Many countries prevent multinational companies from owning more than 49 percent of a subsidiary.

Pros and Cons of Centralization

Some of the major issues a company deals with that relate to its organizational structure are an outgrowth of whether the overall structure is centralized or decentralized.

Drug companies that develop drugs at two or more sites may be organized to emphasize centralized or decentralized features. The value of centralization in a multinational company is that it provides standardization and conformity across all business units or across all similar units (e.g., production, research) in policies, procedures, and practices. Centralization decreases unnecessary duplication of effort and allows for cost savings, while insuring that good business practices are adhered to by all parts of the worldwide company. A team of highly skilled and competent experts may be assembled at the central site who are also available to subsidiaries that could not ordinarily afford their services. Apart from the many administrative and personnel services that may be centralized (e.g., purchasing, training), systems analysts, industrial engineers, and other types of experts may also be assembled at a central site.

Other advantages of centralization include decision making by senior managers who (1) generally have the most experience in the company, (2) generally have the broadest perspective of what is occurring in the company, and (3) are best able to balance the resources and power amongst the various functional groups. The decision about which products are to be sold in which countries is usually either a central or local one, although a certain amount of negotiation must occur. There are numerous advantages to either approach.

Disadvantages of centralization include a potentially excessive bureaucracy, slow response time because many decisions must be passed higher in an organization, and lack of sensitivity to local issues. Decision making becomes more personalized, based on the judgments of a few senior executives who wield a great deal of power. Most other managers have less of a sense of participation and the most creative ones will tend not to stay.

Advantages of Decentralization

Decentralization involves a delegation of authority, power, and responsibility from a central group to lower level managers. This tends to decrease the work load on the senior managers and motivates the lower level managers to work harder and be more productive. More rapid decisions may be made in a decentralized organization because decisions do not have to be passed as high in an organization. Because the lower level manager is usually more familiar with the conditions concerning the issue, better decisions are often reached.

Distribution of Services—Centralization Versus Decentralization

The major issue in organizing a company relating to many services is whether to centralize them as a department or decentralize them into the functional areas where they are most needed and used. The answer for several services is clearly one of centralization. This applies to groups such as patents, mailroom, toxicology, printing, photography, and so on. Decentralization is generally used for other services such as secretarial support and intragroup coordination. Most services fall into a gray zone that may be handled in many different ways, including various combinations of both centralization and decentralization.

Library and Computer Services

Most medium and large libraries usually have the bulk of their materials centralized, but have decentralized satellite libraries in various departments as well. Libraries also exist in individual offices that are tied to a central library. Books purchased for individuals to keep on an extended loan basis are often subject to recall for use by others.

Computer services are handled differently in many companies, as well as within companies over time. The actual services provided are evolving and companies are continually exploring the optimal means of utilizing groups of computer experts to provide services. They may be centralized at either a corporate or functional level (e.g., production, marketing, research and development) and/or decentralized within specific departments.

Coordination of Drug Development

Coordination of drug development activities across departments and functions is discussed in Chapter 13 on the matrix approach. Most companies have established a separate department within the last decade to coordinate project activities. There are also coordinators who work within the line function of each separate division at the divisional, department, and/or section level. These vertically oriented coordinators usually interact with horizontally oriented coordinators who work in the central matrix group.

APPROPRIATE SIZE OF A DRUG COMPANY

How Large Is Large?

Organizations usually grow in size as their products are commercially successful and profitable. Large drug companies are arbitrarily defined as those with annual sales of over one billion dollars. Medium-sized drug companies are defined as those with sales varying from 100 million to one billion dollars per year. Small drug companies are defined as those with smaller annual sales.

Small companies that are successful often have a well-defined corporate culture that is credited with bringing them success. They usually try to retain this culture as they grow in size. Nonetheless, compromises are forced on all growing companies, and their atmosphere and culture almost always changes as their size increases.

The issue sometimes arises as to how large a company wishes to become. This may seem to be a bizarre question to those who view unlimited growth as a desirable goal. Some people believe, however, that each drug company has an optimal size and to surpass that size has an adverse affect on efficiency of developing drugs, in addition to adversely influencing company values and atmosphere. Many drug companies are highly successful financially and must decide how to deal with their profits. When profits mount, they may be put back into the company to strengthen and build the core business to an even greater size. Profits may also be invested in many other ways, such as to purchase-related (or unrelated) businesses. The vision of a com-

Table 5.1. Selected factors that tend to increase drug company growth

1. Larger number of patients use drugs as the demographic profile of industrialized countries changes toward an older age distribution
2. Additional life-span of patients with chronic diseases
3. Increasing demand for drugs in less-developed countries
4. New innovations and technology (e.g., drug delivery systems)
5. Greater number and availability of effective OTC[a] drugs
6. Highly attractive commercial returns from major breakthrough drugs
7. Development of new diagnostic tests that can detect biochemical changes indicative of early stages of disease. This will then provide a target for drugs that reverse or suppress the progression of these changes

[a] OTC, over-the-counter drugs.

pany's future objectives and goals should have a major bearing on the specific ways that profits are dispersed. When a company faces strong threats to its core business, its profits must be spent in a defensive manner (e.g., to buy outstanding stock, emphasize work on line-extensions).

Is Larger Better?

Many executives believe that "larger" is not necessarily "better" for a drug company. The efficiency with which a company is able to operate is usually compromised as its size increases beyond a certain point. This will undoubtedly slow the company's ability to complete clinical studies and register new drugs in a timely manner. If certain functions such as research are divided and two heads rather than one are appointed, it may lead both to competition between them and decreased efficiency. Of course, two or more separate research and development groups may be established if there is an appropriate way of dividing the group. A number of types of research and development groups that could logically be established as separate entities are (1) human research and development, (2) animal research and development, (3) pesticides, (4) biologicals, (5) diagnostics, and (6) market-support activities in technical development. These and/or other categories could be organized as two (or more) separate research and development groups, as long as each of their heads reported to a single research and development head. The purpose of having a single overall head would be to (1) encourage cooperation, (2) minimize competition, (3) improve communications, (4) improve coordination, and (5) provide a scientific arbiter when necessary between the groups.

Scaling up the size of a company not only requires new buildings, but also demands new departments to provide services where a single person or small group was previously able to handle the work load. Adding new levels of supervisory personnel is usually unavoidable, but this step should be kept to a minimum. Nonetheless, the ways of conducting work that were effective when performed by a certain size group may be impossible when the group's size increases. Totally new approaches to maintaining efficiency often have to be found. Factors that tend to increase or decrease the rate or extent of drug company growth are listed in Tables 5.1 and 5.2.

Benefits of Being Smaller

Benefits of smallness are obviously desired by most companies that decentralize their management, whereas those which consolidate and centralize usually desire

Table 5.2. Selected factors that tend to diminish drug company growth

1. Increased costs of research and development
2. Increased risks of research and development
3. Reduced length of effective patent life
4. Increased regulatory requirements
5. Increased controls on prices that companies are able to charge for drugs
6. Customers becoming more cost conscious and making decisions based purely on economic grounds
7. Fewer independent doctors, pharmacies, and hospitals as customers
8. Greater constraints on sales promotion activities
9. Negative attitudes about the drug industry created by consumer groups
10. Fewer significant new drug discoveries[a]

[a] Points one to nine affect most research-based drug companies in a country where these primarily external factors occur. The last point is primarily internal and depends on the success of specific companies.

the benefits of larger size. A major issue for each company is to find the size that balances advantages obtained from being both large and small and minimizes disadvantages. People often join a company when it is relatively small. Marked company growth often changes their personal interactions with other staff and their work in a major way that some staff perceive as undesirable (e.g., separation into different buildings, lack of being involved with as many different activities).

Advantages of a smaller size include (1) being able to respond rapidly to new opportunities, (2) having greater flexibility in modifying operating procedures and organizational structures, (3) having fewer managerial levels, which often translates into less bureaucracy, (4) having a greater chance of an intimate work environment, and (5) enhancing communications and cooperation through personal contacts. As a company grows, many critical factors that contributed to its original success will change or disappear. Many of these factors (e.g., knowing everyone by name, interacting with many or all company functions on a daily basis) are impossible to achieve in larger companies. Significant growth in overall size does not necessarily correlate with growth in profits. Some larger companies divide into smaller autonomous (or semiautonomous) companies to achieve increased efficiencies, a greater esprit de corps, and competitive advantages present in many smaller companies.

Methods to Achieve Company Growth in Head Count

Growth in head count at a company is appropriate when it is based on greater profits and leads to a competitive advantage for the company. The probability of achieving greater head count and/or profits should be carefully assessed prior to a decision to initiate steps for expansion and growth. The two most important competitive advantages a company may attain for their drugs are product differentiation (i.e., a unique feature of a drug that serves a medical need not served by other competing drugs) and cost advantage.

An important question in the drug industry is how growth in the number of employees is best achieved and managed. One desirable method is to add people when a new drug is discovered that brings "megabucks" into a company. Growth in head count funded by sales of an increased number of drug units because of a new promotional campaign is also desirable. Increased production of drug units achieved by cutting wholesale drug prices may not increase profits sufficiently or at all. This method may become an inefficient and costly approach for a company to stimulate growth. Growth that is based on one or two major drugs leads to a potentially vulnerable position for a company. When those drugs go off patent and generic substitution occurs, the sales will usually drop. For example, Roche Laboratories laid off approximately 1,000 workers at about the time when Valium's patent expired. If an unexpected and serious human adverse reaction or animal toxicity is reported for a major drug, that company may be placed in a precarious financial position.

Methods to Decrease Head Count

Many successful drug companies, in addition to all unsuccessful ones, experience times when the number of employees must be decreased. This may occur in a particular business or group of a company for any of many reasons, or it may occur across the entire organization. Depending on the number of people involved, the urgency of change required, and levels of people within an organization affected, a number of approaches may be followed. Staff may be decreased by (1) firing them directly, (2) allowing them to resign, (3) allowing them to transfer within the company, (4) encouraging some to retire early, (5) finding alternative work, (6) allowing some to work part-time, (7) eliminating unfilled positions, or (8) not replacing employees who leave. The exact method(s) chosen depends on many factors, but the culture of the company often predominates in the choice made.

CRITIQUING THE ORGANIZATIONAL STRUCTURE CHOSEN

Important Questions

A few questions should be considered in evaluating a company's organizational structure.

1. Does the structure reflect the ways in which people operate to conduct work and the ways in which they see themselves (e.g., as a member of group X or Y)?
2. Is the structure most suitable for carrying out the mission of the company (division, department)?
3. Do conflicting structures in different parts of the company lead to problems?
4. What are the real problems or issues with the present structure?
5. What problems may be anticipated with the structure and how may they be addressed?
6. Have all relevant managers had an opportunity for input into the structure and a chance to critique it?
7. What are the plans to disseminate information on the organizational structure plus receive feedback and to review suggestions?
8. How will changes in the organization's structure be implemented?

Once these questions are considered, ways to address each issue should be determined.

Developing Standard Operating Procedures

An organization's structure is in some senses a static picture of where people and functions are placed. What breathes life and activity into this picture are the operational guidelines that inform people of how they are to behave to get work accomplished and goals achieved. Standard Operating Procedures (SOPs) differ greatly for all companies, and within a single company, they differ greatly over a period of time. All companies attempt to balance flexibility and rigidity in developing SOPs that will enhance activities and efficiency, rather than inhibit and squelch them. Drug companies have experience in developing policies, guidelines, and SOPs that attempt to achieve their goals.

6 / *Corporate Management*

The key element in developing a shared purpose is mutual trust. Without trust, people will engage in all kinds of self-centered behavior to assert their own identities and influence coworkers to their own ends. Under these circumstances, they just won't hear others, and efforts to develop a shared vision are doomed. Nothing destroys trust faster than hard box attitudes toward problems that don't require such treatment. David K. Hurst. From *Harvard Business Review* (May–June, 1984, p.85).

Good ideas and good products are a dime a dozen. Good execution and good management—in a word, good people—*are rare.* Arthur Rock. From *Harvard Business Review* (November-December, 1987, p. 63).

COMMUNICATING WITH AND INFLUENCING OTHERS

Introduction

Nonscientists are usually unable to understand the details of work of most technical specialists (e.g., computer programmers, scientists). Some specialists therefore claim that nonscientists cannot really appreciate the significance or meaning of their work. This statement should not be accepted by nonscientists, regardless of whether they are managers or have other positions. Every scientist should be able to explain the nature of his or her projects, goals, strategies, and other issues in simple and clear terms that any educated individual can understand. When a scientist retreats into jargon it is a statement that the speaker does not truly want to communicate with the listener, or that the speaker is unable to do so. Many scientists who are unable to communicate effectively with nonscientists are also unable to communicate with other scientists. In dealing with such scientists, managers must adhere to good manners, which means that they should not give offense unintentionally.

Why Do Nonscientists Sometimes (or often) Have Difficulty Communicating with Scientists about Scientific Issues

A wide gulf often appears to exist between the thinking of scientists and nonscientists. There is much more to explain about the gap between scientists and nonscientists than to merely state that their training is different and nonscientists are not trained in the scientific method. One important difference between these groups may be illustrated with an example.

Assume that a particular disease is either present or absent in people. The disease appears to be associated with a particular symptom. The question to consider is whether the symptom and disease are truly related. Experimental data to investigate this association will fit four categories.

These four categories are:

1. Patients in whom both the disease and symptom are present.
2. Patients in whom the disease is present but the symptom is absent.
3. Patients in whom the disease is absent but the symptom is present.
4. Patients in whom both the disease and symptom are absent.

This example is also referred to as a two by two contingency table.

It is common for nonscientists to rely primarily on information in the first category when reaching a decision as to whether there is a relationship between the disease and symptom, especially if the numbers in the first category are much larger than in other categories. This approach is incorrect. People who only pay attention to two (or even three) of these categories may also be misled in their conclusion. For example, if more people with the disease lack the symptom than have it, nonscientists may conclude that there is no association between the two. Scientists are taught that a valid conclusion may only be reached by considering all four of these categories. Statistical techniques can readily compare relative proportions in all four categories to arrive at a conclusion of whether there is an association.

Another important reason why scientists and nonscientists may interpret information differently is that scientists are taught to be skeptical because of the many types of bias that may enter an experiment or clinical study. Many subtle (or obvious) types of bias may greatly affect design, conduct, analysis, and interpretation of an experiment or clinical study. We have all heard many examples of data that suggest one interpretation, only to be told later about a previously unsuspected bias or problem that greatly affected that interpretation. As an example, "In 1978, a Los Angeles study was released that showed that persons living in areas where jet plane noise was greater than 90 decibels had a significantly increased death rate." The popular press got some mileage out of this: *Time* magazine headed its article "Sonic Doom-Can Jet Noise Kill?" Shortly thereafter, the study was published in a scientific journal, where its merits could be more closely examined. The strong possibility of a secondary association was raised by the fact that people who live in the devalued housing close to airports are often poorer, older, or otherwise different from the general population. A subsequent study reanalyzed the data from Los Angeles and controlled for the confounding effects of age, race, and sex. When those differences were taken into account, jet noise was found to have no effect on mortality. (Michael et al., 1984). A more detailed discussion of biases is given in *Guide to Clinical Interpretation of Data* (Spilker, 1986b).

How Can Nonscientists Evaluate Medical Claims?

The most widely accepted answer to this common issue is that nonscientists must consult trusted scientists or clinicians who are knowledgeable in therapeutic areas of interest. If the professional evaluation received is not satisfactory to the nonscientist, then it is useful to obtain a second opinion. This second opinion may be obtained from an individual, committee, or task force from inside the company. If the question has major implications for a company, then it may also be useful to involve outside consultants.

Communicating between Two Sites in an Organization

Two (or more) semi-independent research and development sites of a company may each (1) duplicate work of the other group, (2) have totally separate functions or areas to study and work on, or (3) have some overlap in their assigned areas and functions. Although there is not a single best approach for all companies to use in dividing work between two (or more) sites, it is necessary that the missions of each group be clearly established and known by all relevant people. For example, drug discovery research could be handled in several ways. This research could be conducted at only one site. Research in certain therapeutic areas (e.g., on parasites and bacteria) could be conducted at one site and all other research conducted at a second site. Another possibility is that some or all research could be contracted to universities. In deciding how to divide the total research and development effort between two sites of one company, it is important to consider that certain groups of people may perform specific activities better than other groups, and that people are generally much happier doing what they do best. A related issue is deciding which activities should not be conducted in-house and which activities should be contracted to universities, consultants, or independent contract houses.

Techniques Used by Managers to Influence Others

Basic approaches to exerting influence on others include using the following techniques: (1) authority, (2) bargaining, (3) persuasion, and (4) intellectualizing.

In choosing one or more of these approaches there are several factors that a manager should weigh. As one moves from techniques utilizing pure authority (point 1) to pure intellectualizing (point 4):

1. It takes more time to use the procedures.
2. The vulnerability of the manager increases.
3. The impact on subsequent behavior increases.
4. The flexibility of how the approach is used tends to increase.
5. Resentment in the listener tends to decrease.
6. The quality of the other's performance after the discussion tends to increase.

In using one (or more) of these approaches to influence someone, it is important to understand and use the sources of one's power or ability to influence. These can be summarized as:

1. *Rewards* This category is not meant primarily as monetary or material rewards, but includes such benefits as (1) sharing information, (2) introducing the other person to "important" individuals, (3) praising the person to others, and (4) writing positive comments and statements about the individual in reports.

2. *Punishment* Similar concepts apply as for rewards, although with the opposite approach.

3. *Expertise* This includes not only technical knowledge, but also the knowledge of how to accomplish tasks in the organization and knowledge of the proper sequence of activities to follow.

4. *Legitimacy* This derives from one's position of being higher in an organization compared to another person.

5. *Interpersonal Skills* The power of one's personality may be the only means available to influence others.

Improving Communications

It is important for relevant people to have the most complete and accurate information possible. One alternative to accurate information that unfortunately occurs is that people create their own stories, fleshing out areas where information is skimpy or absent. During periods of early discussions, it is important to either keep the topic 100 percent secret or keep all relevant people fully abreast of the current status. While plans are being developed it is likely that gossiping and rumors will occur. This leads to people hearing incorrect or distorted information, which in turn may lead them to become upset and to negatively criticize other people in the company. Sometimes it is worth initiating a rumor of a planned decision or action to determine what reactions it engenders.

One easy means of improving communications within a company is to send important memos and reports to all people that should have the information. Spreading information not only builds good will, but prevents others from having to try and obtain the same information for themselves. In addition, it often leads to greater efficiency and helps prevent misunderstandings.

Another easy means of improving communications is to keep a list of action points and points of agreement at meetings. Formal minutes of most meetings are rarely referred to or used. Action points state what is to be done and who has the responsibility for doing it or leading the effort. Follow-up of these points at future meetings can usually be handled easily and efficiently. At the end of any meeting, the chairperson or another person should review major points of consensus and major items to be dealt with in the future.

MANAGEMENT MODELS AND STYLES

Before discussing management styles that are particularly appropriate for the drug industry, it is worth mentioning some of the basic approaches and models of management presented in recent years. A few representative systems are mentioned to show the variety in styles that may be conceptualized and to illustrate that several authors have tried to boil down a great deal of information to a few simple concepts. These systems have the advantage of being easily understood, although that understanding does not on its own enable managers to easily change their beliefs or basic approach. In fact, it is amazing how many managers are unable to recognize their own style after reading one of these books, even when their style is transparent to many others.

The Spectrum from Autocratic to Committee Styles

Many managers' styles may be viewed as lying at one or more places along a continuum from autocratic/dictatorial at one end to a democratic committee approach at the other end. Some of the other styles that may be described along this spectrum are:

Passive consultation

Where a manager passively listens to colleagues' and others' views, if offered, before reaching a decision.

Active consultation

Where a manager actively seeks ideas and input from others before reaching a decision.

Consensus management

Where a manager actively seeks ideas and input from others and also insures that discussions continue until a general consensus is reached about the most appropriate decision.

A single manager or committee may function along the lines of two or more of the five styles mentioned.

When a manager is promoted to a new position it is important for that person to take the necessary time to learn about the style and desires of those who interact with and are influenced by that person. Failure to do this has led many new managers into serious difficulties, regardless of their personal style. Additional issues arise when a manager's style differs markedly from that of a predecessor. This may be an advantage, but often raises more caution signals for the manager to heed.

Four-Dimensional Model

The book *Improving Productivity Through People Skills* by Lefton et al. (1980) describes four styles of management. These are autocratic, unassertive, easygoing, and collaborative styles and are based on two scales: warmth to hostility, and submission to dominance. This system describes management styles in terms of "Q's," a short-cut system used to describe complex concepts.

Social Style

Four social styles (analytical, driver, amiable, expressive) are described in the book *Social Style/Management Style: Developing Productive Work Relationships* by Bolton and Bolton (1984).

Other Styles

Other styles, approaches, and models focus on a "hard" rationale using elements such as structure, people, tasks, strategies, and decision processes, or on a "soft" intuitive model using elements such as roles, groups, networks, rewards, shared vision, and common purpose. Hurst (1984) describes each and shows that both hard and soft approaches are necessary in a company and may be combined to work more effectively.

A large amount of material has been written about advantages of the Japanese approach to management. Their approach is briefly and succinctly presented by Tsurumi (1982). He stresses the "human side of labor" and stresses that American managers have focused on the wrong methods of improving productivity. The correct approach according to Tsurumi is an easy one to utilize, and his brief article is highly recommended.

Measuring One's Leadership Skills

There are many books and articles about differences between leadership and management (Geneen [1984]; Bennis and Nanus [1985]) and how an individual can easily measure his own leadership skills (Martin [1985]). One example is shown in Fig. 6.1. This simple test may be taken by individuals who wish to rate either themselves or the effectiveness of others. A summary of characteristics of leaders and managers is given in Fig. 6.2. Commonly encountered relationships of leaders to their group is shown in Fig. 6.3. The potential scenarios shown in Fig. 6.3 become much more complex when multiple leaders are involved, as well as consideration of other factors that influence a group and its leader.

Boards of Directors

Boards of directors of pharmaceutical companies primarily deal with large business issues and allocation of resources. Its members are often chosen because of their knowledge about such matters; however, they should also be instructed in the methods, concepts, and issues of drug discovery and development. In addition, these groups must reach important decisions about many scientific and medical issues. Therefore, representatives of both science and medicine should be present on the board. It is not sufficient to have only scientists on the board of directors, since most scientists do not adequately understand medical aspects of drug development or the thinking processes of physicians. Chapter 3 describes how scientists and clinicians are trained to think differently. The management styles of boards of directors vary along the spectrum described earlier in this section of autocratic rule to democratic committee.

Entrepreneurship in the Drug Industry

The term "entrepreneurship" has become a widely used buzzword in all industries. It is difficult to find a current journal on management techniques that does not discuss entrepreneurship. Two representative articles are by Stevenson and Gumpert (1985) and Shays and de Chambeau (1984). Within the drug industry some departments tend to form and develop around successful scientists. This is clearly an

LEADERSHIP EFFECTIVENESS SCALE

Instructions: This rating form describes 30 practices that are commonly demonstrated by acknowledged leaders. Please read each statement carefully. Then decide the extent to which the person being rated demonstrates that practice. Indicate your decision by checking the appropriate box to the right of each practice. (To score the results, see next page.)

The person being rated:	Usually If Not Always	Fairly Often	Occasionally	Rarely If Ever
1. Keeps group members informed.				
2. Expresses thoughts clearly and forcefully.				
3. Speaks well from a platform.				
4. Is a good listener.				
5. Attracts others to want to hear what he/she has to say.				
6. Communicates a sense of "being in charge."				
7. Encourages upward communication from followers.				
8. Demonstrates compassion for others.				
9. Provides rewards that are important to followers.				
10. Is sensitive to the needs of others.				
11. Attracts others to want to join his/her group.				
12. Has the full backing of all those who work under him/her.				
13. Provides enough structure to create a cohesive feeling among his/her subordinates.				
14. Establishes an authority line that is clear, consistent, and appropriate for the situation.				
15. Strives to win by allowing subordinates to also win.				
16. Gets tough when necessary.				
17. Is respected by subordinates when authority is used.				
18. Uses the power that he/she has with firmness, but also with sensitivity.				
19. Consults with others before making important decisions.				
20. Has a strong track record for making solid decisions.				
21. Follows a logical pattern in making decisions.				
22. Communicates decisions with pride and decisiveness.				
23. Is able to admit mistakes when he/she makes them.				
24. Faces up to and makes hard decisions.				
25. Gets others caught up in his/her positive force.				
26. Creates an active tempo that others emulate.				
27. Communicates a positive attitude during difficult or tough times.				
28. Always puts his/her best foot forward.				
29. Articulates an inspiring mission for the group.				
30. Generates a feeling of pride and accomplishment in his/her followers.				

Fig. 6.1. A scale to measure leadership practices. From Martin (1985) with permission of Penton Publishing Co.

HOW TO RATE

To calculate your score on the Leadership Effectiveness Scale, give yourself 4 points for every U/A, 3 points for every FO, 2 points for every OC, and 1 point for every R/E. Record the subtotal of each category in the corresponding section below.

SUBSCALES

Communicator (Questions 1-6)	Subtotal ______
Mutual Rewarder (Questions 7-12)	Subtotal ______
Power Figure (Questions 13-18)	Subtotal ______
Decision-Maker (Questions 19-24)	Subtotal ______
Positive Force (Questions 25-30)	Subtotal ______
LEADERSHIP EFFECTIVENESS	**TOTAL** ______

INTERPRETATION

105-120	Strong Leader
90-104	Good Leader
75-89	Fair Leader
Under 75	Improvement needed

Fig. 6.1. (Continued)

example of entrepreneurship, especially when a department's function partly or completely overlaps with that of an already existing department.

Burroughs Wellcome Co. is a midsized drug company, which evolved to the point approximately 15 years ago, where it had a small research group within the larger research division that actually duplicated several functions (e.g., synthetic chemistry, biological testing, metabolism, pharmacology, and even toxicology). This group, headed by Dr. Gertrude Elion, was remarkably productive and successful as an entrepreneurial activity. This approach probably would not work at all drug companies. If this approach is utilized today it could most easily either focus on one scientific discipline (e.g., biochemistry) or on one therapeutic area (e.g., psychiatry) where several disciplines are represented.

It takes a special talent to function as an entrepreneur in a drug company. Whereas artists are often characterized as dreamers and workers as doers, entrepreneurs may be thought of as people who are both dreamers and doers. They want their ideas to be tested and to succeed in the real world of patient care. They are not the types of scientists who are always saying "let's study it further."

Most drug companies that believe the entrepreneur concept has value understand that there can only be a small number of entrepreneurs. The entrepreneur primarily functions either as an individual or as leader of a small group, whereas to get drugs developed efficiently it is necessary to have mostly *team players* working in synchrony.

LEADERS' BOLDNESS CONTRASTED WITH MANAGERS' CAUTIOUSNESS

LEADERS	MANAGERS
Who They Are	
Leaders are heroes. Their strong sense of personal mastery compels them to direct affairs. Leaders use power to influence others' thoughts and actions. They are driven by a grand design and have intuitive flashes of insight that lead to dramatic breakthroughs.	Managers are problem solvers. They achieve results through persistence, tolerance, and good will — three useful traits in large, conservative organizations. They achieve their goals through a cautious process of trial and error.
How They View Themselves	
Leaders seek to profoundly alter human, economic, and political relationships. Their sense of who they are does not depend upon their job titles or other social indicators of identity.	Managers strive to protect the existing order of affairs. They identify with the status quo. Strengthening existing institutions heightens their self-worth.
How They View Their Work	
Leaders seek risk and danger, especially where opportunity and reward appear high. They question established procedures and create new concepts. Leaders create excitement and inspire co-workers. They want results.	Managers fear uncertainty. They prefer to manipulate co-workers and to use established policies to reach organizational goals. Managers are more concerned with the processes that achieve results than with the results themselves.
How They View Their Goals	
Leaders are driven by their personal goals. They are innovators who strive to alter established policies that they feel uncomfortable with. Leaders alter expectations and change the way people think. They create ideas instead of merely reacting to them.	Managers focus on the organization's goals. They are driven by a need to conform rather than a desire to change existing systems. They are passive individuals whose goals are shaped by their organization's history and culture.
How They View Others	
Leaders arouse intense feelings of admiration and devotion. They care about people and their needs.	Managers relate to people according to their job titles and social status. They are more concerned with people's roles in a process than with their needs.
How They Achieve Respect	
Leaders' authority derives from their personal relationships.	Managers' authority stems from their positions.
Where They Are Found	
Leaders may be found anywhere in an organization — from the loading dock to the CEO's office.	Managers are supervisors, department heads, and administrators.

Fig. 6.2. Characteristics of leaders and managers. From *Business Week Quarterly* with permission.

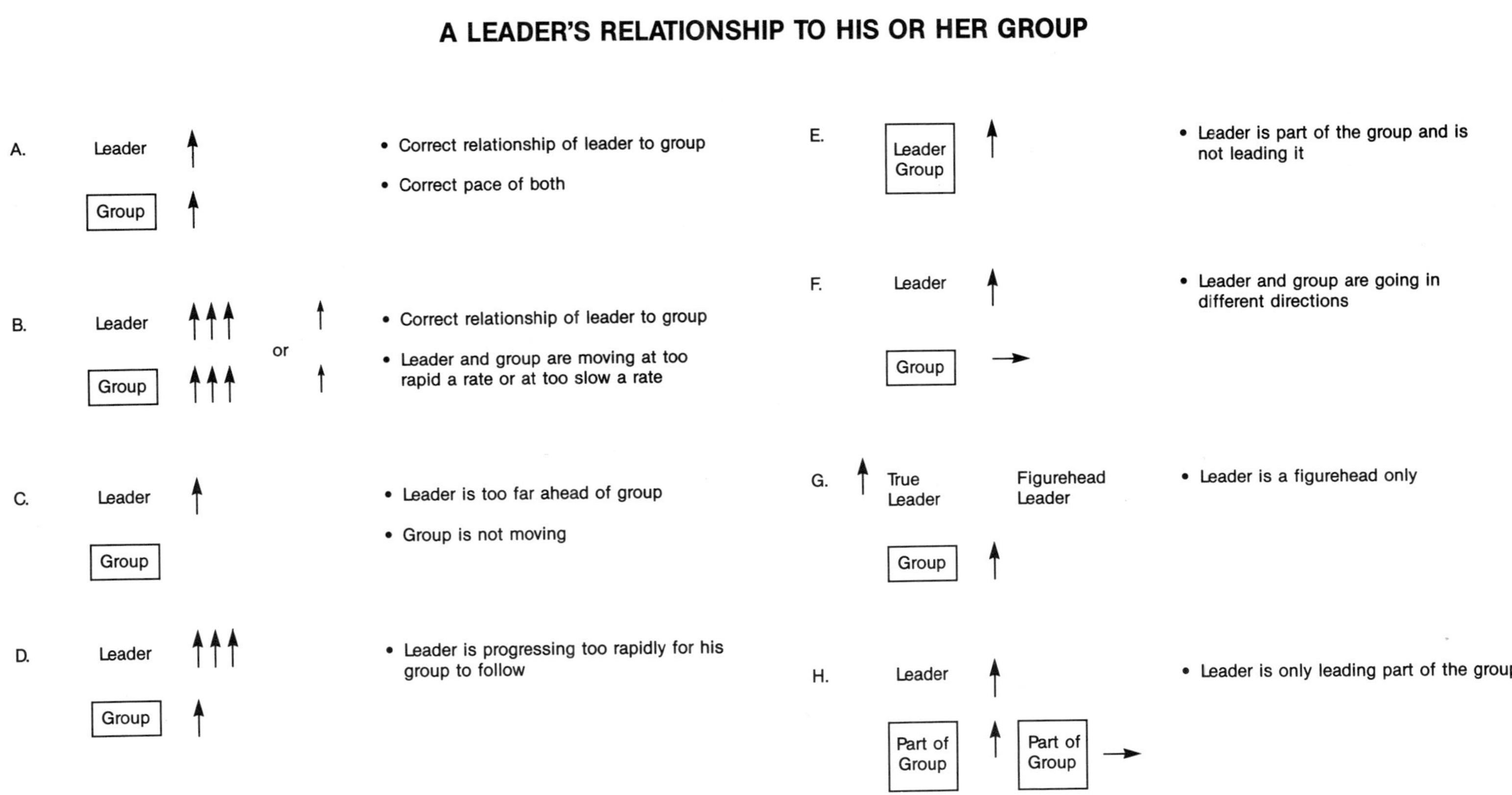

Fig. 6.3. A leader's relationship to his or her group. The reasons for problems in B through H may be that the leader is out of touch with his or her group, is unable to control it, has lost interest in some or all of the group, or another reason. The *arrows* are the direction of movement. Three *arrows* are used to show rapid movement and a short *arrow* is used to depict slow movement.

Individualists in the Drug Industry

Some individualists in drug companies are not entrepreneurs and create problems within a drug company. Each company desires to have individualists who have a positive influence within the organization, as well as have team players. Individualistic scientists who vigorously attempt to opt out of the drug discovery process, refuse to screen drugs, and/or are unwilling to participate in drug development are often counterproductive. These scientists usually define their role in industry solely in terms of their own freedom, professional career, and reputation. Many people believe that this group of scientists do not belong in the drug industry and would function more effectively in an academic environment where being a team player is usually less important.

Different types of project teams exist in drug discovery and development, depending on the nature of the task and the professional discipline or department of the members. Keidel and Umen (1984) describe different teams in terms of analogies to baseball, football, and basketball. They point out various management issues relating to the team's function.

APPROACHES TO MANAGEMENT

A number of basic characteristics and issues relating to management are described.

Are the Right Questions Being Asked?

An important issue to consider is whether managers are asking the most appropriate questions to help meet a company's needs and goals. If only partially correct questions are asked or the questions asked are not phrased properly, then even the best obtainable answers may be irrelevant to answer the most pertinent questions. Thus, it is essential to insure that the questions asked are the correct ones and to discuss relevant assumptions and definitions before embarking on the quest for the answer. If assumptions and definitions underlying a question are not clear, and especially if the question is not explicitly stated, then the exercise may be destined for failure from the outset. The ability to (1) pose the best questions, (2) have the right timing, (3) interpret data appropriately, (4) not procrastinate, and (5) reach the best decisions, all depend on the quality of drug company personnel. One reason why the specific questions asked are so important is because a great deal of time and effort are spent by many employees on analyses, reports, memoranda, meetings, and information gathering that are all designed to answer questions posed by managers and senior executives.

The problems a company tackles may be real, potential, or imagined. Potential problems have a greater or lesser probability of occurring. Some of them are important for a company to deal with, but many others waste valuable resources and time. Real problems must be assessed for their importance and urgency, while potential and imagined problems must be identified as such and carefully discussed before allocating resources to their solution.

It is important and often essential to ask whether or not a question need even be asked. Alternative means to obtaining answers sometimes exist. For example, if a clinical group is intending to initiate a study to answer a well-phrased specific objective, it must be determined whether the data already exist in a company's archives or elsewhere (e.g., a government archive). In verbal communication, the tone in which a question is asked is also important to determining the answer obtained.

The Multiplier Effect

All managers and committees throughout an entire company from the board of directors down pose appropriate questions. One difference between a question posed by a chief executive officer (CEO) and a manager of a small group at a low level in the company is that there is a large multiplication effect when the question is posed by the chief executive officer. This is analogous to a model of moving gears. If the largest gear on top of a pyramid of gears (i.e., CEO) moves one notch (i.e., raises a minor point or question), his lieutenants' gears move several notches in the amount of activity they conduct to review the question, in the decisions they make on how to delegate work to answer the question, and then in the process of actually delegating the work. Each of their movements of several notches is sufficient to move the gears of several or numerous workers below them through a complete rotation and so on, until many people lower in the organization, who are doing most of the actual work to address an important (or idle) question, are scurrying around, sometimes frantically. The managers at a lower level in a company do not generally create a large multiplier effect, except in a limited way with their subordinates.

Quality of Management

In situations where managerial competence is good at senior levels and poor at lower levels, much of a company's work is often not implemented or conducted properly and many problems are not appropriately solved. There are also situations where the quality of management and decision making is poor at upper levels and excellent at lower levels. If leaders do not impose bad decisions and directions on their subordinates, this situation may be compensated for by having an excellent staff. If leaders take a company in an undesirable direction, however, then even the best staff in the world may be unable to correct this error. Two examples of bad directions include:

1. Diverting a company's resources too widely away from the core business, especially to areas where little expertise is present and where the company may become too widely dispersed geographically.
2. Concentrating a company's resources too heavily in a narrow area of drug discovery and development, which makes the company vulnerable to unexpected changes in the marketplace and to changes in medical practice.

These relatively extreme, but opposite, approaches to management are reminiscent of the Japanese board game of "Go". In this game, either too strong a defensive or offensive posture usually leads to weaknesses in one's position and to eventual defeat.

Table 6.1. Some major functions of management

Function of management	Committee and/or individual usually responsible
1. Establish overall corporate mission, objectives, goals, and strategies. Provide leadership and direction	Board of directors or chairman of the board
2. Determine allocation of resources for various functions of the company	Board of directors or chairman of the board
3. Determine overall research policies	Research policy committee, head of R and D and/or head of research
4. Determine research approaches to be used and allocate resources	Research and development management committee, head of R and D, and/or individual heads of research and development departments
5. Monitor and review progress of drug development strategies	Project steering committee, various individuals, or committees
6. Implementation of strategies	International project team, project team leader or manager

[a] R and D, research and development.

Functions of Management

Many functions served by management vary between different levels in a corporation. While individuals on several levels deal with generally similar or identical issues, conflicts often arise when a group attempts to deal with the functions of another group. Some major functions of management are shown in Table 6.1, with a focus on research activities. The major group(s) usually responsible is also indicated.

Management of Subsidiaries

Ideally, each subsidiary should be managed according to a plan or strategy that is tailored to that subsidiary. Adopting a single approach to all subsidiaries will force some of them into uncomfortable and ineffective ways of conducting business, not to mention creating strains between the groups involved.

The management plan developed must consider central headquarters' objectives, importance of the subsidiary, and various conditions within the industry and country (e.g., economic, social, political, cultural). Past performance of the subsidiary plus future expectations will help shape this plan, which focuses on budget, growth, profitability, return on investment, and specific goals to be achieved.

One alternative to the approach of using a single management strategy for all subsidiaries is to allow each subsidiary to be an autonomous entity and establish its own plans. A second alternative is to govern all subsidiaries in the same manner. A third approach is the management by crisis philosophy. Only subsidiaries with current crises become actively involved with the central corporation. A fourth approach would be to invest money in those subsidiaries that submit proposals for using money in ways consistent with the corporation's goals.

Subsidiaries have a resemblance to children in that they are often born through the parent company's efforts to start a new group. This group may consist of one person or only a few people. The group usually begins to grow in size and soon demands more and more independence from the parent company. Offspring may develop in ways that are unexpected or undesired by the parent company. Eventually, some subsidiaries may become bigger than their parent and a few may attain independence. A subsidiary that has grown up and is then purchased by another company, according to this metaphor, could be viewed by the new parent as an adopted child. The parent company hopefully knows both their bad traits as well as their good ones.

Another means for multinational drug companies to obtain a wholly owned subsidiary is to acquire an existing domestic or foreign company. This method is a more rapid means of establishing a viable company than building onc *de novo*. Other advantages of this approach include the contacts, market information, and roots in the community that are likely to be present in the acquired company.

Duplication of Efforts

In examining activities conducted at separate research and development sites of a large drug company, it is clear that a certain amount of duplication will occur. Duplication is of several types:

1. *Worthwhile duplication* that is synergistic and contributes to progress on drug discovery and/or development.
2. *Unnecessary duplication* that may not be valuable, but does not delay progress on drug discovery or development.
3. *Unnecessary duplication* that is not valuable, but delays progress on drug discovery or development.
4. *Counterproductive duplication* that is competitive in a negative sense and may actually be detrimental for a company.

Several variations of these possibilities occur. The challenge is to foster an appropriate amount of the first type and to eliminate the last two types of duplication. One of the reasons for the third type of duplication is poor organization and/or poor planning. Poor organization would be responsible if duplication were a part of a company's operations, whereas poor planning might be responsible if a duplication occurred primarily on one or a small number of drugs, projects, programs, or activities.

Counterproductive duplication arises from many causes. One cause is different philosophical approaches to an issue that orients the sites in different directions. Each site may use a different template to view and interpret the same data and thus reach conflicting interpretations. Another philosophical difference might relate to a highly conservative individual who supports the status quo ("If it ain't broke, don't fix it") versus a person (or group) who seeks change and appears to thrive on it, regardless of its real value.

Ideal Drug Company Environment

Each individual has their own idea of what constitutes an ideal drug company environment. Three aspects of an ideal environment are presented, along with possible means of moving toward those goals.

Mutual Respect and Trust

The first aspect is that there should be mutual respect and trust between professionals and between employees and their managers, including senior managers. There are many ways to achieve this state. On a general level this includes being honest at all times and using a policy of openness in dealing with people, where problems and issues are frankly discussed. Specifically, there are many forums and methods that may be used to increase and maintain the type of communications where this atmosphere will develop and flourish. These include: (1) holding periodic seminars for an entire company where current status of the company and/or a specific function (e.g., marketing, research and development) are presented, (2) holding periodic seminars for senior managers with the same purpose, (3) providing training programs of various types, (4) promoting employees from within the company, and (5) encouraging formal and informal presentations about (and by) staff at meetings, in company magazines, in newsletters, and on bulletin boards.

Positive Values and Goals

The second aspect of an ideal environment is where the corporate mission, objectives, and goals emphasize positive values that employees believe in and will work hard to support. The corporate mission should serve as a unifying mechanism that makes employees feel positive about working for that company. Discovering, developing, producing, and marketing new drugs to treat human disease and relieve suffering is a valuable goal and is a strong motivating factor for most employees of a drug company.

Positive Company Culture

The last aspect of an ideal environment to be discussed is that of maintaining a positive company culture. This is more controversial than the former two characteristics and certainly is not viewed the same way by all drug companies. A positive culture may be defined as one where (1) employees are guaranteed employment as long as the company is financially stable, (2) benefits provided are at least at a reasonable (if not better) level in comparison with the drug industry and with local industry, and (3) the company shows in many ways that it cares about its employees. This culture and outlook must emanate from the most senior managers. If they believe in and promulgate these principles, then these principles will become the established culture of the company.

Level of Technical and Administrative Support Services to Provide Employees

The issue is how to determine the appropriate balance for a company, between providing the minimal level of technical services (e.g., photography, graphics, laboratory assistants) to professionals who are discovering, developing, manufacturing, and marketing new drugs and providing so many services that corporate profitability is seriously eroded. Clearly, if internal staff support is too lean the professionals must either do without important services, obtain them through other means, or perform the tasks themselves. In any of these cases their productivity will suffer. One clearly does not want PhD chemists spending their time washing glassware. A comparable issue relates to hiring administrative assistants, secretaries, and clerks for each group of professionals.

A lean professional staff that is well motivated and working hard is often more productive than one where a larger number of ancillary services are available. So many people may be hired to provide services that what was once a single service job becomes divided into multiple jobs and many people are underutilized and underemployed. This is the so-called "fat organization" with duplication of services and activities. The excessive levels of bureaucracy that are created usually lead to inefficiency and disgruntlement.

Management by Fad

Every year or two new books appear in the field of management that are extremely widely read. These are often hailed as a major step forward in one or more aspects of business. These books apparently have had a significant impact in the management of many drug companies. Usually, the glow starts to fade after a few years and a new wave of ideas (often from newer books) appear that, if followed, would take the company in a different direction. If each of the ideas proposed were looked at clearly and calmly and senior managers were not pushing hard to implement the latest fads in management, then fewer faddish ideas would be imposed on many companies. Some of these ideas *do* have value, but usually they must be thoughtfully processed through the company's culture and current conditions to determine the best way to incorporate the concept. Some of the many faddish concepts include:

1. *Sloganeering* The negative rebound is usually substantial when companies decide that "We Stand for the Best" or some other slogan is ideal for the company. The company often extensively promotes the phrase. Few professionals in the drug industry are truly motivated by slogans, which at best are viewed in a neutral context and at worst as highly counterproductive forces.
2. *Use of management by objectives techniques* This concept was fairly widely explored a decade and more ago. Its value for the drug industry, especially within research and development, was not found to be positive. This resulted in large measure from the high degree of uncertainty and frequent changes in plans and strategies required for efficient drug development.
3. *Formally identifying and grooming candidates for many senior positions* The many drawbacks of identifying "high potential candidates" make it difficult to understand why this concept was ever seriously considered. Although the identity of candidates should remain secret, this information has a way of leaking out. This knowledge demotivates those who are not chosen and creates expectations of rapid promotions in those who are. This is an example of a lose-lose situation (i.e., where everybody loses).

Whatever the theme of the book of the year (e.g., *Theory Q, The One Minute Manager, Megatrends, In Pursuit of Excellence, The Changemasters*) it is essential to evaluate thoroughly and clearly whether any aspects have relevance for a specific company before a concept is endorsed and implemented.

Who Is in Charge?

If someone outside your company viewed the research and development activities as a whole, would he say that senior managers were appropriately making the major decisions and delegating others? Or, would that person say that senior managers were watching and not directing what is going on, apart from providing minimal input and review. Who determines whether drug development on each drug should proceed along broad or narrow lines? Are management decisions on resource allocations and other issues followed efficiently, or is better focus and control needed?

Some line function groups try to control as much decision-making responsibility as possible, even in areas in which they are not directly involved. When these line managers are asked about whether they can handle another project or a different responsibility with their current staff, their answer is always "yes." Several months later senior managers usually receive an urgent request from these line managers for additional head count positions. These managers are usually empire builders. One cure for this problem is to insist on well thought-out estimates of personnel requirements at or near the outset of each project, another is to reassign staff according to current priorities, and a third is to avoid the multiple tangents that some managers are always proposing to follow. Still another approach is to insist on the group doing all the work without any increases in head count. This usually forces the manager-in-charge to look for more efficiencies in his or her group.

Awareness of Activities One Manages

Only some activities of a department, division, or unit are known to senior managers. Their information comes through reports and other forms of communications. Although it is not important for senior managers to know details about most activities that would not affect their decisions, there is invariably some information that should be known but is not. One issue to consider is which system will minimize this category of unknown (but important) information. An ideal system would probably include a combination of both formal and informal methods. Formal methods should avoid placing strong pressure on people, while still auditing relevant activities. It is important that all or almost all work being conducted in departments is conducted with the knowledge of the relevant department heads.

Time Management

Five major problems relating to how managers spend their time were stated by Humble (1980) to be (in order of importance):

1. *Telephone interruptions*—Both in number of calls and length of time spent on many calls.
2. *Meetings*—Managers often attend too many meetings that last too long, often are unnecessary, and often are poorly run. Everyone could add an Amen here.
3. *Unexpected visitors*—Too many people drop in without an appointment or any notice.
4. *Poor delegation*—Work that could be and should be delegated is often done by the manager.
5. *Crises*—Unexpected problems often upset one's work plans.

Managers who are efficient usually attempt to minimize the time that they spend or waste on these (and other) activities.

Minimizing Risk to a Drug Company

Senior executives at drug companies that are spending up to hundreds of millions (dollars) on research and development wish to develop drugs that are both commercially and medically rewarding. Although many companies can afford to develop a small number of medically but not commercially important drugs, this potential (or desire) must be balanced by the need to minimize risks to the company of not developing profitable drugs. There is a popular belief in the drug industry that by only developing drugs that are within established clinical classes (e.g., beta-receptor antagonists) or are likely to reach the market, a company minimizes the chance that it will have a huge commercial success. Another way of expressing this view is that conservative companies that do not take risks will not reap a major commercial success and that big rewards go to big risk takers. Although this axiom is true in some cases, there is no reason why it should be true for any particular company or situation. In fact, some companies have achieved enormous financial success and strength by being second to reach the market with a new type of drug (e.g., Glaxo Inc. with ranitidine for treating patients with duodenal ulcers). In addition, a methodical, conservative, low risk-taking company may discover an ideal artificial sweetener or a safe drug for weight reduction. This one drug may catapult the company into a strong financial position. The point is that major new drugs do not necessarily involve more commercial or scientific risk in their development than drugs of lesser importance.

Most of a company's risk in terms of investing money occurs during the drug discovery period. A highly conservative posture is usually noted in those companies that primarily or solely develop licensed-in drugs and also concentrate on line-extensions of their current products. If the latter approach is used as a major strategy, it generally represents a short-term effort to improve the company's financial health, but will probably not reap the greatest profits over the long term.

APPROACH TO MAKING MAJOR CHANGES IN A COMPANY

Approach to Making Major Company Changes

An approach that may be considered when major (or even some minor) company changes are considered is shown in Fig. 6.4. This approach usually requires that

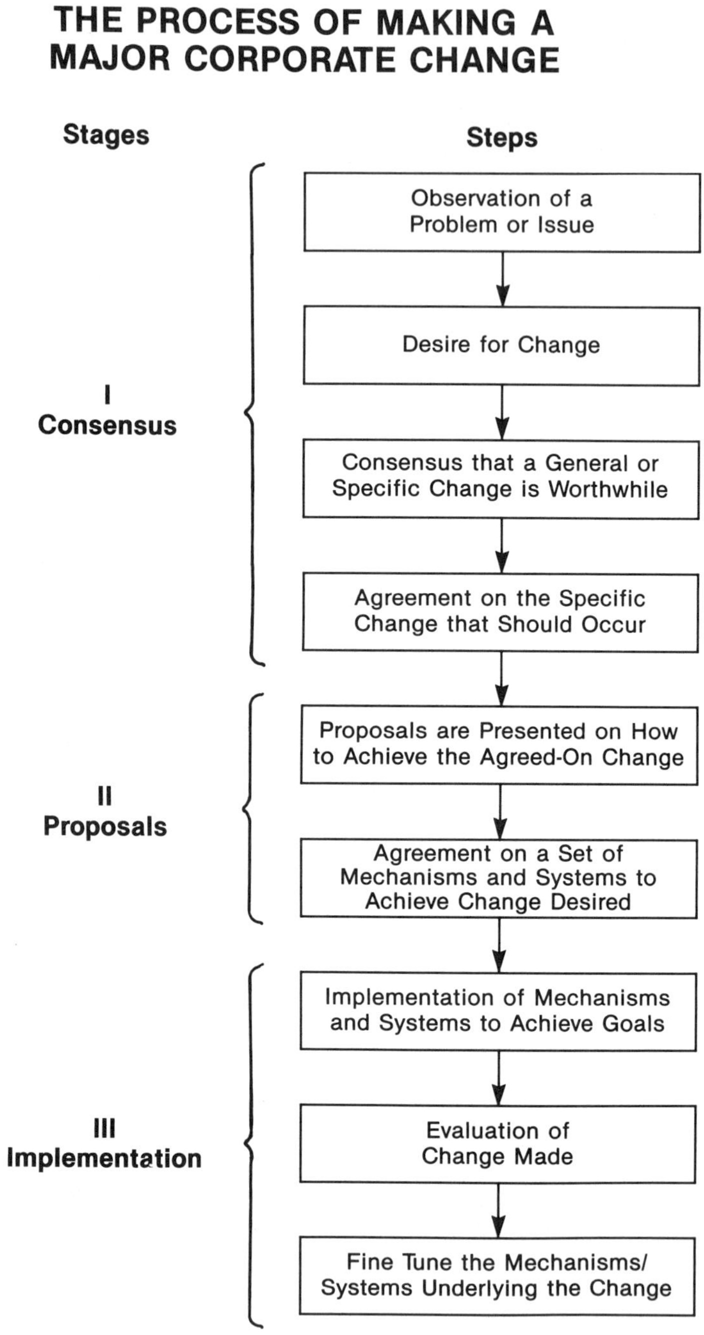

Fig. 6.4. Steps that are often involved in making major corporate changes.

each step be considered in the order shown, although modifications may be appropriate for specific situations. Each step in the figure may be proposed or evaluated by external consultants in addition to (or in lieu of) in-house experts and managers.

Some individuals may progress in their thinking rapidly and in a stepwise order through each of these phases. That process is rarely adequate, however, to achieve a major company change, because most or all relevant executives must be brought through this process. It is often best to bring them along as a group. If this attempt is rushed it usually leads to a counterreaction, and the proposed changes are likely to be turned down. What many people refer to as "timing" is in reality having all key people in agreement about one stage so that they may proceed toward the next stage together. The nine stages shown are really part of three larger processes. These three processes are (1) consensus that a specific change is desirable, (2) agreement on which mechanisms will be used to achieve the change, and (3) implementation of the mechanisms required to achieve the change. A few additional comments on each of the steps are given below.

Observation of a Problem or Issue

The initial observation is made either by a person or group, but usually the same observation must be made by a number of people before additional steps are taken. A relatively long period of time may elapse between successive attempts to bring about the major change.

Desire for Change

The concept of the desired change will vary along several spectrums. These include the spectrum of (1) general to specific ideas about what change is needed, (2) vague off-the-cuff to well-thought through ideas about the change, and (3) short-term to long-term changes desired.

Consensus That a General (or Specific) Change Is Worthwhile

It is necessary to build a consensus among relevant people to insure the success of changes made. Changes have a better chance of being accepted and lasting if they are not forced on people. As many people as practical should be allowed and encouraged to participate in developing the proposed change.

Agreement on the Specific Change That Should Occur

General goals must be established relating to the specific change desired. Relevant analyses should be conducted to obtain as much information as possible to help in the decision-making process.

Proposals on How to Achieve the Agreed-On Change

Each available option is described. The data are presented and the pros and cons of each option are discussed.

Agreement on a Set of Mechanisms and Systems to Achieve the Desired Change

Once a specific proposal is accepted, plans must be established to implement it. All hierarchical levels in a company must be considered in terms of whether they will be affected, if so, how, and what influence that will have on the proposed mechanisms and systems.

Implementation of Mechanisms and Systems to Achieve Goals

The implementation phase may begin with a pilot project. This is especially worth considering if resources and time constraints allow this approach. The time lost in conducting a pilot study is often more than made up for in improvements incorporated into the fully implemented plan.

Evaluation of Change Made

Evaluations of the change made may occur at periodic intervals, preset intervals, on an ad hoc basis, or on a crisis basis. In some situations it is important to plan evaluations when the mechanisms and systems are being implemented. It is almost always relevant to question and assess whether the goals of the change are being met. But, this aspect is often ignored after a change is implemented. The importance of these postchange evaluations is to modify changes made to bring them more in keeping with the original goals. If the change was mandated by an executive pronouncement rather than the process described, it is even more critical to follow up and evaluate whether the change was enacted.

Fine-Tuning the Mechanisms and Systems Underlying the Change

Fine-tuning usually occurs as a result of the evaluation conducted. Some important and basic differences exist between companies or between two subsidiaries of the same company that may influence the approach taken to bring about change. Nonetheless, differences between drug companies are sometimes exaggerated. It reminds one of the differences between capitalism and communism. Some people state that in capitalism, man exploits man, and in communism it is the opposite.

DEVELOPING AND IMPLEMENTING STRATEGIES

Companies have overall missions, whether stated or not, as well as goals and/or objectives. In addition they have strategies or plans of how they will achieve those goals. These concepts are discussed in greater detail in *Guide to Planning and Managing Multiple Clinical Studies* (Spilker, 1987c). The rest of this section primarily discusses a company's objectives and strategies for achieving them.

Defining a Company's Objectives

Drug companies should have an overall strategy or direction to follow. It is amazing to learn that some drug companies do not have one. A strategy refers to a company plan that is used as the company travels toward a specific objective or goal. If that goal is to become a highly diversified health care company, of which pharmaceuticals are a small part, the path will be quite different from a company that has decided to focus entirely on prescription pharmaceuticals. Goals of another drug company might be to focus on (1) over-the-counter (OTC) and prescription drugs equally, (2) to diversify so that approximately 50 percent of revenues come from non-health care businesses, or (3) to enlarge the medical device and diagnostic part of their business until it contributes 20 percent of total sales. Many drug companies are owned by a nondrug business and their goals may be phrased differently.

Once the overall corporate objective is established, it is easier to consider and respond to many issues that a board of directors often have to deal with. Typical issues include deciding how much money can be allocated to (1) buying a new business and diversifying the company, (2) expanding present manufacturing capacity and facilities, (3) expanding basic research in hopes of finding a novel drug, or (4) investing in new opportunities of various types.

Developing the overall company strategy may be done by (1) the CEO dictating which direction the company will take, (2) the CEO and board of directors debating this issue and reaching consensus, or (3) having a specific group (e.g., task force, planning committee) develop recommendations and present them to the board of directors for discussion. Other alternatives such as hiring management consultants may also be followed. A strategic planning model is shown in Fig. 6.5.

Which Businesses Should a Drug Company Be in?

Every company will answer this question differently, which is appropriate. Furthermore, the most appropriate answer for any company will change over the years. It is essential for senior management to pay close attention to new opportunities and the changing health care environment so that the company is appropriately positioned. Most large research-based drug companies are primarily focused on discovering and developing drugs, even though they may own numerous other businesses. Some of the businesses that are relatively close to the core business of ethical pharmaceuticals are shown closest to the center of Fig. 6.6. Other businesses that are somewhat less related to ethical drugs are farther from the center. This does not imply that those businesses closest to the center are preferable, or that those further away are to be eschewed. The right blend for each company differs and must be determined by its own senior managers and/or owners.

A company's core business is one that (1) is an essential part of the company's image and reputation, (2) generates a large portion of the company's sales and profits, and (3) utilizes the knowledge and expertise of the company.

Determining Strategies

The company's strategy determines where the company should be in X years and what type of company it wants to be. Once that decision is made, each group within

A STRATEGIC PLANNING MODEL

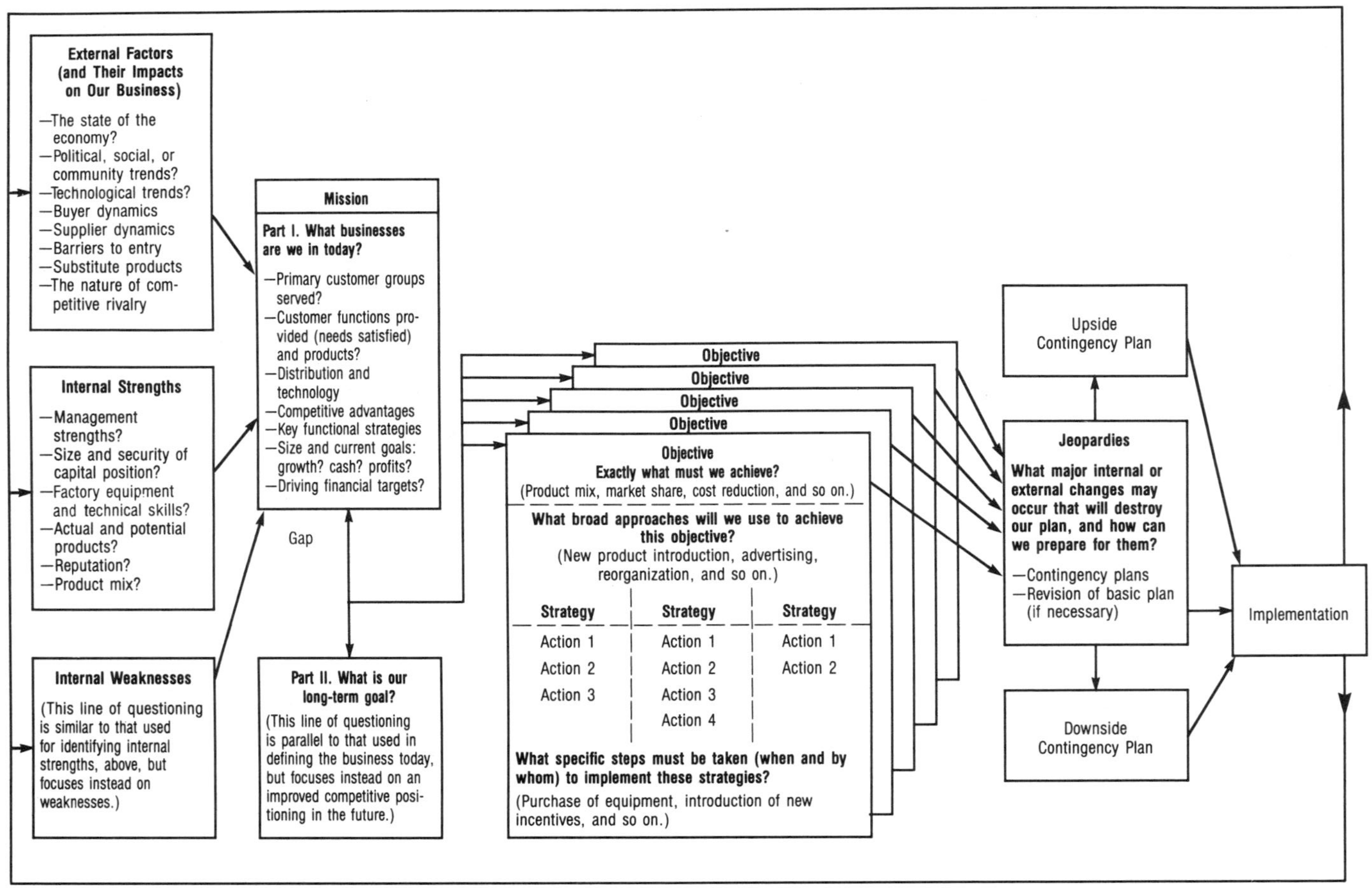

Fig. 6.5. A strategic planning model. From Stringer and Uchenick (1986) with permission of Lexington Books.

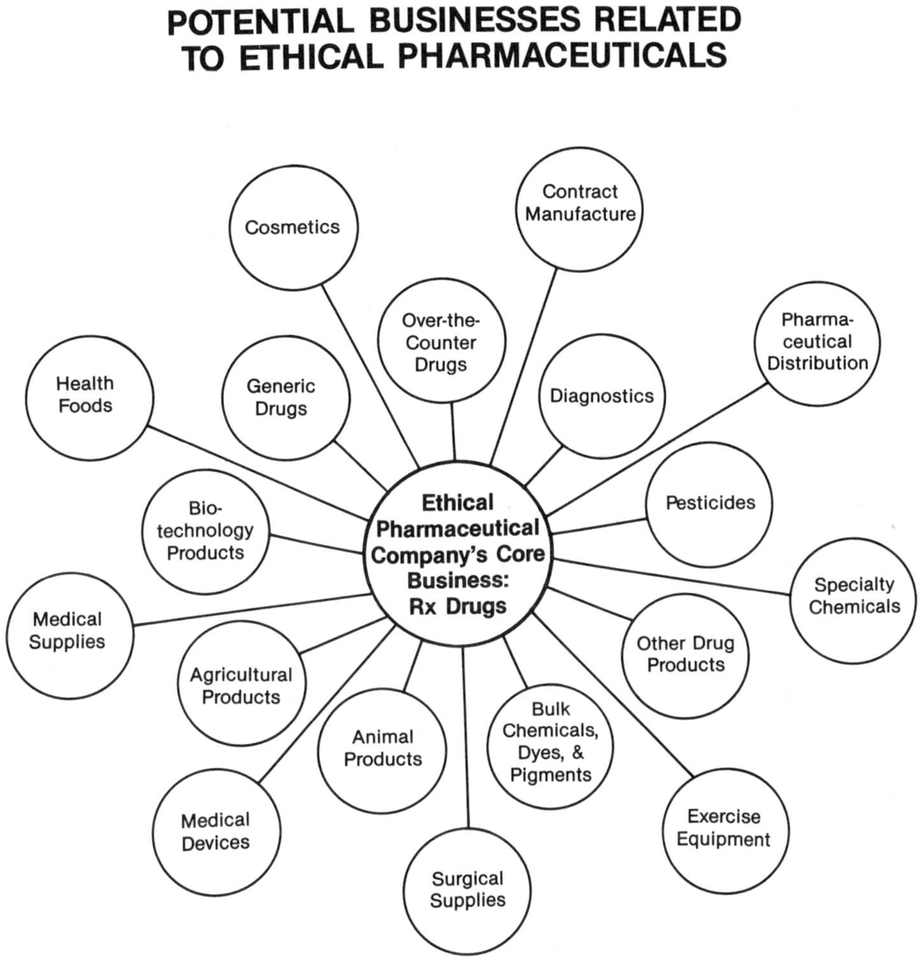

Fig. 6.6. Selected businesses related to ethical pharmaceuticals.

the company, whether an independent business unit, function (e.g., research, production), department, or matrix group can determine their own strategies, which will further the attainment of the overall company strategy.

Companies without an overall strategy have additional difficulties when important opportunities present themselves. Company officials must decide which opportunities to exploit and which ones to reject. If there are a variety of potentially conflicting goals amongst people who determine the company's response, then it will be quite difficult for a series of important decisions to be made using the same criteria. Major company decisions should attempt to (1) lead to change that is constructive, (2) build on previous decisions, and (3) help move the company toward its objectives.

As an exercise on how to choose strategies, consider the following situation. Assume that there is approximately a 5 percent chance that a new project on an experimental drug in early Phase II studies will be a breakthrough drug and an overwhelming success. The chance of it being a small or moderate success is approximately 60 percent, and the chance of its failing and not showing activity is assessed as 35 percent. How should one prioritize this drug's development and set company objectives?

The answer certainly depends on (1) other drugs in the company's portfolio, (2) their stage of development, and (3) the specific resources needed to develop this drug. The need for resources could potentially put the drug in conflict with other projects. In the example given, to purchase expensive raw materials and make a large amount of drug stock based on a 5 percent chance of the drug's being a breakthrough drug is usually too high a risk for most companies to take. In fact, unlike some old wine, the profiles of most drugs do not improve with age, rather they usually tarnish and become spotted with adverse reactions and stories of patients and populations in whom the drug does not satisfactorily work.

Communicating Strategies

In communicating the company's strategies to staff and workers, management must insure that the strategies are clear to everyone. The first group to consider are the senior managers and others who will be promulgating the strategy. Unless the entire concept and purposes it serves are totally clear in their minds, they will be unable to communicate effectively this information to others. Differences in presentation or hearing someone give different messages on different occasions must be avoided. Sufficient detail must be presented to allow relevant individuals to understand the overall strategy. The information must be presented so that employees have an opportunity to discuss and question the ideas. People want to know what the strategy is, why the strategy points were chosen, what difference it will make for the company, and what the strategy means for them. Hopefully, when all of this is complete the employees will agree with and support the strategies presented.

In addition to providing a written document, a company's strategy may be communicated via large conferences and/or a series of smaller meetings where relevant issues are discussed and questions answered. This is a critical step in having the strategy adopted by employees. If this is not done, the strategy may remain the manager's strategy without sufficient acceptance by employees.

Implementing Strategies

The major activities that lead strategies from paper to reality should be clear. Goals and objectives that strategies are designed to accomplish should also be clear. Some of the steps to conduct are:

1. The people who are responsible for conducting each of the activities should be identified.
2. A plan to communicate the strategy should be in place.
3. Potential problems that are inherent in the plan should be known prior to its dissemination. Counterarguments should be prepared and some of these should be presented, even if the anticipated criticisms are not raised.
4. Potential sources of employee resistance to the plan should be anticipated and counterarguments prepared.

5. A follow-up monitoring plan should be developed and agreed on before the strategy is widely disseminated.
6. Future meetings to review progress made on the strategy should be scheduled.
7. Methods for updating the strategy should be outlined.

Contents of a corporate strategy may sometimes turn out to be less important than the processes used to generate and communicate it and the reactions it engenders in employees.

ESTABLISHING PRIORITIES

Once decisions are made on important drug development priorities, the information must flow both upwards and downwards through a company. Systems should be used to disseminate this information that insures all relevant people are informed in a timely manner about decisions that affect their work. Regardless of the system used to establish priorities (i.e., formal or informal) and to disseminate information in a company, the methods used to reach decisions on priorities should be consistent for all drugs.

Every professional in a drug company has some of their priorities (1) established entirely by themselves, (2) set in conjunction with others (primarily supervisors), and (3) imposed by others. Decisions on priorities are therefore made at multiple levels and requests for decisions on priorities flow both upward and downward in the company. An individual who is uncomfortable with making a decision about a priority, or is comfortable but desires agreement from others, will generally either refer the decision upward or make the decision in conjunction with others. Some decisions rise all the way up to the chief executive officer before a final decision is made. Some companies like to push decision-making responsibility down to lower levels in the organization. This correctly suggests that the appropriate level for making the identical type of decision varies in different companies. The actual situation is far more complex because even a single type of decision is often made at different levels within each drug company. One of the reasons for this additional complexity is that certain individuals at all companies attempt to avoid making decisions, whereas others make many decisions that are not strictly within their prerogative or purview. Thus, it is usually too simplistic to say that company A makes its decisions at a higher organizational level than company B.

LONG-RANGE COMPANY PLANNING

Functions of a Planning Staff

What a variety of tasks are put under this title! Every company that has a long-range planning office defines it differently and places it in different parts of the organization. To some companies, long-range corporate planning is a strictly financial position staffed by one individual or by an entire department. The primary function is to prepare corporate budgets and/or forecasts of sales and profits. The time limit or horizon of these forecasts may be one year or may extend to approximately seven years. Although there is no limit on how many years may be forecasted, the benefits of extending forecasts in the drug industry past five to ten years should be seriously questioned. A financially oriented corporate planning group may also examine the previous year's performance or that of several previous years each time the budget is prepared. This allows a better view of past trends to be coupled with future directions (or at least projections).

Other companies define long-range planning in a more broad manner. For example, the planning group could focus on defining, critiquing, and reevaluating the company's mission, objectives, goals, and strategies. The person or group who has this function acts in some ways as the company's soul. It is their responsibility to insure that senior company managers have appropriate templates against which they make decisions and chart the company's course. Junior managers and workers should be given a sense of corporate direction, as well as company values and strategies that are utilized to achieve the goals. Some of these corporate attributes (e.g., mission, values, objectives) may only have to be reevaluated every several years. But, specific goals and strategies should be reevaluated on an annual or semiannual basis, utilizing an agreed on set of procedures.

A third role for a long-range planning group would be to analyze business opportunities. They would evaluate current businesses and propose (1) new business opportunities that should be sought and (2) businesses that should be divested. Opportunities that the company has in terms of business acquisitions, mergers, or divestitures could be evaluated by this group. It is also possible for them to evaluate licensing opportunities, joint venture possibilities, and other product-related issues. In fulfilling this role they may produce explanatory material and/or analyses. These could be highly detailed and comprehensive, or summarize materials prepared by other groups.

Procedures of Strategic Planning

Numerous references describe the process of strategic planning for a company to use. It is interesting that the methods presented are remarkably similar in various references (Stringer and Uchenick, 1986; Porter, 1980, 1985; Waddell, 1986; Guth, 1985). The reader is referred to these or other references for details, but the basic approach is shown in the model illustrated in Fig. 6.5. This approach may readily be fitted to a drug company. There are many viewpoints to consider, either before strategic planning is started or when it is reviewed (e.g., see Gray, 1986; Hayes, 1985). Strategic planning is one area where the basic methods do not have to be modified because of differences between the drug industry and other industries.

Assessing the Value of Strategic Planning

No matter which of the above roles (or others) is served by a corporate planning group, it is essential to periodically ask "What is the value of the group's outputs?" Planning groups sometimes grow with a company and their size may become large and their operations geared toward producing reports for others. Materials they generate may become voluminous, giving the appearance of a worthwhile activity.

But, the real value of thick reports must be carefully assessed. Sometimes, totally eliminating periodic or other types of reports causes a sigh of relief and no complaints about a loss of important information. These people may be free to *do* their work rather than being obligated to document and write about work they have already done or are planning to do.

7 / Selected Personnel Issues at the Corporate Level

You can issue directives and policy statements and messages to staff until the wastepaper baskets burst, but they are nothing compared with promotions. Promotions are the one visible, unmistakable sign of the corporation's standard of values, an irrevocable declaration of the qualities it prizes in its staff, a simultaneous warning and example to everyone who knows the nature of the job and the qualities of its new incumbent. Men who have worked diligently and successfully and then see those who have worked less diligently and less successfully promoted above them start to read the management want ads in the paper the following morning. Antony Jay. From *Management and Machiavelli.*

PERSONNEL ISSUES AT THE CORPORATE LEVEL

Basic Characteristics of a Wise Chief Executive Officer

Drug companies are potentially faced with many problems when the chief executive officer does not understand basic issues of drug development, marketing, or production and yet insists on being actively involved in decision making in these areas. A wise chief executive officer who does not have a background in these areas (and even if he does) will delegate responsibility to his most senior managers. By doing this the chief executive officer usually enhances his own image within the company and enables it to be run more efficiently. If the chief executive officer does not have adequate confidence in his senior managers' ability to make sound decisions or does not trust them in other ways, then those managers should be given different tasks, transferred, or encouraged to resign.

Choosing Senior Managers in the Pharmaceutical Industry

To become a truly effective senior manager in the drug industry, it is essential to understand how drugs are developed and how the industry operates. Even the heads of personnel and human resource departments require this knowledge. Clearly, many companies either do not believe this principle or believe that it only takes a short while to learn about the drug industry. For example, some companies hire academicians with (1) impressive reputations, (2) solid understanding of science, and (3) important contacts, for senior managerial positions within research and development. These people often have little or no industry experience, and have only interacted with a company as a consultant. Another comparable example occurs when government executives are brought to a company because of their contacts and knowledge about the Food and Drug Administration (FDA). It is ironic that a company's board of directors sometimes turn over important senior research and development (R and D) responsibilities to people with little or no knowledge about drug discovery, drug development, and the drug industry. Nonetheless, both scientifically sophisticated academicians and knowledgable government employees often add important characteristics and input to a company, but not as new senior managers of a highly complex system they know little about.

Companies should primarily promote experienced managers or leaders from within the drug industry to their most senior positions, even if their scientific reputation is not as illustrious as some academicians, or whose connections may not be as impressive as some government employees. The mistake of hiring inexperienced senior managers from outside the industry is often dramatic in its impact on the productivity of a company that it is surprising that it occurs on so many occasions. The author's observations are that it usually takes new managers from outside the industry several years to fully learn the basics of industrial drug discovery, drug development, and marketing activities. During this period their company's research effort may stagnate, go off on tangents, make many mistakes, or at the least, not move forward aggressively in a desired direction. In addition, many outside scientists who are hired to head research and development groups overly emphasize the research function they are usually most familiar with and pay insufficient attention to maintaining a balance with other functions that they are usually less familiar and comfortable with. Moreover, drug discovery activities in industry are quite different than drug research in academia, and many academicians never learn the basics of industrial research.

Who should a company want to hire as a director of research in charge of new drug discovery? This person could be a top administrator, a top scientist, a top leader, or someone with other qualifications and characteristics. If so, which characteristics are most important? These questions are answered differently in different companies because each company's needs differ, the people making the selection have their own biases, and the characteristics of potential candidates will also differ.

Determining an Appropriate Staffing Level, or How to Avoid Over- and Understaffing

A major personnel issue concerns whether to staff an organization based on peak periods of activity, lean periods of activity, or some middle position. In groups, departments, or companies where staffing is based on meeting anticipated (or actual) demands experienced during peak periods, there is almost invariably a problem encountered during slack periods. The problem is that a significant amount of staff time is underutilized and unproductive. Employees may be fired or forced to take early retirement in organizations that are less concerned about employee well-being and are not "paternal." In other organizations, personnel may be reassigned or allowed to "weather mild storms." When an organization expands its staff during good times and trims back during lean periods, the process is sometimes referred to as an "accordion effect." This phenomenon is often observed in small consulting companies. After they win a large contract they rapidly hire new staff to help conduct the work. When the contract is over, many staff members are let go or fired if a sufficient number of new contracts have not been obtained to provide adequate employment. In extreme cases, companies are forced to go out of business. This latter phenomenon is relatively common for small consulting companies.

Chronically understaffing a company is usually an unsatisfactory approach because it creates a large backlog of work and places heavy pressures on the staff. One alternative to avoid undo pressure is to contract work that cannot be conducted in a timely manner in-house to outside groups. Contracting work to outside groups is often more expensive for a company than if the work were done in-house. Nonetheless, if additional work occurs sporadically and may be satisfactorily performed by contractors, then the contracting approach makes good business sense.

Advantages of understaffing are that people generally (1) work hard because they have a large workload, (2) become more efficient in performing their work, and (3) put aside less important work (this may also be a disadvantage). This type of lean and efficient organization often (4) develops a positive esprit de corps, and (5) almost everyone cooperates with each other, because they feel that they are playing an important part in a group effort. On the other hand, the staff may be overburdened for a long period with an excessive amount of work, or employees may believe that their employer is cheap, purposely keeping the group understaffed, and is profiting unfairly from their difficult conditions. Workers often become burned-out or disgruntled in this situation and their efficiency markedly decreases. To achieve the desired balance between under- and overstaffing, one should analyze staffing issues in the context of a cost-benefit analysis.

The cost side of the cost-benefit analysis includes both actual direct costs (e.g., low unemployment keeps the unemployment tax rate low), and less indirect costs (e.g., training of staff). The benefits of understaffing include steady employment. But, if a company understaffs by too many people, it can lead to situations where important errors are made by overworked staff or inexperienced temporaries. A major problem with overstaffing is that it threatens steady employment over a long period. One rough measure of whether a firm is over- or understaffed is to examine the ratio of total company revenues per employee, for several companies. This figure does not indicate whether the staff are deployed appropriately, and these numbers are also influenced by the nature of the marketed drug portfolio. Nonetheless, there may be valuable information in a comparison with competitors to indicate the degree of over- or understaffing.

Changes in Work Load Over Time

The level of drug development activities (i.e., work load) in a specific department or group varies as a single major drug travels through the development pipeline. The work load of a group also varies over time as more or fewer drugs are being developed simultaneously. The numbers of permanent staff may be adjusted to account for long-term changes in the total work load. It is more difficult, however, and it makes little sense to continually adjust a department's staff based on temporary changes in their level of activities. Two major types of changes occur over time. First, there are changes in work load that are of long duration and may be viewed as relatively permanent. Second, there are transitional changes which fluctuate over a shorter time span, on the order of weeks or months.

Staffing needs for long-term changes are usually viewed as permanent. Staffing options for fluctuating changes usually require a different approach. Some possible solutions to meeting short-term staffing needs involve temporary adjustments, such as (1) adding temporary help, (2) contracting work to outsiders, (3) allowing backlogs to temporarily develop, (4) reassigning personnel, or (5) using special deployment teams.

Trade-offs between Quality and Quantity of Staff

In the long term, no drug company can combine overstaffing and overpaying its employees. To do so would put the firm's cost structure out of line with competitive firms. The company should carefully analyze which positions are most critical to its success and set its pay levels high enough to attract and retain individuals with sufficient skills to create and maintain competitive advantages for the firm. Conversely, the firm should be careful not to overpay positions where high skill levels are not critical to the success of the enterprise. In such areas, quantity of staff may be more important than quality.

Companies can purchase many ingredients of drug development (e.g., rights to a drug, services of contractors to develop a drug, consultants, people to design and monitor studies). One key ingredient that companies cannot easily purchase is a talented and loyal senior management group that understands the subtleties of drug development, knows the professional people within the company, and works together as a team. On the other hand, it is often easier to replace a senior manager than a middle level manager who has specific skills and experience necessary for drug discovery or development.

Orientation and Training of New Employees

Orientation

Each drug company has its own corporate culture, which is largely influenced by the company's mission, values, objectives, beliefs, and goals. The aspects of corporate culture that vary most between drug companies are generally each company's myths and traditions. The orientation of new employees is an ideal opportunity to present that culture and to initiate a specific type of corporate thinking.

Orientation programs should also include various other relevant aspects of the company and new employee's division (e.g., research, marketing, production). This includes a review of the company's history and its contributions to medicine and science, plus personnel issues, information about the company's products, and other appropriate information. It is also important to discuss procedures that are used to derive the philosophy and approaches that a company uses in reaching decisions. These objectives are usually addressed using a combination of talks, tours, brochures, videos, and slide presentations. Factors that have a positive or negative effect on employees' motivation should be considered not only in creating the initial orientation program, but in other interactions between a company and its employees such as training programs.

Training

Current staff may be offered or required to have training in new areas of responsibility, as well as to improve skills in various aspects of their current position. Courses focus on manual, technical, managerial, personal, psychological, and/or communication and decision-making skills.

When new staff are hired to meet a crisis, replace staff, or enlarge a group, it takes time for them to develop sufficient experience to contribute fully to the company. It is important to consider the rate of growth in staff size, so that new employees may be assimilated well into the company. One means of expediting their learning curve and minimizing the orientation time is with well-thought-out training programs.

Training programs should be as well tailored to the individual as is consistent with efficient use of time and the efforts of others. There are so many options available that are both cost and time effective that to allow only on-the-job-training (OTJ) makes little sense and may be largely counter-productive for many employees. Scientific, clinical, marketing, finance, and production staff usually have a wide variety of both internal company and external training opportunities. The staff's problem is mainly one of choosing the right formats and finding the time to take courses or attend meetings. Courses sponsored by the company may be either on- or off-site.

There are many obvious advantages to run a course off-site, when it is practical to do so. This issue is discussed in greater length relating to project leader training in *Guide to Planning and Managing Multiple Clinical Studies* (Spilker, 1987c). Courses have the best chance of being successful when they are developed or modified to suit the specific participants and also are evaluated in a pilot program.

MOTIVATION AND PRODUCTIVITY

Motivating Factors

Motives of professional staff vary in different areas of a drug company. Obviously, money is an extremely important motivator, but its importance varies for different people. For those in marketing it is usually relatively more important than for scientists in research and development. Scientific achievement and professional recognition are also extremely important motivators for scientists and clinicians in drug companies. For business staff, power and authority are often extremely important motivators. One of the corollaries of these differences is that mechanisms to improve productivity and morale vary greatly in different professional areas within a drug company. For example, characteristics of high scientific performers are listed in Table 7.2. Points designed to increase productivity and quality in a company are listed in Table 16.2. These refer primarily to a production facility. Recognizing differences between groups in terms of their interests, training, perspective, and manner of working as well as the motivational factors discussed, allows a company to derive more effective use of employees' abilities and skills.

Some people believe that the motivators described in the paragraph above (e.g., money, recognition, power) only relate to senior managers. Although these motivators are most obvious in terms of their use for senior management, they also exist at lower levels within a company. The degree to which they are present at lower levels depends primarily on whether managers throughout a company desire to pass such benefits down through the company and also on whether they are allowed to do so. Even when certain managers are prevented from providing additional money to lower levels as salaries or as a bonus they may be allowed to provide additional responsibilities. If this too is prevented, they may always provide additional recognition to staff below them in the form of public thanks, notices on bulletin boards, articles in company publications, dinners where the employee's spouse is also invited, or various other mechanisms that are known to be meaningful. Trinkets, certificates, or other approaches should only be used when they are known to be valued by the recipient, because recognition in a form that is distasteful to the recipient may be counterproductive. A few factors that have a positive or negative effect on employee motivation are listed in Table 7.1.

What Do Workers Really Want?

Surveys of managers and workers usually turn up highly different views of what each thinks that the workers really want. Although specific details of each survey differ, the most important points generally reported by workers are:

Table 7.1. Factors influencing motivation of employees[a]

A. Positive motivating factors
   1. Flexibility in work schedules
   2. Flexibility in vacation schedules
   3. Ability to discuss issues with people at all levels in the company
   4. Recognition for contributions
   5. Ability to attend professional meetings
   6. Ability to help plan in-house scientific meetings
   7. Awareness of how one's work fits into the "big picture"

B. Demotivating factors
   1. Unethical approach to drug development and/or marketing
   2. Insufficient staff to conduct relevant activities
   3. Overstaffing and resultant idle time
   4. Lack of any decision making
   5. Promotion of individuals considered to be unqualified
   6. General lack of information about the relevance of one's work

[a] An excellent article on motivation (Herzberg, 1987), originally published by the *Harvard Business Review* in 1968, has sold more reprints (1.2 million) than any other article published by that journal.

1. Appreciation for work done. Employee attitude surveys consistently show that managers neglect to meet workers needs for psychological recognition. Most people have an almost unlimited capacity for being recognized when they have done a good job. Managers too often fail to take advantage of this no-cost means of improving worker morale.
2. A feeling of being "in" on things, i.e., being "part of the action" or at least aware of the major activities going on in their group. This involves both downwards communication to workers from management and upwards communication from workers to management.
3. Job security.
4. Good wages.

When surveys are made about workers' attitudes, or other personnel issues, it is important to propose recommendations or solutions as well as describing the results.

Improving Productivity

Many personnel issues are directed toward increasing productivity. A few additional comments are made here of points not discussed elsewhere. These are not presented in any particular order. Additional ideas for increasing the productivity of technical professionals are presented by Griggs and Manring (1986). Characteristics of high scientific performers are listed in Table 7.2, and a number of reasons for low employee productivity are given in Table 7.3.

1. The number of people who work together in a single office is usually inversely related to their productivity. At both junior and senior levels, each professional should have their own office space with privacy. Putting two people in the same office markedly diminishes productivity, unless they are working in a laboratory or in an environment where their work does not require privacy. When people find it difficult to hold meetings or even telephone calls in their room and must spend time going elsewhere to conduct business, it creates problems. It may become a major

Table 7.2. Characteristics of high scientific performers[a]

1. *Freedom*: Is coordination compatible with freedom? Best performance occurred when both were present
2. *Communication*: Effective scientists both sought and received more contact with colleagues
3. *Diversity*: In both research and development, the more effective scientists undertook several specialties or technical functions
4. *Dedication*: Several simple questions showed that high-performing scientists and engineers were deeply involved in their work
5. *Motivations*: Among various motives characterizing high performers, an outstanding trait was self-reliance
6. *Satisfaction*: Effective scientists reported good oportunities for professional growth and higher status, but were not necessarily more satisfied
7. *Similarity*: Colleagues of high performers disagreed with them on strategy and approach but drew stimulation from similar sources
8. *Creativity*: Creative ability enhanced performance on new projects with free communication but seemed to impair performance in less flexible situations
9. *Age*: Performance peaked at midcareer then dropped—but less among inner-motivated scientists and those in development labs
10. *Age and Climate*: As age increased, performance was sustained with periodic change in project, self-reliance, and interest both in breadth and depth
11. *Coordination*: In loosely coordinated settings, the most autonomous individuals did poorly—perhaps because they were isolated from stimulation
12. *Groups*: Groups declined in performance after several years, but less if the members became cohesive and intellectually competitive

[a] These are the chapter headings from the book *Scientists in Organizations* by Pelz and Andrews (1976.) Reprinted with permission of the Institute for Social Research of the University of Michigan.

problem of decreased productivity if many people have to conduct their business under crowded conditions.

2. When professionals spend a significant portion of their time handling routine matters that could be dealt with by a clerk it compromises their productivity. If many people in a company operate in this manner, the efficiency of drug development may be significantly compromised. One assistant may handle time-consuming activities of several professionals, allowing the professionals to utilize their time on more important and/or complex issues. The question is to determine how many assistants to hire. Hiring too many assistants may be counterproductive and adversely affect a group's efficiency.

Table 7.3. Possible reasons for low employee productivity[a]

1. Boredom
2. Lack of clear responsibilities
3. Individuals never see a finished product of their work
4. Bureaucratic rules, excessive paperwork, and red tape
5. Supervisors who do not encourage and support employees
6. Lack of adequate physical comforts in the environment
7. Frequent transfers of personnel
8. A new supervisor
9. Incompatibility between the supervisor and his employees
10. Poor communication between staff or between managers and employees
11. Lack of openness and honesty in the environment
12. Benefits that have not kept pace with those of other companies
13. Political maneuvering of senior managers, which creates stress and pressures on employees

[a] These may also be applied to an individual employee. These are not listed in any particular order.

3. Encouraging professionals to ride to work in carpools and company-owned vans is a means of facilitating intellectual sparks and original ideas. This is one type of the intellectual turbulence described in Chapter 4, where imaginative people help each other solve problems or define new approaches to issues.

4. A few of the more recently developed tools to help individuals improve their productivity include: (1) electronic mail, (2) electronic conferencing, (3) voice mail, (4) calendar management, (5) calendar scheduling, (6) computer filing system, and (7) numerous other computer software packages.

Many other issues relating to productivity are discussed in Chapters 4 and 16.

ATTITUDES OF WORKERS TOWARD DRUG DEVELOPMENT—NEGATIVE, OVERLY OPTIMISTIC, AND REALISTIC

General Attitudes

When someone is discussing a particular aspect of drug development, listen closely. Is he saying "what if all of these negative things happen with a drug" in a way that says he does not want to take a chance and develop a drug, even though others believe it to have a reasonable chance of success? Is the person always saying "let's try this, I know it'll work," after many previous trials have failed. Is this optimistic person always wanting to try one more thing before a dead drug is finally buried? On the other hand there are realistic people who say "why not try such and such to overcome the problems we face or the potential problems that may occur?" Attitudes differ, but at some companies (and perhaps in some countries) there is a preponderance of people who have a generalized form of "negative disease."

Negative Disease

It is important to be objective and to evaluate carefully and critically new ideas. Being skeptical of many new claims is prudent (see, for example, the section on advertising claims in Chapter 21). The pertinent question is whether this attitude is manifested as objectivity or as negativity. The author has met relatively few people in the drug industry who are overly optimistic and positive about most new drugs under development. Many do develop myopia, however, about one or two particular drugs for a variety of reasons. But, numerous individuals in the drug industry have "negative disease" and have usually found it safer to raise objections than to agree or take a realistic approach. Companies are fortunate if they are dominated by a realistic group of senior managers.

Other aspects of "negative disease" are where people are (1) more comfortable repeating old work than starting new work, (2) more comfortable starting one clinical study after another without having a clear regulatory endpoint in focus, (3) always attempting to answer basic questions about how a drug works rather than initiating studies to move the drug forward toward regulatory approval in the most straightforward manner possible, (4) certain that if they have not done all relevant work themselves they must repeat the work before it can be believed, and (5) certain that their country is the true center of the world for drug development.

Foxhole Mentality

Foxhole mentality is another cause of negative disease in staff members. This refers to people who are afraid to stick their heads out of their foxhole, because they have been "shot at" in the past. Once someone is shot at they usually become gun shy, or they stock up on ammunition and plan their next assault more carefully. Some people operate entirely in a foxhole. They listen to the "big guns" blasting overhead and occasionally (or often) see flares and lights in the nighttime sky that indicate a battle occurring some distance away. People who operate in isolation in individual foxholes probably have a higher incidence of negative disease (a form of trench fever) than do other workers.

Overly Optimistic Disease

The author has met fewer people with this condition than those with negative disease. Optimistic disease folks are prone to make comments such as:

- "Our data look great, let's write up the New Drug Application (NDA) now."
- "The FDA will *have* to approve this promptly."
- "Let's use all European data. After all, the FDA accepts it now."
- "Let's take the Product License Application (PLA) from England and send it to the FDA."

These comments are often naive, but those who make such statements with force and have positions of power may be viewed as strong, forceful leaders. These traits are really counterproductive in a senior manager who believes he is inspiring and leading his troops.

Difficult Individuals Who Either Create Problems or Prevent Their Resolution

Unfortunately, many individuals who personally hamper solutions to problems desire to be the center of attention, even of negative attention. Some of the people who either place themselves or are placed in a central position where a problem or issue exists have been in a company for many years. Some may have positions of authority but have been bypassed for more senior positions. They obviously derive a great sense of enjoyment and/or importance from creating bottlenecks and difficulties for other people in the company. Alternatively, the obstreperous people may simply be used to doing their job in the "old way" and may be unable or unwilling to change and adapt to new situations.

If this type of individual is found to be responsible for an important problem, then spending a significant amount of time to resolve one situation will usually not lead to a long-lasting solution. Related situations will often arise within a number of months, if not sooner. In such cases it is generally desirable to replace the person. This individual may be moved to a position outside the mainstream of the company's activities. Alternatively, a mechanism may be developed which would force the person to accept a system which he or she could not (or at least, not easily) alter, block, or delay.

Using a Balanced Perspective

In dealing with many drug discovery and development issues and problems it is usually wise to remember that there are more than a dozen ways to do almost anything. There are also many perspectives on most issues. Thus, when hearing that someone has done something "outrageous," it is best to avoid accepting that conclusion easily. It usually turns out that their perspective is also valid. This is especially true for people who are generally considered to be reliable.

Companies would do well to have a few basic rules and policies to help guide their behavior and reactions to various situations. This is similar to the concept of adopting some principles of living, such as: (1) never eat in a restaurant called Moms, (2) never eat in a restaurant with more than four calendars on the wall, (3) never play cards with a man named Doc, and (4) never shoot pool with a man named after a city.

LIAISON BETWEEN DIFFERENT FUNCTIONS

All companies require different groups to cooperate and to function well together. One factor that differs between companies is how well different functions cooperate and conduct work for each other.

Examples of One Division Doing Work for Another

There is often a desire or need in one group to have someone in another group perform work for them. A few examples of this are listed.

1. Research and development wants someone in marketing to evaluate the current status of competitive drug projects and drugs already in the market.
2. Marketing wants someone in research and development to develop planning charts and flow diagrams to assist them in scheduling the launch of a new product.
3. Production wants technical assistance from chemical and analytical development units to assist with problems of a recently transferred process.
4. Research and development wants production to manufacture clinical study drug supplies for a large upcoming clinical study.
5. Marketing wants specific medical studies conducted on soon-to-be-marketed and currently marketed drugs to support promotional claims.
6. Research and development wants marketing research data to assist in reaching various decisions.

Many other cases could be listed. These examples require coordination and cooperation between different functions in a company. When the quality and rapidity of service provided by one group on major priority items are not acceptable, strains develop and alternative solutions are often sought. Some of these are described below.

Reconciling Problems When Work Done by Another Division Is Not Satisfactory

Alternative solutions usually exist for a group or unit that is displeased with the quality, quantity, or timeliness of services received from another group or unit within the same company. These may involve (1) discussing the issues involved and agreeing on what work will be able to be handled over a given period, plus identifying necessary conditions for its completion, (2) contracting the work to outside groups, and (3) developing the capability within the group that is displeased to handle the necessary work themselves.

Developing the capability of conducting work usually performed by others solves problems in some situations. The value of this approach varies from a positive duplication of effort to an unnecessary if not a counterproductive duplication. The decision of whether the duplication is positive depends on many factors that are not enumerated here because each situation is quite different. A few specific cases are discussed below.

Another approach that is sometimes followed is for the group that is providing the service to hire one or more additional people who are dedicated to helping the other function. This approach sounds reasonable, is logical, and may be a satisfactory solution. Nonetheless, the author has observed that in several situations where it has been tried, the people hired to do work for another group spend less and less time on that work. This has occurred even when their salary comes from the group that desires the work. These people become involved in work directed by their administrative superiors, rather than their "clients."

Case Studies

Case I

The marketing division desires to have some clinical studies performed which will help them support advertising claims they would like to make on both new and old drugs. In addition, there are several line-extensions to existing products that they want to have developed, as well as obtaining an increased shelf life for other products. Each of these items is requested of research and development through appropriate channels. Much of the work, however, never seems to get done, and other work gets done much more slowly than marketing believes reasonable. In an extreme case, marketing's highest priorities are not completed by research and development. Marketing executives are now thinking about how to deal with this situation.

Case II

The department of pharmacokinetics and metabolism conducts various studies on animals to determine the profile of new drugs. The priorities within that department are set by the head of that department, who believes that drugs at a later phase of clinical development should receive much higher priority than drugs currently in an early phase.

The medical department relies on the department of pharmacokinetics and metabolism to help plan the pharmacokinetic aspects of drug protocols and also to assay biological samples (e.g., blood) for determination of drug levels. The particular problem is that the medical department wants certain assays performed as soon as possible on a completed Phase I study. These data are necessary to help design the next Phase I clinical study for that drug. Nonetheless, this work is given a low priority by the department of pharmacokinetics and the work does not seem to get done.

Discussion of the Two Cases

The particular cases cited are representative of innumerable examples that could be described where staff in one reporting group are requesting work or service from another group. They illustrate division-to-division differences (case I) and department-to-department differences (case II). These types of problems also exist at both higher and lower levels within a corporation.

The easiest way to solve many such problems is for relevant individuals to communicate (by telephone, meeting, or memo) and to reach an amicable solution. Unfortunately, this approach is not always used or may not be sufficient to solve a problem. Other methods must often be sought. Another common solution is for the aggrieved parties to take their case to an arbiter, usually an individual who is above them in the company's hierarchy. This person may resolve the issue, either amicably or by imposing a solution. But, this more senior individual may not be willing to settle the issue or may not settle it so that both parties are pleased. In such situations, the problem(s) generally continues to brew and may boil over again in the future. In thinking about differences between one's approaches and those of others one is reminded of Mark Twain's line from *Pudd'nhead Wilson*: "Nothing so needs reforming as other people's habits."

Another approach to resolving differences is to establish formal and/or informal mechanisms to deal expressly with problems. A mechanism that might be proposed in case I would be for the marketing division to establish its top priorities on an annual (or semiannual) basis. These would then be communicated to research and development via an established route. This would avoid having numerous individuals within marketing each attempt to have their own plans carried out by individuals within research and development. This standardized approach would allow research and development groups to deal more uniformly and effectively with drug development requests from marketing.

Marketing may make reasonable requests that are within the capabilities of research and development, but cannot be accomplished because of insufficient resources. One means of solving this problem is for research and development to increase its resources so that it may adequately provide all reasonable services requested. Another alternative is for the marketing division to establish their own medical department, whose priorities would be determined solely by marketing interests. A third alternative would be for the marketing division to place some or all of their studies with outside contractors who would either conduct the studies themselves or act as middlemen and place them with investigators. A fourth alternative is for the marketing division to contract with the research and development group and to pay for such studies. A combination of these or other alternatives is possible. Many of these approaches have analogous solutions for case II. There will always be many complex or difficult issues between departments and between divisions, but most can be resolved if there is genuine interest in doing so.

8 / *Differences Within and Between Drug Companies*

The best person to decide what research work shall be done is the man who is doing the research, and the next best person is the head of the department, who knows all about the subject and the work; after that you leave the field of the best people and start on increasingly worse groups, the first of these being the research director, who is probably wrong more than half the time; then a committee, which is wrong most of the time; and, finally a committee of vice-presidents, which is wrong all the time. C.E.K. Mees. Former head of research at Eastman Kodak Co. Quoted by Pelz and Andrews (1976, p.322).

My way of doing business was never entirely scientific, but I think the emotional, dramatic kind of manager can hold his own with a scientific manager. Thomas Watson, Jr., former chief executive of IBM. From *Fortune* (August 31, 1987).

INSTITUTIONAL CULTURE AND MEMORY

Background

Within any company there are many philosophical and other differences concerning the methods that are the most efficient, most ethical, most practical, and most cost-effective for developing drugs. It is a happy but unusual occasion when there is total agreement among all managers about how to develop even a single drug.

This issue becomes more complex when a company is simultaneously developing a particular drug in two or more countries. This is especially relevant if the company is not run as a centralized "dictatorship," and each company site running a development program for the drug has a voice in the decision-making process. There are a number of issues that are generally addressed differently in various countries, and these differences often place strains on any unified development plan. Differences within a company are usually a reflection of the types of differences that also exist between companies. Although many of these differences are discussed throughout the book, some overall areas where differences exist are reviewed in this chapter.

Company Culture

The culture of a drug company influences the approaches used in drug development. A highly conservative approach in drug development is where each major question that could be raised by a regulatory agency has been studied and discussed. A less conservative approach could be to conduct a minimal number of studies and to assemble a lean NDA in terms of quantity of data. Proponents of the lean approach hope that various potential issues about the drug are not raised and that the quantity of data submitted will be sufficient to obtain regulatory approval. Other aspects of the impact of a company's culture on drug development relate to whether a company is prone to challenge Food and Drug Administration (FDA) requests for additional data or whether the company accepts FDA requests without comments. Some companies attempt to achieve a close "alliance" with the FDA on a drug's development from the time the initial plan is formulated through each stage of its development.

Culture may be viewed on at least three separate levels. The *first level is the overall company level* where one may focus on aspects that distinguish each company. These include the internal company environments, traditions, values, image, and reputation, plus personalities and style of the most senior leaders. Cultures might differ in the relative roles of marketing and research and development in major decisions made about identifying therapeutic areas to research and specific drugs to develop and prioritize. Either marketing or research and development might have a major role in establishing company goals and objectives.

The *second level is that of the entire function* (e.g., research and development, marketing, or production). This level of culture depends on the same aspects as the corporate level plus the nature of present staff, most senior manager or leader, and characteristics of the specific function. The *third level relates to the specific people each worker directly interacts with in his or her daily activities*. This level of culture depends on all of the above noted factors plus the specific attributes and environment of the person or group involved and those with whom they interact.

Knowledge of a company's culture is essential. It allows people to know (1) who to go to when you want things done, (2) where the real power lies, (3) who to avoid, and (4) how to build a consensus in achieving one's objectives. It allows people to function more effectively in their various roles.

Institutional Memory

The term institutional memory refers to the nature of the drug company in terms of its traditions, values, myths, and information that have value and should be preserved and handed on to future employees. Institutional memory is really the wisdom of a company, which is a distillation of the people's experiences. Each company should have both formal and informal methods for collecting, storing, and passing on information, knowledge, and data obtained by company employees. These data, which are important for historical purposes, future evaluations, and future analyses, enable the company to preserve its individual and collective wisdom and the company's identity. This information includes various reports and analyses that contain lessons that could be extracted and used (see Chapter 4). The information would be collected, coded, and stored in a facility with ability for rapid retrieval. This historical data base could also be stored on hard copy (i.e., paper) or in a deep-freeze facility (i.e., warehouse), where it would be less accessible for rapid retrieval.

Another aspect of institutional memory resides in the minds and memory of longer term employees. Those who have been at a company for a long time often serve as a repository for various types of information and as internal consultants as well as mentors for newer and also for younger employees. A company with rapid turnover risks losing important people who retain part of the company's identity and can help train new employees in many cultural, as well as methodological, aspects of the company.

A company's institutional memory includes (1) old equipment, relics, photographs, and souvenirs of past events and buildings; (2) reports and analyses, especially those which present a broad overview of the company and may be useful to mangers who are able to utilize the data; (3) specific analyses and reports created for the purpose of developing an institutional memory, such as lessons gained from terminated projects and important measures and trends in productivity; and (4) professional know-how that is often lost when scientists, clinicians, marketing or other professionals leave the company. The latter may be captured by carefully structured interviews and through other means, such as retaining certain individuals as consultants after they retire or leave.

Information that is part of institutional memory is valuable for drug discovery and development for several reasons. Many questions frequently arise that may be answered with already existing company data. But, before these data can be used, they must have been collected, processed, and archived in such a manner that they are retrievable. People must be trained in the best methods of retrieving it. Lessons of the past must be transmitted to new employees. Information from the past will help current staff steer the best path through the course of drug development, hopefully avoiding wrong turns and tangents.

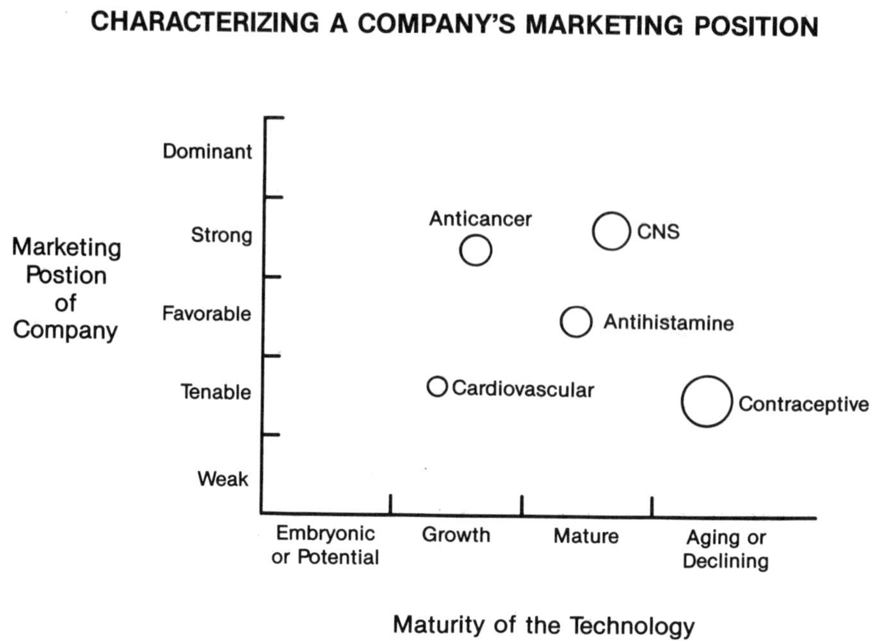

Fig. 8.1. Characterizing the marketing position of a specific company. The size of the circle is proportional to the relative size of sales. CNS, central nervous system.

ATTITUDES AND APPROACHES TOWARD DRUG DISCOVERY AND DEVELOPMENT

Factors Influencing Attitudes toward Drug Development

Widely differing attitudes toward drug development exist both within and between companies. One scale along which attitudes vary is from optimistic, positive, and enthusiastic at one end of the spectrum to pessimistic, negative, and discouraged at the opposite pole. Factors that affect attitudes of managers and employees include the (1) number of medically and commercially exciting drugs in the development pipeline, (2) opportunities for career advancement and enhancement, (3) working conditions, (4) attitudes of superiors, (5) attitudes of top management, (6) financial health of the company, (7) personalities of the people involved, and (8) overall trends of the company's performance.

The style that is generally used to develop drugs differs between different companies. The choice of a company's style is usually a reflection of the personality of the most senior manager or group of managers. Some may emphasize pharmacokinetic studies, mechanism of action studies, or have a desire to explore many different indications for each drug. Other aspects of style relate to the degree of caution or risk usually taken. Differences may exist in different businesses or divisions of a company because of differences between the managers that direct each. In large companies the chief executive officer needs a strong personality to influence the entire company. This may be accomplished in many different ways from group meetings with hoopla to quiet sessions with one or a few individuals.

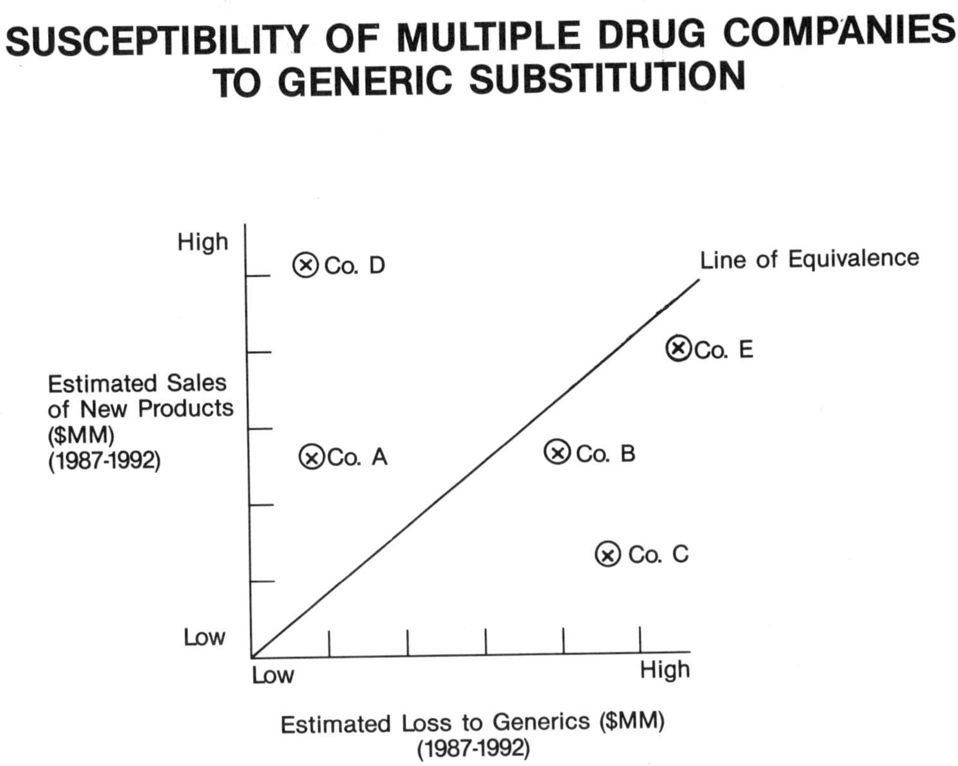

Fig. 8.2. Susceptibility of various drug companies to generic substitution. This factor varies for different companies at a specific point in time. Those below the line are more susceptible than those above the line.

Strengths and Weaknesses of a Company in Different Therapeutic Areas

Many approaches to developing drugs within a company depend on how the company perceives its own strengths and weaknesses. Marked differences between companies are often based on the relative strengths in different therapeutic areas, and whether the therapeutic areas represent growing, mature, or dying areas for future drug development (Fig. 8.1). A method to illustrate the susceptibility of companies to competition from generic substitution is shown in Fig. 8.2 and that of a single company over a period of years is shown in Fig. 8.3. In Fig. 8.2 each company's position is indicated by a single point on a grid of estimated future sales of new products over an arbitrarily chosen number of years versus estimated future sales losses of current products over the same period because of competition from generic drugs.

There are proponents in each company who strongly espouse the view of building on the company's strengths. A great deal of common sense underlies this proposal, and this approach is often essential for companies to follow if they wish to remain viable. Nonetheless, there is a danger that if a company concentrates all of its efforts and resources on building its strengths, the company may become too narrow in its focus. This in turn could make it more vulnerable to competitive forces. Building up highly selected areas of weakness is also important if those areas have been

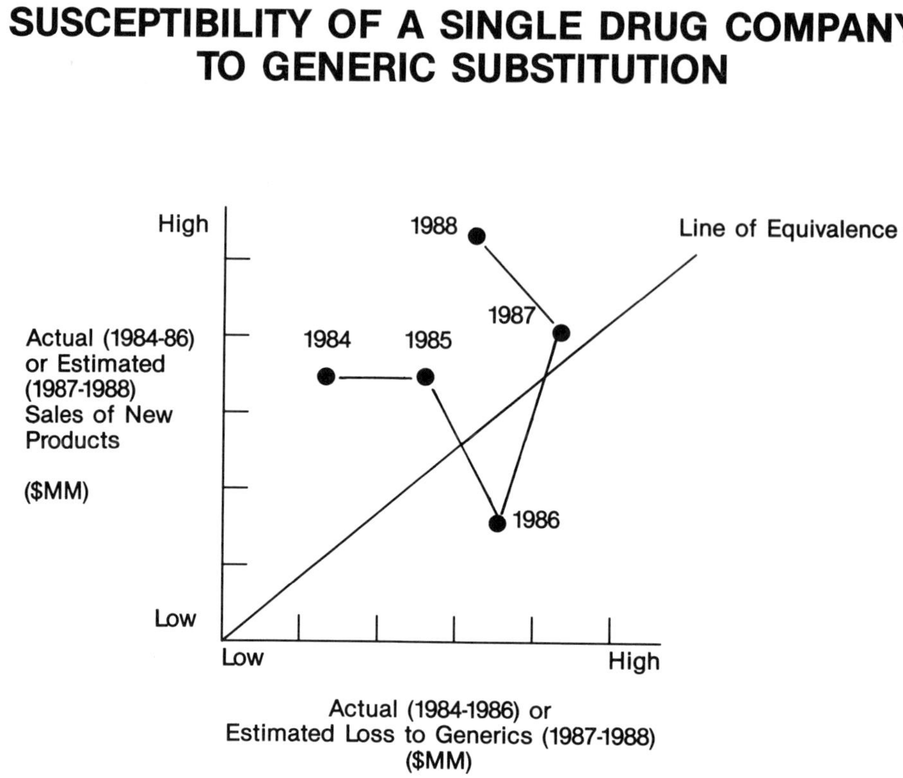

Fig. 8.3. Susceptibility of a particular company to generic substitution over a period of years.

targeted as future areas of strength. This pendulum must be continually balanced because a company that becomes too diversified also becomes vulnerable to its competitors. The most appropriate balance between building on strengths versus developing weaknesses changes over the years and must be continually reassessed.

Approaches to Drug Discovery and Development at Various Companies

Developing an Overall Concept of Drug Development

If several companies each discovered or licensed the same drug, they would each develop it in a somewhat different manner. The basic approaches to development would differ as to the number of indications to pursue, whether to conduct them simultaneously or sequentially, how to prioritize each of them, and how much resource to assign to each. The same would be true for determining the number of dosage forms and routes of administration to pursue and whether to pursue them simultaneously or sequentially. Differences between companies might emanate from sources within research and development, marketing, or both groups.

It is desirable for a company to chose an overall concept for a drug's development before development is actually initiated. One method to do this is to discuss a drug's development in terms of a visual model. This would enable each manager to have

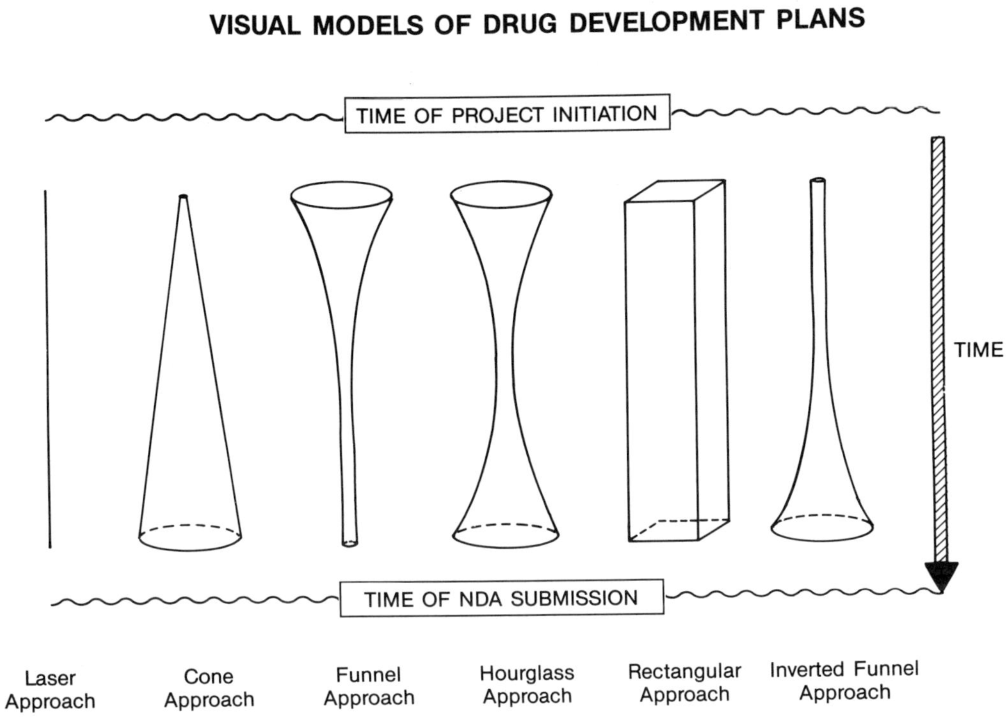

Fig. 8.4. Visual models of drug development illustrating different types of plans or approaches followed. The width of each figure equals the total number of dosage forms, indications, routes of administration, and dosage regimens. From Spilker (1987c) with permission of Raven Press. NDA, New Drug Application.

the same mental image of how the drug's strategy will be applied to its development. Figure 8.4 illustrates general types of approaches that may be followed to develop a new drug. The width of each figure is proportional to the total number of dosage forms, indications, routes of administration, and dosage regimens. These figures may serve as a frame of reference when planning the development of a new drug, and are described in more detail in Chapter 3 of *Guide to Planning and Managing Multiple Clinical Studies* (Spilker, 1987c). Most drug companies focus on reviewing and refining the plan that is proposed for a drug's development. This is appropriate to consider *after* a general concept is adopted.

Allocation of Resources

In terms of how each specific indication of a drug would be developed, the greatest difference between companies would probably be based on the amount of resources applied. Some companies have adopted the strategy of applying many resources to a few drug development projects, whereas in recent years, more companies have tended to apply fewer resources to more projects. The general procedures used to plan, monitor, and manage the development process have become rather standardized and are generally similar between companies. Nonetheless, some companies are more efficient than others in how well they conduct their development activities.

Another consideration concerning the allocation of resources relates to the amount of risk that a company is willing to take. High-risk projects usually take more time and require more resources to be expended than a low-risk project, before a decision point is reached that a drug has an acceptable profile and will be marketed.

Setting and Using Target Dates

Attitudes toward target dates for completion of defined drug development activities are generally viewed similarly in production plants at most companies where schedules are adhered to as closely as possible. The same approach occurs in most technical development laboratories. Attitudes about target dates, however, differ at various companies in research, medical, or marketing departments. At some companies, dates are used in some of these departments as a means of establishing work schedules and assigning responsibilities. At other companies, dates are considered as convenient targets and as a guide to help plan work. Dates may be established for completing project activities using knowledge of other conflicting project work going on or to be conducted in the same department. Alternatively, dates may be set independently of any other project work. It makes most sense to use the former method as the latter approach represents an ideal case and will make dates of little practical use. A few companies place so much stress on achieving target dates that the quality of work produced or reports written is compromised. There are many advantages to gain by allowing some slippage in dates if a better output from the responsible department is attained.

Business Sources of New Drugs

Companies place a different emphasis on various methods used to obtain new drugs. Companies may emphasize any combination of proactive in-house drug research programs, licensing, purchase of products, or joint ventures. These topics are dealt with below and also in more detail in various other chapters. Most companies sell drugs that come from multiple types of business sources. These sources include:

1. *Internal research and development* This may be entirely conducted at a single drug company based in one location. When a company is able to develop a full and adequate portfolio of investigational and marketed drugs from their own research, less need and emphasis is placed on points 2 to 4.

Internal research and development may be conducted at two or more independently functioning sites of a single drug company. Many possibilities exist of how two sites work together, even within the same company. For example, a drug may have been discovered at one site and developed at the other, the drug may have been synthesized at one site and originally tested at the other, or there may be joint development. Chapter 19 discusses global drug development in more detail.

2. *Licensing* Drugs may be licensed-in at any stage of development. This ranges from licensing a general concept or idea for a new drug where specific molecules may not have been designed, to licensing a compound that is in an early, middle, or late preclinical stage. A drug could be licensed that is in any stage of clinical

investigation or have achieved regulatory approval and be marketed in one or more countries (see Chapter 26).

Companies may adopt a reactive or proactive stance to licensing. In the former mode, the company responds to offers made from external sources and in the latter case, they actively seek to license drugs into the company.

3. *Purchase* The ownership of marketed or investigational drugs may be bought and sold. This is more common for over-the-counter (OTC) nonprescription drugs than for prescription drugs.

4. *Joint venture* Two or more companies may jointly develop drugs that either has discovered. They may also establish a third company, or identify an existing third company, which is then asked to develop a drug. The joint venture mechanism is especially useful when the companies each bring something unique to the agreement. This should lead to a complementary relationship in terms of expertise, capital, resources, patents, and/or ideas. This mechanism allows a very large and a very small company to participate on an equal, or nearly equal, basis in developing and marketing a drug (see Chapter 26). Certain drugs may be developed by a joint venture that could not otherwise be developed by the separate partners.

Marketed drugs may come from the same company, other companies, private entrepreneurs, academicians, government laboratories, or other sources. Nonetheless, numerous studies show that approximately 90 percent of drugs come from the drug industry and that the percent is increasing. This topic is reviewed by Kahn et al. (1982; see p. 109, 110).

Internal Company Hype and the Emperor's New Clothes Syndrome

One of the greatest dangers faced by all drug companies is that the hype of new investigational drugs inside a company will affect decisions made about its development so that nonobjective and incorrect decisions are made. A description of hype includes perceiving a drug in a nonobjective way and believing, or at least expressing, unrealistic expectations for the speed of a drug's regulatory approval and the magnitude of its commercial success. On the other hand, a drug can rarely be described by a single image that is totally objective and universal. This is because a drug's characteristics are complex and may be viewed from many perspectives. Even though an objective view of a drug's profile and expectations should be sought, there is obvious value to a company when its employees are enthusiastic about all drugs currently being investigated.

Individuals who present data about a drug to senior managers often promote and extol the drug far more than can be supported by current data and results. This may lead those managers to repeat the praises and high expectations of the drug to others, even though some may have serious unexpressed doubts about the drug's qualities. This is what is referred to as the "Emperor's New Clothes Syndrome." This is the story where the Emperor is sold a set of clothes that do not exist. He puts on the imaginary garments and the Emperor's closest advisors, staff, and townspeople are afraid to tell him the truth. Only a small boy has the courage to express it.

Reasons for Internal Company Hype

A common reason for hype about a new drug is because one or more individuals in a central position relative to a drug (e.g., the project leader) are ambitious and desire additional recognition or power within their company. These individuals may also believe that senior managers only want to hear good news. These reasons lead them to "accentuate the positive and de-emphasize the negative." The desired outcome is to make their drug (and indirectly, themselves) the center of attention. They continually request more resources and personnel to develop the drug. They attempt to investigate as many additional indications, dosage forms, routes of administration, and dosing regimens as possible. Their recommendations may appear to be sound and clearly planned. The most questionable aspects of their behavior often are inappropriate acceleration and expansion of plans, plus failure to present potential (and actual) drawbacks of the drug. Most competent managers in reviewing these recommendations can determine when wrong answers are given, but it takes a creative manager to identify when the wrong questions are being asked.

Another reason for internal hype is that some senior managers believe strongly in the value of their own pet project and discourage criticism of its efficacy or safety profile. They generate an inflated profile of their project to keep resources allocated to it at a high level and to prevent (or at least minimize) either criticism or a careful appraisal of the project's true value. Whatever the reason for internal company hype, it is an indication of problems within a company. This problem reflects (at least in part) an inability of senior managers to be honest and open about the quality of their projects.

The Importance of Minimizing Internal Company Hype

It is rarely in a company's interest for individuals to accept positive statements about a drug without asking questions, requesting data, and when relevant, expressing doubts. Unless people are willing to do this, and usually few are, it will often lead to a company's unnecessarily spending a lot of money and resources. Major discouragement and disappointment will occur at a later time that might have been avoided. Resources expended could have been better spent on other drugs and projects. If scientists and clinicians believe that management is pushing a dead horse around the track, then this view may also lead to serious problems in employee morale and to decreased productivity. This in turn can have an even more widespread negative impact on a company.

All companies should strive for an open dialogue on the attributes of a drug and the best way to develop each drug, so that all views may be heard and judged. It is sad when no one is willing or feels able to express their views. Fear of retribution often inhibits open and appropriate critical comments. In extreme situations a company may delude itself for years. The FDA sometimes has to play the role of the young boy in *The Emperor's New Clothes* who states that the emperor is not wearing any clothes.

Another form of this syndrome of internal hype concerns the true market value of a drug. Marketing estimates may have been inflated for various reasons and the eventual sales picture may turn out to be a major disappointment. Alternatively, the marketing estimates may be unrealistic because of assumptions made. Individuals who claim the emperor is being sold a suit of exaggerated figures are usually brave. The project being touted may be the "pet idea" of a senior manager. The lack of objectivity may be concentrated on the drug's efficacy, safety, technical problems, manufacturing, market potential, or a combination of these. It is hoped that the types of problems described are rare occurrences.

Discussion of Issues on New Drugs

Companies should encourage open and continuous discussions of relevant issues on investigational drugs. Most, if not all, senior managers believe that they do this. The issue is whether most middle and lower level managers believe that this is being done. Many individuals may have mixed or even negative feelings as to one or more drugs' value to the company. The question is whether that individual is openly discussing his or her concern. If a drug has inherent problems it is better to identify them sooner rather than later. On the other hand, encouraging an objective approach does not mean that a company should seek to evaluate various types of *potential* problems or allow a drug to be tested in nonessential studies where a negative outcome is likely.

When minimally accepted criteria of a drug's profile or commercial potential cannot be achieved, it is usual to terminate the drug's development. Some individuals appear to require absolute certainty that criteria cannot be achieved before they are willing to terminate a project, whereas others reach this decision more rapidly. Many dollars, resources, and time may be saved when this decision is reached expeditiously, before every minute point or remote possibility is explored in detail.

Politics (i.e., personal interactions and relationships) have the same role in the drug industry as in other industries or settings. The political strength of people depends on their real or perceived power in a company. One way to discuss this topic is in terms of gaining or losing influence. A good book on this subject is *Power! How to Get it, How to Use it* (Korda, 1975).

Not Invented Here Syndrome

NIH is the usual abbreviation for the National Institutes of Health, but it is also used for another widely known term, "Not Invented Here." In this context, the NIH syndrome refers to the lack of enthusiasm, commitment, and even activity on a project that did not originally come from the group currently responsible for working on it. For example, an original concept or drug may be licensed-in from another company or it may have been originally developed by another branch of the same company. The department or group responsible for performing certain work is saying, in effect, "We do not want any ideas or projects in our department that are not ours." One can recognize this syndrome when referring to new ideas by comments like: "That's not the way we do things here," or "We've tried it once that way and it didn't work," and "Don't let Mr. X know you're working on that approach." When referring to new drugs, various disparaging comments are made or else the project is virtually ignored. It is clear that insecurity and jealousy are two key ingredients that often lead to the NIH syndrome.

Whatever the origin, it is management's responsibility to minimize and eliminate this type of thinking and behavior. If not eradicated it can compromise a group's performance or a drug's entire development program. This problem is best prevented in advance by fostering a spirit of cooperation between different parts of a company and by stressing advantages gained through cooperation. To do this it is often valuable to invite participation of all professionals associated with a new project at an early stage in decision-making to discuss how to create or modify the development plan. This should enhance the commitment of all people to the plans reached.

PHILOSOPHICAL ISSUES THAT VARY BETWEEN COMPANIES

Studying Drugs That Will Never be Marketed

The attitude with which companies take new drugs into humans for testing differs between companies and often between different locations of the same company. At some companies, there is a clear understanding, usually unwritten and often unstated, that all compounds taken into humans will be pursued as far as possible toward regulatory submission and marketing. In other companies, this attitude may only apply to some drugs, while other compounds are taken to humans on an experimental or research basis. This concept usually means that a drug will be studied in humans to determine whether it has activity or to answer a specific question. In this experimental situation it is known that the compound tested in humans will never be marketed. If the experimental drug possesses sufficient efficacy, the company may feel more secure about committing additional resources to synthesize and evaluate related chemicals that would be expected to be more active, more potent, less toxic, or have other properties that are not considered adequate in the original compound. A few of the reasons why the original compound tested in humans may be inadequate for marketing are that it may (1) not be absorbed orally, (2) have a short duration of action, (3) be too weak, or (4) have toxic metabolites. One reason why this approach rarely works as planned is that evaluating the hypothesis in humans requires so much time and money that it usually makes more sense to devote those resources to preclinical efforts attempting to discover a drug with the desired characteristics.

Studying Multiple Related Compounds in Humans

One variation on the theme described above is to take several related compounds to the clinic simultaneously. This practice is not as common today as it was 20 or more years ago. When several compounds are studied side-by-side, a choice as to which specific compound should be pursued further is made after Phase I and/or some Phase II data are collected. Government regulations have increased so dramatically over the last few decades that the time, effort, and cost needed to evaluate compounds in this manner is so great that the approach is no longer feasible or productive in the United States. If costs of developing new compounds through part (or all) of Phase II were less and regulations were less stringent, there is little doubt that many companies would utilize this approach more often. The approach has a major advantage in that similar compounds differing in only one or a few vital respects (e.g., effect on an enzyme of potential significance) could be evaluated and the clinical importance of that aspect evaluated.

Determining How High a Dose Should be Evaluated in Phase I Studies

Companies vary in how they determine the point at which to stop a Phase I safety study where the dose is progressively increased. Some conservative companies only evaluate doses that they believe will be studied for efficacy in Phase II studies. Other companies increase dosage to the point at which some patients experience mild to moderate adverse reactions. Although the term patients is used throughout this book, it also refers to normal volunteers who enroll in most Phase I studies. If a study is stopped at the first signs of an adverse reaction, then the maximal dose that patients can tolerate will not be learned. This occurs because initial adverse reactions observed in a gradual dose escalation study are probably mild and may not even occur at higher doses. Moreover, adverse reactions may have been (1) observed in the most sensitive volunteers or patients, (2) really an artifact or a placebo response, or (3) confounded by other factors that may or may not be understood.

If Phase I studies are continued after mild adverse reactions occur, it is possible that the drug's higher doses may cause severe adverse reactions. In this situation patients given those doses may be exposed to unnecessary risks, which is both unacceptable and unethical. The balance between prematurely stopping a dose escalation study or unacceptably pushing a dose higher is to establish, prior to initiating the study, the criteria on which dose escalation will be stopped. This usually relates to seeking the dose at which adverse reactions occur that would not be tolerated by patients who are given the drug during actual treatment. For anticancer drugs this endpoint will differ greatly than for mild analgesics (pain killers), because there are already safe drugs available in the latter case. Of course, all of this preparation may be jettisoned when the first patient has a clinically important problem that lies in the gray zone and a rapid (or even slow) decision must be made about whether to expose other patients to a higher dose, or even to continue dosing patients with the drug.

Phase I Studies in the United Kingdom Versus the United States

There is a striking difference between requirements that must be satisfied prior to studying a new drug in humans for the first time in the United Kingdom and the United States. At present, a drug may be studied in the equivalent to Phase I in normal volunteers in the United Kingdom without obtaining regulatory approval or even informing government authorities. In addition, the drug may be studied without obtaining any approval from or even informing any ethics committee. British pharmaceutical companies obtain permission from an ethics committee, even though they are not currently required to do so in all situations.

In the United States, the FDA's awareness of all studies of investigational drugs in humans is assured through regulations. A sponsor is obligated to submit a large quantity of preclinical and manufacturing data, as well as detailed plans for clinical evaluation, information provided to the investigator, and the curricula vitae (résumés) of all investigators, prior to initiating a study. Additional details of information presented in an initial regulatory submission are given in *Guide to Planning and Managing Multiple Clinical Studies* (Spilker, 1987c). All studies must also be reviewed by an ethics review committee (Institutional Review Board) at the site where the study will be conducted.

Most initial Phase I studies in the United States are considered as dose-ranging tolerance studies and adhere to the policy of progressively increasing the dose until moderate adverse reactions are observed. This policy is much less often used in the United Kingdom, where initial studies are considered as primarily pharmacokinetic studies. British scientists study doses of a drug expected to yield efficacy in Phase II studies. This difference in approach sometimes leads to different doses of a drug being evaluated in Phase II, and helps explain why different doses may eventually be recommended for patients and marketed in various countries.

It is an interesting side note that scientists in the drug industry must obtain formal licenses to operate on or use animals in the United Kingdom, whereas no such formal requirements exist in the United States.

Fat Versus Lean Development Programs

Some drug companies traditionally design their master development plan to be extremely lean and only include those studies and number of patients believed absolutely required to obtain regulatory approval. Other companies design a full (i.e., fat) development program that includes numerous studies (e.g., metabolic, toxicological, clinical) that are nice to have, but presumably will not be required for regulatory approval. It is not clear how many companies distinguish between these two types of development programs and make a conscious decision to include or reject most or all studies that are nice to have, but are not required.

Problem Situations and Danger Signs

A few situations that represent potentially serious problems for a drug company are briefly mentioned. Each of these issues would be handled differently within different companies. Great variations also exist in how these situations are handled within a company, depending both on the perceived importance of the problem and on the personality of the people involved. When any of the situations described are spotted, senior managers should initiate plans to address the issue.

1. *Insufficient communications between different levels or functions of a company* This problem is noticed when senior managers observe that two or more groups are not working well together, are not holding necessary meetings to resolve issues, or are not appropriately transferring information and reports upwards, downwards, and across functions.

2. *Inaccurate communications between different levels or functions of a company* This problem is noted through similar methods as those mentioned above.

3. *Deteriorating or poor staff morale* One sign of this problem may be an increase in staff turnover, but the problem may be recognized in many different ways (e.g., increases in absenteeism, complaints about a wide variety of issues, requests for transfer). The reasons for this problem must be determined and addressed.

4. *Poor cooperation between different departments or functions* This is often

part of another problem such as those mentioned above. This issue should not be approached in isolation. Poor cooperation may result from high walls being erected between departments (see Chapter 4), from a manager's attempts at empire building, or for other reasons.

5. *Negative disease* (see Chapter 7)

6. *NIH syndrome* (see description in this chapter)

7. *Creating problems* There is value in anticipating problems that may arise in moving a project forward or in attempting to carry out any plan. Alternative strategies may then be thought through and evaluated prior to the need for such contingencies. This is a positive example of "what if" exercises. On the other hand, this approach can be taken to extremes when too many potential problems are imagined or a few *potential* problems are thought of as *actual* problems. In either situation, a group may become paralyzed or move in one or multiple tangents. This may be a part of the "woe is me" or "woe is us" syndrome and usually reflects an ineffective leader.

8. *False belief syndrome* Many companies fall in the trap of believing a drug to be effective, primarily based on their faith in one or more positive reports by outside scientists or the company's own scientists. Sometimes this belief persists for several years and costs the company many millions of dollars in fruitless research, clinical studies, and technical development. What many of these companies lack is an individual or group who is asked to look at the evidence objectively. This issue is discussed in the sections in this chapter that discuss "hype."

9. *Judging people by their activity level and not by their results* In most situations in a drug company (except for aspects of drug discovery), individuals should be judged by the results they achieve and not by how busy they appear to be. This refers to analyzing the quality and not merely the quantity of work attained. Professionals in the personnel office, for example, should be judged by whether the right people are hired and not by the number of applicants screened and interviewed. Professionals in training departments should be judged by the education and benefits that course participants achieve, not by the number of classes held.

10. *Systems that become ends in themselves* As the size of a company increases, it is necessary to develop and institute more systems for senior managers to know what is occurring and also to allow line managers to handle more activities efficiently. In some departments and even companies, the importance of systems becomes too great. Instead of their being used as tools to asist drug discovery and development, they become ends in themselves. Reports are written that are unnecessary and excessive time is spent on activities with little meaning and could be readily eliminated.

Many other differences exist between companies in the ways in which they go about discovering and developing drugs, in their marketing activities, and relationships with the public, press, and other external groups. Many of these differences are described throughout this book.

Achieving High Standards

It is worth remembering the principle that "excellence exists" when drugs are being developed. Excellence can be found in (1) the quality and abilities of people the company hires, (2) the principles and values these people espouse, and (3) the standards used in developing drugs. Companies differ in how they value and how close they come to achieving these three standards of excellence. Unfortunately, not every company aims at achieving the highest standards possible. Some try to cut corners whenever possible. It is suggested that by adhering to high standards, companies will actually increase their chances of making major commercial profits. For example, "me-too" drugs usually do not generate great profits, and sloppily conducted and analyzed studies usually delay regulatory submissions much longer than the additional time that would have been spent conducting a study the proper way. It is important at all levels of a company to carefully and thoroughly review plans proposed and work conducted, rather than superficially approving whatever information and data are proposed.

9 / *Future Environments for Drug Discovery and Development*

The only solid piece of scientific truth about which I feel totally confident is that we are profoundly ignorant about nature. Indeed, I regard this as the major discovery of the past hundred years of biology. It is, in its way, an illuminating piece of news. It would have amazed the brightest minds of the eighteenth-century Enlightenment to be told by any of us how little we know, and how bewildering seems the way ahead. It is this sudden confrontation with the depth and scope of ignorance that represents the most significant contribution of twentieth-century science to the human intellect. We are, at last, facing up to it. In earlier times, we either pretended to understand how things worked or ignored the problem or simply made up stories to fill the gaps. Now that we have begun exploring in earnest, doing serious science, we are getting glimpses of how huge the questions are, and how far from being answered . . . It is not so bad being ignorant if you are totally ignorant; the hard thing is knowing in detail the reality of ignorance. Lewis Thomas, American physician and essayist. From *The Medusa and the Snail.*

May you live in interesting times. Chinese Proverb.

WILL CHANGE IN THE DRUG INDUSTRY BE REVOLUTIONARY OR EVOLUTIONARY

Introduction

It is important to look at future environments for drug discovery and development in a broad section on corporate issues relating to drug discovery and development. Decisions made about where to allocate resources, which businesses to enter or leave, and what strategies to use are in large part based on the corporate perception of future environments. Each of us views the future with a somewhat different perspective and reaches different conclusions about the relative importance of various factors that will influence it. This chapter identifies many factors that will undoubtedly play a significant role in shaping the future environment. Some important questions to consider about these factors will also be discussed.

What Future Are We Talking About?

The *near-term future* (i.e., over the next one to two years) is not discussed in this chapter. The *midterm future* (i.e., from two to twelve or so years, which is the time necessary to develop drugs that have already been discovered) may be assessed with some assurances, and several aspects of this period are discussed. The more distant *long-term future* cannot be visualized and predicted with as much clarity, but this is the major period described in this chapter. No conclusions will be reached about what distant future environments will be like (e.g., in the year 2020). A number of trends that will influence the distant future world of drug discovery and development are already underway and will be discussed.

What Will Drugs Be Like in the Year 2020?

Two general types of answers are usually given to this question, revolutionary and evolutionary.

The type of future forecast that any particular scientist, clinician, or marketer favors undoubtedly says more about their own personality and beliefs than about the likelihood of one of these scenarios being closer to the truth. The revolutionary view is most often held by optimistic upbeat managers and the evolutionary view by conservative and more pragmatic managers. As an aside, the author believes the future will be closer to the evolutionary answer.

Revolutionary Answer

Numerous individuals and groups are predicting a new revolution in drug discovery and treatment of many diseases (Wells, 1983; Faust, 1984a,b; Taylor and Voivodas, 1987; Unger, 1987). A representative quote of the revolutionary style answer is taken from Unger (1987): "Sometime in the early part of the next century, it is generally felt that we will be relatively free of disease and that the new drug development research will focus more on cures and on the correction of deficiencies . . . Drugs will be "engineered" rather than "discovered," and therefore the process will be more efficient . . . it seems likely that virtually any receptor or enzyme will be able to be characterized (both functionally and structurally) by the year 2000."

The temptation to predict widespread changes in the future is based on a few assumptions:

1. The rate of drug discovery in the past can be extrapolated into the future.
2. New techniques of biotechnology (see Table 2.9) plus sophisticated computer modeling techniques of molecular structures will lead to a large number of new drugs.
3. Most new drug discoveries that may potentially occur, will actually occur.

The problem with the first assumption is that great discoveries do not occur according to a time schedule. Just because one can usually know with reasonable certainty that the next generation of an electronic device or computer hardware or software is possible to design and build, it does not mean that truly novel drugs are going to be found at a predetermined rate. This lack of predictability, however, means that changes and discoveries may occur either faster or slower than anticipated. The ability to extrapolate from past successes (and failures) in drug discovery to major long-term future discoveries is obviously unknown. Almost any scenario could be vigorously defended with many facts and figures. Nonetheless, such extrapolations are made using personal judgment and guesswork.

The problem about the potential of recombinant and other methods of biotechnology to supply new drugs (second assumption) is that at present, this potential cannot yet be evaluated accurately. For one thing, these techniques are primarily applied to protein drugs, which must be used parenterally (primarily intravenously). Most proteins will only be therapeutically useful until smaller molecules are discovered that are clinically equivalent and may be taken orally.

The third assumption is difficult to assess, except that there is little reason to believe that the current intensity of competition between drug companies will diminish, unless the drug industry in certain countries is nationalized. Therefore, every attempt will be made by companies to exploit both potential and actual opportunities for drug discovery, development, and marketing advantages.

If it is possible to combine biotechnology with electronics and create a new hybrid, then a new revolution would be at hand. The marriage of microchips and biochips would have potential that is difficult to fully imagine. At this time we must consider this possibility as remote and only unfettered speculation.

Evolutionary Answer

The evolutionary answer to predicting the future is based on the belief that the rate of discovery of important new "miracle" drugs will remain about the same as that over the last decade, or may decline slightly. Drugs with small but real improvements will gradually replace some older drugs. Although new types of drug delivery forms (e.g., edible whips, transdermal patches) will be found useful for some drugs, they will not be used for most drugs. Capsules, tablets, and intravenous solutions will still remain the most common types of drugs.

Future Environments Affecting Drug Discovery

The single aspect that will probably have the greatest influence on drug discovery from today through the year 2020 is the additional scientific and medical knowledge gained about health, disease, and functions of cells and organs. Research scientists in academic, industrial, and government laboratories seek this knowledge every day. This information is critical to the future success of the research-based drug industry because scientific breakthroughs are often converted into new approaches for drug discovery.

Future Environments Affecting Drug Development

There are multiple environments in which drugs are developed and which in turn influence drug development. These environments include the (1) internal environment or milieu within a company, (2) commercial and business environment outside a company in which drugs are manufactured, distributed, and sold, (3) regulatory environment in which drugs must be approved and in which their progress is monitored, (4) social and political environments in which drugs are developed and sold, (5) academic environment in which drugs are clinically evaluated, and (6) medical and health care environments in which drugs are used. Each of these six environments are discussed below. Several factors that will influence future environments are then discussed. Additional information and perspectives on the future of drug development may be obtained in *Pharmaceuticals in the Year 2000* (Bezold, 1983), *The Second Pharmacological Revolution* (Wells, 1983), and other books listed in the references about the drug industry at the end of the text.

INTERNAL COMPANY ENVIRONMENT

There are major differences in the environments within drug companies today. Future changes will be based primarily on the same factors that affect the current environment. These factors include (1) size of a company, (2) nature of a company and its organization, (3) personalities of key individuals who control and manage a company, (4) current success of a company's products and the company's degree of financial solvency, (5) expectations for major new products in the therapeutic areas being studied, and (6) traditions and heritage. These factors will change to a different degree and in different ways over time within each company. Numerous interactions occur among these factors. For example, there is usually a strong correlation between the current success of a company's products and the size of the research and development budget.

COMMERCIAL AND BUSINESS ENVIRONMENT

Competition between Companies

Competition between companies is intense in many disease areas. This competition results from many factors such as generics and multiple brands available in some drug classes. Profits are being squeezed by cost containment measures and increased research budgets. These and other reasons are raising pressures on drug companies to succeed or possibly face buyout or extinction. This pressure is most squarely placed on research and development units in research-based companies.

Most research-based companies are working at the frontiers of knowledge and are competing with each other. When drugs are discovered and are undergoing development, the competitive intensity heats up. The intensity of competition that has always been strong in the marketing area is becoming stronger during the drug development period. One reason is that the first drug to reach the market usually is able to retain the greatest market share, even after other drugs are approved and marketed. Threats of therapeutic substitution and actual generic substitution add fuel to this fire of competition. See Chapter 26 for an additional discussion of competition between companies.

Number of Disease Areas in Which Drug Companies Are Seeking New Drugs

There is an extremely large number of disease areas where new drugs may be discovered and developed. Nonetheless, most companies are searching for new drugs in a relatively small number of disease areas. There are several reasons why most companies are concentrating on a limited number of therapeutic areas. First, there is a lack of suitable animal models in many areas, and also a lack of sufficient scientific information about cellular problems and the causes of many diseases. A third reason that reduces the number of areas in which most drug companies are active is that the potential for profit is limited in most therapeutic areas. Few companies are willing to invest (i.e., risk) millions of dollars looking for beneficial drugs unless there is a reasonable expectation of profit.

Number of Independent Research-Based Drug Companies

There has been a long-term trend toward decreasing numbers of research-based drug companies. This trend has been more apparent in some countries than others, but has been fairly universal in industrialized countries for more than 25 years. The trend toward decreasing numbers of manufacturers of drugs has not been as consistent. The former trend will probably continue despite the fact that a number of bulk chemical companies new to drug discovery have moved into this area (e.g., Eastman Kodak, E.I. du Pont de Nemours & Co.), and also a number of companies have started from scratch in the last decade (e.g., many biotechnology companies). Mergers and buyouts of biotechnology companies by major drug companies will reduce the number of independent biotechnology companies. This trend is already apparent, as is their relatively high failure rate. Japanese drug companies are expected to become more active in international markets in the future.

The impact of fewer research-based drug companies on drug discovery and development is not clear. A smaller number of companies may employ the same number of professionals at current levels, although it is more likely that the total number will be reduced. It is impossible to know how successful these companies will be at discovering new drugs. Many different scenarios could be hypothesized.

Increasing Pressures on Research and Development

The factors that are primarily responsible for the overall trend toward fewer research-based drug companies include (1) increased costs of discovering and developing a drug, (2) decreasing life of patent protection for most drugs, and (3) decreasing economic return from sales because of generic manufacturers and cost-containment issues. These latter issues force drug companies to deal more with Health Maintenance Organizations (HMOs), Preferred Provider Organizations (PPOs), and mail-order companies to sell their drugs, rather than with physicians who prescribe them. The erosion of a drug's sales to generic competition is occurring more rapidly today than in the past. One to two decades ago it took about 10 years for a brand name drug to lose most of its market. Today, because of more rapid entry by generics onto the market and more substitution within pharmacies, markets are being lost within a few years. This trend may even accelerate in the future. Other factors include progressively restrictive government regulations of those agencies that approve and control drugs used. These factors also place a greater emphasis on the need for drug companies to discover new chemical entities (NCEs) with commercial value to remain in business. This tends to pressure most research-based companies to explore the same therapeutic areas, many times using the same animal models and biological endpoints.

REGULATORY ENVIRONMENT

Regulations impact drug development much more than they do drug discovery. Only a few of the many areas influenced by regulations are mentioned. Examples are chosen to illustrate that costs of meeting regulatory standards are increasing, even though initial movements toward international harmonization of regulatory requirements are occurring. Accurately predicting the regulatory environment that will be present in the year 2020 for any country or group of countries is simply impossible.

Requirements for Postmarketing Studies

Adverse reaction reporting requirements for marketed drugs currently differ in many countries. Over the last decade, there have been steadily increasing requirements for companies to conduct more postmarketing studies to measure the incidence of adverse reactions of newly approved drugs. At least a dozen countries already require information on adverse reactions that occur in other countries. This has led to a virtual explosion of new requirements for companies to supply such data to regulatory agencies in many countries. This type of information must be supplied using different forms and definitions of important terms. In addition, the amount of data required as well as the frequency of reporting also differ between countries. Although this recent trend toward increased complexity is quite alarming, there are encouraging signs that the situation will improve. One such sign is that a group of regulatory agencies and companies have met and derived common definitions, forms, and approaches that would simplify this issue. A pilot study utilizing these standardized forms is starting.

The future world of 2020 will likely involve reporting of all serious adverse reactions to a central source that will communicate with national regulatory agencies. Alternatively, companies will utilize a standard form to provide this information to national regulatory agencies on a single agreed-on frequency with standard definitions of terms and standard methods. Most companies will have centralized these operations.

Standardization of New Drug Dossiers Worldwide

There is a growing trend for national regulatory agencies to communicate more with each other and to share more information than ever before. This is taking place both prior to and subsequent to the time of drug approval. A trend toward increasing uniformity among regulatory agencies is noted in the efforts of the European Economic Community (EEC) to standardize applications for drug approval in their member countries. This procedure has been implemented, but its success or failure will take a number of years to assess. The trend toward greater harmonization of regulatory requirements and possibly a single regulatory dossier for most countries seems inevitable. Nonetheless, this trend is currently moving at a rather slow rate. Present differences in the practice of medicine between countries are likely to remain, although these differences may become somewhat less.

Standards for Drug Approval

Perhaps the greatest influence of regulations on drug development will result from the standards used to approve drugs in terms of efficacy, safety, or quality of life. It is conceivable that regulatory authorities may require data that demonstrate the superiority of a new drug over existing therapy before the drug may be approved for marketing. This type of change would be vigorously protested by the drug industry.

Advantages of a new drug may be demonstrated not only in terms of efficacy and/

or safety, but also in terms of quality of life, compliance, pharmacokinetics, cost-effectiveness, or in another area. Standards for having a new drug added to the formulary of many hospitals, HMOs, and PPOs already require this type of data to be presented. Drug companies vigorously attack such requirements in most situations for numerous reasons. These reasons include the impossibility of knowing for many years whether or not a drug in development will actually be demonstrated to be superior to existing therapy. New areas of clinical usefulness or superiority over existing therapy have sometimes been found for newly introduced drugs that were originally considered to be "me too" drugs.

The standards for drug approval resemble a high jump where the bar is constantly raised as improved drugs are approved. The standards are actually set by the drugs themselves that are available, not by an arbitrary ruling of a regulatory authority. Nonetheless, at some point the bar will be so high for many therapeutic areas that it will cease to be profitable for drug companies to develop new drugs that are not greatly superior to existing therapy.

SOCIAL AND POLITICAL ENVIRONMENT

The social and political environment in which drugs are developed overlaps to a large degree with both regulatory and medical environments.

Current Trends toward Increased Patient Responsibility for Their Own Care

The current trend toward increased patient responsibility for their own care is expected to continue and become even more widespread in the future. One aspect of this trend is that patients want more medical information than they are receiving on drugs that are prescribed or available over-the-counter (OTC). Drug manufacturers may decide to provide patient package inserts for their drugs. This type of information sheet could present (1) useful suggestions for taking drugs, (2) information about recognizing adverse reactions, and (3) answers to commonly asked questions. These sheets could be dispensed at the time the prescription is written or at the time it is filled (see Chapter 21 for additional discussion on this topic).

Other potential directions are for more drugs to be marketed over-the-counter. OTC drugs usually bypass the physician's influence in that other sources influence a patient's choice about which drug(s) to purchase. Future OTC drugs will come from currently available (and future) prescription drugs. It is unlikely in the United States that NCE drugs will initially be granted OTC status. An additional offshoot may be for more diagnostic kits to be developed and marketed directly to patients, similar to the current marketing of pregnancy kits, occult blood detectors, ovulation predictors, urine glucose tests, and blood glucose tests. Future diagnostic kits will probably include tests to diagnose strep throat and urinary tract infections. Kits to monitor treatment may be marketed to enable patients to insure their blood levels remain within the therapeutic range.

Drug tampering (i.e., poisoning of capsules) should be less prevalent in the future because of tamper-resistant capsules, gelatin-banded capsules, caplets, and the elimination of all capsules by some manufacturers. This issue is discussed further in both the marketing and production chapters of this book (Chapters 21 and 22).

Current Trends in Characteristics of the Population

There is a trend in the population of developed countries for a steadily larger number and percent of their population to be older. The increased number of older people will undoubtedly focus increased attention on (1) the number of drugs prescribed for older patients, (2) the appropriate doses to prescribe, and (3) the duration of drug treatment. These considerations in turn will raise other issues of patient compliance, drug interactions, and adverse reactions. One likely result of this overall issue is for physicians to prescribe drugs more carefully for older patients. From both an economic and medical viewpoint this is highly desirable and should reduce the number of hospitalizations resulting from drug interactions and other drug-related causes. From a company's commercial viewpoint, any decrease in sales that result from more careful medical treatment will be more than compensated for by the increased number of patients expected to use the drug.

Public Pressures for New Regulations

Politically, it is difficult to predict whether future events will trigger major changes in drug legislation as occurred in 1906, 1938, and 1962. The regulatory pendulum has swung toward insuring state-of-the-art purity, safety, and efficacy of drugs. The chances are therefore diminished for a national tragedy occurring through human callousness or ignorance on the scale of those that triggered the passage of the Pure Food and Drug Act of 1906, the Food, Drug and Cosmetic Act of 1938, or the Kefauver-Harris Amendments of 1962 (to the 1938 Act). Nonetheless, a major drug tragedy may still occur. If one does occur it is vital that political reactions be rational and balanced. If standards for drug approval are increased further, they could easily go beyond realistic levels and prevent or markedly delay many medically valuable drugs from being approved. Risks of further withholding valuable new drugs from patients would probably not be worth any small medical benefits to society achieved in terms of increased safety requirements for new drugs.

The drug approval process could undergo a large change if the United States Congress mandated that the FDA rapidly approve all new drugs that have demonstrated therapeutic value and an acceptable risk to benefit ratio. The FDA has no current mandate to *approve* drugs. Finally, the *Congress should provide the FDA with sufficient resources to allow them to review New Drug Applications (NDAs) expeditiously. Alternatively, Congress could enact a new system to approve drugs* (see Chapter 25 for a discussion on this point and a proposal).

Industry Pressures for New Regulations and an Improved Relationship with the Food and Drug Administration

A movement toward partial drug industry deregulation in the United States may occur in the future, although at the moment this possibility appears remote. Certain aspects have already been proposed, such as allowing companies to use some or all Institutional Review Boards (IRBs) to approve Phase I studies without first submitting an Investigational New Drug Application (IND) to the FDA.

The relationship between the FDA and the drug industry is primarily adversarial. Nonetheless, there have been some drugs where drug development was marked by a spirit of cooperation (e.g., Retrovir). It is hoped that the number of cases of collaborative drug development between the American government and the drug industry will increase. There is a great amount of progress that could be made in this area. Improved relationships between national regulatory agencies and the drug industry should be encouraged in every way possible. This issue is further discussed in Chapter 25.

ACADEMIC ENVIRONMENT

Competition for Funds and Grants

A major trend that will probably continue in the academic environment within the United States is increased competition for grants and financial support. In recent years this had led to increased requests from academicians for financial support by the drug industry. The drug industry has generally responded, although much more so in some areas than others. It is only natural that drug companies support work that is of primary interest to them. This has occurred through a variety of programs and mechanisms that are discussed in Chapter 24. A major cutback of government support for academic research in the future would probably intensify the same trends present today. Any major increase in government funds for academic scientists and clinicians would probably have a relatively small effect in terms of affecting academic interest in collaborating in drug development. This is because many studies sponsored by drug companies are of great interest to academicians in terms of career enhancement, or as a relatively secure source of funds. On the other hand, many new drugs of minor clinical importance might have a more difficult time being developed if fewer clinicians need financial support.

MEDICAL AND HEALTH CARE ENVIRONMENT

The Changing Concept of Health Care

At the beginning of this century, medicine was limited in the range of effective treatments it could offer patients, and the term health care was primarily used to describe caring for the sick. As a result of the antibiotic revolution and development of many other drugs, by the 1960s the term health care had come to include the concept of treatment, plus some cures for many bacterial diseases. Current research and medical emphasis has been shifting the pendulum of health care toward earlier diagnosis and prevention of disease. This change is being accompanied, and in part caused, by greater interest in self-care by patients. People are accepting a greater responsibility for their own health. Fitness, exercise, use of vitamins, and other practices associated with healthy lives have all become part of many people's desire to optimize their health and prevent disease. Thus, health care in the 1980s and 1990s will place a heavy emphasis on fitness and prevention of disease. The drug industry has responded to this trend in many ways (e.g., providing methods to stop smoking, developing various combinations of vitamins and minerals). Future trends in this direction will be fascinating to observe.

The public is learning much more about health care and is more oriented toward evaluating medicine and medical care as a commodity. As a result, there will probably be (1) more advertising directed to the public, (2) greater choice of health care providers, and (3) greater demands made of health care providers. How each of these relates to a specific drug company will differ and must primarily be addressed by marketing and public relations groups.

The Changing Nature of Medical Practice

The nature of medical practice and the types of patient treatments influence which drugs and dosage forms are developed. The opposite is also true (i.e., drugs and dosage forms developed influence medical practice). For example, inpatient treatment for some diseases encourages parenteral dosage forms to be developed, and new technologies including transdermal patches influence the ways physicians treat their patients.

The way in which medicine is practiced has constantly changed since 1900, and the rate of change has clearly accelerated over the last decade. The number of physicians practicing by themselves has decreased as the trend toward group practice has accelerated. More physicians are also joining HMOs, PPOs, and other prepaid groups that provide health care to a growing percentage of the United States population. The impact of these groups on the practice of medicine is being felt at a national level and has encouraged several large companies, such as General Motors, to enter the health care market themselves to provide services for their employees. There is no doubt that if this trend toward managed health care continues, the practice of medicine will be entirely different in another decade or two than that of just a few years ago.

Many models of HMOs exist (e.g., staff model HMO, open access HMO, individual practice association HMO). Other models of health care include PPOs, exclusive provider organizations, managed fee for service, and unmanaged fee for service. Over the next 10 or so years many models will likely persist and the field will not be reduced to a few winners. Some large hospital chains and HMOs are now offering many health plans instead of the one or few plans that they used to offer.

HMOs and large hospital chains are oriented to cost containment and are able to purchase the drugs they need in more economic ways than can a single hospital or group of physicians. One reason that drug costs are closely examined by many groups is that other hospital costs such as nursing care, pharmacy services, and many other aspects of running a hospital must be present and available 24 hours a day. It is not as easy to cut back and control these costs even though the extent of their utilization may vary widely from day to day. Potential savings in these areas would probably be much greater than for drugs, because drugs constitute a much smaller percent of a hospital's expenses. It has been calculated that only approximately 6 to 8 percent of total medical costs within the United States are for drugs.

Because HMOs and other prepaid groups currently utilize more generic drugs than non-HMO groups, the trend toward greater use of generic drugs will also increase. Goldsmith (1986) has described various aspects of the future health care system in more detail.

Sales of Future Drugs

Hospitals, large department stores, and professional associations are starting to enter the mail-order drug business. These groups are specializing in selling drugs to patients who require long-term chronic use or periodic use. This practice will undoubtedly have a growing impact on the business of small pharmacies. Drug companies will probably have more national purchasers and fewer small stores to sell to. This will further increase price competition, especially on multisource (i.e., generic) products and on products where therapeutic equivalents (i.e., different drugs that act the same way) exist. There is even a trend in some areas for physicians to dispense the drugs they prescribe. Although this is the current practice in Japan it has elicited a major debate in the United States. This event has pitted pharmacists versus physicians in extremely acrimonious legislative battles.

Major Factors Influencing Health Care Over the Next 3 to 30 Years

The most important factor that has brought about the changes in health care over the last decade is probably the switch from the concept of "quality care for everyone" to "cost containment." The driving force behind this switch was the rising percent of the Gross National Product spent on health. Interestingly, the amount of money spent on drugs as a percent of the United States health budget has fallen over this same period. For example, the percent was 14 in 1960 and had decreased to seven percent by 1984.

A list of important factors expected to influence health care and its delivery over the next two decades includes the following. A brief comment is included of a likely way in which drug discovery or development will be affected. Although a number of possibilities are given, current trends in health care delivery may have a minimal influence on future fruits of the drug discovery process.

1. *Rapid growth in expenditures on health* The rate of increase in national health expenditures is slowing, but in 1987, it reached over 500 billion dollars, or 11 percent of the Gross National Product (GNP). Health expenditures are estimated to reach 15 percent of the GNP by the year 2000, primarily because the United States' population is aging. These sums demonstrate a growing market for useful drugs.
2. *Additional cost-containment measures* This factor could make it more difficult for expensive new drugs to be widely used, unless the drug provides a major benefit in terms of financial savings, efficacy, safety, or quality of life.
3. *Increasing age of the population* This factor should provide continued stimulation for companies to invest heavily in research and development. The total market for drugs will undoubtedly increase in terms of the number of units sold.
4. *Reduced demand for institutional care* This factor is not expected to have a major impact on research and development.

5. *Increase in health care companies (e.g., HMOs)* This factor is discussed elsewhere in this chapter.

6. *Decrease in number of independent hospitals* This factor is discussed below.

7. *Increase in self-care by patients* This factor will affect some therapeutic areas and types of drugs (e.g., OTCs) more than others. This is also related to an increased emphasis on health and fitness.

8. *Increase in organizations focusing on health* More groups are forming with specialized purposes. They are already attempting to influence how research funds are spent by government, academia, and industry in looking for new drugs and other types of cures for diseases.

9. *Oversupply of physicians in some specialties and locations* This factor is not expected to have a major impact on research and development, except possibly to stimulate more physicians to consider careers in the drug industry.

10. *Increasing government regulations* This factor could easily become a major one in decreasing company incentives to invest heavily in research and development. The specific influence will result from interactions among many aspects of the regulations and may vary from drug to drug.

11. *Increasing number of multisourced drugs (i.e., generics)* This factor will lead to increased competition and is discussed elsewhere in this chapter.

12. *Improved packaging and product development* This factor (e.g., better needles for patient use, unit-of-use packages, time-release drugs) will encourage public acceptance of greater drug use that is medically appropriate.

13. *Increase in government price-setting policies* This factor is already squeezing company profits in many cases and may negatively influence a company's ability to invest in research and development.

14. *Improved technology* The ramifications of improved technology are difficult to predict but should allow many processes of today to be done more easily.

15. *Changes in values* This factor is possibly the most difficult one to predict. Although many values go through historical cycles, they usually return in altered forms and have different influences on society.

Putting the Factors Together that Will Influence Future Health Care

In attempting to decipher how this mix of real and possible influences will affect a company, it is useful to determine both a best-case and worst-case scenario. Based on those assessments, some steps may become apparent that should improve chances of achieving a positive outcome. It is important for managers who are charting the company's course to pose many difficult questions, even though the answers cannot be known with great assurance. The best guesses as to future trends will enable various decisions to be made. In fact, some of these trends may not occur or may be reversed, which will greatly alter the predicted outcomes. Thus, overall strategies developed must be flexible if they are to deal effectively with a rapidly changing environment.

If the theme of cost containment continues, and most indications are that it will, there will be further competition between drug companies based on price and increasing generic drugs. At the present time, most of the 200 most widely used drugs are not protected by patents. Shortly after the turn of the 21st century, none of the presently patented drugs will remain covered. This means that only drugs yet to be discovered will still be covered by patents in the year 2020. If that group of drugs is to be prescribed, the drugs will have to offer improved benefits over current therapy, which by then will be available in less expensive generic versions.

Future trends toward consolidation of medical care providers will continue, possibly at an increased rate. There will probably be fewer owners of hospitals, pharmacies, nursing homes, physician offices, and pharmaceutical manufacturers. This trend may extend to HMOs and PPOs as well. This will tend to increase pressures on drug companies to demonstrate advantages of their drugs over their competitors. This in turn will influence the clinical studies conducted and tests used in the future. Areas that will become more important in this regard are quality of life, compliance, and cost effectiveness.

FACTORS UNDERLYING ENVIRONMENTAL CHANGES

Each environment discussed will change over the next 30 years based on a number of underlying factors. To better understand the likelihood of each potential change described for these environments, it is necessary to understand how each of the underlying factors may themselves change. These factors will be major influences on drug discovery and drug development in the future.

Communications

The recent and still ongoing revolution in communications has been largely triggered by developments in computer hardware and software. There is no reason to expect that this movement will not continue. This will influence all environments, but the potential impact on the regulatory environment may be particularly noteworthy. This is because computers are underutilized in respect to regulatory review of submissions, as well as in their communications with the drug industry.

Information

It is difficult to predict if future directions will change qualitatively from those that are apparent today. One change will likely be an increased accuracy of data and reports, given the enormous room for improvement in these areas. See *Guide to Clinical Interpretation of Data* (Spilker, 1986b) for a more detailed discussion on this topic.

Cooperation

Future improvements in cooperation between national regulatory agencies will most likely lead toward a single regulatory dossier. Increased pressures for research-based companies to discover novel drugs may lead toward more collaborations between drug companies in the areas of licensing and joint ventures. Whether cooperation between drug companies and regulatory authorities will improve in the future is uncertain, but clearly desirable. Many industries presently have positive relationships with government agencies in the United States. Why not the drug industry?

Political and Social Pressures

There is little doubt that strong social pressures lead to relatively rapid political responses. One need only look at the reasons why major regulations have been passed. The first regulatory law in the United States was the Biologics Control Act. This was passed after diphtheria toxin accidentally contaminated with tetanus was given to protect children and ten children died as a result. This regulation established standards for the preparation of serum and vaccines. The Pure Food and Drug Act was passed in 1906 as a result of public outrage over adulterated products described in *The Jungle* (by Upton Sinclair) and other books. The Food, Drug, and Cosmetic Act was passed in 1938 as a result of public horror over approximately 100 deaths of Americans from a toxic solvent used to prepare a liquid form of the antibiotic sulfanilamide. The Kefauver-Harris Amendments to the 1938 Act were passed in 1962 because of public reaction to the thalidomide tragedy.

Although each of those examples of public opinion's impact led to stronger regulations, there is no reason to believe that social and political pressures could not be exerted in different directions regarding drug development. For example, if the plight of the drug industry became more strained and this story became widely known, political pressures might mount to provide the FDA with a mandate to approve drugs, require the FDA to review NDAs and NDA supplements more rapidly, or to develop a new system to have drugs approved.

It is incumbent on the drug industry to place far greater emphasis on influencing the political system than it has done in the past. These actions should be made through legislators at the local, state, and federal levels; through regulatory agencies; and perhaps most importantly through the many publics with which they interact (see Chapter 29).

Scientific Discoveries

Future scientific breakthroughs will influence each of the six environments. The magnitude of this influence is impossible to gauge accurately. Experimentation with new life forms may lead to important changes in social and political environments. The major influence on drug discovery will be in the internal company environment. Future discussions about human disease, animal models, physiological processes, biochemical mechanisms underlying drug effects, and other areas will all direct the search for new drugs in directions that cannot be accurately known today.

Fads

There is no limit to the number or pervasiveness that fads may play in influencing each of the various environments. This is not a totally negative influence, because it often targets public and political attention and resources toward important areas, although often for the wrong reasons. A number of fads in management are described in Chapter 6.

Section III

Research and Development Organization and Management Issues

10 / *Organizing at Research Division and Department Levels*

> *The success of a corporate R&D program becomes visible only in the light of its mission and purpose. If the choice is to adopt a generic, loosely market-coupled approach, then organization requires a strong discipline orientation and close attention to the number and excellence of contributions to the technical literature. If the choice is to adopt a targeted, tightly market-coupled approach, then organization needs a project orientation and must link its rewards to ultimate business success. Failure inevitably comes from trying to organize, appraise, and reward according to one approach while expecting results typical of the other.* Roland W. Schmitt. From *Harvard Business Review* (May–June, 1985, p. 128).

ORGANIZING RESEARCH AND DEVELOPMENT

Multinational drug companies are often organized in two parts, focused on the United States and the rest of the world. This occurs regardless of whether the headquarters of the company are in the United States or not. The reasons for this two-part division are numerous and include the large drug market in the United States and the relative importance of the Food and Drug Administration (FDA) worldwide.

Most companies approach organizational issues at the research and development level in ways similar to those described for the entire company. The reader is referred to Chapter 5 on organizational issues at the corporate level for this discussion.

Determining Whether to Utilize a Centralized or Decentralized Research and Development Organization

Large multinational companies usually conduct research and develop drugs at two or more sites in different countries. If a company has two or more such groups, their organization and coordination may either be centralized or decentralized. Some advantages and disadvantages of decentralization are described below. Those for centralization at a corporate level are discussed in Chapter 5.

Advantages of a Decentralized Approach

Some advantages of a decentralized approach for conducting research are:

1. Scientists with different educational, scientific, and cultural backgrounds often approach a research problem in different ways. Multiple groups, either together or independently, may be more likely to solve problems and to discover drugs than those from a single site who share a common background. In addition, the managers at one site may tend to have a single approach.
2. A lively exchange of opinions between individuals at different research centers may be fostered. This tends to generate ideas, support fact finding, and stimulate drug discovery.
3. Each particular type or area of research may be performed at the site(s) where the best experts and best facilities are located.
4. Local development and support facilities can usually provide more rapid and more appropriate assistance for patenting drugs. Local staff usually negotiate more effectively with government authorities than do staff operating from a foreign country.

Numerous other advantages exist for a decentralized research organization in terms of management and also in training of staff. Advantages include reducing the number of steps of communications required to have decisions made, involving more people in decision making, dispersing power and authority, and training more executives for other positions.

The same type of advantage exists in development of new drugs. These include the probability of improved negotiations with local registration authorities, development of dosage forms, dosage strengths, and use of colors that are most desired.

Disadvantages of a Decentralized Approach

Disadvantages of a decentralized approach include difficulties in (1) planning an overall direction to follow when different philosophies of drug development exist at each site, (2) coordination of activities at each site, (3) decision making on a single project being developed at multiple sites, (4) development of intergroup rivalries, (5) existence of different standards, policies, and basic approaches, (6) lack of highly trained and competent managers, and (7) greater cost to the company. Conflicts may develop between the headquarters and its subsidiaries because autonomy of local sites tends to increase at the expense of the central group's authority. Autonomy at multiple locations is often valuable and may even be essential for some companies to conduct effectively basic research and discover drugs. But autonomy is much less essential and may be counterproductive for conducting preclinical, clinical, and technical development studies on new compounds and drugs. Moreover, autonomy of multiple sites in drug development activities may be counterproductive in this era of global drug development.

Decentralized companies or territories may be run like a series of walled cities, each governed by a ruler who makes all decisions and rarely communicates with the central palace. Another decentralized model is where there is a loose confederation of independent cities that band together when necessary for mutual protection and benefit. The mayors of these cities may be wary of each other but tend to have even less trust of the state's leader.

Organizing Research and Development by Scientific Discipline

The research effort at most companies is more formal and organized today than it has been in past decades. Like most industries, drug companies are primarily organized around basic functions such as research, marketing, finance, legal, personnel, and manufacturing. There are two general approaches that drug companies have followed in organizing their overall research and development activities. These are to organize by discipline (Fig. 10.1) and by therapeutic teams (Fig. 10.2). In the more common approach, scientific disciplines such as pharmacology, toxicology, medicine, and organic chemistry are established as separate departments (Fig. 10.1). Progress of a compound through the three stages of discovery, development, and marketing involves "passing" the compound along from department to department, but activities also persist for a long period within any one department. Also, multiple departments must work closely together at most stages of a drug's development. Even when a drug's application for regulatory approval is submitted to a government agency, the organic chemistry department may be synthesizing additional compounds for patent protection, and the pharmacology department may be learning more about the drug's mechanism of action. Other departments are also involved in studying the drug and are equally busy. Individual departments may be grouped into multidepartment groups (e.g., divisions, units) of research, technical development, medical personnel, and support services (Fig. 10.1). Another way of grouping departments is to divide them into drug discovery and drug development divisions.

Large departments may be divided into sections that each reflect specific therapeutic areas or on another basis. For example, both pharmacology and medical departments are usually divided into sections specializing in therapeutic areas such as cardiovascular, central nervous system, gastrointestinal, or respiratory therapy. If size warrants, these groups may be further subdivided, generally by specific diseases. For example, a cardiovascular section could be divided into separate groups working on hypertension, angina, and congestive heart failure. Another type of subdivision is based on the type of drug under study. For example, a cardiovascular section could have separate groups working on calcium channel blockers, beta-receptor antagonists, and angiotensin-converting enzyme inhibitors.

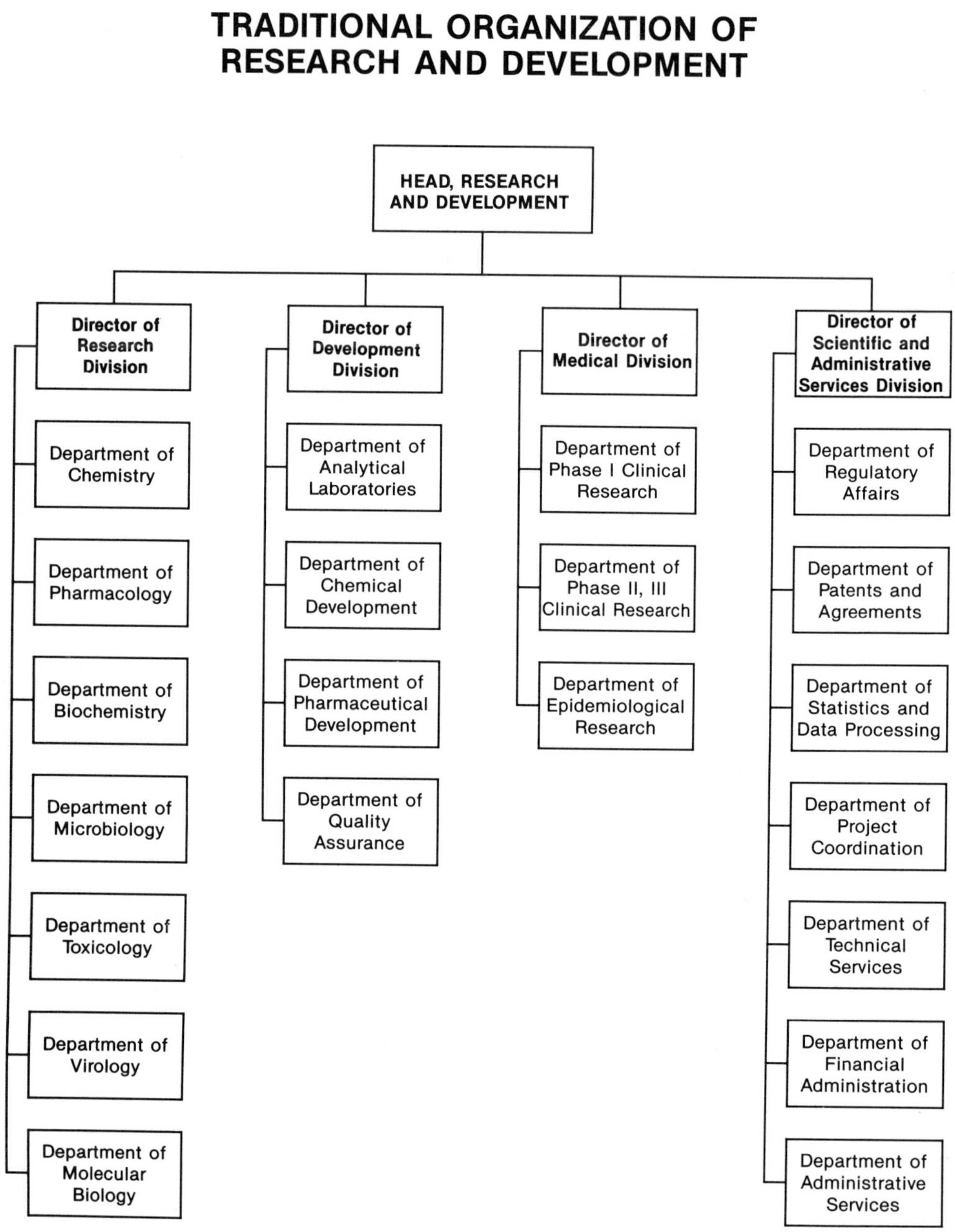

Fig. 10.1. Traditional discipline-oriented organization of research and development activities in a drug company.

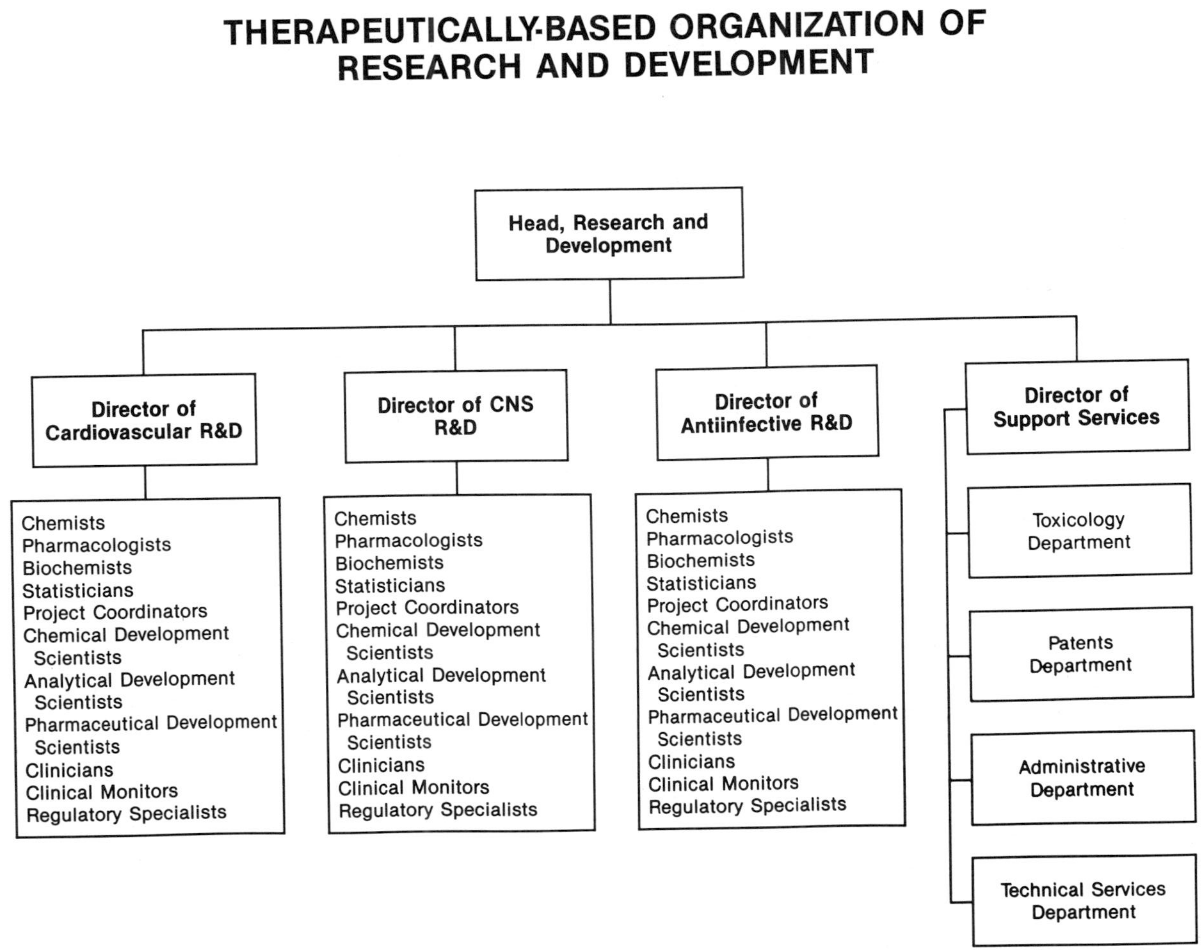

Fig. 10.2. Therapeutically based organization of research and development activities in a drug company. R&D, research and development; CNS, central nervous system.

Organizing Research and Development by Therapeutic Team

Another major organizational structure is the therapeutic team. In this approach the entire research and development unit involving both drug discovery and development functions is divided into therapeutic areas like cardiovascular, gastrointestinal, or central nervous system (see Fig. 10.2). This approach was used by The Upjohn Company for many years. Their experiences over the first five years of this approach have been summarized (Weisblat and Stucki, 1974). In this general model each group contains representatives of all scientific disciplines (e.g., biochemistry, pharmacology) and medicine while other groups (e.g., patents, regulatory affairs, and toxicology) are centralized and provide general services to all therapeutic groups. The major advantage of this approach is that it brings people together from numerous disciplines and increases their collaboration and hopefully their productivity. People from various disciplines within the larger group (e.g., cardiovascular) can easily be assigned to develop a specific drug.

Organizing Research and Development by the Matrix Approach

A third approach to the overall organization of research and development involves the matrix concept (Fig. 10.3). Most large research-based companies organized by scientific discipline have incorporated matrix concepts into their organizational structure. Each scientist reports to a superior through the traditional "vertical"

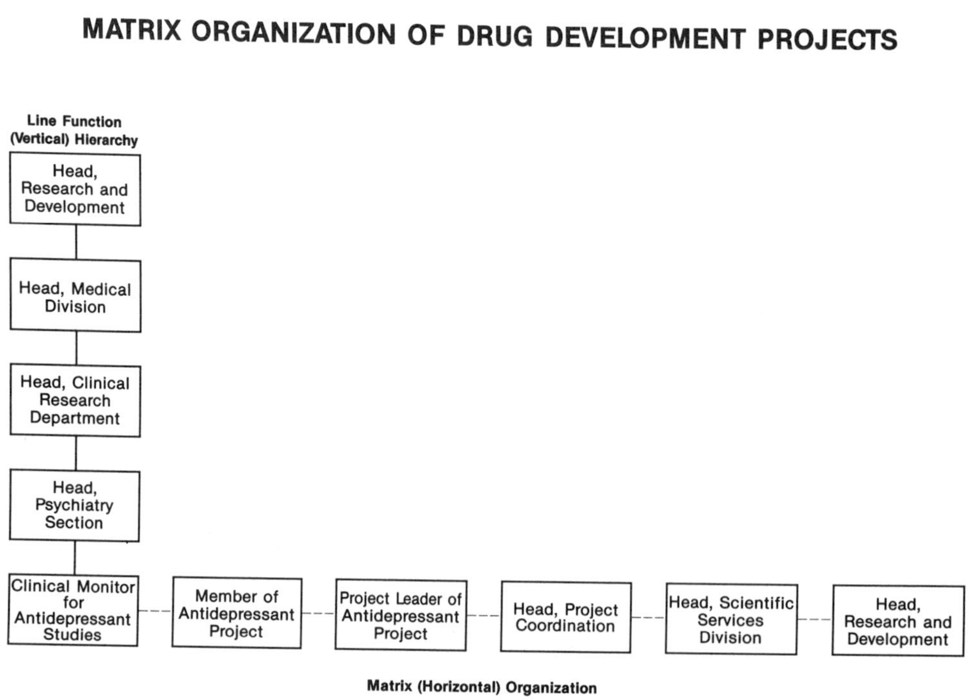

Fig. 10.3. Matrix (horizontal) organization of drug development project activities in a drug company.

hierarchy. Some scientists are also assigned to a project and report in a "horizontal" structure to the project leader or project manager. A strong matrix system requires professionals working on a project to have a formal or semiformal reporting relationship to both a line manager and a project leader or manager. In a weak matrix, dual reporting relationships are more informal. Matrix systems are described more fully in Chapter 13.

What Is the Critical Mass Necessary to Have an Independent Research and Development Function?

The actual size of the overall research and development function that constitutes a critical mass for drug discovery and development is a difficult number to derive. This figure depends on many variables. Nonetheless, several senior research and development managers from various drug companies have estimated the number to be on the order of 600 to 800 people (Bartholini, 1983). The size of the essential core for either the discovery or development function is even more difficult to estimate, because many departments support both efforts. On the other hand, a research and development group can grow much larger before its size per se begins to decrease its efficiency.

It is important to consider this concept on several levels. At the overall research and development level, critical mass refers to having sufficient personnel and skills within a company to handle the important activities necessary to discover and develop a drug. It does not preclude an occasional need to contract highly specialized work to outside contractors, because no company would ever desire to have in-house all of the equipment, staff, and facilities necessary to handle every contingency that could arise. That would be a foolish goal. But, it is a worthwhile goal to be able to rapidly respond to most or all common situations and problems that arise. A rule of thumb is that commonly required functions should be available in-house if contracting them would decrease performance quality and/or substantially increase the time to complete the task. Some less frequently required functions that are of particular interest to a company should also be present in-house. This might include tests conducted infrequently on one of the company's major products.

Drug Discovery

At an individual research department or discipline level (e.g., organic chemistry, pharmacology) the concept of critical mass could be defined similarly. In drug discovery, the term is often used to describe the amount of research effort believed necessary for each research project. If the effort is too small, there is a danger that the approach would be too superficial to have a high likelihood of discovering a drug or achieving the research goal. This would result in wasting time, energy, and money. If a large number of appropriate resources are applied to a small number of research topics, there will usually not be a question of achieving a critical mass, but of whether the resources could be more efficiently allocated to explore a larger number of topics. Regardless of the quantity of resources placed on any research program, the chances are quite limited for discovering a compound that will reach human studies, because only approximately one out of every 1,000 compounds achieves that goal. Of those that reach human testing, only 10 to 20 percent ever reach the market.

Drug Development

Each company should evaluate whether its development activities (in addition to research activities) have achieved a critical mass. This implies that all important activities needed to develop a drug may be efficiently conducted in-house except for a small number that are cost-effective to contract to outside groups. If there are severe bottlenecks in the drug development pipeline and resources to correct the bottlenecks are not available, it may indicate that the company has not yet achieved a critical mass. Some individuals have suggested that a research and development budget of between 100 and 175 million dollars per year (1988 levels) is the minimum amount of money necessary for a research-based drug company in the United States to obtain and maintain a critical mass in its research and development activities.

Support Services

Critical mass cannot only be viewed as a total number or overall concept. There is also a critical mass that exists within technical development, medical, research, and support services. Appropriate numbers of staff that constitute a critical mass could be judged on many bases, including (1) number of people in each area per project, (2) amount of drug sales per research and development employee, and (3) number of people in each area at other drug companies of a similar size.

Figure 10.4 illustrates one means of conceptualizing the various levels and types

TYPES AND LEVELS OF SUPPORT FOR DRUG DEVELOPMENT ACTIVITIES

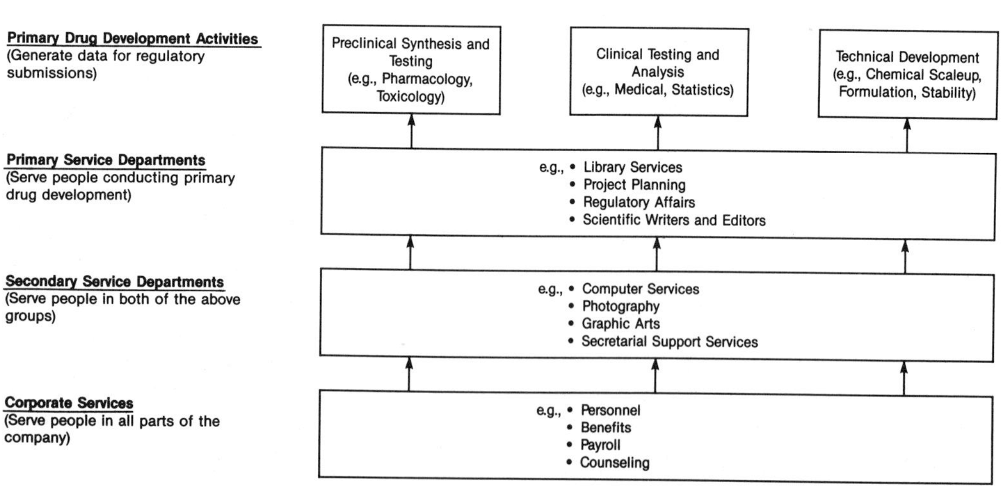

Fig. 10.4. Types and levels of support for drug development activities.

of support services provided for drug discovery and development activities. Scientific support departments include toxicology, metabolism, patents, regulatory affairs, scientific planning, and library services. Technical support departments include chemical development, analytical development, and pharmaceutical development.

ORGANIZING BASIC SCIENCE DEPARTMENTS

Most newly synthesized compounds are initially intended for evaluation in a single biological system or therapeutic area. The compound may also be tested in numerous additional biological tests or therapeutic areas at the chemist's (or biologist's) suggestion. Assume that three different and unrelated chemical compounds are all made for biological screen 1 by chemist A. Also assume that these three compounds each had activity in other biological test screens for various projects. The ways in which additional follow-up compounds would be made for each project varies substantially between companies. Fig. 10.5 illustrates common systems used by drug companies to deal with this situation.

Rigid Organizational Structure

Panel A in Fig. 10.5 illustrates a highly rigid organizational structure in which a research chemist is assigned to act as a leader within chemistry for each biological program or project. In this situation, if one of Chemist A's compounds is found to be active in another biological project, Chemist A must turn over all ideas and chemical leads for that project to the appropriate chemist who is the liaison for that project. Taken to an extreme, this could mean that two or more chemists could be making similar (or even identical) compounds, although they would be intended for different biological projects.

Another disadvantage of this system is that chemists would have to become familiar with an extremely wide variety of synthetic chemistry techniques, depending on what chemicals were found to be active in the biological screens and tests for which they had chemical responsibility. This approach could present problems because the expertise of most chemists is limited to selected areas of chemistry. On the other hand, this problem is usually not too serious, because good chemists may convert to a new area in approximately six to twelve months. This structure is being used in some drug companies although it is felt to be an inefficient system.

Totally Open Organizational Structure

Panel B in Fig. 10.5 illustrates the opposite system as in panel A. In situation B, a chemist follows up on all biological leads himself or herself. On the positive side, each chemist has the freedom to pursue drug discovery paths of interest. It is more difficult to control and coordinate this totally open system and to direct resources to those biological projects of greatest interest and priority to the company. Unless the people involved in this system have many chemical leads of interest to work on, a sense of competition and even jealousy may also develop. This situation could occur because all groups of chemists are essentially competing for attention of the

ORGANIZATIONAL RELATIONSHIPS FOR CHEMISTS AND BIOLOGISTS TO DISCOVER NEW DRUGS

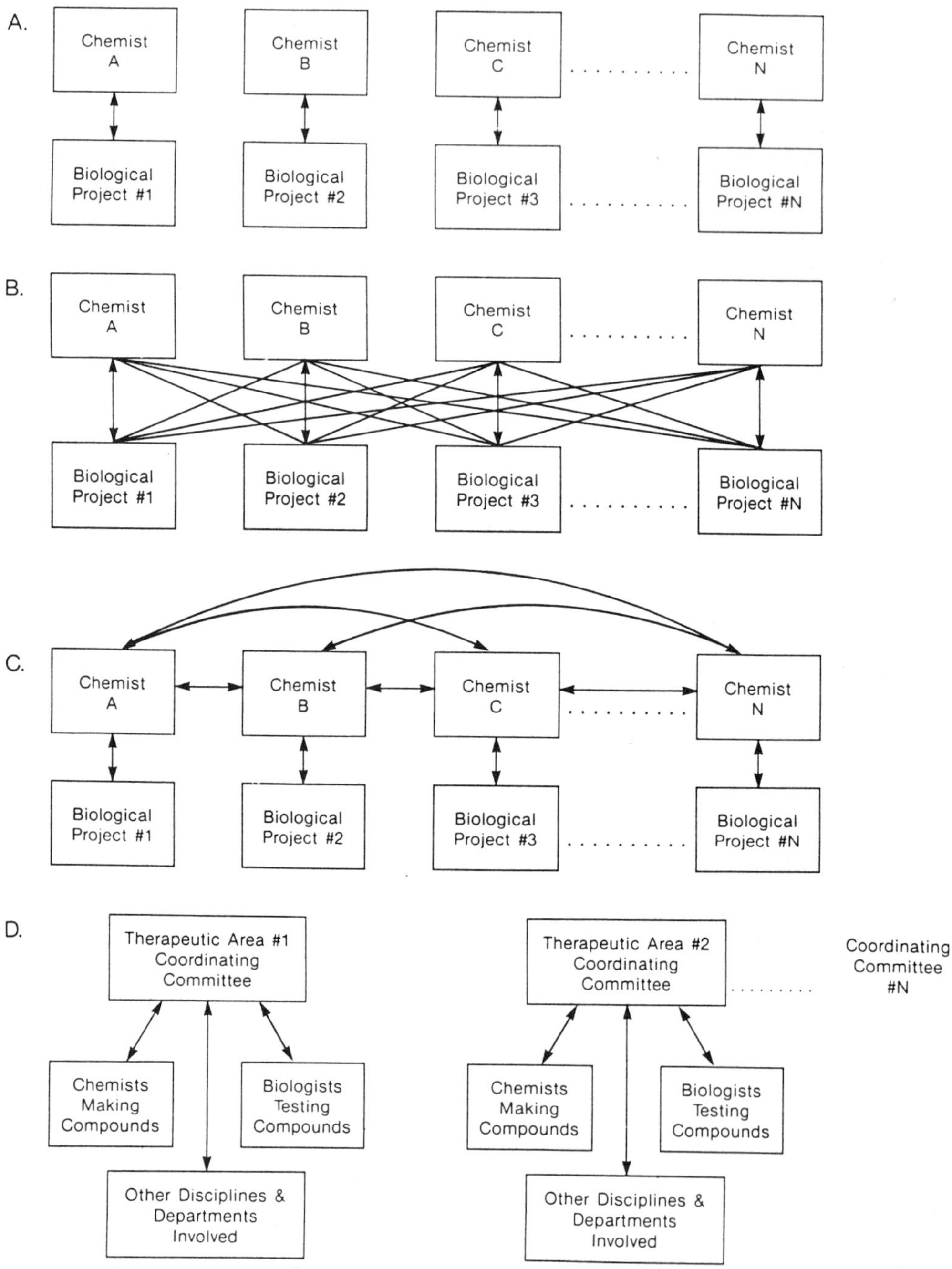

Fig. 10.5. Organizational relationships and interactions between chemists and biologists in drug discovery activities. Companies usually adopt one of these systems, although hybrid systems are also possible. Interactions are for (1) setting priorities, (2) planning new chemical structures to synthesize, (3) choosing old compounds to study, (4) collaborating on compound synthesis, and (5) other functions. Individual panels are described in the text.

biologists who are testing and screening compounds. Because the biological groups have limited resources to test compounds and have to prioritize their efforts, this open system (i.e., panel B) is likely to create problems. This is because compounds of some chemists will be tested before those of others, even though the delayed compounds may have a higher priority.

A Hybrid Approach

Panel C in Fig. 10.5 illustrates one of numerous hybrid systems possible. In this system, chemists coordinate their work with other chemists, but limit their interactions to the single biological project (or projects) that they are primarily supporting. This approach readily allows for coordination of all efforts within a single project. Priorities and allocation of resources are easier to establish and control. Multiple chemists may prepare compounds for a single project, especially when the synthetic techniques require different types of chemical expertise. A single chemist is assigned to coordinate the various activities amongst the chemists who are involved with a specific project. This individual in conjunction with the chemistry section and department heads, plus the senior biologists establishes the priorities within chemistry.

Coordinating Committee Approach

Panel D in Fig. 10.5 illustrates approaches in which each pharmacology project or therapeutic area has a committee to coordinate the various activities within the disciplines involved. This committee identifies or at least approves the compounds to be made and their relative priority for synthesis. The committee decides when to request additional tests (e.g., advanced pharmacology, toxicology) and when to recommend that the compound be studied in humans. If a therapeutic area is organized in this manner, the committee may have authority over a single or many pharmacological projects. The committee may be a small group of a few senior individuals or it may contain a relatively large number (i.e., 10 to 15) of members.

The committee approach may also be grafted to one of the preceding types of organizations (i.e., panels A to C). In one of those situations, the personal interactions illustrated would operate until a chemical "lead" was discovered that met certain criteria. The committee structure would then be used to plan and direct additional work either on that chemical series, or on that specific compound. A committee approach seems worthwhile for larger drug companies. It enables a company to have an efficient system while utilizing ideas of a number of scientists on a specific topic.

Basis of Establishing a Research Project or Program

Within a department, the projects or programs of particular interest may be based on a disease, target, enzyme, physiological function, chemical class of compounds, and/or therapeutic area. The author prefers the therapeutic area in most situations. One advantage of using therapeutic areas as a basis for organizing the company's research activities is that it encourages more interaction with groups in other departments studying the same therapeutic area. Whichever model is chosen as the basis for defining research projects or programs, it is generally desirable to be consistent. A company should have a strong rationale if it mixes projects based on different criteria.

How Are Preclinical Departments Established?

Most companies establish preclinical departments and organize their research based on major scientific disciplines (e.g., chemistry, biochemistry, physiology). Others utilize hybrids of scientific disciplines (e.g., molecular pharmacology, metabolism and kinetics, molecular biology), and still others use therapeutic areas (e.g., cardiovascular, gastrointestinal), or arbitrary titles usually depending on historical tradition or people around whom a scientific department is constructed (e.g., investigational science, experimental biology, exploratory research). Departments may also be created around one of the company's successful drugs. Another approach is to organize research according to the function of drugs (e.g., prophylactic, therapeutic). These companies may also have a group primarily assigned to conduct exploratory research.

Size of Individual Departments

The size of individual departments may be an issue. Some companies divide their chemistry department into two or more smaller size departments, whereas other companies prefer to keep them intact, even if they contain over 200 people. The motivation to divide or remain whole should be based on logic, plus efficiency of drug development. Nonetheless, decisions are usually based on views and opinions of key personalities within the company.

ORGANIZING A MEDICAL DEPARTMENT

Many of the same type of organizational questions exist within clinical areas as for basic research departments. A company may be organized with a single medical department where the staff are involved with all clinical studies from Phase I to Phase IV. Alternatively, walls may be erected and different departments established which only plan, initiate, monitor, and analyze clinical studies in one, two, or three clinical phases or in certain therapeutic areas on specified projects. The United States pharmaceutical industry has examples of almost all of the possible permutations of dividing medical departments to work on specific phases of drug development. Medical departments have been established to conduct only Phase I, II, III, or IV studies, or Phases I and II, II and III, or I, II, and III studies. A rationale of some validity may be described for each of these choices and many pros and cons of each alternative presented. One important principle is that the fewest number of walls possible should be established between clinical departments. Methodologies and objectives differ most for Phase I and Phase IV studies. Therefore, any division of a medical department into two or more separate departments should preferably be to divide one or both of those phases from the others.

If a drug company assigns medical staff to specific therapeutic areas this is usually done for Phases II and III, but not for Phases I and IV. Phase I studies are usually conducted in normal volunteers and the question of a drug's ultimate use is not usually critical to the study design and methodologies used. There are, however, a few exceptions to this principle (e.g., anticancer drugs and antiarrhythmic drugs are originally studied in patients).

11 / *Management of Research and Development*

There is, indeed, a specific fault in our system of science, and in the resultant understanding of the natural world . . . This fault is reductionism, the view that effective understanding of a complex system can be achieved by investigating the properties of its isolated parts. The reductionist methodology, which is so characteristic of much of modern research, is not an effective means of analyzing the vast natural systems that are threatened by degradation. Barry Commoner, American writer. From *The Closing Circle.*

Never make a threat. Reason with people. Don Corleone (the Godfather)—Mario Puzo. From *The Godfather.*

INTRODUCTION

Levels and Issues of Research Management

Various levels of research and development management are illustrated in Fig. 11.1. This figure stresses the functional responsibilities (e.g., discovery, development) rather than specific disciplines. It is intended to show that management principles, beliefs, and philosophies may be (and often are) extrapolated from one level of management to another. Some of the basic issues that frequently arise in the management of research and development are listed in Table 11.1. Some of these issues are discussed in this chapter.

Most research, development, and medical department heads and many individuals

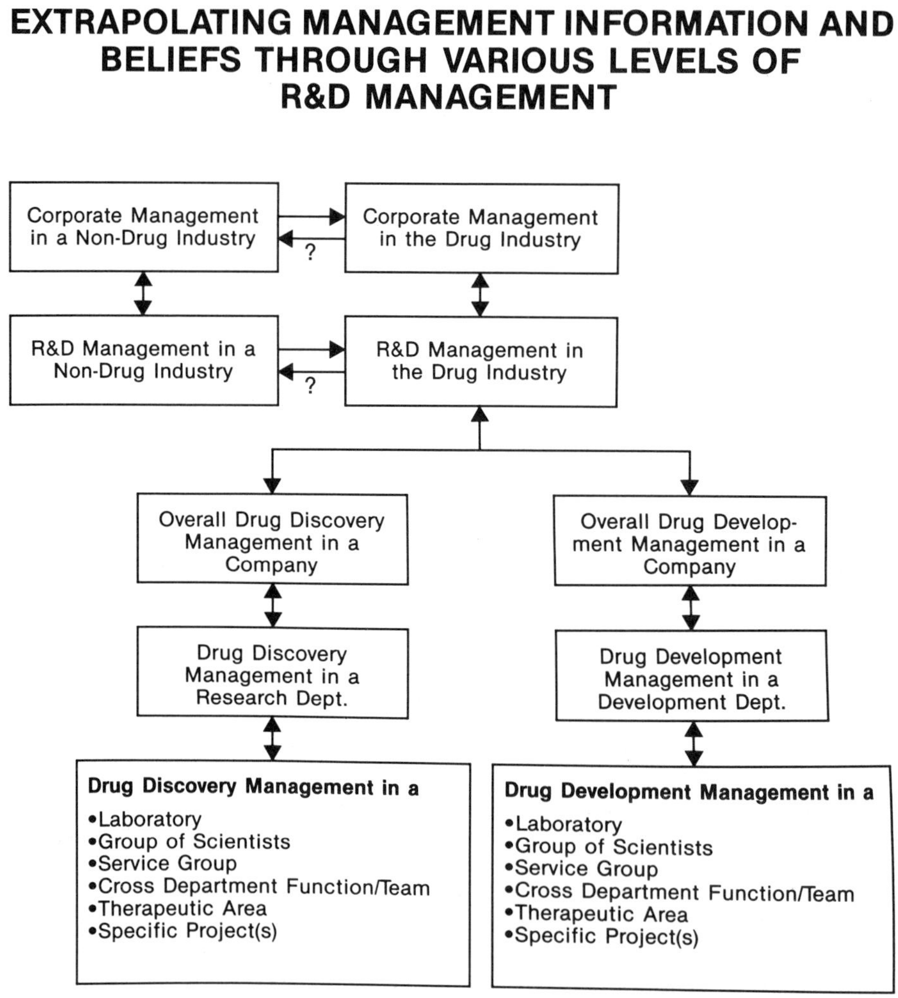

Fig. 11.1. Extrapolating management information and beliefs through various levels of research and development (R&D). Arrows represent extrapolations. The question marks (?) from drug industry to nondrug industry indicates that the extrapolation is usually in the other direction.

Table 11.1. Basic issues frequently considered in the management of research and development

1. Should drug discovery be centralized or decentralized?
2. Should drug development be centralized or decentralized?
3. Should drug discovery be conducted entirely internally (i.e., within the company)?
4. How much and which parts of drug development should be contracted out?
5. How productive is the entire research and development group?
6. Are the activities of drug discovery, drug development, and line-extensions in balance?
7. How much money should be spent on research, development, and line-extensions?
8. How may communications and interactions be optimized at all levels within research and development and between all relevant departments?
9. How may communications and interactions be optimized between research and development and marketing (and production)?
10. How may activities be appropriately prioritized and resources allocated?
11. How much authority should be given to the matrix system of project management?
12. How closely should activities be monitored and leaders held accountable for meeting estimated dates for completion of activities?

within those departments tend to believe that the company's research and development activities revolve around their own axis. It reminds one of traveling to different countries and noticing world maps, that place their own country in the center of the map. Science is a sensitive plant and scientists must often be careful gardeners. Many management questions arise everyday, and managers must be careful about how they respond. Although one or two approaches may suggest themselves at once, there are almost always many ways of approaching any question or issue.

In addition to the levels of research management described in Fig. 11.1 there are other levels at which basic decisions are made about research. These decisions include (1) whether a company should do any research to discover novel drugs, (2) which therapeutic areas (e.g., cardiovascular, central nervous system) should be researched, (3) which diseases should be researched, (4) which biological targets should be chosen to define activity, and (5) which methodologies should be used to approach each target? There are also issues of how much effort and resources should be expended on each research project and who should make the decisions on the five questions listed above.

The decision to pursue research in specific therapeutic areas may be made by scientists who are actively conducting and directing the research and/or by senior managers who review and supervise those scientists. Some companies allow scientists more freedom than others in this matter. If a company encourages its scientists to make decisions on which diseases to study and which approaches to use, then the managers of the scientists are probably more concerned with allocation of resources, priority setting, and review of progress, rather than controlling the specific research direction that each scientist is taking.

At most companies, however, the decision of which therapeutic areas to pursue (level 2 above) and often which diseases to research (level 3 above) are made by senior research managers. The decision of how to approach each disease (levels 4 and 5), however, is often left to senior scientists. Managers may not only control the broad therapeutic areas and specific diseases that are researched, but may also control each target established within each of those diseases. The determination of specific methodologies to be used is commonly delegated to scientists at most companies.

Information Flow

It is important for managers to consider the means whereby they receive and disseminate information. This will allow them to determine whether currently used mechanisms should be modified. If so, then means to do this may be determined. Each person who reports directly to a manager should be providing information on both a periodic and ad hoc basis. People who have a dotted line (i.e., informal) reporting responsibility, have special relationships, or are peers of the manager, are other sources of information. If insufficient or inappropriate information is being received, then steps must be considered to rectify this situation.

Delays in the flow of information may occur anywhere along the path, and this is another aspect that may have to be addressed. Senior managers should utilize several different systems to expedite both upward and downward flow of information to themselves. Likewise, careful attention should also be given to methods used to disseminate information to others who are both higher and lower in the company, as well as at the same level. It is hoped that readers of this book are not hoarders of information, but want to share it with all relevant people within their company or organization.

The Meaning and Use of Target Dates

Target dates are usually established for achieving major milestones (e.g., New Drug Application [NDA] submissions, product launches) as well as for completing many of the individual activities and tasks that must occur for major milestones to be achieved. Target dates are used differently in different companies and sometimes by individual groups within the same company. Dates may be used (1) as a specific formal tool to develop work schedules and responsibilities, (2) as an informal guide to plan activities and work, or (3) as a general guide to assist people in establishing priorities. Production groups and some highly technical departments tend to use the formal "specific tool" approach and scientific researchers use the "general guide" approach.

Dates may be estimated on an *ideal or theoretical* basis. On this basis, dates indicate when activities could be completed if all resources were available and no conflicting activities were competing for priority. Alternatively, dates may be estimated on a *realistic* basis that includes consideration of all projects being developed. Even using a realistic approach, dates may be chosen that are optimistic, pessimistic, or in-between.

Optimistic dates are sometimes used in plans to spur and encourage the people working on a particular project. Although this method may be effective for a few activities, it is usually counterproductive over the life of a project. Most people prefer to gauge their work using target dates that are achievable without a superhuman effort. It is important for all project dates (e.g., time for Investigational New Drug Application (IND) or NDA submission, time of drug launch) to be established using the same approach and for all drug projects to use the same approach. Dates are useful guides for most people to use in planning their work, even though the targets established are not always met. Dates for obtaining regulatory approvals on various submissions are particularly difficult to set accurately. They may be expressed with confidence, however, as long as the year of approval is not listed.

BALANCING WORK EFFORT ON DISCOVERY, DEVELOPMENT, AND LINE-EXTENSION ACTIVITIES

The optimal balance between efforts expended on each of these three functions is influenced by the overall health and goals of the company. The pressures on research and development to stress either short-term or long-term horizons depends on the view of stockholders, board of directors, research and development managers, plus input from marketing. If a company's goals are heavily oriented toward short-term profits or the company is in poor financial health, it will tend to emphasize work on line-extensions. If a company's orientation is toward long-term scientific breakthroughs and novel drug development, it will often emphasize discovery research. If a balanced concept is stressed, then efforts will be approximately balanced on all three functions.

A long-term company commitment to drug discovery is necessary to have an efficient, effective, and motivated professional group of scientists who are attempting to discover and are actively developing drugs. As a company grows in size and it markets more novel drugs, the time spent on developing line-extensions and on other activities necessary to support marketing activities generally increases. A drug company and its research and development managers need flexibility to adjust and maintain an appropriate balance between these three functions. The process of balancing these functions should be performed at least every two or three years, if not annually or more subtly on an ongoing basis. The drug discovery function cannot be turned on and off easily like a water tap each time a reassessment is made. Nonetheless, additional funds can almost always be spent on specific research activities of particular interest or on development activities where a bottleneck has occurred.

Should Drug Discovery Research Activities Be Isolated from the Rest of a Drug Company?

When scientists are worried about their jobs and/or the attitudes of company managers, it becomes difficult for most to think creatively. Some people have suggested that it is desirable to remove drug discovery research from the company environment and to place it in an isolated research institute. This would theoretically allow scientists to concentrate on their research activities. The record of drug discoveries made in such research institutes of drug companies, however, is not impressive, even though these centers often contribute significantly to basic research. If criteria of success are based on research publications then such groups have been successful.

There is another approach that emphasizes creation of a positive work environment for basic research scientists (see Chapter 4). Scientists are not isolated from other activities and are encouraged to interact with development-oriented scientists and marketing-oriented personnel. Some discovery-oriented scientists also have the opportunity (if desired) at most companies to participate in drug development activities as members of project teams.

Preventing a Drought of New Products within a Company

There is no magic formula to achieve the goal of having a continual flow of new drugs. All companies are bound to have periods when few, if any, new products are developed. This is an important issue in all companies and a critical concern in some. In fact, much of this book is directed toward this concern. Some of the factors that tend to minimize the chances of this problem (i.e., a drought of new products) occurring are to (1) hire the best staff possible, insuring that a sufficient number of highly creative people are present, (2) develop and maintain a positive atmosphere and environment, where people are encouraged to be bold and imaginative, (3) utilize licensing as an important adjunct to supplement in-house drug discoveries, (4) organize the company and its research departments to encourage flexibility, (5) maintain a critical mass of skills and talents, (6) build and maintain up-to-date equipment and facilities, and (7) maintain high ethical standards.

Within the project portfolio there should be an appropriate mix of short-, mid-, and long-term projects. These groups of projects may be defined in many ways, but the specific definitions per se are not important to this discussion. What is more important is that the projects not only have appropriate medical and commercial value, but also reach the market at a steady rate. Any big gaps in this respect should be addressed through licensing, acquisition, or some other approach. Research programs should also be established to provide an appropriate mix of short-, mid-, and long-term research programs.

Reviewing Projects

There are many groups that review projects in a company. Reviews occur at different levels and for different reasons. A number of important considerations and questions for review groups are presented below.

1. *Purpose of meeting* Are the meetings held to review projects intended as an information sharing exercise or as a time to discuss issues, set strategies, and/or solve problems? If issues are to be discussed, it may be useful for the reviewers to identify the issues before the project leader or others are invited in to the meeting.
2. *Asking the right questions* In reviewing potential research activities and projects and making decisions, it is important to ask the best questions. The question "Is this something we can do," may elicit a different answer than if the managers ask "Is this something we should do."
3. *Reaching decisions* Are decisions reached by consensus, by vote, or by the chair making a ruling? The first method is usually best since unpopular executive decisions often are not enacted or meet great resistance and may adversely affect morale.
4. *Where is the focus directed* Do reviewers focus both on basic objectives of the project and the specific details and issues? Or, do they sometimes lose sight of the former and thereby allow the project to head in an inappropriate direction away from its goals? Are goals reassessed at appropriate intervals?
5. *Focus on past versus future activities* Do reviews focus solely on the project's past achievements and current status (i.e., a retrospective review) or do they *also*

focus on the next steps in the project and on future activities (i.e., a prospective future-oriented review)? Do reviewers evaluate the overall direction in which the project is moving? Do reviewers confirm (insofar as possible) that several years into the future the market potential for the anticipated drug will still be adequate to justify the drug's development?

6. *Allocating priorities* Priorities in the overall portfolio often change, and a project may have to be slowed to allow others to speed up. How does the group handle this? Unless this step is carried out carefully it may be demotivating to a company's staff. If this occurs, a project's momentum may slow or even come to a complete stop.

7. *Sharing of information* Since information is power, how do senior and other managers deal with information? Do they share it openly or guard it carefully and only provide it to others as necessary? Is it easy or difficult for each group to obtain the information it needs to operate effectively?

8. *Preparation for meetings* Do reviewers come to meetings prepared to conduct their reviews? Have they read and digested material sent to them ahead of time or do they spend time being walked through material they should already know?

Assessing the Reality Level of Plans and Proposals: How to Spot Unrealistic Plans

Various types of unrealities either creep into plans or are purposely put there. It is essential for all professionals and all managers to be able to recognize problem zones and to eliminate them where possible, and to question them where not.

The first type of problem is familiar to everyone who understands statistics. That is the problem of using numbers incorrectly, such as describing the effects of a drug on affecting heart rate or any of hundreds of other parameters by terms such as 5.434 percent or 5.434 beats per minute. This practice gives the veneer of being highly precise and accurate, but is often misleading and may be deceptive. Two examples of where this occurs in drug development plans are:

1. Planning to complete a drug study in 15.33 months.
2. Planning to submit a particular NDA in 5.72 years.

Given the number of years and number of uncertainties in drug development, the 5.72 years is misleading and the .72 should be dropped or the date changed to 6 years. Alternatively, the time to NDA submission may be expressed as a range of 5 to 6 years.

Another type of unreality in drug development plans is where an excessive number of events are described in minute detail. This is highly unrealistic because all development plans are usually modified several times before they are completed. In fact, it is more accurate to say that many drug development plans are modified several times per year. One example of an unrealistic plan is when a highly detailed clinical plan up to the time of a drug's marketing is established before the drug is ever put in humans. Another example is where a highly developed plan of all steps from Phase I through NDA submission is formulated at the time when a compound is made a project and the plans for the IND are also being developed.

Unrealistic plans may sometimes be identified by discussing what each of the outcomes would be based on the proposals and recommendations. Unrealistic ideas may be found through contradictions, unrealistic outcomes, or conflicting logic. It is always disheartening when this type of problem is discovered by a retrospective analysis instead of a prospective one.

Planning for Meetings

A calendar of all important company meetings should be established about a year in advance. This provides various advantages to individuals who must attend and assists in organizing which meetings should precede or follow others. Thus, a group or committee that presents their results to another group may schedule their meeting(s) appropriately. An international as well as national calendar may be developed. This may be done at the level of the entire company, a specific function, (e.g., marketing, production), a department, and/or a section within a department.

Quid Pro Quo

A long-term company commitment of resources to research and discover drugs includes the responsibility for an appropriate number of research activities to succeed. This means that the heads of research and research departments, plus section heads of research departments accept accountability for discovering new drugs. Their budgets may be lightly tied to their productivity in extreme cases. This could mean that the amount of increase in a budget from year to year would depend (in part) on the number and quality of compounds that reach development. For example, there could be a minimum budget established, plus an amount based on performance within research, research and development, or within the entire company. If this practice were followed it would be necessary to prevent wide fluctuations in budgets and in head counts. Care would also have to be taken to insure that productivity was real and that compounds were not advanced primarily to increase the research budget. One means of preventing abuses and establishing a fair system would be to use a moving five-year average in determining the number of compounds advanced for development. This approach is not specifically recommended.

Subcategories of Drug Discovery, Drug Development, and Line-Extensions

In addition to balancing drug development efforts between drug discovery, drug development, and line-extension activities, it is necessary to balance efforts *within* each of these three major categories.

Drug discovery

Subcategories primarily relate to the number of therapeutic areas and diseases being researched and the depth to which each is pursued (see Chapters 2 and 4 for discussion of this topic).

Drug development

Subcategories refer to the number of drugs being developed, the resources applied to each, and the current stage of each project.

Line-extensions

The subcategories used for drug development may also be applied to line-extension activities.

Because development costs increase as a drug progresses through the pipeline, a larger sum of money is generally spent on all of a company's drugs in Phase III than on drugs in Phases I and II. If this is not the case, a serious review of the situation should occur. It may mean that the company has (1) an insufficient number of drugs in Phase III, (2) a surfeit of drugs in Phases I and II, or (3) a serious imbalance in the allocation of resources.

Contracting Drug Development

Many aspects of drug development may be contracted to outside groups. For the last 10 to 25 years it has been common for research-based drug companies to contract a number of their clinical studies to contractors for completion. These contractors either conduct the studies themselves or act as middlemen to place the studies with other investigators. In the last decade there has been a gradual increase of the types of contracting services available and a steady increase in the amount of work that companies place with contractors. The major motivation in using contractors is to save time, which is especially important during periods of peak work load. In other situations (e.g., specialized toxicology studies) a company may be unable to do the work itself.

Contractors Versus Consultants

Although contractors could be considered to be consultants (and vice versa) a sharp distinction is drawn between these two groups. Consultants provide advice, opinions, evaluations, and recommendations, whereas contractors provide a service that is usually more tangible (e.g., a specific report or study). Consultants are mainly discussed in Chapter 4. Contractors are considered as for-profit businesses and therefore must also be differentiated from academicians, government agencies, and institutions that interact with drug companies.

Locating Contractors

Locating contractors is not usually a problem for any drug company because, most contractors advertise heavily. Each relevant group (e.g., clinical, toxicological, regulatory) should retain files of available contractors. Evaluations of their past performances, plus references and other related information should be kept in a readily accessible place and available to appropriate staff. Ex-employees of a company often make excellent contractors for certain purposes (e.g., writing final medical reports) if they are not employed at a competing company and conflict-of-interest issues do not arise.

Services Provided by Contractors

In general, contractors are pleased to tailor their activities to the needs of the companies. A few contractors offer to provide the entire clinical study process including preparing a protocol, conducting the study, editing data, entering it into computers, quality assuring the data, preparing a statistical report, and preparing a medical report. Other contractors specialize in only certain of these processes, such as entering data and preparing statistical reports. Contractors also conduct toxicology, other preclinical studies, and prepare regulatory submissions, especially if there is a model for them to work from. Another role they fill is to prepare final medical reports for numerous studies using one company-prepared report as a template or model. A few contractors are willing to develop a company's entire program on a new dosage form or totally develop a new chemical entity (NCE) all the way to a finished regulatory submission.

Choosing a Contractor

Issues that arise in dealing with contractors include how best to measure the time saved by using their services (before the contract is signed) versus the amount of effort required on the part of internal staff to help the contractor initiate the project and to monitor their efforts to assure high quality work. In some cases the efforts necessary to train contractors and to monitor their activities is almost the same as having the company's staff conduct the work themselves. In this situation any time gained by using the contractor would be minimal because company staff would have to fit the training and monitoring activities into their busy schedules. Any contractor that has previously conducted similar work for a specific company would generally require less training and should be able to conduct the work in a timely fashion. Turnover of the contractor's staff is only one of many reasons that could mitigate against this advantage.

Another issue is the importance of requesting references from potential contractors. It is relatively easy for many contractors to put a polished presentation together and give the appearance of being able to meet a company's needs. Carefully checking references of other drug companies who have used the contractor provides invaluable information on areas to pay particular attention to and means of insuring a successful relationship. Most professionals at drug companies the author has contacted have been quite willing and open about providing references on consultants, contractors, or investigators. In some situations it would be worthwhile having several contractors bid for the same project. Bids should usually be judged primarily on the basis of their overall quality rather than strictly on price.

ALLOCATING RESOURCES

The most important control over allocation of resources is the initial decision to undertake a research or drug development project. Another area of control occurs at the time of project review, which occurs on both an ad hoc and periodic basis. Reviews to discuss specifically the allocation of resources may occur at an annual, semiannual, or quarterly meeting. This review is held in addition to various others within departments and divisions (e.g., medical, technical development, marketing).

Essential questions to pose in considering allocation of resources include (1) what will it take to achieve a specific goal, (2) are resources actually allocated according to the major criteria used, and (3) what are the rate limiting steps in progressing toward each project?

Methods to Allocate Resources

There are several ways for senior research and development managers to review the allocation of resources on different projects and to reallocate those resources when priorities are revised. For example, in the clinical area, managers may initially focus on projects, staff, or indications when they conduct this exercise.

1. Start with a list of all areas where professional staff are currently allocated. Review each project and other areas (e.g., medical services, education and training, computer services) and decide if the number of MDs, PhDs, and junior level staff is appropriate for the next 6, 12, and 18 months. Other time periods could be used. Identify staffing needs that are anticipated to occur if the project moves forward as expected. Determine the increases and decreases per project at each time point. At the end of the exercise, add up the additions and deletions of head count and determine if the net change is realistic to implement. If not, review the changes to bring them in line with totals that are considered realistic.
2. Start with the total number of MDs, PhDs, and junior level staff available. Apportion staff to each project for the next six months, year, and two years. Any shortfall of staff will require hiring additional staff, cutting some projects, and/or reapportioning staff assigned to different projects. This list may then be compared with how staff are currently allocated. Discrepancies must be discussed and resolved.
3. Start with all of the indications pursued for all projects. This number will be greater than the number of drugs being developed. Then assign a priority rating to each indication and followup by conducting the exercise described under point number two above.
4. Allocate available money to each project, therapeutic area, or indication after one of these staff allocations is made. This financial allocation is not done in some companies and is a way of life in others. A variation of this exercise is to limit the allocation of funds to money spent for external clinical studies or for all external grants (e.g., including toxicology).

To help achieve a balance in the allocation of funds to different research or development projects under development, one may rank order all projects according to money spent over the last one, three, six, twelve, or other number of months. This list of money spent and name of each research or development project may be reviewed to see if the relative amounts of money spent is in accord with the desires of research management. The same data could also be expressed for each research or development project as (1) a percent of all money spent, (2) the total work effort in terms of months of effort, and/or (3) percent of total work effort. Any of these analyses could be presented by individual department, division, or other group.

Achieving a Balance between Discovery, Development, and Line-Extensions through Allocation of Funds

When a company undergoes a period of rapid growth (or decline) in size, the balance between the three areas of research and development activity may be adversely affected. Either new staff will have to be employed (or cut) or activities conducted will have to be modified. Research may be initiated in new therapeutic areas. The traditions of a company as well as its current strengths will provide useful benchmarks to help decide where new funds should be allocated.

In allocating funds to these three functions (i.e., discovery, development, line-extensions) money may be sent to the separate divisions responsible for conducting drug research and development. On the other hand, the entire research and development function may receive a single pot of funds, and the head of the entire group may then allocate money to different groups. If the money allocated to research and development by the company is given as a lump sum then money may be allocated by research and development (R and D) managers to those departments or projects that create the loudest noise. These are usually departments and activities closest to commercialization of products. They usually emphasize the near-term benefits to the company if funds are allocated to certain development or line-extension activities. If there are no spokesmen for research or means of protecting their resource allocation, then there may be a temptation to cut the research budget or have it grow at a low rate. These actions may appear to be reasonable, but when the total mass of the research effort decreases below a critical level, the negative impact on research productivity will usually be disproportionate and far greater than anticipated.

Allocation of Resources Based on a Drug's Commercial Potential

Resources in research and development may only partially be allocated based on a drug's commercial potential, assuming that a company wanted to do this. There are several reasons for this. First, only a limited number of people can work on a drug at certain stages of its development regardless of its commercial potential. This occurs because many drug development activities must be conducted in a sequential order. For example, if the drug supply is highly limited, little toxicology, clinical, or other studies can proceed until more drug is available. When a drug is in Phase II or III there are usually more opportunities to speed its development by adding resources (i.e., money and people). Second, the commercial potential is closely tied to the eventual clinical profile of the drug. Until this is well known (usually in Phase III), commercial forecasts are usually best guesses and may have to be significantly modified. Commercial estimates sometimes show marked swings and it is generally unwise to crank up or down many R and D activities based on the most recent marketing values. Third, there may be problems with a drug and only a small number of people will be able to sort through the problem and determine the outcome. Until this is done and a solution reached, most other work may have to be placed on hold, either by the company or in some cases by the Food and Drug Administration (FDA).

If resources are allocated to a project on the basis of a drug's commercial potential after the drug has reached Phase II, it is essential that the methods used to estimate commercial forecasts are comparable for each drug. For example, if five projects are each estimated to have third year postmarketing sales of 20 million dollars, it is important to know which (if any) have a much higher potential for sales and which projects have limited potential (e.g., a range of 18 to 22 million). A single number of estimated sales (e.g., 20 million dollars) is usually insufficient information on which to form an opinion of a drug's commercial potential (see Chapter 15). A single number based on a set of clinical assumptions about a drug does not indicate (1) the confidence that the marketing forecasters have in the number's accuracy, (2) the variability associated with the number's accuracy, (3) the drug's potential to become more successful, and (4) how stable or unstable the estimate is likely to be if the drug's profile becomes slightly modified.

Allocation of Resources Based on Therapeutic Areas

It is often desired in drug discovery and drug development activities to focus on and allocate resources to specific therapeutic areas. This approach may be used to emphasize the company's strengths, build up their areas of weakness, or otherwise allocate resources to certain therapeutic areas. Figure 11.2 illustrates one method of how resources applied to areas of strengths and weaknesses may be presented.

If certain therapeutic areas are identified as targets for increased (or decreased) spending over a period of time, it is important to confirm that progress is being made

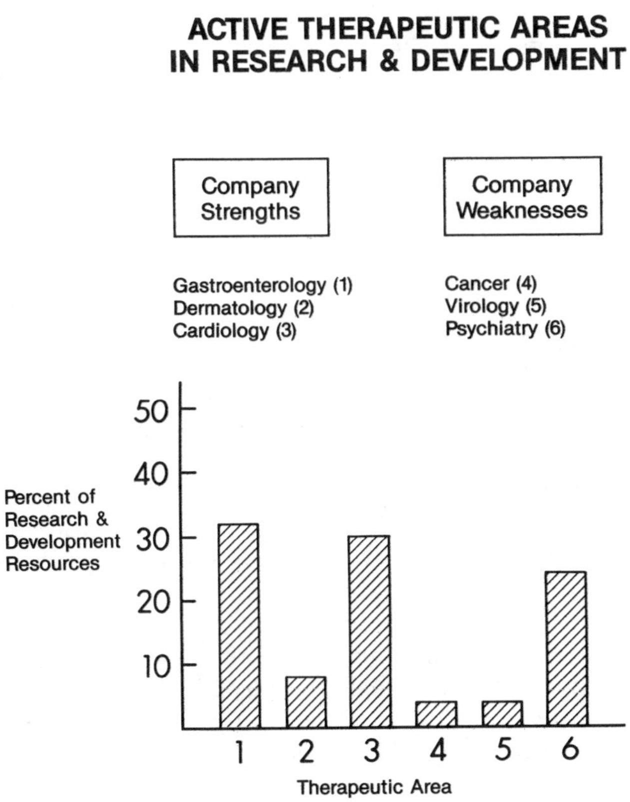

Fig. 11.2. Evaluating how research and development resources are being applied to areas of company strengths and weaknesses. The ordinate could be expressed in terms of money. This figure could illustrate any department or division of research and development.

in that direction. Figure 11.3 illustrates one means of tracking whether or not allocations are made in the desired manner over a period of years.

Evaluating Whether Resources Are Allocated as Intended

The most direct means to evaluate whether resources are allocated as intended is to retrospectively sum up the time and effort reports separately for each group of interest (e.g., project, section, department, division) and to compare their planned and actual work totals. These reports are usually collected as hours or weeks spent on a specific activity and may be converted to a financial total. This information may be plotted or tabulated periodically. In some cases it may be interesting to determine whether a section or department's activities paralleled those of the entire division. In that situation it would be possible to plot the percent of total effort in the entire division on a specific project over time as well as that of the department(s) in question. Other methods of evaluating the allocation of resources are shown in Chapter 15.

It is clear that data of some departments will not mirror the percent allocation of resources of the entire division. This is appropriate, because the top priorities of the entire research and development group are only reflected by time and effort spent in some departments (e.g., medical, statistics, data processing). Other departments spend a larger proportion of their time and effort on projects that are at an early stage of their development (e.g., pharmaceutical development). Other departments vary in this regard (e.g., patents, regulatory affairs).

OTHER ISSUES

Promotions

There are many ambitious people who desire to advance in research management. In choosing individuals to promote, it is essential to determine who puts the company's interests first in their thinking and actions and who puts themselves first. The motives of all individuals being considered for promotions are important to evaluate. As T.S. Eliott wrote about motives in *Murder in the Cathedral*: "The greatest treason is to do the right deed for the wrong reason."

Drug companies usually desire to make most, if not all, of their important promotions from within their company, which is excellent for morale. People who are promoted, however, sometimes rate higher in loyalty and social skills than in their abilities to help the company succeed. Thomas J. Watson, the retired chief executive of IBM wrote (1987) "I never hesitated to promote someone I didn't like. The comfortable assistant—the nice guy you like to go on fishing trips with—is a great pitfall. Instead I looked for those sharp, scratchy, harsh, almost unpleasant guys who see and tell you about things as they really are. If you can get enough of them around you, and have patience enough to hear them out, there is no limit to where you can go."

THERAPEUTIC AREAS TO EMPHASIZE OVER NEXT TEN YEARS

Gastroenterology (1)
Infectious Diseases (2)
Cancer (3)
Dermatology (4)
Pulmonary/Respiratory (5)

ALLOCATION OF RESEARCH AND DEVELOPMENT RESOURCES

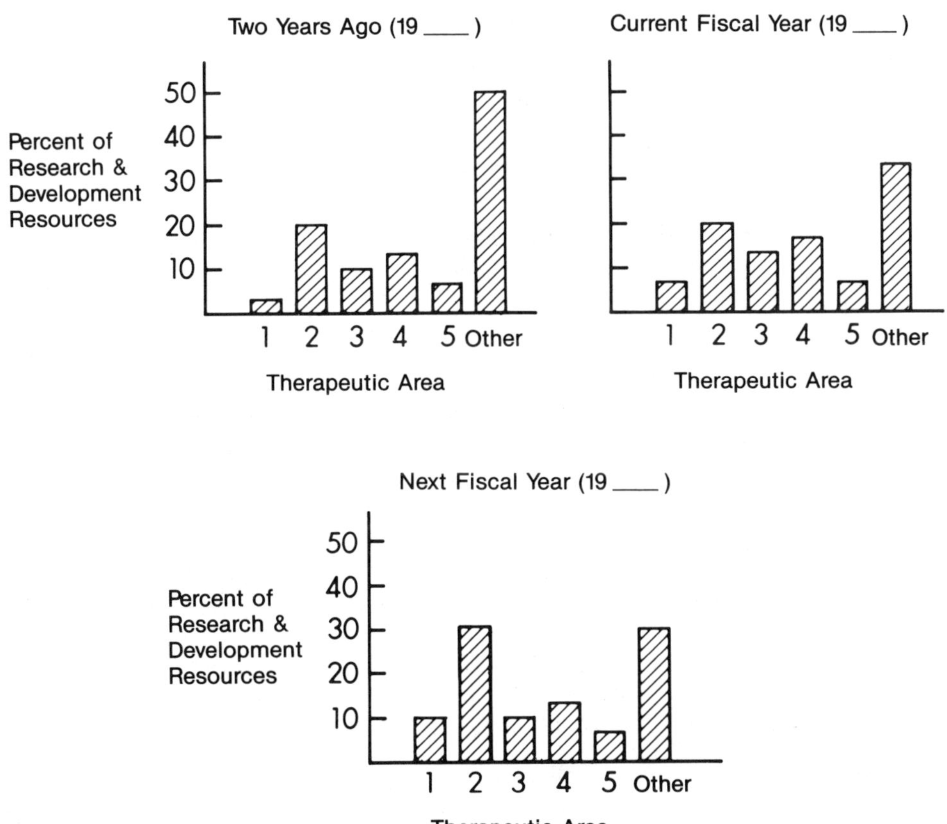

Fig. 11.3. Evaluating how research and development resources are being moved to areas of particular interest. This figure could illustrate just drug discovery activities, medical activities, all drug development, or any particular department or group.

Planning and Documentation

Within each company many documents are generated to provide both general and detailed plans for drug development. Each company has it own types of plans and documents and no single set is *a priori* best. Nonetheless, there are a number of plans that are useful to generate and use.

Strategy documents of various types should be generated (see Chapter 2 in *Guide to Planning and Managing Multiple Clinical Studies* [Spilker, 1987c] and various chapters in this book). Even if they are not widely used, they force the people who prepare them to focus and organize their thoughts on critical issues. Reports to senior managers are also a useful means of keeping managers abreast of current activities, even if the reports are quite general. Various types of schedules dealing with the overall project system, individual drug projects, and parts of drug projects are important. Plans of current allocations and future needs for additional staff, facilities, and money are also important to document and review in a systematic way. Representative documents are described in various chapters of this book.

What Options Exist When Work on Important Projects Cannot Progress at Top Speed?

This is a common problem for productive companies and also for those able to license-in important new drugs. Some options include the following:

1. *Place some projects in a slower development mode* This may entail using a priority system. One drawback of this approach is that it may discourage scientists to whom the delayed project has great importance.
2. *License the project to another company* This has the disadvantage that it usually provides little revenue and is not usually worth doing if it is possible to develop the drug oneself at a slower rate. This approach, however, may be more attractive to a company if it includes a cross-licensing, joint venture, or other business opportunity.
3. *Proceed with all projects a bit more slowly* This view is predicated on the fact that drugs that fail cannot be predicted in advance, and a slight delay in each (or most) may be less damaging to the company's future sales and to employee morale than other alternatives.
4. *Contract out part or all of the development program for some investigational drugs* For discreet smaller projects this may be a viable option. Otherwise, only one or a few aspects (e.g., statistical analyses) may usually be contracted out.

12 / *Personnel Roles and Issues in Drug Discovery and Development*

Basic research is very competitive . . . The competition starts at the lab bench. Alfred W. Alberts, Merck & Co., Inc.

If you have bright, highly motivated people who feel responsible for their work, they will discover great things. Dr. Edward M. Scolnick, Merck & Co., Inc.

[A] venture capitalist I know says, somewhat in jest, that the first thing he looks at in a business plan is the financial projection. Frankly, how anyone can figure out what sales and earnings and returns are going to be five years from now is beyond me. The first place I look is the resumes, usually found at the back. To me, they are the essence of any plan. Arthur Rock. From *Harvard Business Review* (November–December, 1987, p.63).

PERSONNEL ISSUES AT THE OVERALL RESEARCH AND DEVELOPMENT LEVEL

Numerous issues relating to personnel are discussed in Chapter 9 (e.g., consultants, special deployment teams, task forces, hiring professionals). Although those issues relate to corporate (i.e., general company) issues, they also relate to research and development (R and D). Issues in this chapter primarily relate to R and D.

Roles of Scientists

Scientists who discover and develop drugs have many different roles to play in a drug company. Some are assigned one of these roles and do not deviate throughout their professional career. Others are assigned two or more distinct roles (either simultaneously or sequentially) or through their own initiative take on additional roles because of apparent needs in their company.

Roles of scientists may be classified as follows:

1. *Generator of new drug discoveries* This is usually applied to someone in a chemistry department, although some scientists who generate ideas for new drugs work in a biological department (e.g., pharmacology, microbiology) and collaborate closely with chemists to design new compounds.
2. *Evaluator of biological activity* These scientists are by definition in a biological discipline and test compounds for activity. A series of biological tests is designed to systematically progress the evaluation of new compounds over a series of hurdles (i.e., compounds that are active in one test proceed to the next test(s), and so on).
3. *Technical development scientist* Evaluations and improvements in several scientific areas come under this heading (e.g., formulation development, stability testing, chemical scaleup, analytical evaluations).
4. *Project leader or project manager* One or more individuals lead the development team that takes the compound from the laboratory to the clinic and to the market.
5. *Administrator and manager* Some scientists direct the work of other scientists, review progress, and monitor activities associated with drug development.

Scientists need to have many skills to conduct any one of these activities effectively. These skills, which include those of the entrepreneur, teacher, and diplomat, in turn usually depend on an individual's personality, interests, and abilities. These interpersonal skills may be developed, but they are not readily taught.

Metamorphosis of One's Role within a Company

Few drug companies allow their scientists and other professionals in research and development a great deal of flexibility in defining their roles. People who are unhappy with their roles may request a transfer to a different department, join a different company in a new role, or retrain themselves through education. At those companies that allow some professionals to redefine their roles, people who see an unmet need that they could fill may move slowly in that direction by an amoeba-like growth. Amoeba send out a small part of their cell body to explore a new area. If they do not encounter resistance they may move their entire cell in the new direction. A positive aspect of this approach is that the person who is exploring a new area is highly motivated to do a good job and the company will probably benefit from their activities. The negative aspects are that many people may be seeking new areas to work in and creating numerous conflicts throughout the company. If an individual is successful in the new area, he or she may be engaged in activities for which they were not hired and their original job function(s) may be inadequately performed or covered.

Career Development Opportunities

Many scientists perceive their careers as a stepwise building process where each advance made in their professional discipline (e.g., professional publication, positive contribution to the company) is viewed as helping in their career advancement. Scientists often have overlapping careers within their drug company, as well as within their general discipline of science or medicine. Outside their company they may (1) teach courses, (2) present lectures, (3) author manuscripts, (4) conduct research, (5) engage in patient treatment, (6) serve as officers in professional societies, (7) work for a trade association, or (8) help organize and chair meetings and symposia of various types and groups.

It is ironic that the most effective and creative scientists in a drug company may only be promoted at most drug companies by giving them administrative responsibility and taking them out of the laboratory. This is a major issue, because they are often of greatest value to the company working actively in the laboratory. This has always been a difficult personnel issue in drug companies among ambitious senior scientists whose professional career growth has outstripped their administrative career growth. In a pyramid type of organization there are usually few positions and even fewer opportunities for promotion available that will satisfy ambitious scientists. Some companies have addressed this issue by creating a system of "half-level" promotions. This approach, however, merely serves to increase the company's bureaucracy and often complicates the career problems and possibly drug development as well, rather than solving these issues.

Dual Career Track within a Company

To recognize differences between scientific and administrative career paths, many drug companies have formally established two separate career tracks. A series of professional ranks are often created, possibly comparable to those of Instructor, Assistant, Associate, and Full Professor in academic institutions. This approach is usually not completely successful on its own if a promotion merely represents a new title and does not bring with it other forms of recognition or changes in job responsibilities. Promotions should be accompanied by public recognition (e.g., an announcement in a company publication, a notice on the bulletin board) plus tangible benefits (e.g., dinner for the employee plus his or her spouse, raise, bonus). In addition, a dual career track should allow scientists to remain active in the laboratory without taking on additional or undesired administrative functions or being penalized financially.

Another solution to the problem is to promote senior research scientists to be heads of therapeutic areas for drug research. They are given the responsibility of supervising and directing several scientists in different scientific disciplines under a matrix approach, while at the same time remaining active as a creative scientist. This type of matrix approach is superimposed on traditional department line functions. Chapters 5, 10, and 13 discuss the matrix approach further. Panel D in Fig. 10.5 illustrates one type of therapeutic area committee.

Who Are the Creative Scientists?

Creative scientists often develop an individual approach or style in how they develop their ideas and seek to reach their goals. They differ greatly from each other and do not fit a single pattern. Each desires certain freedoms to pursue their own ideas, though the paths they follow are often extremely different. General goals should be established by managers for their efforts and activities. A large majority of scientists (as well as others) prefer having a clear goal and direction to follow that is supported by the company's managers and will enhance the company's overall health.

Scientists are motivated by different factors. Some of the factors that influence employees' motivation are listed in Table 7.1. One of the most frequently mentioned factors is freedom. The word freedom, however, has many definitions and applications. These include freedom to (1) choose their research topic, (2) conduct research in their own manner, (3) attend scientific meetings, (4) publish scientific research, and (5) direct a number of laboratories. Other factors that motivate scientists are the same as those affecting all employees. These include the possibility of achieving a high visibility in the company and obtaining a salary commensurate with their talents, and in line with salaries paid at other companies.

The Core Group of Highly Creative Scientists

It has been stated that a drug company with 2,000 scientists has most of its best ideas come from approximately one percent of its scientists, or approximately 20 people. Loss of a significant number of those important staff members would have a major impact on any drug company. Most of these scientists are well known to other scientists and managers in a company, and their identity can easily be learned by managers in other companies who are interested in obtaining this information. This means that every company is potentially vulnerable to raids on their most outstanding and important scientific staff, much as entire academic departments are sometimes raided by other universities. These creative scientists should be supported fully by the company because they are so important and valuable.

Other scientists should be encouraged to be creative, but no one can be commanded to be innovative. All scientists should be helped to achieve their highest level of creativity. From a management perspective, one means of achieving this goal is by encouraging and rewarding risk in scientific thinking and by not punishing failures. It is usually clear which people are seeking new challenges and which people are trying to avoid them. It is also usually clear which people are always advertising and promoting themselves within a company and which are primarily promoting the company's interests.

It is the author's view that a company is better off with a mediocre drug (or idea) and great people to develop it, than to have a great drug (or idea) and mediocre people to develop it. In drug development (or in life) there is not sufficient time to make every mistake, even once. A company must have managers and staff who can anticipate and avoid as many problems as possible. This emphasizes the importance of hiring the best people a company can identify and attract.

Influence and Control of Scientists

Many enlightened research and development executives adhere to a more lax policy of influencing or controlling employee activities during the drug discovery period and adhere to a more regimented policy during the drug development period. This issue is discussed more fully in other chapters. During each of these periods, it is necessary to balance a laissez-faire attitude in which scientists are given little supervision and a regimented approach in which their efforts are tightly controlled. The balances relating to loose versus strict territorial limits and the types of barriers between departments are discussed in Chapter 4.

Control of Science by Nonscientists

There is often a strongly negative influence felt within research and development offices and laboratories when nonscientists with MBA degrees or business backgrounds become managers of research and development. Nonscientists often use an excessive amount of "foreign" jargon and apply "foreign" concepts (from the scientist's perspective) to measure and also to *control* what is going on. These efforts usually create a strongly negative reaction in scientists, similar to the fur rising on a cat's back (i.e., piloerection). It is usually in the area of control of research where most serious issues and problems arise with nonscientist managers of research.

PERSONNEL ISSUES AT A MEDICAL DEPARTMENT LEVEL

In staffing a medical department there is need for a wide variety of personnel with different backgrounds and orientations. There is a need for professionals with MDs, PhDs, PharmDs, and other degrees and training.

Training of Physicians

MDs are trained (in medical school hospitals) to make rapid decisions even though the information available on which to make a decision is often incomplete. This occurs frequently in the hospital care of patients and not only in medical emergency situations. Treating patients in private medical practice usually requires that treatment plans are also initiated before all relevant data can be obtained. MDs are taught to develop and use the skills of clinical judgment. This judgment is heavily based on one's prior experience and knowledge of clinical probabilities of outcomes in various situations.

Training of Scientists

PhDs and other scientists are trained quite differently than MDs. As scientists, PhDs are taught to withhold judgment(s) and decisions until they have sufficient information of adequate quality to solidly defend their position. They are taught to logically approach a problem and to solve it systematically, collecting all necessary and appropriate information.

Awareness of these general differences in training of MDs and PhDs enables one to better understand the perspective of a scientist or clinician in both approaching problems and answering questions. It also helps explain why PhD scientists have become important staff members of medical departments at drug companies, and why a coterie of traditionally trained MDs is usually insufficient on its own to develop drugs efficiently. Both clinical and scientific perspectives are needed in medical departments. In recent years more MDs have received training in science and can now better appreciate and utilize both the clinical and scientific approaches in dealing with issues of drug development.

Utilizing Staff Time Efficiently

Most of an MD's time at a drug company is not spent on work that requires an MD degree to accomplish. The same is true for PhDs, although probably to a lesser extent. The issue of how companies utilize their MD's time is answered differently at various drug companies. Some companies put their MDs on the "front lines" and have them lead important projects, with or without responsibility for administrative duties that could be delegated.

Some companies assign a PhD to assist each MD, because the PhD is able to provide high-level scientific support. Administrative control of a project is often given to an MD. Companies with a small number of MDs often utilize them as general (or specific) consultants to deal with important medical questions or issues. In this situation, each MD assists non-MD staff on several drug development projects at the same time. Even using these approaches, most of an MD's activities in the drug industry do not require an MD degree to complete successfully. On the other hand, some companies tend to put experienced PhDs in charge of medical sections and have MDs report to them. Experience has shown that this approach works well when the appropriate staffs are present.

MDs may be assigned to projects or other activities that require all of their time and are extremely challenging and fulfilling. On the other hand, this situation often does not occur, and many physicians may not be utilizing their time in a fully productive manner. One alternative to assigning each physician to a single project is to assign each to two or more different projects. This approach may also be used for clinical research assistants and other staff working in the clinical area. It often provides advantages to both the individual and the company to have them working on multiple projects, especially when there is insufficient work to do on one of those projects at all times.

Primary Roles of Physicians in Drug Development

Physicians serve many functions in drug development:

1. Physicians serve as an important internal source for clinical opinions and advice on a wide range of issues, including (1) medical emergencies that arise involving the company's drugs, (2) serious adverse reactions to investigational or marketed drugs,

(3) strategies for the marketing of the company's drugs, (4) ethical concerns that arise in various situations, and (5) medicolegal evaluations regarding product liability.

2. Physicians serve as internal experts for various aspects of clinical research, including (1) clinical feasibility of the experimental design, (2) study conduct, (3) clinical interpretation of data, (4) extrapolation of data, and (5) generation of new hypotheses to test.

3. Highly trained and experienced physicians who are both clinicians and scientists have an important role in bridging the gap in understanding that often exists between basic research and therapeutic challenges in medical practice. This role is manifested, in part, through evaluation of the potential need and place for new drugs or medical products. The MDs can comment on anticipated reactions in the medical community to proposed drugs, services, or other products.

4. Physicians function as administrators, which includes such responsibilities as project leadership and providing medical input on numerous committees at all levels within an organization. Many drug companies have at least one member of their board of directors who is a physician.

5. Physicians represent the company at many meetings outside the company with regulatory authorities, other government agencies, academicians, professional societies, trade associations, the media, and various other groups.

Many functions of a physician involve interactions with statisticians to help plan studies, analyze the data, and interpret the results. Interactions may be complicated when colleagues in a second, third, or even more countries are involved. Figure 12.1 illustrates a simple example to indicate some possible interactions.

Secondary Roles of Physicians in Drug Development

Efficiency is believed to be enhanced in medical departments, as in almost all other departments in a drug company, when individuals are working in areas where they are most experienced. Because of the need of clinical expertise in many areas of a drug company, MDs are often asked to deal with issues that are outside the area of clinical studies. These activities are usually not secondary in importance to the company, but are often secondary in importance to the clinician in relation to his or her primary functions. Secondary functions of physicians in industry include some or all of the following:

1. Analyzing legal cases relating to the company's products, and liaising with the legal department and its outside attorneys.

2. Reviewing and approving the medical content of advertisements, compendium submissions, and various other documents prepared either inside or outside the medical department.

3. Corresponding with health professionals on medical questions raised by the outside health professional.

4. Holding telephone conversations with health professionals who raise medical questions and/or other problems.

5. Reviewing and approving (or denying) requests from scientists for drug samples to be used in animal or human studies.

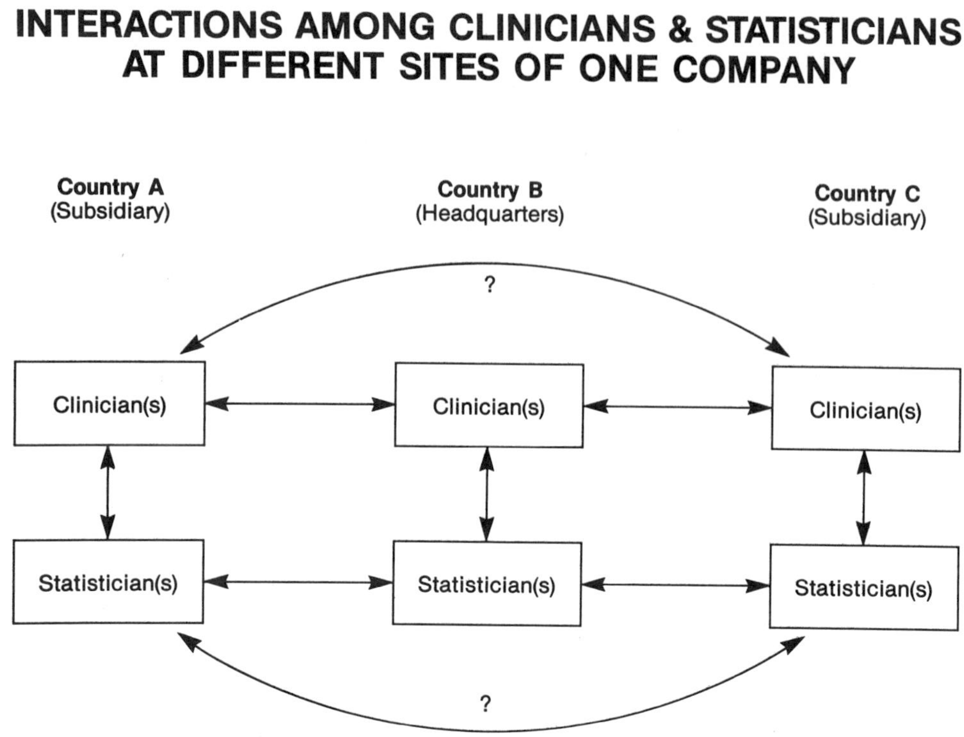

Fig. 12.1. Interactions among clinicians and statisticians at different sites of a single company.

6. Reviewing and approving (or denying) requests from physicians who desire investigational drugs for compassionate plea protocols or use.
7. Corresponding with sales representatives on questions about marketed and/or investigational drugs.
8. Communicating with medical or other representatives of regulatory agencies.
9. Providing a medical review of compounds or drugs being evaluated for potential licensing.
10. Training new staff in the medical department.
11. Preparing annual reports on marketed drugs for the Food and Drug Administration (FDA).
12. Hosting guest speakers and other visitors from outside the company.
13. Speaking to various organizations on medical aspects of drug development.

In many larger drug companies some or all of these issues are handled by specialized groups, either within or outside the medical area. Although it may improve efficiency to have a separate group of non-MDs handle most of these issues, difficult questions should still be handled by the company's medical experts. Non-MDs who concentrate on these areas often perform these activities as well as or better than trained medical personnel, who often view these requests for assistance as interruptions of their major work.

Maintaining Clinical Skills

Over a period of years, it is natural for physicians in the pharmaceutical industry to become less sensitive and aware of many medical issues and subtleties faced by practicing physicians with their patients. In fact, clinical skills atrophy over time when they are not actively used. In addition, medical practice changes rapidly in many therapeutic areas. Thus, as the physician in industry becomes more skilled within his administrative and research-scientist roles, he or she simultaneously loses those clinical skills that were developed during medical training and practice. Many physicians function less skillfully as clinical researchers and medical consultants over time, because they have been away from the trenches and direct hands-on activities with patients. These were the very experiences that originally provided them with the knowledge and experience they needed and used in designing protocols, providing medical advice, and interpreting data.

Companies handle this problem in a variety of ways. One of the most common approaches is to hire numerous physicians and to accept a relatively rapid or frequent turnover of personnel. In this manner, it is always possible to have some recently trained clinicians on hand. Obviously, such an approach has substantial drawbacks and cannot meet all of a company's needs for current information.

A short period of intensive clinical exposure would enable some company physicians to retain and further develop medical acumen and skills. These skills are critical to the optimum functioning of their clinical and advisory roles. This goal could be achieved in several ways, including a one- to three-month ward rotation every number of years. These short sabbatical periods would provide benefits both to the company and physicians that could not be achieved by attending professional meetings, conferences, and seminars. Another possibility is for the company to encourage its physicians to spend one or even two days per week at a local hospital where their clinical skills could be maintained. These approaches would stimulate the physicians in addition to accomplishing several other goals (see Chapter 24 on Industry-Academic relationships). There are already drug companies that follow this practice (e.g., Burroughs Wellcome Co., Boehringer Ingleheim Corp.). Other companies offer their MDs a half or whole day per week at a local hospital, but some discourage their MDs from fully utilizing this time.

Cascade Effect of Hiring a New MD or PhD

The effect of an additional person hired into a drug company differs depending both on the specific department and on the person's position. The general effects of hiring an MD into a medical department are indicated in Fig. 12.2. This illustrates that other departments are affected. The MD who is initiating clinical studies probably requires more additional support throughout the company than any other single person hired into a drug company at an entry level. This additional support is in terms of work generated in other departments. Hiring a single MD would probably not require additional staff to be hired in other departments, although their work load would increase.

An MD who is hired into a medical department will (under most situations) plan

SUPPORT AND SERVICES REQUIRED WHEN AN ADDITIONAL MD JOINS THE STAFF

WITHIN THE MEDICAL DEPARTMENT:

Added Administrative Support

*Secretarial Services
*Administrative Services

Added Technical Support

*Monitors
*Technical Assistants

WITHIN THE RESEARCH & DEVELOPMENT DIVISION:

Added Statistical Support

*Planning Studies
*Reviewing Protocols
*Analyzing Data

Added Management Support

*Reviews of Any New Projects Assigned to MD

Any Project Added for MD To Develop

*Many Other Departments Affected

Drug Development Laboratories

*Synthesis of Study Drug
*Packaging of Study Drug
*Shipment of Study Drug

Information and Data Processing Support

*Data Editing and Entry into Computers
*Data Tabulations
*Library Services
*Data Documentation, Storage, and Retrieval

Other

*Regulatory Affairs
*Preclinical Sciences

OUTSIDE THE RESEARCH & DEVELOPMENT DIVISION:

Corporate Affairs

*Personnel/Benefits
*Employee Health
*Payroll
*Parking and Local Transportation
*Cafeteria
*Printing
*Photography
*Purchasing
*Travel
*Design Graphics
*Engineering
*Training Programs
*Others

Other Groups

*Legal
*Marketing
*Patents

Fig. 12.2. Support and services required when an MD joins the staff of a drug company. This illustrates the cascade or pyramid-like effect of hiring an MD to initiate clinical studies.

and initiate clinical studies. These studies in turn demand additional services and technical support in many areas of the company. A PhD scientist hired into a research department at a comparable level to the MD usually has much less impact on the resources of a company. If a company hires two or more additional MDs at one time, they have to be prepared and willing to deal with the cascade effect seen in other departments that occurs approximately six months to a year later.

13 / *Balancing Line Function and Matrix Approaches*

Because change is so rapid it is not uncommon for an individual in midcareer to find that the hierarchy is passing him by. In other words, he has climbed part way up the ladder and feels competent. He stops to rest, but rapid technological change goes on. He intends to catch up, but when he tries he is technologically obsolete. He has become uneducated for his job simply by standing still. Laurence J. Peter. From *The Peter Prescription.*

DEFINITIONS AND BACKGROUND

General Description of a Matrix

The management hierarchy present in almost all companies is referred to as line management. This is the so-called pyramid or vertical system where people report to others above them in a chain of command. There is a second management system referred to as the matrix or horizontal system that is used for drug development by most medium and large drug companies, as well as by some smaller drug companies.

In this system each new drug or line-extension of a drug that is being developed is called a project. The progress of each project is planned, facilitated, and reviewed by an interdisciplinary group of members referred to as the project team. People who perform the work on a drug, or who are responsible for the work, may be the project team member or may informally report to the team member from their department or discipline. The disciplines represented on most projects include pharmacology, toxicology, technical development areas (e.g., chemical development, pharmaceutical development), statistics, regulatory affairs, project planning, and medicine. At some drug companies the project team also includes marketing- and business-oriented members. Each team has a leader who reports (possibly on an informal basis) to an individual who then reports either through line management or directly to the head of research and development.

The matrix system represents a second reporting relationship. At some companies this reporting relationship is formal, and this may lead to conflicts with line managers. A major technique used to avoid these conflicts is to have matrix-reporting relationships loose and informal. Interpersonal skills, diplomacy, tact, and, above all, a desire for this system to work are required to have a successful system.

The major aspects of developing drugs using a project-driven matrix management approach may be broken down into various components. Cleland (1984) has proposed nine elements in this philosophy, which are shown in Fig. 13.1.

Levels within an Organization at Which Matrix Groups May Function

The matrix function usually is most visible in a company when it is used to develop new drugs toward an Investigational New Drug Application (IND) and a New Drug Application (NDA). A matrix approach to management also functions at several other levels within a company. At the most general level, the matrix concept may be used to organize an entire company. Chapter 5 describes various organizational aspects of this approach. Figure 5.3 illustrates how this concept can be used to organize a company, and Fig. 10.3 illustrates the use of a matrix approach for organizing a research and development group.

Internationally

At the international level, members from various countries, who are part of a multinational company, work on teams (or committees). Such teams exist and operate at different levels of the company's hierarchy. This topic is discussed further in Chapter 19. These teams may be concerned with international policies, strategies, plans, and/or activities. These groups or teams may focus on one or more of the following functions: establishing, monitoring, reviewing, problem solving, or coordinating. In many ways, the board of directors, which is composed of both staff members and senior line managers from different countries, is a matrix function. It is the team that operates at the company's highest level.

Nationally

Many types of matrix groups function at the national level. There are numerous areas where people from different disciplines get together outside the traditional

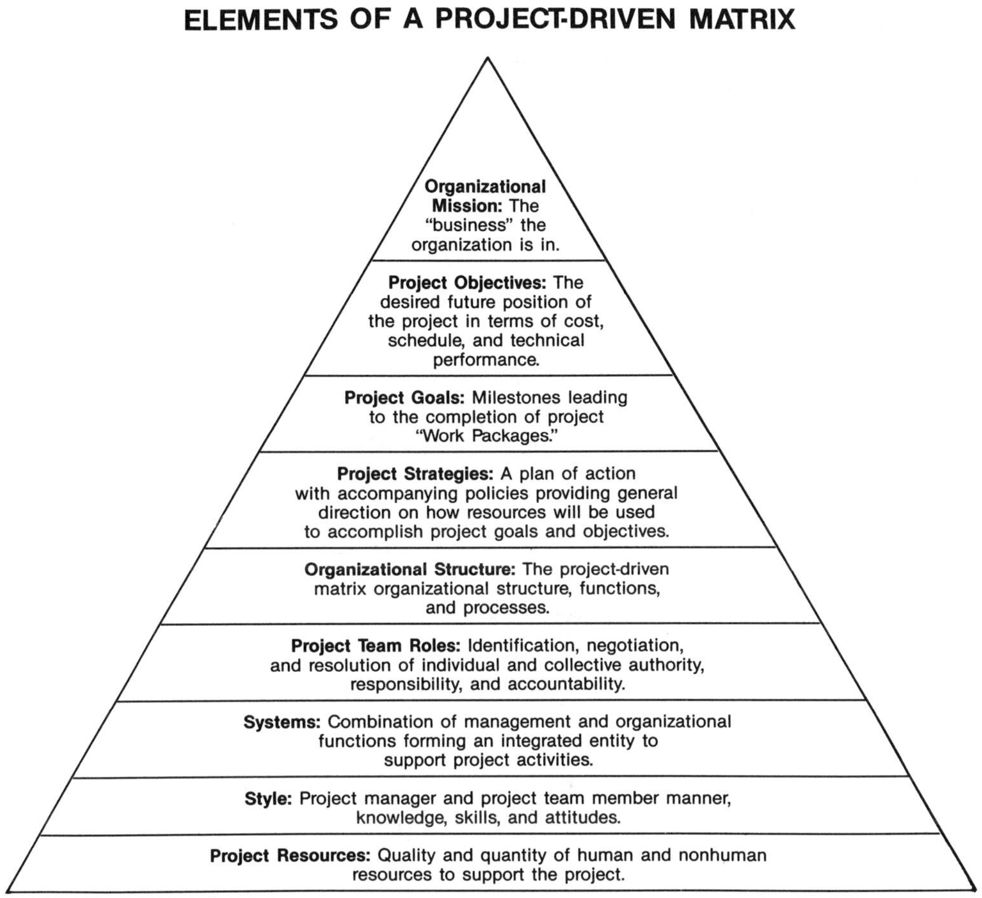

Fig. 13.1. Elements in the project-driven matrix management philosophy. From *Project Management Journal* (Cleland, 1984) with permission of Project Management Institute.

hierarchical structure of the company. Most of these groups have other names, such as task forces, and many are used on a temporary basis. All issues and functions described under the international level may also operate at the national company level.

Drug Development

This level relates to the project groups (i.e., teams) that are planning and carrying out the many activities of drug development. Project teams may be national and/or international in their makeup. Figure 10.3 illustrates how project teams report in a matrix organization. This is the activity that is usually referred to when one reads about project groups or teams in the drug industry.

Research Projects

The matrix approach within research and development may be used to assist drug discovery as well as drug development activities. For drug discovery, an independent team of scientists from different disciplines and/or departments (e.g., chemistry, biochemistry, pharmacology, microbiology) may work together on a formal or informal basis. This group may focus their efforts and goals on one or more therapeutic areas (e.g., cardiology, gastroenterology), diseases (e.g., angina, sickle cell disease), physiological effects (e.g., to shift the oxygen dissociation curve to the right), biochemical effects (e.g., to stimulate or inhibit a specific enzyme), or pathological effects (e.g., to prevent necrosis from developing in ischemic tissues). This group may have a member who helps the team by (1) coordinating their activities, (2) monitoring their progress, (3) communicating their activities and results to senior management, (4) drawing up plans for advanced testing of active compounds, and (5) helping to facilitate the resolution of disputes or other issues. Various organizational structures used for drug discovery are shown in Fig. 10.5 and are discussed in Chapter 10. The matrix approach tends to be more informal at the early stages of drug discovery and more structured at later phases of preclincial research when a specific compound is being evaluated and considered for further development.

KEY PLAYERS IN A MATRIX SYSTEM

Overseeing a Matrix System

At both national and international levels, it is generally valuable to have a small department oversee the matrix system. The functions of this department would include planning, monitoring, troubleshooting, and facilitating solutions to problems. Other major activities could include generation of financial records (e.g., tracking project costs), conducting analyses of the project system, and serving as a source to collect and analyze archival information.

At each level where one or more matrix groups function, there may be an individual who is assigned the role of coordinating activities. This person may or may not be a member of the individual project teams. If no one is assigned this coordinating responsibility, it becomes the function of the groups' leaders and/or line managers. In addition to the person who coordinates activities, any department with a representative on the team may also have a separate individual (or group) that coordinates all activities and all studies conducted within their department.

Most drug companies benefit if they have an individual who has few line managerial responsibilities in charge of coordinating and improving the efficiency of international drug development and project-related activities. This person receives information about activities and problems from all drug development groups. He or she provides input where needed to keep communications lines operational and insures that all relevant groups are communicating effectively.

Project Team Leaders

The leader of a project team is usually appointed by one or more senior managers through either a formal or informal mechanism. A project team may have a single leader for its entire life, but often there are two or more leaders, although at different points in the project's life. One common pattern is to have a preclinical scientist lead a project until an IND is filed and clinical studies are initiated. The project is then turned over to a clinician who leads the project until the NDA is approved. After that point a marketing oriented individual is appointed to lead the project. A separate project team of primarily different members who focus on production and marketing issues may be created at any time, but this is likely to occur during Phase III (Fig. 13.2). The advantage of forming a separate team in production and/or marketing is that it enables each group to function more efficiently, because each is primarily concerned with different activities. A few people, especially the project team leaders should be on both (or all) teams. This helps insure close coordination of efforts. The same principles apply to a research and development team established in two separate countries where the drug is being developed (see Chapter 19).

Project leaders are often viewed as project champions. To obtain project leaders who are effective project champions it is important that project leadership be viewed as a privilege and honor rather than a burden or as a reward for other services or work. If people are merely rewarded for their hard work in their own discipline by being made a project leader, it is more likely that they will not do as effective a job as those people chosen because they are the best candidates. Individuals who are most highly motivated to act as project champions are often chosen as project leaders.

Numerous advantages and disadvantages of this approach exist. See *Guide to Planning and Managing Multiple Clinical Studies* (Spilker, 1987c) for details.

Project Team Managers

A totally different approach to providing project leadership is practiced by those companies that have project managers. These individuals are not primarily scientists or clinicians, but are full-time managers of a small number of projects. Managers are chosen for their administrative ability to move projects ahead rapidly, efficiently, and in the desired direction. Good project managers are independent, aggressive, objective, pay attention to detail, and have a high level of interpersonal skills. They usually have a scientific or medical background because some scientific training is usually important for their success with new chemical entity (NCE) projects. People with a PhD or MD are desirable candidates, if they also possess the other characteristics described. Individuals with a business, production, or marketing background could also be suitable candidates for selected types of projects (e.g., over-the-counter drugs, marketed prescription drugs, Phase III drugs), especially if they have demonstrated the requisite skills and talents.

Utilizing Project Managers Versus Project Leaders

Major advantages of having project managers rather than project leaders are that the managers do not have commitments to line-function managers, and do not have the responsibility of also running a program in their own discipline (e.g., the drug's entire clinical program). Therefore, they have more time to devote to administrative issues and other matters outside their discipline than project leaders. Project managers also will tend to be more objective and independent about decisions they make.

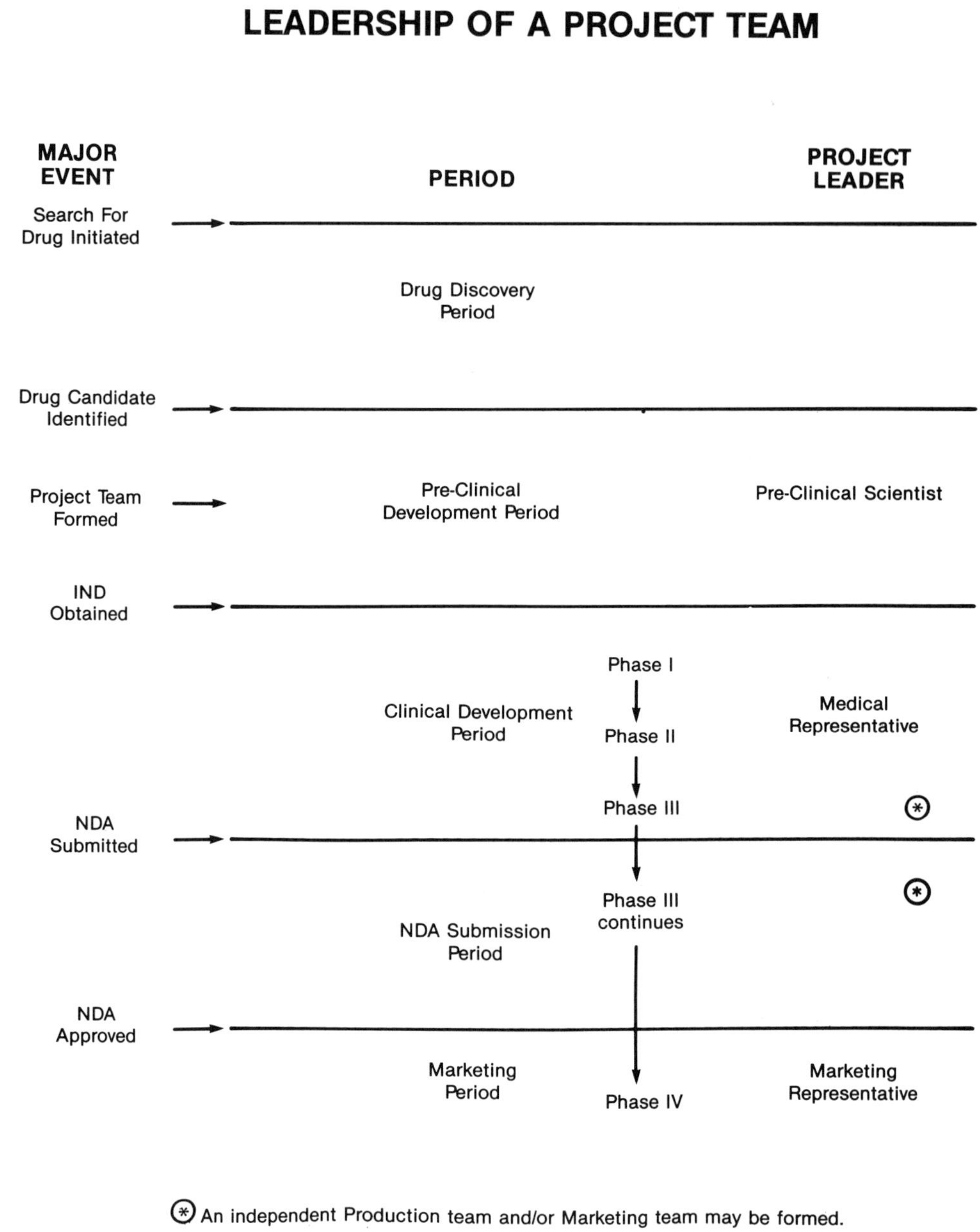

Fig. 13.2. Leadership of a project team as it changes from a preclinical scientist to clinical scientist and to a marketer. IND, Investigational New Drug Application; NDA, New Drug Application.

Managers are also desirable to use when a company has too few project champions or when it is difficult for champions to cross department boundaries to have work accomplished.

It is the author's opinion that most companies will utilize project managers rather than project champions/project leaders in the future. The project managers are professionals whose job is to achieve the project's goals and whose performance is judged by the success of this effort. The project leader is often an "amateur" at leading the project, and his line managers (i.e, supervisors) may resent time spent on directing a project, especially if it interferes with higher priorities of the manager. It is inefficient for a company to continually train new champions for a long period before they become effective project leaders. Moreover, project leaders focus their energies on achieving their discipline or function goals. It is ironic that many of the best project leaders have insufficient time to devote to running their project because of their almost total commitment to their line-function responsibilities.

Alternative Approaches

Two alternative systems to utilizing a pure project leader or project manager system are:

1. *A transition system* One example of a transition system is when project leaders head projects from their inception through the Phase II go-no go decision point. Once this decision is reached, the project is turned over to a project manager who leads the project administratively until the drug is marketed. The ex-project leader usually continues to remain active on the project within his or her discipline (e.g., clinical research). This system has the disadvantage that the transition occurs at one of the busiest times in the project's life.
2. *A combination system* An example of a combination system is to have project leaders focus on scientific and policy issues (e.g., strategies, objectives) and an assistant project leader who focuses on administrative issues (e.g., planning, tracking, writing reports, troubleshooting). Each person who has this role could assist from one to six or so project leaders, depending on the work load within each project.

Project Team Members

It should be clear to the project leader (or manager) why each member of their team was appointed. Reasons could include (1) providing invaluable expertise, (2) providing an opportunity to learn about a new activity or therapeutic area, or (3) being drafted because no one else was interested, available, or willing to serve. Some teams change their membership rather frequently as the project goes through various stages along the drug development pipeline. If there is any confusion about who is actually on the team, this issue should be rapidly settled by the project leader. This is usually resolved through discussions with project members, department heads, or senior managers. Some companies appoint department heads to serve as members of a project team, but most companies appoint more junior personnel.

Project Coordinators/Planners

An important member of the project team is the person who serves as navigator for the project. Whereas the project leader serves as the captain, each project needs an individual to draw up plans, track progress, and help insure that the project remains on course. This individual raises a red flag when the project goes astray or runs into problems. This individual usually reports to a separate department of Project Coordination or Project Management and has limited authority to facilitate a solution to problems or issues.

The role of project coordinator is not clearly defined at most companies, which has both advantages and disadvantages. Advantages include the ability to be more effective in expediting those services most needed by the project (e.g., tracking the writing and reviewing of various reports, tracking drug use and need, following competitors' activities). Disadvantages include the ability of the project leader (1) to exclude this individual from information needed to perform his or her role effectively, (2) to ignore their role and work, and (3) to have another individual in the project leader's discipline carry out much of this work. Solutions for the coordinator often relate to finding those services that the project leader desires and can utilize in running the project. If a project manager is running the project, then a project coordinator may act as an assistant project manager. Another approach to a solution is to strengthen the matrix system so that the responsibilities of the coordinator are more clearly defined.

INITIATING NEW PROJECTS

Initiating Projects in a Multinational Drug Company

One of the most basic issues in a project system is whether or not a compound must meet formal criteria prior to elevation to project status. These criteria could be established in terms of scientific profile, medical need, and commercial value. If a multinational company develops drugs at two or more separate sites it is possible that new projects may be only established or initiated by the central headquarters, or initiation may occur at each of the semi-independent sites developing drugs. If the latter situation prevails, then it must be determined how each site is to react to projects initiated by the other sites. Their reactions could be to do nothing except to follow the new project's progress, to form an independent group that would also develop the drug, or to develop an international project team. Another approach to establishing new projects is to require joint approval of new projects by all sites where the drug will be developed.

Types of Projects Initiated

Some companies believe in one type of drug project, i.e., all investigational drugs are intended to be marketed unless work is terminated by toxicity, lack of efficacy, or for another reason. Other companies or even a different site within the same company may believe that some projects should be established to test a theory, even though it is known that the compound being tested will not become a marketed drug. The author believes that this second type of project should not be initiated by drug companies, except if considered extremely important, and then only on a limited basis.

Getting a Project Off the Ground and Moving Ahead

Some of the many issues that must be dealt with in starting a new project and maintaining the momentum of existing ones include:

1. *Authority* Where is it and how will it be used? How much is the direct authority of those involved and how much is indirectly derived by personal or reporting connections to those who have direct authority? Also, are there people who exert authority although there is no evidence that they have a right to do so, i.e., that authority was delegated to them from more senior managers? If a project team is composed of department heads or more senior managers, this will not be an issue, whereas if junior people are members it may represent a major problem.
2. *Communication* What are the processes and mechanisms to be used communicating both to higher and lower levels in the company? Are they operating efficiently? How could they be improved?
3. *Decision making* Who makes decisions at each level in the company and how are they made? Are issues raised for debate as a "front" after the real decision has been made? For example, does the medical representative ask for views about conducting a certain study at a project meeting after the protocol has been written and the investigator chosen?
4. *Review* How are activities reviewed by managers at various levels in the company? How does the project group review its activities?
5. *Priorities* How are priorities established and by whom? Are they in harmony at different levels of the company and between different departments at the same level?
6. *Resources* How are resources allocated? How are conflicts handled? Conflict-of-interest issues are discussed separately in this chapter.
7. *Commitment* What is the real commitment by senior managers to the project? Where does the project fit on the scale ranging from "no interest" to "vital for the company's survival."
8. *Team assessment* Are members assessed by how well they represent their function as a sort of ambassador, or by how well they push the project ahead within their discipline and meet their responsibilities? Are project members and leaders only assessed by line managers or is there an additional assessment through the project system, i.e., by an appropriate manager of the matrix system?

Each project tends to develop its own style and rhythm after it has been operating for a period of time. This style is influenced by individuals on the team, the importance and nature of the drug being developed, and many other factors. There is often a striking difference between the project leader and line managers in how they view a particular project. Senior research and development managers must view the entire project portfolio and assign a priority and resources to each. Priorities may be given in an informal understanding or using a formal system. Many projects often receive a lower priority and fewer resources than the project group and project leader believe appropriate. This same discrepancy sometimes occurs at the corporate level, where the board of directors and/or chief executive officer may not view the project portfolio, or a selected project, with the same degree of enthusiasm or caution as senior research and development managers. If this occurs, the reasons should be evaluated.

Valuable opportunities for the company could be lost if corporate executives are not provided sufficient information and appropriate education to understand relevant scientific and clinical information. On the other hand, it is also important for senior research and development managers to fully understand the overall corporate perspective. These topics are discussed in more detail in *Guide to Planning and Managing Multiple Clinical Studies* (Spilker, 1987c).

Keys to Project Team Success

The project team is the central concept underlying the matrix system. The team depends on cooperation for success, as does the entire matrix concept. Without cooperation within the team and within the company, the matrix system tends to break down. One or two senior managers who place their own power base and personal considerations above the company's interests can severely damage or even destroy a matrix. This is especially true for a weak matrix.

Successful project teams have the appropriate people on them in terms of experience, skills, and authority. It is also desirable, although not essential, that members work within close physical proximity. The team's overall performance depends on several factors that relate to the team.

1. *Roles and relationships* Each person on a team should understand his or her role in having the project progress and achieve its goals. Their relationships with other project team members should be clear as well as their relationship with the department they represent.

2. *Goals* The goals of a project team should be clearly defined and communicated, both to its members and to others. It is usually preferable, although not mandatory, for the team to propose their goals and to request the endorsement of senior management.

Alternatively, goals may be established by more senior managers. Even in that situation, the team itself would establish many of the more detailed goals that would be required to achieve the major ones. For example, if the major criteria for the drug to achieve in a certain disease state are established by senior managers, the components of those criteria and the appropriate paths to reach those goals may be established by the project team.

3. *Processes* Processes refer to the mechanisms utilized to achieve a team's goals. They include the plans, schedules, and procedures that a team uses. Although the general approach may be dictated by a company, it is still possible for a team to utilize creativity and imagination in how they achieve their goals. A suitable motto for many teams would be "Whatever it takes", i.e., they will do whatever it takes to achieve their goals. This may involve putting in longer hours, working weekends, brainstorming to find a creative solution to a difficult problem, or reaching a compromise solution with the team working on the same project at a different company site.

4. *Relationship with the company* The team must operate in the context of the company's environment. To work effectively it must work in harmony and not at cross purposes with the company's structure, culture, and lines of authority and power.

Project Team Meetings

Team meetings are held periodically at some companies and on an ad hoc basis at others. The author favors the latter approach, although a minimum number of meetings may be required each year. A more pertinent issue is whether project meetings are held for the purpose of (1) information exchange, (2) problem solving, or (3) strategic planning. In the former approach, each relevant person usually presents a brief or full report of the project's status in his or her department. This is generally an inefficient use of people's time and there are other ways (e.g., reports) to fulfill this need. It is better to use people's time discussing and debating either problems or project strategies, plans, tactics, and goals. This latter approach helps to build consensus. Nonetheless, it is vital that the discussion is directed by the project leader and is not allowed to wander aimlessly. The project leader should usually establish alternatives and determine the pros and cons ahead of time. He or she may have already chosen the "best" approach and may have lobbied several members prior to the meeting.

Brief action items or points should be used as minutes, along with a list of who is responsible for each. These could be reviewed at the end of the meeting and then sent with copies of relevant overhead projections, or other material, as project minutes. It is well known that traditional project minutes are filed and rarely read or referred to by most project members.

ESTABLISHING A STRONG VERSUS WEAK MATRIX

The terms strong and weak refer to the relative importance and power of line managers and project managers. In a strong matrix the balance of power favors the project manager and in a weak matrix it favors the line manager.

Characteristics of a Strong Matrix

There is a continuum from strong to weak matrices. A strong matrix is usually characterized by (1) a formal dual reporting relationship, (2) authority of project leaders to control resources and make decisions on resource allocation, (3) assigning budgets to each project where the funds are controlled by individual project leaders, and (4) having project leaders reviewed by the head of the matrix system. Target dates are more meaningful to use as goals in a strong than in a weak matrix. A strong matrix requires more documentation of activities and more time spent on administrative matters. More emphasis is placed on costs and accountability for costs. People are also held accountable for slippage in time as well as cost overruns.

Advantages of a strong matrix are that it (1) gives a clear organization and direction to the project, (2) avoids ambiguity for project members, (3) allows for judging progress more clearly against a plan, and (4) minimizes the chance of people going off on tangents.

Characteristics of a Weak Matrix

A weak matrix is characterized by almost none of the above characteristics, except that an informal dual reporting relationship exists. The head of the matrix system has no real authority in a weak matrix. Relationships in a matrix between project leaders and (1) project members, (2) project coordinators, and (3) the head of the matrix are weak and almost totally controlled by line managers.

Advantages of a weak matrix are that it (1) is highly flexible, (2) avoids problems of dual reporting relationships, (3) works well if everyone cooperates, and (4) allows people to operate in their most effective manner and utilizes their internal drive.

Problems and Issues of a Weak Matrix

A major disadvantage of a weak matrix is that individual project leaders cannot easily obtain resources. In addition, they have little or no authority when they negotiate for additional resources with line managers. If a project leader also has a position of line authority this issue is less important. But, for those project leaders who do not have the "requisite" line authority it may become an even greater issue (see conflict-of-interest section below).

Another issue in a weak matrix is that project leaders feel less need to inform the head of the matrix system about their problems or to solicit help in addressing them. As a result, less information about problems may filter up through the organization. This may lead to various other problems because an important responsibility of a matrix group is to supply information, as well as to help a project move forward. It is easier for project leaders and project members to hide or suppress information if the matrix system is weak. This suppression is usually intended to be "temporary, of course," until the problem is resolved within their department, but the problem may become worse and a crisis situation occur. Thus, project leaders may take their project in an unapproved direction (purposely or inadvertently) and not inform relevant people.

One way of determining if a matrix is too weak for a company is to ask if senior managers are promptly informed about problems or if they are often surprised. Are senior managers informed about problems by line managers who hear the news directly from the project leader? Does the project leader also inform the head of the matrix system?

There are many possible approaches to consider in addressing the issue of a weak matrix. One is to have the central matrix group continually track the progress of all projects and periodically report on any significant delays or problems. Another possibility is for the project leader or project manager to periodically report any and all delays in the project's timetable plus any significant issues to senior managers.

Conflict-of-Interest Issues in a Matrix Organization

The matrix system has a number of inherent characteristics that sometimes lead to conflict-of-interest situations. One of those situations involves section heads who are also project leaders or managers. Conflicts of interest result from the desire of some managers to assign a disproportionate number of available personnel to their own project and fewer head count to other projects in their section. This bias exists when assignment of personnel would not be considered appropriate by an independent reviewer. This bias can generally be easily justified by the section head with numerous rationalizations. If a department head is also a project leader, the temptation to move his own project rapidly ahead at the expense of other projects will generally be strong. It may be difficult for senior managers to perceive how the biases of section or department heads have affected the allocation of resources among projects because of the many rationalizations and justifications that may be raised.

Another conflict-of-interest issue derives from the fact that a matrix gains its strength at the expense of line managers. There is an inverse relationship between the authority and power of line managers and matrix managers. This means that line managers must agree to give up some of their "turf" when a matrix system is either established or strengthened. This places an obvious conflict-of-interest issue out in the open. If line managers agree to strengthen the matrix system, it is clear that they will lose at least some of their power and influence. Thus, they usually present reasons why the matrix should remain unchanged or even be weakened. It takes an extraordinary line manger to recommend strengthening the matrix system. This person is usually one who places the company's interests above his or her own territoriality. Usually that individual is a secure, self-confident person whose main motive is not personal "empire-building," but rather productive corporate building.

Having Little Turf or Line Authority May Be a Source of Strength

Managers in an organization are almost invariably concerned about retaining and expanding their power. Because many people believe that a good defense is a strong offense, there is usually a great deal of maneuvering, posturing, and infighting within any large company in an attempt to secure one's power base and to gain additional power. In a weak matrix system there is little power along the horizontal axis so that matrix managers do not have to be as concerned as line managers about protecting their turf. These managers may therefore spend more of their energies identifying problems and also finding solutions to them.

14 / *Choosing the Number of Drugs to Develop Simultaneously*

We thought that if we didn't grab the business, someone else would, and that we would never have this kind of opportunity again. We always thought of an order lost as a disaster. So we decided to push the company as rapidly as the market would permit. Thomas J. Watson, Jr. Former chief executive of IBM. From *Fortune* (August 31, 1987).

IDENTIFYING TYPES AND NUMBERS OF PROJECTS TO DEVELOP

Introduction

The major reason to consider this topic is that drug companies want to improve their ability to discover and develop drugs that will keep the company viable. Every company experiences fruitful periods where increased numbers of new products are introduced and dry periods when fewer new products are developed and marketed. If a critical number of viable projects are able to be kept in the drug development pipeline (i.e., in basic research, preclinical development, and clinical systems), it will help increase the number of fruitful years and minimize the number of dry years. Another method to achieve this goal in addition to in-house drug discovery is through licensing-in worthwhile drugs that meet the company's needs.

The number of drugs or projects a company undertakes at any one time depends on many factors that must be periodically reassessed. The number of projects that a specific department within a company may undertake simultaneously must also be periodically reassessed. Nonetheless, each department must balance its capabilities (e.g., number of staff, amount of budget, equipment, and facilities) with current and future requirements of actual and potential projects. This balance may usually be assessed and controlled more precisely in a single department than in the entire company. This situation is somewhat analogous to the budgets of the United States and the individual states. Almost all states (analogous to individual departments) must have a balanced budget each year and therefore know which activities are possible to carry out. On the other hand, the federal government (analogous to the company) has the ability to borrow money and go into debt to take on activities that are of interest to them. So too, an entire company may borrow money to carry out affairs of interest, whereas individual departments are limited by their budget and usually have a fixed amount of resources to apportion.

Research Projects and Full-Scale Development Projects

The appropriate number of projects to keep in the pipeline depends on whether preclinical research projects or full-scale clinical development projects are being discussed. The number of preclinical drug discovery projects may be further broken down into active projects involving exploratory nonfocused studies in broad therapeutic areas and research projects on highly targeted diseases. Research projects may or may not be required to have a chemical lead before they qualify as an official research project.

Once a commitment is made to take a compound to humans for clinical testing, it may be considered as a full-scale development project. Some companies divide this group of full-scale development projects into two categories, those which will be taken to market (if possible) and those which will only be evaluated in humans to address a specific question.

Should the Focus of This Acitivity be on Drugs, Indications, or Other Factors?

Although projects on individual drugs are described as the lowest common denominator between drug companies, each project may also be described in terms of the drug's individual indications, dosage forms, routes of administration, and dosing regimens being studied. An equal or greater amount of work may be expended on studying a minor route of administration for one drug as the entire effort spent on another drug project. Also, a single indication of a major project may require far more resources than all the indications of several other projects. Although the rest of this chapter discusses projects, it is necessary and important to also consider and evaluate within each project the resources allocated for each indication, dosage form, and route of administration currently under study or planned.

APPROACHES TO DETERMINING THE NUMBER OF DRUGS TO DEVELOP SIMULTANEOUSLY

There are two totally different ways to approach this question. The first is to evaluate previous company experience and then to add in new factors that are relevant, and also to consider future goals. The additional factors include (1) consideration of projected growth or diminution of staff and other resources, (2) knowledge of activities that are competing for resources within the company, (3) outside competition, and (4) future medical need for the drugs being developed.

The second method is to develop a theoretical mathematical model. This method requires the developer to make a number of assumptions, and is described below in more detail.

Developing a Mathematical Model to Predict the Appropriate Number of Projects to Develop

One approach to determining the number of drugs to develop simultaneously involves a theoretical approach. This is perhaps best accomplished through mathematical modeling. Mathematical modeling of the appropriate number of projects for a company to develop requires consideration of the company's goal (e.g., a new drug generating 20 million dollars or more is desired every five years). Estimates may also be required of any number of additional parameters that the company wishes to identify and control. These parameters include (1) the rate at which projects will be successful, (2) the average number of projects to be initiated each year, (3) average length of time and costs (resources) required to achieve a successful project, (4) the length of time required to terminate an unsuccessful project, and (5) the total costs to be spent on unsuccessful projects. Instead of using a single estimated average for any of these parameters, it is possible to use two or more different averages, or a range of values (assuming a normal distribution). These estimates should be derived from past company experience, present trends, and future goals. When the past, present, and future estimates for a parameter differ greatly it would be desirable to derive the model using each set of values, or to use the two extreme values.

When this type of mathematical simulation is run, wide fluctuations are observed in most of the outputs. Because of uncertainties of assumptions used in the model and variations in numbers used, the appropriate number of projects to develop simultaneously turns out to be a relatively wide range.

Keeping the Pipeline Full

Any company's portfolio of investigational drugs may be improved in quality by adding better projects in terms of medical and commercial value. An issue discussed later is when should less attractive projects be trimmed from the portfolio. An important issue for a research and development-based company is to determine how many clinical development projects and how many research projects with chemical leads are required to keep the drug development pipeline full. No one can answer this question with certainty at any one company, because many factors determine whether compounds and drugs will be successful. Moreover, only some of these factors are able to be controlled. One means of attempting to keep the pipeline full is to determine mathematically the steady-state number of projects necessary to achieve one's goals, as previously described. It is then the responsibility of senior managers to insure that this number of projects is present. A more practical means is to evaluate the contents of the company's portfolio to determine whether the pipeline is full. This may be done by investigating the activities of all departments involved in drug discovery, development, and sales.

Many managers believe that each component part of research and development should be operating at or near maximal capacity in a highly efficient and productive manner. By keeping the overall research and development system (as well as individual departments) taxed beyond their capacity to handle the current work load, it will be more likely that the system is being used efficiently. The drawback to this approach is that it insures that every department is busily working, but does not insure that they are working on the most important projects, on the most important activities within those projects, or in an efficient manner.

Allocating Many Resources to Few Drugs Versus Allocating Few Resources to Many Drugs

There has been a controversy for many years within the pharmaceutical industry about how to proceed most rapidly toward a New Drug Application (NDA). Some people advocate concentrating all of a company's available resources on a few projects, hoping to expedite their progress. Other people advocate distributing available resources among several or many projects and therefore trying to move a greater number of potential drugs toward the market, and increase the chances of commercial success.

The specific path chosen by each particular company has depended on several factors, including the following:

1. The philosophy of the individual(s) in charge. The views of that person or persons usually affect the entire research and development organization more than any other factor.
2. The historical experience and culture of the particular organization.
3. The quality of the specific projects that are available at a given moment within the company.

Specific methods used to allocate resources are discussed in Chapter 11.

TO TRIM OR TO ADD—IS THAT THE QUESTION?

Project Costs

The most expensive projects are those that (1) are nearing NDA submission (i.e., are in Phase III of development), (2) have had their NDA submitted, or (3) have had their NDA approved and new indications or dosage forms are being studied. Most major new drugs that successfully reach the market continue to require large sums of money to support research and development activities for several additional years. As a result, the most expensive projects are usually the most promising and advanced ones. The converse is also true, in that the youngest projects are usually the cheapest ones. Expensive lifetime toxicology studies and expensive Phase III clinical studies are almost always begun after the drug's activity has been clearly demonstrated.

Are Chances of Commercial Success Increased by Trimming or Adding Projects?

No one has ever devised a satisfactory formula to predict which investigational projects will be commercially successful. Thus, it must be concluded that no minor project can ever be dropped from a company's portfolio with full assurance that it might not someday have become a "major" corporate asset. Cutting the number of projects to a select few will primarily affect projects in the early phases of development that will not cost significant sums of money, except in future years, should those projects prove promising and merit further development.

No drug can ever be totally written off as always remaining a minor player, having no chance to grow in medical importance, or to become highly profitable. Some drugs launched with little fanfare or for orphan indications have later been found to possess significant activity in diseases with large markets and have made significant contributions toward corporate wealth. It must, however, be said that this course of events is uncommon.

Focusing Activities on an Appropriate Number of Projects

At some point a company may have too many projects in its portfolio. This situation can threaten efficient drug development if scientists do not concentrate enough of their energies on an appropriate number of the most promising projects. These individuals may work randomly on different drugs, or try and push too many research and development projects ahead simultaneously. Perhaps the most extreme situation would occur if there were so many projects that there was only a single clinical study being conducted on most projects at any one time and no studies on others. Although this is an unlikely scenario, there are many enthusiastic scientists and clinicians at most companies who eagerly seek and/or accept all new challenges for developing new indications, new dosage forms, and new drugs. These enthusiasts sometimes lose their ability to focus attention on accomplishing critical project activities and sticking to their commitments. This is a real problem, regardless of the underlying psychological reason why they jump from project to project, or from indication to indication within a project, or from study to study within an indication. These people are always looking for new challenges to take up, rather than finishing tasks they have started.

The opposite extreme is also counterproductive. This is exemplified by individuals who tenaciously adhere to a previously accepted development plan when everyone else is convinced about the need to move on to a new study, new indication, or new project.

SPECIAL CASES

How Many Orphan Drugs Can a Company Afford to Develop?

Numerous answers have been given to this question that vary from specific responses (e.g., none, one, three) to functional replies (e.g., only those with commercial potential, only those with medical potential, only those with commercial and medical potential). The correct response primarily depends on the company's financial condition. Companies in a financial crisis can ill afford any funds going toward nonprofitable ventures. The traditions of the company and outlook of the most senior executives will clearly influence a company's perception of this issue.

The most important characteristic of orphan drugs from a drug development perspective is that they are a heterogeneous and not homogeneous group of drugs. Their widely differing characteristics and potential for profit have been described as well as their pros and cons from an industry perspective (Spilker, 1985, 1986a).

Sexy Drugs With Pedestrian Effects

Everyone at a drug company gets excited when a novel drug is discovered and is found to be active in treating a disease that had previously been either untreatable or inadequately treated. If the drug has a totally new chemical structure and mechanism of action, then the excitement it generates is much greater, both within the company and medical community.

Situations also arise when a drug has an exciting new chemical structure and mechanism of action, but the clinical usefulness does not offer any significant advantages over currently available therapy. Drugs of this nature may be characterized as sexy drugs with pedestrian effects. They usually have little chance of being incorporated into most physicians' armamentarium. Some companies may still choose to develop this type of drug and to promote it heavily. These companies largely predicate their decision on the appeal that the novel chemical structure and mechanism of action will have for some physicians. This decision may represent wishful thinking by company executives and must be carefully evaluated. Marketing research can be asked to assess how well the drug will eventually do in the real world of clinical medicine.

AN APPROPRIATE ANSWER TO THE QUESTION POSED BY THE CHAPTER'S TITLE

Reasons Why It Is Better to Place Many Projects in a Portfolio

There is no doubt that if a company only had a few projects with positive potential, then it would of necessity concentrate its efforts on a small number of projects. It is clearly a moot point to discuss the number of projects that should be in a portfolio when a company has little choice because of limited research results and limited licensing opportunities. Nonetheless, in an era where it is recognized that an average drug requires 8 to 12 years to reach the market, a policy that places all efforts in a concentrated way on a few "big players" is generally imprudent. That approach would be virtually a guarantee for insuring long dry spells of new drugs in the future. Moreover, the long and complex path a drug follows to reach the market makes it unlikely that several projects in different stages of development will compete for the same resources. Concentrating corporate resources on the few potentially best compounds and drugs increases the corporation's risk if those drugs should fail. Including more projects in the company's portfolio is generally viewed as a more prudent and conservative approach.

Do Increased Resources Always Speed a Drug's Development?

An important consideration in deciding whether or not to place more funds and resources in certain projects relates to whether the increased funds would significantly increase the rate at which the drug could progress toward an NDA. There is no doubt that for some projects a large increase in personnel and money would have a significant effect on the rate at which the project would proceed. This is especially true if the work can be contracted to outside groups for assistance, or if the additional staff could be dedicated to a rate-limiting step, such as writing final medical reports.

Developing a drug is primarily a sequential activity, and there are only a limited number of things that can be done during Phases I and II to increase the speed of most drug development activities. One important step is to assure that the quality of all work performed meets acceptable standards. Another is to have a clear clinical path established that does not meander or deal with less relevant issues. In a typical Phase I drug evaluation, a single-dose study is followed by a multiple-dose study where volunteers receive doses for a specified time up to approximately one month. In Phase II, pilot efficacy studies are conducted double blind and then a major well-controlled efficacy study is conducted. If the personnel and other resources put on a project prior to Phase III are excessive, it may mean that (1) a variety of ancillary studies are conducted that are not required for an NDA submission, (2) other therapeutic indications are pursued, often too early in a drug's life for maximal efficiency and benefit, and/or (3) some studies (e.g., metabolism, toxicology) are being done earlier than necessary in a project's life, and may not speed the overall process. In addition, Phase III-type studies may be initiated before Phase II studies have clearly demonstrated drug activity. If the drug is later found to be toxic, insufficiently active, or is terminated for another reason, then many studies and efforts will have been "wasted." Of course, if the drug turns out to be active, then some time will have been saved. The trick is clearly knowing (i.e., guessing) at an early stage of development which drugs will reach the market and determining which steps will result in saving the most time.

A whole web of inefficiencies and unnecessary problems often develop in a project that has too many activities going on simultaneously. A sound approach has always been to emphasize, insofar as possible, an efficient, streamlined approach toward the company's goals, applying resources where they have the greatest benefit. Ironically, additional resources would often have most value or effect if put on those projects that are being slowed due to a low priority and are the most likely candidates to be trimmed from an overfilled portfolio.

15 / *Evaluating a Portfolio of New Drug Projects*

Trying to assess basic research by its practicality is like trying to judge Mozart by how much money the Salzberg Festival brings in each year. Konrad Lorenz, Austrian naturalist.

OBJECTIVES AND PERSPECTIVES OF A PORTFOLIO ANALYSIS

What Does Portfolio Analysis Mean?

The term portfolio analysis is used to describe an examination of a group of compounds and/or drugs using medical, scientific, commercial, financial, and/or other parameters. Drugs that are evaluated may be (1) investigational, (2) marketed, (3) a combination, or (4) may focus on any subset of those groups (e.g., the 10 most important projects in terms of commercial value or effort). The analysis of any parameter may vary from a subjective appraisal to a precise quantitative evaluation using standard financial or other methods.

A portfolio analysis may be conducted as a special one-time exercise or as part of an annual or other periodic review. If the analysis is conducted as a special one-time exercise there is a greater likelihood that it will be performed (in whole or in part) by outside consultants rather than by internal company staff.

The analysis may be limited to assessing medical and commercial values, or it may include other aspects as well. Although there is substantial information to be obtained from analyzing the previous year or half-year, the most important information usually comes from comparing results with those obtained on several past occasions. This allows trends to be identified and may raise issues that should be addressed. An analysis will have value if (1) the information used is valid, (2) the information used is current, (3) appropriate methods are used to conduct the analysis, and (4) a sufficient effort is expended on the exercise.

What are the Purposes of a Portfolio Analysis?

The purpose(s) of the portfolio analysis must be defined in advance of the exercise. A portfolio analysis may be used to provide characteristics of the therapeutic areas and even the businesses the company is in. A company may thus evaluate whether the therapeutic areas being researched and targeted with new projects match those that they wish to pursue. The analysis may also be used to demonstrate whether the company is actively engaged in businesses that provide long-term growth opportunities. Another purpose may be to identify potential gaps in the portfolio over various periods of time when new products are not expected.

A portfolio analysis may also be used to decide which projects should be retained and which should be pruned. If the analysis is not limited to looking at each project as an overall entity, but examines each of the indications, dosage forms, and routes of administration separately, then it is possible to evaluate which of those aspects should be retained and which should be pruned. Projects may be pruned or temporarily allotted minimal resources to reallocate finite resources to higher priority projects.

Pruning projects from a portfolio does not necessarily mean that the projects clipped are to be terminated. Another possibility is that pruned projects may be licensed-out or used as trading material (*quid pro quo*) for cross-licensing with another company. If drug discovery becomes less fruitful for a company, it will have a much stronger motivation to increase licensing-out of its pruned projects or even pruned dosage forms. An intermediate step is to diminish resources allocated to a project so that it barely remains alive or progresses at a minimal pace.

Lowest Common Denominator

The principle focus of thinking about a portfolio is in terms of the individual project. It is, nonetheless, insufficient to focus solely on projects as the lowest common denominator in analyzing a portfolio. Each indication, dosage form, route of administration, and dosing regimen studied should be evaluated independently in terms of its medical and commercial importance. Resources applied to their development should be appropriate, both in terms of quantity and also in terms of timing. For example, it may be appropriate to ask if development of some indications of a drug should be delayed. Each of several indications pursued in a large project may utilize the same quantity of resources allocated to the sum of five (or even more) small projects. Only through a thorough analysis of a project's individual parts can the value of the overall project be adequately ascertained.

When discussing secondary indications of a drug, it is relevant to consider whether they are spin-offs and closely related to the primary indication or whether they are in different therapeutic areas. An indication that was originally secondary in importance may become the primary one for a drug in medical and/or commercial terms. As the number of indications being evaluated increases, it is essential to determine whether a fixed quantity of resources is being divided into smaller pieces or whether there is an incremental growth in resources. The answer to this question should have a significant impact on the strategy developed for each project.

Portfolio Gaps

Numerous types of gaps may exist in a portfolio. For these to be adequately addressed they must first be identified by type (see below). Each of these gaps is based on the company not achieving its goals. Goals must be identified prior to determining that a gap is actually present or is projected to occur sometime in the future.

1. *Gaps in research activities* Inadequate drug discovery activities are being conducted in therapeutic areas of importance to the company. Alternatively, research may be ongoing in areas of interest, but research goals may not be met.
2. *Gaps in discovering novel compounds of importance* An inadequate number of important chemical leads have emerged from research that have entered the drug development system (i.e., project system). The company is not meeting its drug discovery goals.
3. *Gaps in developing compounds of importance* Inadequate or no projects are active in the drug development pipeline in certain therapeutic areas. Alternatively, no projects are active in specific phases of development, or other drug development goals (e.g., number of projects in the system) are not being met.
4. *Gaps in submitting New Drug Applications* Research and development is not meeting its goals of submitting X number of NDAs per year of new chemical entities (NCEs) and Y number of supplemental NDAs for line-extensions.

5. *Gaps in financial forecasts* Products to be marketed plus current products are not expected to meet the company's financial goals.

6. *Gaps in licensing activities* Goals set for licensing activities to fill any of the above noted gaps are not being met.

7. *Gaps in marketed drugs* Various types of gaps may exist in specific therapeutic or disease areas.

Portfolio gaps resulting from lack of new products could also be viewed in terms of potential financial shortfalls over a specific number of future years. If short-term gaps are identified (i.e., within a four- or five-year period) an attempt may be made to fill them through (1) acquisition of new products, (2) acquisition of another company, (3) corporate merger, (4) licensing-in of marketed and/or investigational drugs, or (5) rapid development of line-extensions. Long-term gaps (i.e., greater than an eight- to ten-year period) could be addressed through changes in basic research, proactive licensing, joint ventures, or acquisition of other companies.

Perspectives of Various Groups Conducting a Portfolio Analysis

The group conducting a portfolio evaluation may be based in research, marketing, finance, or another section of a company. Their approach, methodologies, and orientation will undoubtedly be affected by their training and the purposes of the review. Any of these groups could conduct the entire portfolio exercise without soliciting help from other groups. This means that the medical value may be assessed by marketing personnel and the financial value by research personnel. But, this approach would generally yield data that would be less believable to most reviewers and corporate officers than if the analyses are conducted by those who are most expert in that field. If asking help from other groups creates a problem (e.g., too much time required), then a nonpartisan person or group may be chosen to conduct and direct the entire exercise. This may require the services of an outside consultant who has the requisite capability and credibility. Another alternative is to have internal staff generate the report, and to have either staff at a separate company site or a consulting group audit and review the results.

An important part of the perspective used in approaching portfolio analysis includes consideration of (1) which drug businesses (e.g., prescription, over-the-counter drugs (OTC), generics, biotechnology) will be considered (2) the scope of projects, drugs and/or research compounds to be considered, (3) which geographical area is being considered (e.g., single country, single development site, single company, worldwide operations), and (4) who is making the decisions at each level. Separate portfolio analyses could be conducted on marketed drugs, investigational drugs, and research compounds. Other types of portfolios are described in the next section.

Reviewing a Multinational Company's Overall Portfolio and Those of Individual Sites

Multinational drug companies often conduct research and develop drugs in two or more countries simultaneously. Each of the major sites for these activities may have relative autonomy and independence, although their efforts are coordinated to some degree with the other sites. In this situation, the portfolio of one country's projects will undoubtedly overlap with that of other sites. In addition to the portfolios of the individual sites, the portfolio of the company as a whole should be analyzed. Comparisons may be made between these site-specific portfolios as well as comparing portfolios with industry averages. Managing directors within each country where a company's drugs are sold may also conduct portfolio analyses.

Even if portfolios of two separate sites developing drugs for the same company contained the exact same projects, the commercial value of each portfolio could be completely different. Imagine that one site was developing drugs for the American market and the other site was developing the same drugs for the rest of the world. The commercial value of drugs being developed to treat tropical diseases would clearly differ between the two sites. The value of drugs for many other diseases would also differ markedly between sites because of other factors. These factors include (1) the status of existing and projected competition, (2) the way that medicine is practiced in different countries (e.g., whether certain types of drugs are or are not commonly used), (3) the size of the drug market(s), (4) the ability of each site to sell the drug, and (5) numerous other factors.

DEVELOPING A PORTFOLIO

Determining an Ideal Portfolio

There may be occasions in reviewing the company portfolio, evaluating the portfolio of another company, or planning in which direction to develop a company's portfolio when it is important to consider what the ideal drug portfolio would look like.

The ideal portfolio for one drug company would differ from that of another company depending on the businesses they are in, their mission, and traditions. Although some characteristics would be identical (e.g., the importance of long patent life of investigational drugs), most will vary to a small or large degree from company to company. A portfolio of prescription drugs under development may be viewed as consisting of three separate types of investigational drugs: (1) innovative drugs, (2) "me-toos" (NCEs), and (3) line-extensions. The ideal portfolio, according to the director of research, may differ from that defined by the director of marketing or the director of production. There is therefore no single concept of an ideal portfolio, except possibly in the most general terms.

Determining a Realistic Portfolio

Factors that must be considered in choosing new compounds or drugs to include in a portfolio are:

1. *Patent life remaining at the time of a drug's launch* This estimated period

should be adequate to recoup development costs and to make a profit. Exceptions may be included if agreed to by relevant managers.

2. *Regulations* Regulations that must be followed to have drugs developed and approved must be attainable.

3. *Time to develop and market drugs* This time should be near the lower end of the average range, insofar as possible. Drugs vary greatly in this regard, so that a more reasonable goal might be to have a mix of short-, mid-, and long-term projects.

4. *Costs to develop and market drugs* Projected costs should be reasonable, unless the anticipated return on investment justifies larger development costs. Spending huge sums to develop an orphan drug is rarely realistic.

5. *Social attitudes about drugs* These should be positive or neutral. If problems are anticipated then an educational campaign or another approach should be considered. If this is not feasible or would not be cost-effective, then the drug's development plan should be reassessed.

6. *Clinical feasibility* Drugs should be possible to study in terms of patient availability and clinical parameters to measure. It may be possible or even necessary to utilize new efficacy parameters to evaluate a drug. But, the credibility of such parameters to the Food and Drug Administration (FDA) and prescribing physicians must be assessed.

7. *Medical value* This should be high, although it can not be accurately established for most investigational drugs until after a number of patients have been studied.

8. *Commercial value* The portfolio's overall value should be appropriate from the perspective of meeting the company's financial goals. Financial goals should allow room for a limited number of less commercially attractive drugs to be included in the portfolio when they contribute high medical value and have a high likelihood of being marketed.

9. *Probability of achieving marketing* This should be high for most drugs in the portfolio. Longshots from a medical efficacy or safety perspective should generally have high commercial value if a decision is made to develop the drug.

10. *Legal considerations* There should not be significant legal issues (e.g., probability of product liability suits) or social issues (e.g., potential for drug abuse) for most, if not all, drugs in the portfolio. Oral contraceptives are a group of drugs where numerous social issues have been raised (e.g., use in underdeveloped countries, religious sanctions), as well as a major issue on the changed benefit to risk ratio over the last 25 years.

11. *Competitive value* Two aspects of competitive value should be considered. *First*, drugs in the portfolio should offer a real advantage over existing drug therapy. This advantage may be in terms of an improved benefit to risk ratio or another advantage such as improved absorption, quality of life, convenience, compliance, or acceptability to patients. If the drug will compete with one of the company's own products, competition may enhance sales or lead to severe cannibalization of the marketed drug's sales. *Second*, the number of competitors present in the therapeutic areas where drugs are being developed should be determined and their potential impact assessed. Assessments should be in terms of expected time to market, as well as important advantages and disadvantages of competitor's drugs in comparison with the company's drug.

ANALYZING THE VALUE OF A PORTFOLIO

Comparison of Scientific Versus Medical Value

There is an overlap between parameters used to assess scientific and medical value of a portfolio. Medical value refers to the actual need for the new drug in medical practice and includes consideration of direct benefits it will provide to patients and indirect benefits it will provide to health care providers. Scientific value relates to the interest in a new drug from an academic and research perspective. This includes consideration of the drug's scientific novelty and mechanism of action. Drugs with high scientific and low medical value are described in Chapter 14 as "sexy drugs." Few new drugs have high medical and low scientific interest, because the mechanism of how an important new drug works would usually be of great interest to academic scientists. Nonetheless, one possible example of a drug that has high medical and low scientific value was the discovery that mannitol was an important new treatment for brain edema by producing an osmotic diuresis. The mechanism of this effect was believed to be known, and there was relatively little scientific interest generated by this important medical discovery. "Me-too" drugs are in a different category, because they have little scientific and little medical value but may achieve significant commercial success.

Judging the Scientific Value of a New Drug

Scientific value of individual drugs may best be gauged on a relative scale from low to high. Determining where a drug fits on this scale is usually straightforward and noncontroversial. As a drug's medical value changes, there is often, but not always, a concomitant change in its scientific value. Scientific value is based to a large degree on the scientific novelty of a drug's mechanism of action and chemical novelty of its structure. Drugs that are unique in how they act have a high scientific value, but unless they have desirable clinical properties their medical value may be low. A drug that is found to be toxic and is withdrawn from the market (i.e., loses its medical value) may retain its scientific value and interest if it is the only known drug to stimulate or inhibit a receptor of interest.

Drugs with high scientific value may be marketed in part on that basis. Marketing claims may state that drug X is the first of a new type of drug to treat disease D, or that drug X is the only commercially available drug to inhibit the Y receptor, or that drug X is the first drug to stimulate enzyme Z. Whether the latter two claims are accompanied by desirable clinical effects or remain merely pharmacological activities must be assessed by physicians who read these or related claims.

Rating the Medical Value of a New Drug

Medical value in terms of benefit to patients and the practice of medicine may be most easily described for each project in the portfolio according to one or more simple scales. Examples of such scales include the following.

1. The drug has high, moderate, or low medical value (based on a subjective assessment, questionnaire, or other method). This assessment is made with a three-point scale.
2. The drug has extremely high, high, moderate, adequate, little, or no medical value. This is a six-point scale.
3. Benefits of the drug are expected to reach: Over ten million patients/year, over a million patients/year, over ten thousand patients/year, or another number of patients/year. These numbers may be estimated by marketing groups using input from research and development about the drug's characteristics.
4. The drug is viewed as providing life-saving therapy, relief of a debilitating disease, high or moderate relief of a chronic disease, or high or moderate relief of an acute disease.
5. Percent of all patients with the target disease who are expected to use the drug: 75 to 100 percent, 50 to 75 percent, 25 to 50 percent, or 0 to 25 percent.
6. Overall medical benefits of the drug may be rated by a group using an arbitrary scale of 1 to 100.
7. Ability of the drug to displace current therapy for a disease.
8. The likelihood of physicians prescribing the drug for their patients.

Almost all of these scales assess a drug's medical value relative to existing drug and nondrug therapy. Only scale number four can be rated independently of existing therapy.

Another method of determining medical value of a drug is to compare the therapeutic ratio of a drug with those of existing drugs. The therapeutic ratio equals the dose that causes adverse reactions divided by the dose that causes a beneficial effect. The larger the number, the safer is the drug. This approach would only be practical for drugs that have completed Phase II. Prior to that point it would be impossible to assess a drug's therapeutic ratio. The therapeutic ratio of some drugs entering Phase III studies is still difficult (or impossible) to determine accurately.

What is Therapeutic Utility of a New Drug?

The therapeutic utility of a new drug depends on the perspective of the group that is asking the question.

1. *To a drug company* How do perceived medical benefits compare with perceived commercial benefits? Do benefits sufficiently outweigh risks so that the drug will be able to be marketed?
2. *To a regulatory agency* Can benefits of a new drug be demonstrated in an adequate population of patients? Benefits and risks are considered on a level of the entire society, i.e., for all patients who may use the drug.
3. *To a physician* How will the physician's ability to treat patients be affected? The answer is usually phrased in general terms.
4. *To an individual patient* Will the treatment diminish the intensity of symptoms, improve chances for a longer life, and/or provide a better quality of life than was available with prior therapy? Risks and benefits are considered strictly for the single patient affected. Direct effects of a drug on a patient may lead to indirect effects on others (e.g., family, friends, business associates).

Evaluating the Commercial Value of a New Drug

There is no doubt that commercial value is usually the most important parameter at drug companies for judging individual projects, as well as the overall portfolio. The commercial value of a particular investigational drug project (or the overall portfolio) may be expressed in many ways but is always based to some degree on numerous unknown factors. It may be expressed as a forecast of:

1. Third (or other) year sales of the drug after it is marketed.
2. Total sales for first three (or other) years on the market discounted to its present value.
3. Estimated range of sales for third (or other) year sales.
4. Net profit after taxes for the first five (or other) years on the market.
5. Number of years to pay off the research and development costs from the stream of net earnings after taxes.
6. Third (or other) year sales times the probability of success. This is a risk-adjusted forecast.

The above forecast may be based on the drug's achieving an optimistic profile, expected profile, or minimally acceptable profile. Alternatively, multiple forecasts may be given for each drug.

It is essential that all project forecasts in a portfolio be made using the same approach for all projects. This can usually be best accomplished by a single person or group that evaluates all projects. Any of the above forecasts may be compared with opportunity costs of using the money invested in research and development in other ways.

New product forecasting is an inexact science that is subject to many changes in the market as well as changes in a drug's profile. Most of these changes cannot be accurately defined or predicted early in an investigational drug's development. In some situations, the number of patients to be treated after the drug is marketed is extremely difficult to estimate and any forecast may be highly inaccurate. This situation may occur when a new drug is to be used for an as yet untreatable disease. Each year that most drugs are on the market it generally becomes easier to forecast their sales with greater accuracy.

There is usually pressure for marketing groups to provide a forecast early in a project's life. Providing a range of numbers based on a drug's attaining either the ideal or minimally acceptable profile is desirable. This range allows others to determine whether the minimally acceptable profile would affect the expected sales (based on the projected profile) by up to 10 percent or by 10-fold. A range also allows others to understand the degree of variability and confidence placed in the numbers provided by those who developed them. If marketing reports estimate third year sales of 40 million dollars for the *expected* drug profile, it is uncertain whether their calculations are ± 10 percent or ± 100 percent. Even if a range is provided as a forecast using the expected drug profile, it is uncertain how the minimally acceptable drug profile would affect the forecast. Marketing forecasters must be cautious about clinicians who provide them with overly positive attributes about the drug and glorify the compound's profile.

ANALYZING A PROJECT PORTFOLIO IN FIVE STEPS

Steps To Follow

The first step in evaluating a portfolio of investigational and/or marketed drugs is to determine which projects should be considered as part of the portfolio. The second step in evaluating a portfolio is to evaluate each project in terms of its individual characteristics. The third step is to evaluate the overall balance and composition of the portfolio using the methods desired. The fourth step is to interpret the results. This interpretation is based on changes, trends, progress toward goals, and various comparisons. The last step is to use the results to modify the company, or business area.

Projects to Include in a Portfolio (Step One)

Categories of the portfolio include (1) marketed drugs, (2) investigational drugs, (3) drugs that are both marketed and investigational, (4) investigational drugs that have past their go-no go decision point and are definitely going to be developed, and (5) research compounds. Other categories could also be defined.

The current phase of development or status may be illustrated for each project in the portfolio in several ways. A common method is to use a horizontal bar for each project listed along the left margin (ordinate) to show whether it is currently pre-Investigational New Drug Application (IND), or in Phase I, Phase II, Phase III (pre-NDA submission), Phase III (post-NDA submission), or is marketed. Another method is to have years along the ordinate (X axis) and to show dates of regulatory submission and approval for each project. Many alternative categorizations may be used depending on the makeup of the drugs in the portfolio.

The total number of projects or drugs in the portfolio can be easily illustrated on a year by year basis with a line graph or histogram. This type of graph may also show the number of projects terminated per year. The number of projects initiated may be (1) expressed as a number per year, (2) compared with a standard goal, or (3) described on a moving multiyear average (Fig. 15.1).

Parameters to Measure Individual Projects in a Portfolio (Step Two)

Some of the methods that may be applied to the measurement of individual projects are described below.

1. *Probability of submitting an NDA, Product License Application (PLA), or other regulatory submission* Minimal criteria for which a regulatory application will be submitted should be established for each drug. Based on these criteria, a probability may then be established for submitting each project in the portfolio. This probability provides a useful single means for estimating the likelihood of marketing each drug. The major disadvantage of this measure is that with few exceptions, it is directly related to a drug's phase of development, i.e., drugs in Phase I usually have a low probability of being marketed, those in Phase II have a higher probability, and those in Phase III have the highest probability. Probability may be assessed as quartiles

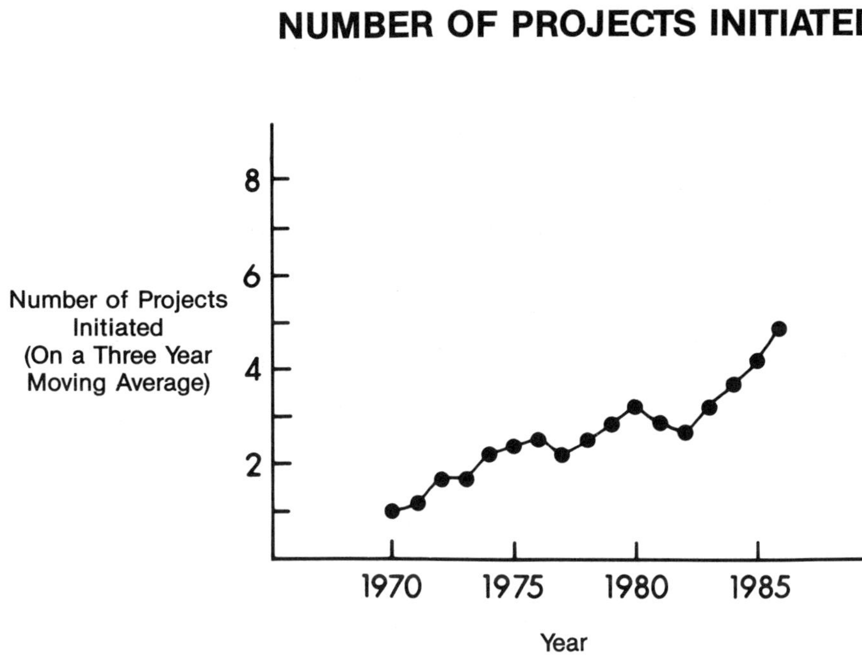

Fig. 15.1. Number of new projects initiated per year. This graph could be a histogram, or could only illustrate the actual number per year instead of a moving average. The term "three year moving average" means that the value(s) of the year in question plus those of the previous two years are averaged.

(i.e., 0 to 25 percent, 25 to 50 percent, 50 to 75 percent, 75 to 100 percent), deciles (i.e., in tenths), or even on a scale from 1 to 100. The 100-point scale is clearly too detailed because small differences would not be meaningful. If a drug's profile becomes tarnished, it is worthwhile establishing at what point a regulatory submission would not be submitted.

2. *Probability of achieving clinical goals* This probability is assessed in terms of safety, efficacy, and other important targets (e.g., pharmacokinetics, quality of life). This point and that listed under point three below are subsets of point one and may be expressed numerically in any of the ways discussed under point one.

3. *Probability of achieving technical goals* This probability relates to issues of formulation, chemical scaleup, stability on storage, and numerous other considerations mentioned in Chapter 20. Goals are usually expressed as the minimally acceptable standards that allow continuation of a drug project.

4. *Number of staff* Is the number of staff working on each project sufficient? This question may be assessed in purely subjective or objective terms. An objective assessment is shown in Fig. 15.2, where a balance is sought between staff allocated and potential value of the drug. Several other scales that could be used are also indicated in Fig. 15.2, such as percent of total staff or percent of anticipated sales to come from current investigational drugs. The percent of staff could refer to all development staff, total staff working on projects, senior staff, medical staff, or any other defined group. Cumulative scientist or clinician years of effort expended could

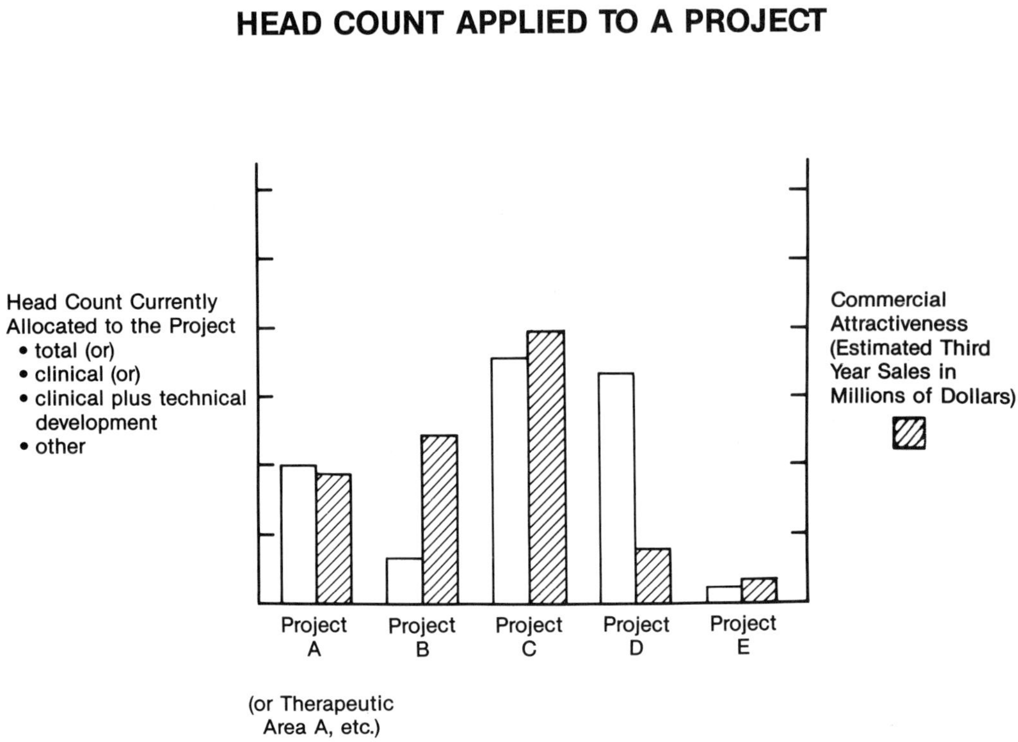

Fig. 15.2. Head count currently applied to a project and its commercial attractiveness. This type of graph could also be used to illustrate specific therapeutic areas.

be plotted for each project, for high versus low priority projects, or for projected versus actual values.

Another aspect of staffing could be graphed as the number of people needed per project versus number available per project. The best means of graphing this comparison might be as two vertical bar histograms per project plotted alongside each other. This approach would enable a rapid comparison to be made for each project.

5. *Market attractiveness (i.e., value) of the project* Each project should be commercially attractive to the company, or else there should be some other compelling reason to develop the drug (e.g., an orphan drug may enhance the company's prestige and also enable patients to be helped who previously had no effective treatment). Various scales may be used to measure market value. These include (1) third (or another) year's sales forecast, (2) total of first three years forecasted sales discounted to present value, or (3) broad ranges of third year sales. An example of the ranges could be (a) up to 5 million dollars, (b) 5 to 25 million dollars, (c) 25 to 50 million dollars, and (d) above 50 million dollars per year. The percent of current projects in each range may be determined.

Many marketers prefer a single point of value to a range of values. Their reasoning is that a single number minimizes the confusion that may occur in determining where in the range the project actually lies. Profitability of a drug may also be measured in numerous ways: (1) specific dollar amounts, (2) profits of a drug in the third year

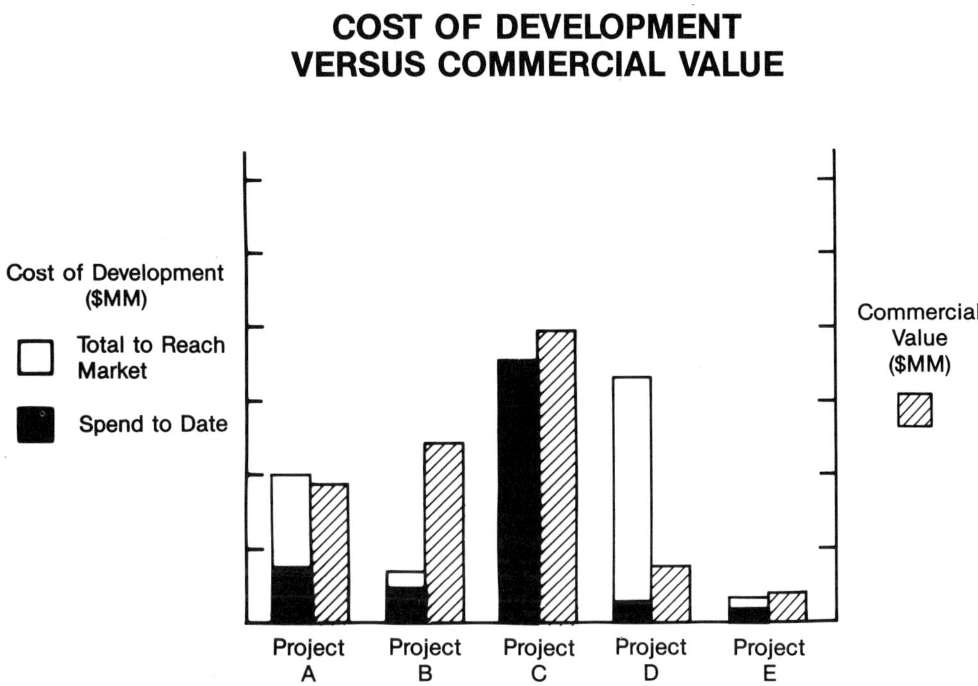

Fig. 15.3. Cost of development (i.e., research and development) and commercial value of individual projects. Commercial value is the net present value or the net profit stream before or after taxes. This type of graph could also be used to illustrate specific therapeutic areas. Other research and development parameters could be medical utility of each drug and time to get to a New Drug Application (NDA).

(or fifth year) after marketing, (3) number of years until the project begins to make a profit, and (4) total profits on a drug.

6. *Money spent on each project* What is the rate of spend and how does it compare to previous projections? How much money still has to be expended? The percent of the total spent may be followed and tracked in many ways (Figs. 15.3 and 15.4, for examples). Numerous additional means of tracking and presenting expenditures are shown and described in Chapter 23.

7. *Competition* What is the status of competitive products that might impact on each project? How much of a competitive race is each project in? What is the level of competition in terms of quality of their products and intensity of activities in the field? Will resources allocated by a company to a drug's development be sufficient to meet or bcat the competition? If not, what options and strategies are available?

8. *Project fit* Does each project fit the company's culture, long-term plans, and strategy for drug development? These should be easy questions to answer for most projects. Projects that lie outside the company's comfort zone may present problems that could be addressed in such ways as cross-licensing, comarketing, or using other alternatives.

9. *Uniqueness of the concept or risk* There are two types of risk that may be measured for each drug in a portfolio. The first type relates to the probability that the drug will reach the market. This is primarily related to its phase of development

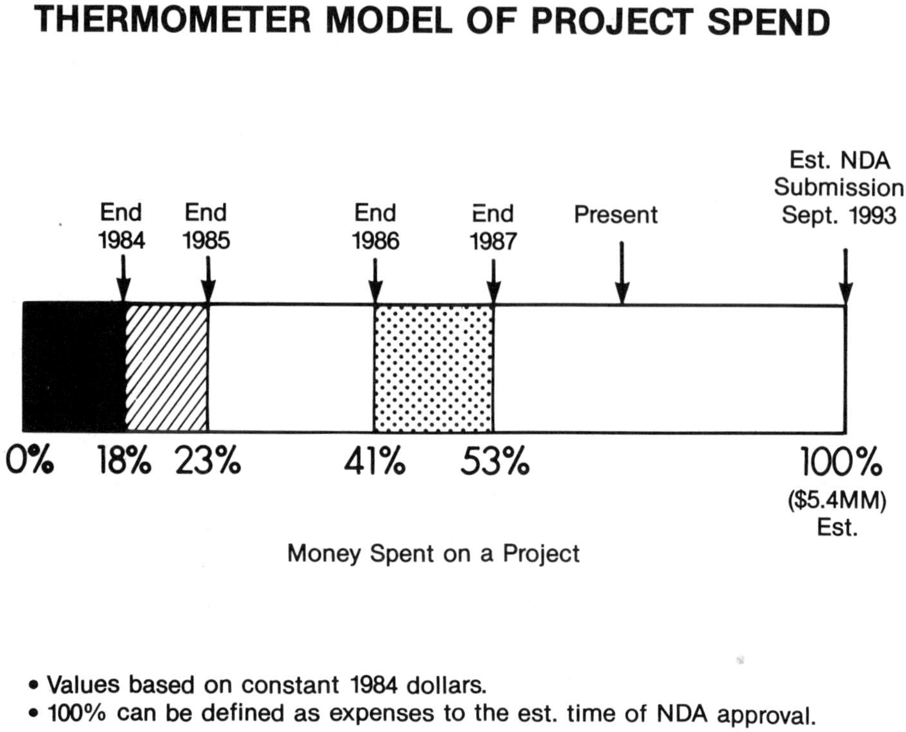

Fig. 15.4. "Thermometer" model used to illustrate the proportion of money already spent on a project. NDA, New Drug Application.

and is covered under points 1, 2, and 3 above. The second type relates to the uniqueness of the concept and whether the drug represents an untried or unproven theory or a known concept. For example, a new cephalosporin antibiotic represents a low-risk drug, whereas a new enzyme inhibitor designed to treat a disease where no treatment is available represents a high-risk project. Figure 15.12 can be used to identify how much resource is going to projects of high risk and low risk. A company that has a great deal of basic research underway in disease areas where high-risk projects exist usually decreases its overall risk. The risk in high-risk projects also diminishes after clinical efficacy and safety are established. Therefore, this type of risk is also related to the phase of a drug's development.

Parameters to Measure Groups of Projects in a Portfolio (Step Three)

The third step in analyzing a portfolio is to evaluate the entire group of projects in the portfolio, or possibly only a specific subset of projects. The methods used either illustrate each project separately in a scattergram, table, or other format, or combine all values into a cumulative or overall figure. This may be done with some of the following methods.

A histogram, table, scattergram, grid, or other visual depictions may be made to illustrate the amount (or percent) of resources (e.g., head count, money) allocated

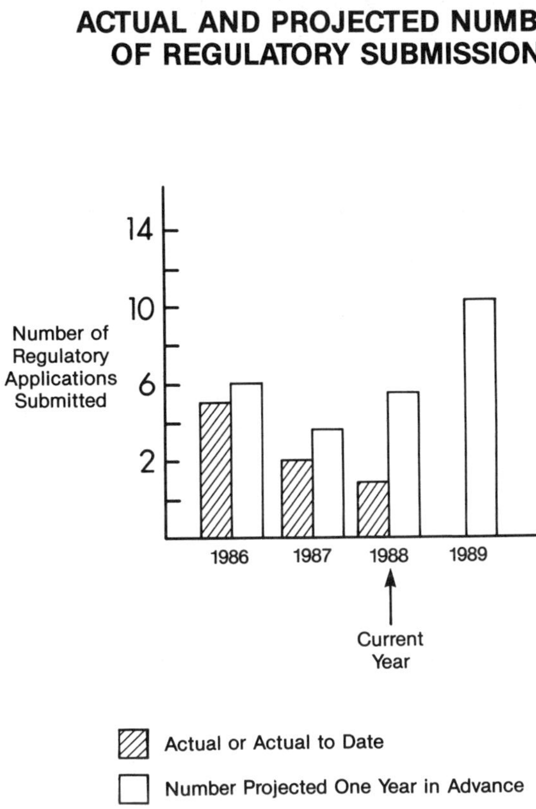

Fig. 15.5. Illustrating the number of regulatory submissions made per year. This plot may be made for specific types of submissions and may be made on a semiannual or other basis. The precise category (categories) of submissions to be tracked must be defined.

to each project. The number of regulatory submissions may be followed (Fig. 15.5). The commercial value (Figs. 15.6 to 15.9) or the competitive position (Fig. 15.10) could be shown. Using the histogram format shown in Fig. 15.6 it would be simple to determine if any projects were out of balance as to the number of staff working on it. This assumes, of course, that the allocation of staff is to be based on a project's commercial value. Other values or an index could be created as a basis for staff allocation. An apparent imbalance might be acceptable to a company and certainly does not mean that staff should definitely be reassigned. A similar histogram could be constructed for cost of a project and commercial value illustrating both the amount already spent and the amount forecasted to either complete planned activities or to get the drug onto the market. Another histogram could illustrate the current phase of development of each investigational compound and drug in the portfolio.

Allocation of Resources

Figure 15.11 illustrates how resources are actually used on some or all projects. This type of graph can also be used to illustrate planned allocation of resources. The specific way in which resources are measured (e.g., total dollar allocation, months of effort, number of head count, external grants, percent of total effort) will have some impact on how data appear. The parameter chosen to plot as a measure of

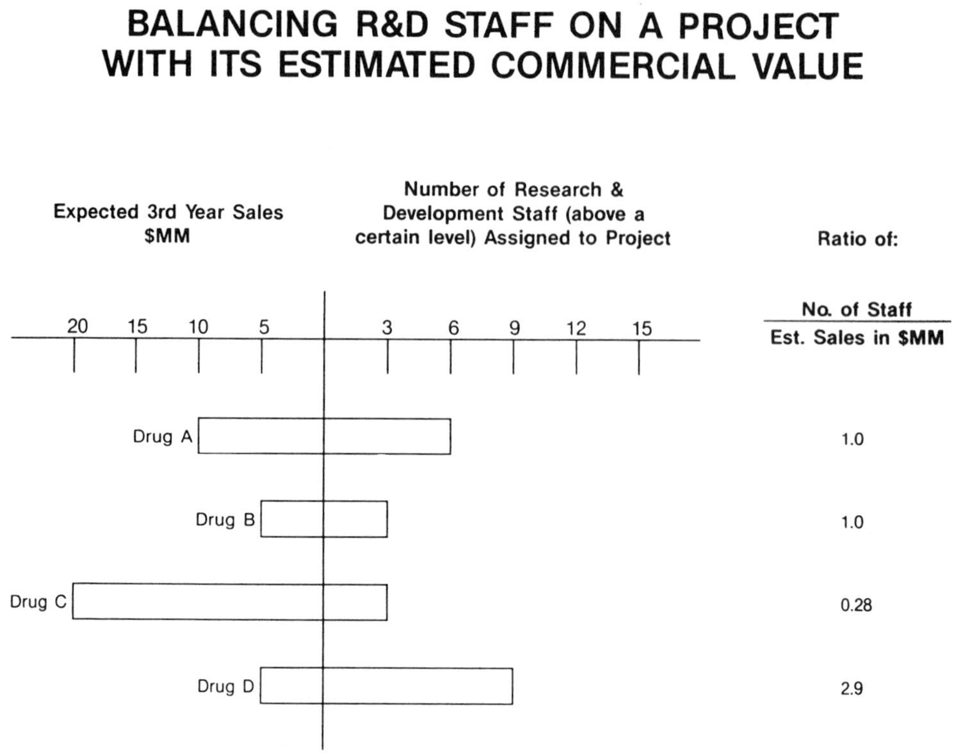

Fig. 15.6. Comparison of staff allocated to a project and expected sales of that project. Changes from a previous year could be shown as a hatched bar. The number of staff could be current resource allocated or the total number of person years to complete a project. Each drug could be illustrated with multiple bars to show different indications or dosage forms. Effort expended to date could be shown with a dotted bar.

resource allocation or resources used is often important in influencing the type of conclusion reached. Projects may be listed in order of expenses incurred over the preceding X number of months, percent of effort, or chronological formation of the project. Projects may be grouped by therapeutic area or by priority (if one is assigned) and expenses or another parameter relating to resources graphed along the ordinate. Each project could be represented by a bar, or dot on the abscissa. Plots of actual versus projected allocations of resources may also be prepared.

Figure 15.12 illustrates allocation of resources according to the level of a project's risk. Risk is usually defined in terms of the probability of marketing a drug. This, in turn relates primarily to the drug's phase of development, but also includes consideration of patent status, licensing issues (if any), and the likelihood for early phase projects of demonstrating efficacy and safety.

Commercial Parameters

Commercial parameters (e.g., expected third year sales) are generally used to analyze the overall portfolio. Examples of other commercial parameters include: (1)

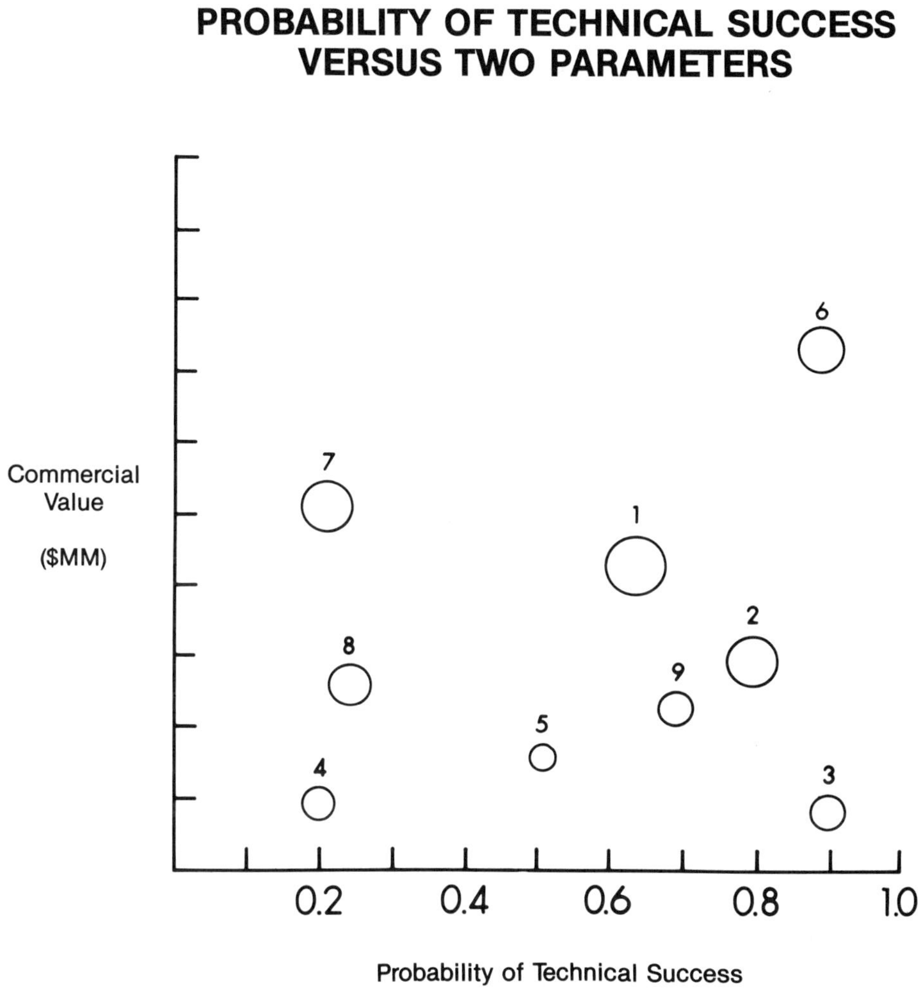

Fig. 15.7. Probability of technical success versus commercial value of individual projects. The size of each circle is used to indicate a third parameter. This third parameter may be the cost of the project to develop, the medical need for the particular drug, or any other parameter of interest. Numbers refer to a particular project which would be identified on a separate list.

return on investment, (2) expected sales over the first two or three years, (3) expected contribution to profit, and (4) amount of money saved per year on hospitalizations through use of the drug.

The ratio of commercial value to (1) headcount, (2) total cost of development, or (3) another parameter may be determined for each project. These ratios may be plotted for a project from year to year to illustrate trends. A scattergram of these ratios at any one point in time would illustrate any projects that are outliers. Outliers may be acceptable and may not require any adjustments, but the method would flag them for attention. A combined ratio for all projects could be determined and compared with ratios from previous years.

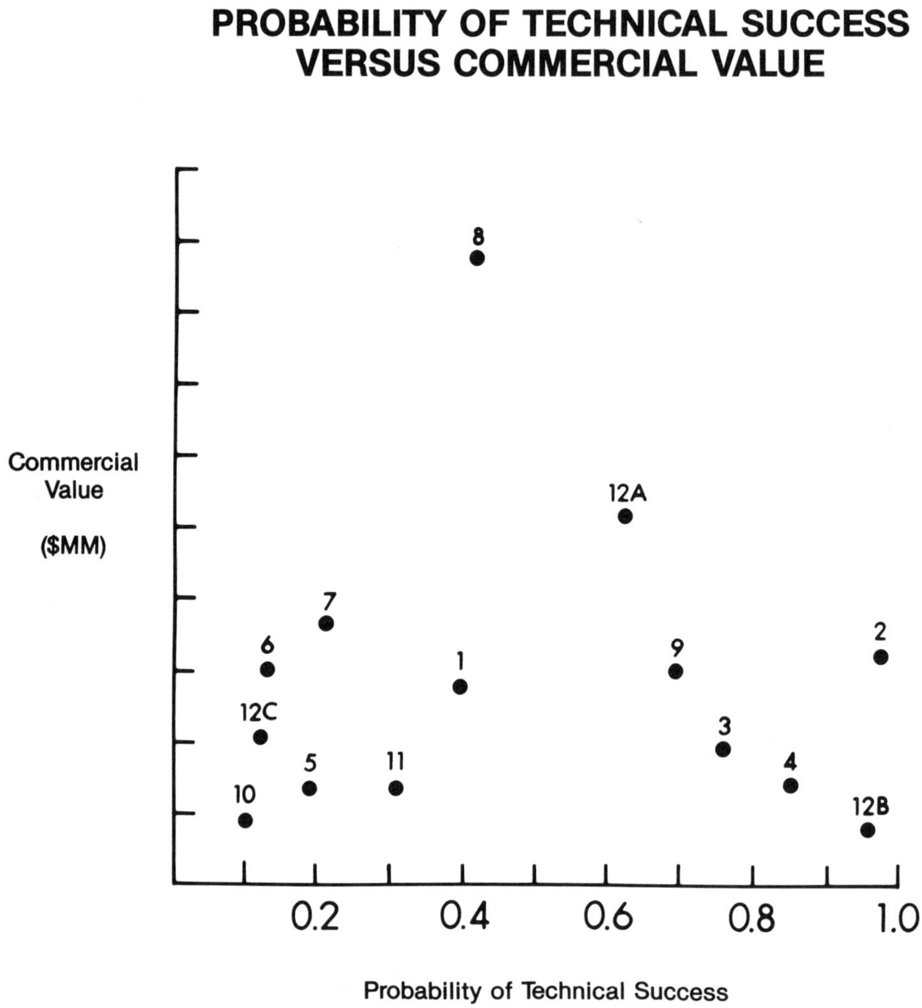

Fig. 15.8. Probability of technical success versus commercial value of individual projects. Each dot represents a different project, except for 12, where each letter represents a different indication studied for the same project. A separate key must be provided to identify the projects. Technical success and commercial value may be defined in several ways. The probability of submitting a Product License Application (PLA) or New Drug Application (NDA) could be used as the abscissa.

Medical Parameters

Relative medical value could be expressed as the (1) number of patients to be treated, (2) percent of total patients to be treated, (3) number of surgeries avoided, (4) number of hospital days avoided, or (5) using various other parameters.

Financial Methods to Analyze a Portfolio

1. Determine the total value of the portfolio. This concept could be illustrated as a graph depicting several years' values, preferably with dollars expressed in constant

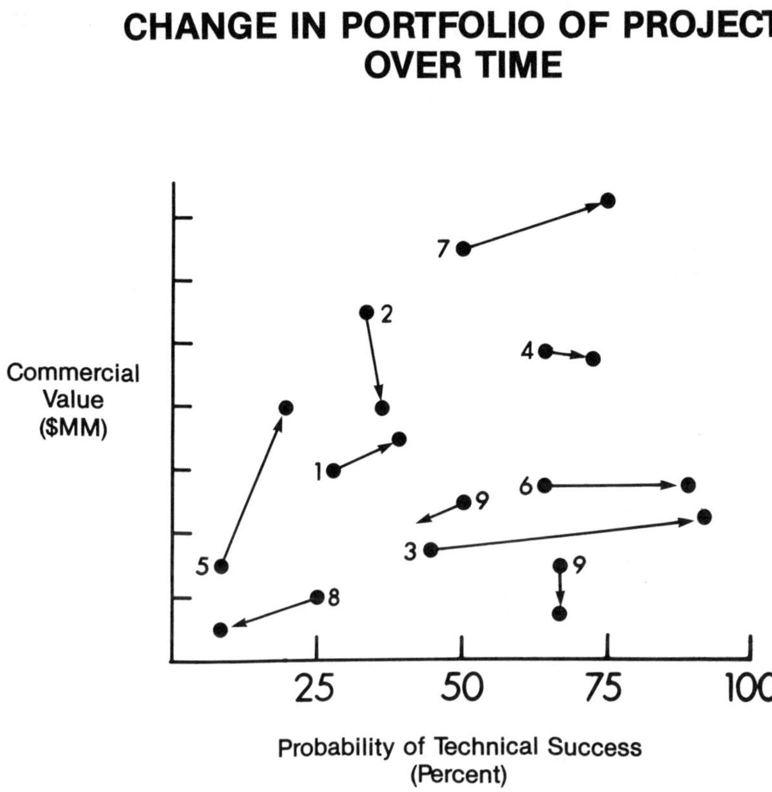

Fig. 15.9. Illustrating change in a project portfolio over a period of time (e.g., year).

amounts. This graph would clearly show how the overall portfolio's value is changing.

2. Return on investment (ROI) may be graphed as a percent versus the probability of exceeding ROI (Fig. 15.13). Although it is important to set high financial goals for a company, the higher they are set in terms of ROI, the less likely it is that they will be achieved.

3. How the overall portfolio's value changes from year to year. This may be simply illustrated or it may be shown how results meet or exceed certain financial criteria or goals (e.g., amount of sales generated from new products, yearly increase in sales targeted). Figures 15.14 to 15.16 illustrate sales and profits generated from new products.

4. Evaluate the ratio of net income after taxes, for marketed drugs over a one- to five-year period since it was marketed, to the total research and development costs for that drug. This ratio can be constructed for all drugs of a company, for drugs grouped into major therapeutic areas, or for drugs grouped by line-extensions and research based new chemical entities. This ratio will give an idea about the drug(s) value.

5. It is also possible to evaluate profits on a drug since initial marketing. In addition to determining the total value for a drug since it was marketed these evaluations can be determined for each year of the drug's marketing, for every two to three years, or on a moving two- to five-year average.

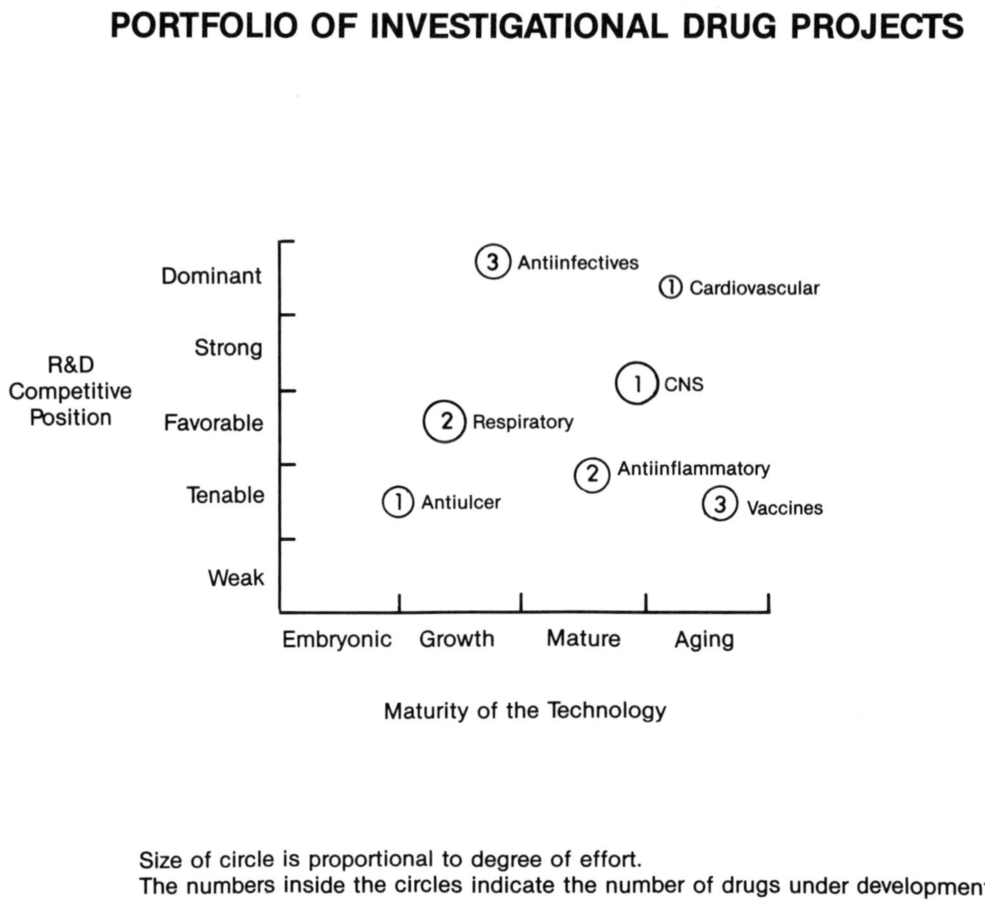

Fig. 15.10. Illustrating a portfolio of new drugs on the basis of the technology's maturity. The size of the circle is proportional to the degree of effort. The numbers inside the circles indicate the number of drugs under development. Although this figure illustrates therapeutic areas, the same format could be used to illustrate individual drug projects. CNS, central nervous system; R&D, research and development.

6. The cost of research necessary to generate each IND, project, and/or NDA may be calculated in constant dollars. This number may be calculated for separate two- or three-year blocks or by using a moving average (see Fig. 15.17 upper graph for an example).

7. The average number of dollars spent per project per year and/or the average number of staff hours or months expended per project per year or on drug discovery are also useful indicators to track (Fig. 15.17 lower graph).

Visual Grids or Scattergrams of Various Types

Selected grids or scattergrams are shown in Figs. 15.7 to 15.9.

Axes of the figure generated could include almost any two of the following:

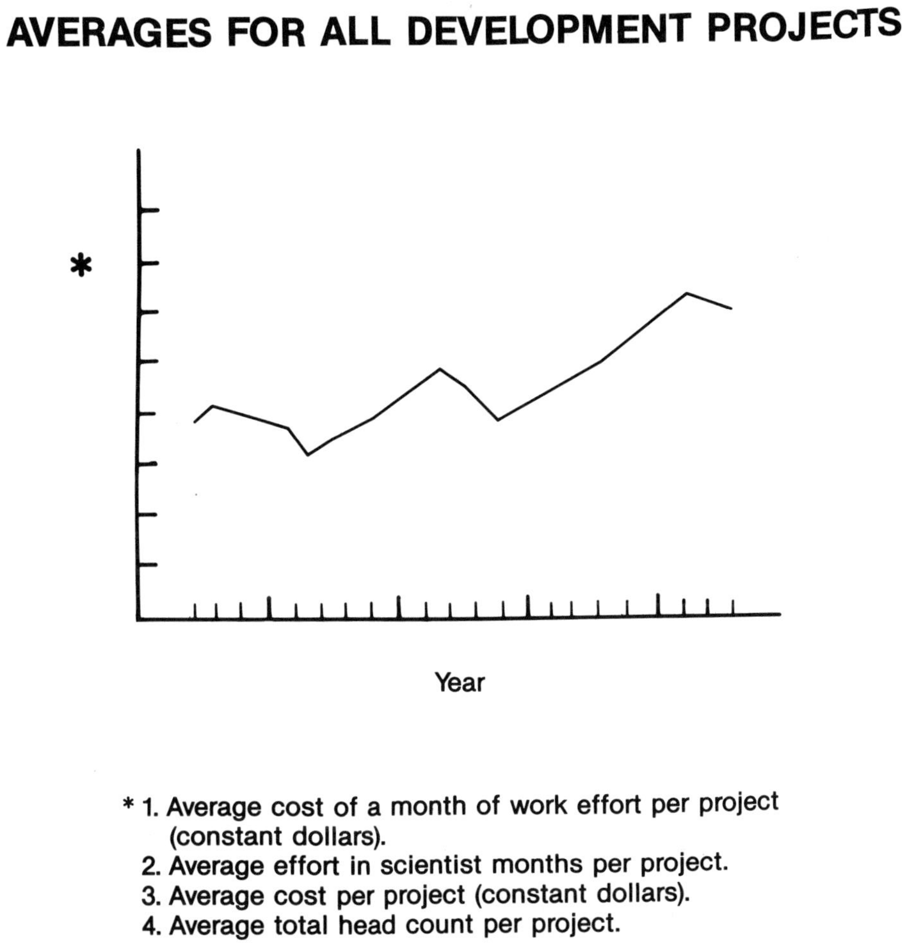

Fig. 15.11. Average cost of work effort on a project. The ordinate may also be average effort, average cost in constant dollars, or average total head count per project.

1. Total time required to develop each product (in years), or time needed to develop each drug, starting at the present.
2. Projected commercial sales for each drug over a period of X years. X usually equals from two to five years.
3. Projected profits for each drug over a period of X years. X usually equals from two to five years.
4. Staff needed to develop each product in terms of total years of effort. This may be calculated separately for junior and senior staff. Other breakdowns of expressing staff requirements could be used.
5. Total financial cost to develop each product. This may be broken down as internal costs and external grants.
6. Cost of additional capital equipment and facilities required to manufacture each product.
7. Current resources allocated to each project in terms of money, staff, or both. The changing amount of this cost, or effort, for each project over a period of several

PORTFOLIO OF INVESTIGATIONAL DRUGS (i.e., Projects)

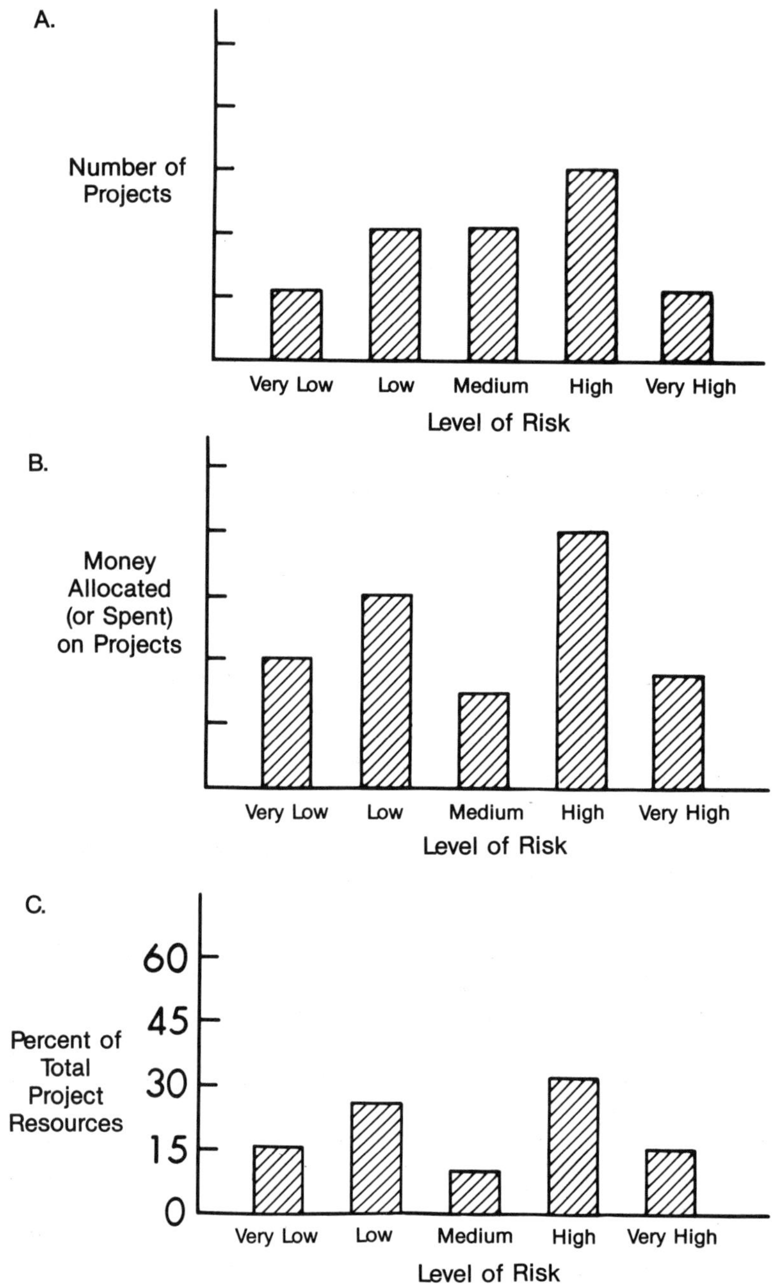

Fig. 15.12. Illustrating a portfolio of new drugs on the basis of risk. The five categories of risk would have to be defined prior to creating this figure. Risk might be defined in terms of probability of success. Changes from year to year could be illustrated.

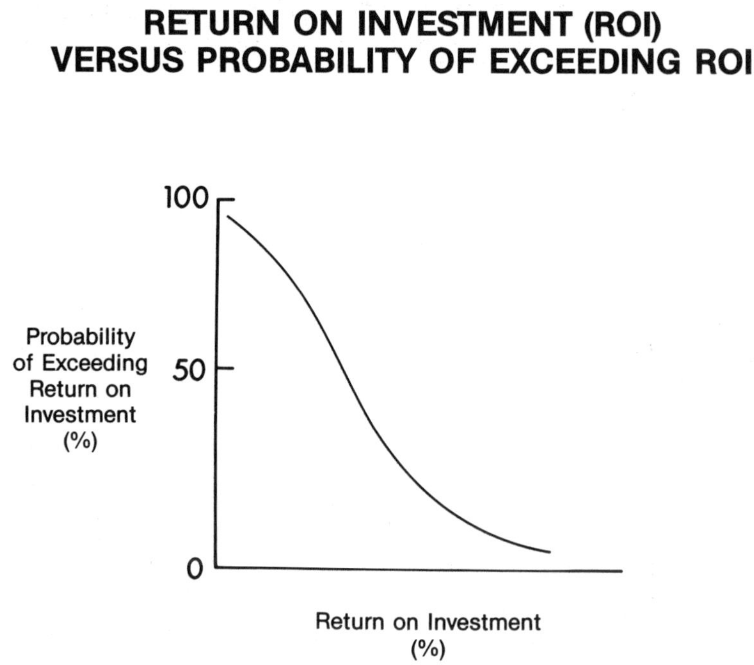

Fig. 15.13. Return on investment in a portfolio versus the probability of exceeding the return on investment.

years could be shown to demonstrate (1) how the total has changed, (2) how the percent of the total expended on that project has changed, or (3) how accurate were the forecasts that were made.

8. Medical value of each investigational and/or marketed drug.
9. Probability of achieving the minimum criteria on each investigational compound or drug to obtain a marketed product.
10. Probability of submitting a regulatory dossier on each drug. This parameter could be illustrated separately for each indication and dosage form being studied.
11. Intensity of competition in relevant disease areas. The quality of competitor's drugs could be illustrated as well as their status.
12. Comparison of investigational compounds or drugs with other companies' investigational drugs, in terms of regulatory approval, medical value, commercial value, or another parameter.
13. Anticipated date of filing the initial (or any) regulatory application.

Three-dimensional graphs could be plotted with three of the above axes. Grids may consist of discrete points (e.g. one point per project or one point per indication being pursued). It is also possible to divide most axes into three or more ranges (e.g., high, medium, low; Fig. 15.18).

It is important to identify the major assumptions made in compiling any of these grids. This should prevent, or at least minimize, misunderstandings about what the data represent and how they should be interpreted. A few examples of assumptions that could be identified include:

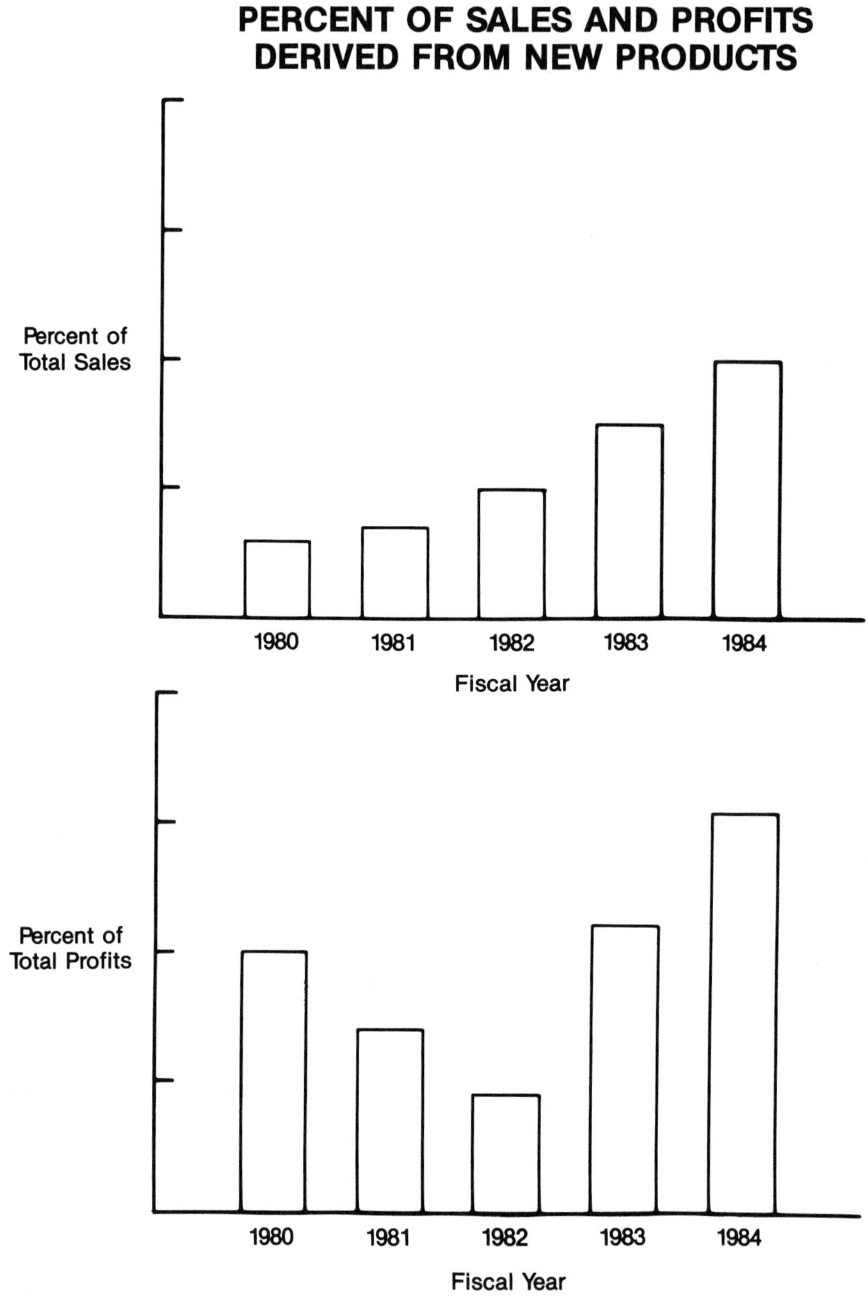

Fig. 15.14. Percent of total sales and profits derived from new products in each of several years. The term "new" is usually defined as three, four, or five years from the time of product launch. Products may be defined as a new dosage form (e.g., capsule, ointment, solution) or only as the first dosage form launched. If multiple countries are considered then additional assumptions must be made. Future projections may also be illustrated on the figure.

SALES AND PROFITS FROM NEW DRUGS

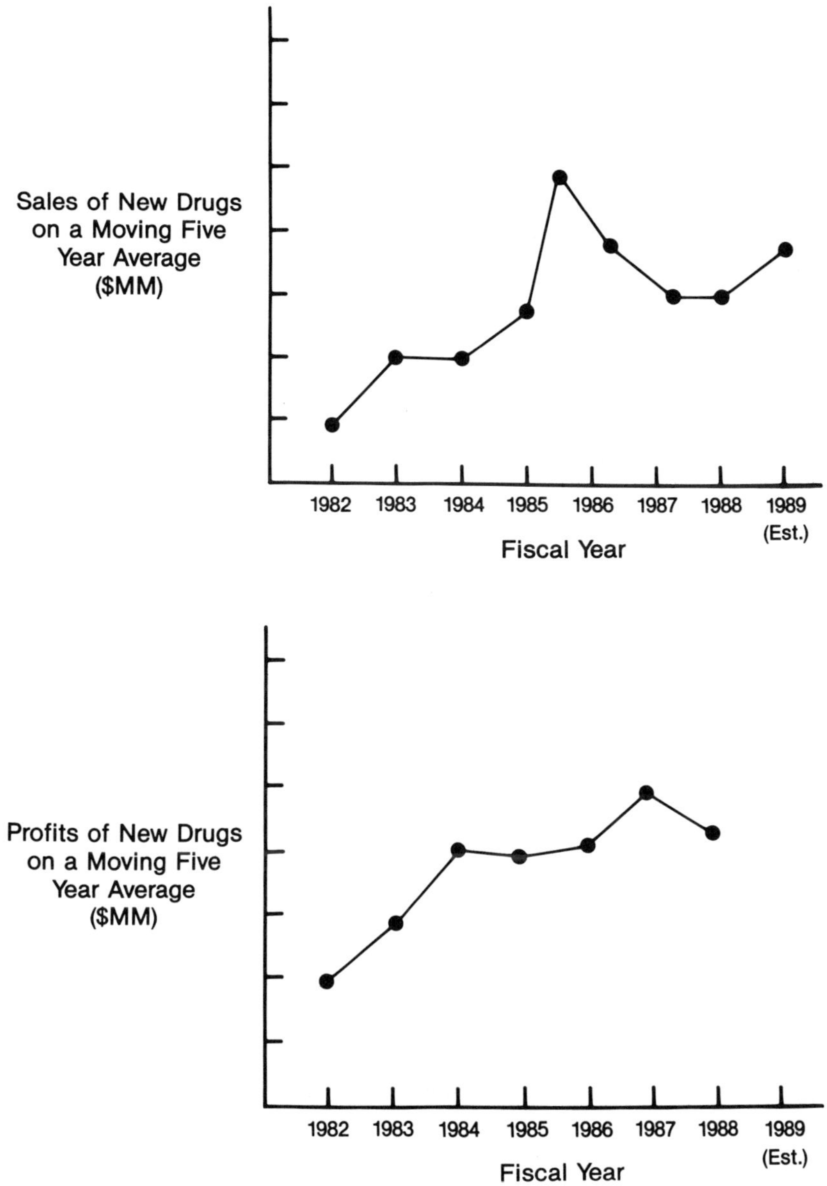

Fig. 15.15. Sales and profits of new drugs per year. The values may be calculated on a per year or moving three- to five-year average.

PERCENT OF SALES AND PROFITS FROM NEW DRUGS

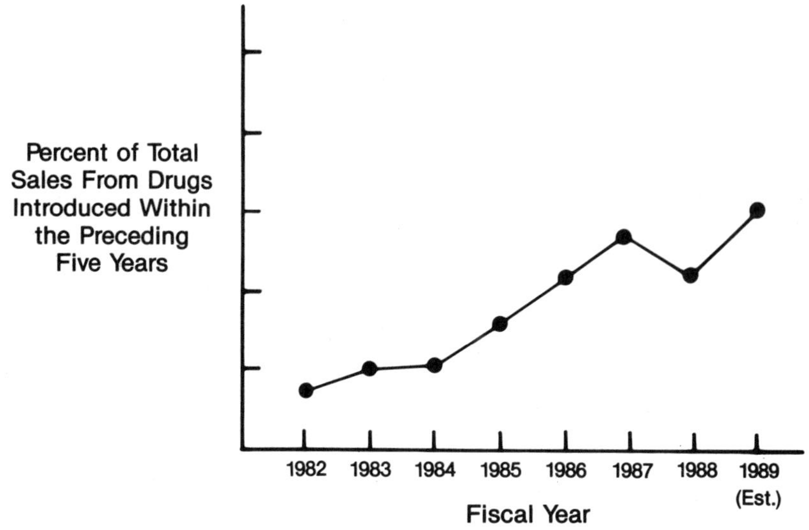

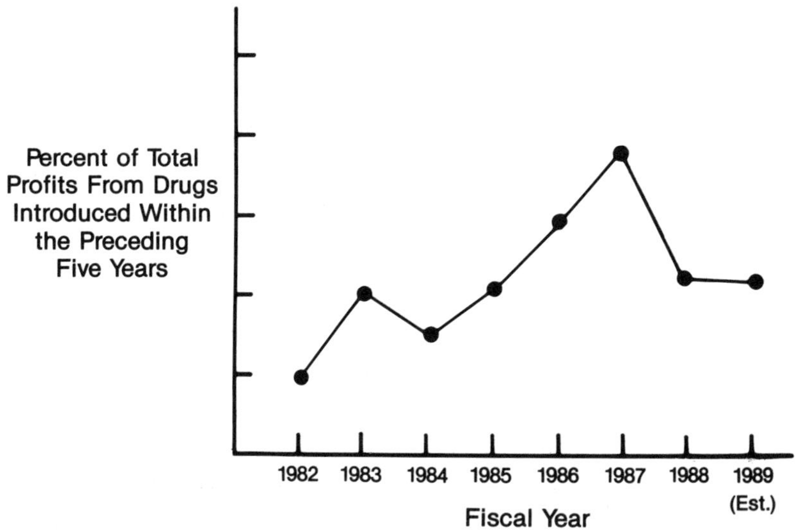

Fig. 15.16. Percent of a company's total sales and profits derived from new products. The values may be calculated per year or on a moving three- to five-year average. Both actual and projected data (i.e., past and future years) may be shown. "New" products must be clearly defined.

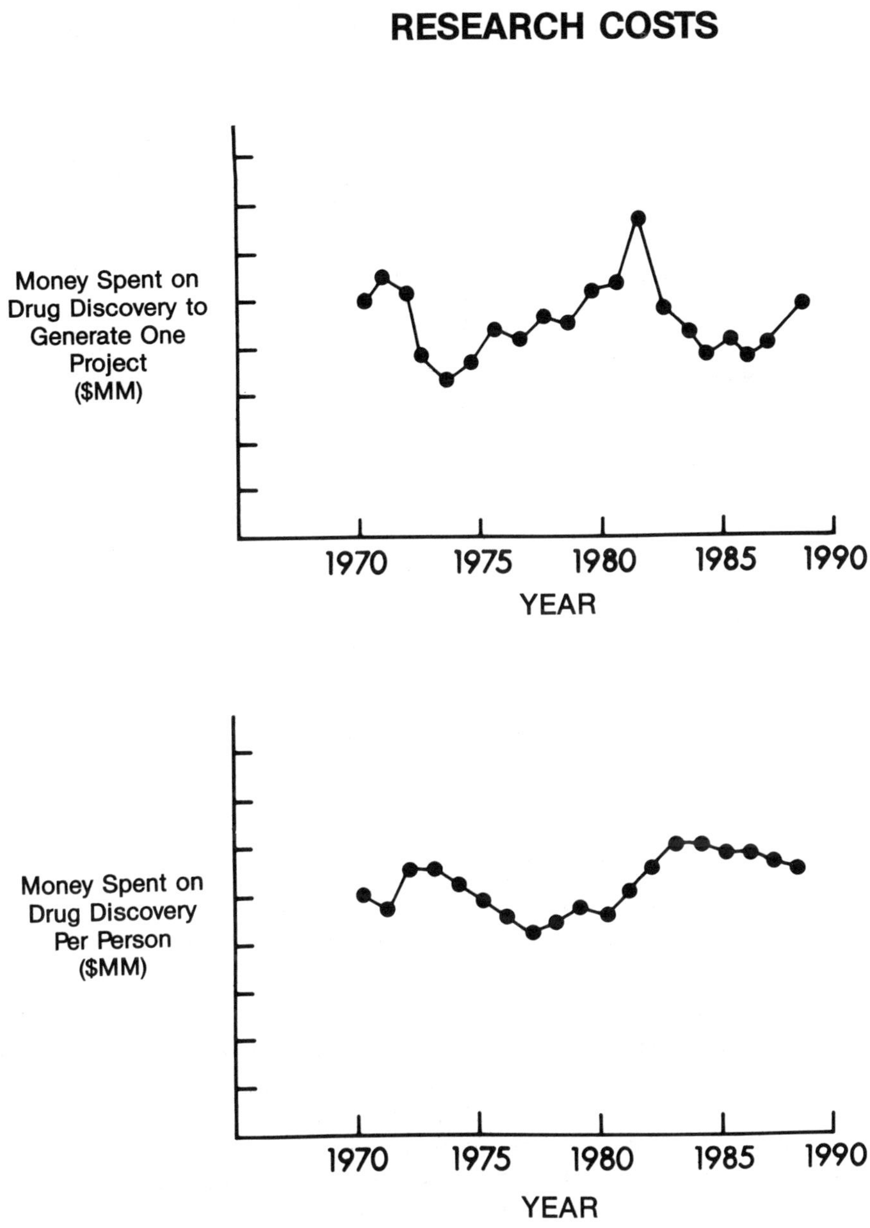

Fig. 15.17. Research expenditures on drug discovery activities required to generate a new chemical entity (NCE) project. A three- to five-year moving average may be used.

1. Market value is based on 19XX dollars and reflects actual (or potential) market size in 19XX.
2. Projected project costs do not include research expenses spent to identify the compound or development expenses on earlier lead compounds.
3. Competitor's projects are (are not) considered in this analysis.

Scales such as market attractiveness may be presented in terms of a score (e.g.,

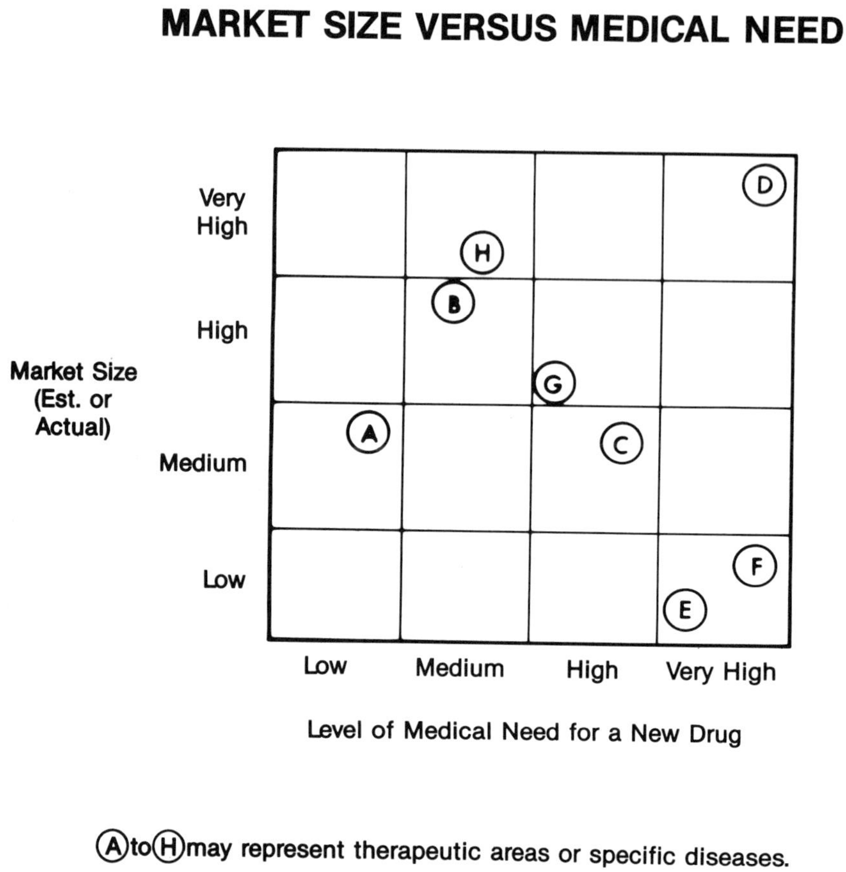

Fig. 15.18. Grid of market size versus level of medical need. The size of the overall market in dollars, pounds, marks, or other currency will dictate what the labels along the ordinate mean.

one to 100; high, medium, low) or as money. If a score is used it may be quantitative where each factor is identified and a weight assigned. It is important to identify the person or group that is completing these scales. If both marketing and research and development personnel are involved it would be interesting to compare their views. This topic could be the basis of a fruitful discussion.

An interesting alternative would be to weight all relevant parameters and to create a single score for each drug in the portfolio. Although this approach would simplify the assessment, drugs are too complex to be reduced to a single figure, especially if research or business decisions will be based on that score.

Other grids may be used to illustrate an overall portfolio. These vary from simple ones (Fig. 15.19) to much more sophisticated ones (Figs. 15.20 to 15.22). Each of these grids have different goals and are clearly more suitable for illustrating certain types of data. For example, the grids shown in Fig. 15.20 to 15.22 are usually used to illustrate businesses a company is engaged in, rather than illustrating a collection of drugs. Each project or drug on a grid may be rank ordered by its position along either axis, or as a combination of the two axes. Variations on each of these approaches are possible, such as by assigning different weights to each axis. Figures

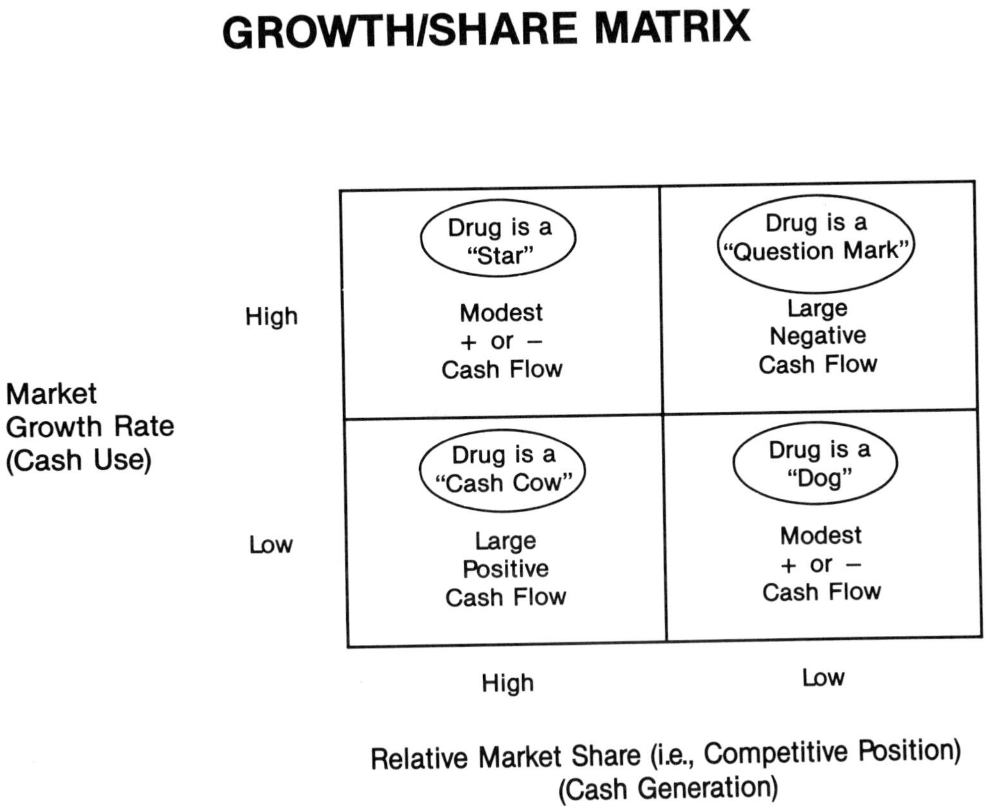

Fig. 15.19. Growth share matrix illustrating four basic types of drugs or businesses.

15.20 and 15.21 could illustrate therapeutic areas of marketed drugs where each pie shape would be the market share of the separate market.

The grid in Fig. 15.22 may be used to assist a company that desires to allocate resources to businesses on the basis of their overall importance to the company. The grid may also be used to evaluate whether a company has businesses that are appropriately positioned. Related diagrams of the same businesses may be made where each square illustrates current, planned, or forecasted (1) sales, (2) profits, (3) location of businesses, (4) characteristics of the labor force, or (5) other characteristics of each business.

Interpretations of a Portfolio Analysis (Step Four)

After all of the analyses are conducted and the tables and figures completed, the data must be interpreted. These interpretations will enable important decisions to be reached at different managerial levels relating to budgets, resource allocations, and other issues. If the managers who are interpreting the results lack the expertise to understand the meaning of the data (e.g., probability of a compound becoming a success), they might allocate an excessive (or inadequate) amount of resources toward developing a particular drug.

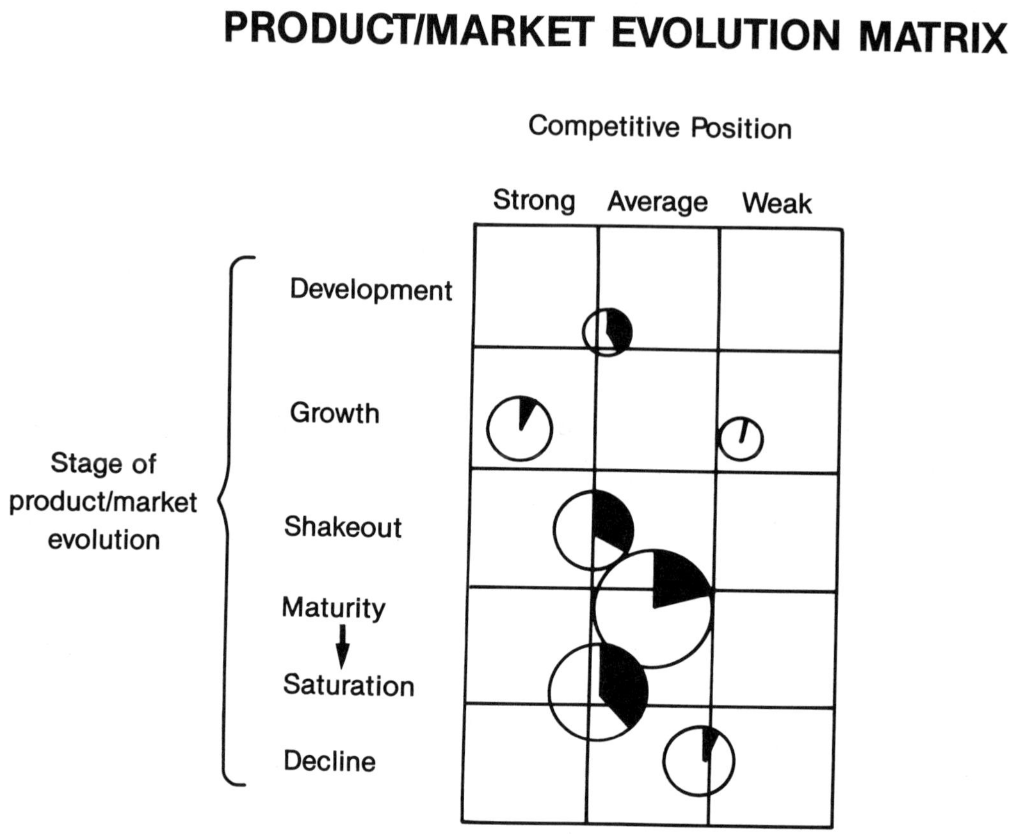

Fig. 15.20. Product market evolution matrix. From Hofer and Schendel (1978) with permission of West Publishing Co. Area of circle is relative to size of market. Pie section shows proportion of market controlled by company.

The above discussion has considered the situation where all investigational projects will be successful and the products marketed. However, this is clearly not the case. Industry-wide averages show that only about one in seven drugs tested in humans is ever marketed. For some companies this ratio is either higher or lower. *The value of this ratio per se does not indicate that a company is either more or less productive than the industry as a whole.* This is because different companies define projects differently, are more or less conservative about elevating compounds into project status, and may easily manipulate this ratio if they wish to do so. The portfolio analysis may be based on the assumption that only one project in seven, five, or any other number will be successful. This number is derived by a historical review of what has transpired within that company.

The overall value of any drug is an evolving concept that develops during the years that the drug is studied. This value relies heavily on the interpretation of the drug's profile in relation to both its desired clinical profile and its minimally acceptable profile. Knowledge of a drug's commercial potential also must be factored in to determine a drug's true value.

Once the portfolio analysis is complete, it may be compared with:

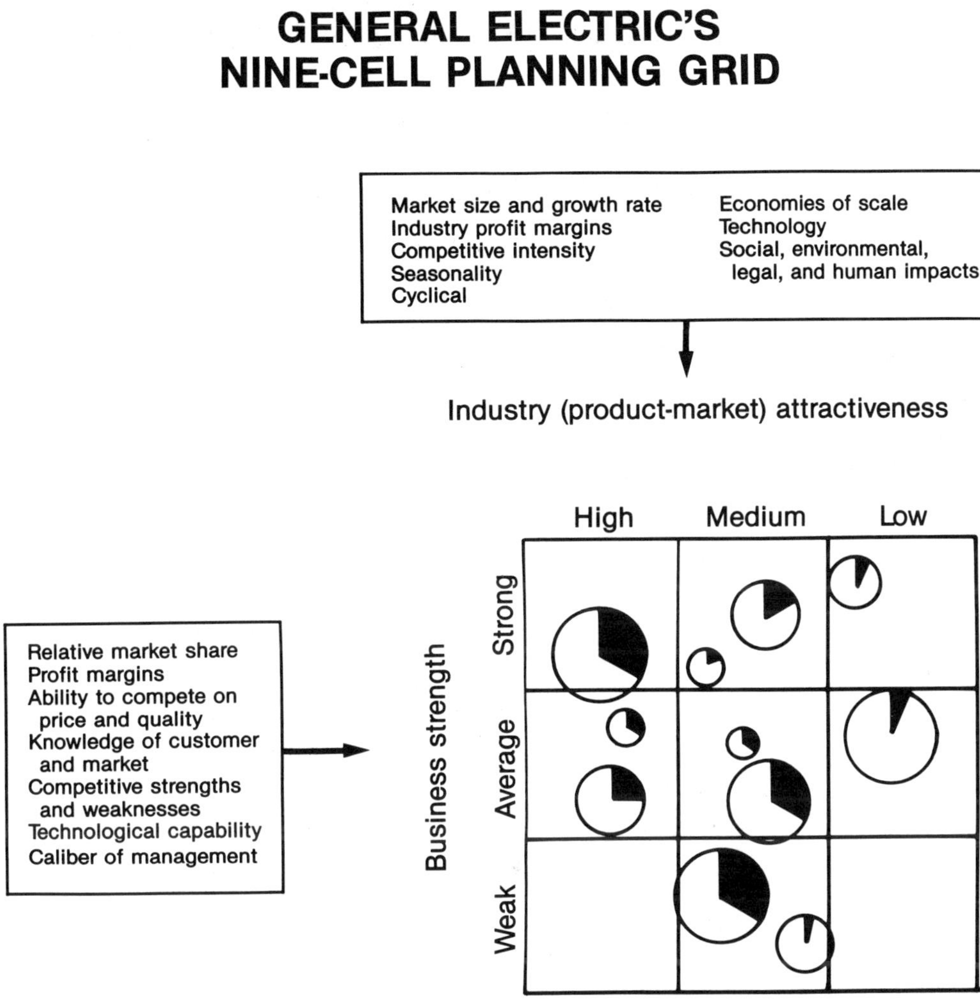

Fig. 15.21. General Electric's Nine-Cell Planning grid of business strength versus industry (product market) attractiveness. From Hofer and Schendel (1978) with permission of West Publishing Co. Area of circle is relative to size of market. Pie section shows proportion of market controlled (i.e., market share).

1. Similar data obtained in previous years.
2. Other semiautonomous research and development groups within the same company (i.e., two separate sites of research and drug development).
3. Available data on the industry's performance. This data may be obtained from trade associations, publications, or other sources.

Data may then be compared with previously established goals to identify whether these goals were achieved. Trends in the data may be evaluated, especially if goals were not met, and in the final step mentioned below, plans of how to maintain, improve, or reverse the trends may be proposed.

PORTFOLIO OF MULTIPLE BUSINESSES

Strength of Each Business Relative to Competitors		High	Medium	Low
	Strong	1	1	2
	Moderate	1	2	3
	Weak	2	3	3
		Attractiveness of the Industry		

1 = Develop businesses within these areas.
2 = Maintain businesses within these areas.
3 = Consider divesting businesses within these areas.

Fig. 15.22. Company position versus industry attractiveness figure.

Utilizing a Portfolio Analysis to Modify a Company (Step Five)

After the portfolio analysis is completed and the data interpreted, it remains a sterile exercise unless it influences future decision making. This may be in context of issues that arise independent of the portfolio analysis, or attention may be directed toward using the interpretation to modify the company in a specific way. Senior managers may revise their strategy(ies) in many ways. For example:

1. They may decide to reallocate resources to emphasize certain therapeutic areas or projects.
2. They may decide that certain projects do not fit their portfolio and license them to other companies.
3. They may decide that the company is spread too thinly across many therapeutic areas.
4. They may decide that certain gaps in the portfolio must be addressed by any of several techniques.

OTHER PORTFOLIO ISSUES

Financial Analyses

To conduct portfolio analysis on a strict financial basis as is done in numerous industries requires sophisticated cost-accounting systems. For each project such systems consider the (1) investment required, (2) degree of risk, and (3) return on investment desired. It is not realistic to utilize this sophisticated financial system in a number of companies because the degree of accuracy required for the calculations is not possible to attain.

Mathematical Models of a Portfolio

A model may be created using all available company data to estimate what the ultimate return is or should be for each dollar spent on research (or research and development). This model may provide a basis for estimating the minimal research budget required to maintain an adequate number of projects in the development pipeline. This approach would also provide data to justify maintaining or changing the amount of money spent on research.

A mathematical model may be created in either a forward or backward manner. In the forward approach, current budget allocations are used and future outcomes are predicted, usually based on a best-case prediction. This model is evaluated over a number of years to assess its accuracy and to fine-tune (i.e., improve) the model. In the backward approach, one or more goals are identified that were achieved. Working backward from those goals data are then derived to calculate the quantity of resources that were required to achieve the target. In either the forward or backward case, it does not follow that the next project will be discovered with X dollars and Y years of effort. But, over a 10- to 30-year period with average productivity (based on retrospective data) it may be possible to obtain an approximate indication of these numbers and make reasonable predictions.

If the amount of money spent on research that generated a new project (or new marketed drug) were calculated, this value could be tracked on a moving three- (or five-) year basis. This trend would be one indication of whether productivity in research was changing. This analysis would require that constant dollars were used.

Should New Drugs be Developed Only if Their Forecast Achieves at Least a Minimal Value?

Some companies reportedly have a magic cutoff number for what dollar value constitutes a minimally acceptable third year sales forecast. If a drug's forecast does not achieve this figure, then its development is terminated or at least significantly slowed. This is a narrow-minded approach for several reasons. First, it is a drug's profit and not its sales that should be important to a company. Development costs may be low for some drugs (e.g., orphan drugs). Second, some drugs may not initially appear to be commercially attractive because the right questions have not been asked (e.g., the patient population may be greater than perceived, the drug may have desirable benefits in terms of compliance or quality of life that were not appreciated). Third, a commercially unattractive drug at the time it is initially evaluated may become more valuable over time. Fourth, there may be other reasons to develop and market a drug (e.g., company image, entrance into a new therapeutic field, high medical value, filling out a franchise or product line, keeping a competitor out of an area).

A Potential "Danger" of Creating a Portfolio Analysis

When enormously complex projects are reduced to a few numbers, it becomes relatively easy for some senior managers to look at the "bottom line" or another number and say that a specific project should be cut or de-emphasized. The appropriate time for seriously questioning whether a specific project should be established is when the project is initiated. That is also the time to establish the minimally acceptable standards each project must meet for its development to continue. At some companies the head of research and development has the final say about this point, whereas at others it is the chairman of the board and board of directors.

Other Pitfalls Regarding a Portfolio Analysis

Other pitfalls to avoid in developing and analyzing project portfolios include (1) unnecessary complexity, (2) flashy presentations, (3) analyses that focus solely on "where we're at," and do not adequately address, "where we're going" and "how are we to get there," and (4) one-shot exercises that fail to establish an ongoing process of portfolio analysis, review, and evaluation.

Additional information on pharmaceutical prognostications are found in an article by Balthasar et al. (1978). In conclusion, aspects of the portfolio analysis may be used to evaluate productivity of research and development (see the next chapter) and to plan the commercial development of new drugs (see Chapter 21).

16 / *Measuring Productivity, Innovation, and Project Success*

Science when well digested is nothing but good sense and reason. Stanislaus, King of Poland. From *Maxims*.

Measures of productivity are like statistics on accidents: they tell you all about the number of accidents in the home, on the road, and at the work place, but they do not tell you how to reduce the frequency of accidents. W. Edwards Deming. From *Quality, Productivity, and Competitive Position.*

DEFINITION AND DESCRIPTION OF PRODUCTIVITY AND INNOVATION

Introduction

Virtually every organization and group, regardless of their functions and goals, desires to improve their productivity and number of innovations. For research-based drug companies, productivity of their research and development function is vital for corporate prosperity and often, for its survival. Measuring and tracking a company's productivity and innovations enable senior managers to assess whether the funds they commit to research and development are well spent and are insuring the future success (and even existence) of their company. It is also relevant for senior research and development managers to measure, analyze, and report on the productivity and innovativeness of the groups they manage when justifications are required to support their annual budget requests or to defend the effectiveness of research and development. Evaluations of a group's productivity or innovativeness may also be used as a means to identify problem areas and as a guide to improve the effectiveness of drug discovery and development activities.

Productivity and innovation are commonly used terms in the drug industry that everyone understands. Or do they? Dictionary definitions of these concepts cannot be directly applied to drugs or the drug industry without making numerous assumptions and decisions about what factors to consider and how they should be applied. One of the reasons for this situation is that both words (productivity and innovation) have several definitions with various shades of meaning. As a result, both terms are defined operationally in this chapter, and other definitions could be proposed. Unfortunately, most discussions of productivity and innovations in the scientific and medical literature do not clearly specify the precise definitions used.

Definition and Description of Productivity

Chambers 20th Century Dictionary (Cambridge University Press, Cambridge, UK, 1983) defines productivity as "the rate or efficiency of work, esp(ecially) in industrial production." *Webster's New International Dictionary of the English Language* (2nd ed. Merriam-Webster Inc., Springfield, MA, 1953) includes the phrase "yielding or furnishing results, profits, or benefits." These definitions indicate that productivity is a rate or ratio. This is usually viewed as an output divided by some type of input.

In the manufacturing area the most traditional definition of productivity is output per labor hour. In marketing, finance, and other disciplines, definitions generally emphasize how well the company earns money and is able to accomplish the same or an increased number of tasks with fewer people, less time, and/or less money. The most important aspect of productivity in research and development is the number of commercially viable new drugs that were discovered, developed, and marketed. This number may be expressed per dollar spent on research and development or by another parameter (e.g., per 1,000 people—years of work). A productive company will be able to demonstrate this quality through the number of new drugs it "produces".

Productivity of research and development is evaluated in many different disciplines and areas (e.g., number of patients who complete a given study per month, number of keystrokes of data entered per hour by a data entry operator). The term *productivity* includes consideration of the efficiency of an activity or operation, whereas the term *innovation* does not.

Definition and Description of Innovation

The definition of innovation in numerous dictionaries is (1) something new or different and (2) introduction of new things or methods. Although there may be many innovations relating to the process of drug development (e.g., an improved method of conducting any one of thousands of activities), in this chapter the term is restricted to the discovery and development of new drugs.

The process of innovation was described as having four separate functions or components (Scherer, 1970). These functions may be modified to fit the drug industry.

1. *Invention* Conceptualization of a new drug, at least in a rudimentary form, plus the demonstration that the compound or drug possesses either biological or clinical activity of interest.
2. *Investment* This involves the risking of funds and commitment of resources for a compound or drug's development.
3. *Entrepreneurship* Management's decision to pursue a compound or drug's development and the commitment to efforts required for efficiently organizing and carrying out the development.
4. *Development* This involves the lengthy and complex steps required to bring an investigational compound to market. If a drug is already marketed, then new development activities may be necessary to attain regulatory approval for the newly discovered activity.

This description indicates that innovation involves much more than just drug discovery. The primary quantitative measure of innovation, however, is the number of new drugs or drug forms (e.g., dosage forms, creative packaging) developed. This number is often expressed on a per year basis. It is unclear whether a drug must be marketed for a company to count it as an innovation. A drug that is sold in country A and is rejected by regulatory authorities in country B would usually be considered as an innovation in country A, but not in country B. A different endpoint than drug marketing should be used to define an interesting compound as an innovation. A logical endpoint would be to use the time a compound becomes a drug. This has been defined as the moment when the first human is given a compound in a drug study. On the other hand, it is also possible to define a chemical compound as an innovation at the time that a company's management has made the commitment to invest money and to pursue the drug's development (i.e., the step of entrepreneurship). This is usually the time when a compound is elevated to project status. Whichever of these three time points is chosen as a criterion of defining a new chemical entity as an innovation (i.e., commitment to development, first human exposure, or initiation of marketing), that criterion should be consistently applied. Other time points are possible to define.

Although the preceding discussion was written as if each drug represents a single innovation, there are several reasons why this is not always true.

1. There may be innovations in different therapeutic indications for a single drug, where new and important uses are discovered. These discoveries may occur almost anywhere along the drug discovery and development pipeline from preclinical studies to testing of clinical theories, to serendipitous events. A major innovation has little or no precedent in the drugs used for that indication, and represents an improvement in therapy.
2. Innovations may occur in marketing and production, in addition to research and development. Novel manufacturing processes may allow a drug to be produced that otherwise would be impossible or would be too expensive to be competitive in the market.
3. Medicine is practiced differently around the world and some drugs used, even in industrialized counties, vary greatly. A number of well-known and highly used drugs in one country may be little-known and little-used, just across the country's border. Thus, an innovation in one country will not always be considered as an innovation in all countries.
4. Numerous creative ideas contribute to the development of virtually all drugs. These "innovative" ideas are not innovations in the sense that the overall drug is a single innovation. Nonetheless, some creative ideas leading to advances in a drug's development (e.g., discovering a new route of chemical synthesis) could be defined and considered as innovations.

Productivity and Innovation Versus Value

Many definitions and descriptions of productivity and innovation do not consider the value of the drugs developed. Value may be measured and/or judged in both commercial and in medical terms. Numerous aspects of these values as well as scientific value, are described in Chapter 15. A company may wish to judge its research and development group, not solely by the number of drugs under development and how well they are being developed, but also by their value. Methods and parameters that include both commercial and medical value should be considered.

A research and development group may work hard and efficiently in developing drugs, but through no fault of its own, most or all of their important investigational drug projects may have to be terminated. This could occur for many reasons, such as toxicity in animals, adverse reactions in humans, or lack of sufficient efficacy in human patients. A research and development group in this situation might still be rated as highly productive and innovative, depending on the specific definitions used. It is also possible that the number of their innovations would be zero, and their productivity would also be zero, if the definitions used required a drug to be marketed.

Drugs may have a high medical value but low commercial value and never repay their development and marketing costs. It may be debated as to whether these drugs contribute to a company's productivity. On one hand they clearly do because of all the benefits that patients will receive, but on the other hand, a company that is highly productive but only markets this type of drug will eventually go out of business.

GENERAL METHODS TO MEASURE PRODUCTIVITY

Levels at Which Productivity is Measured

It is usually important to measure productivity at multiple levels, including that of an individual scientist, a group of scientists, an individual research department, a project team, all research departments, all development departments, all research and development personnel, an entire company site, or an entire multinational company. Some methods that are appropriate for one level are not suitable for others.

Productivity of individual scientists is usually measured as part of their annual performance review. This chapter is concerned with judging productivity of the entire drug research or drug development effort, not that of the individuals who plan, conduct, and supervise this effort.

Establishing a System to Evaluate Productivity

One approach to evaluating productivity is to divide the evaluation into the following questions:

1. What is to be assessed?
2. What general tools and techniques are available to evaluate productivity?
3. What are the pros and cons of each method for the specific tasks intended?
4. Which tools and techniques are best to use and which parameters are best to measure?
5. How many parameters should be measured and is it worth combining the results into an overall index?
6. Will greater precision in measurement make any difference in actions taken to improve productivity?
7. What comparison data are available?
8. How will these evaluations be conducted?
9. Who will conduct this evaluation and interpret the results?
10. Who will review and approve the results?
11. How will the results be applied to the company (e.g., to improve productivity)?

A number of additional questions and issues should be considered before setting up the exercise.

1. Are there preconceived endpoints or results that the evaluation is supposed to

demonstrate or attain? If so, are these results hidden or clearly stated? Are there mechanisms to prevent this type of bias from influencing the evaluation?

2. Does the staff in charge of the evaluation have vested interests in having the outcome fit a predetermined pattern? How may these vested interests be controlled so that they do not bias the outcomes?

3. To what depth will the measure(s) be used to evaluate productivity, i.e., is a superficial or an in-depth analysis being conducted?

4. Is this activity a one-time analysis or is it intended to become a periodic (i.e., ongoing) activity?

Making "Snapshot" Evaluations at a Single Point in Time Versus Developing Trends Over a Period of Time

Comparing the effectiveness or productivity of a research and development function with similar groups in other companies often compares activities and situations at a single point in time. This is analogous to evaluating a photograph of the research and development function at a specific moment in time. It is also important to judge changes over a period of years to determine whether a company's performance is improving, deteriorating, or remaining constant. Evaluating changes over time could be viewed as analogous to studying a movie version of research and development or whatever function is being assessed.

Who Will Conduct This Evaluation?

There are basically three answers to this question. The analysis may be conducted primarily (or solely) by (1) internal company staff, (2) external consultants, or (3) by a joint effort of both. There are a number of consulting groups with experience in reviewing all or part of a drug company's research and development organization. External consultants will require significant assistance in time and effort from the company's staff, even when the consultants perform all of the analyses and evaluations themselves.

In the situation where both company staff and outside consultants are involved in performing the analyses, several scenarios may be followed. The first is where members of the evaluation group are chosen from both the company and consultants to work as a unified team, perhaps being instructed in the general approach to follow by the consultants. Another possible scenario is for the consultants to adopt a more passive role and serve as facilitators helping guide the company staff and keeping them on-track as they gather information and conduct the analyses in-house. The opposite situation, where company personnel serve as facilitators for the consultants is possible but unlikely to occur.

SPECIFIC PARAMETERS TO MEASURE PRODUCTIVITY

What Components of Research and Development May be Assessed to Measure Productivity?

A company may evaluate the productivity of a highly specific part of their research and development division or they may wish to conduct a sweeping evaluation of the entire research and development function. In either case, each of the components that are to be assessed must be identified. If a highly specific part of research and development is to be evaluated it may consist of a single component. If the entire division is to be assessed, it may be desirable to choose some global measures or to examine separate components. Data on any parameter obtained at different times may be plotted to evaluate trends.

Parameters to Measure Overall Research and Development Productivity

Research and development productivity may be globally measured using parameters such as (1) number of Investigational New Drug Applications (INDs) filed, (2) number of projects started, (3) commercial value of projects started, (4) number of New Drug Applications (NDAs) filed, and (5) how closely the total group met their annual goals in terms of the first four parameters listed. The first four parameters may be expressed on a per year basis and trends analyzed over time. In addition, these parameters may be evaluated on a per research and development person basis (per year) to make the comparison a bit more fair from year to year because the company's total research and development effort is likely to change from year to year in the number of people employed and money spent. Only professional staff above a certain level could be considered. A three (or other) year moving average could be used to further smooth out differences that often occur from year to year. Money spent per person per year on the three major functions of research and development groups (drug discovery, drug development, and market-oriented activities including line-extensions) could be determined separately or together. See Chapters 15 and 23 for examples of figures that illustrate research and development expenditures.

A number of other objective parameters that may be used to measure productivity are listed in Table 16.1. A variety of grids or scattergrams could be produced to illustrate the status of investigational drug projects. Grids from two or more years could easily be compared to determine whether the movement of projects was in a desirable direction and was adequate in amount (see Fig. 15.9).

A highly gross and imperfect measure of productivity would be the number of months taken by a regulatory authority to approve NDAs or Product License Applications (PLAs) (Fig. 16.1). The number of months taken for a drug or the average number of months for all drugs approved in a given year or group of years could be compared with the company's previous performance. These values could also be compared with those of the drug industry. Numerous caveats are required for this comparison, because the time taken by the Food and Drug Administration (FDA) to approve drugs depends on many factors. These include the type of drug, medical need for the drug, and specific reviewers involved. This measure would be related to a company's productivity if there is a correlation between quality of the data submitted and speed of regulatory approval. The author believes that this correlation is relatively high for initial NDA applications. This measure is less indicative of productivity when evaluating supplemental NDAs.

Another criterion of overall productivity would be degree and quality of the liaison between research and development (R and D) and other functional areas in a company. Feedback from other groups that frequently interact with research and de-

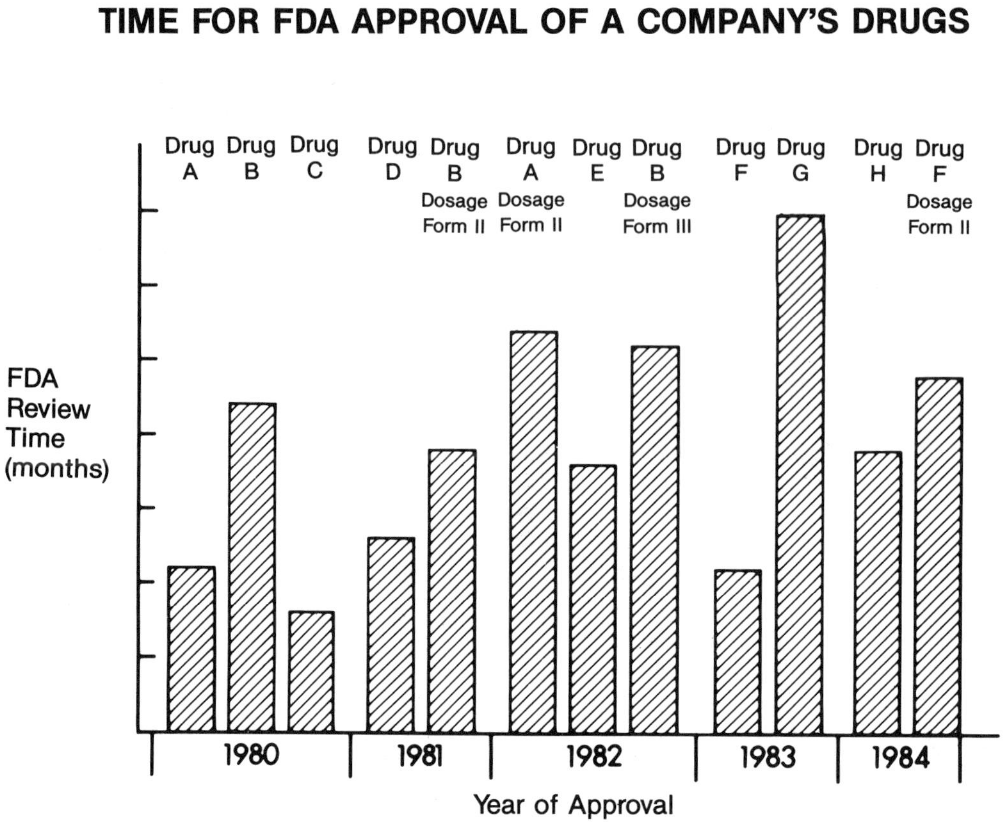

	1980	1981	1982	1983	1984
Company Average: (months)	A	B	C	D	E
Industry Average: (months)	L	M	N	O	P

Fig. 16.1. Tracking the time required for regulatory review and approval of new drugs. A similar graph could track regulatory supplements.

velopment (e.g., marketing and production) would be important to judge how well the liaison was being accomplished. It would be ideal to measure both the number and value of good ideas and good decisions made as an assessment of productivity. Unfortunately, this cannnot be accurately done.

Parameters to Measure Various Aspects of Research and Development Productivity

In addition to evaluating productivity of the overall research and development function described above, it may be relevant to measure the productivity of component parts. Various parts (e.g., drug discovery, medical group, technical devel-

Table 16.1. Parameters for measuring productivity of research and development activities[a,b]

A. Regulatory parameters
   1. Number of new products reaching the market in X years
   2. Number of new regulatory submissions for NCEs[c] in the United States and/or several specific countries
   3. Number of countries approving specific drugs
B. Commercial parameters
   1. Amount of sales and/or profits generated from products that reached the market within the last three years[d]
   2. Percent of sales and/or profits generated from products that reached the market within the last three years[d]
   3. Number and value of drugs licensed-in within the last three years[d]
   4. Number and value of drugs licensed-out within the last three years and how the company benefits
   5. Potential commercial value of all investigational drugs (e.g., total of estimated third year sales times the probability of marketing the drug)[e]
   6. Potential commercial value of projects established within the last year
   7. Number and value of line-extensions currently being developed
   8. Average cost to complete each stage of development[f] (e.g., preclinical, Phase I, Phase II, Phase III)
   9. Average research cost to discover an NCE that reaches project status
   10. Ratio of new drug sales over X years divided by research and development expenditures over that same period
C. Research and development parameters
   1. Medical value of all projects with investigational drugs
   2. Medical value of projects established within the last year
   3. Number of new projects established within the last year
   4. Number of compounds reaching human studies within the last year
   5. Rapidity with which unsuccessful projects have been terminated within the last three years (i.e., the number of months from project formation to termination)
   6. Degree of congruence between projected goals and actual accomplishments
D. Personnel parameters
   1. Number of senior staff who left the company within the previous three years
   2. Evidence of positive staff morale
   3. Number of publications by staff
   4. Image of the research and development departments
   5. Number of staff with academic appointments

[a] Effectiveness or productivity would be assessed by comparing the value of a parameter with those obtained for an equal preceding period or with values obtained in previous years. Trends would be of particular importance. If the parameters had not been previously measured, then a new analysis of older data may be conducted. All of these values could be presented in tabular or graphical form. Two or more of these parameters could also be combined.

[b] Not all of these parameters are considered worthwhile measures of productivity. The use of some would depend on the specific situation.

[c] NCE, new chemical entity.

[d] A different number of years could be used.

[e] These numbers may be reduced by multiplying by the percent of drugs put in the project system that historically reached the market (i.e., success rate).

[f] Financial comparisons should be made using dollars of comparable value to correct for inflation. Other corrections may also be used, but must be clearly defined.

opment) or departments may be evaluated with some or all of the following parameters. Numerous caveats will be necessary in using each of these measures.

1. The number of therapeutic areas or disease areas being researched.
2. The specific choices of therapeutic areas being explored for new drug discoveries in terms of medical need and commercial value.
3. The number of compounds and drugs, or new chemical entities in the project system.

4. The speed and efficiency with which drugs are moving through the drug development pipeline. Evaluate the number of months from project formation to IND submission, the duration of Phase I, Phase II, Phase III, and total development time to NDA submission.

5. The time from IND filing to NDA submission. This may be evaluated on a moving three year average and compared to the company's previous performance as well as the industry average.

6. The percent of regulatory submissions (i.e., NDAs and PLAs) that are in each category of therapeutic importance (i.e., 1A, 1B, 1C).

7. The relative portion of total R and D resources hypothetically allocated to each project versus that portion actually used by each project.

8. The relative portion of resources spent on (1) drug discovery, (2) drug development, (3) product support, and (4) other activities compared to previous years and to an ideal industry-wide or company standard.

9. The relative commercial and medical value of projects under development compared with previous years.

10. The status of activities on licensing-in drugs.

11. If the licensing function is based within research and development, then the status of licensing-out or cross-licensing activities may be assessed.

12. The quality of currently used systems may be evaluated for (1) coordinating efforts among different drug development sites, (2) choosing compounds for development as drugs, (3) obtaining new technologies, (4) communicating results, (5) avoiding unnecessary duplication of efforts, and (6) making decisions in a rapid yet effective way.

13. The organization of research and development activities may be assessed in terms of effectiveness.

Within any company, the appropriate responses to these and many other related issues change over time. In addition, there is rarely just a simple answer or approach that is adequate for any issue, and different sites of a single company often address these issues independently. Also, many individuals have differing opinions on each of these issues. Therefore, drug companies are almost constantly reassessing their responses, even when it appears that a consensus was reached only a short time before. When a new president is appointed or a new director of research and development takes charge, one of their first steps is often to reexamine one or more of these issues. The ways that they choose to approach the examination are discussed below.

Choosing the Best Methods to Assess Productivity

Both hard and soft measures may be used to assess productivity of research and development. The most important single measure from a company's perspective is the commercial value of all new marketed products developed over the last X years. The value of X should probably be based on a moving multiyear average, usually three, four, or five. This technique avoids the ups-and-downs that often occur from year to year. In addition, limiting the number of years to five is important because it does not extend the focus so far back in time that sales of newer products contribute relatively little to this category because of the presence of some financially important "old timers."

The parameter of commercial value may be used for both marketed and investigational drugs. A research and development group may be judged to be productive if its portfolio of investigational drugs and line-extensions are commercially valuable. To assess their value it is often desirable to consider drugs in a number of separate categories. Investigational drugs that were developed in-house may be evaluated separately from drugs that were licensed in. Line-extensions may be evaluated separately from new chemical entities. The portfolio as a whole may be analyzed and judged in many different ways (see Chapter 15 on portfolio analysis).

Commercial Parameters

The approximate value of each investigational drug may be estimated by multiplying the probability of marketing the drug by the total forecasted sales for a given period. The probability of each investigational drug's being marketed at some point is estimated by the people who are most knowledgable about that probability, i.e., usually senior managers in research and development. The total forecasted sales for the first three (or other number) years of marketing are estimated by the appropriate staff in marketing. This is based on many factors in addition to the drug's profile, including (1) current market size, (2) projected market trends, (3) ability of available methods to treat the disease, (4) severity of disease symptoms, and (5) nature of the population to be treated (e.g., children, debilitated patients).

Values for each investigational drug are calculated to provide an estimate of the total projects' portfolio value. This number may be easily graphed on an annual basis to illustrate how the overall portfolio's value is changing in commercial terms. If a company's productivity and progress is strictly measured in commercial terms, then this value, and its comparison with values from previous years, is particularly important.

Medical Parameters

The above method does not consider the portfolio's medical value. Each investigational (or marketed) drug may be evaluated on a crude or sophisticated scale to judge its medical value. A qualitative four- or five-point scale (e.g., little = 1, moderate = 2, strong = 3, exceptional medical value = 4) is usually adequate to express the medical value of most drugs, especially investigational drugs. This is because the clinical profile of investigational drugs is incomplete. The numbers corresponding to medical values for each drug in the portfolio may be added to obtain a total score. The average medical value score per drug may also be determined. The values obtained with either of these methods could be plotted on a year to year basis. The trend of these analyses would indicate how the portfolio's medical value is changing over time. This trend would also relate to a company's productivity in research and development.

Precautions

The approach described in the above two sections is oriented toward a global commercial and medical view of the portfolio. This approach is insufficient on its own, however, to present the status of research and development. Moreover, the results may be misleading. From a commercial perspective, one major new drug may skew the picture of the portfolio in a highly positive manner and tend to mask the fact that few other commercially attractive drugs are in the development pipeline. That fact should generally act to stimulate more licensing activity to be conducted to fill potential future therapeutic and financial gaps. If the major drug in the pipeline falters (e.g., new adverse reactions arise, efficacy is not as good as anticipated) or stronger competition arises from other companies, then the entire company may be vulnerable and its future could be placed in jeopardy.

Parameters to Avoid in Measuring Productivity

There are a number of parameters that should generally *not* be used to measure the productivity of research and development. This is primarily because they relate to *output* and not *productivity*. The former is merely a tabulation of effort and activity that may bear no relation to productivity. These parameters include:

1. *Number of chemicals synthesized* The amount of work required to synthesize new chemicals varies enormously from compound to compound. The difficulty of synthesizing each chemical varies from those prepared using well-established and straightforward synthetic steps to those requiring creativity, long hours, and repeated attempts, with low yields. The importance of each new chemical made varies greatly. Some are made to complete a series for patent protection, others to evaluate a structure-activity relationship, some are from new series, and some are believed to represent a major therapeutic advance. Merely evaluating the numbers of new chemicals synthesized would generally be a highly misleading measure of productivity. If this parameter was to be used in a drug company, then at least some chemists would probably generate larger numbers of less important chemicals in order to demonstrate their high degree of productivity. The company's true productivity would suffer as a result.
2. *Number of compounds screened for a specific or general biological activity* This parameter is inappropriate for analogous reasons as those described above for the chemistry department. Screening is usually carried out in biological departments.
3. *Number of patents filed or obtained* The number of patents filed or obtained on new chemicals would also superficially appear to be a reliable indicator of productivity. Unfortunately, this parameter could also easily be manipulated by chemists or others who might attempt to patent more compounds than would be prudent from the company's perspective. Given the high costs of obtaining and renewing patents plus the large amount of work involved in filing patents in many countries, using this approach to measure productivity could be an expensive mistake.
4. *Number of clinical drug studies conducted* Many clinical studies are conducted for product support, to replicate prior studies, to increase statistical validity,

or to increase the patient population treated as part of Phase III or postmarketing surveillance. All are legitimate practices but are poor indicators of productivity in research and development. The size of a study varies greatly and there is often little correlation between a study's size and its relative importance to a company.

5. *Number of patients evaluated in drug studies* Parameters number 4 and 5 may be easily manipulated if desired, and are not inherently useful as measures of productivity. While some studies are able to process relatively large numbers of patients through a clinic, others evaluate few patients in great detail. If determining the total number of patients studied was strongly desired as a parameter, then it should be modified to measure the total number of patient days (or weeks, or months) of treatment, to improve its reliability. The drawback of even this particular modification of the parameter is that a few long-term studies of many patients, where little effort was expended, would strongly influence the results. One way of preventing this would be to divide studies into categories based on the length of patient treatment (e.g., less than one week, between one week and a month, between one and six months, over six months).

6. *Number of publications authored by staff* Although the connection between the number of publications authored by company staff and the research and development productivity seems farfetched, some people and publications have proposed this parameter (and each of those above) as appropriate tests of productivity.

What Comparison Data Are Available?

Each drug company would like to compare the results and conclusions of its own internal analyses with those of other companies. This is rarely possible for several reasons, only one of which is company secrecy. The large number of variables used to conduct any comprehensive evaluation in a company illustrates that data from another company would probably have been obtained using different assumptions and methods. Publicly available data about other drug companies are not usually adequately detailed and reliable enough to base important judgments on them. Most data from other companies would therefore have limited usefulness for direct comparison. Differences do not only include the assumptions and methodologies used but also definitions of terms (e.g., project, success) and specific questions asked. These could all differ markedly between companies. In addition, it is generally believed that most companies are not internally consistent in their definitions of these terms from year to year or from department to department.

In terms of drug discovery, it would be useful to compare the productivity of in-house discovery efforts and that of other companies. The value of licensed-in drugs to a company may also be assessed in comparison with in-house drugs. This issue may be evaluated through several approaches. One is to determine separately the return on investment for drugs discovered by in-house research and drugs that were obtained as a result of licensing activities. Another is to focus on how well each of these groups of drugs achieves the goals established for that function. For example, if drugs are licensed-in to fill certain financial gaps or to utilize available staff time in most development departments, then the success of the drug in meeting those goals must be assessed.

Pharmaceutical Trade Associations

One alternative is to compare the values of a company with the industry average. This latter type of information is collected by the Pharmaceutical Manufacturers Association (PMA) in the United States and by numerous other pharmaceutical trade associations around the world from their member companies. The advantage of this type of comparison is that the trade association usually collects and processes the data in the same way for each company and is consistent over a period of years. This consistency means that differences in definitions used by different companies tend to become less important. On the other hand, there could be inconsistencies in trade association data from year to year if (1) different companies are included in the data base, (2) the questions posed to the companies are modified or changed, or (3) companies answer questions somewhat differently each year because the company's respondents use different assumptions, interpretations, or definitions.

A pharmaceutical trade organization is in a good position to collect data in a uniform format from many research-based companies. The associations would then circulate industry-wide results so that each company could compare itself with the industry mean (or range). In fact, this is being done at present (e.g., *PMA Statistical Fact Book*), and the amount of industry-wide data available from trade associations appears to be increasing. This is generally a satisfactory source of comparison data, if the data addresses questions of interest.

Other Sources of Industry Data

Other useful sources of industry data include the FDA, other regulatory agencies, the World Health Organization, drug industry financial analysts, Scrip, and organizations like the Centre for Medicines Research in the United Kingdom (Woodmansterne Road, Carshalton, Surrey, England SM5 4DS) and the Center for the Study of Drug Development in the United States (Tufts University, 136 Harrison Avenue, Boston, MA 02111). Activities of the Center in Boston have been described (Anonymous, 1987b). Various sources of marketing data are also useful places to obtain such information. The single most appropriate and useful source of data for comparison purposes is that of the company itself. Older records, data, and reports provide material that may be analyzed and used for comparative purposes (see the section in Chapter 8 on institutional memory).

IMPROVING PRODUCTIVITY

General Principles

The most important principle to improve productivity is the necessity to pay attention to both the details and the big picture in developing drugs. It is necessary to be concerned with all aspects of drug development and to maintain an objective view. There have been many techniques and tools proposed to help improve productivity. Some of these are only applicable for one or a few levels at which pro-

Table 16.2. Points designed to increase productivity and quality[a]

1. Create constancy of purpose toward improvement of product and service, with the aim to become competitive and to stay in business, and to provide jobs
2. Adopt the new philosophy. We are in a new economic age. We can no longer live with commonly accepted levels of delays, mistakes, defective materials, and defective workmanship
3. Cease dependence on mass inspection to achieve quality. Require, instead, statistical evidence that quality is built in, to eliminate need for inspection on a mass basis
4. End the practice of awarding business on the basis of price tag. Instead, depend on meaningful measures of quality, along with price. Eliminate suppliers that can not qualify with statistical evidence of quality
5. Find problems. It is management's job to work continually on the system (design, incoming materials, composition of material, maintenance, improvement of machine, training, supervision, retraining)
6. Institute modern methods of training on the job
7. Institute modern methods of supervision of production workers. The responsibility of foremen must be changed from sheer numbers to quality. Improvement of quality will automatically improve productivity. Management must prepare to take immediate action on reports from foremen concerning barriers such as inherited defects, machines not maintained, poor tools, fuzzy operational definitions
8. Drive out fear so that everyone may work effectively for the company
9. Break down barriers between departments. People in research, design, sales, and production must work as a team to foresee problems of production that may be encountered with the product or service
10. Eliminate numerical goals, posters, and slogans for the work force, asking for new levels of productivity without providing methods
11. a. Eliminate work standards that prescribe numerical quotas. Substitute leadership
    b. Eliminate management by objective. Eliminate management by numbers and numerical goals. Substitute leadership
12. a. Remove barriers that rob the hourly worker and his or her right to pride of workmanship
    b. Remove barriers that rob people in management and in engineering of their right to pride of workmanship
13. Institute a vigorous program of education and retraining
14. Create a structure in top management that will push every day on the above 13 points. Put everybody in the company to work to accomplish the transformation

[a] From *Quality, Productivity, and Competitive Position* by Deming (1982) with permission of MIT and C. Edwards Deming. A few modifications of these points were made based on changes by Dr. Deming in his book *Out of the Crisis*, also published by MIT.

ductivity may be assessed (see earlier discussion in this chapter). The tools often change as technology changes and must be continually reassessed.

A major means to improve productivity is to adhere to simple principles, such as honesty and openness, and to create a desire for people to want to be productive. People usually desire to understand what activities they are supposed to perform in a company and how their work assists the company. It is useful to assume (at least initially) that all of the staff are highly motivated and want to conduct their work in an efficient manner and desire to have positive relationships with their co-workers. Most workers are better able to adjust their own work to achieve the company's objectives rather than for a manager to direct them closely. All good managers learn how much independence each of their subordinates can handle.

Productivity in production and elsewhere in a company increases as quality improves, because less reworking is necessary. Less reworking reduces waste of employee time, equipment time, and materials. Deming (1982) proposed 14 points to increase the productivity in production areas. Many of these points (Table 16.2) are also applicable to research and development. His book elaborates on these points. He states that quality is everyone's job, but the effort to improve quality is led by management. Many of the chapters in this book contain principles that (if followed) will lead to improved productivity. It is the responsibility of senior mangers to implement these points.

Numerous personnel issues that are intended to improve productivity are discussed in Chapter 7.

Factors Influencing How Rapidly a Project Moves through the Drug Development System

The following are major factors that influence the speed of a project's movement.

1. *Priority of a project in the organization* Although this point is obvious, there is sometimes a distinction between a stated priority and an actual priority.
2. *Resources applied* Increasing the resources placed on a project does not necessarily increase the speed with which a project moves. Nonetheless, there is a direct relationship during much of a project's life between the number of staff and amount of money spent with rate of progress. Whether the change and movement that occurs is in the desired direction and represents progress is another issue.
3. *Sound development plan* The development plan refers to individual preclinical, clinical, technical development, marketing, and production plans that are all coordinated on a national and international basis. Without a carefully crafted and detailed blueprint of a project's strategy and direction, it is easy for various people to direct the project in new or multiple directions. Some of these directions may be conflicting, raise problems, or at the least decrease efficiency.
4. *Monitoring of progress* It is critical to keep a company's stethoscope on the pulse of its projects. This is accomplished with an appropriate number of plans and schedules that are followed. These plans and schedules allow a company to measure the *progress* of a project and not merely the *activities* conducted. Any group within a company may be extremely busy and highly motivated, but if the group is pursuing tangents or are "spinning their wheels" and not moving forward, the project is not benefitting. In fact, many tangents are actually counterproductive to the drug's development (e.g., resources may be drained from the major activity, new problems may be created).
5. *Effectiveness of management* Managerial effectiveness is required to make decisions with appropriate input and speed. Managerial effectiveness in keeping a project on track and avoiding most tangents is also essential to move it rapidly toward its goals.

Identifying Company Problems That Affect Productivity

In dealing with issues relating to company problems, it is critical to identify whether the problem is one of structure and organization or one of personalities independent of the structures. Some people blame organizational structures and systems used when the real problem involves attitudes and styles of some people. Another issue is whether the organizational structure itself is the problem or if it is the way it is functioning and is being utilized. Sometimes, altering the way people are working may be sufficient to elicit a desired change, without need to modify the company's organizational structure.

MEASURING THE SUCCESS RATE OF A COMPANY'S PROJECTS

A research and development group's rate of success may be defined in several ways. A common definition of success refers to the percent of initiated projects that become useful drugs. The precise definitions and assumptions used in characterizing projects greatly influence the rate of success that is calculated. The types of analyses performed also may skew results in one direction or another.

Definitions Used in Determining the Rate of Success of a Company's Portfolio

Number of projects and compounds

Each single compound developed as a drug is only counted as one success or one failure. The terms success and failure are mutually exclusive. Each compound or drug is considered separately, even if more than one compound was designated as being in the same project.

Successful drug

A drug where at least one formulation has been approved by a regulatory authority for marketing. Alternative definitions are possible, such as including drugs where at least one NDA has been *submitted* for approval. The project associated with a successful drug may either be terminated or kept active.

Unsuccessful compound or drug

A compound or drug where no formulation or indication studied has resulted in approval of a regulatory application. Also, work on the compound or drug has been terminated or suspended.

Investigational compound or drug

A compound or drug that is currently being evaluated preclinically and/or clinically. This may include marketed drugs that are being tested (1) in new indications, (2) with new dosage forms, or (3) using new routes of administration. The decision of whether marketed drugs may also be considered as investigational drugs depends on whether the categories of successful drug, unsuccessful compound, and investigational compound are defined to be mutually exclusive. If they are not, somc compounds or drugs could fit into two or even all three of the categories.

Stage of development at the time of termination

Multiple formulations and indications have been (or are being) pursued for some compounds and drugs. The highest stage achieved by any formulation for any indication is considered to be the stage of development at the time of project termination.

Table 16.3. Analyses used to calculate success rates of compounds developed as drugs

Analysis	Type of success rate[a]	Type of compounds	Number of projects in the analysis
A	Cumulative	NCE[b]	All[c]
B	Cumulative	NCE	Completed[d]
C	Cumulative	All	All
D	Cumulative	All	Completed
E	Individual phase	NCE	All
F	Individual phase	NCE	Completed
G	Individual phase	All	All
H	Individual phase	All	Completed

[a] See Fig. 16.2 for an illustration of these two concepts.
[b] NCE, New Chemical Entity.
[c] All projects includes currently active projects.
[d] Completed projects were completed either successfully or unsuccessfully.

Description of Methods Used to Calculate the Success Rate of Compounds

Calculating the success or failure rates of compounds entered in a project system appears to be a straightforward matter until a number of additional questions are considered:

1. Should all compounds be included in the analysis or just the new chemical entities (NCEs)?
2. Should the group of compounds considered in the analysis include currently active projects or only those already judged as successful or unsuccessful?
3. Should success (or failure) be evaluated separately for each stage of development (e.g., preclinical, Phase I, II, III), i.e., independent of other stages; or should rates of success be determined cumulatively from the onset of designating an investigational compound as a project?

If each of the possible analyses using these three questions is conducted, there will be eight separate analyses. Table 16.3 enumerates these analyses. A graphic depiction of question 3 is shown in Fig. 16.2. Because the success and failure rates are complementary and together equal 100 percent for all analyses except A and C, only the success rate will be discussed. The success rates of compounds and drugs shown in Fig. 16.2 are listed in Table 16.4.

Analyses A to D ask the question: Of all the projects formed, how many were successful at filing an IND, completing Phase I, Phase II, or filing an NDA?

In analyses A and C, the cumulative success rate for any specific milestone is illustrated in Fig. 16.3. This shows the number of active projects at each stage. The percentages shown in this figure are based on the total number of compounds entering the project system minus the cumulative number of active compounds.

In analyses B and D the cumulative success rate for any specific milestone is calculated by using as the denominator the total number of compounds entering project status in the set of terminated or successful projects. The numerator equals this total minus the cumulative number of failed compounds. Therefore, if 50 compounds had entered the system and five were terminated before IND filing, seven

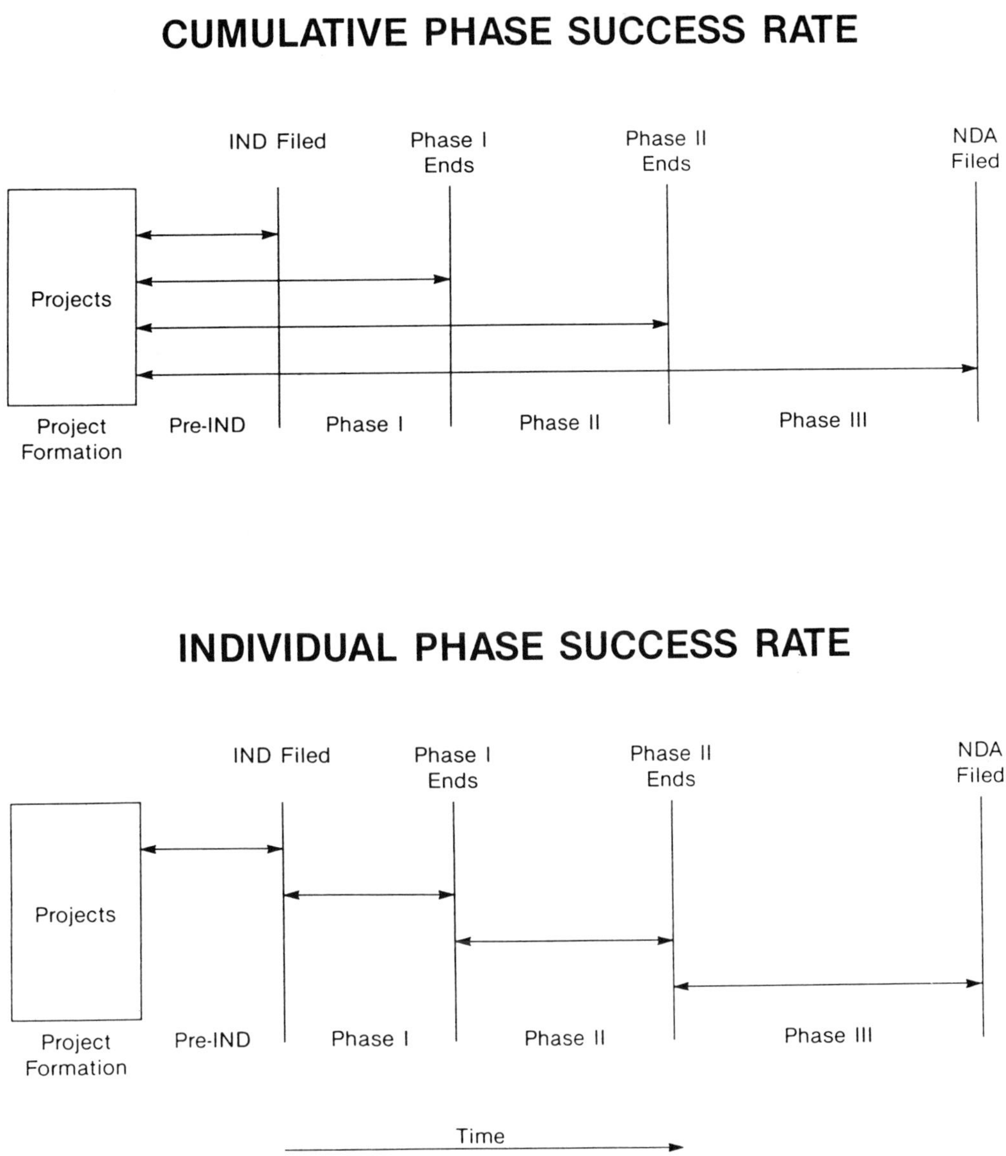

Fig. 16.2. Illustration of the cumulative phase success rate for compounds reaching a milestone and individual phase success rate for compounds entering each specific phase of development. IND, Investigational New Drug Application; NDA, New Drug Application.

were terminated in Phase I, four were terminated at Phase II, and the remainder have gone past Phase II, then: The cumulative success rate through

$$\text{Phase II} = \frac{50 - 5 - 7 - 4}{50} = \frac{34}{50} = 68 \text{ percent.}$$

The cumulative failure rate equals the complement of this number, or 32 percent.

Table 16.4. Calculating the success rates for compounds and drugs shown in Fig. 16.2[a]

Phase	Cumulative success rate[b]	Individual phase success rate[c]
Pre-IND[d]	$\frac{79}{95} = 83\%$	$\frac{79}{95} = 83\%$
Phase I	$\frac{59}{90} = 66\%$	$\frac{59}{74} = 80\%$
Phase II	$\frac{27}{72} = 38\%$	$\frac{27}{41} = 66\%$
Phase III	$\frac{15}{64} = 23\%$	$\frac{15}{19} = 79\%$

[a] The failure rate is equal to 100 percent minus the success rate.
[b] Active projects in that phase and previous phases are excluded from the analysis.
[c] Active projects in that phase are excluded from the analysis.
[d] IND, Investigational New Drug Application.

Analyses E to H ask the question: Of all the projects entering a specific stage of development (e.g., Phase I, Phase III), how many successfully completed that stage?

The individual stage success rate equals the number of compounds that completed that stage successfully, divided by the number that entered, minus the number now in that stage. From the illustration above, 38 compounds have entered Phase II, three are now in that stage, and four were terminated in that stage. The remainder (31) were successful. Thus, the individual Phase II success rate is:

$$\text{Phase II} = \frac{38 - 4 - 3}{38 - 3} = \frac{31}{35} = 89 \text{ percent.}$$

The individual failure rate of that stage of development equals the complement of this number, or 11 percent. The success rates are summarized in Table 16.4.

There are published success rates of one in five (20 percent) to one in ten projects (10 percent) in the drug industry as being successful. Success is defined as a drug that is marketed. The considerations discussed in this chapter, plus the various definitions and characteristics of projects at different companies, make success rates unwise to compare across companies. Within a single company these rates may be compared. But, most companies would be more pleased with a low rate that produces an occasional blockbuster drug, as opposed to a high rate of successful "me-toos" that are commercial failures. Obviously, there is a large middle ground between these two extremes.

Reasons Why Research and Development Groups often Fail to Achieve Complete Success

The title of this section uses the term *complete success*, because it is often difficult to state that a group has had no success. The pertinent question is whether their success could have been substantially greater through their own efforts, given the same opportunities. The major aspects affecting success are considered to depend on research and development management and in some situations on senior corporate management. A few convenient categories of reasons are (1) capabilities, (2) organization, (3) portfolio, (4) attitudes, and (5) atmosphere.

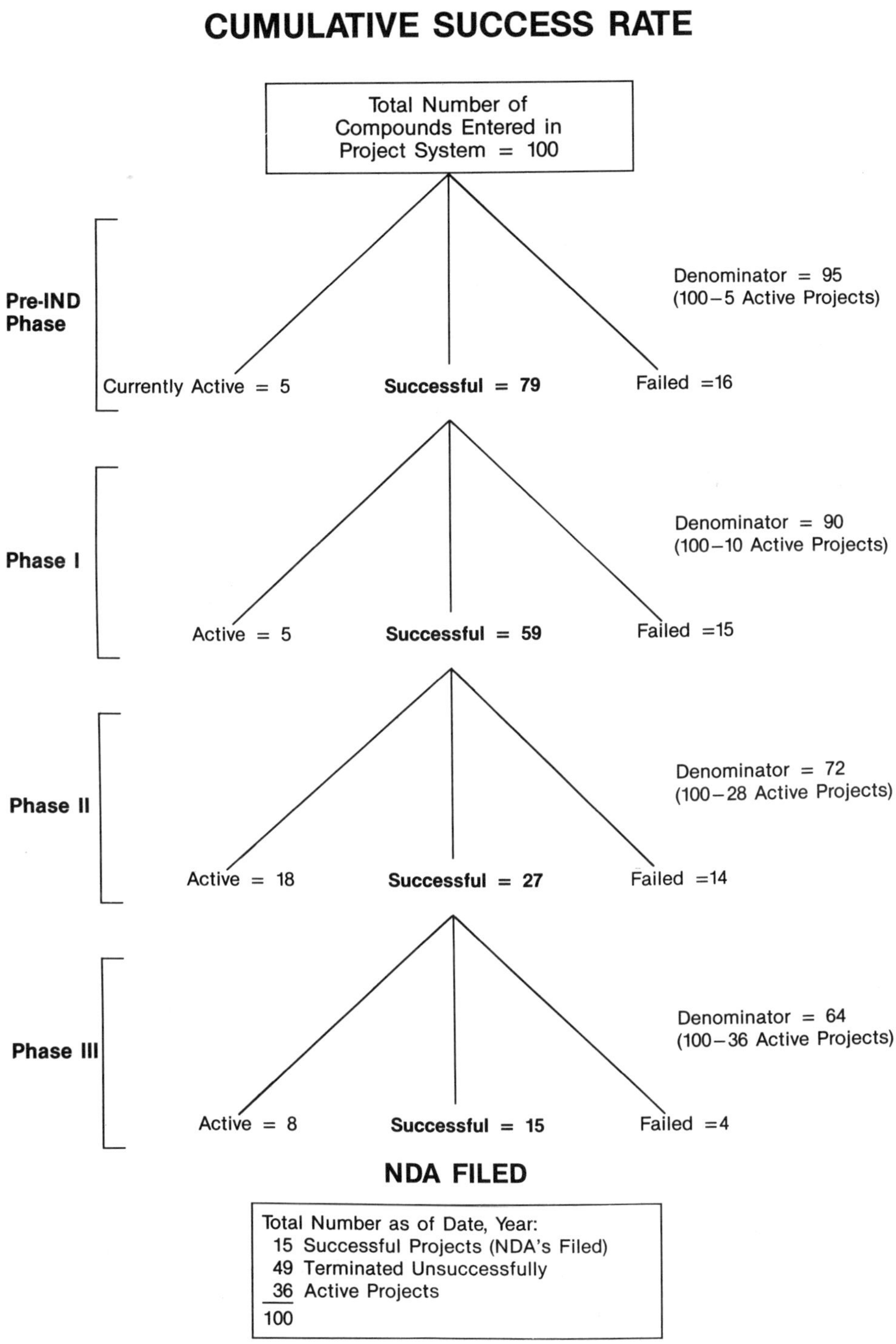

Fig. 16.3. Example of determining success of projects based on the individual phase success rate. IND, Investigational New Drug Application, NDA, New Drug Application.

Capabilities

Capabilities include consideration of the strength of all important departments. Are department heads and senior executives capable and competent managers? Is there a critical mass present in each department, in terms of equipment and personal expertise? Are there weak links? Are some departments perennial bottlenecks or trouble spots?

Organization

Does the company's organization facilitate communication between people at the same level as well as up (and down) the hierarchy? Does the organization facilitate the transfer of a drug from department to department? Is there an excessive number of administrative levels in the company? Do people complain about the amount of paperwork? Are barriers being raised between groups or do existing walls hinder communication and productivity?

Portfolio

Is the portfolio being built and maintained in a systematic or in a haphazard way? What types of projects are going into the portfolio? Is the portfolio analyzed on a periodic basis and is it analyzed appropriately? What is done as a result of the analysis?

Attitudes

Is there a positive attitude throughout the company toward drug development? Are people anxious to progress a drug's development or do they raise objections, pursue tangents, or digress into unnecessarily detailed or extraneous points and experiments? Are there conflicts between preclinical and clinical personnel, or do they and other groups cooperate appropriately?

Atmosphere

What is the work environment like? Is there a positive environment? Do people receive recognition for important accomplishments? Are senior managers trying to improve the work environment?

The above are a few of the considerations and factors that are necessary to achieve a successful and productive research and development group. Other factors relate to the emotional and financial support of company management, and a relative independence of the research and development function from manipulation and control by senior company managers.

Section IV

Technical and Function Issues

17 / *Information, Data Management, and Statistics*

The very first principle of Systems-design is a negative one: Do It Without A System If You Can . . .

Systems are seductive. They promise to do a hard job faster, better, and more easily than you could do it by yourself. But if you set up a system, you are likely to find your time and effort now being consumed in the care and feeding of the system itself.

New problems are created by its very presence. Once set up, it won't go away, it grows and encroaches. It begins to do strange and wonderful things. Breaks down in ways you never thought possible. It kicks back, gets in the way, and opposes its own proper function. Your own perspective becomes distorted by being in the system. You become anxious and push on it to make it work. John Gall. From *Systemantics*.

INFORMATION SERVICES AND ISSUES

Types of Information in a Drug Company

Pharmaceutical companies are extremely information-intensive enterprises. A large quantity of information is obtained and relied upon from external sources and is also generated internally throughout drug discovery and development processes. Information is systematically recorded for easy retrieval to support each product's survival, from its conception through its life in the market.

Information generally falls into the following categories:

1. *Raw data* Preclinical, clinical, and technical data are processed, analyzed, and illustrated in tables and figures. Analyzed data and the reports produced form the backbone of regulatory submissions. Analyses also enable appropriate decisions to be reached on important issues. Financial, marketing, production, and other non-research and development (R and D) data are necessary both for drug development and for operations of a company.

2. *Published literature* Scientific or technical books and journals housed in company libraries meet most basic information needs of employees. Access to the published literature and various data bases is facilitated by many computerized on-line bibliographic and other data bases.

Literature on company products receives special attention. Articles from the world-wide biomedical literature are gathered, analyzed, indexed and entered into in-house, on-line computer data bases. These references must be rapidly available for consultation for detailed information. These data bases also support periodic reports to the Food and Drug Administration (FDA) or other regulatory agencies.

3. *In-house company documents* These include a wide variety of meeting minutes, reports, analyses, regulatory submissions, archives supporting Good Manufacturing Practice (GMP) and Good Laboratory Practice (GLP) procedures, litigation records, and other material. These are usually kept in one or more repositories, and some documents are entered on computer. Important materials are often also indexed and key terms are identified for computer searches. Microfiche and microfilm may be used to condense data and to avoid storing large quantities of old data and reports. Optical storage facilities are used by an increasing number of companies.

4. *Information on chemicals synthesized* Records may contain a great deal of information beyond the chemical structure and its physical properties, such as amounts synthesized in each batch, amounts remaining from each batch, physical location where the material resides, and specific chemical and biological test results obtained with the material. The topic of computer modeling of new compounds is discussed in Chapter 2. Data about chemicals used as raw materials often may be purchased on magnetic tape from manufacturers.

5. *Media references to the company's products* This can be organized by product and will contain newspaper, news magazine, and other media references. This file may be started when a compound is first tested in humans, passes an efficacy go-no-go decision point, or is marketed.

6. *Competitive intelligence* Relevant information may be collected on the competitors' activities, status of competitive drugs, size and nature of relevant markets, trends in those markets, plus any other useful information. It is easy to collect huge

amounts of data on competitor's drugs. The challenge for any company is to keep this file limited to the true essentials and to periodically update the material so that it remains current. This is usually too expensive or possibly too arduous a task to perform on any but the most important products of the competitors. Addressing selected questions and focusing on specific topics are two methods that may be used to accomplish this task.

7. *Institutional memory* See Chapter 8.

Flow of Information

Figure 17.1 illustrates general ways of visualizing the flow of information. Many variations of this flow exist depending on the type and uses of information involved. This figure is a simplified theoretical approach to illustrate the steps involved. The real situation is usually much more complex, primarily owing to numerous feedback loops and cycles that occur among different stages in this scheme. Computer and other systems may be targeted to deal with particular stages of the flow.

A few of the many types of considerations and aspects associated with each stage are described.

1. *Obtaining information* Information comes from scientific, clinical, and other experiments; sales data; production information; and many other sources both within and external to the company. Data arrive electronically, verbally, and/or in hard copy.

2. *Confirming the accuracy of information* This may involve editing data via various means. Computer programs may be able to check the accuracy of some scientific data, raising "flags" when data are outside preset limits or have internal inconsistencies. The topic of artificial intelligence is becoming more important each year and has numerous applications to confirming the accuracy of information and to drug development. This is discussed in the following chapter section on data management.

3. *Categorizing and organizing information* Information must be categorized and organized to some degree by knowledgable people prior to being processed and indexed for storage.

4. *Processing and indexing information* Processing information involves putting it into a computer, photographing it on microfiche or microfilm, and indexing it for eventual retrieval. Data must be processed so that the company retains the ability to combine and/or analyze it at a later date.

5. *Storing information* Information may be stored as hard copy, electronically in a computer, on microfilm, on microfiche, and/or on optical disks. Each of these methods have particular features that make them desirable for use in active files, archival files, or files that have both functions. Specific systems and equipment are usually purchased based on factors listed in Table 17.1. This table does not list various general criteria such as servicing, number of units sold, availability, reliability of the equipment, and so on. Companies usually have a backup system for protection, or at the minimum they store important information in at least two geographically distant places.

6. *Retrieving information* It is essential to separate the topics of information

INFORMATION FLOW

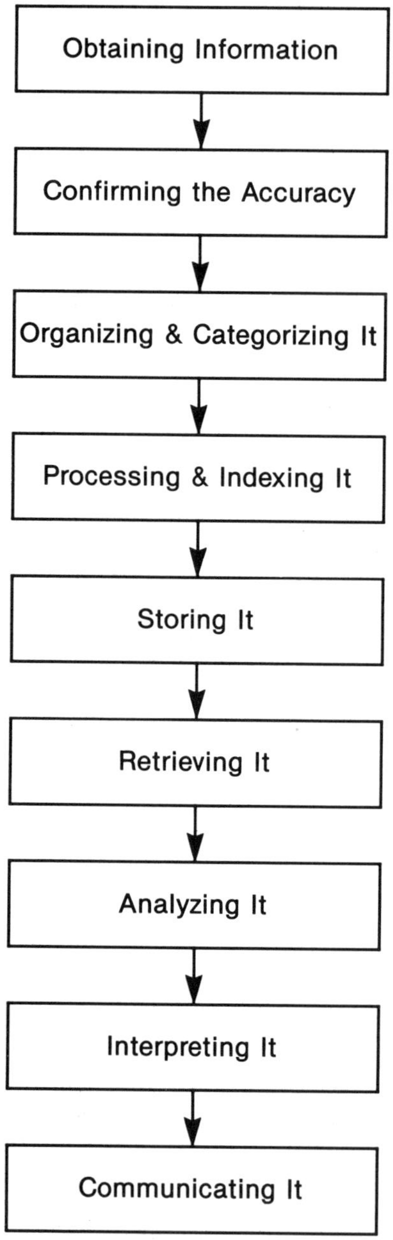

Fig. 17.1. Pattern of information flow. Many variations exist of this generic pattern.

Table 17.1. Primary factors used to select systems and equipment to store information[a]

1. Time to store information
2. Ease of storing information
3. Time to access information
4. Ease of access to information
5. Degree of control of the system or equipment
6. Cost of hardware
7. Cost of maintenance
8. Degree of security
9. Erasability of disks or tapes
10. Capacity for storage
11. Flexibility for different uses
12. Ability to integrate with other systems

[a] Many general criteria relevant to purchasing any equipment (e.g., reputation of manufacturer and vendor, service guarantees, availability) are not included in this table.

storage and retrieval, because the solution to one may not aid (and might actually hinder) the solution to another. Different types of access to data exist (e.g., physical access, logical access). These types of access and other related topics are discussed by Blair (1984). Information indexed with key terms is easier to retrieve. A variety of indexing terms usually need to be searched to obtain broad coverage of topics. Skilled information scientists are usually necessary to retrieve relatively complete information on complex questions.

A critical issue about retrieval sometimes concerns the people who have access to stored information. A common question is whether the person who is requesting data or a report has a *desire* or a *need* to know the information.

7. *Analyzing information* This may be done by many techniques varying from casual observation to formal statistical analyses. Analysis often means selecting, combining, or organizing the information into tables or figures so that it may subsequently be interpreted.

8. *Interpreting information* The meaning of the information is gleaned using the analyses as the basis of the interpretation. After the interpretation is made, it may be extrapolated to other situations.

9. *Communicating information* Information must be effectively communicated to achieve appropriate and full impact. If all of the above eight steps are conducted, but the results are either not communicated or are not communicated well, then most of the value in the above exercise (i.e., steps 1–8) may be lost.

Offering Information to Professionals

Service and education are major functions of providing information. Exploring ideas is another function. For information from central data bases or other centralized sources to be used by professionals, a number of steps must be followed. First, the various uses of information (in a general sense) must be known by potential users. Second, the groups of potential (and actual) users must be identified. Third, information about available resources must be disseminated. This may be done by providing an easy to understand menu of the types of information available and typical uses of the information, plus services provided by those who have or control access to the information. One useful method may be to illustrate which types of information would be helpful at each stage of drug discovery, development, and marketing. This approach could be emphasized with illustrations. One of the essential principles for many information services to follow is that providing a few "pearls" to assist users in reaching a decision or solving a problem is preferable to a large data dump. Large quantities of nonimportant information primarily disheartens the recipient and may be counterproductive to the goals of the data search.

Selected Issues Relating to Information

1. Access to information is a constant issue within a company. The confidential nature of internal data dictates different levels of access to various data bases. One means of achieving this goal is to have different passwords for a single data base. Different passwords control access of each part of the data base.

2. How may a company efficiently deal with the enormous amount of published data, some of which is critically important? Some companies categorize all data into different classes. For example, one system uses three categories with the following definitions: Priority-1 reports apparently have a direct and immediate impact on marketing or medical strategies. Priority-2 reports would add to product knowledge, and priority-3 reports would be the least important and serve as supporting knowledge. The priority of any report or piece of information is not static, but may change drastically and suddenly in unanticipated ways (e.g., an old regulatory letter may acquire new importance based on recent information).

3. Other issues include (1) who owns what data, especially if it resides in a central source, (2) who maintains the data, (3) in what format should data be kept, (4) how detailed should summary data be made.

DATA MANAGEMENT

The Universe of Data Management

Data management is a general phrase that has many meanings within a drug company. A number of years ago fewer areas were concerned with data management than today, and issues were much less complex. Large quantities of data are generated by all functions of a company. Data must be processed, combined, interpreted, and used in ways that are clear, efficient, and designed to achieve one's goals. The term data management refers to the processes whereby some or all of these steps are handled, monitored, and controlled. This section describes major areas in research and development where large amounts of data are generated.

1. *Research* Drug discovery activities utilize computers to an increasingly greater degree to generate, store, and analyze data. This category includes many preclinical activities in chemistry, pharmacology, and other biological sciences. Results obtained on each of a company's compounds should be stored and made readily available to scientists. Molecular modeling is an area requiring sophisticated data handling.

2. *Toxicology* The flow of toxicological information and data into formal reports suitable for registration dossiers is becoming more automated. In many individual studies there is a large number of animals involved, a large number of parameters is measured in each animal, and evaluations are made at numerous scheduled time points. This means that efficient systems must be developed and utilized to handle an enormous quantity of data. GLP regulations require high standards of data management in addition to high standards of animal care and treatment.

3. *Clinical studies* The huge amount of data generated in even a single clinical study requires sophisticated data management systems. Data management involves many aspects including data collection, data transmittal to the sponsor (this is done by remote entry methods in some studies), data editing, data entry into computers, data verification, data analysis by statisticians, and data interpretation. For large scale multicenter studies, special groups and monitors at both a central site and the individual study sites are often required in addition to the sponsor's staff.

4. *Regulatory affairs* Compiling regulatory dossiers involves numerous data management techniques. These include collating and completing reports, numbering pages, transferring data to another medium (e.g., microfilm, microfiche), and submitting different subsets of data to numerous regulatory agencies around the world in a variety of different formats and languages.

5. *Technical development* Numerous aspects of technical development generate large amounts of data (e.g., stability tests conducted under various conditions, with samples obtained and analyzed at numerous time points). Capsules can now be weighed individually and their quality assured. Complex clinical study drug labels and bottles may be prepared and the bottles filled with capsules or tablets using sophisticated systems requiring computer-assisted data management. Chapter 20 describes other examples of technical development where large amounts of data are generated.

6. *Data and information storage* Keeping up with all of the company's reports, minutes, and other documents is a major effort requiring a variety of systems to keep these records in order. Documents must be indexed for retrieval and other uses. Published literature on the company's drugs and other topics of interest must also be systematically analyzed and referenced for easy retrieval.

7. *Postmarketing surveillance* Reports on adverse reactions to marketed drugs reach companies from many sources as described in Chapter 19. The quality and relevance of those data vary to an incredible degree. The data must nonetheless be dealt with rapidly and accurately because of its importance, as well as regulatory requirements.

8. *Quality assurance procedures* Quality assurance (QA) procedures are used in many areas of a company in relation to drug development, including toxicology and drug manufacture. The large volumes of data generated require automated computer-assisted systems to help in this effort.

General Issues in Data Management

Although each functional area of a company has particular issues with regard to data management that are unique to their function, many issues are common to several areas. General issues, plus a few more specific ones, are mentioned.

Table 17.2. Selected drug development areas that may be automated

1. Accounting and budgeting at a company or smaller level of organization
2. Statistical analyses
3. Data acquisition from laboratory instruments
4. Production procedures
5. Data processing of clinical and other areas
6. Investigational drug inventory control
7. Personnel deployment
8. Project planning
9. Remote data entry of laboratory data
10. Evaluations of investigators
11. Clinical data storage, maintenance, retrieval, and analysis
12. Same as item 11 above for toxicology, metabolism, pharmacology, chemical stability, or other types of data
13. Registry of compounds made and test results
14. Quality assurance results of samples tested
15. Published reports of interest
16. Adverse reactions from various sources (e.g., company, other sites, regulatory agencies)

The most important point about data management is that it must be a planned process where a great deal of forethought has gone into the creation of systems, flow of information, checks and balances, and other aspects of the plans that are implemented. Rushing any part of this process may easily cause complex problems to develop that can take years and significant effort and money to unravel. This process cannot be allowed to develop on its own in a topsy-turvy manner. Many data management issues involve reassessing an area where the company has fallen behind the state of the art or believes it can handle data in a better way. New systems must be evaluated, chosen, and then implemented.

Few areas of data management are not intimately connected with computers and computer uses. The use of computers in data management is undergoing rapid change because advancements in both hardware and software have had a dramatic effect on the roles that computers can play in data management (Tables 17.2 and 17.3). Because of this ongoing change, most general issues relating to computer hardware or software are not discussed here, nor are the myriad of more technical computer issues.

Choosing Systems and Equipment and Establishing Policies for Their Use

How may companies best determine the amount of money, time, and staff effort to devote to data management? The rapid change in computer software and hardware make decisions about purchasing equipment more difficult. Lease arrangements have become more attractive in many situations. Many of the primary factors used to select systems and equipment to store data are listed in Table 17.1. Other functions of equipment require different considerations.

After an elaborate system is installed, what should a company do about encouraging employees to use that system? Should the company make the system mandatory, i.e., modify their standard operating procedures so that everyone must adhere to and use the new computer approach? If the company makes the system optional, then few people will use it in some cases. This could mean that a great

Table 17.3. Selected clinical areas of drug development that may be automated[a,b]

1. Protocols (e.g., per drug, per department, per key elements of study design)
2. Data collection form library
3. Contracts with investigators
4. Payments to investigators
5. Patient enrollment information
6. Adverse drug reactions[c]
7. Laboratory data
8. Patient visit data
9. Drug inventory control (e.g., supplies on hand, where supplies went, where supplies are located in a warehouse)
10. Clinical study materials (e.g., orders, status of orders)
11. Cross-study tabulations
12. Labeling of containers for drug studies
13. Information on investigators
14. Information on study centers (e.g., reliability, performance)
15. Time allocation of staff spent on various drug projects

[a] Certain areas may be automatically flagged (i.e., brought to the users attention) when data exceed certain limits or meet certain criteria (e.g., serious adverse reactions, laboratory values that exceed a prespecified number).
[b] Some of these functions may be integrated into a network as described in the text.
[c] These may be integrated from various sources (e.g., investigational studies, marketed studies, foreign sites).

deal of effort and money may have been "wasted." Clearly, the answer to this problem is to evaluate the needs of the potential users ahead of time and to give priority to those systems that are most important to the company, rather than of particular interest to a small number of protagonists. This often turns out to be difficult to identify accurately in practice. Choices often have to be made between competing systems, with different characteristics, or between a well-known system and a newer one that could be far superior, but would require a great deal of effort in installation, maintenance, and/or reeducation of staff.

Should a Company be among the First to Use a New System?

A common problem arises for a company when a vendor is attempting to sell a new system that has all the features desired by the company, but the vendor has not sold any of the units or has sold only a few. A company should generally not be one of the very first clients to purchase and operate a new system. It is virtually certain that the system will have many bugs and will require much more time and effort to become operational. In some cases, highly touted systems never become operational. Another problem about being among the first companies to purchase a system is that the system's concept may not be feasible in practice, or in the drug industry, because of a large input required in time and effort compared to a relatively small gain or output, or because of other factors.

On the other hand, there is a strong temptation within many people and companies to be first to get new systems. This is to get ahead of or to gain on their competition. Another motivation is that most computer or technically oriented people like to have the newest gadgets available. These urges and requests must be controlled because there is a certain probability that the company's progress may actually be slowed in one or more areas by a new system that has many bugs. On the other hand, it is not advisable to be the last company to purchase a new system, because by that time it will be fully operational and helping other companies to develop drugs.

Specific Data Management Issues

More specific data management issues currently being explored within the drug industry include the following:

1. Validation techniques for the many steps in the handling and use of data. How to validate vendor-supplied validation systems?
2. Tracking movement of data from process to process. It is important to establish an audit trail to be able to track data movement at a later date.
3. Minimizing or avoiding poor quality data submitted to regulatory authorities.
4. Copying data efficiently and rapidly using high technology (e.g., microfiche, microfilm).
5. Numbering data and pages rapidly and correctly in a regulatory submission.
6. Remote data entry from investigator's sites to a company or to central laboratories. All clinical data or a small subset (e.g., laboratory data) may be handled in this manner.
7. Planning and tracking multiple project activities on a worldwide basis.
8. Developing and utilizing adverse reaction dictionaries for clinical data.
9. Submitting periodic reports on time to the Food and Drug Administration (FDA) and other agencies.
10. Collecting only relevant data in a study. Any study that collects too much data is in jeopardy of compromising the study's value to the company. Careful consideration must be made of each parameter measured and the amount of data obtained on each parameter. This includes questioning the total length of data collection forms and the amount of data to be collected.
11. Planning production activities in many different geographical areas.
12. Developing artificial intelligence systems. This primarily involves expert systems that try to capture the decision-making ability of an expert within a specific domain of knowledge. It is attempted for areas where algorithms are not appropriate. Some potential uses include (a) molecular modeling, (b) interpreting biological screen data, (c) statistical design analysis and interpretation, (d) automating quality assurance procedures, (e) scheduling production activities, (f) developing marketing plans, (g) controlling complex manufacturing procedures, and (h) predicting drug interactions.

Integrated Systems: Small, Big, and Giant

Other terms for small, big, and giant networks are local area systems, integrated systems across departments or functions, and company-wide integrated systems.

Many scientists and managers have established data bases of various sizes. It was realized many years ago that there were many advantages to be gained by linking some of the data bases with networks (i.e., programs and hardware), so that cross-data base communication and cross-tablulations are possible. Links between data bases are referred to as network systems. Networks enable new questions to be addressed, additional problems to be solved, and in general improve communications. All of the data bases that are linked together by a network constitute an integrated system. Another term used is umbrella system. Small integrated systems have been available for a long period.

The trend toward putting more data bases within the same integrated system has been rapidly increasing. Many large integrated systems cover function-wide data and may be accessed from multiple computer systems using multiple types of data management. The linkage between desktop personal computers and large mainframes, plus networks among various users has been expanding. The linkage between various information data bases at a department level has also been increasing. Companies that are unable to communicate between their various sites efficiently are behind the state of the art. It is important to integrate both the various pieces of hardware and also the various software packages. If only the former is integrated, then the system will not usually be treated as an integrated tool by the users.

Although the trend toward developing large integrated systems is progressing rapidly, there is presently no overall giant system that can cover and link all of the research and development data bases. This type of integrated system would enable a professional to tap and use any data at his or her level of clearance. This futuristic possibility may not be a completely desirable goal because of possible problems of misuse, security, and difficulties if the system is not operating properly. The largest data base possible within a company would involve information from most, if not all, divisions. This too may not be feasible because of security, practicality, and the limited number of people who should have access to all information.

Non-Research and Development Integrated Systems

In addition to research and development data bases, other functions are developing the means of linking some of their data bases in areas where they share interests. These functions include finance, marketing, and production. Examples of uses include better production planning, marketing forecasts, financial reporting of results, and so on. Uses of large data bases that are maintained outside a company are discussed in Chapter 19 under postmarketing surveillance. Such data bases include those tracking individual patients, drugs being used, hospital admissions, diagnoses, and other information. Questions on a company's drugs may be posed to these data bases.

Levels of Integration between Data Bases

There are several levels at which systems or people are integrated.

1. *Physical connection of hardware* Machines from different manufacturers and also from a single manufacturer must be connected or networked if they are to be integrated or operate as part of a single system.
2. *Compatibility of software* Even after the equipment operates as a single system, the software used must be made compatible.
3. *Data structure—compatibility bridges* This is the most important level of in-

tegration. It requires that the data being handled by the system are compatible, so that pieces may be combined.

4. *Translation bridges* This relates to making different applications work together in a single system. It is hard to maintain bridges (linkages) between in-house software and commercial software. Many drug companies seek commercial vendors to provide this software. Each company requires different bridges for their systems.

5. *Application system* A system may be designed to unify many data bases. This is the most overall view of what is developed. Another way of viewing issues of integration are as two types: integrating people to work together and integrating technology to perform as desired. The five levels presented all relate to the technology aspects, but require the people developing, using, and maintaining the system to be integrated (i.e., work together).

Developing an Integrated System

Probably the most important principle is to keep the system simple and make it work. An important corollary of this principle is that it should be developed from the outset by technically oriented people working closely with those who will be using the system. It is also imperative that the concept of the system be supported, if not championed by one or more senior executives with enough clout to insure that the work is completed. After the system has proved its worth, it may be expanded to take on other functions or it may be joined to another network.

It is, ironically, those companies that did little or nothing to develop data bases in the past that have an advantage today. They do not have many established pieces (data bases) that have to be integrated into a system. This allows them an opportunity to develop a more ideal system than those companies that made large financial investments in developing systems and data bases that are less readily connected by networks and integrated into a total system.

The first step in getting started to develop an integrated system is to insure that the people who will be using the system are working cooperatively with the technical people who will set it up. The person who will use the system often must be willing to do his or her work in a different manner after the system is established. This may require a major selling effort by computer-oriented professionals who make recommendations about the type of integrated system to develop. At the same time it is essential for the user to insure that the right issues are being addressed by the technical staff. This is where the commitment from relevant senior managers is important.

Without adequate attention to these steps it is possible for computer people to design and build integrated systems that no one really wants. Whether computer staff develop a new system quietly (i.e., without prior knowledge of the eventual users) or not, the end result is the same—the system will not be used.

The plan proposed must be critiqued to see if it is cost-effective, i.e., if the effort is worth the expected outcomes. Benefits must be judged in terms of timeliness, accuracy, and comprehensiveness of information obtained.

Problem Areas and Issues in Developing an Integrated System

1. A large amount of software and hardware is present in a company that is too valuable to discard and too difficult to integrate into an efficient system.

2. The justification for establishing a new system is usually based on cost savings. These estimates are difficult to establish and involve many assumptions, which may be challenged.

3. Numerous vendors of computers must be dealt with, especially across different disciplines (e.g., production, marketing) and among different countries.

4. Few reliable vendors of application software exist. This often forces companies to write their own.

5. Different sites of the same company often have different beliefs about what are the most important issues and how to address them.

6. There is a balance between developing adequate security for an integrated system and still retaining user friendly systems.

7. Technical personnel to develop and maintain the systems may be centralized, peripheralized into individual functions (e.g., marketing, production) or some combination (e.g., distribute maintenance personnel to peripheral functions, but centralize systems development).

Other Issues about Integrated Systems

Many data management issues have little to do with either hardware or software. The same type of data at two sites, in different departments at one site, or from study to study at one site may be collected in different formats and at different depths, or expressed differently. The perfect computer system cannot readily combine data that have such differences. This problem may be readily addressed in some cases by senior managers making decisions about company policy (e.g., regarding forms to be used to collect clinical data). But, if the end-users differ either in their philosophy or in their uses of the data, there may be greater difficulties resolving this issue. For example, preclinical animal test results may be desired by some users in a format indicating merely that data are positive (+) or negative (−), but others will desire exact data (e.g., doses used, results in detail).

There is usually a great reluctance to establish data bases when they are initially suggested. This is because the owners of the separate files have a vested interest in systems they have developed and territory they try to protect. On the other hand, this reaction is appropriate in many situations. Ownership of a data base usually means responsibility and commitment to its appropriate use.

When a new integrated system is being established a great deal of education may be necessary for the staff who will eventually use it. It usually takes time to get all relevant people to accept the need and the characteristics of a new system. Many technical issues must be determined and agreed to, including (1) system requirements, (2) data base design, (3) record structure, (4) material to be included, (5) who will set up the system, (6) formats for printing outputs, (7) the thesaurus to be used, and (8) who will maintain the system.

Other related questions include (1) how user friendly the system will be, (2) may the information be transferred (i.e., downloaded) from a central mainframe computer to user's individual terminal for manipulation, (3) if the answer to question 2 is yes, may manipulated data now be uploaded back into the central computer with or without an audit trail, (4) how many people outside the core group who establish and maintain the system will have access to it, and (5) should information stored be solely what is needed or should it contain information that would be nice to know?

The future in this area promises to be even more exciting and challenging. A skeptical attitude, however, will serve companies well; that attitude will force them to focus their approach and to utilize their resources most effectively. This will enable them to take best advantage of data management technologies and to learn from other people's experiences and mistakes. Utilizing integrated software from outside the company is usually desirable, even when internal resources are available to develop a unique software program.

STATISTICAL CONSIDERATIONS

Someone once said that there are "liars, damned liars, and statisticians." This has been attributed to Benjamin Disraeli and Winston Churchill, as well as Will Rogers (and possibly others). Whatever its source, it conjures up the image of a statistician being able to make the numbers say whatever you want them to say. Another similar comment relates to the joke about three people who were asked the sum of two plus two. The first was a banker and he answered "four". An accountant was second, and he gave the same response. But, when a statistician was asked the sum of two plus two, he took the questioner aside before responding "What do you want it to equal?"

Roles of Statistics and Statisticians in Drug Development

Before describing some of the many issues concerned with statistics, it is useful to broadly define the universe of statistics in drug discovery and development.

In the preclinical area, scientists utilize statistical principles and methods in the design, execution, and analysis of their experiments. The statistics department may be asked to become involved in individual experiments where sophisticated analyses or concepts are required. Statisticians may also act as consultants to departments that need advice or assistance with data analyses, data automation, or another function.

The largest role of statistics in the drug industry in terms of assignment of personnel is in the clinical area. Regardless of whether statisticians are organizationally part of a clinical group, there are close interactions between them. These focus primarily on clinical studies in the areas of study design, protocol development, data analysis, and statistical report writing. Statisticians are often asked to analyze special problems or issues and to accompany clinicians or scientists to regulatory meetings.

A third area where statistics has intimate involvement is in the quality assurance area of production. A number of the roles played by statisticians in quality assurance are described in Chapter 22.

Broad Issues Involving Statistics and Statisticians

A few representative issues are indicated to provide a flavor of the many types of issues that are encountered.

1. Is it required for statisticians to review all clinical protocols *prior* to their implementation? Over the last 30 years, the pendulum has swung from an almost total "no" to an almost complete "yes." There are still drug companies, particularly outside the United States, where this practice is not required.

2. How much interaction and discussion is there between the clinician and statistician about how to analyze the data collected? Is the decision on which groups and subgroups to compare reached by mutual agreement or does one group have total authority in this matter?

3. Are statisticians integral members of each project team? This is an accepted and standard practice at most drug companies.

4. Are statisticians involved in any research activities seeking new or improved methods of analysis, or are they methodically turning out cloned reports on drug studies?

5. How may company statisticians convince regulatory authorities about the appropriateness of utilizing a specific approach in a specific situation? Even nationally respected statisticians in academia have been unable—at least on some occasions—to change the minds of nonstatisticians at regulatory agencies who insist on having companies use the "FDA approach" to data analysis.

A problem faced by drug companies in dealing with regulatory agencies is that some regulators who are untrained in statistics unilaterally decide on statistical issues, even though prominant academic and drug industry statisticians strongly disagree with their approach. Moreover, some regulators have arbitrarily created new statistical rules that have been enforced as FDA policy. On the other hand, a major issue often arises between two (or more) valid approaches to a set of data from a statistical perspective. Too often, individual statisticians claim that their analyses are the "best" way to handle the data. Nonetheless there are often multiple ways of analyzing data and pros and cons to each.

Some statisticians believe that *all* data obtained in a study must be analyzed, because no matter whether patients should have been treated, met protocol requirements, or never even received the drug, there was an intention to treat. A more clinically oriented approach is to analyze data of patients that make clinical sense, and delete data of other patients from the analyses. The author believes that all relevant statistical analyses should be conducted and some or all presented to regulatory agencies. The analysis that the company believes to be most relevant should be noted and its appropriateness defended and supported. This may save time if a single analysis is presented and a regulatory agency then asks a company to conduct others.

Another issue relates to two development sites of a company each wishing to analyze data from a single clinical study using different statistical tests. Unless agreement is reached on a joint position, the company may be placed in a difficult position if different interpretations of the study are reached.

One of the greatest difficulties in clinical studies regarding statistics are the large number of biases that may enter a study and affect the results. Bad statistics lead to incorrect conclusions about cause and effect relationships (e.g., did the drug cause the adverse reaction) and to a flawed understanding of the relationship being studied.

Examples of Poorly Applied Statistics

The newspapers are full of statistical distortions every day. For example, one study claimed that older automobile drivers are safer than younger adults. But that study was based on the number of accidents per year. Because older people drive less, they have fewer accidents. But, if the comparison was based on the number of accidents per mile driven, then older drivers were the second to worst category of all drivers.

Another problem that is frequently noted occurs in advertising. Numbers and data are often twisted beyond recognition. A long history of distorted use of statistics in marketing claims is so pervasive that it has helped create generations of skeptical people and has destroyed a great deal of trust both between physicians and drug companies and between drug companies and regulatory agencies.

Two commonly reported situations where more information is required to understand a situation are presented below.

1. As a holiday weekend approaches and commences, we are given results in the media of the precise number of people killed locally, statewide, and nationally. The assumption is made that it is more dangerous to drive on holiday weekends. A careful review of traffic accident data illustrates that approximately one-third more deaths occur on holiday weekends compared to an average weekend. But, there are at least one-third more cars on the road during holiday weekends, so that the probability of any car having an accident resulting in death is no greater than on other weekends. In fact, the probability may be somewhat lower because of increased driver awareness and the visible presence of more police officers on the highway.

2. Women are often reported to earn less than men for comparable work. But, there are many factors involved in how people accept positions and are paid. One situation experienced by many couples where both are highly paid professionals is when the husband looks all over the country to select the best job possible to advance his career. Then, his wife looks for a job in the specific area chosen by the husband. In most situations she will earn less money than if the area of her search was not as restricted. The point is not to challenge the initial claim, which is probably true, but to illustrate some of the factors that complicate its interpretation.

18 / *Toxicology Issues*

It has been stated that animal toxicology has as much predictive value in terms of a compound's potential toxicological profile in man as the ritual hepatoscopy practised by the Babylonians using sacrificial goats in their attempts to foretell the future. This practice is referred to in the Old Testament in Ezekiel Ch. 21. It was also practised in the Roman era during the siege of Jerusalem in 70 AD and was documented by Josephus. Before dismissing this ancient practice as having no predictive value, it might be well to note that the goats' livers on both occasions accurately predicted the fall of Jerusalem. It would be even more foolish to dismiss the predictive value of animal toxicology studies so lightly. John P. Griffin, English physician. From Predictive Value of Animal Toxicity Studies in *Long-Term Animal Studies: Their Predictive Value for Man.*

All substances are poisonous, there is none which is not a poison; the right dose differentiates a poison from a remedy. Attributed to Paracelsus, 16th century.

INTRODUCTION

Newspapers are often replete with stories about the latest chemical or environmental pollutant or drug that is found to be toxic. The news is blasted forth in the media and sales of the drug plummet; sometimes the company's stock falls as well. Although some of the news stories are justified, others distort a complex relationship by representing it in black and white terms. For example, are vitamin A and selenium toxic? This question may seem silly, but arctic explorers sometimes developed serious vitamin A toxicity from eating too much whale blubber or other local foods. Also, reports that selenium was carcinogenic at high concentrations led to its being purged from some people's diets. As a result, it has been claimed that "many human deaths have occurred from selenium deficiency" (Berry, 1986). At low doses, selenium is an important nutrient. It is therefore incorrect to state that humans should avoid all chemicals that may cause cancer at high doses.

Toxicology studies can never demonstrate that a drug is safe. They can only define the toxicity of the drug under the specific conditions of the study. Toxicity is a characteristic of all substances, when studied in sufficient doses. Some studies show that a drug is not toxic under the conditions tested. New human or animal data may be uncovered at any time before or after a drug is marketed that demonstrate a drug to be more or less safe (at least under the conditions studied) than previous toxicology studies indicated.

Types of Drug Toxicity

One classification of drug toxicity considers two major types. The first are those toxicities that result from an extension of the pharmacological activity that is related to the drug's therapeutic effect. This may be viewed as a continuation of the dose-response relationship beyond the peak beneficial effect. The other major type of toxicity is unrelated to a drug's beneficial effects, and may either be predictable to occur in patients (e.g., gout caused by thiazide diuretics) or unpredictable (e.g., hyperplasia of the gums caused by phenytoin, retroperitoneal fibrosis caused by methysergide).

Types of Long-Term Studies

To evaluate chronic drug toxicity, three major types of long-term animal studies are conducted. The first is chronic testing to evaluate gross (i.e., large) and microscopic changes in the body, plus behavioral changes. The second type is carcinogenicity studies that last for the natural life-span of rats and mice (approximately two years). The third type is reproduction studies that include three subtypes: fertility, teratology, and perinatal evaluations. It is often useful to retain some animals from chronic toxicology studies when the exposure phase is finished. These animals are used for evaluating the reversibility of specific adverse effects. This information enables the potential significance of positive toxicity findings to be better assessed.

Studying Higher Versus Lower Dosages in Toxicological Studies

There are numerous well-known reasons why high doses of a chemical or drug may produce entirely different effects than those produced by a lower dose. For example, at high doses the body may be unable to metabolize a drug that is handled in a therapeutically useful and safe way when lower doses are given. Toxic metabolites may be produced at exaggerated dose levels that are not formed at therapeutically useful dose levels. Alternatively, the body may be unable to eliminate large doses of a drug and the drug may buildup (i.e., accumulate) to levels that cause toxicity in safety tests but would be unlikely to occur in humans taking recommended doses. There may also be marked differences in effects noted in different species with high doses of a drug.

PLANNING A TOXICOLOGY PROGRAM

Core Studies

There is a core number of toxicology studies that are usually conducted with few if any modifications. It is essential for most drugs to perform subchronic tests (e.g., 30-, 60-, or 90-days exposure) in two species. The information obtained is used as a starting point to plan further studies. Core studies contain both short-term and long-term studies.

The specific studies conducted for a drug depend on its eventual route of administration to patients, the duration of patient exposure, and previous clinical and toxicological information on related compounds or drugs, plus regulatory requirements and requests. Depending on these factors, a number of additional studies are usually added to the core group of studies to be conducted. Beyond this group of studies are a large number of potential studies that could be considered. Some companies are more conservative than others in their approach to toxicology and usually go beyond what would be considered to be a minimum number of studies by most regulatory agencies.

Specialized Studies

In addition to long-term toxicology studies and the appropriate battery of short-term studies, a number of specialized studies often must be conducted. The nature of these studies depend on the nature of a drug, i.e., its therapeutic use, chemical class, and specific clinical and pharmacological characteristics of its profile. These studies could involve additional species of particular interest or special strains of animals with certain genetic characteristics. Also, specific routes of administration, new parameters, or various formulations of the drug could be evaluated. For example, if analyses for impurities in a drug undergoing stability tests demonstrate that 15 percent of a specific breakdown product is formed, it may be useful to conduct toxicology studies on that breakdown compound, either as part of the parent drug mix or when tested independently. In addition, the biological activity of breakdown products should be measured. If breakdown products are either isomers of the parent drug or biologically similar to the parent drug, then it may be possible to obtain regulatory approval for a shelf life that would permit this degree of degradation in the final drug product.

Timing of Toxicology Studies

There is one major "Catch-22" situation that often arises in determining the appropriate timing for conducting toxicology studies. This relates to the general desire to wait for efficacy of a new drug to be established in Phase II studies before initiating the long-term toxicology studies (i.e., one-year studies and lifetime carcinogenicity bioassays, each done in two separate species). These studies are not only extremely expensive to conduct (approximately a half million dollars for each rodent bioassay used to assess carcinogenic potential), but they also consume large quantities of investigational drug. The drug may not yet have been synthesized in sufficient amounts to allow such testing to occur at an earlier stage, and there may be various problems associated with obtaining sufficient drug. Nonetheless, if the go-no go point in Phase II is used as the time to initiate long-term toxicology studies, the clinical studies on some drugs could be completed and ready to submit to a regulatory agency before toxicology reports are ready. It is undesirable for toxicology reports to be a rate-limiting step in submitting a regulatory application.

In practice, there are generally ways to provide for adequate time to complete the toxicology program necessary for a regulatory submission before all clinical reports are finished. One way of dealing with the "Catch-22" situation with long-term studies is to make every effort with computers, scheduling, and other techniques to reduce the lag, commonly six months to one year or more, between completion of long-term dosing and availability of the final report. If a problem of timing seems to be likely, then long-term toxicology studies can be initiated earlier in the development program, with the understanding that the money to pay for these studies would possibly be wasted if the drug had to be terminated. The term possibly is used because if the drug's toxicology profile demonstrated the absence or presence of specific findings, it could provide important information to help plan the future development of the entire chemical series.

Some research and development managers desire to start many toxicology studies on all new investigational compounds as soon as drug supply is available. This makes sense if there are few drugs undergoing development at the company and the company is in the fortunate position of having abundant resources. Most drug companies are clearly not in this position. But, if a company is effectively prioritizing the development of its investigational drugs and if it is concerned about not wasting dollars and resources, then it is generally wise to delay the start of long-term toxicology studies until after some Phase II studies are completed. These studies should clearly demonstrate efficacy, confirm that the safety profile is adequate, demonstrate acceptable pharmacokinetics, and provide an overall indication that a regulatory submission (e.g., Product License Application [PLA], New Drug Application [NDA]) will probably be prepared for the drug.

Are All Toxicological Studies Conducted According to One Standard?

There is great variation in the quality of contract toxicological laboratories that conduct studies for the drug industry. A drug company that bargain shops looking for the cheapest place to conduct a toxicology study is usually foolish. There is no faster way to kill a promising drug unnecessarily, or to delay its progress, than by raising toxicological questions that must be addressed. Clinical programs are often put "on hold" by the Food and Drug Administration (FDA) and/or by the company itself when toxicological issues arise.

Quality studies are essential and corners should not be cut. In situations where specialized toxicology studies are required, there may only be a few laboratories qualified to do the work. These groups may be unable to schedule a company's work as soon as desired. This presents a potentially serious dilemma. It is usually better to wait for the best group, provided that the development program is not unacceptably delayed. When delays are unacceptable and the study must be contracted to another group, the contracted study must be monitored intensely.

Cost of Toxicology Studies

Drug company executives are aware that toxicology studies are often extremely expensive. There are a few occasions when these studies are the single greatest expense in developing a new drug. This situation could arise either if questions arose that required numerous additional studies or if the costs of clinical studies and technical development were rather modest. For example, if a new drug was being developed for a rare disease, the clinical studies might rely heavily on a few case studies, whereas the toxicology "package" of studies could be quite extensive and expensive. Although orphan drugs are usually approved with abbreviated efficacy data compared to a drug intended to treat a large patient population, the amount of safety data required for approval may not be commensurately reduced by the FDA. Although toxicology studies are expensive, they usually account for a relatively minor portion (approximately 11 percent) of the total drug development cost (see Chapter 23).

ISSUES IN STUDY DESIGN

Representative Factors

Many factors relating to the drug substance, animals, and intended clinical use of a drug must be considered when designing toxicology studies. These will not be enumerated or described in detail, because they are adequately discussed in the toxicology literature. A few general factors, however, will be mentioned to provide a flavor of issues encountered. Diet is an important consideration because it can affect tumor incidences and the animal's longevity; therefore, it must be carefully controlled. The specific strain of rat or mouse used also has an influence on tumor incidences and duration of carcinogenicity bioassays (i.e., some strains live longer than others). Choosing a species to study is sometimes difficult when it is known that animals metabolize a drug differently than humans, or have unique toxicities not observed in humans. In addition, not all animal species exhibit toxicities that may be specifically sought to evaluate (e.g., rats do not vomit). The more one delves into the field of toxicology, the more variables one observes that may affect a study's outcome and interpretation.

Three dose levels of a compound are often chosen to give to animals. The low dose is expected to be a no-effect dose and is set at least five times the expected or known therapeutic dose (if possible). The high dose is chosen to identify toxic effects, but is not set so high as to jeopardize completion of a study. An intermediate dose is usually set at the mean of the high and low dose. The amount of a dose received by animals depends in part on whether it is physically given to the animal (e.g., by injection, by placing it in their stomach) or placed in their food (e.g., once a day for a specific period, provided *ad lib.*).

Reasons Why Multiples of the Anticipated Peak Human Dose Are Used in Toxicology Studies

The major reason why large multiples of the anticipated peak human dose are studied is to determine what might be the worst possible scenario of the drug's toxicity. That belief, based largely on empirical observations, is that if 100 times the peak human dose does not produce unacceptable toxicity in laboratory animals, the dose given for therapy in clinical practice should be safe. A second reason for using large multiples of the anticipated peak human dose is to avoid using large numbers of animals. For example, if a toxic event actually occurs in 5 percent of all animals (or humans), it is necessary to study 60 animals in order to be 95 percent certain that you will observe a single case in the sample you are studying, or 100 animals to be 99 percent certain that you will observe one case. It is assumed, primarily on a statistical basis, that the use of higher doses will help identify potentially important toxicity using smaller numbers of animals. This assumption may (or may not) be valid. Dose-response relationships are therefore vital to the process of safety assessment.

Dose-Response Relationships

The dose-response pattern often provides more useful information than that gathered by preclincial testing at excessive dose levels. Various toxic dose levels may be determined to provide a profile of a drug's safety in animals.

1. *No-observed effect dose.* No effects of any type noted.
2. *No-observed adverse-effect dose.* Effects noted, but judged minimal and unlikely to cause significant toxicity in patients.
3. *Adverse-effect dose.* Moderate toxicity observed.
4. *Frank-effect dose.* Severe toxicity noted.

These four levels of dose-response relationships in toxicological studies provide a comparison with doses shown or projected to be used and safe in humans.

There is no magic formula that states a drug must not produce toxicity in laboratory animals at X times the dose needed for therapy if the drug is to be clinically useful. The same principle applies to the human situation. The ratio of the toxic dose to the therapeutic dose (i.e., the therapeutic ratio) should be as high as possible. The magnitude of this number clearly depends on the particular disease and situation. Serious adverse events in humans are often acceptable with a new anticancer drug, but would be totally unacceptable for diseases where relatively safe drugs already exist, or for diseases characterized by low morbidity.

Studies of Biologicals and Biotechnology Products

As a compound's structure progressively departs from a natural chemical found in humans, the initial toxicological requirements of regulatory agencies increase. This means that a company planning a toxicology program for a natural substance it is developing may shift the bulk of the work to a later time. This usually occurs *after* the drug's efficacy and safety have been identified. This is important because drug supply is usually a major issue early in a biotechnology derived drug's development. This does *not* mean that natural sequence proteins or other biologicals are necessarily safe for use in humans or do not require extensive toxicological tests.

Biotechnology products are evaluated in both acute dose studies for up to a few days and in chronic dose studies for up to four weeks. In addition to more traditional aspects of toxicity, animals are examined for antibodies, effects on the immune system, and local tolerance. Most natural products can be given in either physiological or pharmacological dosages. *Physiological doses* are relatively low doses given to replace absent or low levels of that substance in patients (i.e., to bring patients' own levels to normal). Adrenal steroids, thyroid hormone, insulin, and human growth factor are examples of hormones that may be replaced by physiological doses in patients who are deficient. *Pharmacological doses* are usually multiples of physiological doses given to patients to elicit an effect. These relatively high doses may cause marked toxicity. Examples of natural products used in this way include interferon, tissue plasminogen activator, and heparin.

REGULATORY ISSUES

Regulatory Guidelines

Guidelines for conducting toxicological studies on most new drugs are relatively straightforward (Table 21.15 in Spilker, 1987c). Those guidelines, however, are both directly and indirectly controlled and influenced by regulatory agencies around the world. As a result, the guidelines established for choosing the basic experimental design, as well as the numbers, species, sex, age, and feeding conditions of animals to be studied, are not always the same for each country. The doses of drugs to be studied are usually based on dose-ranging studies. These are pilot studies of short duration used to evaluate toxicological effects at several prespecified dose levels. Definitive toxicological studies of many kinds utilize the information obtained in dose-ranging studies.

Methods and parameters used are also indicated and described in the protocol. Specific measurements and evaluations conducted on live animals are generally well established, as are the methods of necropsy and obtaining both gross and microscopic tissue samples. Measurement of drug levels in blood is an important part of toxicological testing, because this information is often useful in extrapolating results of preclinical tests to humans.

Interpretation of results obtained in preclinical toxicological tests requires extensive experience if the testing is to be used to maximum advantage in the drug development process. Disagreements are inevitable when lesions or other adverse events do not fit accepted clear and unambiguous criteria. Pathologists often reach different diagnoses of the lesions they "read" in microscopic slides. There may also be great differences of opinion among toxicologists who interpret the significance of findings reported in any specific test. Even when two or more toxicologists agree about the diagnosis of a lesion or the nature of another adverse event, there are often great differences in how they assess the potential significance of the data for humans.

Regulatory Requirements in Different Countries for Toxicology Testing

Differences between countries are sometimes based on political or social rather than scientific considerations. Unfortunate experiences with a drug or class of drugs can be the source of some of these differences. For most countries except Japan there are relatively minor differences between toxicology requirements. Japanese requirements are identified more precisely and are itemized in greater detail than in other countries. In some situations a study or two may have to be redone or added by a sponsor to provide additional information required for a Japanese regulatory submission.

Differences in toxicology requirements between countries include (1) the number of studies to be done as part of a regulatory submission, (2) the type of studies to be done, (3) the design of each study (e.g., duration of treatment, manner of feeding animals, parameters to be measured), and (4) the rate at which studies must be conducted during the drug development process. For example, if a study to evaluate a drug in humans for three months is to be conducted as part of a Phase II clinical plan, the regulatory requirement for a specified duration of already completed toxicology studies to support the safety of the human study varies between countries.

Decisions of regulatory agencies in requesting or recommending (but not requiring) toxicology studies are often questioned by drug companies on the basis of scientific rationale. Nonetheless, most companies comply with all regulatory requests for studies from those agencies that are considered less flexible. Some regulatory requests do not appear to be based on science, but either on a desire to complete a checklist or for obscure reasons.

Regulatory Requirements in Different Countries for Mutagenicity Testing

One of the current issues in toxicology concerns different regulatory requirements and guidelines for mutagenicity testing. Mutagenicity tests are short-term tests that are thought useful by some people to predict the carcinogenic potential of compounds. These tests are hotly debated as to their relevance for predicting a drug's carcinogenic potential (Clive, 1987). The major problem is that a high rate of false-positive results are obtained in some of the most widely used *in vitro* tests. This means that although a drug may be found to be a mutagen in one or more tests, it may later be found not to cause cancer in laboratory animals. Tests to evaluate cancer in animals involve dosing animals for approximately two years and are considered a more reliable indicator than mutagenicity tests as to a drug's potential to cause a cancer in humans.

One of the major reasons for requiring mutagenicity tests at an early stage of a drug's development is to better protect normal volunteers and patients exposed to the drug. Because carcinogenic studies are often not initiated until after a drug's efficacy is demonstrated, demonstrating that a drug is inactive in mutagenicity tests is believed by some to reduce the likelihood that patients in clinical studies are being given a carcinogenic drug. Some patients might receive long-term treatment with a mutagenic drug if this property is not evaluated at an early stage of drug development. On the other hand, the significance of this point is often unknown, and because the false-positive rate for demonstrating mutagenicity is relatively high, a more likely consequence is that potentially useful drugs are dropped unnecessarily.

One of the counterarguments for conducting long-term (i.e., two year) carcinogenicity studies focuses on the fact that most drug-induced cancers are observed rather early in the course of lifetime carcinogenicity bioassays, usually within the first six or twelve months. Some people believe that a shorter period of drug testing than two years could be used to assess drug safety in animals (Walker and Dayan, 1986).

The FDA does not *require* that any mutagenicity tests be conducted to have a new drug approved. It may, however, either *request* or *recommend* that certain specific mutagenicity tests or a general battery of such tests be performed. Because of the requirements for mutagenicity testing outside the United States, most American-based drug companies routinely conduct such tests, and almost all drugs approved by the FDA have data from some of these tests.

The European Economic Community (EEC) does *require* a battery of mutagenicity tests to be performed. They have established various categories of tests and allow each company to choose the specific tests it desires to conduct from each of the separate categories. Requirements in Japan are even more extensive. Their attitude appears to be a desire to identify the dose that causes mutagenic effects and to describe these effects, rather than to test drugs in such tests at reasonable multiples of the actual human dose. Thus, their emphasis appears to be on characterizing a drug's toxicity rather than testing for its safety. This difference is important to consider when observing how different regulatory agencies interpret safety data.

MUTAGENICITY ISSUES

Categorization of Mutagenicity Tests

One categorization of mutagenicity tests includes evaluations of the following three situations.

1. *Point mutations* (i.e., single gene mutation that is undetectable microscopically). These are usually evaluated in bacteria. This is most frequently evaluated using the well-known Ames test.

2. *Chromosomal breakage* in vitro.

3. *Chromosomal breakdown in whole animals.* The assumption is made that if a drug causes chromosomal breakage, then future generations of cells may be abnormal. A major issue is how extensive chromosome repair is in humans and what role it can play in reversing chromosomal damage. Unfortunately, little information is currently known about chromosomal repair.

Selected Issues Involving Mutagenicity Tests

Each compound must be tested separately in mutagenicity tests, because two compounds with similar chemical structures may yield entirely different results. Chemicals with similar structures may have opposite potencies as mutagens and carcinogens. This makes it difficult to extrapolate mutagenicity data to humans. Even if a drug is positive in both mutagenicity and carcinogenicity tests, it may not be concluded that the same mechanism is involved.

Assume that a new metabolite is discovered in human studies late in a drug's development and that the metabolite is present in relatively large amounts. If large amounts of this metabolite were present in the animal species evaluated, then its toxicological profile would be known. If this metabolite was not present in the animal species evaluated for the long-term toxicological effects of the parent drug, its toxicological profile would not be established and a difficult situation could arise. One question is whether new mutagenicity tests must be performed. The new compound may have to be tested in several mutagenicity tests to register the parent drug in EEC countries, whereas these tests might not be required in the United States.

Given the possibility of a false-positive response in mutagenicity tests, would it be worthwhile at this relatively late date for a company to conduct these tests? Would it be preferable to conduct the more predictive (and much longer) carcinogenicity studies instead? The risks of a false-positive result would be to (1) give strong ammunition to any competitors, (2) delay launch of the drug, and (3) put an albatross, perhaps permanently, around the drug's neck. Of course, some regulators might not require mutagenicity testing of all metabolites formed, especially if small amounts of the compound were present in animals that were part of the carcinogenicity studies; or, if the company committed itself to conduct new carcinogenicity studies on the metabolite. Many options exist in this scenario and input must be received from many functions of a company before a decision is reached.

19 / *The World of Clinical Studies and International Drug Development*

The history of medicine has never been a particularly attractive subject in medical education, and one reason for this is that it is so unrelievedly deplorable a story. For century after century, all the way into the remote millennia of its origins, medicine got along by sheer guesswork and the crudest sort of empiricism. It is hard to conceive of a less scientific enterprise among human endeavors. Virtually anything that could be thought up for the treatment of disease was tried out at one time or another, and, once tried, lasted decades or even centuries before being given up. It was, in retrospect, the most frivolous and irresponsible kind of human experimentation, based on nothing but trial and error, and usually resulting in precisely that sequence. Bleeding, purging, cupping, the administration of infusions of every known plant, solutions of every known metal, every conceivable diet including total fasting, most of these based on the weirdest imagines about the cause of disease, concocted out of nothing but thin air—this was the heritage of medicine up until a little over a century ago. Dr. Lewis Thomas. American physician and essayist. From *The Medusa and the Snail.*

PRINCIPLES AND APPROACHES OF CLINICAL STUDIES

Types of Clinical Studies

Although there are numerous classifications that have been proposed about how to categorize clinical studies, they are generally similar. *Safety* studies are discussed in this chapter, and in fact all clinical studies contain some safety considerations, even if safety per se is not an objective of the study. The other major category of clinical studies is *efficacy*, which usually is evaluated during Phases II and III. Other categories of clinical studies include *pharmacokinetics* (absorption, distribution, metabolism, and excretion), *cost-effectiveness*, *compliance*, and *quality of life*.

Levels of Clinical Studies

Different sets or levels of clinical studies exist. Five discreet levels of clinical studies are shown in Fig. 19.1. A number of sublevels of each of these levels are also indicated. These levels and sublevels may be used to understand the types of clinical studies. Any particular clinical study will be a part of multiple levels and may be viewed from different perspectives. This is especially important to consider when data from different studies are compared and possibly combined.

LEVELS OF CLINICAL STUDIES

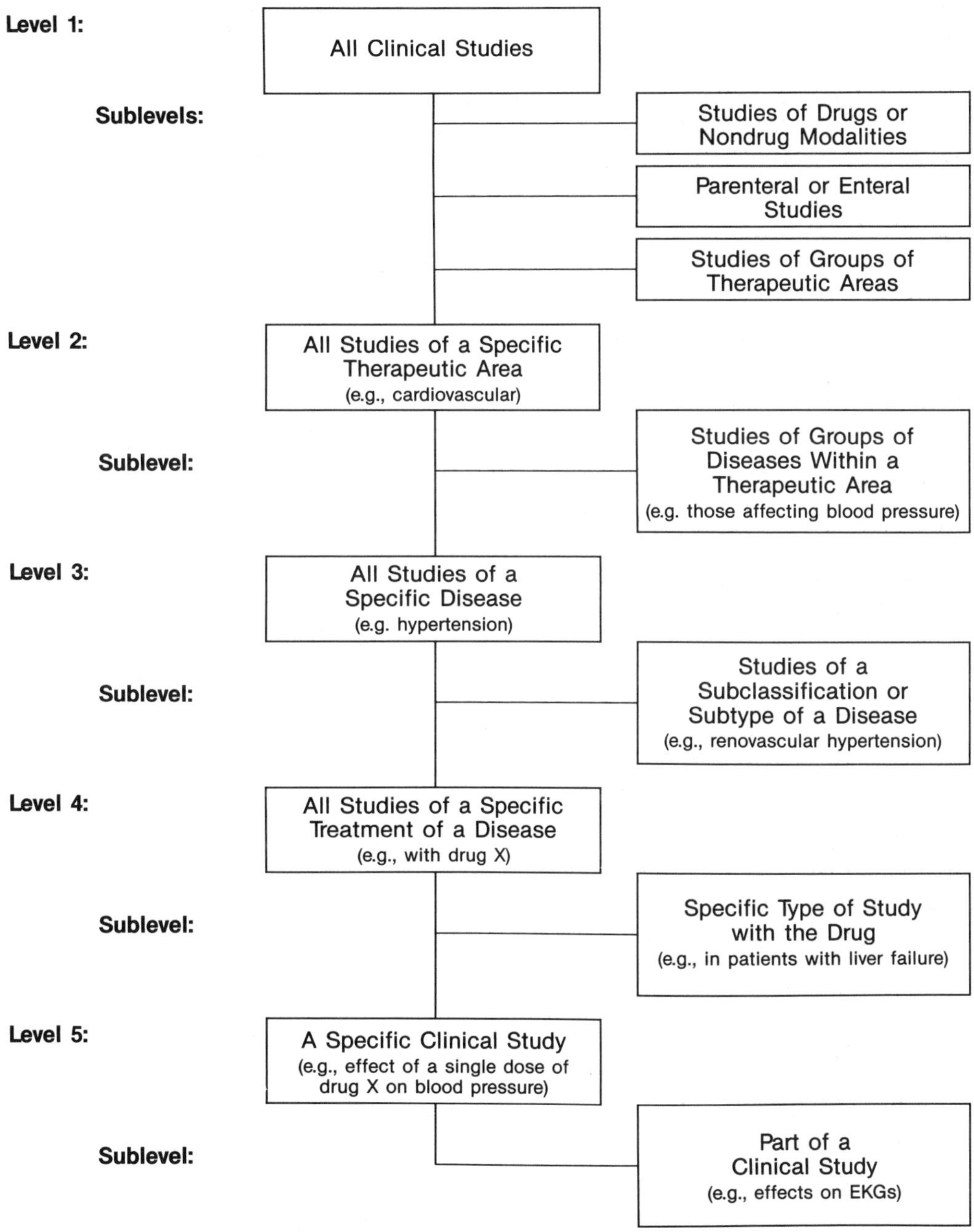

Fig. 19.1. Levels and sublevels of clinical studies.

This book cannot go into detail about the design and conduct of a single clinical study, the interpretation of data resulting from clinical studies, or the planning and management of multiple clinical studies. Readers who desire this information are referred to the *Guide to Clinical Studies* trilogy (Spilker, 1984, 1986b, 1987c). That series of books focuses on level 1 of Fig. 19.1, although numerous examples are given from all levels. Many books are written about methods, data, or drug treatment at levels 3 and 4. There are few references of practical information on clinical methods at level 2 (see Spilker, 1987a for an example). This chapter presents general concepts and principles relating to clinical studies for individuals who seek an overview of this field.

Categories of Clinical Indications

Virtually all drugs are evaluated for activity in more than one indication (i.e., disease or medical problem). For any drug this usually occurs sequentially for some diseases and simultaneously for others, although a company may decide to study numerous indications for a drug either sequentially or simultaneously. To plan the clinical development for a drug it is important to develop a strategy of how the drug's activity (i.e., efficacy) will be determined in terms of timing of studies and order of regulatory submissions. This is done for each indication of interest. This strategy is a critically important decision in terms of how a drug is to be developed. This decision is usually made before the drug has been studied in humans, even though it may be revised at later times. To assist in this effort, the possible indications to study may be divided or categorized into several groups. One such categorization is:

1. Indications already included in the labeling of a comparable marketed drug.
2. Indications that have been submitted to a regulatory agency, for either a marketed or investigational drug.
3. Indications that are currently being evaluated where efficacy is established and there is a firm intention to submit a regulatory application.
4. Indications being evaluated for an investigational drug where efficacy has not yet been well established. A regulatory application is planned to be submitted if safety, efficacy, and other data are acceptable.
5. Indications that will be evaluated in pilot studies when time and resources permit.
6. Potential indications that may be evaluated in the future.
7. Indications for which regulatory approval will not be sought, but where clinical publications are desired.

This same type of categorization could be devised for various routes of administration and/or dosage forms of a drug.

After the categorization is complete, it is possible to prioritize the order in which each specific indication will be pursued, and to begin to allocate resources appropriately to pursue this effort. The overall plan may be only to choose one indication, one route of administration, and one dosage form and not to deviate from the first human exposure until the New Drug Application (NDA) is filed. This has been referred to as a laser approach (Spilker, 1987c). Few drugs follow such a highly targeted path. Most drugs either initially start out with multiple indications being pursued or start out with a single indication and gradually accumulate more indications over time. Different visual models of these (and other) approaches are shown in Fig. 8.4.

Choosing the Indications to Pursue

Different groups of people within a drug company often have different perspectives and opinions on this issue. Scientists usually approach the question mainly from a scientific value point of view. Marketing personnel emphasize commercial aspects. Clinicians consider patient need and the therapeutic utility of a potential new drug. All three views may be in concert, but disagreements and disputes sometimes arise. For example, both marketers and scientists may be enthusiastic about pursuing a new drug to treat chicken pox in children. But, the drug company's clinicians probably realize that practicing physicians would not utilize a new drug in mild cases of chicken pox because (1) the disease is self-limiting, (2) the risk-to-benefit ratio for using the drug in children does not mandate that the disease must be treated, (3) the disease often is either not diagnosed or misdiagnosed in children, and (4) it would be necessary to prove that children treated with the drug prophylactically developed long-term immunity that was at least the same as that obtained after the disease. This is necessary because chicken pox is often a much more serious disease when it initially occurs in adults than in children.

At some companies the indications that are pursued are primarily selected by senior research and development managers, while at other companies, medical personnel have this responsibility. It is important to develop each new drug according to a broad plan that is appropriately reviewed and accepted. Some clinical staff may spend a significant amount of time planning unauthorized studies or evaluating entire indications that lie outside the approved plan. This is usually done in the hope that they will be able to eventually convince relevant managers that the indication of interest to them is worthwhile to develop, or should be evaluated at an earlier point in the drug's development. This practice should be strongly discouraged, because it destroys the resource allocation system and encourages individuals to go in their own direction.

How Is a Clinical Question Posed in a Study?

The way in which a clinical question is specifically worded in the protocol (detailed outline of the clinical study) greatly influences the design of the study that will be conducted to answer the question. The question posed is called the study's objective and is the major purpose for conducting the study. For example, when developing a new antihypertensive drug, many different questions are asked at various stages of the drug's development. Initial questions in Phase I relate to a drug's safety, but in Phase II, questions of efficacy become more important. To illustrate this point, two of the questions that could be the major objective of a study and relate to efficacy are listed, along with a few comments on an appropriate study design chosen.

1. *What doses of the drug cause a lowering of blood pressure by 8 to 15 mm Hg for one month?* A study testing several doses of the drug would be conducted in patients treated for a month after they had been screened, enrolled in the study, had other drugs removed, gone through a baseline period, and then had the drug's dose gradually raised to a stable level. One or more control groups could be included. Patients in a control group would usually receive a placebo or a different active drug.

2. *Is the blood pressure-lowering effect of the drug the same for patients who are treated twice a day as for those who receive the same total dose divided into four individual doses per day?* A study would be conducted comparing effects of two similar groups of patients given the two different dosage regimens. It is possible that at the end of a specific period of time, each patient would be switched to alternate treatment. If the study was to be double-blind, then each patient would take medicine four times a day, but those on the twice a day regimen would take the active drug twice a day and a placebo twice a day. This would either require a special packaging of the drug (e.g., blister pack where each day's dose is labeled) or the use of two different bottles of drugs. The blister pack method is easier for patients to use and would most likely enhance their compliance. A different study design using a separate group of patients for each regimen could also be used.

During Phase III and IV studies more sophisticated questions could be posed. For example, how many years of antihypertensive treatment are required to prolong life for one year? Do patients who receive antihypertensive drug treatment live longer than patients who do not take drug therapy? These examples help illustrate that the study design chosen depends on the question asked and that it is necessary to phrase a study's objectives as precisely as possible.

How Many Questions May be Asked in a Single Clinical Study?

There is a strong temptation when designing a clinical study to ask too many questions. Because it *is* possible to design a study that asks numerous questions, many people from fields outside of medicine (e.g., science, marketing) believe that it is better to conduct a single large study to answer many questions, rather than conducting a series of studies (which may or may not be smaller in size) but only ask one question each. This desire is like the siren luring Ulysses. It is an alluring prospect, but will probably lead to serious problems and could lead to a drug's destruction on the rocky shore. Others may see this issue as deciding whether to gamble the drug's future on a large risky study that will save development time if it works, rather than being more conservative and conducting several smaller studies that will require more time to complete. It is often necessary to conduct several small studies, and this is usually a more sound approach to drug development.

When a number of factors are varied in a single study, the specific reason for a particular clinical outcome is often unclear. For example, assume that two important factors are changed in a study of an active drug. Also assume that the new clinical results do not demonstrate that the drug worked. Then, it is usually uncertain as to which of the two factors was responsible for the failure to demonstrate drug activity. As an illustration, if an investigational drug was shown to be effective when a 500 mg dose was given four times a day, it might be important to learn if a 300 mg dose would be active and also if dosing patients twice a day would be effective. A study that evaluated a 300 mg dose given twice a day could be designed and conducted. If the drug was inactive, however, it would not be known whether the loss of activity was because the dose was lowered from 500 to 300 mg or because the frequency of dosing was lowered from four to two times a day (or both). This simple example illustrates how critical it is to design clinical studies that do not attempt to accomplish too many objectives.

The example given is similar to a situation that occurs thousands of times every day when patients visit their physicians. Assume that a patient is taking a drug that is not working effectively or is causing adverse reactions. The physician may alter several parameters at once and hope that the patient's situation will improve. These parameters could include adding a new drug, stopping the main drug, changing the dose of the main drug, changing the dose of a concomitant drug that may be interacting with the main drug, changing the patient's diet or level of physical activity, and so forth. If the patient improves, it is usually unclear which specific change or combination was responsible. If the patient does not improve, it is still possible that only making a single change would have led to improvement. Further, if an unexpected outcome occurs, then it will be totally unclear as to which factor(s) are responsible. On the other hand, it is frequently difficult for a physician (unlike a scientist) to change only one parameter at a time. Patients are often unwilling to return each week as the physician slowly evaluates many possibilities over a period of months, although this situation does occur when an allergist seeks to identify an offending allergen. A balance between these extremes must be sought.

Posing Questions about Adverse Reactions

Within medical departments, important questions often relate to the objectives of a clinical study. The way a study is eventually designed, conducted, and analyzed relates to that question. If the most appropriate question to ask is not posed, then the best data and answers are usually not achieved. A brief example will illustrate this point. The phrasing of each of the following eight questions about a drug's adverse reactions would influence the study design chosen to answer that question.

1. What types of adverse reactions does drug X cause?
2. Did drug X cause adverse reaction Y in patient Z?
3. Does drug X cause adverse reaction Y in patients with type Z disease?
4. What types of adverse reactions does drug X cause in patient population A?
5. Does the route of administration affect the adverse reactions caused by drug X?
6. Does the dosage form of drug X affect the type (or number) of adverse reactions it causes?
7. Does drug X cause more adverse reactions than drug C?
8. Does drug X cause more serious adverse reactions than drug C?
9. Does drug X cause more serious adverse reactions of type H than drug C?

Many other variations on this theme could be listed. It is apparent that the study designs needed to address these questions would focus primarily on the types of patients chosen, the types of treatment given, and/or the types of adverse reactions expected to be observed.

How are Appropriate Clinical Studies Chosen?

A few basic approaches primarily determine the types of clinical studies conducted and designs used. These include the following approaches for new drugs:

1. Determine the type of labeling desired. This includes identifying the specific indications to be targeted. This points the project in a certain direction in terms of the type of evidence and clinical studies needed to obtain the required data.
2. Determine how many indications, dosage forms, and routes of administration are desired in the first group of regulatory submissions. Evaluate the total amount of suitable resources available and the priority of the drug compared with others in the company's portfolio to determine the amount of resources to be allocated to its development.
3. Determine the types and amount of data needed to get a drug approved. This includes consideration of the patient population(s) to be studied. Then work backward to determine each of the clinical studies needed. Certain assumptions are usually made, such as the necessity in most instances to conduct two well-controlled studies for each indication desired.

Each of these three approaches are logical and allow a clinical plan to be developed that proceeds from one's current position to the goal (i.e., regulatory approval). Not all companies pursue this type of systematic and logical drug development. Some companies initially sponsor academic-type clinical studies (e.g., mechanism of action) or focus on pharmacokinetic studies at an early stage. Others approach study designs in a random manner or follow another pattern (see Figs. 19.2 and 1.4). The number of drugs "developed" in this inappropriate manner is diminishing. When a choice of study designs or approaches to drug development exists, it is usually preferable to conduct a few large studies rather than many small ones. This does not mean that many questions should be posed in each study, but it does mean that an adequate number of patients should be enrolled to achieve sufficient power to detect an effect if one is present. Some people, however, seem to have a talent for asking clinical questions that lead them to pursue tangents and only belatedly (or never) can they achieve their goals. Methods that may be used to speed a clinical program are listed in Table 19.1.

A series of clinical studies may be necessary to evaluate the best way to give a drug (e.g., once or three times per day), the best dose of a drug to give, and the specific type of patients who will respond best (e.g., those with mild versus severe forms of the disease, those with or without certain complications, those with specific subtypes of the disease). With some drugs it is also necessary to determine if the therapeutic effect is related to the peak blood level of the drug, the total dose given, the duration of treatment, or to some other factor. If patients included in an early clinical study evaluating one of these (or other) questions are not appropriate, problems may arise that will literally terminate a drug's development. Thus, caution must be used in choosing how rapidly to permit a drug to be developed. At the same time, a drug's development must not be delayed unnecessarily.

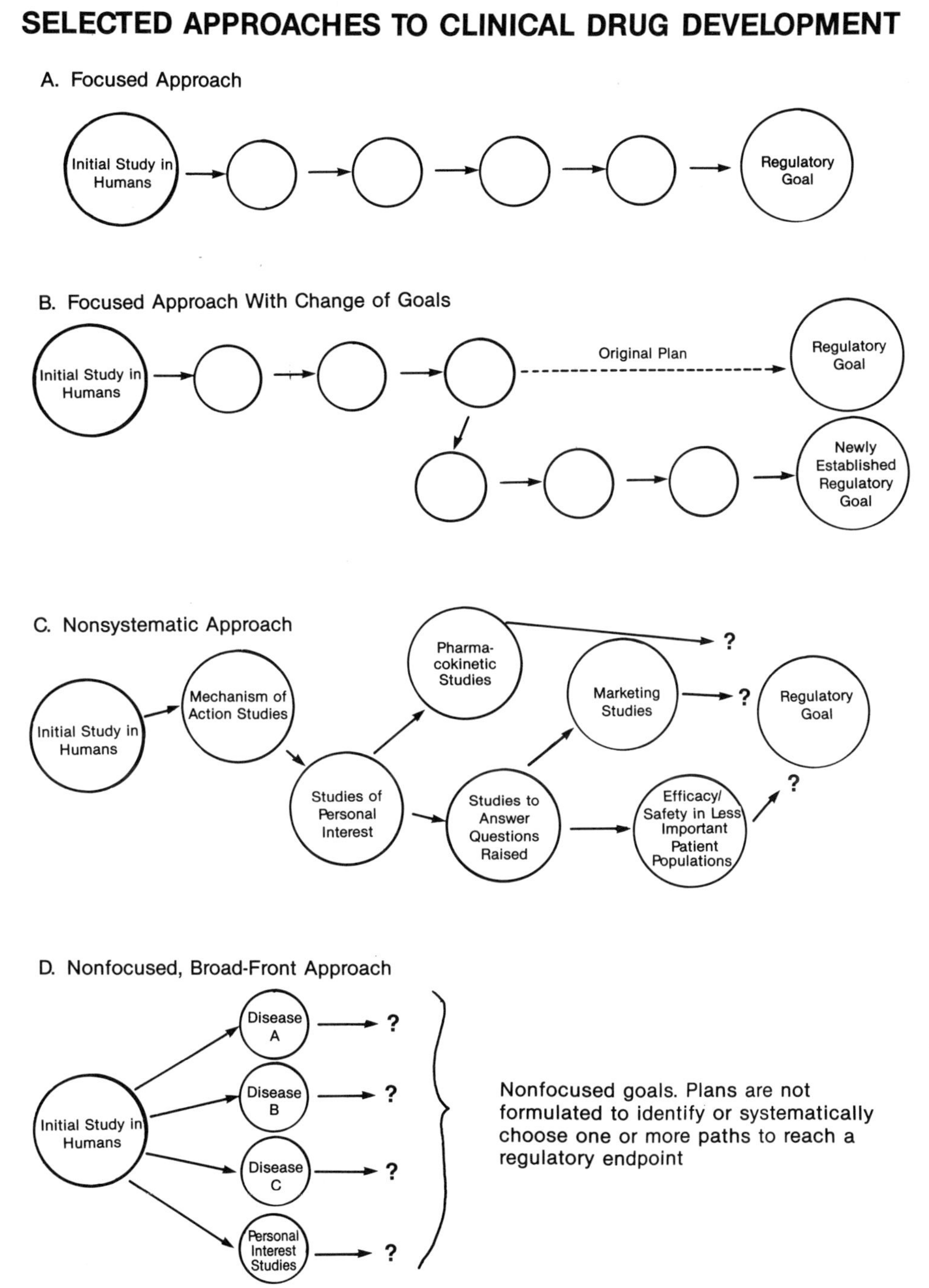

Fig. 19.2. Selected approaches to clinical drug development. Goals are defined in terms of indications, formulations, populations, and other factors.

Table 19.1. Selected means to increase the rate of clinical drug development

1. Increase the number of patients in each study
2. Increase the number of sites conducting each study
3. Increase the number of studies conducted simultaneously
4. Reduce the bottlenecks and rate-limiting steps that are slowing the drug's progress
5. Initiate studies evaluating additional indications
6. Reduce all periods of administrative delays as much as possible (e.g., period between protocol completion and submission to the IRB[a], period between IRB completion, shipment of drug, and initiation of the study)

[a] IRB, Institutional Review Board.

Drugs that have numerous indications and dosage forms under development simultaneously, have them in various stages at one time. One means of illustrating the status of various activities is shown in Fig. 19.3.

Other Principles Concerning Clinical Studies

1. Humans clearly exhibit great variability in their responses to drugs; and, unfortunately (in some ways), clinical studies cannot be controlled as well as animal studies. Many important factors cannot be adequately controlled in most studies. This is especially true in outpatient studies where the patient's diet, exercise, and amount of stress vary and their compliance with the protocol cannot be assured.

2. Pilot efficacy studies conducted early in Phase II have a high likelihood of yielding positive data if they are not well controlled. This may lead a company to believe that an inactive or only marginally active drug is much better than it really is. This in turn could easily lead a company on a wild-goose chase costing many millions of dollars and wasting time and effort of valuable staff who are not available for more productive work. The best method to avoid this problem is to design well-controlled pilot studies, although enrolling only a small number of patients in each. One of the most important clinical principles is that good data in a few patients are far better than mediocre or poor data in many patients. Although this sounds rational and makes good business and good medical sense, it is apparent that many companies do not adhere to this principle.

3. Patients with chronic relapsing or cyclic diseases often enter clinical studies when their disease is at its worst. These patients tend to improve, regardless of whether or not they have been treated with drugs. The statistical name for this phenomenon is regression toward the mean. This is only one of many pitfalls to avoid (or control for) in designing clinical studies. The most common means of controlling this factor is to have a placebo group or no-treatment group of patients. This phenomenon would not apply to patients with a chronic progressive disease (e.g., metastatic cancer).

4. All clinical studies should clearly and fully state the purpose(s) or objective(s) in the protocol. The protocol describes the objective(s) of the study and the means whereby the objective(s) are to be addressed and hopefully answered. Even the interpretation of clinical data is related to how the objectives were stated and the study designed.

5. It is unacceptable to change the clinical endpoint on which the success of a study is based, after a study is complete. It is also unacceptable to change endpoints

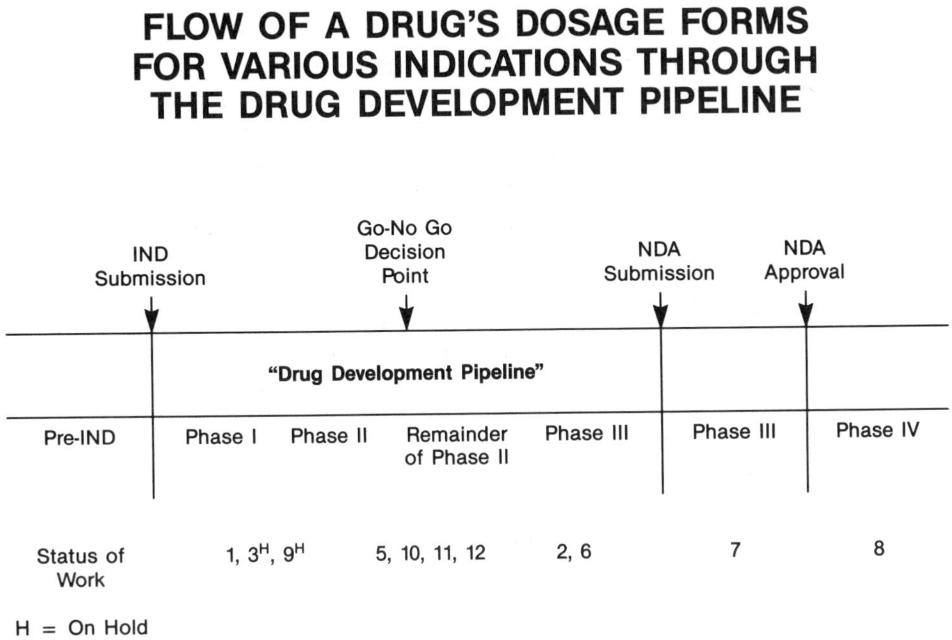

Indications Being Studied

Dosage Form Being Studied	A	B	C	D	E
Oral	1		2		3
Solution	4	5	6		
Transdermal Patch				7	
Cream				8	9
Depot	10	11			12

Fig. 19.3. Planning and tracking the indications and dosage forms studied. The go-no go decision point refers primarily to efficacy. Safety is an ongoing consideration. The numbers to the right of "Status of Work" refer to the exact indication and dosage forms being studied, as shown in the chart below. The numbers are placed under the stage they are at the pipeline. IND, Investigational New Drug Application, NDA, New Drug Application.

during a study, especially if the change is based on results of an interim analysis. Many analyses are sometimes conducted looking for a positive result that was not originally part of a study's objectives. This is called data dredging. An analysis of a new measurement or parameter may be made after the study, however, to form a hypothesis that may be tested in a subsequent study.

6. Drug companies usually spend a great deal of time and energy polishing clinical protocols to the point where they are internally consistent and sparkle like a gem. Unfortunately, in almost all situations, the quality of clinical studies is far from perfect in the way in which they are conducted because of difficulties in controlling human behavior and clinical exigencies that arise. It is rare when a study totally

follows the protocol, although pharmacokinetic studies often approach or may achieve this ideal. There is, therefore, a point of diminishing returns for a company in the amount of time and effort that should be spent fine-tuning the niceties of each protocol's details, when the details are not able to be (or could be but are not) followed in practice. On the other hand, multiple reviews of clinical protocols are necessary to eliminate flaws that might destroy the value of a study. Also, if all relevant measures are not included in a protocol it could become necessary to repeat the entire study at a later date. This could relate to as simple a point as measuring a specific blood test to evaluate renal function at the start and end of a study.

7. More and more protocols at drug companies are written by non-MDs. These people usually lack clinical experience and do not understand what is reasonable to request of a patient in different clinical situations. For example, they often request far too many blood draws and too frequent requests for information from the patient. Although non-MDs may be well-trained clinical scientists, their scientific expertise should be complemented by the clinical expertise of an MD. Their protocols should therefore be carefully reviewed by experienced MDs.

8. A company may place a great amount of resources on clinical studies, to speed its development program. As a result, the company may outstrip its ability to (a) produce the drug, (b) complete toxicological studies, (c) complete technical development work, or (d) solve other drug development problems. This means that an overall coordinated effort is necessary to complete all work in a timely manner. Rushing to complete one part of a development program may be wasteful and nonproductive if other areas are being delayed or are progressing at a much slower pace.

9. All clinical studies that last more than a week or two require a great deal of effort to maintain staff enthusiasm and morale at sites where the studies are being conducted. It has been said that investigators are like radioisotopes, because their interest decays with time. Also, unlike fine wines, most drug studies do not improve with age. Therefore, careful thought and attention must be given to this aspect of clinical studies, which is described in more detail in the *Guide to Clinical Studies* volumes (Spilker, 1984, 1986b, 1987c).

10. Recruitment of patients is a major issue in almost all clinical studies. The steps usually involved in patient recruitment and participation are shown in Fig. 19.4. Investigators almost always promise that more patients will enter their study than they are able to actually enroll. This is so well known that it has led to the phenomenon called "Lasagna's Law" (Fig. 19.5), named after Dr. Louis Lasagna, Dean of Tufts University Medical School.

11. Important clinical studies to conduct from a scientific or medical perspective are sometimes not important studies to conduct from a drug development perspective. If a company's objective is to market a new drug as rapidly as possible, then the former group of academically oriented studies are usually an undesirable diversion to this goal, especially during Phases I and II. In addition, these academically oriented studies may raise questions or problems that must be addressed if the studies are inappropriately designed, conducted, or analyzed. Even if the questions or issues raised are legitimate, they are often inappropriate to address at an early stage of a drug's development. On the other hand, those studies are often extremely important to conduct during Phase III, after a drug's efficacy has been established and it is known that the drug will be marketed.

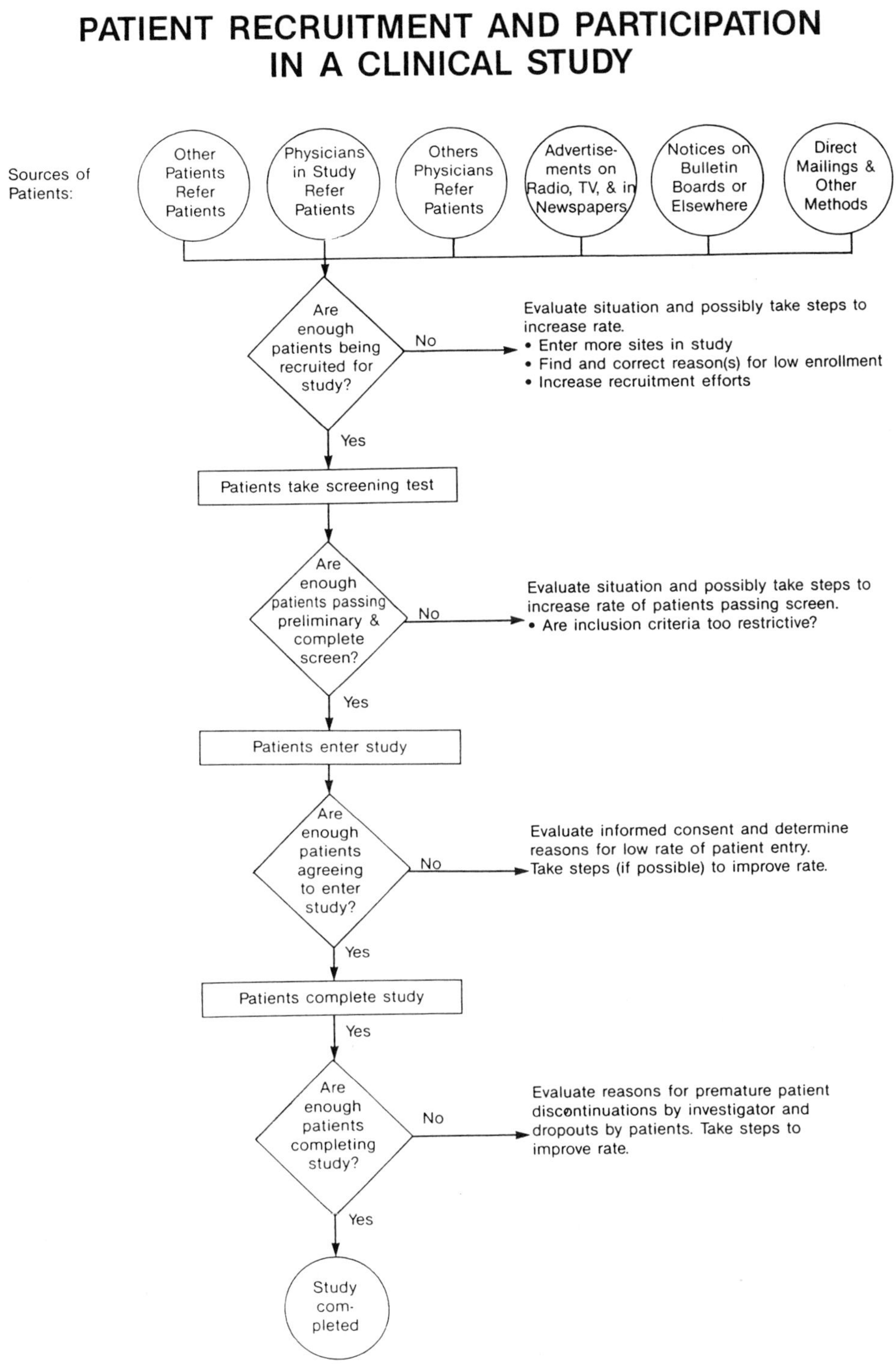

Fig. 19.4. Patient participation in clinical studies.

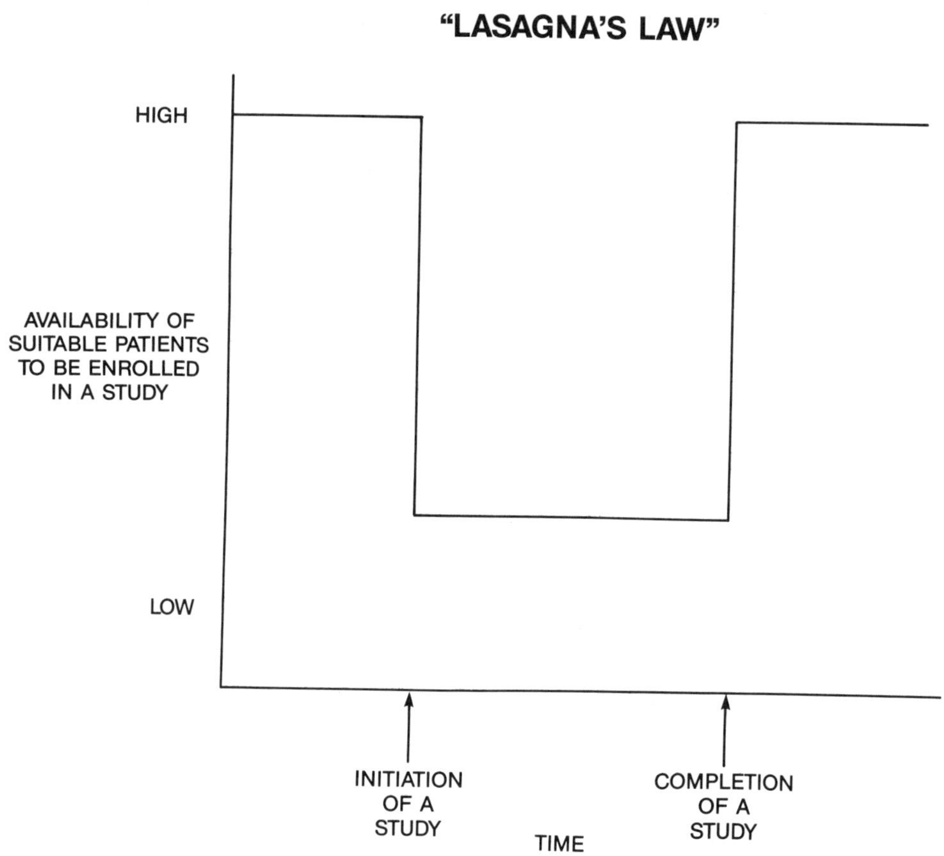

Fig. 19.5. "Lasagna's Law". From Spilker (1984) with permission of Raven Press.

Bringing a Patient Into a State of Clinical Balance: Attempting to Titrate Patients during Clinical Studies

A patient's physical (or emotional) condition is sometimes analogous to a pendulum. Patients usually visit a physician when something has gone too far out of balance. The physician wants to improve a patient's symptom(s) or reduce a risk factor. For example, if a patient has diarrhea, it is necessary to tighten his stools and to decrease the frequency of bowel movements. If a patient's blood sugar is high, then it must be lowered. Too much of an appropriate medicine in such patients, however, often causes too great of an effect (i.e., constipation in the former patient or low blood sugar in the latter patient). Therefore, physicians often increase a drug's dose relatively slowly, i.e., the dose is titrated upwards until the desired effect is obtained. If adverse reactions occur, then the dose is often titrated downwards in the hope that the adverse reaction will disappear while the clinical benefit remains.

These same principles apply when many patients are treated during clinical studies. Although it is possible to evaluate the effects of a fixed dose in patients, it often makes more sense to titrate a patient to a given clinical endpoint (e.g., absence of pain), biochemical endpoint (e.g., decrease in cholesterol in the blood by 15 percent), another type of endpoint (e.g., pharmacological, pathological).

DRUG SAFETY

What Does the Term Safety Mean for a New or Old Drug?

Safety is a relative concept that involves a great deal of judgment. It is relative in that some drugs are safer than others and there is a gradient from drugs that are generally considered safe to those that are generally considered unsafe (i.e., toxic). Safety is a relative concept in another way as well. Over a period of time, more and more information is collected and understood about a particular drug, and therefore a greater proportion of the safety profile is understood. Before a drug is tested in humans, little is known with certainty about its safety in humans, although some reasonable guesses can generally be based on animal experiments. After a drug has been marketed for many years, most of the important information about its safety is known. But, for every drug there is always a chance that unknown toxicities will emerge and alter the benefit-to-risk ratio of using the drug.

Safety is also a relative concept in a third way. A drug that is intended to treat a life-threatening disease for which no adequate therapy is available (e.g., Acquired Immune Deficiency Syndrome [AIDS] in 1985) may be relatively toxic and still be acceptable. The extent of toxicity acceptable would relate to the benefit-to-risk ratio.

Complete safety information is never known on any drug for several reasons. First, new adverse reactions may always emerge that are currently unknown. This is expected for adverse reactions that may result from interactions with future drugs or from changes in the natural history of the disease being treated. Second, some toxicities take many years to develop (e.g., thyroid cancer in people who received radiation of their neck 20 to 30 years before). Third, toxicities may not directly occur in patients exposed to a drug, but may affect a later generation (e.g., vaginal precancerous and cancerous lesions occurred in young women born to mothers who used diethylstilbestrol 20 or so years before). Fourth, the absence of an adverse reaction after a drug is used in many patients may be because the adverse reaction occurs rarely and has not been detected or it may indicate that the drug does not cause that adverse reaction. It is also possible that the drug causes the adverse reaction, but because the problem is relatively common anyway, there is no way to detect the additional cases caused by the drug. For example, if a drug caused lung cancer in one out of 1,000 patients, it would be almost impossible to detect this problem in humans in most situations. The reassuring answer is that toxicology studies would be used to detect this problem and have a reasonably good chance of observing it.

How Rapidly Should a New Drug be Taken to Humans for Testing?

Table 4.2 presents reasons to move new compounds into humans rapidly and Table 4.1 presents reasons to move more slowly. Counterarguments are also given. The correct response to arguments presented in these two tables is that each situation is different and no single approach is always correct. For companies that have a relatively large number of existing drugs under development, higher overall standards should be applied before adopting new compounds for eventual human testing. For a company that has few potentially exciting drugs under development and has underutilized resources, relatively lower standards should be applied. On the other hand, a company that has promising drugs under development should not raise its standards even higher for newer candidates. These compounds require relatively little effort or money for their early development. They may replace other drugs which fall by the wayside or may even be licensed to another company under certain conditions. The number of drugs to study simultaneously is discussed in Chapter 14.

Sources of Information on Drug Safety

Information on drug safety comes from human studies, patient experience, and toxicological studies conducted in animals. From the medical perspective, animal data provide information of *potential* safety problems for humans, whereas data from humans, even though they are often imperfect, usually provides *actual* evidence of safety problems. To improve understanding of drug risks, it is essential to use both actual and potential sources of data. Thus, a drug's safety profile is based on both human and animal data. The extrapolation of animal data to humans is briefly described in Chapter 3.

It is unfortunate and often tragic when patients overdose themselves intentionally. Nonetheless, a great deal of valuable information about a drug's safety profile is often obtained in this way. Information is obtained about (1) manifestations of a drug's toxicity, (2) methods for its diagnosis, and (3) techniques for patient treatment. This information is also sometimes obtained through unintentional overdose of patients. For example, if a patient has an unsuspected genetic deficiency and cannot metabolize a drug, the drug levels may build up and cause toxicity. Also, a patient may misunderstand directions and take too much of a drug, the physician may prescribe too high a dose, or an interaction may occur with another drug that leads to drug accumulation and a toxic event.

After all the safety data on a drug are obtained and analyzed, the risk to a human patient taking the drug must be estimated. This risk may be clear; if not, further studies and discussions are usually warranted.

How May One Determine if a Specific Drug Caused a Specific Adverse Reaction?

Innumerable problems and complexities are associated with establishing the connection between a drug and an adverse reaction that the drug may have caused. Sometimes it is not even easy to identify what is the adverse reaction (Fig. 19.6). All unwanted responses resulting from a drug are defined as adverse reactions, even if they occur in a sort of chain reaction where one leads to another (e.g., orthostatic hypotension may lead to fainting on standing). Medical problems resulting from nondrug events are not considered adverse reactions, even if indirectly caused by the drug. This means that neck pain experienced after an automobile accident is not

IDENTIFYING THE ADVERSE REACTION

A. Drug A interacts with Drug B → Orthostatic hypotension (fall in blood pressure when a patient stands up) → Fainting and fall to floor → Head trauma → Neck pain

B. Drug A → Fatigue → Automobile accident → Whiplash → Neck pain

Fig. 19.6. Identifying the adverse reaction. The *arrow* means "causes" or "leads to".

an adverse reaction, although the accident may have resulted in part from a drug-induced sedation.

Factors that may complicate the association of a drug with a particular adverse reaction include: (1) the natural progression and changes of the patient's disease, (2) other drugs the patient is taking, and (3) other diseases the patient has. Once these issues are sorted out, then there are a whole host of additional factors relating to the patient or drug which may have played a major role in affecting the occurrence or severity of the adverse reaction. A few of these include the patient's age, sex, and genetic makeup as well as the drug's dose, formulation, and age.

Even after all of these issues are completely sorted out (which rarely happens), there is often little assurance that the drug actually caused the adverse reaction. Additional evidence that favors the association is obtained from answers to two specific questions: (1) if the drug was stopped, did the adverse reaction improve? and (2) if the drug was subsequently restarted, did the adverse reaction reappear? This latter technique is called rechallenge, and data from such studies usually provide the best information that a specific drug caused a specific adverse reaction. Nonetheless, it is often impractical, and in many situations it is unethical to consider conducting a rechallenge. Discussions with the patient, physician, and Investigational Review Board (IRB) are required before a rechallenge is attempted.

Some companies use algorithms to answer the question of whether a specific drug caused an adverse reaction. Many have been proposed, but they are not considered reliable by most people. Readers interested in more information on this topic should refer to *Monitoring of Drug Safety* (Inman, 1986) and *Guide to Clinical Interpretation of Data* (Spilker, 1986b).

Evaluation of Drug Safety by Regulatory Agencies

There are no standard acceptable guidelines for regulatory agencies to use in evaluating a new drug's safety. It has been proposed that evidence of safety (and efficacy as well) could be assessed by a group of independent clinical pharmacologists and other specialists. Their judgment would serve as the basis for the government's evaluation.

To some degree this is presently being done by the Food and Drug Administration (FDA) when they convene their Advisory Committees. On the other hand, these panels function strictly in an advisory capacity and the FDA has no mandate to accept their conclusions. Because the FDA is carefully scrutinized by many governmental and nongovernmental groups, they have become overly cautious in most instances and consider worst-case possibilities to a greater degree than is generally deemed appropriate by many outside scientists and clinicians.

The Period between Regulatory Submission and Approval

Phase III clinical studies continue after an NDA or Product License Application (PLA) is submitted to regulatory authorities. For applications that take several years to review, the period between submittal and approval may generate as much or even more data than had been generated prior to submittal. Because of the additional drug exposures, the frequency of adverse drug reactions can usually be better predicted toward the end of this period. Additional patient populations and indications are often also evaluated during this period.

For some drugs this period is the time to establish a compassionate plea protocol. This protocol is intended for patients who do not qualify to enter a clinical study, who live too far from a study site, or who otherwise are not able to be placed in a study. Epidemiological methods may be used to establish a well-designed protocol during this period. The experience with the Phase III compassionate treatment IND (Investigational New Drug Application) for Retrovir conducted by the Burroughs Wellcome Co. demonstrated that good science and data collection can be achieved in this type of study. There is no reason why ad hoc distribution schemes without systematic data collection should be used for lifesaving (or other) drugs given on a compassionate basis in Phases II and III.

CLINICAL IMPORTANCE AND STATISTICAL SIGNIFICANCE

Data in clinical studies are usually analyzed by statisticians who determine the probability that two treatments (e.g., drug and placebo) are different. This is the statistical significance of the data. This does not indicate if the data are also important from a clinical perspective. To determine this, the data and its statistical analyses must be interpreted by someone who is qualified to make this medical judgment. There are situations where data are statistically significant but are not clinically important, and vice versa. Both types of situations are described below.

Situations Where Statistically Significant Results are Not Clinically Important

There are innumerable examples of this situation, and they undoubtedly occur in most clinical studies. Examples include obvious situations, such as:

1. Increases or decreases of three or four beats per minute in mean heart rate in one or more groups of patients.
2. Increase or decreases of one and a half breaths per minute in mean respiration frequency in one or more groups of patients.

In various other safety or efficacy parameters, small changes that are not clinically important are often found to be statistically significant. One reason for this is that many comparisons are usually made and some are statistically significant because of chance alone.

Less obvious examples of this effect include situations where a safety or efficacy parameter's change was unexpected and a group of experts is in agreement that the changes observed are not clinically important. Numerous examples occur in most studies. Another situation is when it is uncertain as to whether or not the statistically significant change is clinically meaningful. Sometimes it requires additional data from new studies to finally resolve this issue. At other times this issue is never resolved and dangles like a loose thread in the medical literature.

Situations Where Clinically Important Results Are Not Statistically Significant

One such situation would be in treating an otherwise untreatable disease. In this situation, a clinical result that approached but did not achieve statistical significance could be immensely important clinically.

In many clinical studies where clinically important data are not statistically significant, better ways to conduct a new study become apparent. It is also possible that the statistical standards established to define drug activity were too stringent and that results were important clinically. Important differences in the second study's design may be in the (1) choice of parameters, (2) ways and times that parameters are measured, (3) duration of treatment, (4) dose of the drug, (5) type of patients enrolled, and so forth.

POSTMARKETING CLINICAL STUDIES

Phase IV is the period when a drug is marketed. Many types of clinical studies occur during Phase IV, including proactive carefully planned active experimental studies to determine the nature or characteristics of actual drug use and passive observational surveillance studies. The term "surveillance" implies a sentinel-like watch on medical practice to learn what is happening with a drug. In informal surveillance studies the world of medical practice is carefully monitored, as with a stethoscope, to learn what is occurring.

Objectives of Postmarketing Surveillance

The primary objectives of postmarketing surveillance are to better evaluate the risk-benefit relationship that must be considered each time a decision is reached to use a drug as therapy and to protect the public health against unexpected consequences of drug exposure. More specifically, this is done to (1) gain a better understanding of these events both medically and scientifically to enable patients to be more effectively treated, (2) prevent individual patients from being treated incorrectly, (3) adhere to regulatory requirements, and (4) protect the company from liability in numerous situations. An underlying principle of these studies is the more a company knows about its own drugs the better it is for the company and for the patient. These objectives are achieved largely by identifying and evaluating the type and frequency of a drug's adverse reactions.

Postmarketing studies are also conducted to evaluate patient populations that were not specifically studied in premarketing studies (e.g., children, pregnant women), and to evaluate the effects of a drug on large scale, long-term morbidity and mortality. The company therefore wants to understand the answers to several questions.

1. *Why is the drug used?* This refers to the indications for which the drug is used, in terms of disease severity, symptoms, and signs. What is the basis for choosing the drug in actual practice?
2. *How is the drug used?* This refers to dosing schedules, duration of treatment, concomitant treatment, and related issues.
3. *In which patients is the drug used?* What are the demographic characteristics of the patient population in which the drug is used? Do they have concurrent diseases or are they using concomitant drugs?
4. *What are the results of the drug's use?* Companies look at the number of adverse medical events in patients receiving their drugs (and possibly other drugs as a control) to evaluate whether there is an excess number associated with the drug. It is also possible that unexpected clinical benefits may be observed.
5. *Are the adverse reactions reported really a result of the drug?* Companies should be able to counter any unjustified associations of their drugs with adverse reactions. They should also understand or be able to determine the true incidence of their drug's adverse reactions when reports come to their attention via the literature, regulatory agencies, internally received information, or from other sources.

Methods of Postmarketing Surveillance

The specific pharmacoepidemiological methods used for any drug in Phase IV depend on the type of data desired and the most rigorous and cost-effective means of obtaining those data. This means that the approach must be custom designed for each particular drug and situation. Methods used to conduct postmarketing surveillance include:

1. Collecting and analyzing reports of adverse reactions reported spontaneously to the company from all countries where the drug is sold. These reports come from physicians, drug company sales representatives, some national regulatory agencies, subsidiary company offices, and even patients. This group of voluntary reports includes the "1639 Forms" sent by physicians in the United States to the FDA and the "Yellow Card Scheme" sent to The Committee on Safety of Medicines (CSM) in the United Kingdom.
2. Following case reports, formal studies, and other published information reported in the medical literature.
3. Questioning physicians in a local or national area on either an ad hoc or systematic basis about a specific adverse reaction. The United Kingdom is undertaking

an important experiment in this context, called Prescription Event Monitoring. This is an example of systematic surveillance.

4. Collecting general information ad hoc from participating hospitals and physicians about a relatively large number of patients treated with a newly available drug. These data may be collected in a prospective or retrospective manner. No matter how elegant these studies may have been, they are extremely expensive and have generally had a modest return of worthwhile information. This approach is being gradually replaced by use of the multipurpose data base described in point 5 below. Nonetheless, this approach could be valuable and even necessary in certain situations where it is impossible to use a data base and it is necessary to find a specific patient group. It is hoped that regulatory agencies will be selective in their requirement for drug companies to conduct such studies on newly approved drugs.

5. Utilizing large multipurpose data bases to address a question of interest formulated as a hypothesis. Multipurpose data bases are automated administrative data bases of large health care plans where data already exist from patients who are members of a group. A major advantage of large automated data bases for postmarketing studies is that patients do not have to be enrolled in a Phase IV study. Patients are studied who are being treated with the test drug under usual or current conditions. Examples of such data bases are in Health Maintenance Organizations (HMOs) (e.g., Kaiser-Permanente in Portland, OR; Group Health Cooperative of Puget Sound in Seattle, WA), hospitals (e.g., automated files and records at the Harvard Teaching Hospitals), Medicaid (e.g., in the State of Tennessee), and a provincial Health Insurance Scheme (e.g., Saskatchewan, Canada). These data bases contain demographic information on patients enrolled, names and doses of drugs for prescriptions filled by the health care pharmacies, hospital admissions and discharge diagnoses, medical problems, and other data. The data bases may be searched to determine whether patients taking a specific drug had more hospital admissions (e.g., for a myocardial infarction or other problem) than did patients with the same disease who were taking a competitive drug. These data bases have been used successfully to evaluate hypotheses (Jick et al., 1985) and have raised the entire field of pharmacoepidemiology to a new level of study design and potential to address important issues.

Record linkage is an important concept that underlies the use of large multipurpose data bases. Record linkage is where two or more record files are linked, usually by computer. This allows questions to be addressed that previously could not be. For example, pharmacy records of outpatients with patient identifier numbers may be linked with hospital inpatient experience of the same patients with a diagnosis code. These records may also be linked with the inpatient drugs prescribed during hospitalization. Many studies may only be conducted with computers that search these data bases looking for specific linkages. For example, the outpatient drug history may be checked for all patients who had an admitting (or discharge) diagnosis of X. Alternatively, all patients receiving a new drug may be tracked to identify their next hospitalization.

Assessing Whether Reported Rates of an Adverse Reaction Reflect the True Incidence

Figure 19.7 illustrates that reported rates of all adverse reactions from a single drug or even the rate of a single adverse reaction from one drug vary throughout a

TYPES OF REPORTING PATTERNS OF ADVERSE REACTIONS

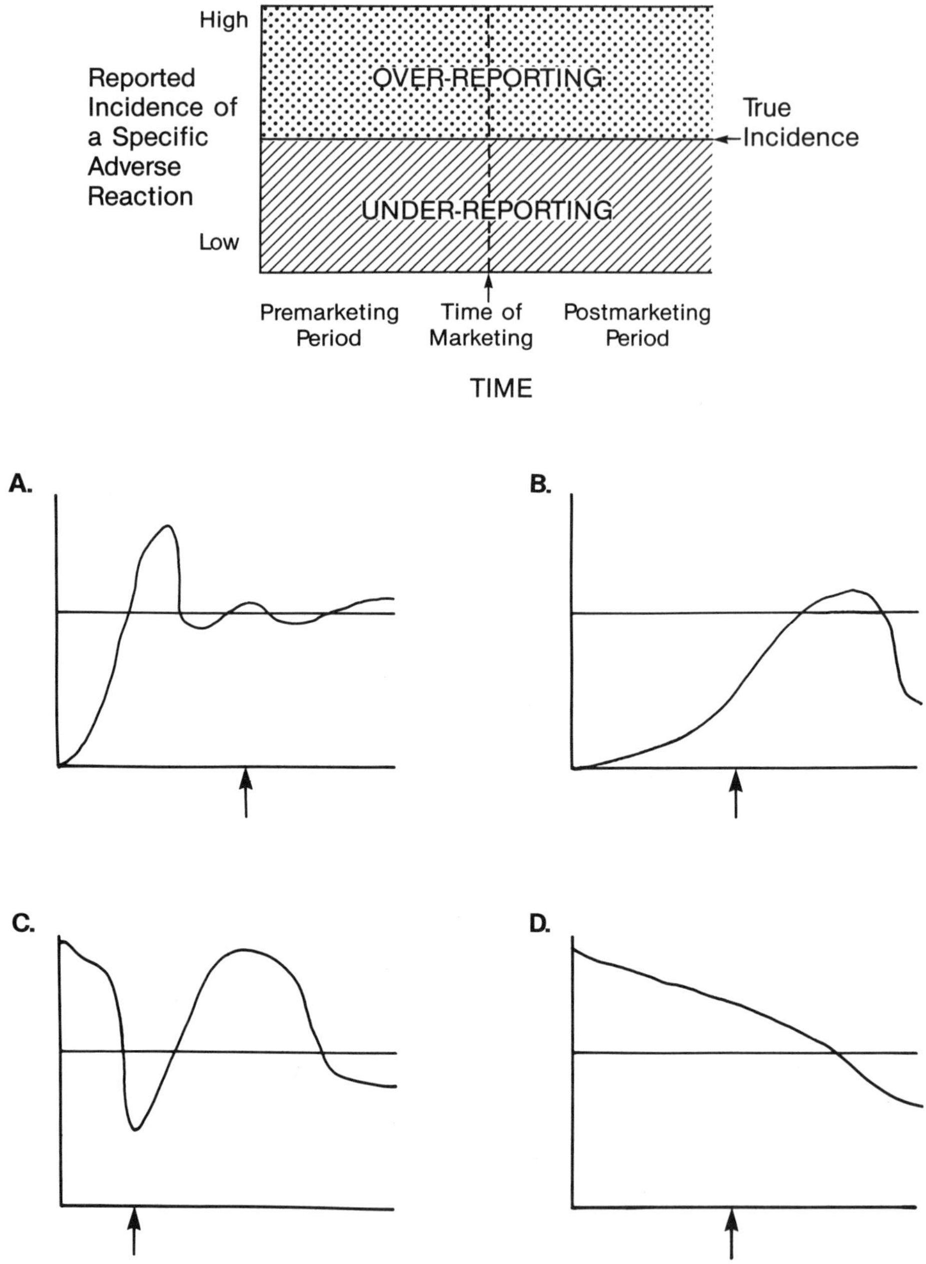

Fig. 19.7. Hypothetical types of reporting patterns of adverse reactions over time. Innumerable variations of these and other patterns are possible.

drug's life. The reasons are generally quite straightforward. Rare adverse reactions (i.e., those that occur less than one time in 10,000 patients) can hardly ever be discerned during premarketing studies where usually a total of only 1,000 to 3,000 patients are exposed to a new drug. After marketing, most drugs are used by many thousands of patients and rare adverse reactions are observed more often. Eventually, those adverse reactions are associated with the drug and are reported in the medical literature. At this point, many physicians are alerted about the adverse reaction. Shortly thereafter it becomes overdiagnosed and widely reported by zealous or naive physicians. Some physicians are anxious to publish reports while others may not be experienced in making an accurate diagnosis of the adverse reaction. In addition, the same diagnosis may refer to different conditions in different countries, or may be referred to by different terms. After a period of time there is often less interest in the medical community about reporting each case of a moderate or serious adverse reaction that is perceived as well known and documented. As a result, the number of reports received by the company and by regulatory authorities represent an underreporting of some or all adverse reactions for a particular drug.

Commonly occurring adverse reactions are observed during premarketing studies. In general, the more common the adverse reaction, the closer the reported incidence is to the true incidence (Fig. 19.7 panel A). After marketing there is usually less incentive for physicians to spontaneously report common adverse reactions or those that are well known (e.g., Fig. 19.7 panel D). Figure 19.7 panel C illustrates a flurry of attention to an adverse reaction after marketing that eventually is reported less often. The premarketing period in panel C could have virtually no reporting of the adverse reaction. It must be noted that the *true* incidence of an adverse reaction is not always characterized by a constant rate, but may vary greatly, further complicating reporting patterns. Many variations on the themes in Fig. 19.7 occur (e.g., some adverse reactions of a drug may be underreported, while others are overreported).

Regulatory Requirements for Postmarketing Surveillance

Until recently, drug companies did not systematically seek to collect postmarketing information. They used the information received spontaneously to adjust a product's labeling (i.e., package insert). This was primarily done by indicating serious adverse reactions that had been reported. Now, several national regulatory agencies are requiring postmarketing surveillance studies as a condition for approving a drug for marketing. In many situations this is a reasonable request.

Data from Phase I to III studies cannot be generalized to all uses a drug will be tried in after marketing, including how the drug relates to different populations (e.g., pregnant women, children) and different conditions of use. One issue arises if a company has already begun a large postmarketing study for country A, and now countries B, C, and D also want postmarketing studies conducted. This exercise could become an unreasonable condition forced on companies who want to have their drug approved.

There are several precedents by regulatory agencies of forcing companies to conduct studies that may not have been necessary. For instance, assume that a company has conducted all required pharmacology, toxicology, and clinical studies necessary to have a new drug approved in an industrialized country with high regulatory standards. The company now wishes to register the drug in several other countries, but learns that country B requires that the pharmacology must be repeated within that country, country C requires that most toxicology and some clinical studies must be repeated, and so on. Although there may occasionally be a rationale for some of the repetition (e.g., to confirm that Japanese patients who weigh less will react the same to a fixed dose of a drug as heavier Westerners), most of these requirements are forced on a company to help the economy of the other country and to feed their national pride. Some people have raised the same issue about the FDA's reaction to drugs developed elsewhere.

Regulatory Requirements for Adverse Reaction Reporting

While exact requirements differ between countries, there is a clear trend for regulatory agencies to mandate receipt of a growing amount of information. In addition to requiring postmarketing studies, many countries are also requiring reports on the numbers, trends, and even details of all serious adverse reactions reported to the company from all over the world.

Some regulatory authorities want reports of all serious and unexpected adverse reactions, whereas others want reports on all serious adverse reactions, whether unexpected or not. Imagine the complexity when each country requires different information on different official forms at different periods of time with different analyses of the data. All multinational drug companies are wrestling with these requirements, which also may change from year to year.

When Should Newly Observed Adverse Reactions be Put in a Drug's Labeling?

There are no simple answers to this issue, only a large number of further issues to consider. The only guide is that each situation must be evaluated independently. Although it might superficially appear that a single universal package insert or drug labeling for each drug would be desirable to better standardize the drug's use, this does not really make sense. For example, different doses may be recommended in different countries. This may occur for any of many reasons (e.g., the drug may be approved to treat different diseases). In addition, different dosage forms (e.g., oral, intravenous) may be marketed in different countries, physicians may use the drug differently (e.g., by itself in one country and elsewhere in combination with other drugs), and so on. The more years a drug is on the market, the greater is the tendency for more adverse reactions to have been reported and therefore to be listed in a drug's labeling.

After Regulatory Approval Why Does the Number of Clinical Studies Usually Stay the Same or Even Increase?

This question is sometimes raised by senior corporate managers, especially those not experienced in clinical drug development. The number of studies on a newly approved drug sometimes decrease, but those situations seem to be the exception.

Numerous types of studies are conducted after drug approval, some of which are unlikely, undesirable, or even unable to be conducted prior to drug approval. These studies include the following:

1. *Clinical studies* A new drug is often compared with its competitors to evaluate differences and detect possible advantages of the new drug. The new drug may be evaluated in special populations to determine their responses in terms of either efficacy, safety, or another aspect (e.g., quality of life, pharmacokinetics). Studies may be conducted to obtain data that can be used to request (1) new indications, (2) improved drug labeling in terms of additional populations in which the drug may be used (e.g., children, elderly, pregnant women), (3) removal or downgrading of a warning, precaution, or contraindication in the drug's labeling, or (4) any other change desired in the labeling. Some studies may be carried out to obtain promotional data (e.g., studies that will hopefully show superiority over the competitor's products) even though no changes in the drug's labeling are requested. These studies may have a different motivational driving force behind them, but they may be well-designed and important clinical studies. Cynics may claim that some of these are solely driven by commercial desires to obtain a publication. Optimists may claim that if the data are publishable that they probably add to our body of scientific and clinical knowledge, irrespective of motivation.
2. *Line-extensions* Developing and studying line-extensions may be considered either as marketing studies or as a separate category. Each line-extension requires a different amount of work and number of clinical studies. Line-extensions include new (a) dosage forms (i.e., solutions, creams, capsules), (b) package sizes (e.g., number of tablets in a bottle), (c) packaging (e.g., blister pack), (d) dosage strengths (e.g., more or fewer milligrams per tablet), (e) flavorings, (f) combinations with other drugs, (g) new excipients (e.g., preservatives), or (h) other modifications.
3. *New indications* Many drugs that are originally approved by a regulatory authority for one or a small number of indications are often evaluated in other diseases or conditions. Regulatory applications that are approved for new indications are usually a valuable source of additional revenue.
4. *Mechanism-of-action studies* Preclinical studies that attempt to delineate a drug's mechanisms of action are often conducted prior to a drug's approval and marketing. Depending on the interest in the drug, academicians and others may continue these studies long after a drug is approved. Clinical mechanism-of-action studies generally tend to be de-emphasized by drug companies during a drug's early clinical development. Such studies are often sponsored by the company as well as by academicians during Phase III or after a drug is marketed.
5. *Postmarketing surveillance studies* The importance of postmarketing surveillance studies is rapidly increasing throughout the world. These studies have various designs and objectives, but are generally intended to improve understanding about a drug's safety in large patient populations. These studies are described in more detail elsewhere in this section.

Reactions of Drug Companies to Postmarketing Surveillance Needs

A few years ago, some forward-looking drug companies hired epidemiologists to address the Phase IV questions that arose in regard to their products. Now, many companies are assembling relatively large departments to deal with these issues. Companies that have major research and development activities being conducted in two or more sites have additional issues brought about by having to link and coordinate their activities. Each site should be sharing their Phase IV clinical data on both an ad hoc basis for important adverse reactions, and on a periodic basis for complete sharing of data. These data are used both for reports to regulatory authorities and for internal company information and analyses.

Some companies have established a single worldwide data base of Phase IV data from spontaneous signaling systems, but there are problems with adopting this approach. For instance, the data from many countries are usually so poor and fragmented that they are hard to combine with better quality data from some industrialized countries. Some reports of adverse reactions are third- or fourth-hand accounts with little detail, while other reports are carefully detailed by treating physicians. Also, a single drug is usually marketed in different formulations and combinations, and may be prescribed in different dosages around the world. As a result of these and other issues, many companies do not want to create a single worldwide data base of adverse reactions. But, these companies usually coordinate all relevant activities between their different sites and share all relevant information on adverse reactions, although they are not put into a single data base.

Coordination between Different Sites Conducting Phase IV Studies

Coordination between two or more different sites of a company in different countries has a number of components. The first is that computer systems used must either be identical or compatible. It makes no sense for a company to have incompatible systems. Yet, there are at least several companies where this has occurred! Second, the systems used to gather, process, analyze, and report data should be compatible. There will definitely be differences in how these steps are conducted in different countries, but there must be easily adapted methods to provide for needs of other important countries. Third, the coordination and cooperation of staff (and management) between countries must be harmonious. Whatever steps are necessary must be taken to insure that these goals are achieved. Without compatible computer systems, a company will be unable to deal effectively with the myriad of issues that always arise during Phase IV.

Specific Issues of Collecting and Processing Adverse Reaction Data

A small selection of issues that arise in regard to collecting and processing adverse reaction data are briefly described.

1. A great deal of data collected are either "bits and pieces" (e.g., grossly incomplete reports) or are obviously full of inaccuracies and may be considered as "junk" data. How are "junk" data handled from around the world, especially when there is no means to go to a specific physician or other reliable source for additional information? Are data of very different quality being combined?
2. How are data of differing qualities handled within a single country for multiple drugs?

3. Reporting rates and procedures differ among nations and over time. To what extent may adverse reaction data from different nations or from different periods be pooled?

4. How can one differentiate between adverse reactions resulting from an overdosage of the drug versus those occurring with normal usage? Also, is it important to differentiate between intentional and unintentional drug overdose?

5. Because the rate of an adverse reaction's occurrence is more important than merely the number of occurrences (i.e., the numerator of a fraction), what characteristics should be placed in the numerator of the fraction used to determine the rate and what should be used as the denominator (e.g., the number of patients treated)? Many different criteria may be used to define the specific categories of patients, drugs, and adverse reactions used as numerators or denominators.

6. Given the enormous bias in collecting adverse reaction data in spontaneous systems, under what circumstances is a comparison of rates justified among different drugs or even for a single drug over time?

7. Should adverse reactions that occur in patients using a drug for unlabeled (i.e., unapproved) indications be considered separately from indications that are approved and recommended? What about adverse reactions that occur in patients who should not have used a drug because of contraindications? Is it appropriate and fair to express a rate of a certain adverse reaction occurring in all patients, when a significant number should not have received the drug? Is it appropriate and fair not to include them?

8. There is almost always some uncertainty about whether a drug caused a specific adverse reaction. How should this issue be handled? No matter what is decided, there will always be many loose ends because important questions will not always be able to be answered if the patient, or even the treating physician in many cases, has to be contacted.

9. How should adverse reaction reports be handled when it appears that the adverse reaction was due to a concomitant drug or to a concurrent disease?

10. Who should decide which reports must be submitted to which regulatory authorities? Should this be the local medical director where the adverse reaction occurred, someone at the central headquarters, or someone in the country requiring the report? On which basis is this decision made? How are serious adverse reactions differentiated from nonserious ones? What about situations when the severity cannot be established? How much effort should be expended to obtain new information? Are important adverse reactions being rapidly and appropriately communicated between sites of a drug company?

11. Does the company, or physician reporting the adverse reaction, determine whether the adverse reaction was attributable to the drug? On what basis does the person decide, because there are many systems available for reaching a decision? Should a company only use a single method?

12. If a situation similar to that in Fig. 19.6 occurs, what would be considered to be the adverse reaction? In most cases, all of the symptoms would be adverse reactions, even though physicians may only see the final outcome which includes the symptom(s) reported.

Many other issues relating to adverse reactions are discussed in Chapter 8 of *Guide to Clinical Interpretation of Data* (Spilker, 1986b).

Benefits of Postmarketing Surveillance

One of the questions akin to that asked by the small boy in *The Emperor's New Clothes* is to ask what is the benefit of the various approaches to postmarketing surveillance studies? Does the information from new techniques have greater value than the older sentinel systems of having alert physicians publish case reports? This is the method that was used to alert the medical community to problems associated with the use of the beta-receptor antagonist practolol after approximately five years on the market in the United Kingdom. The oral form of this drug was then removed from the market. The intravenous form is still available, but only for emergency use. What drugs have been removed from the market because of newer methods and approaches? The answer so far is none.

We are now in a better position, however, to recognize problems with new drugs at an earlier stage and thereby to save patients from having adverse reactions. In addition, we are now able through large data bases to evaluate hypotheses which will provide assurance in some cases that a drug should *not* be removed from the market. Because these data bases exist for other reasons, the cost to test hypotheses is not prohibitive and answers may often be obtained within a short period.

QUALITY-OF-LIFE STUDIES AND ISSUES

Drug companies have been interested in quality-of-life issues for well over a century. Every attempt to reduce adverse reactions of one drug by developing a drug with fewer or less severe adverse reactions is an attempt to improve the quality of life for patients taking the drug. Quality-of-life measures can demonstrate an increased benefit-to-risk ratio and thus make the drug more acceptable to the medical community. This may occur as a result of improving benefits, reducing risk, or both. Sometimes the benefits of a drug on quality of life are not adequately evaluated or assessed from a patient's perspective. Thus, the full information is not always available to the company's marketing representatives who help educate physicians about their drug's benefits.

Quality of life relates to a quantification of human values relating to patients who have a chronic disease. It is a relative concept that differs from society to society and also differs within a society at different times. The patient is in a particular setting in which he influences decisions about initiating, continuing, modifying, or stopping a particular therapy. Measuring the quality of life from a patient's perspective includes consideration of five major areas: (1) economics, (2) psychological well-being, (3) social interactions, (4) physical abilities, and (5) physical state. Economics includes the ability of patients to work and support themselves as they previously were doing. Measures could include days spent at work and days spent in the hospital. Psychological factors, on the part of patients and often their families, are intimately involved in how treatment results are assessed. The same is true for a patient's physical and mental abilities. Physical abilities refer to capabilities and is a more dynamic measure than the baseline status of a patient's physical state. Examples of physical abilities include the ability to dress oneself and the ability to get into and out of a chair or car.

Uses of Quality-of-Life Data

It is becoming increasingly important to evaluate improvement in a patient's quality of life while receiving a new drug and to compare this evaluation with quality of life of patients receiving another drug or placebo treatment, or another treatment modality (e.g., surgery, radiation, biofeedback). This comparison may be made in clinical studies where quality-of-life-issues are the primary objective, or a few quality-of-life measures may be included in clinical studies primarily oriented toward evaluating a drug's safety or efficacy.

There are instances where patient perception of quality of life has had a significant impact on medical treatment (e.g., the trend away from radical mastectomy to limited surgery for breast cancer). The measures chosen to evaluate quality of life should focus on those characteristics that patients most strongly desire. But, many new drugs are unable to elicit an adequate improvement in these parameters. A central issue is whether the drug improves relevant parameters sufficiently to convince hospital or HMO formulary committees that the new drug is worth putting on the formulary and on the pharmacy shelves, either in place of or in addition to currently stocked drugs.

It is clearly a difficult decision to choose or reject a drug for a formulary when the drug has both advantages and disadvantages in comparison with drugs currently on the formulary. Comparisons between unlike measures abound (e.g., drug A provides somewhat greater efficacy, but also increases the risk of minor adverse reactions, drug C makes patients feel better more of the time compared with existing therapy, but increases the risks of a specific serious adverse reaction from one in 100,000 to one in 10,000 cases). If one drug must replace another on the formulary, then the decision becomes much more difficult.

Another difficult decision is when a new drug offers minor benefits over existing therapy, but costs more than current therapy. Whether the additional benefits justify the added costs is often a difficult issue to resolve. This issue must be carefully evaluated before a new drug is officially priced by the company.

Measures Used to Evaluate Quality of Life

Measures of quality of life are multifactorial and may be combined into a single index score of well-being, or they may be used separately as a battery of assessments. The difficulty in the latter case is that some may be positive and others negative or many will vary in their degree of change. Unless one has established a hierarchy of different tests, this may lead to a quagmire when the data are interpreted. Many methods used to measure quality of life have not been adequately validated by careful study. Therefore, claims made about "proven benefits" may later turn out to be incorrect or strongly challenged.

Measures vary from standard validated questionnaires and evaluations using objective and/or subjective parameters to general questions prepared informally as an interview or questionnaire in a clinical study. These latter unvalidated tests or scales may be insensitive to changes brought about by drugs, and responses to the questions may not be reproducible. Future evaluations in this field will undoubtedly lead to greater validation and systematic approaches than exists at present. It is anticipated that both objective and subjective measures will be found essential to use. It is necessary to agree on the different attributes and relative importance of each test ahead of time. In some situations a single overall index relating to quality of life is highly desirable. Until the last decade, the patient's quality of life was generally assessed in clinical studies, if at all, through the filter of the physician.

Many existing quality-of-life scales may be applied to patients with any disease. In addition there are disease-specific scales that are available. Neither category should be viewed as preferable and there are proponents of using general scales even when disease specific scales are available. This is usually based on a greater degree of validation of the scale.

When it is uncertain as to which type(s) of tests to use in measuring quality of life in a specific clinical study, it is usually appropriate to use a battery of tests that measures each of the major aspects of quality of life. This may be done using both standard assessments that are applicable to many diseases and also study-specific measures designed for that particular disease. Caution must be used to choose tests that have been validated. There is a great temptation in this field for people to make up their own test and to not appreciate the importance of validating their test.

Different Perspectives on Quality of Life

From a *health planner's* perspective, the quality-of-life issue is usually one of obtaining the greatest benefits with limited financial resources. The government, HMO, or other planner wants to spend the limited money and resources available where it will achieve the greatest return on the group's investment. The health planner has a predominantly economic perspective. The perspective on this issue from a *psychologist's* point of view is to maximize the social functioning of the individual patient. *Clinicians* focus primarily on a patient's medical health and physical abilities. *Patients* focus primarily on their feelings and any disabilities they may have had. If they are being treated to minimize a risk factor they will focus on the perceived benefits versus the inconvenience, cost, adverse reactions, and risk of the treatment. *Drug companies* want to obtain data to show benefits of their drugs over the competitors for marketing advantages and also to help get their drug listed on hospital, HMO, and other formularies.

Although there is some overlap between these assessments and the quality of life that would be assessed for a specific patient using each perspective, there are also significant differences. One of the most important differences is that health planners are usually oriented to effects that are measured in a patient population rather than on effects in a single patient.

INTERNATIONAL DRUG DEVELOPMENT

Overview

The primary question in global drug development is not whether or *not* a multinational drug company should develop drugs internationally, but on what scale should it be done and how may it best be done. Virtually every major multinational company has moved (or is moving) into the era of developing drugs on an international scale. If the company intends to market its drugs worldwide, then it will develop drugs on a global basis. If it wishes to focus on a number of countries or areas, then its drug development is better described as international. This sharp distinction is not made in this book, unless indicated. Current issues focus mainly on technical details and strategies that enable companies to develop drugs most effectively. Strategies are chosen that reflect the company, its organizational structures, disease areas of interest, and the geographical areas targeted for marketing.

The major goal of global drug development is to have a drug reach the market as soon as possible in all targeted countries. Other goals include achieving a financially stronger company, better staff morale, and more efficient drug development.

Models of International Cooperation and Coordination Between Two Drug Development Sites of a Multinational Company

International cooperation in drug development between two or more sites may exist on multiple levels. Three models are described. The *first model* is loose cooperation with a sharing of results and information on the status of each site's activities. Nonetheless, each site pursues drug development in a generally independent manner. The *second model* is when all relevant sites pursue work jointly on drug development, after a certain point is reached in a drug's progress. This point may be at the initiation of Phase I or Phase II studies, or after drug efficacy is demonstrated by one of the sites. This model keeps drug ownership at the site where work was initiated. The *third model* is when all relevant sites jointly develop a drug from the time when a project is initiated. This leads to joint ownership of all drug projects. It may be desirable for a company to initiate work on only those projects that receive international agreement at the outset. The particular model of drug development chosen should be the one that is believed to be best able to achieve the company's goals. Two or more models may be used by a single company, the choice depending on the nature of the drug or its intended markets.

A certain number of clinical studies function as the core of most, if not all, regulatory submissions. The requirements for implementing and running the global drug development system vary greatly from company to company, depending on their experience, goals, traditions, and the number, nature, and location of subsidiaries. Some companies with centralized organizations have relatively complete international drug development systems and a single clinical plan for international use. A global tracking system is utilized to monitor numbers of patients enrolled at each site and to track whether target dates are being met for each of the milestones (e.g., initiation, completion, report writing) for a clinical study or for various regulatory activities.

Planning an International Clinical Program

Planning an international clinical program for a single drug requires from several months to a full year from project initiation to insure that important points are not missed. This period should be taking place while preclinical and technical studies are underway. This clinical plan cannot be rushed, or the resultant program may create problems and questions that may lead the entire drug's development into serious difficulties.

It is important to review the clinical program with more than a single consultant in each country. These experts in academia, industry, and/or relevant government agencies should be consulted as a feasibility study. The experts should be asked whether the proposed clinical program is appropriately tailored to the needs and nature of the medical practice of their country and is possible to carry out successfully in the proposed time frame. Situations will arise where a special program must be created within one or more countries that must opt out of the global development scheme. At present, Japan is usually viewed as a country that requires special considerations.

In Which Countries Should Clinical Studies be Conducted?

Although many factors enter this discussion, only a few will be mentioned. It is usually easiest to evaluate initially a drug in the United States if it is preclinically developed there. Although regulatory requirements to initiate human tests are generally more involved the United States than in other countries, a company usually achieves reliable data and avoids what is often a time-consuming effort in exporting the drug. Drugs developed in other countries, however, are rarely sent to the United States for their initial testing. Testing new compounds in underdeveloped countries is not usually a good idea because of the (usual) lack of high quality facilities, investigators, and background experience of the staff. Data that result from such studies are usually not reliable. Poor information is much worse than having no information, because it can easily send the company on a wild-goose chase trying to answer questions that were raised. This may last several years and cost many millions of dollars.

Later in drug development, foreign locations are often preferable to sites within the United States and are frequently used (1) to complete core studies in countries where data will then be acceptable to their regulatory authorities, (2) to adhere to various countries' regulatory requirements, (3) for promotional studies, (4) to enlist help from local opinion leaders, or for other reasons. In choosing the countries in which to conduct studies, it may be relevant to consider if there is a national death registry to assist in long-term patient follow-up, and also to determine the stability of the patient population.

Local clinical studies are often required or requested by some regulatory authorities, rather than approving a drug based entirely on foreign data. There are various reasons for this request. For example, most patients in the country may differ from those in whom the studies were conducted in terms of diet, weight, and ethnic factors. Medical practice may differ in the ways that patients are treated. If so, then at least one study should be conducted under the conditions in which the drug will be sold. The regulatory authority may not be readily able to audit the investigator's sites if they are in a different country. Finally, there is what may be the major reason in many cases—chauvinism.

Choosing Project Teams for International Drug Development

Numerous models of project teams for international drug development may be used (Fig. 19.8). The model chosen should obviously be the one that most suits a company's needs at that time.

Panel A illustrates the situation where a project team at the central headquarters is the only one in the company. That team directs development worldwide. It may allocate some studies to be conducted in other countries. Company experts from countries A, B, and/or C may participate in discussions, protocol development, or study implementation and monitoring. One variation of this model is for a member of each country to be on the central project team.

Panel B illustrates where project teams exist at each site where drug development occurs. The dotted lines between different teams indicates an informal or loose relationship and in the cases with a question mark, relationships may not exist. These teams usually share information and coordinate many of their plans, but each team functions independently.

Panel C is the completely integrated model where an international project team is formed at each site that participates in drug development. There is close coordination among all teams. One variation is to have an international project team at the central headquarters and local project teams at the other sites. Each local team may have a representative attend the central headquarters' team meetings.

Panel D illustrates a combination model of panels B and C. This shows the distinction between site or country specific teams (often with eight to 20 members) and international teams (often with two to four members). One variation on this model is to have two major international teams, one based in the United States and the other based in the European headquarters (for European-based companies). The United States team would have representatives from appropriate disciplines plus the project leader (or project manager) from the European headquarters' team. The European headquarters' team would have representatives from other countries working on the project (including the United States) in addition to local members.

There may be an international coordinator who leads the international team's effort, but this individual usually has no line authority for work conducted at a foreign subsidiary. Alternatively, two or more project leaders from different sites may share or rotate the role of international team head.

Reviewing International Development Projects

Progress of each international project team is reviewed by various committees. In addition to the international and/or project teams dedicated to developing a single project, two or more international committees are usually formed to assist global drug development. One review committee usually deals with general policies, priorities, and overall strategies rather than detailed management issues. This group generally meets about every two to six months. If the interval between meetings is too short it take valuable time away from doing work, whereas too long an interval allows groups to drift apart and for the strategies at different sites to move in different directions. It is essential that development strategies at each site be yoked together.

MODELS OF PROJECT TEAMS FOR INTERNATIONAL DRUG DEVELOPMENT

A. Centralized (Controlled/Shared) Model

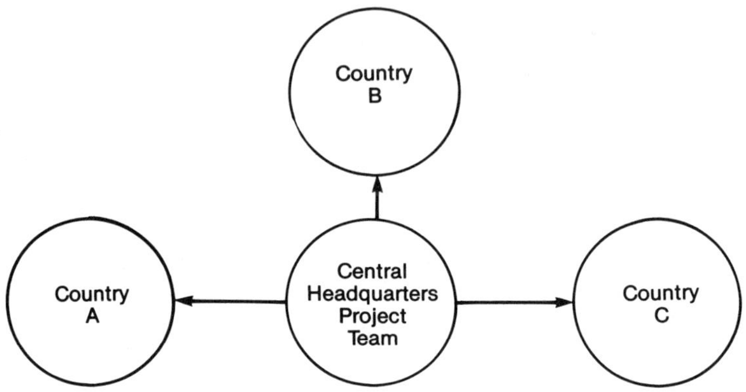

B. Decentralized (Independent) Model

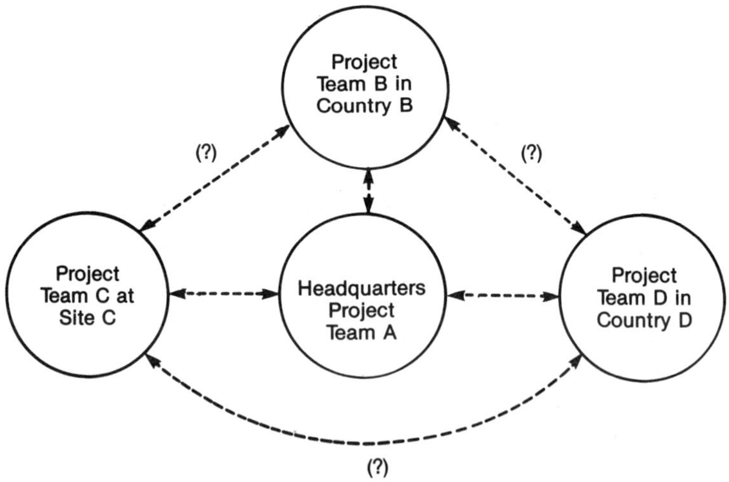

Fig. 19.8. Models of project teams that may be used for international drug development.

C. Network (Integrated) Model

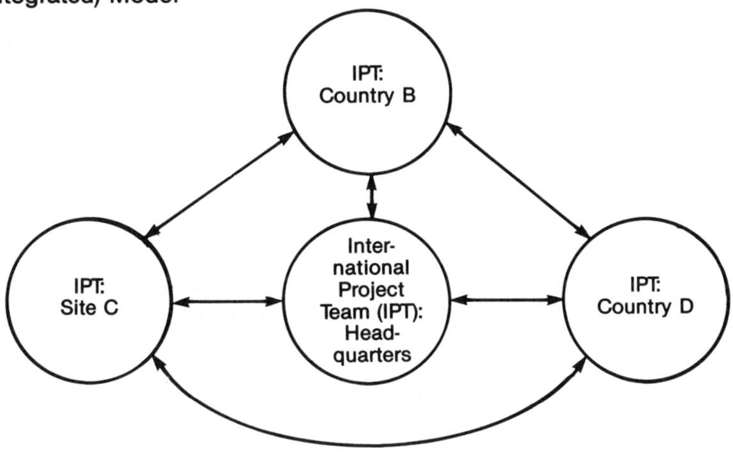

D. Combination Model of Panels B and C

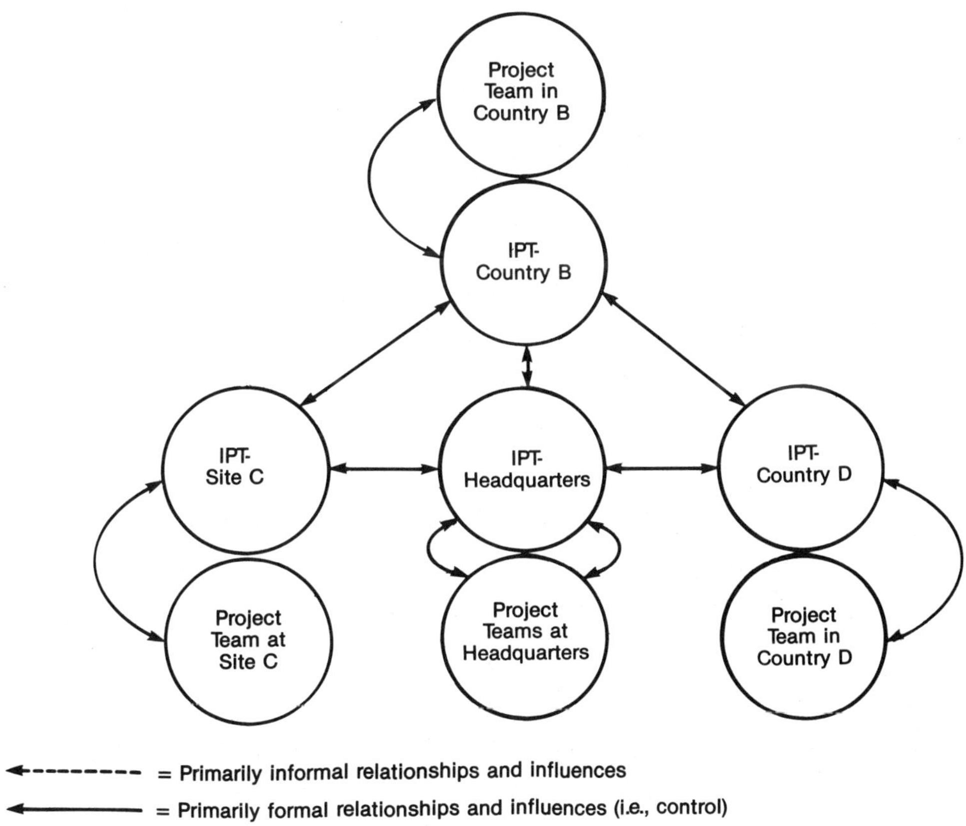

Fig. 19.8. Continued

Another group reviews all international projects for details on their progress and tactics. This committee usually meets more frequently (e.g., every four to eight weeks) and reports to the former committee. International committees that focus on medical activities, technical development, marketing, or other areas may supplement, or even replace the above committees. Many variations on these procedures exist within different companies. The topic of global drug development is discussed in greater detail in *Guide to Planning and Managing Multiple Clinical Studies* (Spilker, 1987c).

Pitfalls to Avoid in International Drug Development

Some pitfalls of global drug development are mentioned above. A few others are briefly discussed.

1. Each research site may have several projects under development in a number of therapeutic areas. Whether there are official priorities or not, each site will have their own priorities for all projects. Unless the central headquarters has absolute authority to dictate priorities to its subsidiaries, it is almost certain that some differences of priorities will occur. If these differences are relatively minor then global development plans on each drug can be effectively pursued. If, however, there are marked differences in priorities, then even having global development plans for drugs will not be sufficient to achieve a coordinated development effort.
2. Different styles in drug development may lead to great difficulties in reaching agreement on a single clinical plan for global development. One site's research and development director may be highly conservative and prefer to develop a project in small steps, being sure of results before progressing to the next step. Another site's director may want to take large steps between clinical studies by making various assumptions to reach the regulatory submission stage more rapidly. These approaches may clash, or at least be difficult to reconcile. The best approach for each drug should be considered individually. To create a successful international development program, a number of people must be willing to give up some of their authority and decision making.
3. Numerous social, academic, and political issues must be considered during a drug's development. These include the views of influential opinion leaders in various countries who have a great deal of say about which drugs are used in their country. This situation occurs in the cancer field where many different approaches exist in terms of dose schedules, combinations of drugs, and nondrug modalities used. Each approach has strong proponents and new drugs are not necessarily viewed in a totally objective way by all investigators and others.
4. Drug companies must insist on drug labeling that is internally consistent across countries. Consistency must be present in such areas of labeling as contraindications, ages of children who may be given the drug, and maximal dose allowable per day or per course. It is unfortunately impossible to have identical labeling worldwide because of legal and regulatory requirements, plus the fact that a company may pursue different indications for a single drug in different countries. One goal is to have agreement on exact wording of critically important sentences that are included in labeling worldwide. A system is needed to achieve input from all appropriate

groups and people when deriving product labeling. An efficient system is also needed to update and revise product labels on both a periodic and ad hoc basis, with appropriate input and reviews. This latter system should indicate guidelines and criteria that may be used to decide whether new data are relevant to incorporate into the label.

5. Compatibility of computers between sites is discussed in Chapter 17 and elsewhere in this book. Many other systems besides computers should also be identical or comparable between sites, including the dictionary used to code adverse drug reactions. COSTART (Coding Symbols for a Thesaurus of Adverse Reaction Terms) is the most widely used dictionary by drug companies in the United States, and the *World Health Organization* (WHO) dictionary is the one most widely used in European countries.

6. Different subsidiaries may not share a common understanding when they use common terms such as "well-controlled clinical studies" or "integration of data bases." This difference is especially likely to occur if one group is very large and the other small, or one group is in Europe and the other is in the United States. Differences in how each group views issues and problems must be sorted out *before* an attempt is made to derive solutions.

7. The program of clinical studies conducted on a new drug must be controlled. If poorly designed or conducted studies are allowed to occur they may compromise regulatory approval in the United States or other countries. The FDA requires information in an NDA on all clinical studies conducted with a new drug. The golden rule in this situation is that it is better to have three well-designed and conducted studies than a mixture of 25 good, average, and poorly designed and conducted studies.

8. Drugs must be developed that local subsidiaries desire to market and sell, or at the minimum, are willing to market and sell. This raises the question of who determines what products each country will register and market. If this is not decided centrally, then it must be established at an early date that drugs being developed are desired by an adequate number of appropriate countries to justify the drug's development.

9. Because each country requires different types of reports and in different formats, it is useful to develop modular-type documents that will simplify assembling a unique PLA for each national regulatory authority where the drug's marketing is desired.

10. PLAs should be submitted to different regulatory authorities as closely together in time as possible. This prevents reports from having to be rewritten and rerewritten because the drug's data base has grown significantly. If this aspect is not carefully planned, then PLA preparation may become an almost continual process of rewriting documents unnecessarily.

20 / *Issues of Technical Development*

I never varied from the managerial rule that the worst possible thing we could do would be to lie dead in the water with any problem. Solve it, solve it quickly, solve it right or wrong. If you solved it wrong, it would come back and slap you in the face and then you could solve it right. Lying dead in the water and doing nothing is a comfortable alternative because it is without immediate risk, but it is an absolutely fatal way to manage a business.
Thomas Watson, Jr., former chief executive of IBM. *Fortune* (August 31, 1987).

INTRODUCTION

Many people in technical development do not accept Watson's view in relation to their problems. They attempt to logically and systematically solve problems correctly and appropriately, even if their approach takes more time than attempting a quick fix. This more deliberate approach is generally appropriate in the drug industry.

A small selection of the many issues and problems that occur during a drug's technical development are identified and briefly described. Most of these could be (or are) the subject of an entire chapter or book. This chapter provides the reader with a flavor of the types of problems that frequently arise in the technical development of drugs. This category includes scaling up the synthesis of a drug substance (i.e., the active ingredient) from milligrams to tons, formulating the drug substance into a drug product (i.e., the finished drug tablet, capsule, or other dosage form) with up to approximately 30 different ingredients, and developing analyses for the drug substance and drug product. Although Good Manufacturing Practices (GMPs) are not specifically discussed in this chapter, they impact on almost all stages of a drug's path through technical development. One of the major issues faced by technical development managers is identifying at what point the GMPs begin to impact on technical activities in a drug's development.

General Activities of Technical Development During Periods of Drug Discovery, Development, and Marketing

Technical development departments play a minor role in drug discovery, although they may carry out some activities to facilitate this effort. Activities focus on providing large amounts of relatively few compounds for preclinical evaluation (e.g., toxicology) or involve preparation of radioactive compounds for specialized studies (e.g., metabolism). Other activities during the discovery period include limited efforts to address specific or general questions in areas such as formulation, stability, or assay development. Finally, patent activities may be handled within the technical development division.

During the drug development period, most types of activities associated with technical development are conducted. Many of these are described in this chapter and include (1) scaling up the chemical synthesis of drug, (2) developing a suitable process for chemical scaleup, (3) developing a drug formulation, (4) developing the process for formulating the drug, (5) supplying compound and the dosage forms (e.g., tablet, capsule, solution) required for clinical and other studies, (6) developing methods to analyze the drug in biological samples (e.g., blood, urine), and (7) transferring the process to production for large-scale manufacture. Other major activities depend on the organization of the particular company (e.g., obtaining drug names, patenting compounds, developing waste-handling methods). Almost all activities require regulatory submissions that describe the work in detail. Regulatory submissions are also required for various compendia (e.g., *United States Pharmacopeia*).

The greatest amount of technical development work occurs after a drug is marketed. This primarily relates to both the large quality-assurance efforts during manufacturing (see Chapter 22) and other support activities to solve problems and keep production on schedule. Technical development is also an essential part of creating new drug formulations and line-extensions during the marketing period.

CHEMICAL ISSUES

Issues Relating to Scaleup of the Chemical Synthesis

One goal of chemical development is to minimize the number of separate chemical steps required in a drug's synthesis. Advantages of fewer chemical reactions are both practical and economical. This goal may be addressed by (1) exploring alternative synthetic routes early in the development process, (2) purchasing raw materials that are closer to the final synthetic step or that allow the chemists to reach the final step more easily, or (3) contracting the manufacture of dangerous, toxic, or highly specialized steps to other companies.

It is rarely possible to go directly from a laboratory scale of synthesizing milligrams or grams to a manufacturing scale where hundreds of kilograms or even metric tons of a chemical may be required. Scaleup often requires chemists and chemical engineers who were not involved in the original laboratory syntheses. Large glassware containers are used to make greater amounts of a drug. Still larger non-glassware reactors are used at the pilot plant scale. This is a stage between laboratory scale and manufacturing scale. Monitoring and testing systems must be developed to evaluate the performance and ruggedness of the various chemical stages. This must be done during the chemical operations and after each step in the synthesis to assure that quality, purity, and yield are maintained. One objective of this process is to fully automate these operations. The number of separate scaleup stages a drug goes through should be minimized.

The number of separate scaleup stages necessary in a pilot plant depends on the drug and problems encountered. One of the many reasons why problems arise is that numerous aspects of scaleup are not directly extrapolatable from one size chemical vessel to a larger size. For example, (1) the temperature gradients may vary more in a larger vessel, (2) there are mechanical differences in stirring (e.g., sheer forces), (3) a loss of visual observation occurs because the metal reactors used are opaque, (4) the changing surface to volume ratio that occurs is critical to heat transfer, and (5) the mechanical handling operations generally take longer on a larger scale. All of these factors may contribute to the variable performance of the process. These factors and others can markedly affect the chemical reaction and results obtained.

Modifying the Route of Chemical Synthesis

The chemical development staff must balance priorities and available resources to successfully complete process development and provide project support work. Chemical development specialists modify or develop new synthetic routes for ultimate use in production. Their goal may be to improve bulk drug yields or purity, decrease costs, or eliminate manufacturing hazards and toxic by-products. At the same time, an adequate supply of drug substance must be generated to continue the various development activities (e.g., toxicology, clinical studies) on the project. Resource issues typically involve shortages in (1) personnel assigned to the work, (2) available starting materials, (3) available equipment, or (4) time to explore fully new chemical technologies. This is sometimes the central dilemma in a compound's development.

PHARMACEUTICAL ISSUES

Formulation—Creating Drugs from Chemicals

There is a big difference between an active ingredient (drug substance) and a drug product. Most chemicals are a single pure compound or possibly a mixture of different compounds, whereas drugs contain added materials called *excipients*. These materials are combined according to a precise formula and each ingredient in that formula has a specific function. Some people refer to the drug formula as a recipe, but this is somewhat misleading as it implies a certain degree of imprecision. Drug formulas specify ingredients to four significant figures, and all changes in the formula for both marketed and Investigational New Drug Application (IND) drugs must be approved both by the company's strict internal standards and by the Food and Drug Administration (FDA).

Agents that should be added to the final drug formula must be determined. Choosing the most nearly optimal list and proportion of ingredients that together make up a drug often takes substantial time and effort. What are the implications of adding each of these substances? Excipients must not react with the drug substance or affect its absorption into the body. Controlled release formulations are one exception where excipients are specifically chosen to delay the drug's absorption.

Most of these issues are handled by pharmaceutical development experts, but sometimes other groups must become involved. For example, a dye color may be banned by one or more regulatory agencies. A decision must be made by marketing experts as to whether to choose a less desirable dye that would be universally acceptable or whether to develop multiple formulations, each with their own dyes that could be sold in specific countries. There may be strong marketing preferences for different tablet or capsule colors in certain countries. This issue is discussed in Chapter 20 of *Guide to Clinical Interpretation of Data* (Spilker, 1986b).

In addition to a drug's color, its size, shape, odor, and taste are usually important considerations from a marketing perspective. Small capsule or tablet size may be difficult to achieve if the amount of each dose is large. Unique tablet shapes enhance product identification, but may cause problems in production. Masking the taste of bitter drugs is often difficult.

It is important to prevent bacterial growth in solutions, suspensions, gels, creams, and other dosage forms intended for oral or topical use. Solid dosage forms do not generally have a problem with bacterial growth owing to their low moisture content. The selection of a suitable bacterial preservative is sometimes difficult because of varying regulations in different countries. Only preservative agents and other excipients that do not interact with the drug are used. In addition, the excipients must be shown not to interact chemically with each other. Excipients are chosen based on the ease of working with the compound in production as well as on scientific considerations.

Parenteral drugs plus most ophthalmic and otic products must be sterile. Parenteral products should also be free of pyrogens (i.e., substances that increase body temperature). The pH (measure of acidity or alkalinity) of parenterals, ophthalmics, and otics is also a consideration and may raise challenging technical issues. For example, to achieve chemical stability and solubility a certain pH may be required, but this pH may not be close to the body's pH, and therefore the drug would cause marked irritation. Another formulation issue of parenteral drugs involves the degree of solubility of the drug in solution. Solvents besides water or saline are often required to enable a sufficient quantity of drug to dissolve in solution. These solvents have their own biological, chemical, and physical characteristics that must be considered.

Stability and Shelf Life

The shelf life of a drug is the time period during which the drug has been shown to remain stable and is therefore acceptable for clinical use. As established in regulatory documents this means that its potency is known to stay within specifications over a defined period of time. A typical drug might have to be within 10 percent of its labeled strength. To evaluate stability for the drug, a company conducts studies under various storage conditions on both the active ingredient alone and on the pharmaceutical preparation (i.e., drug product). These studies are important to determine if the compound decomposes (1) at a rate that would lead to an unacceptably short shelf life, (2) to a toxic by-product, or (3) to a by-product that has synergistic or antagonistic effects on the drug itself.

Chemical stability of all drugs must be tested under various conditions of light, moisture, and temperature for as long a period as is desired for the expiration date. This may be as long as five years for prescription drugs and is even longer for some over-the-counter (OTC) drugs. If the dating is "too short" (usually less than 18 months), then many companies will decide not to market the drug in its present form. In addition, obtaining regulatory approval to market the drug will usually be more difficult. Alternative formulations that achieve a longer expiration date will probably be sought if they are acceptable from a marketing perspective. Each formulation being developed must undergo a separate series of stability tests. Longer dates may be achieved with modified packaging that protects moisture-sensitive, or light-sensitive drugs. Light-sensitive drugs need protective (e.g., amber color) containers. Another method to lengthen dates is to modify recommended storage (e.g., to go from room temperature to 5°C).

Physical stability issues include whether there is absorption of a drug by the cap liner inside the container or binding of an active compound to an excipient. If liquid drugs become absorbed to the cap liner or walls of a container, a different material will be selected for the cap liner (e.g., Teflon, rubber) or container (e.g., glass, one of many types of plastics).

Accelerated Stability Tests

Some stability studies subject a drug substance or drug product to experimental conditions that help predict how much decomposition would occur over a longer time period under more common or extreme conditions of temperature, humidity, and light. This is referred to as an accelerated stability study. Regulatory authorities in the United States and some other countries (e.g., Japan) are moving away from allowing a drug's shelf life to be based on such accelerated tests. The FDA usually now demands "real" time tests, which means that 24 months of satisfactory stability testing will allow a drug to have 24 months of shelf life. Even though accelerated tests for new chemical entities (NCEs) were previously accepted by the FDA, they were always accepted only on a temporary basis until real time tests were completed successfully. The FDA is currently accepting accelerated stability data for minor changes in existing products or for well-characterized products already on the market.

When Does the Dating of Shelf Life Begin?

Another issue regarding shelf life that sometimes arises is identifying the date when shelf life begins. Is this the day when bulk chemical synthesis is completed, the day the drug formulation is complete, or the day the formulation is packaged? There may be reasons why any one of these or other dates would be preferable and would also be logical to use for a specific drug.

Dissolution Studies

Dissolution tests measure rate of solubility of a drug under various conditions of agitation rate, pH, and additional factors. Dissolution studies are conducted because of the assumption that drugs which do not adequately dissolve cannot be well absorbed into the body, and drugs that are not absorbed usually cannot lead to the desired clinical effect. Dissolution tests are a widely used measure of batch to batch variability for newly made drugs, and thus function as a quality-assurance test. Conditions used to study a drug's dissolution involve many factors (e.g., amount of drug, solvent, type of capsule, protective coatings, intensity of stirring, temperature) and may vary enormously in different types of dissolution tests.

Changes in dissolution rates of a known compound or drug may reflect either physical or chemical effects. Physical changes could relate to polymorphic (i.e., crystal structure) changes in the drug substance. Chemical changes could result from interactions with the excipient that causes the tablet to disintegrate. Alternatively, decomposition products of the drug could waterproof the tablet and delay its dissolution.

The correlation of data in humans with rate of dissolution studies *in vitro* depends primarily on the type of apparatus used and its operating conditions. Types of equipment vary in major respects, including both type and intensity of agitation used, plus more than half a dozen more technical attributes. Over 100 varieties of equipment have been proposed (Barr, 1972). Figure 20.1 illustrates a few types of apparatus used for dissolution studies. The major issue is that different methods yield different results, some methods are not suitable for certain drugs, and new methods require extensive review from manufacturers, the FDA, and the *United States Pharmacopeia* (USP) convention.

APPARATUS USED FOR DISSOLUTION STUDIES

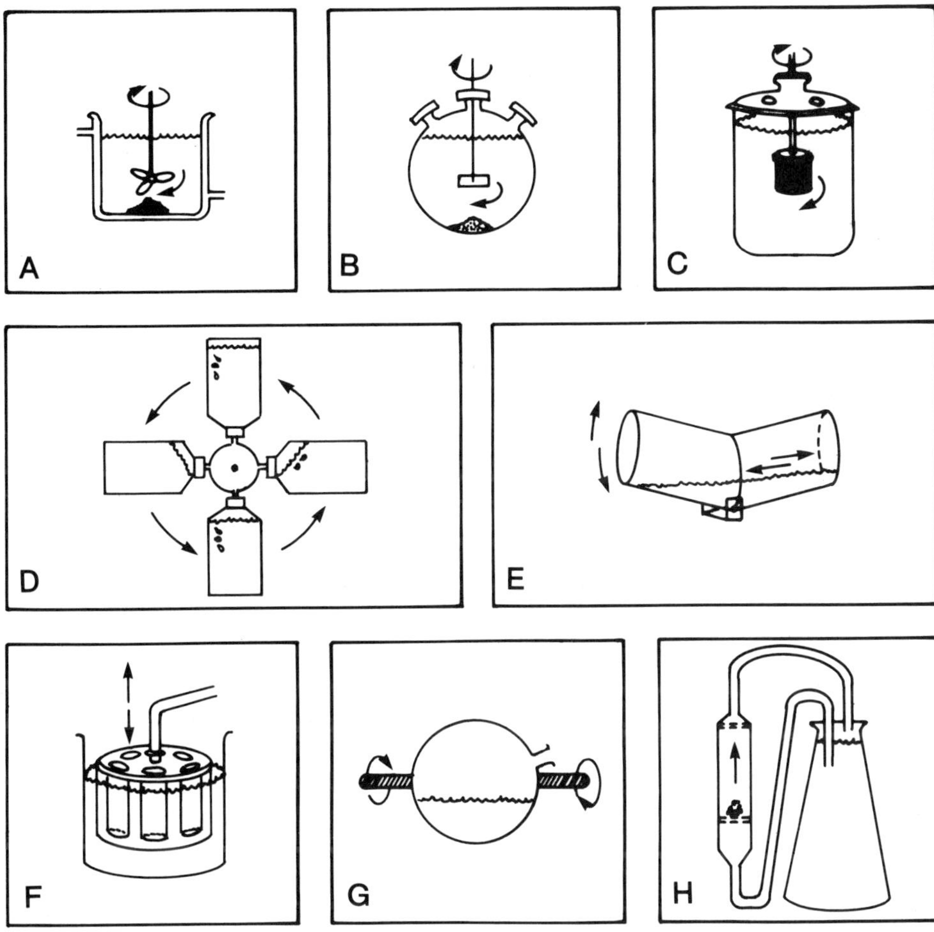

Fig. 20.1. Selected types of apparatus used to evaluate drug dissolution. Reprinted from Barr (1972) with permission of S. Karger.

A company proposes the type of dissolution studies on a new drug to a regulatory agency. The methods proposed may or may not be accepted as suitable. Because variations in equipment and conditions influence results, numerous issues may arise that must be discussed and resolved.

Drug Compatibility

A drug may react with proteins or other chemicals when it enters the blood. Drugs may also interact with substances in other body fluids, or with other solutions being put into the body. It is therefore necessary to confirm that a drug is compatible with and stable in blood and other body fluids. These tests are conducted prior to clinical studies.

Drugs that are given intravenously must be compatible with the solvents that are used to either dissolve or dilute the drug. It must be determined which solvents and which physiological solutions (e.g., saline, sugar and water) may be used with the drug. These tests are routinely conducted. Major issues may arise when incompatibilities are found.

Determining the Number of Formulations, Dosage Forms, and Dosage Strengths to Develop

There are a large number of potential dosage forms that may be requested for development (e.g., creams, ointments, gels, whips, suppositories, sprays, aerosols, solutions, suspension, powders, lotions, tablets, capsules). The need for each dosage form requested must be carefully assessed.

How does a drug company decide how many formulations, dosage forms and dosage strengths (e.g., 50, 100, 250, and 500 mg) of a single drug to develop and market worldwide? Also, which dosage forms should be developed, and in which order? This is a major international issue for most drugs. Local marketing requirements can readily be demonstrated for specific dosage forms (e.g., national preferences for or against certain dosage forms). These often lead to a proliferation of dosage forms being developed, even when the central headquarters desires to minimize this proliferation.

The company may decide on a central policy and approach for each drug and then require local subsidiaries to request an exception. Another approach is to allow each country to decide which tablet and/or capsule size, shape, color, strength, printing, coating, and formulation would be best for their territory and to contract with the parent company or other companies to have it made. The author favors the former approach of having some central control to minimize the proliferation of different forms of the same drug, and to reduce the consumption of valuable technical development resources. A bioequivalence study between two (or more) dosage forms or between two formulations of a drug is usually necessary when the final formulation or dosage form of the drug to be sold is not the same as the formulation used in at least one major clinical study.

Making Final Dosage Forms

The final dosage formulation must be processed through manufacturing equipment without encountering problems and be able to be compressed into tablets, filled into capsules, or made into another dosage form. The physical form of a drug may raise major issues; for example, if the drug is fluffy (i.e., low bulk density) and not compressible into a tablet, if the material occurs in several crystal forms (i.e., polymorphism) which cannot be adequately controlled from batch to batch, or if the active ingredient is not uniformly mixed with its excipients.

At what point during a drug's development does a company switch from the slow and cumbersome method of hand-filling capsules for clinical studies to filling capsules by machine? A machine-fillable method must be developed that utilizes powders of suitable bulk density, particle size, and content uniformity that can be encapsulated without adversely affecting machine performance. Also, there must be a sufficient amount of drug available to develop this method and allow wastage resulting from the use of mechanized equipment. This amount of extra drug may not be acceptable (or available to allocate) early in a drug's development.

Particle shape and size, bulk density, and polymorphic form are affected by the synthetic methods used to make the drug substance. These properties have profound effects on the drug product and may affect (1) uniformity (consistency within a batch), (2) reproducibility (consistency from batch to batch), (3) dissolution rate, (4) chemical stability, and (5) processing and production feasibility. These properties often change as the chemical synthesis method is changed. This means that formulation development is conducted on drug substances with properties that may be different from those of the final commercial product. The formulation developed must be robust to allow for such changes in properties. A synopsis of common issues faced in creating pharmaceutical formulations is presented in Table 20.1.

The mixing of an active drug substance plus its excipients may raise numerous issues. The major issue is whether nonuniform mixing occurs in some or all situations. For example, mixing may be uniform and appropriate for capsules, but not for tablets. Unattractive spots may show on the surface of tablets that were not present in capsules. The search for an attractive drug product that meets all necessary physical, chemical, and biological characteristics may require great efforts to achieve.

Increasing the Duration of a Drug's Action

When should a novel drug delivery system (e.g., transdermal patch, depot injection) or sustained action dosage form be developed to prolong activity of a drug? This approach must be considered in situations where the duration of a drug's clinical effect is insufficient. The determination of a desirable duration of action is largely assessed in terms of technical feasibility, competitive drugs that are available, and perceived benefits for the patient.

This problem, like most others in technical development can be approached in many different ways. Most extended release dosage forms have been developed in an empirical trial and error manner. Several formulations are made and tested *in vitro* and eventually in animals to determine which have the desired characteristics. Technical modifications to a pharmaceutical preparation may be made in terms of (1) excipients, (2) physical form, (3) addition of a retarding agent to slow a drug's dissolution, (4) coating a drug with a different substance to delay its absorption, or (5) other techniques such as using a concomitant drug that slows metabolism of the main drug and thus prolongs its clinical effect. One objective might be to decrease the rate of a drug's elimination from the body by giving another drug that decreases elimination of the major drug. This effect would maintain therapeutic blood (and possibly tissue) levels of the drug thereby possibly prolonging its effect.

Another physiological objective could be to increase the duration of a drug's clinical effect by enhancing the drug's ability to bind with its receptor. This might be accomplished by inhibiting the system that normally inactivates the drug. For ex-

Table 20.1. Selected issues in the development of a drug formulation

A. Appearance
   1. Size
   2. Shape
   3. Color
   4. Odor
   5. Taste
B. Physical characteristics
   1. Sterility – for parenterals, ophthalmics, otics
   2. Pyrogens – for parenterals
   3. pH – for parenterals, ophthalmics, otics
   4. Hardness or friability – for tablets[a]
C. Availability of drug at its site of action
   1. Solid dosage forms – dissolution used as a quality assurance test
   2. Transdermal patches – drug diffusion studies
D. Stability and shelf life
   1. Drug substance (i.e., the biologically active chemical[s])
   2. Drug product (i.e., the formulated drug with excipients)
   3. Compatibility of parenteral products with the solvents used to dissolve or dilute the drug
E. Production feasibility[b]
   1. Uniformity – consistency within a batch
   2. Reproducibility – consistency from batch to batch
   3. Practical considerations (e.g., equipment availability, ability to scale up process from hand-filled to machine-filled capsules, time and efforts required to prepare the dosage forms and dosage strengths requested or required, safety precautions required when handling or working with the unformulated compound and formulated drug)
F. Interaction of various disciplines
   1. Marketing defines product characteristics
   2. Medical determines the number of dosage strengths to develop
   3. Project manager helps plan work effort and allocates drug supply
   4. Chemical development refines and scales up the synthetic method. During these stages the properties of the drug substance may change
   5. Analytical development evaluates the purity of the drug. When problems arise (e.g., low amounts reported in assays) it is not always clear if the problem results from the formulation (e.g., poor degradation, poor content uniformity) or from the analytical method used
   6. Production groups must be able to manufacture the drug and often require assistance during the transition from drug manufacture in a pilot plant to a full production plant

[a] This is a measure of a tablet's ability to withstand subsequent packaging and film-coating processes.
[b] Critical parameters must be defined and controlled.

ample, the enzyme monoamine oxidase (MAO) inactivates drugs known as catecholamines. By giving a patient an inhibitor of monoamine oxidase, the action of catecholamine and other drugs metabolized by MAO can be extended for a longer period.

RESOURCE ISSUES

New Technologies

How may new technologies that are believed to improve drug-manufacturing and quality control processes be best evaluated? Also, how may new state-of-the-art technologies be incorporated into an existing program of drug development and production? A recent example involves the use of robotics (Table 20.2) and other forms of process automation (e.g., autoanalyzers), which are gradually assuming a

Table 20.2. Selected uses of laboratory robotics

1. Nuclear magnetic resonance (NMR) sample preparation and spectral determination
2. High-pressure liquid chromotography (HPLC) tablet sample preparations for analysis
3. Radioimmune assays (RIA) of clinical samples
4. Bacterial endotoxin assays
5. Tests conducted on sterile cell cultures
6. Filling capsules for clinical study material

larger role in technical development. These specific technical issues are not discussed or described in detail.

Each company wrestles with these and related issues on a continual basis. Small teams or task forces are often assembled to evaluate newer technologies, run pilot programs, and make recommendations. There are no general answers to these issues and each new technology must be evaluated on its own merit for each particular company.

Planning the Work Effort

Can technical efforts expended on product line-extensions of existing drugs be balanced with time spent on investigational drugs (new chemical entities)? Also, can technical issues and problems that markedly delay a drug's development be anticipated? Efficient planning requires consideration of department work schedules, backlogs, and priorities. It is often advisable to place project activities in each department's queue as soon as possible. This action may not prevent a project's request from being bumped out of the queue at a later date, but it increases the probability that the work will be done in a timely manner. Most technical departments prefer to work on project activities after it is known that the drug has an acceptable efficacy and safety profile in patients. On the other hand, this situation is not always possible and a great deal of technical work is often conducted at an early stage of drug development.

Sourcing the Drug

Companies must decide where every investigational and marketed drug will be manufactured. This may appear to be a straightforward issue, but often it is not. Multinational companies usually have two or more major sites where drugs are manufactured, and it is usually preferable to choose to make the drug at one of these sites at an early stage in a drug's development. The decision as to where to make a drug will be based on availability of personnel and suitable equipment as well as labor issues, tax issues, ability to export the drug, level of hazard involved, and other factors. Other options besides choosing one of a company's plants to make the drug include (1) having a contract facility manufacture the drug, (2) having one facility manufacture a number of intermediate compounds and then sending the intermediate to another plant to complete the operation, (3) building a new facility, (4) having two (or more) plants make the drug, (5) making some dosage forms at one site and others at a different site, and (6) manufacturing a drug in bulk at one site and compressing it into tablets or filling it into ampuls or vials at another site. Many additional variations exist. Numerous considerations will influence the decisions reached, which may also change during the investigational period, as work loads change and requirements become more firmly established.

Allocating Drug Supply

There are few major issues in the allocation of drug supply when a drug is easily synthesized and a sufficient amount is available. This situation allows drug development activities to move forward at a maximal pace. In the more typical situation, however, drug supply is limited, especially during early stages of development. In some cases, drug availability may be the rate-limiting step that is controlling progress of drug development. This situation requires careful allocation of the available drug to those activities that will move the project forward as rapidly as possible. At the same time, solutions to supply additional drug must be aggressively sought. This may include the development of new synthetic routes.

Drug supplies can be in great demand. Early in its life, supplies of a compound may be required to develop formulations, to develop an assay methodology, to conduct stability tests, to synthesize related compounds, to prepare additional salts, and/or to make analytical reference materials. Later, stronger demands on available drug are often made for large-scale clinical and toxicological studies, developing new dosage forms, and even preparing prelaunch stock.

If drug requests are not prioritized and coordinated, drug supply may be consumed by less important needs and not allocated to work that is critical to the success of drug development. This dilemma may be solved by assessing short- and long-term drug requirements, based on the drug development plan. Most critical activities are planned and drug supply is scheduled according to the time projected for preparation, assay, and formulation. Interesting questions arise when (1) the drug development plan demands more drug than can be reasonably supplied, (2) starting materials are not present and their availability is uncertain, or (3) process development work encounters unexpected problems. For example, if the most critical group involved in a drug's development requires approximately 500 g of drug and only 100 g are available, but future syntheses of 500 g are *scheduled* to occur in six (or twelve) months, should the 100 g be given to another group for their work? It is readily apparent how complex drug allocation issues can become.

Many additional factors can make drug allocation issues even more complex. For example, the dilemma of whether or not to delay clinical studies so that development of a drug's final synthesis can proceed (for its eventual production) is usually settled in favor of maintaining the schedule of clinical activities. It would make little or no sense to perfect a drug's synthesis if the next clinical study showed that the drug was too toxic or lacked sufficient efficacy to be developed further.

Related examples are: should a clinical study be started with capsules if a tablet formulation is scheduled to be ready in four months? Should a large Phase II well-controlled clinical study be initiated with available capsules if capsules with the drug's final formulation are scheduled to be available in three to six months? Will a new formulation be ready on time for a pivotal study (generally the most well-controlled study) that is needed to support a Japanese submission?

Changing Cost of Making a Drug during Its Development

Many drugs are extremely expensive to make during the early stages of their development. Almost all drugs become less expensive to make as the development process continues. This results from a decreased cost of raw goods as larger quantities are purchased, better suppliers are found, or a company manufactures the raw materials themselves. As chemical development continues, more efficient and less expensive routes of synthesis may be found, and increased yields (i.e., percent of active compound obtained from starting materials) may occur.

No matter how expensive (within reason) a drug may be in its early stages, its manufacturing costs may decrease by orders of magnitude. Difficulties abound at an early stage of a drug's life in estimating the ultimate cost to manufacture a compound as a marketed drug. Marketing demand and thus the number of kilograms or metric tons needed cannot be estimated until the clinical profile is known with reasonable certainty. This profile is rarely known prior to completion of Phase II studies and sometimes not until later. The doses required to treat patients are likewise not known with a reasonable degree of certainty until later in Phase II. As a result, it is difficult to estimate the production cost of a day's or week's supply of drug for a patient. Thus, it is important not to terminate a drug's development because it appears to be too expensive to make. Solutions to this dilemma may often be found.

ANALYTICAL ISSUES

Drug Purity

Is the drug's purity adequate? This is really a case by case decision based on the nature of impurities present. Are they toxic? Are they present in the same amount each time a drug is made? Most marketed drugs are well over 90 percent pure. The related substances present include process impurities (i.e., generated during manufacture of the drug substance) and/or degradation (i.e., breakdown) products. The quality and purity of most drugs increase during the course of development. The quality of a drug is a measure of numerous factors including reproducibility of the physical state in repeated batches in terms of particle size, crystal structure, color, density, and other characteristics. The ability of the drug to be processed is another measure of its quality.

Although it is desirable to have a drug's active ingredients and excipients as pure as possible, the effort, time, and cost to maximize purity can become prohibitive after the point of diminishing returns is reached. Moreover, almost all synthetic drugs that are less than 100 percent pure are not toxic in any way to humans because of the trace impurities that are present. These impurities are often inactive breakdown products of the active ingredient. The identity of impurities usually occurs during Phase II or III. Limits are established for the allowable amounts of impurities that may be present.

Purity may be improved by obtaining more pure starting materials. The reliability of suppliers to provide consistent material must be determined and assured. Reliability is usually assessed in terms of meeting dates and providing ordered amounts.

The ability of suppliers to scale up their supply at desired purity levels and at a reasonable cost are also important issues.

The most pure batch of a drug substance is carefully prepared and analyzed at great effort to obtain the reference material with which all batches of production material are compared. This is the "gold standard" and samples of this material are given to the FDA at the time when the New Drug Application (NDA) is submitted. The purity of a drug used in clinical studies and for toxicology studies should be of comparable purity to the drug that is ultimately marketed. If toxicological studies are done with a more pure form of the drug than that marketed, it could raise questions about the toxicity of impurities in the marketed drug.

This raises the issue of whether a small scale synthesis or even an early scaled-up synthesis can be further scaled-up and still produce drug with the same purity, quality, and stability profiles. If clinical and toxicological studies are conducted on a certain purity drug, but the manufacturing process changes or produces variable quality drug, a major issue arises about whether to repeat clinical studies. Some countries such as Japan have far more stringent requirements relating to this issue than do most countries.

Degradation Products

Breakdown products that develop from handling or storing a drug are identified chemically, and are then synthesized if it is important to evaluate them further. Other breakdown products may be isolated biochemically as an alternative to chemical synthesis. Obtaining a sample of major breakdown products is important because each breakdown product has its own spectrum of activities, both in terms of efficacy and toxicity, and these must be understood to insure that a drug's quality, purity, and efficacy are unchanged. Therefore, breakdown products are evaluated in many of the same biological tests used to study the parent drug.

Breakdown products of a drug that are formed by metabolism in animals and humans are also identified chemically and then synthesized. Although breakdown products identified in animals may not be formed in humans, they are important in understanding a drug's metabolic action. Each species metabolizes drugs in somewhat different ways and there is no single best animal species in which to obtain data that can be extrapolated to humans.

Drug Analysis and Bioassays

Identifying and quantifying the amount of a drug present in various biological fluids (e.g., plasma, urine) and in solutions prepared for assay is extremely important. Many different techniques are used to assay drugs. Finding the most sensitive and reproducible method often takes a great deal of time and effort, and the method selected must be balanced with the needs and limitations of the production environment. Some of the most difficult issues involve (1) quantifying extremely small amounts of a drug and degradation products, (2) detecting a chemical compound in complex mixture of excipients, (3) assaying complex biological compounds such as proteins, (4) validating new assay technologies, or (5) setting purity specifications. Bioassays, i.e., assays that use a living system (e.g., animals, tissues, microorganisms) to assay activity, involve many complex issues.

When the same validated assay procedure is performed on the same sample at two (or more) sites of a company, the analysis at each site must give the same result. The degree to which this occurs is a ruggedness test of the assay methodology. Assays may be developed independently at two or more sites, or even in two different departments at the same site (e.g., analytical development and biochemistry), but this is usually an unnecessary duplication of effort and should be avoided. If multiple procedures are used to assay drug levels, different results may occur and lead to many new issues. To cross-validate assay systems it is usual for the sites to exchange both standard operating procedures for conducting the assay and actual samples. If results differ between sites, scientists often visit the other site(s) and hopefully resolve the discrepancies.

Bioassays of Biologicals

Biologicals include genetically engineered drugs, drugs obtained from natural sources, and other types listed in Chapter 2 that are not chemically synthesized. Numerous additional problems are likely to arise in the development of biological products. In part, these problems relate to the fact that biological products are usually much more chemically complex and exhibit more batch to batch variability than most synthesized chemicals. Impurities may include particles of bacteria or yeast, DNA, host cell antigens, viruses, and endotoxins in addition to typical contaminants (e.g., degradation products) seen with synthetic chemicals. Because the activity of biological agents can vary from batch to batch, which affects drug performance, their concentration or strength must be assayed. Assays to evaluate biological activity tend to develop "bugs" and do not always give reproducible results. This problem may also occur with assays used to evaluate synthetic chemicals but is usually less common.

Existence of an assay is a prerequisite for developing a biological product. If an assay is unavailable, there is no means to determine the amount of a product present or to develop the product as a drug. There is sometimes an issue of whether the amount of drug should be quantitated in terms of bioassay units of product or milligrams of protein present. An international reference standard, if available, must be used if bioassay units are necessary to quantitate the drug. Variations in manufacturing procedures will probably make a true international reference standard an impossible objective to achieve for most drugs. In the case of bioassay units it becomes difficult to know if (1) the material assayed is completely pure, (2) the methods used to assay the product are perfectly reproducible, (3) the product will remain stable over time, and (4) the different manufacturing processes used by companies are actually producing the same material. If no international reference standard exists, as occurs for some proteins, then each company working with the product will report results using their own assays. Consequently, there may be little agreement between data obtained by different companies and each drug will need to be evaluated on its own merit.

LIAISON ISSUES

Technical development departments must interact closely with research, medical, production, and marketing departments in the development of new drugs.

Interactions of Technical Departments with Production

Technical development departments are responsible for developing and transferring manufacturing processes for new drugs to production staff. These are usually drugs that development chemists and pharmacists have been producing in a pilot plant stage, prior to the final scaleup to manufacturing scale. Analytical scientists assist in the testing of intermediate and final products and transfer the necessary analytical methodology to quality assurance. To avoid potential conflicts of interest, quality assurance personnel do not report to managers in a production group.

An issue that often arises in drug companies is the desire of production groups to acquire their own technical development staff. Different companies reach different solutions concerning this issue, often depending on logistical considerations (e.g., site location) and how cost-effective the duplication of this effort is viewed. Technical development departments in research and development that assign a low priority to production requests can expect a stronger demand from production managers for technical personnel based in production or for more work to be contracted to outside groups. Normally, support and service to chemical and pharmaceutical production receives the highest priority within technical departments.

Interactions of Technical Departments with Marketing

Interactions between technical departments and marketing groups are mainly concerned with developing investigational drugs and product line-extensions of prescription and/or OTC drugs. Line-extensions include new formulations, dosage strengths, dosage forms, and packages, but not new active ingredients. Technical development work on product line-extensions generally covers the same range of activities that are performed on new investigational drugs, except that issues relating to the chemical manufacture of drug substance are unnecessary.

The issue of allocation of research and development support services to marketing arises when each division reports to different managers in the organization. This is because marketing managers are unable to prioritize research and development work. Some marketing personnel express interest in having a small technical development group under their (i.e., marketing) control. This request often derives from inadequate technical department responses (from a marketing perspective) to marketing requests for services. It makes little sense, however, for a marketing group to establish its own small technical development group. Such a group would not have the expertise of the larger technical departments within research and development. In addition, duplication of scarce scientists, specialists, and expensive equipment is inefficient. The service that marketing would receive from a small group under their control might be more rapid, but it probably would not adequately address many facets of product development because sophisticated personnel in many technical areas would not be present.

The appropriate response to this issue is for the two groups to meet and determine how to improve the technical development department's services to marketing. The service provided to marketing may be judged inadequate or poor on an overall basis, because each marketing professional deals independently with technical staff. In practice, good service may be provided (1) to those who scream loudest, (2) to those who have the best personal relationships, (3) to those with the highest priority projects, and/or (4) by those with the lightest work load. In this system there is no *systematic* approach for marketing to use when interacting with research and development departments.

It would be preferable for marketing groups to present periodically a unified list of priorities and a marketing strategy to technical development and senior research and development managers for review and discussion. The managers would establish (1) those activities that could be conducted in-house within the time frame established by marketing, (2) those activities that could be contracted to outside groups, and (3) those activities that would have to be delayed. This last group of activities could be discussed by the group in more detail if desired. This type of meeting could be held at appropriate intervals (e.g., once, twice, or four times a year) and on an ad hoc basis. To advance line-extension projects along at a maximal rate and to coordinate activities between technical development, marketing, and production, it would be desirable to have a full time professional manager assigned to one or more projects. The number of projects assigned to each manager would depend on the amount of time required to administer each project. This individual would insure timely progression of his or her project(s) through the system. This collaborative effort would prevent unnecessary technical work on line-extensions that did not have the agreement of all relevant managers as to its appropriateness, priority, and timing.

"CATCH-22" SITUATIONS IN TECHNICAL DEVELOPMENT

Many "Catch-22" type (i.e., circular, paradoxical, or no-win) situations involving technical development can be described. A number of these situations are mentioned by Spilker (1986b, 1987c). A few others are mentioned to illustrate types of problems that often arise.

1. *Increasing the drug supply* Assume that the raw materials needed to synthesize a potentially important investigational drug are made by only one or two companies in the world. Also assume the drug company does not have the resources to make the starting material itself. The chemical companies are only able to supply small amounts of raw materials and do not want to increase their capacity, unless a customer (i.e., drug company) contractually agrees to a long-term commitment to buy substantial quantities of the raw material. Obviously, the drug company does not want to give this type of commitment until the drug is known to be safe and effective, and has a reasonable chance of reaching the market.

Many medium and even large drug companies cannot justify spending large amounts of money for a drug that may have only a small chance of being safe and effective. As a result, insufficient drug is available for the development program.

During the period of slow progress on the drug's development, the patent clock ticks away and potential sales in future years are lost and opportunity costs mount. After clinical efficacy is demonstrated, the company willingly makes additional commitments for drug supplies. There is no easy answer to the dilemma of how to increase drug supplies early in a project's life when raw materials are scarce. Companies with greater resources are more likely than companies with limited resources to assume a financial risk at an early stage of a drug's development.

2. *Allocating a small drug supply* A substantial amount of a drug substance or key raw material is required to conduct research, develop new formulations, explore better means of making a drug, develop a production process, or support other technical activities. When the bulk drug is in short supply and that supply is needed to conduct clinical studies, there is a dilemma of how to allocate and use the precious supply. Allocating drugs to clinical studies is often advantageous even at the expense of slowing technical development, especially when the drug is needed for important studies. There is no easy answer to this dilemma except that each situation must be carefully evaluated. This problem is extremely common, because several groups often compete for available supplies of a drug early in its development, and the problem becomes more intense when a drug is targeted for rapid development.

3. *Apportioning work effort* The appropriate amount of technical development work that should be initiated prior to the company's reaching a firm go-no go decision on whether to proceed with a drug's development to an NDA is often difficult to identify clearly. If a company invests its technical development resources on too many projects that later fail, it will create a highly inefficient system of drug development and may compromise the development of drugs that eventually reach the market. On the other hand, waiting for a firm "go" decision on a drug, which occurs somewhere in late Phase II, before investing resources on technical development is impossible. Some technical departments have a rough rule that 80 percent of their work is performed after the go-no go point has been passed. Other departments, however, cannot operate under this rule, especially when technical success influences the go-no go decision. There are also special considerations (e.g., commercial importance, degree of certainty that a specific compound will reach the NDA stage, medical benefits) that may accelerate or delay the amount of technical work required on a specific drug.

4. *Padding drug requests* When clinical, toxicological, and other staff prepare their estimates of drug requirement for the chemical development laboratories to synthesize, it is natural for those requesting a drug to pad their requirements. This makes sense, because many unknown problems may occur that may require more drug to complete their activities. How much additional drug should they request? If their need is for 100 mg or even 100 g and 40 or more kg are being made, they could pad their request by up to 100 percent and it would probably make no difference. If a group requires 40 kg and the synthetic amount to be prepared will be just tailored for that one group, then how much should they pad their request? If they add more than 15 percent or so then their request may affect pilot plant schedules and potentially interfere with the synthetic development of other drugs, besides being wasteful of the company's resources. In clinical studies there are several areas where padding often exists: (1) extra tablets per bottle in case patients cannot return to the clinic for a few days past their scheduled appointment, (2) a few additional bottles for each patient to allow for breakage or additional time on drug, (3) bottles of drug

for additional patients (10 to 50 percent overage is often used) beyond those required by the protocol, to allow for dropouts to be replaced or for additional patients, and (4) additional tablets prepared that are not bottled for a particular study.

This situation is complicated for the chemists who synthesize drugs by other forms of padding: (1) requests for a drug to be made for studies that are tentatively planned but are not certain, (2) requesting a drug sooner in time than really needed, because the staff wants to have a drug available to use when they are ready and believe that the best way to insure this is to place an early request.

These issues should be controlled by an astute project leader and staff from the chemical development group that receives requests. Any suspicious requests and all large requests should be reviewed with appropriate staff. Anyone who abuses company guidelines in regard to these padding issues will eventually be viewed as the boy who cried "Wolf."

It often seems inevitable to technical development scientists that after years of heroic effort spent on solving difficult technical issues, a company toxicologist or clinician announces that a serious safety or efficacy problem has arisen and recommends that the drug's development be terminated. Another way of expressing this point is that if chemical development can make it, analytical development can analyze it, and pharmaceutical development can formulate it, then it's bound to die in the clinic.

21 / *Marketing Issues*

All who drink of this remedy recover in a short time, except those whom it does not help, who all die. Therefore it is obvious that it fails only in incurable cases. Galen, 2nd Century A.D.

In recent times, modern science has developed to give mankind, for the first time in the history of the human race, a way of securing a more abundant life which does not simply consist in taking away from someone else. Karl Taylor Compton (1887–1954), American atomic physicist. From an address to the American Philosophical Society, 1938.

INTRODUCTION

This chapter briefly presents a number of issues faced by marketing personnel in developing new drugs. It does not systematically detail the processes followed by marketing groups to assist in developing new drugs. Interactions that take place between marketing and medical departments are described in Chapter 22 of *Guide to Planning and Managing Multiple Clinical Studies* (Spilker, 1987c). Other sources of information are listed in the references at the end of this book.

General Considerations about New Products

New products are introduced for numerous reasons, but the most widely discussed is to increase company sales in existing as well as new markets. New products are also introduced to provide a means of protecting, if not actually expanding, a company's current share of a particular market. For example, a company may develop and market a new product that merely substitutes for one of their older drugs. This often made sense approximately 20 to 30 years ago when an older drug came off patent or was losing market share because of adverse publicity or problems that the newer drug did not have. Substitution strategies were successful with various classes of drugs including antibiotics, analgesics, and antianxiety agents. In today's market, especially with generic competition and high costs of drug development, it is essential to have a demonstrable added value for new drugs to be successful.

Table 21.1. Assessment of new products by marketing

1.	Sales estimates (third year)
2.	Market potential in terms of number of patients
3.	Patentability and/or exclusivity (e.g., orphan drugs)
4.	Market trend for the therapeutic area or disease area
5.	Development time necessary before an NDA[a] on the drug may be filed
6.	Promotional effort required in cost and its projected effectiveness
7.	Breadth of drug use by medical specialists or generalists
8.	Existing market versus need to create one
9.	Competition in terms of number of companies and drugs, plus how well they are satisfying current and anticipated demand
10.	Effect on other company products (e.g., effect on sales, degree of fit)
11.	Pricing situation in terms of stability and competition
12.	Ability of sales force to promote the drug (e.g., number of staff, training required)

[a] NDA, New Drug Application.

New products that are quite similar to existing products sometimes do extremely well on the market. This is especially true when claims are made for a new drug that differentiate it from existing drugs or expands the potential uses for which it can be sold. Another basis on which new drugs sometimes do extremely well relates to the aggressiveness or the particular approach used by sales representatives who contact and detail physicians. Several parameters considered by marketing when a new product or project is being discussed are listed in Table 21.1. This list is presented to provide a flavor of marketing considerations about new products.

MARKET CYCLE—BIRTH, LIFE, AND DEATH OF A DRUG

Birth and Life of a Drug

Market cycle refers to the life cycle of a product. If the date of a drug's initial marketing is defined as the moment of its birth, then drugs go through many of the growth and maturing phases and steps experienced by humans. The product eventually reaches old age, and is gradually (or rapidly) replaced by newer drugs, by generic equivalents, or by newer medical practices (e.g., nondrug approaches to patient treatment). Eventually, most drugs die and are withdrawn from the market. Marketing-related activities that occur during the market cycle are listed in Table 21.2. Most of this chapter discusses the processes of birth and life in more detail. A drug's death is described below.

Why Do Marketed Drugs Die?

Drugs, like people, may die suddenly and unexpectedly (e.g., from newly observed or reported serious toxicity in animals or patients), or they may have a long lingering "illness" before death occurs. Another analogy with human experience is that the death of some products are totally unexpected and/or extremely painful to the company parents (in terms of lost sales or possible damage to their reputation). The death of other drugs may leave a bitter aftermath in terms of legal wrangles in courts. Finally, many drugs die quietly and peacefully in old age with few patients, physi-

Table 21.2. General types of marketing related activities in the drug industry

A. Advertising and promotion
1. Corporate advertising
2. Product advertising
3. Advertising agency policy decisions
4. Media selection or purchase
5. Sales promotion
6. Product publicity
7. Merchandising
8. Packaging
B. Sales and distribution
1. Sales to major accounts
2. Sales to other selected classes of customers
3. Sales to all other customers
4. Export sales
5. Other foreign marketing operations
6. Distributor or dealer relations
7. Physical distribution of products
8. Sales training
9. Customer service
10. Product service
C. Business research and analysis
1. Research on current and future markets
2. Research on competitors
3. Advertising research
4. Environmental scanning and analysis
5. Economic research and analysis
6. Sales analysis
7. Sales forecasting
8. Marketing information systems
D. Products and planning (excluding R and D)[a]
1. Preparation of marketing plans
2. Product pricing
3. Market development
4. Product line extensions
5. New products related to existing lines
6. New products not related to existing lines

[a] R and D, research and development.

cians, or even company officials to mourn their passing. The comments in this section refer to death of a generic-named drug and not a successful brand-name drug whose sales are eroded by generic competition.

Few studies have examined the detailed factors of why drugs die and are removed from the market. The most common reason is that their sales and profits have fallen to the point where there is little or no business reason to keep them on the market. If there are no compelling medical reasons to keep such drugs available, then they are usually withdrawn from sale.

Sales usually decline for several reasons. These reasons may primarily involve marketing (e.g., poor or inadequate marketing practices by the company, better or more aggressive marketing practices by competitors) or medical aspects of the drug. Medical reasons often relate to the benefit-to-risk ratio of the drug and how it has changed over the years or how it has changed in comparison with other drugs and treatments. Factors may also relate to competitor's drugs. The overall factors affecting the duration of a drug's life may be internal to the drug (e.g., adverse reactions or other toxicity), external (e.g., newer drugs), or a combination of both.

Table 21.3. Reasons for termination of drug projects by Hoechst-Roussel Pharmaceuticals Inc. between 1972 and 1978[a]

Reason	Preclinical	Clinical	Total
Synthesis problem	4		4
Patent problem	1	1	2
Instability	4		4
Toxicological finding	12	2	14
Efficacy less than expected	16	16	32
Adverse reactions	5	3	8
Price problems	1		1
Better competitors	3	1	4
Total	46	23	69

[a] From Seidl (1983) with permission of Raven Press.

Why Do Investigational Drugs Die?

Few studies have been conducted to determine the reasons why investigational drugs are terminated before reaching the market. Seidl reported (1983) the reasons why Hoechst-Roussel Pharmaceuticals Inc. discontinued 69 investigational compounds between 1972 and 1978 (Table 21.3). Twice the number were discontinued for preclinical than for clinical reasons. Prentis and Walker (1986) presented data on 197 compounds evaluated in humans for the first time by seven United Kingdom companies between 1964 and 1980. Table 21.4 lists the fate of the ones that died. The remainder were marketed or were still under investigation at the time of their paper's publication. There are several reasons why these sets of data from Germany and the United Kingdom are not totally comparable and therefore cannot be compared (e.g., different years and countries were evaluated, one study evaluated a single company whereas the other study evaluated seven). Nonetheless, it is interesting that 16 of the 23 compounds that reached the clinic were terminated by Hoechst-Roussel Pharmaceuticals Inc. for insufficient efficacy (70 percent), three of 23 were terminated because of adverse reactions (13 percent), and two of 23 (9 percent) were terminated because of toxicity observed in animals. The comparable

Table 21.4. Reasons for termination of new chemical entities under development by seven United Kingdom-owned companies between 1964 and 1980[a]

	All NCEs[b] studied[c]	NCEs except anti-infectives
1. Problems with human pharmacokinetics	67 (49%)	6 (9%)
2. Lack of proven efficacy		
	15 (11%)	10 (14%)
5. Miscellaneous	12 (9%)	12 (17%)
	12 (9%)	
Total terminated	137	70

[a] This table was modified from a figure presented by Prentis and Walker (1986) with permission of the Pharmaceutical Society of Great Britain.

[b] NCE, new chemical entity.

[c] This category was composed of 67 anti-infective drugs and the data were presented both including and excluding this group of drugs.

data of new chemical entities (NCEs) from the United Kingdom, excluding anti-infectives, were respectively, 41 percent, 19 percent, and 14 percent.

IDENTIFYING THE NEED FOR A NEW DRUG

All research-based drug companies perceive new drugs as their lifeblood. Just how true this perception is may be noted from the following discussion, which indicates the dependence of most drug companies on a small number of drugs for most of their sales.

How Many Drugs Constitute 50 Percent of a Company's Sales?

Some companies make 50 percent or more of their sales from a wide variety of drugs. But these companies are an exception. Most medium and large size drug companies make at least half their sales from a small number of drugs. Table 21.5 was assembled from Intercontinental Medical Statistics (Ambler, PA) (IMS) data of 1985 total sales in United States drug stores and hospitals. The sales included generally represent between 75 and 100 percent of a company's total sales. These data do not include sales of drugs to government agencies, supermarkets, or other sources. Of the 31 companies listed in this table the number with 50 percent or more of their sales coming from one to four drugs are as listed in Table 21.6.

Although the number of companies are fairly evenly divided across Table 21.6, it illustrates that 16 of the largest 31 drug companies made at least half their sales from only one or two drugs and that 22 of this group of 31 companies made at least half their sales from one to three products. Most drugs launched by a company never make a profit for the company and actually never repay development costs. Of all drugs introduced on the market, there is general agreement that only approximately one-fourth to one-third ever repay their cost of development and break even (Virts and Weston, 1980; Grabowski and Vernon, 1982; Drews, 1985; Joglekar and Paterson, 1986). On the other hand, the evidence for this conclusion is not hard, and the true proportion of those that break even or make a profit may be somewhat greater.

Research and Development—Marketing Interface

To be highly productive and successful, it is critically important for companies to have a positive relationship between research and development and marketing. Some research and development personnel do not understand that the commercial success of a drug depends on timely registration and drug differentiation. Others may not believe that marketing personnel are selling the company's products effectively. In these situations relationships are likely to become strained and marketing input will not be sought and incorporated in research and development thinking.

On the other hand, marketing personnel may not (1) understand the complexity of clinical research and technical development, (2) believe that the company's research is adequately focused or concentrated in the most commercially attractive therapeutic areas, or (3) believe that appropriate priorities or allocation of resources are being used. In either situation, relationships will become strained and the two

Table 21.5. Top drugs in sales of leading manufacturing companies in United States in 1985[a]

Company	Product name	Sales millions ($)	Percent of total (%)	Cumulative percent (%)
Merck Sharp & Dohme	Total	1319	100.0	
	Aldomet/Aldoril/Aldoclor	229	17.4	17.4
	Mefoxin	221	16.8	34.1
	Clinoril	135	10.25	44.3
	Timoptic	120	9.1	43.5
	Indocin	103	7.8	61.3
Smith Kline & French Laboratories	Total	1013	100.0	
	Tagamet	482	47.6	47.6
	Dyazide	262	25.9	73.5
	Ancef	97	9.6	83.1
Eli Lilly and Company	Total	932	100.0	
	Insulin (all)	216	23.2	23.2
	Darvon (all)	143	15.4	38.6
	Ceclor	132	14.2	52.7
	Mandol	89	9.6	62.3
The Upjohn Company	Total	737	100.0	
	Xanax	147	20.0	20.0
	Motrin	108	14.7	34.7
	Cleocin (all)	102	13.9	48.6
	Halcion	56	7.6	56.2
Pfizer Laboratories Division	Total	669	100.0	
	Feldene	240	35.9	35.9
	Procardia	180	26.9	62.8
	Minipress/Minizide	111	16.6	79.4
Roche Laboratories	Total	648	100.0	
	Valium/Valrelease	299	46.2	46.2
	Bactrim	50	7.8	54.0
	Dalmane	48	7.5	61.5
Wyeth Laboratories	Total	600	100.0	
	Birth control pills	186	31.0	31.0
	Ativan	124	20.6	51.6
Parke-Davis	Total	550	100.0	
	Dilantin (all)	82	14.9	14.9
	Procan	51	9.3	24.1
	Meclomen	33	6.0	30.1
	Benadryl (all)	32	5.9	36.0
	Erythromycin	29	5.2	41.2
	Anusol	27	5.0	46.2
	Lopid	25	4.5	50.7
Ayerst Laboratories	Total	534	100.0	
	Inderal/Inderide	366	61.6	61.6
	Premarin	97	18.2	79.7
E. R. Squibb & Sons Inc.	Total	521	100.0	
	Corgard/Corzide	113	21.7	21.7
	Capoten	112	21.5	43.2
	Prolixin (all)	36	6.9	50.1
	Velosef	29	5.6	55.7
Burroughs Wellcome Co.	Total	454	100.0	
	Zovirax	58	12.8	12.8
	Lanoxin/caps	51	11.1	23.9
	Septra	48	10.6	34.6
	Actifed	41	9.1	43.7
	Sudafed	38	8.3	52.0

Table 21.5. Top drugs in sales of leading manufacturing companies in United States in 1985[a] (continued)

Company	Product name	Sales millions ($)	Percent of total (%)	Cumulative percent (%)
Schering Corporation	Total	451	100.0	
	Proventil	55	12.1	12.1
	Lotrimin/sone	34	7.5	19.6
	Diprolene/sone	26	5.8	25.4
	Afrin	26	5.7	31.1
	Drixoral	29	6.5	37.6
	Garamycin	21	4.6	42.3
	Valisone	21	4.6	46.8
	Chlor-Trimeton	19	4.2	51.0
Syntex Laboratories, Inc.	Total	436	100.0	
	Naprosyn/Anaprox	285	65.3	65.3
	Norinyl (all)	56	12.9	78.2
	Lidex	38	8.8	87.0
Glaxo Inc.	Total	428	100.0	
	Zantac	303	70.7	70.7
	Ventolin	47	11.0	81.7
	Fortaz	17	4.0	85.8
Dista Products Company	Total	402	100.0	
	Keflex	238	59.1	59.1
	Nebcin	75	18.6	77.8
	Nalfon	49	12.1	89.9
Stuart Pharmaceuticals	Total	392	100.0	
	Tenormin/Tenoretic	231	59.0	59.0
	Mylanta	49	12.6	71.6
	Nolvadex	49	12.5	84.1
Bristol Laboratories	Total	368	100.0	
	Platinol	63	17.2	17.2
	Amikin	32	8.6	25.8
	Polycillin	26	7.1	32.9
	Naldecon	24	6.4	39.4
	Mutamycin	23	6.3	45.7
	Cytoxan	23	6.3	52.0
Ortho Pharmaceutical Corporation	Total	364	100.0	
	Ortho-Novum (all)	257	70.6	70.6
	Monistat (all)	69	19.0	89.5
	Modicon (all)	11	3.1	92.7
Lederle Laboratories	Total	359	100.0	
	Pipracil	64	17.7	17.7
	Minocin	56	15.6	33.3
	Maxzide	29	8.0	41.2
	Methotrexate	24	6.6	47.8
	Diamox	19	5.2	53.0
Abbott Laboratories	Total	350	100.0	
	Tranxene	93	26.7	26.7
	E.E.S.	46	13.2	39.9
	K-Lor/K-Tab	34	9.7	49.6
Sandoz Pharmaceuticals Corporation	Total	327	100.0	
	Fiorinal	50	15.2	15.2
	Mellaril	36	11.0	26.3
	Restoril	35	10.7	37.0
	Parlodel	34	10.5	47.5
	Sandimmune	33	10.0	57.5
Ciba Pharmaceutical Company	Total	327	100.0	
	Transderm-Nitro	122	37.4	36.4
	Ritalin	25	7.7	45.1
	Apresoline	23	6.9	52.0

Table 21.5. Top drugs in sales of leading manufacturing companies in United States in 1985[a] (continued)

Company	Product name	Sales millions ($)	Percent of total (%)	Cumulative percent (%)
Geigy Pharmaceuticals	Total	310	100.0	
	Lopressor	163	52.6	52.6
	Tegretol	60	19.4	71.9
	Brethine	30	9.6	81.5
Private label	Total	307	100.0	
	Small volume generics			
Marion Laboratories, Inc.	Total	293	100.0	
	Cardizem	133	45.4	45.4
	Carafate	39	13.2	58.6
	Os-Cal	30	10.2	68.8
Boehringer Ingelheim Pharmaceuticals, Inc.	Total	281	100.0	
	Catapres	92	32.9	32.9
	Persantine	91	32.5	65.4
	Alupent	52	18.4	83.8
Searle Pharmaceuticals Inc.	Total	276	100.0	
	Calan	49	17.9	17.9
	Norpace	48	17.5	35.4
	Aldactazide/Aldactone	39	14.1	49.5
	Nitrodisc	24	8.6	58.1
Hoechst-Roussel Pharmaceuticals Inc.	Total	266	100.0	
	Lasix	79	29.5	29.5
	Claforan	78	29.2	58.7
	DiaBeta	21	8.0	66.7
Merrell Dow Pharmaceuticals Inc.	Total	365	100.0	
	Nicorette	45	16.8	16.8
	Seldane	30	11.3	28.1
	Norpramin	25	9.6	37.7
	Tenuate	15	5.8	43.5
	Cepacol	14	5.5	48.9
	Novahistine	14	5.2	54.2
McNeil Consumer Products Co.	Total	255	100.0	
	Tylenol	228	89.3	89.3
	CoTylenol	14	5.3	94.7
	Sine-Aid	6	2.3	97.0
Roerig	Total	255	100.0	
	Cefobid	81	31.7	31.7
	Sinequan	39	15.5	47.2
	Navane	35	13.7	60.9
McNeil Pharmaceutical	Total	250	100.0	
	Haldol	86	35.1	35.1
	Tylenol w/Codeine	64	26.1	61.2
	Tolectin	50	20.4	81.7

[a] Sales above 250 million dollars. Data obtained from Intercontinental Medical Statistics (IMS) America, Ambler, PA. Some of these drugs are manufactured by subsidiary corporations.

groups will probably not work smoothly together developing new drugs and line-extensions. If marketing personnel provide a sales forecast on an investigational drug that research and development managers consider too low, it may initiate a conflict between the two groups. Discussions of each group's assumptions and methods will usually resolve this issue and achieve joint support of most plans and actions.

The fate of medically attractive drugs with little commercial value differs depending on the company involved. The factors that determine a drug's fate relate

Table 21.6. Number of drugs constituting 50 percent of a company's sales

	Number of companies
One drug accounts for 50 percent or more of company sales	8
Two drugs account for 50 percent or more of company sales	8
Three drugs account for 50 percent or more of company sales	6
Four drugs account for 50 percent or more of company sales	2
Total	24
More than four drugs account for 50 percent of company sales	7
Total	31

to (1) the company's tradition, (2) the company's current portfolio of projects, (3) how well the drug fits the corporate comfort zone, (4) the power of the drugs' protagonists (and antagonists, if any), and (5) whether there may be alternative reasons to develop the drug. The cooperation of research and development and marketing groups may be severely tested when an investigational drug has a high medical and low commercial value and the project draws resources (or would draw resources) away from projects that the marketing group believes have greater commercial value and are of high or medium medical value.

The Relative Importance of Marketing Versus Research and Development in Influencing Drug Development

Balancing the influence of research and development and marketing forces in developing drugs and driving the corporate business is a major challenge at most companies. One group or the other is usually more influential in decisions made about drug development. One factor that affects which group becomes more influential depends on whether the company traditionally defines success solely in financial terms or whether the equation for success also includes the medical value of new drugs. Another factor relates to whether the company is publicly or privately owned. If the risk to a company's survival or well-being develops, different factors and forces will become dominant (i.e., commercial considerations must dominate).

PROVIDING INPUT TO RESEARCH AND DEVELOPMENT DURING DRUG DEVELOPMENT

Marketing groups often review disease or therapeutic areas that either are currently being explored by research and development, or where new development projects are being considered. Marketing factors included in the evaluation are (1) description of the market, (2) actual trends, (3) potential trends, (4) patient prevalence, (5) current sales data, (6) projected sales data, (7) leading marketed products, (8) prescribing patterns, (9) competitive pressures, (10) competitive products, and (11) market trends.

Periodic Management Meetings between Marketing and Research and Development

Marketing and research and development managers interact on many levels from the board of directors down through the company to the trench levels and on many specialized committees. In addition to these and other formal (and informal) interactions, there should be a periodic meeting to review the priorities of research and development activities conducted for the marketing group. This meeting would review ongoing work, plans for the coming year, and perhaps discuss long-term future requests for assistance. Advantages of this meeting are that:

1. Marketing would assemble a list of all the clinical studies and other activities that research and development is conducting and is requested to conduct for marketing. These would be prioritized from a single marketing perspective, thus avoiding many separate marketers telling many people in research and development that their particular studies are most important to conduct.
2. Research and development can review at a single time, all of the marketing requests for assistance and each of their priorities. Research and development can therefore comment at an early stage if particular studies pose significant problems, should be handled in a different manner, or will require more time to complete.
3. Agreement on the appropriate financing for each of the activities may be achieved prior to a commitment to proceed.
4. Most importantly, marketing would be assured that its top priorities were being addressed and would not "fall through the cracks." Marketing could make alternative plans (e.g., contract work to an outside group) if the research and development departments were unable to conduct specific studies of particular interest to marketing.

Medical Groups Controlled by Marketing

Marketing may desire to control their own drug development function to "more effectively" expand the range of indications on marketed drugs, develop new dosage forms, and conduct studies for promotional purposes. This ability could entail developing both medical and technical development expertise (e.g., pharmaceutical development, analytical development) and groups. Although a number of drug companies have medical groups controlled by marketing, this approach is often extremely controversial. The control of a technical development group by marketing is described briefly in Chapter 20.

CONDUCTING MARKETING RESEARCH

Methods and Types of Studies

Marketing research departments conduct various types of studies, interviews, and literature evaluations relating to investigational and marketed drugs. These include (1) general market evaluations on a drug, disease, therapeutic area, or other category, (2) tests on products (e.g., flavor tests, name recognition tests), (3) pricing studies, (4) environmental studies (e.g., surveys, field trips), (5) tests on packaging, and (6) tests on the value of potential commercial claims.

The methodologies used in marketing research are basically the same as the scientific methods used in sound research and development. First, the problem or issue is defined, next a hypothesis is developed, and then a study is designed to test the hypothesis. The study is conducted and data are then analyzed and interpreted. Finally, recommendations are made and the results are reported in a verbal and/or written presentation.

Another source of marketing data is to conduct telephone or direct physician interviews to better understand their reactions to new and old drugs. These interviews may primarily be oriented toward understanding the need for new drugs, problems of older drugs, or acceptability and desirability of drugs currently under development. Characteristics of an actual or hypothetical drug may be tested with physicians to determine their reactions to its advantages and how often they might prescribe it.

It is sometimes desirable to enlist the help of an outside organization to conduct a market research study. This may be a result of limitations in expertise, contacts, time, facilities, or another factor within the marketing research group. If an outside group is to be utilized, it is necessary to develop criteria to be used in choosing the most appropriate one.

Depth of Market Research

Market research, like research in any other area, may be superficial or comprehensive, may ask highly imaginative and specific questions, or may plod methodically through a general or traditional approach. Each company wants to obtain reliable information in a cost-effective manner, but some are financially able to place more resources in their marketing research efforts than others. Also, some companies are more interested in using these data to make decisions.

There are proponents of a no-frills approach to marketing research (Saltzman, 1985). Saltzman makes the important point that the level of time and expenditure applied to a marketing question should be titrated according to the relative importance of the decision(s) that will be made. One of the keys to reducing costs of market research is to attempt to locate the information needed in secondary sources that are already available. These sources include published literature and computer data bases. Another method is to interview a few selected industry experts and opinion leaders rather than to conduct a broad survey of many individuals. Of course, some companies prefer to place more weight on opinions of physicians who would be the ones to prescribe a product, than on experts who may not be correct in their opinions. No matter which or how many of these (or other) types of groups is approached, it is critical to ask the correct questions, phrased in the correct way, and with proper background information.

Questionnaires used in written surveys, interviews, or on the telephone must be evaluated and validated before they are used. It is extremely easy to introduce substantial bias into the questions asked. A marketing group that desires a certain outcome of their survey may easily bias the questionnaire, even unintentionally. The danger, of course, is that a company may make wrong business decisions based on incorrect marketing data. Marketing researchers are usually aware of this pitfall and take appropriate steps to avoid it.

Sources of Marketing Data Obtained from Outside Groups

Companies with adequate financial resources usually obtain some of their market data from Intercontinental Medical Statistics (IMS) in Ambler, PA. IMS provides actual quantitative data in dollars sold, units of drug, numbers of tablets dispensed, number of prescriptions written, and numerous other categories. These data enable companies to track the size and trends of the market in both drug stores and hospitals for drugs of their competitors as well as to compare those results with their own. Drugs sold in supermarkets and a number of other locations (e.g., beauty aid shops) are not included. Some of the data available include:

1. *Drugstore and hospital audits* These supply market trends, effects of promotional practices, impact of new product introductions, influence of seasonality, and other information.
2. *National disease and therapeutic index* These supply usage patterns of drug use in office-based practices.
3. *National prescription audit* This measures both drugs prescribed by physicians and drugs dispensed by pharmacists. This gives information on pricing, dosages, packaging, promotion, prescription volume, market share, trends, and characteristics.

IMS also conducts a national audit of journal advertising, detailing to physicians, and mailings to physicians. Numerous other related marketing services are available from IMS. Various other sources of marketing data gathered by independent companies (e.g., Pharmaceutical Data Services, Scrip, deHaen, stockbrokers), trade associations, and government agencies also exist.

DETERMINING MARKETING STRATEGY

There is no magic list of factors that constitute a marketing strategy because many types of strategies must be developed before and during a drug's life. The broad areas that are usually considered as part of a marketing strategy are the major headings in the rest of this chapter, plus others that are not discussed or are not discussed in detail, such as drug distribution, financial credit, and drug packaging. Thus, most of this chapter discusses marketing strategies. References to books that provide details and discussions of marketing strategies are listed in the back of this book.

PROVIDING INFORMATION TO CONSUMERS

Providing Patients with Information about Drugs

It is apparent that many patients want to know more about the drugs they take. But, companies are hesitant to provide information directly to patients. This is gradually changing and some companies are starting to advertise about their new prescription drugs in magazines, newspapers, and on television. It is anticipated that these and other patient-related issues will become much more important to drug companies in future years.

Currently, drug companies rely on physicians, pharmacists, nurses, and other health professionals to provide patients with information about prescription drugs. This is correct and drug companies have spent a great deal of effort and money on educating these and other groups. Another means of providing information is via patient package inserts.

Patient Package Inserts

Patient package inserts are information sheets on a drug written for patients and provided to them by a nurse or physician with each prescription or by a pharmacist when the prescription is filled. The use of these sheets for prescription drugs is controversial and there are strong defenders of multiple opinions.

Although most patients want to be guided by their physicians in drug use (and not by a package insert), the author believes that patients have a right to a certain amount of information about any prescription drug they are advised to take by a physician. If the patient chooses not to read a package insert then that is their concern. If a physician chooses to provide additional information, then that is his or her professional prerogative. But, use of package inserts would guarantee that each patient would have ready access to the same standard or minimum amount of information about the drug prescribed. It may also be argued that package inserts are an ethical requirement that accompanies the sale of a drug.

If an insert is being developed for a drug, it is important to understand the range of patients' attitudes as to potential adverse reactions they may experience from the drug. These range from mild to severe adverse reactions that are reversible. It used to be considered that death was the worst adverse reaction imaginable. But, it is clear from patient interviews and the literature that there are several physical and/or mental states that are considered to be worse than death. For example, if patients believe that the risk of a stroke is worse than the risk of a fatal reaction from using a drug, then this is important information in determining how the patient package insert should be written. Numerous social, legal, political, ethical, and regulatory issues must be solved before patient package inserts are widely used.

The Association of the British Pharmaceutical Industry has recently endorsed the concept of patient package inserts (Anonymous, 1987a). They have also issued a series of recommendations that identify each of the elements they believe should be included in the leaflet as well as suggestions for their preparation and dissemination.

Other Vehicles for Companies to Reach Patients

It is possible to provide information about drugs to patients based on the ways in which they obtain drug information. Thus, a different strategy could be developed to try to reach patients who learn about drugs from doctors, friends, news media, magazines, or other sources. This could be done for both nonprescription and prescription drugs.

Patient Participation in Drug Therapy

Some drugs require patients to participate more in their treatment than to just swallow a few tablets each day. The requirements for effective drug use may affect a patient's life-style, such as modifying diet, physical activity (e.g., driving), or personal habits (e.g., smoking or drinking). Examples of such drugs include those that help patients stop smoking, reduce their eating, change the types of foods they eat, and decrease cardiac pain. Special marketing aids to instruct and assist patients and/or physicians are useful approaches to improving patient compliance and benefits. Careful preparation of these aids will greatly assist patient (and physician) education and compliance.

How Much Information Should Physicians Give Patients?

When physicians communicate information about adverse reactions to patients, they must decide how much information to provide and also what type of information. Some details can impart fear, and the patient may not ingest their prescribed drug. On the other hand, physicians who say too little to patients do not adequately inform them about potential risks. The correct balance is to provide each patient with enough of an understanding of both benefits and risks to enable them to make an informed decision about whether to continue taking their drug. This is a difficult goal to achieve.

DECIDING WHERE TO SELL A DRUG

In Which Country Should a New Drug be Registered First?

The most obvious answer is to initially market the drug in that country with the largest market. For most therapeutic areas and diseases, that country is the United States. But most drugs are not initially registered in the United States. Why? The answer primarily relates to the relatively higher standards used by the Food and Drug Administration (FDA) for drug approval and the longer period of regulatory review compared with most other countries. There are numerous reasons why the FDA takes longer than other countries to approve drugs. The FDA usually has a higher "comfort level" that must be achieved by sound data on a new drug. It is generally true that the FDA will more rapidly approve a drug that is already being marketed in another country or countries, although they usually believe that some well-controlled data should be generated within the United States. Preferably, the drug would be marketed in one or more highly developed countries whose standards of approving drugs are also high, and where some postmarketing data has been obtained.

If the company does not immediately attempt to market the drug in the country with the largest market, then should it try to market the drug in the country where it could reach the market fastest? This sounds reasonable, except that those countries where new drugs can generally be marketed most rapidly are countries that would only sell small amounts of the drug. Therefore, those countries could not provide sufficient postmarketing data of high quality to help expedite drug registration significantly in larger markets.

The actual approaches used by multinational companies to target countries for early registration vary, depending on their headquarters, site(s) of drug development, nature of the drug, and anticipated markets. In general, each drug is viewed individually and a strategy is developed to market the drug in as many different countries in as short a time as possible. The particular country in which it is first marketed is often of little consequence to a multinational company, because numerous registration submissions are made at approximately the same time. The factors of market size, speed of approval, accumulation of safety, and possibly efficacy data in a short period are prime considerations in the strategy developed. A company that addresses drug registration in a primarily sequential manner loses a large amount of potential sales in multiple countries.

Although these points hopefully appear obvious, there is an enormous difference in the speed and efficiency with which different large multinational companies bring their drugs to market in many countries.

Who Decides in Which Countries a New Drug Should be Registered?

There are two extreme positions in addressing this question. Those multinational companies that are organizationally centralized usually make this decision at their headquarters, in conjunction with input from regional managers and local directors within each country. Those companies that are decentralized usually make this decision at a local level. What may be a more important issue is whether promotional studies conducted in one country may have a positive or negative impact on drug sales in another country. For example, if patients in an intensive care unit (ICU) are found to respond to a drug in country A, this use may become widely used in country B. If a higher dose of the drug is listed in the labeling in country B, it may lead to serious adverse reactions, resulting in negative publicity for the drug in that country. This raises the question of whether a central group should approve local promotional studies, especially if the studies do not adhere to a centrally approved data sheet on a particular drug or are evaluating a nonapproved use.

POSITIONING A DRUG

In determining how the company wants the drug to be perceived by physicians, patients, and others (e.g., pharmacists, formulary committees), it is essential for marketing personnel to identify an appropriate niche in the market. Although that niche is usually based on broad issues such as safety or efficacy, it may also be based on more narrow or specialized aspects such as drug costs, compliance, packaging, or quality of life.

The group(s) of patients to be targeted must also be identified. A drug may be aimed at all patients with the disease or only to those with a specific disease subtype or characteristic. The drug could also be targeted to older patients, younger patients, those with kidney impairment, or any other specific group(s).

Identifying the Customer

Many business articles and books preach to the American and international business communities that focusing on the customer is essential to improve a company's profitability and market share. Nowhere has this point been more dramatically demonstrated than in the American automobile market. For many years, large domestic automobile companies virtually ignored the public's strong desire to have a small car that worked as well as larger cars. This unwillingness to provide small cars of high quality allowed Japanese and German manufacturers to enter and steadily enlarge their share of the American automobile market.

This general concept is also true for the drug industry. It is natural in the current environment of increased cost-containment efforts and increased competition that greater interest is focused on a drug company's customers. Many companies are trying not only to identify their customers better, but to develop specific strategies to target their promotion and selling to each. Companies that try too strenuously to protect out-of-date drug characteristics such as packaging, unpleasant tastes, large size capsules, and dosage forms eventually have their market encroached upon by more imaginative companies that provide drugs in a way the public wants. This point is particularly true for over-the-counter (OTC) drugs.

Companies that are customer-oriented attempt to determine the services that their customers desire and to provide those services. Companies that are less customer-oriented tend to interact with their clients based on the drugs they have for sale, stressing their perceived advantages. It is often shortsighted to view drugs merely as things to sell rather than as means to satisfy customer needs.

Who Are the Customers?

Ten to 20 years ago the physician was considered to be the customer of prescription drugs. The physician's customer in turn was the patient. Physicians were reached by drug companies primarily through advertising in medical journals and by visits from sales representatives. Secondary customers of drug companies were retail pharmacists, although they were primarily customers for OTC drugs. Other customer groups were viewed as having lesser importance, because a company's activities were focused on causing a prescription for their product to be written.

Today, customers for drug companies include the traditional ones described, but also include purchasing agents for Health Maintenance Organizations (HMOs) and Preferred Provider Organizations (PPOs), hospital formulary committees, distributors, wholesalers, large retail chains, pharmacists, government agencies, nursing homes, ambulatory care clinics, and patients themselves. Patients are no longer considered as a single entity, but are thought of as members of groups, such as the elderly or youth.

Identifying Customer Needs

Customer needs are usually identified by marketing research (Table 21.7). This research may be conducted in several ways. The most limited way is to do the work entirely from literature sources and staff meetings. A preferable approach is to go directly to the customers, interviewing them and soliciting their input. Drugs should be market tested to determine which groups of customers perceive the product in the best light and have the most interest in it. The reasons for their interest as well as lack of interest should provide clues for additional marketing efforts.

Table 21.7. Selected methods used to assess customer needs and satisfaction[a]

1. Toll-free telephone numbers used to obtain comments and complaints as well as to answer questions
2. Focus group meetings on existing or potential products
3. Questionnaire surveys via telephone or mail
4. Customer education materials
5. Employee training in customer relations
6. Interviewing customers in pharmacies
7. Enclosing comment cards in drug packages

[a] A report by the American Management Association edited by Bohl (1987), from which this table is modified (with permission), identified the first three points as the most effective. Whereas the final customer is clearly the public for over-the-counter drugs, customers are primarily physicians for prescription drugs. A further discussion of identifying customers is given in the text.

Creating a Drug's Profile

At an early state of a drug's development, marketing estimates of sales may be based on the drug profile that is minimally acceptable to market the drug. Alternatively, the average profile that is likely to be obtained, or the most optimistic or optimal drug profile may be used. Examples of these types of profile are presented below. Each type of profile could be expressed in terms of various parameters.

Frequency of dosing

A minimally acceptable profile might be to take the drug four times per day. The optimal profile might be to take the drug once a day.

Level of efficacy

A minimally acceptable profile might be to demonstrate that the drug is equally active as drug X, whereas the optimal profile would be to demonstrate drug activity significantly greater than drug X.

Level of safety

A minimally acceptable profile might state that warnings are needed for patients with hepatic or renal compromise. The optimal profile might demonstrate fewer serious adverse reactions in patients with compromised hepatic or renal function than with existing drugs.

Quality of life

A minimally acceptable profile would not lead to any restrictions in the labeling apart from a statement similar to: "Gastrointestinal distress and malaise may persist for up to 10 days but rarely persists for a longer period." The optimal profile might demonstrate that the drug was tolerated better by patients than drugs X, Y, or Z, and compliance observed was better than with those drugs. Quality-of-life issues are discussed further in Chapter 19.

NAMING A DRUG

Almost all drugs have four types of names: chemical, company, generic, and trademark. It is generally believed that good trademarks (i.e., brand names) help to sell a drug and bad names often hurt sales. But, what is a good name? The answer depends on several factors and on which type of drug and name is being referred to. Some drugs also have trivial names. Chemical and company names are neither good nor bad per se. Qualities of generic names and trademarks that are considered positive by companies are described in those sections below.

Chemical Names

A chemical name unambiguously identifies the molecular structure of the drug substance (active ingredient) in the drug product. Although chemists may draw the drug's molecular structure based on the name alone, a single chemical structure may usually be identified in more than one way. Chemical names are rarely, if ever, used by physicians, patients, or even most drug company employees. The names are used primarily by chemists, patent officers, and information specialists.

Company Names

Companies assign internal registration or code numbers to all chemicals they synthesize or otherwise prepare (e.g., extract, isolate). These numbers are a form of trivial names and are assigned for ease of communication both within the company and with external groups until a generic name is formally assigned. There is no need for most chemicals made to receive other names. Marketed and investigational drugs from other companies are also often assigned a code number. Most code numbers have one to three letters that usually identifies the company followed by a series of numbers that usually are assigned in a sequential order. Some companies include the year of original synthesis in this code.

Generic Names

The main criterion in selecting a generic name is that it should be derived in part from previously named structual analogues, the chemical name, or from the intended therapeutic use. Obviously, the name must not duplicate or closely approximate existing trademarks, generic names, or common names. Generic names are not allowed to imply excessive benefits or unproven usages of the drug substance. It usually takes approximately eight months to two years to complete this process. One reason for the long time required is because it is necessary to examine the name in other countries as to various sensitivities (e.g., names may have an undesirable meaning or connotation in another language). There are certain conventions about names and phonetic requirements that are generally followed, such as ending barbiturate names in "al" (e.g., Seconal, barbital, pentobarbital) and ending many alcohol names in "ol". Conventions sometimes change over time, especially when certain syllables and syllabic combinations become overworked, and it is necessary to avoid similar sounding names. The International Nonproprietary Name Committee (under WHO), United States Adopted Name Council (USAN), and other adopting agencies set patterns, and then try to follow them. Each reserves the right to make their own decisions. Companies usually prefer that generic names for drug substances are difficult to pronounce and remember, so that both patients and physicians will better remember the company's more euphonic trademark.

Generic names are formally adopted for all marketed drugs and many investigational drugs. In the United States the USAN conducts this process. USAN is a private agency sponsored by the American Medical Association, the United States Pharmacopeial Convention, the American Pharmaceutical Association, and the FDA. USAN has a mandate from the FDA to conduct its work. The five-member USAN Council works with the company, the International Nonproprietary Name Committee, and various other international agencies to select a single name for the drug substance that will be internationally acceptable.

Trademarks

Trademarks are names assigned by a company after determining that other companies or groups are not using that name or one extremely close to it with which it could be confused. A major issue may arise if the generic name or trademark is not approved at the time when the drug is discussed in public. This situation occurred recently with the names Retrovir and zidovudine (trademark and generic name, respectively). Because of the drug's ultrarapid development only the trivial names AZT and azidothymidine were available for public disclosure after news of early successes were released. After product launch, the old names continued to be used by both the lay press and health care professionals.

The trademark is used in a company's advertising, promotional campaigns, and extensively by the health care industry to differentiate between products. The name may be purposely chosen to be high tech and slick sounding, or scientific and stodgy sounding, depending on how the drug is to be promoted and advertised. Drug companies spend a great deal of time, effort, and money to derive the most appropriate trademark possible. Computer programs are often used by companies to generate candidate trademarks. There is a general trend and desire toward finding a trademark that may be used internationally in most, if not all countries. This enhances name recognition and facilitates use of a single distribution channel. Even a single company used to have multiple trademarks for one drug sold in many countries. This was partly a result of the difficulty in finding a single name that may be used worldwide. Also, local marketing people have their own views on desirable names and in some companies may control the local trademark chosen. Some generic versions of a brand name drug also have their own trademarks, which adds confusion to this area. Several letters of the alphabet have been so frequently used as first letters of trademarks that many companies have elected in recent years to choose these names starting with less commonly used letters to improve recall. Generic names and trademarks are derived by any of numerous approaches ranging from simple brainstorming sessions within the company to hiring outside companies that specialize in inventing names. Table 21.8 lists a number of criteria that have been used to select tradenames.

Table 21.8. Potential methods to select trademarks[a]

Selection criterion	Example of criterion	Trademark
Direct relation to generic name	Tetracycline	Tetracyn
Indication of therapeutic action	A diuretic	Diuril
Sales message or appeal	Ultimate tranquilizer	Ultran
Running theme use of same prefix (e.g., from Company name)	A. H. Robins company	Robitussin Robinul
Literary significance		Soma
Reflect chemical structure	Novrad	Darvon (spelled backward)
Route of administration	Oral administration	Chymoral
Dosage schedule	B.i.d every 12 hours	Combid
Source of raw material	Pregnant mares' urine	Premarin
Not related in any way[b]	Miltown, New Jersey	Miltown

[a] From Smith (1975), with permission of Lea & Febiger.
[b] The example given is actually related in that it is the name of the town near where the drug was developed.

Trivial Names

Some drugs acquire a common or nickname during the course of drug development. This name is usually used for convenience but is often difficult to eradicate, once formal names are approved. One example is zidovudine (Retrovir), which has the trivial name of azidothymidine or AZT. This name (AZT) was widely used in the press because of the drug's great amount of publicity, rapid development, and lack of an approved generic name.

Over-the-Counter Names

In the OTC market, names for similar (or even identical) products such as antacids vary from scientific sounding names (e.g., Gelusil, Mylanta, Amphojel) to more commercial sounding names (e.g., Tums, Rolaids) to old-fashioned, familiar sounding names which have acquired folksy overtones (e.g., Alka-Seltzer, Bromo Seltzer). This issue is discussed further in the *Advertising* section, later in this chapter.

PRICING A DRUG

Pricing a drug is usually considered the most important factor in a marketing strategy. Nonetheless, drug companies are unable to establish a price for a drug on their own in many countries. This is because regulations or guidelines involve government agencies in the price-setting process.

Pricing Strategies

Setting a Price

Setting a price of a drug is a highly complex process, and usually several prices are established for different customers (e.g., retailers, retail chains, wholesalers).

Some of the considerations that enter the issue of how much to charge for a drug include:

1. Costs of raw supplies to make the drug.
2. Costs to manufacture the drug.
3. Costs of distributing the drug to wholesalers and retailers. For example, does the drug have to be shipped under refrigeration?
4. Costs of promoting the drug to reach the target audience.
5. Advantages of the drug over the competition in terms of quality of life, efficacy, safety, pharmacokinetics, convenience, or other aspects.
6. Costs of competitive products and how they are perceived by doctors and patients.
7. Availability of alternative drug and nondrug therapy to treat the same disease.
8. Government registration requirements and various regulations.
9. Requirements necessary to have the drug included in various formularies.
10. Drug's stage in its life cycle.
11. Cost of active drugs used as controls in Phase III studies. This consideration is relevant for several countries that use this factor to help establish drug price.
12. A target return on investment is utilized as a factor to help establish price. Both short-term (e.g., one year) and long-term target goals may be established.
13. Estimated market size at present and in the future.
14. Estimated market share for the drug at different points in times.

These considerations may be used to determine a price that meets the profit goals of company for the drug as well as the sales goals in terms of market share.

The pricing strategy of a drug changes throughout the product's life. Raising prices at some stages of a product's life does not greatly affect the number of units sold. After the point when the drug begins to compete with generic products, raising prices is usually counterproductive, because the volume of units sold will decrease more than can be saved by decreased production costs. This maneuver usually shortens the future life of the product and is therefore not usually done.

Drug prices differ between countries because of many reasons including (1) basis for setting the original price, (2) shipping costs, (3) distribution costs, (4) import duties, (5) taxes, (6) product registration costs, (7) transfer prices, and numerous others. A more detailed list of various factors that enter into a drug's price is given in Tables 6.1 and 6.2 and Figs. 6.2 and 6.3 in Pradhan (1983). This reference also contains a discussion on various issues connected with transfer prices.

Using Price as a Strategic Tool

One reason why physicians choose one drug rather than another when they are approximately equal in medical value is because of a difference in their cost. To gain market share it is necessary either to attract new customers or to increase a drug's use by existing customers. Attracting new customers may be achieved by many promotional techniques or by lowering the price. Although lowering prices below cost may keep potential competitors (i.e., generic manufacturers) out of the market, this is called predatory pricing and is illegal. If the goal is to price a totally novel drug for the first time, a price must be chosen that is consistent with the medical value of the drug in the consumer's view. To increase drug purchases by current customers (e.g., large retail stores, groups of hospitals) it may be important to offer volume discounts and special prices to a select group of customers. New customers may be attracted by special prices on a product line or selected products that are being promoted. It is important for a company to offer the same special price on volume purchases to all customers in a group(s) (e.g., distributors).

The previous discussion is based on the assumption that a drug company establishes the price it is to charge for its own drug. This situation occurs in few countries. Even in countries where this occurs various systems and mechanisms influence or control the price asked. The regulatory authority plays a major role in setting prices in most countries. They may establish a price (1) before (or after) the drug is approved for marketing, (2) totally on their own or in conjunction with information presented by the company, or (3) in a rapid period or in a drawn-out process. The pattern differs greatly around the world. Tucker (1984, p. 130) presents numerous difficulties that confront regulatory agencies in establishing fair prices for drugs.

Drug Costs: Direct, Indirect, and Intangible

Cost of medical treatment for any specific disease may be determined by methods ranging from a rough guesstimate to highly sophisticated techniques. Overall costs of a patient's treatment includes considerations of direct costs, indirect costs, and intangible costs. *Direct costs* of treatment include such costs as the cost of physician's services, hospitalizations (if required), and prescriptions. *Indirect costs* are financial expenses not directly attributed to treatment. They include transportation to and from the place of medical treatment, meals bought at the treatment site, and lost income because of time taken for treatment. *Intangible costs* include discomfort and pain from the disease, plus any embarrassment resulting from the disease or treatment. Although these costs are described for patients, many indirect and intangible costs are also borne by the patient's family, friends, and others who interact with the patient. In addition, there are numerous costs from society's point of view. These costs are not described in this chapter and are primarily in the province of health planners and government officials.

Direct costs are the most easily measured cost. Nonetheless, a study to compare direct costs of two treatments may be conducted in several different ways, and different types of cost comparisons may be made. Calculating and comparing indirect and intangible costs for two or more treatments is much more complex, and no single agreed-on method is available.

Cost-Effectiveness Claims

Most companies desire to demonstrate that their products are cost-effective in comparison with those of the competition. What exactly does this mean? Cost-effectiveness analyses involve comparisons between two (or more) drugs within the same therapeutic category or between a drug and the currently available nondrug treatment. If no treatments are available, then drug costs will be compared to the prevailing therapeutic approach and its costs.

For cost comparisons, it is important to compare drug regimens that yield equal effects. Many factors enter the determination of drug efficacy so that finding equivalent drug regimens is not always easy. Moreover, efficacy may be expressed in many different ways. Also there are many types of costs involved and many ways of expressing those costs.

Issues of Apples and Oranges in Drug Comparisons

When the cost-effectiveness of two drugs are compared, each may claim to be superior based on totally different criteria. Issues of comparing apples and oranges abound. For example, assume that drug A decreases an average patient's hospital stay from ten days to one day, but that it increases the risk of moderate adverse reactions and a fatal reaction compared with an equally effective drug B. How should the costs and risk be assessed and compared? The *cost-to-benefit ratio* is better for drug A compared with no treatment, and is the same as for drug B. The *cost-to-risk ratio* is worse for drug A than for drug B. Also, the *risk-to-benefit ratio* may be worse than originally hoped. If the latter ratio has changed sufficiently to alter the clinical importance of the drug relative to existing therapy (drug B), then the drug's future should be reassessed. If alternative treatment is not available, then the drug should probably be approved by HMOs and other formulary committees for stocking in the hospital. If an existing treatment is available, then a formulary committee may request data on a clinical comparison between drugs A and B before drug A is approved for stocking.

It is easy to understand how several competitors with similar drugs for a single disease may each claim that their drug is more cost-effective than their competitor's drug. For example, the claims of one company may focus on the wider range of disease subtypes treated and a reduced need for pharmacies to stock several different drugs that each only treat a single subtype. Another company may claim better cost-effectiveness based on superior efficacy and reduced duration of hospitalization. A third competitor could claim decreased cost of the drug per week of treatment compared with other drugs that yield the same effect. A fourth competitor whose drug's efficacy and cost are the same as others could still claim cost-effectiveness based on an improved quality of life or improved patient compliance with his drug.

INTRODUCING A DRUG

The real launch date of a drug is no longer a specific day shortly after it is officially approved for marketing. That day used to be the time that the trumpets blared out the announcement of the new arrival. Now, the effective launch date may occur several years ahead of market approval. Many activities are conducted to sensitize physicians to the drug's existence and relevance for their practice. This is done via publications, symposia, and various other events and speeches by thought leaders and industry personnel.

The initial marketing of a drug is an important moment in a drug's life. If the drug is promoted too aggressively and too widely then it will be prescribed to many inappropriate patients and possibly at inappropriate doses. This will probably lead to a large number of adverse reactions, which could be "fatal" to the drug (e.g., benoxaprofen). A more cautious introduction of a new drug is usually a wiser approach than a heavy advertising blitz, although that approach may be acceptable in some situations.

Dr. Grahame-Smith (1987) describes 13 parameters of a typical new drug at the time of its introduction. He scores the understanding of each parameter by a sponsor or developer of the drug on an analogue scale of 1 to 10 and gives high scores (7 or 8) for basic pharmacology, preclinical safety testing, and clinical safety. Low scores (2 or 3) are given to risk, overall benefit, drug-disease interaction, method of use, and types of patients who will benefit most or least from the drug.

Some of the issues associated with launching a drug are described in Chapter 22 of Spilker (1987c). Other issues are described in Chapter 30 of this book, regarding press conferences, press releases, and other types of public relations activities on a drug.

PROMOTING A DRUG

One means of differentiating between marketing and promotion activities in positioning a drug is to consider marketing activities as an attempt to determine people's needs and then to design products that meet those needs. Promotion activities, on the other hand, attempt to change people to meet the attributes of the product.

Advertising Issues

Advertising is considered to be a subset of promotion. Promotional activities also include public relations' efforts and providing product related information to physicians (e.g., using books, journals, newsletters, brochures). This information does not always mention the drug directly and may only be indirectly related to the product. Even indirect promotion, however, helps educate readers about a specific disease or therapeutic area affected by the drug. Scientific exhibits at conventions usually contain product advertising, but also may include or even concentrate on nonproduct approaches to diagnosis, treatment, or prevention of the particular disease associated with the drug of interest. Television advertisements about the disease (rather than the drug used to treat it) are another type of indirect promotion. As a result of this advertising, it is hoped that patients with the disease will visit their doctor to inquire about the advertised treatment.

One of the central issues in drug advertising is to determine and evaluate the payback in sales and profits on a specific product (or product line) for each dollar spent advertising that product (or product line). If spending a dollar on advertising a drug does not generate at least a dollar return in sales, then the only reason to advertise the drug is as a "loss leader" to bring a certain product to the attention of a given audience.

For most products, more than a dollar must be returned in sales for each dollar spent on advertising. As this ratio falls, it eventually reaches a point where it becomes uneconomical to continue advertising a specific product. Either a less expensive medium or a new approach to advertising the drug must be found. A new approach might be to focus better on the content of the promotional message, or to direct the same message to a more selective audience (e.g., to dermatologists rather than to family practice and other physicians who treat skin diseases). In either case, the effectiveness of the drug's advertising must be increased.

Direct to Consumer Advertising of Prescription Drugs

Advertisements in magazines, in newspapers, on television, and on radio that inform the public about a specific disease have become more common in the 1980s. The ads say in essence, "Now there is something that can help you control or treat this disease. See your doctor for more information." Physicians and sometimes patients understand which drug is referred to, even though the drug's name is usually not specifically mentioned. Recent newspaper advertisements for a prescription antihistamine have changed this "no-name" approach and stated the drug's name.

Some of the advantages for a company to advertise a prescription drug directly to consumers are that:

1. It helps patients distinguish when professional input is needed in their care from areas where self-care is appropriate.
2. It informs the public about new products that are available.
3. It provides an update about alternative medical treatments.
4. It indirectly encourages physicians to use a company's drugs.

The specific step in a patient's course of medical treatment influenced by television advertisements is shown in Fig. 21.2. Such advertisements are most effective when there is only a single marketed drug to which the advertisement could be referring. The message will be acted on differently by the audience when there are multiple products that could be referred to in the advertisements.

Future advertisements to the public are likely to increase in number if regulations do not prevent their growth. This might occur if consumer or health-care professional groups strongly object to the practice. Some advertisements will also provide more sophisticated information, because a growing number of people desire to know more about the drugs they take. These people also desire to have a greater role in their medical care. Information on patented drug delivery systems, which increase patient compliance or provide other benefits, may also increase in the future. The FDA, Federal Trade Commission (FTC), and even the public do not have a single clear perception or opinion about this issue, and the eventual outcome of this type of advertising is uncertain.

Assessing Drug Claims

After listening to hyped claims for new drugs made by some company personnel, it is easy to conclude that drugs that have not been tested in patients always seem to have better profiles than drugs that have been tested. Drugs tested in only a few patients also often appear to be better than after they are tested in a larger number. Another way of stating this principle is that drugs usually start their life in a pristine or virginal state, but acquire warts and blemishes as they move toward the market.

Unlike fine wines, most drugs do not improve with age, except in the eye of the drug's promoter.

A small number of reported claims of drug superiority are listed below. The claims are assumed to be true, according to one or more of the possible interpretations given.

1. *Drug A is 10 times as potent as drug B* This claim literally means that one-tenth a given amount of drug A causes the same response as ten times the amount of drug B. This usually means that a tablet or capsule of drug A has one-tenth the number of milligrams of a tablet of drug B and the rest of the drug is made up of various excipients. If the two drugs have the same efficacy and safety profile, then the drug that is more potent usually has no clinical advantage. There would be an advantage for the more potent drug if a smaller capsule size could be used that was more acceptable to patients. For a few intravenous drugs where large quantities have to be given (e.g., the diuretic, ethacrynic acid), development of a more potent drug has practical advantages.

2. *Nine out of 10 doctors recommend the ingredient in drug A* This may be a true statement, but it is not saying that the doctors have recommended drug A per se. If there are several drug products containing the same active ingredient, there may be important reasons to prefer a different drug than A for some patients (e.g., different salt, different dosage form, different excipients). The claim may not indicate how these 10 doctors were chosen and their selection may not have been totally random.

3. *Drug A cured 90 percent of all patients within X days* This may be a true statement, but the disease treated may be self-limiting within X days. Therefore, most patients would have improved without receiving any treatment. This applies to minor colds and other minor ailments. Alternatively, the course of the disease may have been shortened from 20 days to 19 days (on average), which could be statistically significant but would not be clinically important. It would be necessary to examine the data and study design(s) to evaluate the clinical relevance of this statement.

4. *Drug A causes improvement in 90 percent of all patients with disease X* But, what happens when the drug is stopped. Do problems recur? Is there actually a rebound effect (i.e., return or exacerbation of the original symptoms)? Is there a withdrawal phenomenon? How does the drug compare with others in these regards? Numerous related questions could also be posed.

5. *Drug A has the following three activities. It does X, Y, and Z* But, are any of these activities related to how the drug works clinically? Do these activities explain the drug's beneficial effects in patients? It is also possible that these activities were only observed in animal studies, were only observed at toxic doses, or were only observed in a small number of patients.

6. *Drug A is as good as the most powerful drug available to treat disease X* But, can one treat disease X with more mild drugs? How good are any drugs in treating this disease? How do physicians usually treat patients with this disease? What adverse reactions occur with drug A versus others used to treat patients with disease X?

7. *The competitor's drug B was not as active as drug A in patients when each was tested at equal doses* But, if higher doses of the competitor's drug were given,

Table 21.9. Profile of traditional and professional types of over-the-counter drugs

Professional OTC[a] drugs	Traditional OTC drugs
Rationally based	Emotionally based
Sophisticated upper income orientation	Middle-America lower income orientation
Advertising intensive	Advertising insensitive to a degree
Contemporary state-of-the-art image	Folklore based, used by one's parents

[a] OTC, over-the-counter drug.

would it have been more active and equally safe? Equal doses of two drugs in terms of number of milligrams may not be relevant to compare unless it is known that the two drugs are equally effective or at least have comparable efficacy.

8. *Drug A has fewer side effects than the competitor's drug* But, were the two drugs compared (1) at comparable equi-effective doses, (2) in the same study, and (3) in an identical patient population? Also, was a comparison of a single entity and a combination drug made? This would be an especially unfair comparison if the side effect profile on one drug was affected by the second drug in the combination product.

9. *Four out of five hospitals use drug A more than drug B* Hospitals usually choose one drug over another generally similar drug of the same type because of price. The drug manufacturer may have supplied the drug at a lower price particularly to obtain hospital use. Were all hospitals in the sample in one geographical area, possibly the one where the company promoted its drug heavily? How many hospitals were in the sample? Was it 5, 10, or 410? Many additional factors could also have influenced this statement.

The issue of possible medical questions asked and interpretations drawn is complex. From the advertiser's perspective, a major issue is what type and how much information should be provided to medical readers. An appropriate approach to this issue is to provide the information that a reasonable physician would want to know. The quantity and quality of this information can easily be determined in most situations by discussing the issue with physicians, either inside or outside the company. From a physician's perspective, many marketing claims unfortunately remind one of the title of Shakespeare's play—*Much Ado About Nothing*. It is the task and goal of marketing personnel to avoid this problem and to explain claims in ways that meet the physician's needs, and answer the most frequently posed questions.

Professional Over-the-Counter Drugs

There appears to be a new group of OTC drugs that are promoted and perceived differently than older established ones. These are sometimes referred to as professional OTCs. Their characteristics, as compared with traditional OTCs are listed in Table 21.9. It is clear from this table that professional OTCs share many characteristics with prescription drugs. They usually come from prescription drug manufacturers, are packaged and promoted in a more high-tech and professional manner, and are named more like prescription medicines than heavily advertised popular drugs like Tums, Rolaids, or Alka-Seltzer.

Marketing data demonstrate that the total market share of professional type OTCs is growing at the expense of traditional OTCs. Some of the reasons for this include

(1) increased sophistication of consumers, (2) increased self-medication by consumers, partly as an alternative to expensive physician visits, and (3) availability of new OTC drugs that are perceived as more effective and usually safer than older traditional OTCs. Whatever approach a company takes toward characterizing and advertising each OTC drug, it is probably most essential to be consistent to avoid confusing consumers.

Most OTC drugs cannot be placed entirely in just the professional or traditional group. OTC drugs vary along the spectrum between these extremes. A number of examples of antacid drugs that fit the general category of popular, heavily advertised, traditional OTCs are Tums, Pepto-Bismol, Rolaids, Alka-Seltzer, and Bromo Seltzer. More professional OTCs are Gelusil, Maalox, Riopan, Mylanta, and Gaviscon. Differences exist within each of these two groups as to how scientific or folksy the drug is presented.

DISTRIBUTING AND SELLING A DRUG

Drug Distribution

Companies distribute their drugs in a wide variety of ways that include some or all of the following:

1. Direct to retail stores, such as (a) drug store chains, (b) supermarket chains, (c) mass merchandisers, (d) individual drug stores or supermarkets, and (e) other outlets.
2. To hospital chains and individual hospitals.
3. Through wholesalers to the above retail stores.
4. Through mail-order organizations to the public.
5. To underdeveloped countries and other groups via specific charities. This last channel is used with guarantees by the charity that the drugs donated will not reenter the markets of developed countries.

Accuracy of Market Predictions of New Product Sales

Drug companies attempt to forecast future sales on every drug they sell. Forecasts are made for the next fiscal year, as well as for two or three years in the future. These figures are the critical numbers that production groups use to determine how much of each product to manufacture. If the forecast for any product is much lower than customer demand, it results in back orders and customer dissatisfaction. Forecasts that are much greater than sales result in a high inventory of unsold drug, in addition to tying up manufacturing equipment that could possibly have been used to make other drugs. Either of these situations may create significant additional problems for a company. Some of the factors that may lead to inaccurate market forecasts are listed in Table 21.10.

It is common at some companies to hear disparaging comments within research and development departments about the relative inaccuracy of many marketing predictions. These comments are generally unfair, because marketing estimates often have to be made long before the clinical profile of a drug is established. In addition,

Table 21.10. Factors that may lead to an inaccurate marketing forecast

1. OTC[a] competition increases substantially causing sales of marketed products to fall
2. Prescription drugs face increased competition
3. New products fare poorly and do not reach forecasted sales
4. Marketing costs rise more than anticipated
5. National and international economies do poorly
6. Regulatory delays are longer than anticipated
7. Sales representatives did not promote the drug sufficiently, accurately, or appropriately
8. Marketing forecaster was inexperienced

[a] OTC, over-the-counter drug.

marketing estimates are often made before the target population size or makeup is known, especially for novel therapeutic agents. The extent of nonlabeled drug use for a new drug is also uncertain.

Moreover, the methods used to predict a drug's sales are not precise, especially for a new drug. This is even more pronounced for the initial drug marketed for a new indication. Forecasts are based on discussions with physicians about why they prescribe certain drugs, the problems they see with those drugs, attributes of a new drug that would make them change to a new drug (or at least to try a new drug), and other factors. Physicians who are interviewed, however, may not be representative of the total population of physicians or may not follow through on their own pronouncements.

Other factors that go into marketing forecasts include the quality of clinical data and opinions of scientific (and nonscientific) people, both within and outside the drug company. Part of the inexactitude of marketing estimates therefore relates to uncertainty within research and development as to identifying the precise indications and populations the drug will work on, how well it will perform, and the characteristics of its safety profile.

Where Does a Company Focus Its Activities on the Physician-Patient-Pharmacist Chain?

After a new prescription drug is approved for marketing and launch, it has the *potential* to help patients with one or more diseases. Before patients may be helped there are many activities that must occur. Activities involved in the drug's production, quality assurance, packaging, shipping to wholesalers, and distribution to pharmacies will not be discussed. Activities at the other end of the spectrum (i.e., relating to the patient, pharmacist, and physician) are briefly reviewed.

Figure 21.1 illustrates the usual chain of events that leads to a physician prescribing a drug for patients and for patients obtaining and following medical treatment. Drug companies have traditionally attempted to influence two of the three parts of this relationship, i.e., they have provided the physician with information and education hoping that a prescription for their drug will be written. Companies encourage the pharmacist to stock their drug and encourage them to dispense their drug when generic equivalents are also available. With generic drugs taking a greater share of the overall market, the relationship between company and pharmacy is becoming more important for all manufacturers. The threat of therapeutic substitution (i.e., having a pharmacist dispense a different drug than the one prescribed, but one which

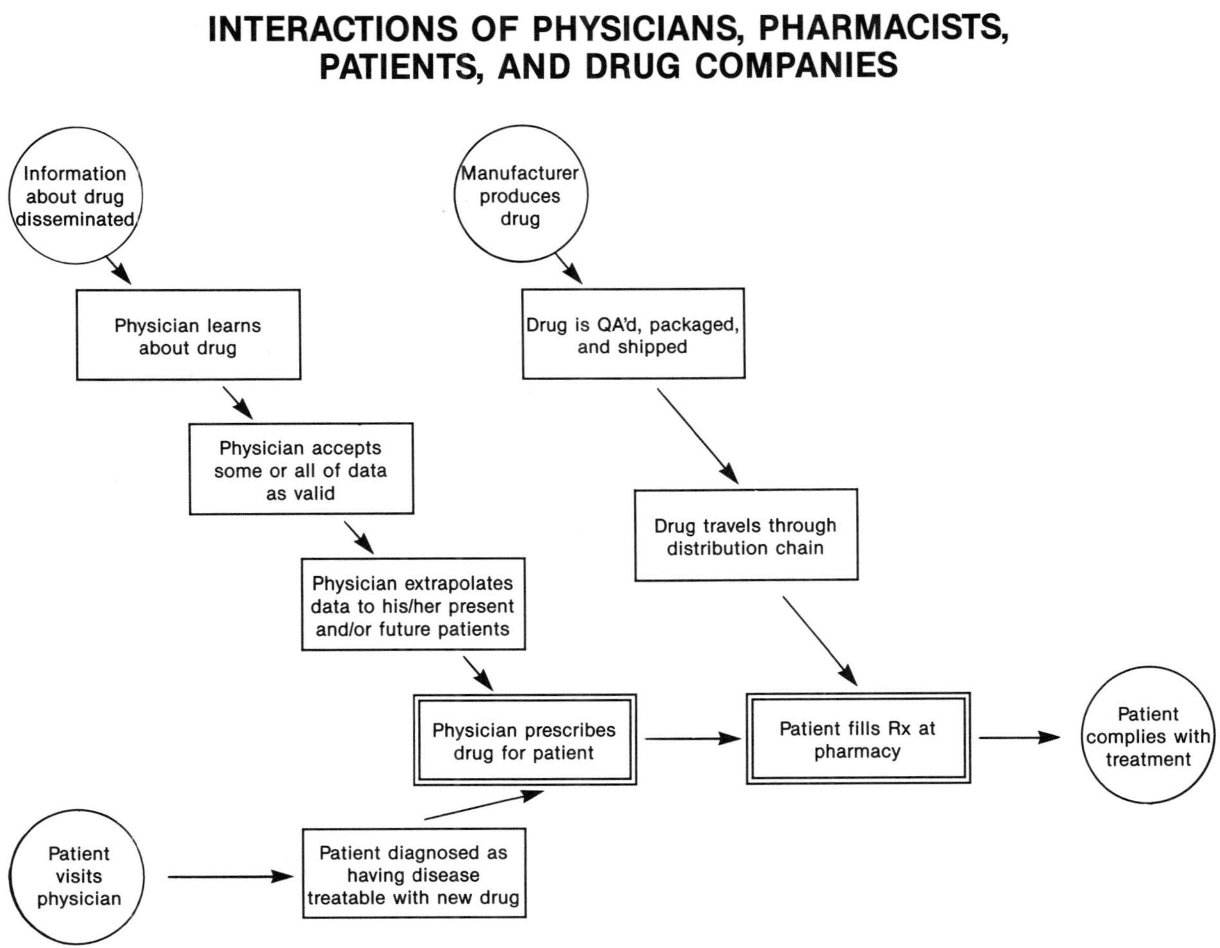

Fig. 21.1. Interactions of physicians, pharmacists, patients, and drug companies. QA, quality assured

is theoretically equivalent to the drug prescribed) will exponentially increase the importance of this relationship.

Companies did not approach patients to influence prescription drug use until recently. Contacts via direct newspaper, television, and magazine advertising is becoming more common and is discussed elsewhere in this chapter. Steps followed by patients in obtaining and following medical treatment are shown in Fig. 21.2.

Promoting Drugs to Physicians in Primary, Secondary, and Tertiary Care Practices

Academicians in tertiary care hospitals (i.e., referral centers) and primary care practitioners treat most diseases in generally similar or identical manners. For a few diseases the differences in treatment (or diagnosis) are great. This usually relates to (1) the use of sophisticated equipment that is often not readily available to primary care physicians, or (2) to situations where clinical practices espoused by physicians in teaching hospitals are not adhered to or followed by private physicians in the community. The reasons for this latter gap are many and may have a major impact on a company's drug sales (either positively or negatively, depending on the particular situation). Companies are therefore forced to promote some drugs differently to various groups of physicians. This distinction is also observed in how physicians in different specialties use the same drug. These differences may relate to the types of patients treated, the usual dose range used, or to other factors. It is often important for a marketing department to help educate physicians in private practice about medical practices in tertiary care academic centers. Not only can this education help increase sales of a particular drug, but it will disseminate current state-of-the-art opinions about a given therapy.

PROTECTING A DRUG

Impact of Marketing Decisions in Other Countries

Marketing decisions made in one country are having a continually greater effect on marketing issues and decisions made in other countries. There is a current trend toward more uniform pricing of a single product in multiple countries. The European Economic Community (EEC) and World Health Organization (WHO) are looking at and comparing prices set in different countries in an attempt to achieve greater uniformity across national boundaries. Because most countries have agencies that control prices charged for drugs, this is also being done at the national level.

Protecting Drugs from Tampering and Counterfeiting

In recent years several well-publicized cases of drug tampering have led to unfortunate deaths of innocent victims. Some of these cases have had a drastic impact on a company's sales and on sales of the entire drug industry. The industry's response has been swift, responsible, and positive. Some companies have totally given up manufacturing drugs in capsule form in favor of using more tamper-resistant dosage forms such as caplets and tablets, and have increased their use of blister and bubble

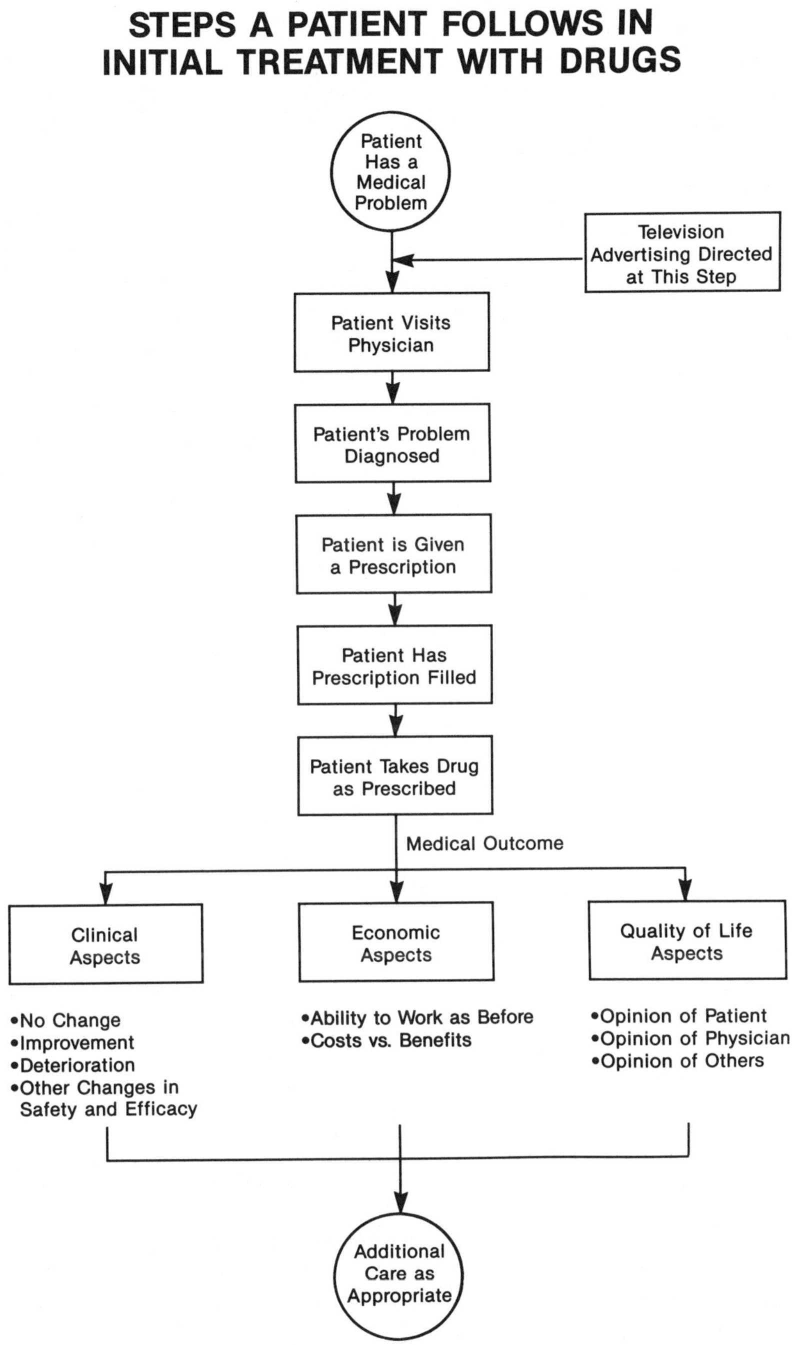

Fig. 21.2. A patient's steps in obtaining and following medical treatment with drugs.

packs. Other firms have begun placing gelatin bands as a sealing device around each capsule joint. No totally tamper-resistant method is available to protect drugs. Present techniques, however, including shrink seals on containers, seals on cartons, and many other methods provide a major advance in assuring patients about the integrity and safety of marketed drugs.

Another problem that is sometimes encountered by successful drugs is that of counterfeiting. Capsules without printing and tablets without imprinting may be counterfeited most easily. Therefore, the printing or imprinting on a capsule or tablet of a company's name, logo, or a drug name provides some protection against counterfeiting. Caution must be used when determining the exact name, symbol, code number, or other information to be printed on the capsules. If too much material is printed on a capsule, patients may perceive that they are ingesting an excessive amount of ink and become upset instead of reassured. Tablets are harder to manufacture than capsules and thus they add additional protection for a company against fraudulent manufacturing, especially if a unique tablet shape is used. Coloring or film coating of tablets are other processes that help in this regard.

These processes do much more than merely make counterfeiting more difficult. Each of these steps helps create brand recognition and hopefully brand loyalty. Patients offered generic versions of their branded drugs sometimes insist on sticking with the "small round orange ones" because of the patient's experience and knowledge that they work.

EXPANDING A DRUG'S MARKET

Increasing Market Share

Measuring Market Share

The term *market* is a measure of the actual or potential commercial value of a drug or group of drugs. A market may refer to (1) a specific drug in which multiple companies are competing with generic and/or brand drugs (e.g., the market for propranolol), (2) a group of drugs of one type (e.g., the market for beta-receptor antagonists), (3) a specific disease (e.g., the market for drugs that treat hypertension), (4) a specific therapeutic area (e.g., the market for drugs used in cardiology), or (5) all drugs in all markets. When two or more drugs are sold in a market they each have a certain share of that market. The most common measure used to define market share is percent of the total market, which is usually based on sales dollars. Other measures of a market include the (1) number of new prescriptions, (2) number of new plus refilled prescriptions, (3) number of units of drug sold, and (4) number of tablets and capsules dispensed. Each of these four measures may also be expressed as a percent of the total market.

Total Market Size and Its Fluctuations

Most therapeutic area markets remain relatively flat from year to year in terms of constant dollars (i.e., adjusted for inflation). The effects of inflation may give

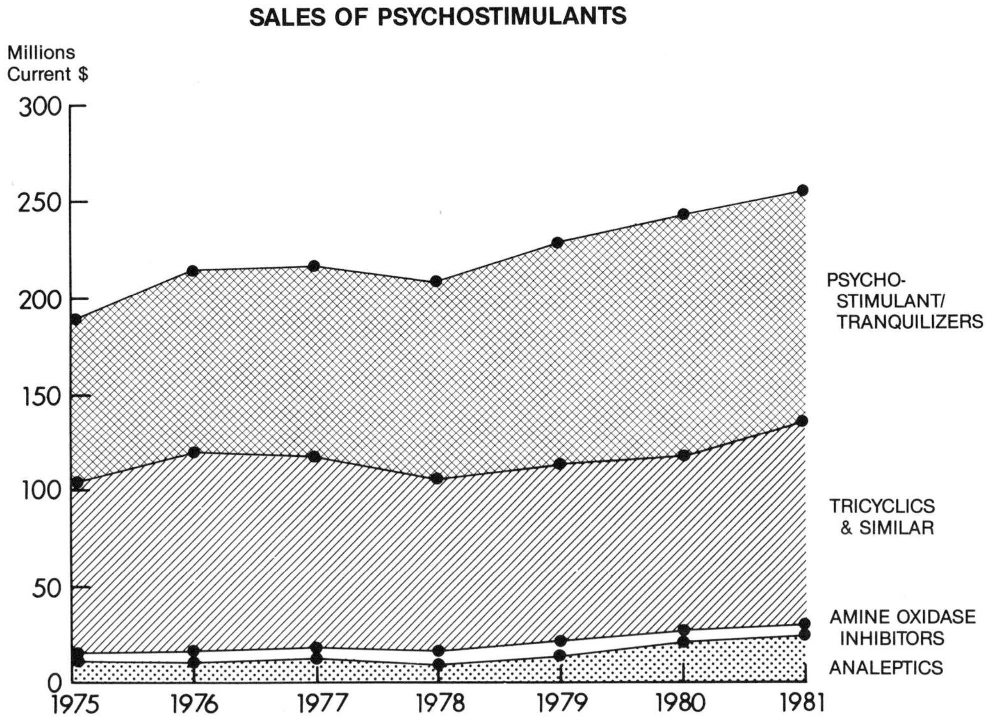

Fig. 21.3. Market share for psychostimulant drugs over 1975 to 1981, illustrating a stable market.

monetary data the appearance of slow or rapid growth. The number of units sold or prescriptions written is less influenced by inflation. In this type of a relatively flat market, new products must compete with existing drugs for market share and sales. When a new drug is introduced into the market, the total market size may remain unchanged and the market share of competing products is redistributed. Figure 21.3 illustrates this situation.

Another possible situation is shown in Fig. 21.4. This illustrates that the introduction of newer anti-arthritis drugs expanded the total market over the period shown (1976 to 1981). In this type of expanding market, new products do not need to take major sales volume or dollars away from existing products.

Some possible reasons for the phenomenon of an expanding market are:

1. There is a larger patient population from year to year. This may occur for many reasons. For example, the disease that the drug treats may be spreading (e.g., the Acquired Immune Deficiency Syndrome (AIDS) patient population is growing).

2. Patients are using the drugs to treat other medical problems. For example, the nonsteroidal anti-inflammatory drugs introduced for arthritis may be used to treat pain resulting from other causes.

3. The patient population is not growing, but more patients are being diagnosed as having the disease. There may have been a public health awareness campaign aimed at physicians or patients because of long-term underdiagnosis, or availability of new diagnostic methods. For example, the number of patients treated with an-

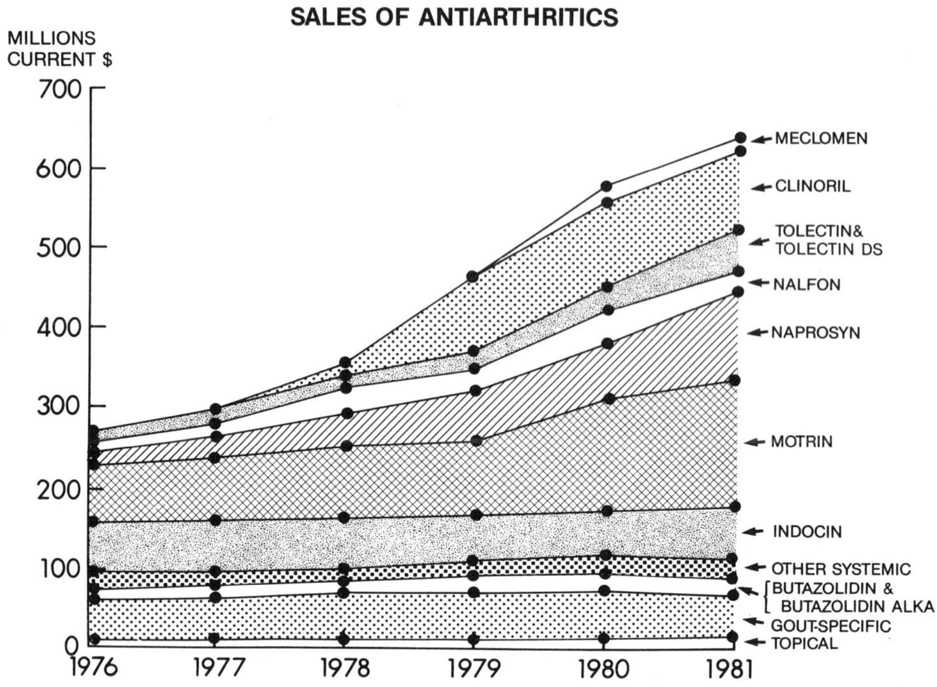

Fig. 21.4. Market share for antiarthritic drugs over 1976 to 1981, illustrating an expanding market.

tihypertensive drugs increased during the 1960s and 1970s because previously undiagnosed patients were being diagnosed and treated.

4. Some patients who are unable to tolerate existing drug therapy are able to tolerate newly marketed drugs. This occurred with nonsteroidal anti-inflammatory drugs.

5. Some patients who did not benefit from previous drugs are benefiting from newer ones.

When the size of a particular market is noted to change, it is important to determine if this occurred because (1) there are more (or fewer) products on the market, (2) there are more or fewer units of the products being sold, or (3) the prices are changing. It is important to track these parameters (as well as those listed above) when trying to understand the reasons underlying changes in a market. Other analyses that may be conducted are to compare commercial trends of (1) older drugs versus more recently introduced drugs, (2) more expensive drugs versus the least expensive drugs, or (3) any two other categories. This type of analysis helps a company better understand what is influencing the market changes observed.

Approaches to Increase Market Share

Basic approaches to increase market share may focus on any or all of the following means of positioning and promoting the drug: developing a new or improved (1) product formulation, package, or line-extension, (2) sales approach and pricing strat-

Table 21.11. Possible reasons used to explain poor sales performance

A. Drug related
  1. New adverse reactions reported
  2. Efficacy was perceived to be less than anticipated
  3. Difficulties encountered in manufacturing the drug
  4. Other problems encountered with the drug itself

B. Market related
  1. Prices set at too high a level
  2. Estimate of potential patients was too high
  3. Competitors were more firmly established in the marketplace than was anticipated
  4. The advertising and promotion campaigns were unable to position the drug as planned
  5. Other competing drugs were introduced
  6. The drug was backordered for a prolonged period
  7. Misdirected distribution, sales, and/or promotion efforts
  8. Difficulties encountered in distributing the drug

C. Other reasons
  1. Medical practice shifted in an important aspect
  2. Problems related to the company's image emerged

egy, or (3) promotional approach. Some of the specific approaches used by drug companies to increase the market share for their products include:

A. Product related

1. Develop more line-extensions in terms of dosage forms or routes of administration. These must be chosen to minimize cannibalization of a company's own products. The timing of the product's launch must be chosen to minimize return of products from pharmacies.

2. Change the drug's packaging to achieve an advantage over the competition. Some OTC drug packages are similar to detergent boxes and almost jump off the pharmacy shelf with bright colors and striking patterns. Others are designed to be more quiet and "professional."

B. Sales approach and pricing strategy

1. Increase the amount of activities and time spent by marketing representatives detailing (i.e., promoting) the product of interest.

2. Develop a specialized sales force to handle the product, either specifically or along with a small number of other drugs. This specialized sales force could be targeted to a specific type of physician (e.g., psychiatrists) or to a specific type of institution (e.g., hospitals).

3. Utilize a new distribution system, for some or all of a company's drugs.

4. Give drug samples to physicians and hospitals to familiarize them with the drug and its uses.

5. Identify the reasons for a drug's poor sales performance (e.g., Table 21.11) and then address each of the possible points.

6. Decrease drug price, either as a short-term promotion to pharmacies and others or as a long-term strategy.

C. Promotional approach

1. Increase advertising in quantity, change the advertising's message, or upgrade (or downgrade) the advertising's quality.

2. Develop more public relations activities for the product (see Chapter 30).

3. Develop data to better differentiate the drug from its competitors. This may be in terms of cost benefits, quality of life, or other characteristics.

4. Target advertisements and other promotions more closely to those specialists who have the highest use of that class or type of drug. A company could, for example, decrease their advertisements for ophthalmic anti-infectives placed in general medical journals and increase their advertisements in journals specifically oriented to and read by ophthalmologists.

5. Increase the number of exhibits at medical meetings. Emphasize presentations of posters and talks by company and noncompany personnel.

6. Develop and distribute (or only distribute) medical literature, texts, or other material that is educational and only indirectly promotes a product, or does not promote the product at all. The distribution of authoritative medical information on a disease treated by the drug is valuable from the company's perspective, even if the drug's name is not mentioned.

7. Sponsor clinical studies that would be of interest to physicians and could be promoted by sales representatives. Other publications of clinical studies may stimulate sales for both new uses as well as the drug's original use(s), even if sales representatives may not distribute reprints or promote the uses.

8. Change the name of a product to reflect the image that the company wants to project. Is the image of the product better achieved with Foot Guard or Tinactin? Icy Hot or Myoflex? Gas-X or Mylicon? Daycare or Comtrex?

Conversion of Prescription Drugs to Over-the-Counter Status

The migration of drug brands from prescription to OTC status has been accentuated over the last decade. The reasons for this primarily reflect the fact that drug sales are greater when they are off-prescription. One reason is that patients are able to choose the specific drug brand they want to buy, and the pharmacist is generally not in a position to have the patient switch to a generic brand. There are no established regulatory or other criteria for switching from prescription to OTC status although the FDA usually requires at least three years of marketing experience and documentation of at least 5,000 cases. Nonetheless, every case is unique and must be evaluated by the sponsor as well as the FDA on its own. FDA approval is necessary to make this conversion to OTC status.

A number of reports have claimed that the public saves a large amount of money when prescription drugs are sold OTC (Vickery, 1985). This money appears to primarily relate to a decreased number of physician visits. For example, MIT economist Peter Timmon estimated that the availability of hydrocortisone OTC saved Americans over a billion dollars between 1980 and 1982 (Vickery, 1985). These are strong arguments in favor of the prescription to OTC conversion of relevant drugs in this era of medical cost containment.

Sales of a Drug for Unapproved Uses and Obtaining Regulatory Approval for Those Uses

Drugs are used to treat patients with one of two types of diseases or indications: indications that are approved and indications that are not approved by regulatory authorities. This latter group of indications are often referred to as unlabeled indications. The amount of a drug's use that is for unlabeled indications varies from drug to drug and also varies for any one drug during the course of its marketing life. Physicians often experiment on their own and use drugs for unapproved indications. Alternatively, some new uses for drugs are discovered through serendipity (see Table 2.2).

Companies must decide whether to seek regulatory approval for unlabeled indications of a new drug. One aspect of this decision relates to whether the drug works in some or all patients with the disease. Another aspect is whether the drug effect is as strong as clinicians think necessary before they would incorporate the drug into their own practice.

22 / *Production Issues*

We can no longer live with commonly accepted levels of mistakes, defects, material not suited to the job, people on the job that do not know what the job is and are afraid to ask, handling damage, failure of management to understand their job, antiquated methods of training on the job, inadequate and ineffective supervision. Acceptance of defective materials, poor workmanship, and inattentive and sullen service as a way of life in America is a roadblock to better quality and productivity. We have learned to live in a world of mistakes and defective products as if they were necessary to life. It is time to adopt a new religion in America. W. Edwards Deming. From *Quality, Productivity, and Competitive Position.*

A number of production issues that are relevant for many drug companies are discussed. As with the marketing and finance chapters, the issues covered represent a select sample intended to provide a general overview. Issues are grouped into a few broad categories.

WHAT IS PRODUCED?

Differences between Producing Drugs, Foods, and Other Materials

The major difference between producing drugs and other materials is that government regulations are more extensive and the standards are higher for producing drugs. Most of the relevant manufacturing regulations are referred to as Good Manufacturing Practices (GMPs) in the United States. Some of the differences between producing foods and drugs are fascinating. For example, most foods that are produced by humans (as opposed to natural foods such as fresh fruits) are not produced aseptically (i.e., under sterile conditions). Nonetheless, most foods are made or prepared in clean conditions. People rarely become ill from food that is nonsterile. The stomach and intestines contain numerous bacteria that are not harmful to us and some produce vitamins that are even essential for our good health. Injected drugs, however, must be sterile and pure because the injection of nonsterile or nonpure preparations (e.g.,with glass or pyrogen contamination) into the bloodstream could create significant medical problems for a patient.

When Does Production Become Involved with Investigational Drugs?

There appears to be a trend at many drug companies for production personnel to become involved with investigational drugs at an earlier point in the development process than they did approximately 10 to 15 years ago. Traditionally this involvement was sometime during Phase III, but it is now generally during Phase I or II. When a number of formulations are being considered for development, it is important to consider production's ability to manufacture each formulation. There may be significant differences in the investment in equipment required, the degree of risk involved, the amount of hazardous waste products produced, the labor required, or other important factors associated with their production.

Dialogue between production and technical development personnel should be established as early in a project's life as is convenient and practical. A committee structure is often an appropriate mechanism to insure that relevant questions are both posed and answered satisfactorily. This allows production at an early stage to begin monitoring a project's progress, develop an awareness of potential future events, and consider various options for facilities and equipment that may be used to make the drug.

Balancing Production Effort with a Drug's Value to a Company

Is it logical to believe that the effort expended on a drug's production should relate to the amount of sales a product generates or is expected to generate? This question may be interpreted as either referring to each unit of drug made or to the total effort for the entire drug's production. In fact the number of units of a drug produced often do not correlate well with the drug's sales. Some drugs have extremely low prices and a high number of units are sold, and the opposite situation also occurs. In addition, small volume products (i.e., when few units are produced) may require a relatively large amount of plant capacity and resources to manufacture them. This places pressure on those resources (i.e., equipment and labor) that are also needed to manufacture other products. Potential solutions to this problem include (1) having small volume products synthesized and packaged by other manufacturers, (2) increasing the number of work shifts, (3) expanding plant capacity, and (4) selling or dropping the product from the company's line.

A new drug may require equipment and processes at more than one plant for its production. This issue may be addressed in several ways.

1. A new facility may be built to focus primarily or exclusively on the new drug.
2. An existing facility may be "beefed-up" to handle the drug.
3. Several existing company manufacturing facilities may each handle certain parts of the manufacturing.
4. Part or all of the manufacturing may be contracted out to other companies.

Contract Manufacturers

All companies that manufacture drugs periodically have to decide about whether to utilize contract manufacturers to make certain drugs. This question becomes particularly important when new techniques or equipment are required to make a new drug and it is uncertain whether a company desires to bring that technology in-house. A company may have a tradition of manufacturing all of their own products, but it makes little sense to rigidly adhere to this principle when it is economically preferable to have other manufacturers make a new drug.

HOW IS IT PRODUCED?

Transferring a Manufacturing Process from Technical Development to a Production Group

The sense of urgency with which the manufacturing process is transferred from technical development (i.e., research and development) to production varies greatly from drug to drug. If the sense of urgency is high, there may be insufficient time to develop a robust process (i.e., a reliable, reproducible process that is insensitive to minor changes in conditions) where all of the relevant parameters have been optimized.

Some of the issues that determine when a process is ready to be transferred to production include (1) is the process robust, (2) have all of the important manufacturing factors and possibilities been considered and worked out or at least evaluated, and (3) is the batch to batch variation acceptable in terms of the specifications that must be met? It is desirable to increase the drug's yield to a significant degree before manufacturing begins. Most of the work on this issue is usually completed prior to transferring the process to production.

In most situations when a technical development department turns over a process to production, that process is well defined and has been tested on a full-scale production basis. Personnel from both development and production groups will have tried the manufacturing as an "EX" (experimental) batch using the actual equipment that will eventually be used. During the later stages of technical development's experimentation, they often "borrow" production equipment to test the best method.

Which Equipment is Used to Produce Drugs?

Drugs may require new or highly specialized equipment for their manufacture. A decision has to be reached about whether to invest in new equipment. The pertinent issue is to determine which criteria to use when deciding about purchasing or leasing new equipment. It is often helpful if a standard approach has been developed that may be applied to a new situation so that a decision may be reached rapidly. The main alternative is to redefine the criteria and procedures to follow each time an important question arises. This would result in unnecessary delays and a great deal of frustration.

Return on investment is the primary criterion used to address the issue of obtaining new equipment. This is determined using cost accounting procedures. The total cost for the purchase of new equipment plus drug manufacture is determined and contrasted with the total cost either using existing equipment or following another course. If the new equipment will lead to a savings over the current methods, then the time to reach a savings equal to the equipment's purchase and installation price is calculated. This is the payback time. If the payback time issue is not relevant, then other factors must be considered (e.g., competition, time to install the equipment, production downtime) in reaching a decision on whether to purchase the new equipment.

Another aspect relating to new equipment is how should a company optimally utilize automation and remain current with state-of-the-art technologies. These technologies include use of computer-controlled production, robotics, and other equipment. These issues are a continual concern to companies because there are always new procedures and equipment to evaluate and new drugs or line-extensions to manufacture. In addition, the competition between companies in many therapeutic areas and with generic drugs places a high premium on achieving greater cost-efficiencies in production.

WHERE IS IT PRODUCED?

Companies often make most of their drugs in more than one manufacturing plant, or at least they develop contingency plans to make each drug at multiple plants. Companies must protect themselves against unknown situations that could threaten, decrease, or eliminate a plant's ability to make one or more drugs. One reasonable approach to reduce threats and the dependency of a company on a single plant is to build, lease, or occupy a second backup plant. Alternatively, a second manufacturing source could be approved to manufacture one or more drugs, if necessary. This plant must become licensed by the Food and Drug Administration (FDA) to manufacture drugs of interest to the company, and could be a contract manufacturing facility.

HOW WELL IS IT PRODUCED?—QUALITY CONTROL AND QUALITY ASSURANCE

The quality of a finished drug product is not an all-or-none question, but requires conscious decisions by a company as to what quality is to be used as a minimum standard and as a goal. These decisions must consider both compendial (e.g., *United States Pharmacopeia* [USP]) and regulatory requirements.

Roles of Quality Assurance and Quality Control

The quality assurance department is often viewed as a ''policeman'' in reviewing production activities. This relationship varies enormously, not only between companies, but also within a single company. Quality may be described in terms of (1) purity of raw materials, (2) ability of drugs to meet chemical and physical specifications, (3) consistency of manufactured products from batch to batch, (4) validation of procedures, (5) validation of systems, and other factors. Companies may determine that they want a goal of absolutely no product recalls, even for minor issues. This goal implies that the company's regulatory strategy is to avoid even small issues arising with the FDA. This is however, an unrealistic standard for even the most conservative drug company because of the many ways of interpreting federal regulations and GMPs and the uncertainty of what may happen to drugs in actual use situations. Nonetheless, all companies must determine goals and standards in terms of product quality.

A few decades ago, quality control (QC) was the process used to insure that drugs met official specifications (Fig. 22.1, panel B). It became apparent, however, that just because a drug met the final-stage specification requirements did not mean that it also met requirements at each intermediate step. The only tablets or other dosage forms tested that one was certain of were the ones actually tested. If a group of 20 tablets were tested out of a batch of six million made, it did not provide adequate assurance that the entire batch met the standards used. Also, if the final requirements were not met and the product was flawed it was difficult, if not impossible to identify the source and reason for the problem. Therefore, the concept of quality assurance developed as an ongoing evaluation process of most (or all) of the individual steps

QUALITY ASSURANCE AND QUALITY CONTROL

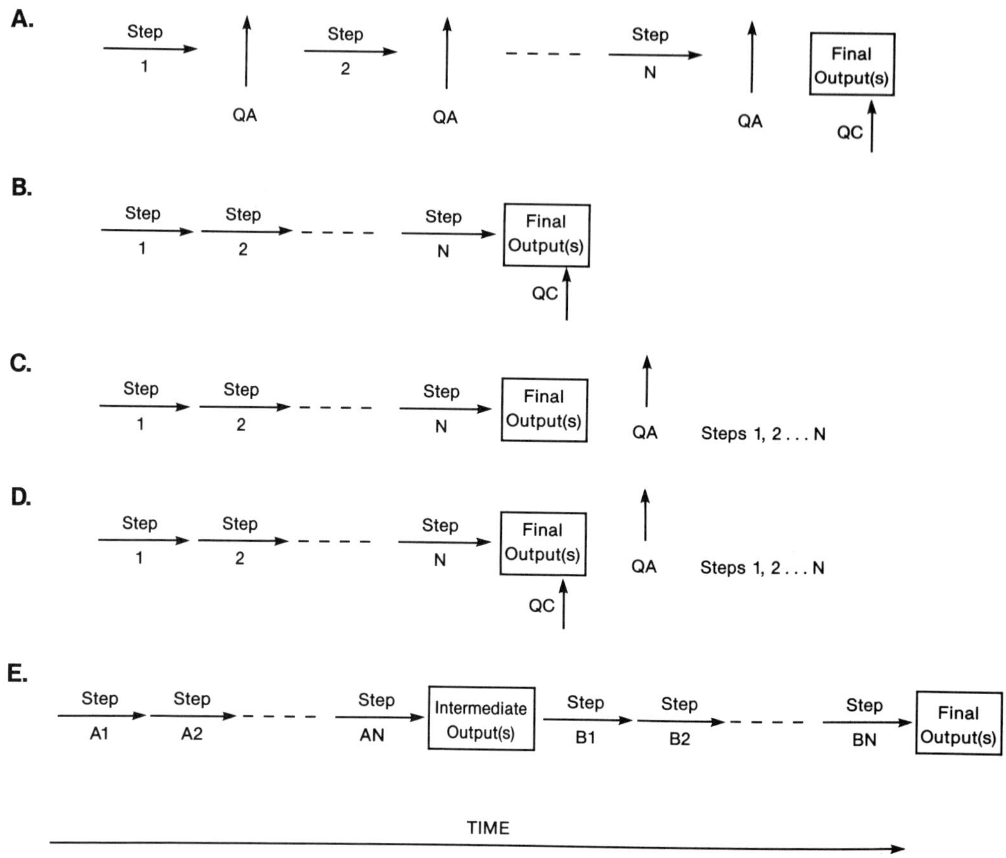

Fig. 22.1. Procedures of quality assurance and quality control. The final output for a clinical study is when the last patient is completed. The final output for production is when the finished drug is made (or packaged), and the final output for toxicology is when the final report is written. Panels are discussed in the text.

(Fig. 22.1, panel A). Quality assurance (QA) also means that the methods used to audit the manufacturing processes are validated. QA depends on interpreting the GMPs plus state-of-the-art practices in industry. Most companies have one set of QA standards for all drugs that pass through a plant, whether produced for a contract, to supply a generic manufacturer, or to provide a brand name product. Many drugs have over 100 separate steps evaluated as part of their QA testing procedures.

Panel A of Fig. 22.1 is the most conservative method of conducting QA and QC operations, because each step in the process is quality assured and approved before the next step is initiated. An example could be in manufacture of certain sterile products, where steps such as assays of sterile water, pyrogen tests, material tests for contamination, filling procedures, and final sterilization are each evaluated. Panels C and D show operations where QA is conducted after the products are made.

These approaches would be considered reasonable only for highly reliable products and procedures, because if the product fails the test then the entire batch must be discarded. A hybrid of panels A plus C or D is also possible. Panel E would be appropriate for chemical syntheses where intermediates en route to the final chemical are evaluated. Many variations exist for conducting QA procedures in panel E including A to D, plus various hybrid-type models.

Reporting Relationships and the Potential for Conflict-of-Interest Issues

Because of the sensitive nature of the work conducted by the quality assurance department and the potential for conflict-of-interest issues, it is essential that QA managers not report to the head of production. QA workers might feel pressure to approve a step in a process, whether the pressure was present or not. This pressure would be much stronger if someone in production had the authority to determine the final outcome of a "gray" issue relating to QA. GMP regulations require separate reporting through to the senior management level.

Sterility Testing

One of the most sensitive issues between quality assurance and production involves the evaluation of products produced in a sterile environment. Eliminating sources of contamination in manufacturing and minimizing environmental contamination in drug testing are two important goals for all companies that manufacture sterile products. Unfortunately, these goals are usually difficult to achieve. When evaluating a product for sterility, it is extremely easy to introduce environmental contamination. The issue is whether a product that fails a sterility test does so because of manufacturing problems or of contamination introduced by quality assurance personnel during the testing procedure. The issue involves much more than just egos, because a great deal of money is usually invested in the suspect drug batch. If a drug batch is discarded unnecessarily, a loss of significant effort and money can result.

Until recent years, most sterile products were manufactured under generally clean, but nonsterile, conditions and then were sterilized at the end of their processing, usually by heat. A number of samples were taken for sterility testing and if only one failure was observed, another set of samples was tested. If the second set were all acceptable (i.e., without failures) then it was assumed that the entire batch was sterile and the sterilizing process was effective.

A recent change in the above sterility-testing procedure was brought about by the USP. The new procedures do not allow a repeat test unless the failure can be shown to be related to a laboratory error. One of the reasons for this change is that some products are not stable enough chemically to be sterilized by heating to a high temperature. At the present time many products are prepared under aseptic conditions over a period of days and are not sterilized at the end of the procedure. As a result of this change, a simple test for sterilization is inadequate. To further insure sterility, samples are taken of the environment for parts of each day of manufacture. These include samples of (1) air in the room, (2) wall surfaces, (3) whatever settles out of the air onto special culture dishes placed on tables, and (4) finger daubs of the operators in the aseptic areas. In the last test, the operators touch their fingers to an agar plate that is then incubated to check for bacterial contamination.

There are two major issues that have arisen in regard to this change. First, there are no fixed limits or guidelines as to what degree of environmental contamination is sufficient to pass or reject a batch. Thus, the decision about rejection is based on the comfort level felt by individuals who evaluate the data. They typically look for trends or spikes in the data. Each case is separate and it may not be possible to establish clear guidelines. The second issue is that environmental samples are placed in an incubator for three days. Thus, it is three days after contamination occurs that anyone is aware of a problem, whereas with the original system, it was suspected almost immediately and in many cases was remedied by a retest or a resterilization. The consequences to a company in terms of wasted time, resources, and effort are greater in the second situation. These issues have significantly raised the pressures on both production and QA departments to produce drugs in an environment that is as close to microbial-free as possible. The cost of approaching this state is so expensive that all sterile drugs are likely to continue to escalate in price, and if greater steps in this direction are taken, probably for relatively little gain in sterility, costs may increase even faster.

A related issue that may become more important in the future is the environmental conditions under which nonsterile products are produced. One of the specific questions concerns bacterial contamination of tablets, capsules, and liquids. It is clear that the stomach and intestines provide adequate protection for patients in most situations. Any changes in regulations governing this aspect must be carefully evaluated to insure that the interests of patients are truly served by any regulations proposed.

Process Validation in Manufacturing Steps

A validated procedure is one that is proven to do what it is stated to do. This is an important part of GMPs. Validation lies at the heart of quality control systems. Ongoing evaluations and checks insure that all equipment is properly calibrated, operating appropriately, all appropriate materials are identified, and all materials are handled correctly at all stages of manufacturing. Validation procedures are conducted with up-to-date monitoring equipment, modern statistical designs, and tests that demonstrate the integrity of the procedures. The validation procedures and data generated from tests and monitoring activities are thoroughly documented.

Validating computer systems used in manufacturing drugs is a major issue in the drug industry today. The Computer Systems Validation Committee of the Pharmaceutical Manufacturers Association (PMA [1986]) has issued a report with additional information. Substantial effort continues in this area at numerous organizations (e.g., FDA, Drug Information Association).

Sampling of Tablets for Testing

When companies manufacture tablets it must be determined that the tablets are acceptable for sale. The quality control/assurance group must pass the material, i.e., certify that it meets agreed-on standards. One of the first standards to consider is the potency of the material. The assay methods that evaluate a tablet's potency destroy the tablet in the process of evaluation. Thus, no matter how rapid and inexpensive an assay system is developed, only a sample of an entire drug lot may tested. Thus, rules must be established as to how many tablets to sample and the basis on which specific tablets will be chosen for testing. Criteria are also established that tablets must meet to pass inspection. For example, the active ingredient in a tablet might be required to be within ±10 percent of the amount stated on the label of the drug. This variation might represent true tablet to tablet differences, but there are also variations in the amount measured owing to the assay variability. Major factors affecting assay variability are the skills of the person who is running the test, instrument variability, and week to week (or shift to shift) variability in assay results obtained.

Acceptance Quality Level

The highest percent of defective units (e.g., tablets) that is acceptable as a production average is called the acceptance quality level. The unacceptable quality level is the percentage of defective units for which there is a low probability that the batch will be acceptable. Different types of sampling plans may be chosen to select random samples for testing. The selection of the method to use depends largely on statistical considerations. Because of the great importance of sampling a manufactured drug appropriately, expert statisticians are usually involved in the choice of a sampling design. Their goal is to design a method to obtain samples that are representative of the entire batch or lot. Sometimes, interval samples (e.g., every nth tablet) are studied instead of random samples to evaluate the production run.

Disintegration and Dissolution Characteristics

The disintegration and dissolution characteristics of tablets must be tested. In both of these tests, six tablets are tested under identical conditions and must meet standard specifications. If one or two tablets do not meet specifications, the test is repeated on 12 additional tablets using higher acceptance criteria.

Dissolution tests are time consuming and expensive. Figure 20.1 illustrates some of the standard methods used. The USP and other formulary requirements specify which of these specific methods must be used in dissolution testing.

Tablet Weight

Sample tablets must be weighed to confirm that their weight is within a prespecified range. The general standard for uncoated tablets in the USP is: "Weigh individually 20 whole tablets, and calculate the average weight: the weights of not more than 2 of the tablets differ from the average weight by more than the percentage tested and no tablet differs by more than double that percentage." See Table 22.1 for example.

Table 22.1. Measurement of tablet weight

Average weight of tablet (mg)	Acceptable difference in weight (%)
130 or less	10
130 to 324	7.5
More than 324	5

Other Tests

Other tests that must be conducted (when relevant) include tests for metal particles in ophthalmic ointments and for pyrogenicity in biological products. Pyrogenicity refers to the ability of the material to raise body temperature in a sensitized animal. Pyrogenicity is a rough measure of the amount of foreign protein in the product and the product's potential to elicit an allergic or anaphylactic reaction in humans. Other tests include microbiological tests to evaluate sterility.

In-Process Testing and Control

The discussion above describes the testing of a drug after it is manufactured. Although these procedures are currently followed, they are insufficient when performed on six or so tablets to assure the acceptability of lots of up to ten million tablets. In addition, if serious problems occur it would be extremely expensive and potentially disasterous for a company if an entire lot had to be destroyed. The major alternative procedure is to test a drug at all stages of its manufacture. This is referred to as in-process testing and control.

Some of the relevant issues involved with in-process testing and control are:

Potency. The active compound must be evenly dispersed throughout the dry powder before it is compressed into tablets or filled into gelatin capsules. Also, a precise amount of the powder must be compressed into tablets or filled into the gelatin capsule.

Control charts. These are graphical depictions of performance data that illustrate how well samples perform on some important measure. They illustrate whether the process is operating within its capability and at an acceptable level. Different types of control charts are used in the drug industry. These charts are a valuable tool to use in identifying batch to batch trends.

Cosmetic Issues of the Drug Product

This category includes consideration of the following questions: (1) may any of the dyes or inks used to print a name and/or number on a capsule or tablet be smudged or illegible, (2) may the drug packaging and/or cartons be used if the color tones are somewhat different from the standard, (3) may the cartons be scuffed or scratched, (4) may the printing be slightly off-center, or (5) may other aspects of the cosmetic appearance of the drug be less than perfect? If a high standard of cosmetic appearance is used to pass all individual drug tablets and capsules intended for sale, then the rejection rate after the drug is manufactured plus the cost of the passed product will both be relatively high.

People who work in a quality assurance department usually express concern about these or other relatively minor cosmetic flaws. Nonetheless, if the drug itself is in compliance with all regulations, then marketing considerations must dictate what decisions are made about cosmetically flawed products. This is almost always addressed on a case by case basis.

The standards used by a company for judging a drug's cosmetic appearance may be lowered after a brand name drug goes off patent, because the drug must now compete in price with those produced by generic manufacturers. Passing drugs with an adequate but not perfect appearance is one means of controlling the cost of manufacturing. Most companies want to establish and maintain uncompromising high quality for new chemical entities while they are protected by patent.

Improving Drug Quality with New Equipment

New state-of-the-art equipment may sometimes produce drugs with more consistent quality than with older equipment. There might be fewer impurities when new equipment is used to synthesize the active drug substance. There might be more consistent moisture content of drug granules if the equipment is used to dry granules prior to compressing them into tablets. Most companies conduct careful analyses to determine the cost- effectiveness of new equipment. Comparing costs from outside contractors is usually also taken into account before a decision is reached on whether to purchase major pieces of new equipment. Product quality is also considered when new production processes are evaluated as a means to cut manufacturing costs. There is a certain point at which the cost savings are not economical because of an unacceptable decline in a drug's quality. The exact balance or trade-off between quality and cost differs for each drug and is greatly dependent on the company's attitudes.

Drug Tampering

The wave of tampering with drug products in the 1980s has sent a shock down the spine of the American public and others around the world. No longer can all drug capsules be viewed the same way. The drug companies involved and the entire industry handled this massive problem in a completely appropriate and responsible manner. The industry has developed several alternative methods for producing capsules, which has had a marked effect in decreasing (and hopefully eliminating) this problem. Improvements include (1) taping boxes, (2) putting heat shrink seals on bottle tops, (3) putting a band around the joint of gelatin capsules, (4) sealing capsules by spot welding, (5) using capsules of a different shape that are more difficult to separate, (6) using more blister packs, and (7) eliminating capsules altogether.

The concern with capsules has carried over to other dosage forms, where additional security measures (e.g., heat shrink seals, wrapping containers) have been implemented. The methods developed have cost significant sums of money to implement. These costs must ultimately be passed on to the consumer. Marketing aspects of the drug-tampering issue were discussed in the preceding chapter.

HOW MUCH IS PRODUCED?

Number of Manufacturing Plants

There are several aspects to this particular topic. The first is the issue of how much of one or multiple drugs *can* be physically produced at a single plant. Another issue, which is usually more difficult to answer, is how much of a drug *should* be produced at one plant? To address the latter issue, one must consider both the present and future (projected) size of the labor force at a plant plus the amount of manpower that is available or is possible to recruit. Other major criteria relate to (1) total volume of products produced at the plant, (2) available and total plant capacity, and (3) considerations of specific drugs manufactured at the plant. This information is necessary to help determine the appropriate size of a plant. The issue of deciding when and where to build a new manufacturing facility is particularly complex.

Level of Service to Customers

Another issue that affects the amount of drug produced at a particular plant relates to the type and level of service that is to be provided to customers. This service relates in part to the turnaround time necessary to ship goods. This depends in turn on the amount of the drug kept in inventory. The types of methods and systems used to track and process both inventory and orders are critical to determine how much a company's inventory may be decreased.

Use of Marketing Forecasts

Marketing forecasts indicating the number of units of each product to be sold are necessary for production planning. These forecasts are issued for the next 12- to 18-month period and also on a long-range basis (e.g., five years). The long-term forecast is prepared using one to three cases: a base case (i.e., most likely scenario), a pessimistic case, and an optimistic case. These allow long-term production planning in terms of equipment and labor utilization. Using pessimistic assumptions or considering "what if . . ." exercises allow senior managers to plan contingency operations more effectively. Some of these assumptions are listed in Table 21.11 as general comments. More specific assumptions along these lines would have to be made in a "real life" situation. Shorter term forecasts are used for master scheduling of products, materials' planning of parts, and capacity planning of time.

Production Capacity

A related issue concerns utilization of a plant's capacity. Most companies attempt to utilize plant capacity at a predetermined optimal level. If the operating level is low, then there will always (or almost always) be an excess of spare capacity. If the operating level is set at an extremely high level, it may threaten the ability to manufacture important new products after regulatory approval or to deal with serious problems that arise. A clear policy and set of goals must be established on this issue. After that is done, plans may be developed to reach that goal.

Adjusting production capacity to appropriately meet demands placed on production is a constant issue for all companies. This balance will fluctuate over time. It may either fluctuate within a narrow range or fluctuate widely, as the demand for products rises and falls. Seasonal cycles of some products are able to be anticipated, but a sudden marked increase or decrease in number of units sold may upset this balance. In practice there is rarely an excess of capacity in all areas of a plant. There will commonly be a small excess in some areas and a greater excess in others.

Companies that have excess plant capacity may perform contract work for other drug companies, the government, or other customers. When excess plant capacity still exists, a company will usually scale down their capacity to save money (e.g., a second or third shift may be eliminated) or utilize the capacity through other means. Plant capacity is often increased as older equipment is replaced or supplemented with newer equipment. For example, many new state-of-the-art machines operate much more rapidly than the machines they replace.

If excess plant capacity has been sold by a contract with a customer, and the company has a sudden and unexpected need for new capacity, a severe problem could easily develop. A company must insure that filling excess capacity with contract work, for example, will not affect its most profitable product lines. If this problem develops, one temporary alternative is to go to outside contractors to produce some products. Outside contractors, however, may be limited in the capacity that they have for sale, since they may be committed to other companies and may not be able to accept additional contracts. In addition, regulatory approval must have been previously obtained to have the contractor produce the company's drug(s).

WHY ARE PRODUCTION COSTS SO HIGH?

This is clearly a relative question and does not apply to all companies equally and does not apply to all drugs manufactured by a single company. There are many reasons for high production costs which may include:

1. New construction, remodeling, and maintenance of facilities.
2. Labor costs.
3. New state-of-the-art equipment.
4. Quality assurance and quality control systems implemented to insure high production standards.
5. Packaging of drugs in more technologically sophisticated containers and methods (e.g., blister packs).
6. Disposal of waste products according to all local, state, and federal regulations.
7. Protection of the public from tampering by utilizing more expensive manufacturing and packaging techniques.
8. Maintaining inventories at a level that insures ability to supply customer's needs rapidly.

Each of these issues has been discussed in numerous articles and books. In this overview only a few points of general interest are briefly described.

Administrative Costs

Administrative costs are often an area where some progress may be made in cost trimming. Some drug companies build large staffs to provide services to professional workers. The functions of many of these service personnel may often be combined with those of other workers. Administrative systems may also be simplified or streamlined in many situations.

Location of Manufacturing Facilities

Manufacturing facilities situated in large urban areas usually produce goods at a higher costs than plants situated in rural areas. Several American drug companies have taken advantage of reduced taxes in Puerto Rico for several decades. The favorable tax status of Puerto Rico, however, may be removed by Congress at any time.

Plant Size

The size of a plant is another major factor influencing cost of goods produced. Cost advantages are gained with a large-sized production plant, but only up to a certain size. Once a plant exceeds a certain size there are no longer benefits to be gained from further expansion. It is not always apparent to company managers when that size is being approached, although it usually becomes obvious when that point has been passed.

Inventory Size

Inventory issues relate to the entire production pipeline, from raw chemicals and supplies (e.g., bottles, labels) to finished products. Companies must determine the appropriate balance between a sufficiently large inventory of drugs that allow a company to supply its customers rapidly, and a small inventory that requires a lower investment of working capital. Are criteria used to establish a policy for one drug suitable for others, or should different policies be adapted? Companies usually have a single policy regarding inventory for all their prescription drugs and a separate one for over-the-counter (OTC) drugs. The number of inventory turnovers per year is calculated by each company. This number comes from the cost of goods sold per year divided by the average inventory. This number varies between companies for various reasons. First, generic companies usually maintain high inventories because their customers are not likely to back-order drugs, but will turn to another manufacturer or distributor of generic drugs. New products tend to be stocked at high levels if a company is able to make sufficient amounts of the drug, because forecasts may be highly inaccurate. Companies also like to maintain large inventories of lifesaving drugs. Thus, inventory strategies for some drugs often differ within a single company.

One extreme approach is to adopt a flexible system called "just-in-time inventories." In this system, raw materials arrive at a company's plant just in time to

Table 22.2. Selected production issues relating to a physical plant and its equipment

1. Determine at what rate and in what manner old equipment should be replaced
2. Determine how well each of the facilities and major equipment are operating
3. Determine on what schedule older plants should be closed, modernized, or expanded
4. Determine if automation, robotics, and computer-controlled equipment can be installed in a cost-effective way
5. Determine how much capital is available to purchase additional and replacement equipment
6. Determine if new drugs are being developed that will require new equipment or facilities
7. Determine if it is possible to improve the layout and product flow in the plant
8. Determine how equipment may be modified to reduce set-up time between production runs
9. Determine how to protect plants from the danger of catastrophic events (e.g., sabotage, natural disasters) and protection from other problems originating inside or outside the plant

produce the number of products that were ordered. No inventories are maintained. Most companies do not use this approach, and are more concerned about how they may shift their inventories from finished products to bulk materials (e.g., drug powder, drug capsules) that may be rapidly packaged into whatever size unit is most needed.

Other Questions and Issues on Production Costs

What additional means could be used to reduce costs? Are a company's costs comparable to those of others in the industry? Which products, if any, could be made more cheaply by outside contractors? What are the reasons for this? Could the answers be applied to internal costs? If not, then are there plans to contract out the work? If so, are they being implemented and if there is no implementation, why is this so?

These are just a few of the additional questions that may be raised on this topic. Clearly, it is critical for companies to raise and focus attention on the most important questions for their situation. Focusing on less important or even irrelevant questions will dilute their corporate effectiveness and allow their competition to gain or overtake them.

CHALLENGES FOR PRODUCTION

Many production techniques and tricks-of-the-trade are not published in any journal or book. Nonetheless, much of this information is available and many state-of-the-art ideas are freely traded between companies. Production staff members acquire this information at professional meetings and by visiting facilities of other companies. Every company wants to learn how the competition does it. Many ideas are non-transferable because they reflect one-time operations designed to custom fit a specific production line or to solve a specific problem. Current and ongoing challenges for production groups are mentioned in Tables 22.2 to 22.5.

Planning and Scheduling Issues

A few issues faced in planning production runs are: How tightly may the runs be scheduled? How much slack time is necessary to build into the plan to avoid problems

Table 22.3. Selected production issues relating to the processes conducted

1. Evaluate if technical support from research and development in terms of expertise and priority are adequate to transfer drug manufacture from the pilot plant to full production
2. Determine if technical support from research and development is adequate to support various other issues (e.g., troubleshooting, quality assurance)
3. Determine if demands on production equipment by research and development to manufacture clinical study supplies are greater than anticipated
4. Determine if government regulations are requiring more time and money to meet and validate
5. Evaluate if inventory systems may be improved to increase turnover and decrease current inventory
6. Evaluate if improved systems may be implemented for planning material requirements, aiding manufacturing with computers, streamlining paper flow, and evaluating quality control
7. Evaluate if improved technology may be introduced to improve drug manufacture

at a later date? How much lead time is necessary when scheduling production runs in different areas of manufacturing? Are these times growing? Are lead times too long? If so, at what point should additional production lines be established?

In terms of drug development and transferring new drugs into production, two major questions are: One, are investigational drugs integrated into production in an efficient manner? Two, is the project leader in production working closely with project leaders in marketing plus research and development? Project plans and scheduling issues are reviewed by various groups. It is useful to have summaries of production-oriented issues for the review of projects. Maintaining a synopsis of production issues on each project would include tracking points listed in Table 22.6.

Issues between Production and Marketing

Production groups need to know how much of a drug they need to make. They ask their marketing colleagues for an estimate. Marketing personnel know that the market share they can capture and the amount of drug they can sell depends on how effective and safe the drug is. Effectiveness and safety cannot be known until clinical studies are well into Phase II or even Phase III. Other factors also affect this estimate, such as price of the drug and the ability to be good salespeople. Therefore, marketing does not want to provide estimates prematurely to production because they may be highly inaccurate. But, these estimates are necessary for production to determine whether they will be able to manufacture the drug in-house or will have to have it

Table 22.4. Selected production issues relating to people involved

1. Determine if higher standards should be used to hire new employees
2. Determine which training programs are most effective
3. Determine which training programs should be added
4. Determine if the number of employees may be reduced through improved processes, new equipment, or other methods
5. Determine how labor disputes may be handled most effectively
6. Determine how threats to production facilities may be handled
7. Determine how the company may deal with a labor pool that is inadequate to provide enough highly competent employees
8. Evaluate team building programs that may be instituted (e.g., quality circles)
9. Determine how employees may be given more responsibility

Table 22.5. Selected production issues relating to products made

1. Marketing forecasts may either be too high or too low, resulting in unsold inventory or large backorders
2. Suppliers of important raw materials may be unreliable as to delivery dates
3. Suppliers or contractors may not be totally reliable in meeting agreed specifications and quality of raw supplies or finished products
4. A sudden increase in demand for products may exceed the plant's capacity
5. Quality assurance procedures and standards may change, resulting in a greater number of rejected tablets or other dosage forms
6. Less expensive starting or intermediary materials may be possible to use
7. Assembly line procedures may be improved in speed or efficiency
8. Product recall or tampering may have a marked effect on production schedules

made by outside contractors. A new plant may possibly have to be constructed and dedicated to producing the drug. Alternatively, new manufacturing equipment to make the new drug may have to be purchased. If marketing personnel wait until the clinical profile of a new drug is well established before providing estimates to production of the number of kilograms and units required for launch and year one, then production may not have sufficient time to gear-up their operations and iron out "bugs" in their system prior to the product's launch.

One approach to solving this dilemma is to develop a series of alternative plans, each with different assumptions. Then, as each major new piece of information is gathered, the most suitable decision will become more clear. In reality, a drug's career often changes suddenly by a new finding of toxicity in animals or humans, or because of another problem (e.g., another drug approved for the market, technical problems). Plans often have to be greatly changed, sometimes with little warning. Fortunately, most drugs that are terminated prior to marketing die before passing the go–no go decision point that is usually reached sometime during late Phase II.

Competitive Pressures

In some disease areas (e.g., hypertension, angina) there is often a great deal of internal company pressure to reduce the cost of branded drugs, because of the need to compete in the marketplace. During the period when a company has a patent on

Table 22.6. Items to include in a synopsis of production status for individual drugs

1. Date of report
2. Project name, number, and leader
3. Accomplishments
4. Marketing requests and schedules
5. Meetings with marketing and research and development
6. Critical uncertainties
7. Problems
8. Resource status
9. Quality assurance and validation issues
10. Inventory issues
11. Packaging issues
12. Major action points and time schedules for completion
13. Summary

a unique drug, they may concentrate on producing the best product possible and pay less attention to manufacturing costs. If other companies also have drugs in the same therapeutic class that are equivalent, or even better, then there is more incentive for a company to compete on cost.

As soon as its patent expires a drug becomes subject to generic competition. At this point, producing drug at minimal cost is always critical. It is important to develop improved manufacturing processes continually during a drug's life and not wait until these pressures mount. Efforts to improve the manufacturing process are often handled jointly by both technical development and production departments. New technologies, equipment, and ideas must be evaluated to help improve a drug's manufacturing processes.

Standards That Spiral Upwards

Various government inspectors that tour manufacturing plants impose their own subjective interpretation of the regulations on the company they are inspecting. This is almost unavoidable because regulations are often vague. Regulations must be interpreted because they cannot cover or anticipate every situation. As a result, the inspector may decide that a company is out of compliance with a regulation. The company may be requested to purchase new equipment or somehow modify their manufacturing process. Alternatively, the company may decide on their own to upgrade their systems to take care of a situation described by the inspector. When the inspector returns, he or she notices that standards are raised, even though up to this time, no other company may have followed or implemented the new standards. This inspector and others may now confidently tell other companies that they too must raise their standards, to meet those achieved by the original company. Thus, a new state of the art has been created. This cycle may continue in many different ways, and the result is that production costs escalate for the companies affected. These costs are eventually passed on to the consumer in most situations.

Deciding on an Appropriate Level of Risk

There are always major questions of risk involved in manufacturing new drugs. At one extreme, a company could await FDA approval before ordering the equipment they will need to manufacture a drug. At the opposite extreme, this equipment could be ordered when a project is initially established, based solely on results in animals. In either case the company is almost always being risk-foolish. Finding the right balance, however, is often difficult and always requires sound judgment.

As a drug progresses from project initiation to market approval, and as more information becomes known, the risk to a company in purchasing equipment and/ or building facilities clearly changes. Educated guesses must be made in terms of how soon the drug is expected to reach the marketplace and also in terms of what type of drug labeling the company expects to have. A company that establishes its market forecasts based on one set of assumptions and finds that the approved labeling is much more restrictive will have to greatly reduce their forecast. If the original forecast was used to justify a new building dedicated to manufacturing the drug or to purchase new expensive equipment for the same purpose, then there may be some extremely embarrassed people around. If the company resisted the urge to make these moves, then the same people will be greatly relieved (although also disappointed at the bad news about labeling). One of the few guidelines for determining when to go ahead with the decision to risk significant capital is to carry out a dialogue among the people involved, allow time for thoughtful judgment, and obtain the most accurate forecasts possible of quantities needed and dates that decisions must be made.

Vertical Integration

Vertical integration refers to a company obtaining control of additional steps in the process of turning raw goods into finished products and having them sold to the final customer.

Each drug manufacturer purchases supplies and raw materials used in manufacturing, packaging, and shipping their products. Many companies contract these activities for some or all of their products to other companies. There are trends within some companies to bring more of these activities "in-house" to gain control over the processes involved. Other companies are moving in the opposite direction and are attempting to have contractors prepare drugs for them, or to synthesize key intermediates. Two of the factors that influence these trends and a company's decisions are the costs of various approaches and the capacity of a company's current manufacturing plants to perform the necessary operations. Changes in tax and other laws will influence each company's perception of which approach is preferable for each of their products.

Backward Vertical Integration

There are two types of vertical integration, backward and forward. Backward vertical integration means that a company manufactures or controls the supply of starting chemicals they need instead of buying them. If a raw product is mined it might mean that the company purchases a mine. The driving forces behind this move are to save money and to gain control over the availability of supplies.

Forward Vertical Integration

Forward vertical integration means that a company becomes active in the distribution chain of its finished products. This might include operating wholesale or retail sales businesses in those countries where it is legal. Owning retail pharmacies or distribution networks would allow greater control over marketing activities. The primary driving forces behind a decision to move a company in this direction are to earn greater profits and gain better control over marketing of drugs.

Issues of Vertical Integration

Some of the issues that affect decisions about forward vertical integration are whether to sell competitors' products in a distribution network or a retail store. In the former, the answer is usually no. In a retail pharmacy, the answer is yes; otherwise, it would be difficult to attract customers to a pharmacy that only sold drugs of a single company. An issue faced by new entries into these areas is that other retailers and distributors are likely to consider this practice unfair and will react in a strongly negative way to this new type of competition.

Backward vertical integration may require a large investment to achieve the necessary financial return. Gradually adding additional syntheses to a company's repertoire, however, may be a relative inexpensive and painless way to approach this goal.

A Summary of Current Challenges for Production

Some of the current challenges that production plants must cope with are listed below.

1. Construct and maintain an appropriate number of modern facilities for manufacturing drugs on a worldwide basis.
2. Introduce state-of-the-art techniques and equipment for manufacturing and packaging drugs.
3. Manufacture, package, and ship new products almost immediately after they are approved by the FDA, and/or other regulatory agencies.
4. Meet unexpected challenges in a rapid, efficient, and ethical manner (e.g., to develop tamper-resistant packaging).
5. Produce products in a cost-efficient manner.
6. Improve emissions, effluents, and waste products leaving the plant in a socially responsible yet economic manner.
7. Develop contingency plans in case of major catastrophes or emergencies.
8. Sell excess production capacity while retaining the ability to expand production of one's own products if the need arises.
9. Achieve a low rejection rate of finished drugs of high quality.
10. Produce investigational drugs to assist chemical development groups while utilizing resources for manufacturing.
11. Track time and effort of all employees while not spending excessive resources on this activity.
12. Develop a cadre of motivated and dedicated employees.
13. Turn inventory a sufficient number of times per year (based on cost of goods sold).
14. Utilize sophisticated computer inventory systems so that it is no longer necessary to physically segregate materials passed by a quality assurance group from materials that have not yet been passed.
15. Process, ship, and invoice all orders within a preset time period.

A summary of production issues are listed that relate to a physical plant and its equipment (Table 22.2), processes conducted (Table 22.3), people employed (Table 22.4), and products made (Table 22.5).

23 / *Financial Issues*

We demand that big business give the people a square deal; in return we must insist that when any one engaged in big business honestly endeavors to do right he shall himself be given a square deal. President Theodore Roosevelt. From *Autobiography*.

CORPORATE ISSUES

This chapter does not present or discuss detailed financial aspects of running a company, how to improve a company's financial performance, or detailed analyses of financial issues. Rather this chapter identifies some of the important financial issues a company faces. This chapter is written for the neophyte in financial matters who is interested in an overall view of financial issues within a drug company.

Joining Financial Policies to Corporate Objectives

A company's corporate objectives and goals include financial objectives and goals. These may be used to help insure that the company's detailed financial policies and procedures are directed toward meeting these goals. If they are not, then it would be essential to redirect the financial policies and procedures or to establish new ones. Progress toward financial goals must be monitored and reviewed. Procedures to conduct various financial activities must be developed that are in concert with policies.

Accounting practices should be changed whenever necessary to better reflect company practice within the limits of generally accepted accounting principles. Accounting procedures should be viewed as to their true purpose of helping to record and communicate business transactions. They are most useful in doing this when they are closely tied to actual business practice, and are expressed in easily understood terms. The "numbers" are an aid in decision making, and should be used as a tool and not as an oracle or as an end in themselves.

Degree of Acceptable Financial Risk

The degree of financial risk that is acceptable to a company is a policy issue decided by the chief executive officer or the company's board of directors. The risk deemed acceptable varies widely between companies and within a company at different periods. Companies determine acceptable risk based on numerous factors including (1) stability of the core business(es), (2) current rates of return on the company's investments, (3) financial and other corporate goals, (4) degree of solvency, (5) degree of operating leverage (relationship of fixed to variable costs), (6) personalities of the senior managers, (7) preferences of certain important outside groups (e.g., bankers, shareholders), and (8) opportunities available. The answer to this question of acceptable risk influences many other business decisions made by a company and reflects itself in the company's reputation in the business community as relatively risk-oriented or risk-averse. Financial risk issues are even more complex within multinational companies, especially during periods of rapidly fluctuating currency exchange rates.

Financial Forecasts

How far into the future should a company attempt to extend its financial forecast and plans? The horizon in some businesses (e.g., dress designers) is short and even a single year may be too long. In others, a 20-year cycle is necessary (e.g., forest products, because of the life cycle of trees that are harvested). For drugs, a three to seven year time period is reasonable, given that the usual length of time required to bring a new drug to market may be up to 14 years. The major parameters used to develop a financial forecast are sales forecasts, promotional expenses, capital items, head count, and noncapitalized expenses (e.g., clinical study costs, grants to investigators). These categories are also accounted for at the end of each year. At that time the previous year's forecast is compared with the actual expenses incurred.

In addition, most companies compare spending and sales against budget on a monthly basis. Finally, all personnel, capital, and noncapital items from all company functions may be folded together to give an overall expense and capital investment picture of the short-term budget and the long-term forecast.

Early discussion of potential or likely financial problems to be faced during the prospective three to seven year period is important. This discussion would allow senior managers to take preventive steps to avoid problems and also to determine how tightly to control head count and other expenditures.

Sources of Financing

There are three usual approaches to financing a company's activities. These are to use internal, external, or a combination of financial sources. The overall degree to which each is used depends on many factors that are well known to financial professionals. Actual choices, however, are often based on personal decisions of the chief executive officer, or are politically influenced by the board of directors and/or key outsiders. Carefully developed criteria are sometimes used to establish the basis for reaching a decision. Even if this logical approach is followed it will be necessary to adjust the criteria used to meet each specific situation. This is because conditions relating to criteria change, and there are specific situations for which certain criteria may not be appropriate. The question of whether to finance multiple businesses of a company separately or collectively generally depends on the company's objectives, as well as on the overall organization of those businesses.

Allocation of Resources

Corporate resources are allocated to various activities in a complex manner that differs greatly from company to company and from time to time within any company. Decision makers who allocate capital and other resources to capital equipment and facilities, acquisitions, spending on core businesses, and dividends to stockholders are the most senior managers of a company.

A closely related issue is that of forecasting the availability of future resources, especially capital resources. Standard financial techniques used to determine these numbers are available in financial textbooks. Monitoring previous forecasts within the company will indicate the degree of accuracy of methods used and ways in which methods were used. Ongoing monitoring of resource allocations and utilizations is another integral part of being able to forecast future needs for resources. Ongoing monitoring is usually conducted within the overall corporation as well as within each subsidiary company business or division. It is also possible to conduct this activity at a department or even section level.

Senior company managers must decide how much risk they are willing to take when they approve the research and development budget. Regardless of a company's current financial performance, rationales are readily available and are used to justify spending more, less, or the same amount of money on research and development in the future. This is discussed later in this chapter. The amount of risk that the top research and development managers want to take and their plans for the money included in the budget request should be explainable to the company's top nonscientists. Nonscientists should never accept comments along the lines of "This is too technical to explain to this group," or "The scientific reasons are too complex to simplify." Senior managers were hopefully chosen for their superior intelligence and their ability to understand principles. These nonscientists may request or hire other scientists to evaluate any detailed scientific hypotheses, concepts, or rationales. This could be handled either by contacting noncompany board members who are scientists or by approaching independent consultants.

Senior company managers should also assure themselves that there is an appropriate balance between resources allocated to drug discovery, drug development, and market support. Without an appropriate balance (which will likely change over the years) for the entire company, it is easy for a company to stray in the wrong direction. This is a major pitfall to avoid.

Psychological Aspects of Spending Money on Questionable Projects

One particular issue will be addressed. This is the question of deciding whether to spend additional money on a project about which serious questions have arisen after a moderate or large amount of money has already been spent. This important issue appears to arise quite often at all levels of decision making. Arkes and Blumer (1985) investigated this phenomenon, and they reported that there is definitely a greater tendency to continue work and spend money on a highly questionable endeavor after some money and effort has been expended and invested. More importantly, they observed that the chances of success of the undertaking are inflated by those who have incurred the sunk cost as opposed to those who have not.

Projects and other activities develop momentum once they are initiated and after a period of time take on a life of their own. It therefore takes more courage for managers to question and stop a project after it is initiated than before it is begun. There is also a strong theoretical basis to the fact that people are often willing to "throw good money after bad." This is why one frequently reads statements such as "To terminate a project in which $1.1 billion has been invested represents an unconscionable mishandling of taxpayers' dollars" (Senator Denton, November 4, 1981, quoted by Arkes and Blumer, 1985).

Some research and development directors require virtually 100% certainty that a project has no potential to succeed before they are willing to terminate it. This means that they will be investing money when the chance is over 90 percent that success will not be achieved. Other directors are willing to terminate a project at an earlier stage and place resources on other projects with a higher likelihood of success. The difference in behavior between two such directors could be viewed as one company moving ahead in a series of competitive races with one or more albatrosses around their neck. If one assumes that each company began each race with approximately equal resources (which is rarely true) then the one who sheds albatrosses, or does not acquire any, has a better chance of winning an important race against their competitors.

Transfer Pricing

Different businesses, divisions, or departments within a company often provide services for other parts of the company or to other business units. In addition to services, chemicals, drugs, or intermediate products may be "sold" within the company or overall business entity. The value to set for these services or goals (transfer price) and the manner of handling these transactions varies widely between companies, and also between different business groups within the same company.

Labor charges for employees in one business doing work for another business may be sold at cost. This cost usually includes an amount for overhead. The amount one business or function charges another may be based on (1) actual hours of time spent, (2) standard costs for products, (3) an average number of hours per year, (4) a percent of one group's budget for negotiated services, or (5) a contractual basis that deals with each request for services as a separate contract to be negotiated. Tax considerations are often a critical factor in choosing which method(s) to use.

A major issue that arises in transfer pricing relates to the amount of money charged and how this figure is derived. There are many implications relating to these decisions. One concerns the amount of duty paid to customs for importation of a drug. The greater the declared value, the greater (generally) is the customs duty, and vice versa. But, if the declared value is set at a low figure, then the amount the company may eventually be allowed to charge for the drug in many countries will also be impacted. In some situations it is possible to set a relatively low value for an investigational drug and to raise it at a later date, after the drug has been approved for marketing. Tax paid on a higher profit will be higher, so that tax rate differentials need to be considered.

Drug supplies are transferred from one part of a company to another, as (1) finished goods ready for sale, (2) bulk drug needing packaging, (3) raw drug needing packaging, (4) raw drug needing formulation, or (5) as a chemical that may or may not require additional synthetic steps. Major issues relating to drug transfer changes involve customs, taxes, import and export valuations, and duties. When a drug is manufactured at one site and shipped to another country for sale, the subsidiary country receiving the drug pays the manufacturing company. This payment is usually done by adjusting the current account ("the books") between the two companies.

Cost-Effectiveness Data

Future large-scale purchasers of drugs at Health Maintenance Organizations (HMOs), Preferred Provider Organizations (PPOs), and hospital chains will demand to see more cost analysis data before they are willing to put a newly approved drug on their formulary. Cost-benefit and cost-effectiveness analyses are not discussed in this section. A brief review is included in Chapter 27 of *Guide to Clinical Interpretation of Data*, (Spilker, 1986b). The calculation of costs involved in conducting medical studies and in developing an entire drug from start to finish are described in Chapter 24 of *Guide to Planning and Managing Multiple Clinical Studies* (Spilker, 1987c).

Differences in Accounting Principles between Functions of a Company

Combining financial statements from multiple subsidiaries into a consolidated single company statement is a complex endeavor with multiple accounting issues. Different countries handle many accounting issues using different systems and definitions that make consolidation of various figures extremely difficult. The way that is usually taken to get out of this dilemma is to utilize a number of assumptions and conventions, and to follow them consistently. By adhering to the same approaches each year, one year's set of numbers may be compared with others.

RESEARCH AND DEVELOPMENT BUDGET

Essential Questions to Address

The major financial question in research and development for most companies is how much money is the company willing to invest to generate new drugs. Concomitantly, another issue is how will the funds be spent (i.e., on internally generated drugs, licensed drugs, or purchased drugs)? Most other considerations about what can be afforded flows from decisions reached on these two questions.

Although most of this section concerns a research and development budget as a whole, there are various other budgets that could be and are often prepared. These include business area budgets (e.g., diagnostics, over-the-counter drugs (OTCs), pesticides), therapeutic area budgets, and individual project budgets.

Organizing the Research and Development Budget

The research and development budget may be organized by individual department functions, or by products (i.e., projects), or a mixture of both. If the department approach is used, each department may be subdivided by projects they are working on and/or by their functions.

The amount of detail and effort to put into a budget must be carefully evaluated. Too much time, energy, and paperwork devoted to completing budgets may not be productive. Part of the reason for this is that many factors and activities will change before the budget year is completed. Projects will be added and dropped or new responsibilities may totally reshape how the allocated money is being spent. In viewing the appropriate amount of time to spend preparing a budget, it must be decided "if the juice is worth the squeeze."

The law of diminishing returns is very steep in this area, in terms of the effort expended and increased accuracy or benefits obtained. It takes moderate effort to develop a reasonable plan and often a great deal of effort to make it fairly accurate. Additional accuracy usually requires a disproportionate amount of time and money and even then may not achieve the goal, because of the reasons stated above. It is virtually impossible to create totally accurate plans (or budgets). The only thing one knows for certain about a plan is that it is wrong. It is desirable to assess in hindsight in what ways it was wrong, and by how much. This may help the planning process improve its accuracy in future cycles.

Accountability for the Research and Development Budget

On a retrospective basis, senior managers within research and development (or at the corporate level) may ask for a synopsis of progress achieved with money spent over the last "X" years. This accountability for moneys allocated to research and development may be handled in several different ways. Ultimately, the issue boils down to one of trust. Either the most senior managers trust their subordinate managers and delegate them responsibilities and resources or they do not. If not, confrontational and uneasy situations are likely to occur within management, and the morale of the organization may become adversely affected. Tension created by management uneasiness over financial matters may filter down to staff and affect or even disrupt scientific creativity and productivity.

Determining the Size of the Research and Development Budget

The question of how much money is necessary or advisable to spend on research and development certainly could be dealt with in several long chapters, if not a book. The most appropriate answer for a research-based company depends on numerous factors, many of which change from year to year. Most importantly, science requires a long-term company commitment to maintain an appropriate spending level to keep scientists both productive and happy. Spending levels that do not achieve this result can have devastating effects on a company's morale and productivity that may be extremely difficult to repair in the short term. Scientists, as others, understand that there are sometimes compelling reasons to cut their budget (e.g., for the company's health), but they expect cuts to be applied fairly and appropriately throughout the organization.

The amount of research and development's budget relates to considerations of the past, present, and future nature of a company's internal environment as well as to the external environment that affects the company. Approaches to determining the size of a budget for research and development may focus in a major or minor way on one or more of the following:

1. Identifying an appropriate percent of sales to allocate to research and development. Some companies follow this approach in part because it allows them to easily calculate the size of the budget and track changes and trends.
2. Identifying a percent of profits. This parameter is more reflective than percent of sales of a company's financial health. On the other hand, profits are often highly volatile and do not provide as stable a base as sales.
3. Comparing a company with its major competitors. The research and development budget of comparably sized companies of the same general type (e.g., research-based) and productivity are used to help determine an approximate range of spending needed to support research and development activities.
4. Developing mathematical models to extrapolate past research and development expenditures required for maintaining an acceptable level of productivity into the future. This approach requires a large amount of data to develop a valid model, depends on many assumptions regarding the nature of future productivity, and may not be more accurate or appropriate than using either of the above methods.
5. Taking the current budget and increasing it by a percentage that accounts for inflation and what is considered to be appropriate growth. This is the method apparently used by United States presidents in calculating certain parts of the nation's budget.

6. Identifying all major activities to be conducted over the coming year and adding the costs together to derive a total. This approach has the disadvantage that activities planned and conducted often differ.

Justifying the Size of the Research and Development Budget

The author's opinion is that each of the approaches described above can be used to justify any given amount of money considered necessary to spend on research and development. The question is whether a company picks a number and works backward to justify it, or works forward to identify what an appropriate number should be.

If a company is doing well financially, then a strong case could be made for any of the following possibilities: (1) maintain research and development (R and D) spending at the present level to keep the company prospering, (2) increase R and D spending to further fuel the company's development and growth and exploit the productivity of R and D, or (3) decrease R and D to use some of the money "saved" to fund other ventures.

If a company is doing poorly financially, then arguments could also be made to (1) maintain R and D spending at the same level, because the company cannot afford more funds and it is important not to cut back on the budget at a time when a successful drug is desperately needed, (2) increase R and D spending, because if a new significant drug is discovered, it will provide the company with the greatest potential economic benefit, or (3) decrease R and D spending, possibly by cutting out research in those areas least likely to be productive and thus increase the chance of continuing in those areas with the greatest likelihood of success.

These brief comments indicate only a few of the many arguments that may be used to support any position on how to determine and justify the research and development budget, regardless of the financial position of the company. The exact reasoning chosen may be utilized before the budget is selected, to help determine its most appropriate size. Alternatively, this exercise may be undertaken after a draft or final budget is established, as a means of justifying the size of the budget chosen. Licensing-based companies that solely develop drugs discovered by others or are generic manufacturers with little research or development costs have somewhat different considerations. There is usually a greater degree of certainty that their planned activities on drug development will be actually conducted.

Allocating Research and Development Funds

There is a common misconception that drug companies have broad flexibility to use the many millions in their research and development budget much as a gambler uses poker chips. In this metaphor the company places more or fewer chips (i.e., resources) on one project or another. That scenario would generally be liked by senior managers if it were true. It would allow them to move resources easily to have one or more projects move rapidly ahead. The facts, however, are that fixed costs plus management and administrative costs take up a substantial portion of the research and development budget dollars. Even after all fixed costs are allocated, there are many types of technical support services that must be financed before the relatively few discretionary dollars may be placed on the hot leads or exciting projects. Furthermore, even applying large resources of money and professional staff on a project cannot always move important projects ahead more rapidly. There may be rate-limiting steps that take time to complete before further work may be conducted. In addition, almost any type of preclinical, clinical, regulatory, or technical problem may arise that delays progress.

Fixed costs in a budget include salaries of permanent employees, their fringe benefits, rent on space, lease payments on equipment, utilities, taxes, depreciation, and any allocated costs passed on from the overall corporation (e.g., computer services, other company costs). Administrative costs include the many services provided by non-research and development groups including: personnel, payroll, finance, employee benefits, graphics, purchasing, engineering, maintenance, counseling, and training. Technical support services that are usually placed within research and development include: animal maintenance, library and information services, regulatory affairs, data processing, statistical services, project planning and tracking, computer services, analytical laboratories, and formulation laboratories. All of these costs must be allocated regardless of the specific work they perform.

The remaining funds that are available to pay for emphasizing one project versus another are rather limited when expressed as a percent of the total research and development budget. If a company reemphasizes or reallocates their efforts on projects, it would be desirable to confirm that desired changes have in fact been appropriately initiated and followed. This may be done by evaluating time and effort reporting forms that track actual time spent by scientists and other personnel.

Tax Implications of the Research and Development Budget

A tax credit is granted to a company for moneys spent on research and development in the United States and most other countries. In the United States some companies may obtain a small additional percent tax credit for money spent on clinical studies of officially approved orphan drugs. This is described in the Orphan Drug Act of 1983. This tax credit applies from the time that the orphan application is approved until the time that the New Drug Application (NDA) is approved. Part of the research and development budget may therefore be viewed as being "paid" by taxes saved, because of various tax deductions the company takes.

One question that arises is whether money used to fund research and development should come from company profits, borrowed funds, or stock sold to generate cash. Research-based companies usually use company profits, whereas start-up companies often fund research and development from proceeds of stock sales and borrowed money.

RESEARCH AND DEVELOPMENT EXPENDITURES

Definitions of Categories Used to Track Expenditures

Actual expenditures for a drug's development vary depending on many factors, not the least of which are the various definitions used of categories to track those expenditures. Some of these issues are discussed in Chapter 23 of *Guide to Planning and Managing Multiple Clinical Studies* (Spilker, 1987c). Actual development costs vary greatly from drug to drug, year to year, and company to company, depending on whether the definitions used are uniform or change, in addition to actual changes.

Two published reports of the percent of research and development money spent on various functions of drug development are illustrated in Fig. 23.1. The percent figures shown are based on averages of many drugs. These data are expressed in generally similar categories, although there are some differences between them. Despite any caveats about definitions, there is quite close agreement between the two sets of data. One interpretation of these data is that money to be allocated for drug development may be planned for various functions or categories with some degree of accuracy. Each drug will have a different profile of expenditures from these average figures, but overall expenditures at most research-based companies probably resemble this composite picture.

Accounting for Research and Development Expenditures

If a company desires research and development to account for money spent, then this may be done in a number of ways. Efforts and progress reported by research and development may be described in general terms or to any level of detail required. Data indicating where money was spent may be organized and expressed in terms of one or more of the following categories.

1. Research projects, development projects, and product support activities. This refers to drug discovery, drug development, and market support functions.
2. Research division, development division, medical division, and scientific support division. Administrative expenses may be identified separately or folded into each of the four divisions.
3. General and specific activities that require the largest resource commitment and expenditures.
4. Activities which involve marketed products or products close to the market.
5. Specific therapeutic areas.
6. Functions of drug development (Table 23.1).
7. Business areas the company is involved in (e.g., agricultural products, veterinary drugs, human prescription drugs, human OTC drugs).

Presenting Data on Research and Development Expenditures

There are innumerable ways to present data on research and development expenditures for a specific company. A few are shown in Figs. 23.2 and 23.3. In addition to presenting these data according to the functions of research and development (Fig. 23.3), similar graphs could be presented to illustrate expenditures according to therapeutic classes of drugs studied (e.g., cardiovascular, anti-infective, anticancer, gastrointestinal) or drugs in different stages of development (e.g., preclinical, Phases I through IV). Although these figures illustrate changes from year to year, it is also possible to explore a single year's expenditures for departments, business units, or groups within a specific department. Data may also be presented on an

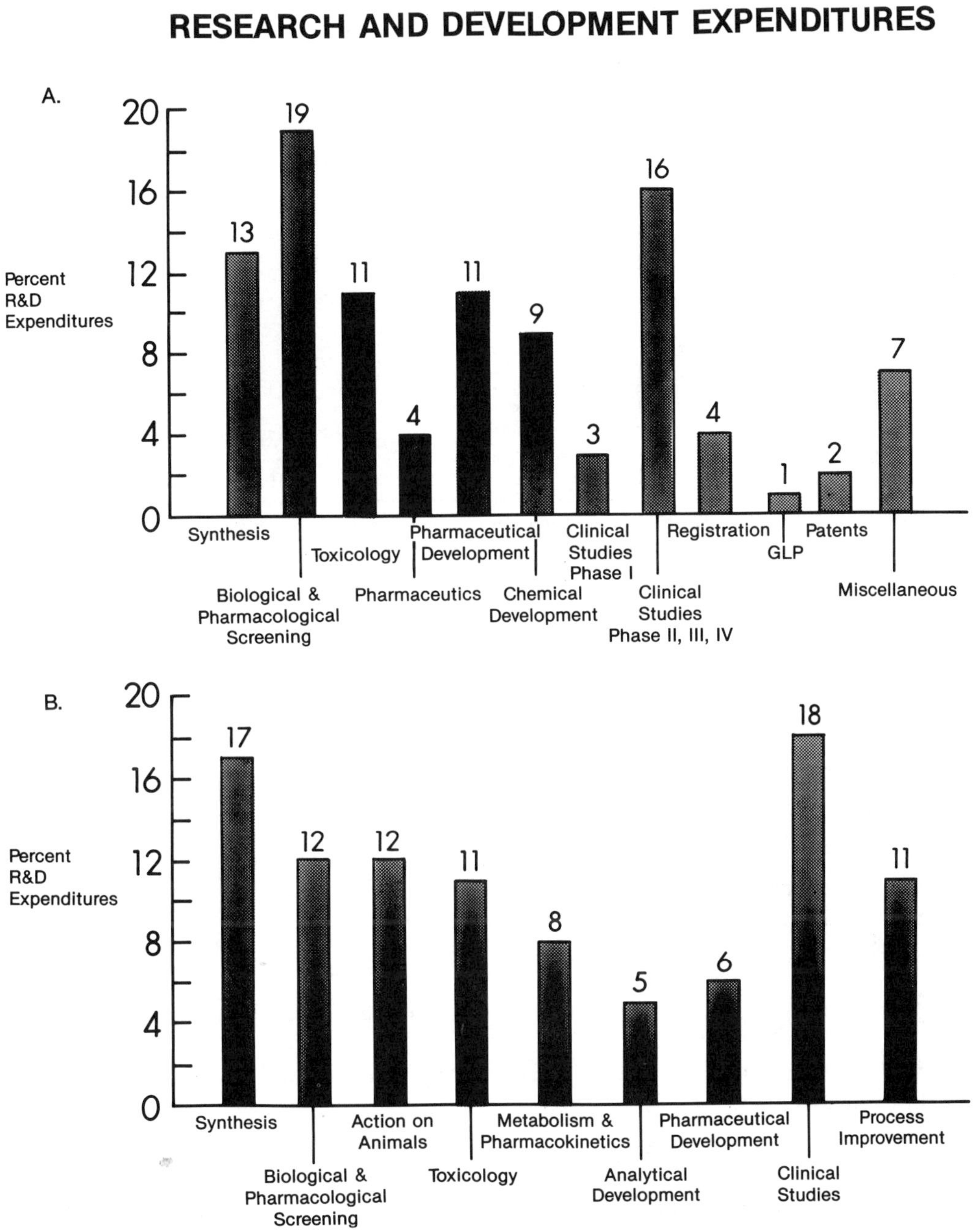

Fig. 23.1. Research and development expenditures by function. Panel A reprinted from Prentis and Walker (1985) with permission of *The Pharmaceutical Journal.* Panel B reprinted from Seidl (1983), with permission of Raven Press. R&D, research and development, GLP, Good Laboratory Practices.

Table 23.1. Research and development expenditures by function in West Germany and the United States

		Percent of total costs	
		West Germany[a]	United States[b]
1.	Synthesis of chemicals and isolation of natural products	17	11
2.	Pharmacological screening	12	18
3.	Secondary testing	12	—
4.	Toxicology	11	9
5. a.	Metabolism and pharmacokinetics	8	—
b.	Bioavailability studies	—	3
6.	Analytical development	5	—
7.	Pharmaceutical development	6	10
8.	Process development for manufacturing and quality control	11	10
9.	Human studies	18	24
10.	Other	—	15
		100	100

[a] From Seidl (1983) with permission of Raven Press. This breakdown is based on data from seven major West German drug companies for 1980. The four types of expenditures in a research budget were for personnel (65 percent), material (20 percent), capital (8 percent), and a reserve of 7 percent.

[b] From Table 20 of *PMA Annual Survey Report 1980–1983*, with permission.

annual basis as five year growth rates or percent of sales. When comparing distant periods, data should be adjusted for inflation. Figure 23.4 illustrates another approach to presenting expenditures on projects in research, development, or both. This type of graph may also be used to present sales or profit of marketed drugs according to therapeutic area.

Expenditures may be tracked during a period and illustrated by comparing projected with actual costs (Fig. 23.5). This approach may be used in many different ways in most areas of a drug company. For example, sales are often tracked by comparing forecasted and actual monthly sales.

Interpreting Data on Research and Development Expenditures

Caution must be used in interpreting these graphs for numerous reasons. A few examples are given.

1. A decrease expressed in percent from one year to the next may in actuality represent an increase in money spent.

2. Definitions of categories may change from year to year or between countries whose data are combined.

3. A specific reason may readily explain an otherwise unexpected change in any numerical figure.

Fig. 23.2. Selected methods of illustrating overall expenditures within research and development (R&D). Similar graphs could be prepared to illustrate production or marketing expenditures.

OVERALL R&D EXPENDITURES

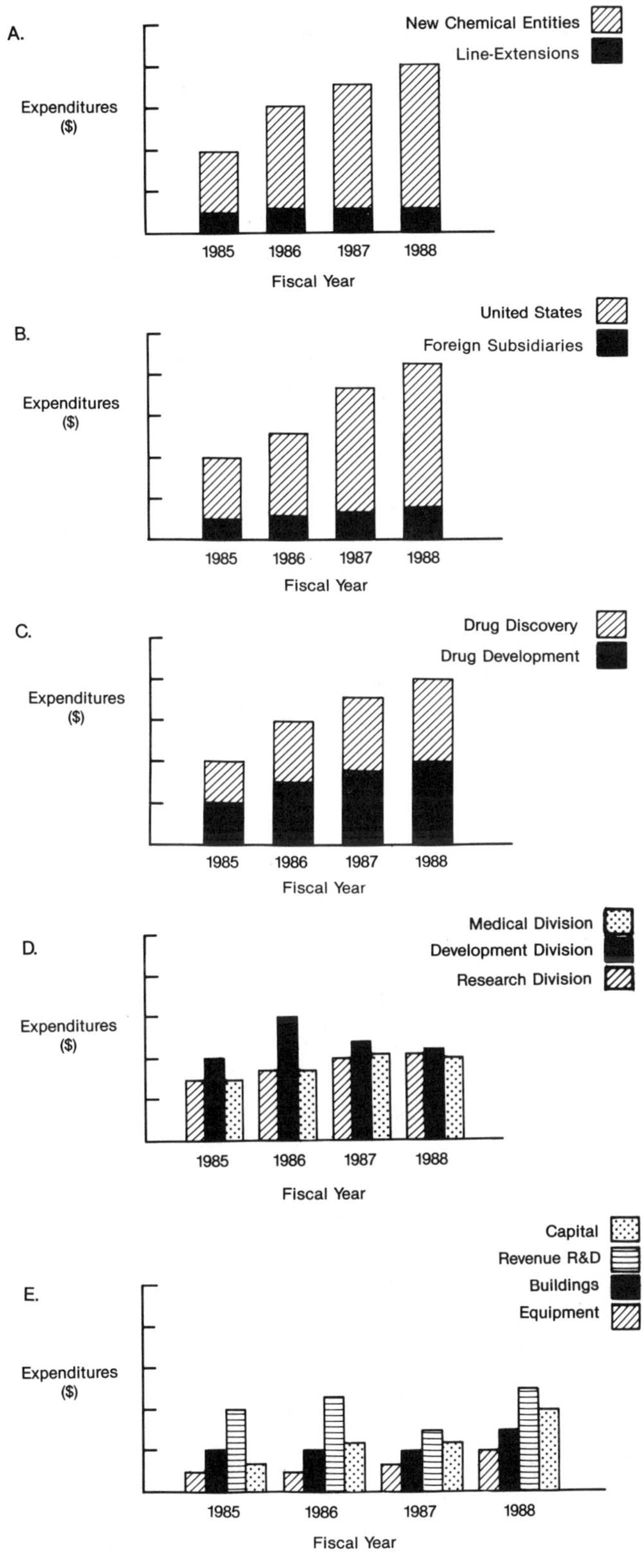

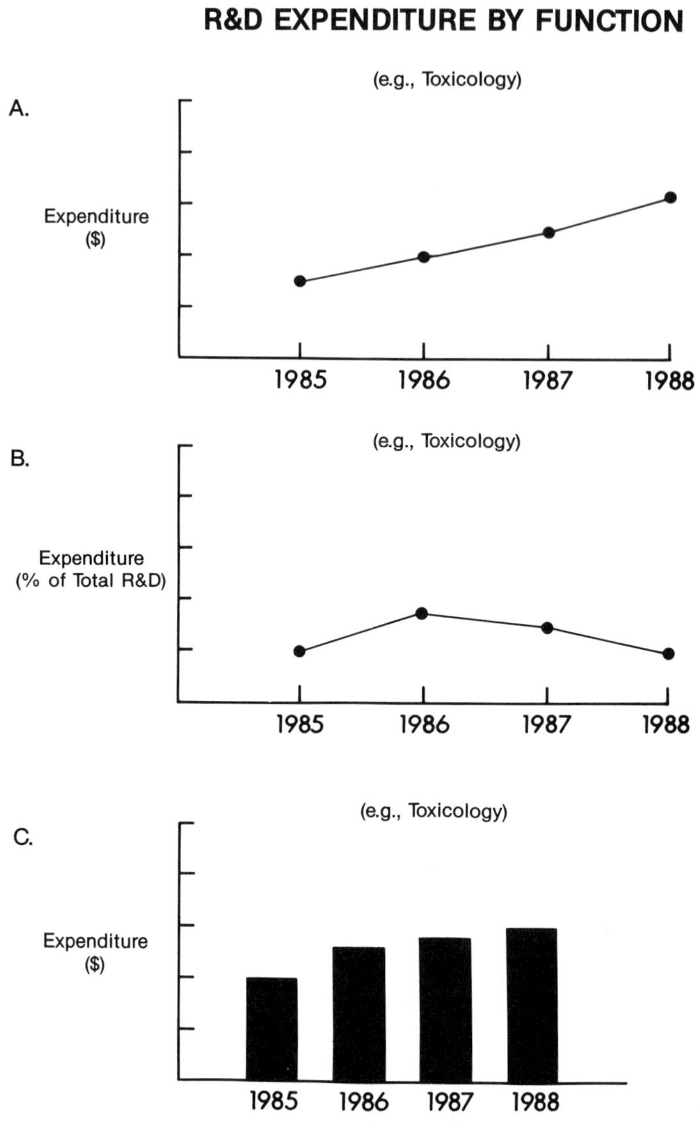

Fig. 23.3. Selected methods of illustrating expenditures within research and development (R&D) according to function. Each function could be presented separately as in panels A to D or combined as in panels E and F. Most panels could also be presented as percent of the total amount spent in addition to exact sums of money. These types of graphs may also be used to illustrate expenditures based on therapeutic area of drugs studied, phase of development, specific department or division involved, country involved, or with another parameter. Similar graphs could be prepared by marketing or production groups.

4. Money spent may not have been discounted to express all numbers in constant units of currency (e.g., dollars, marks, pounds).

5. Data may have been collected differently from year to year, or from country to country.

6. Money spent may not have been adjusted to account for inflation.

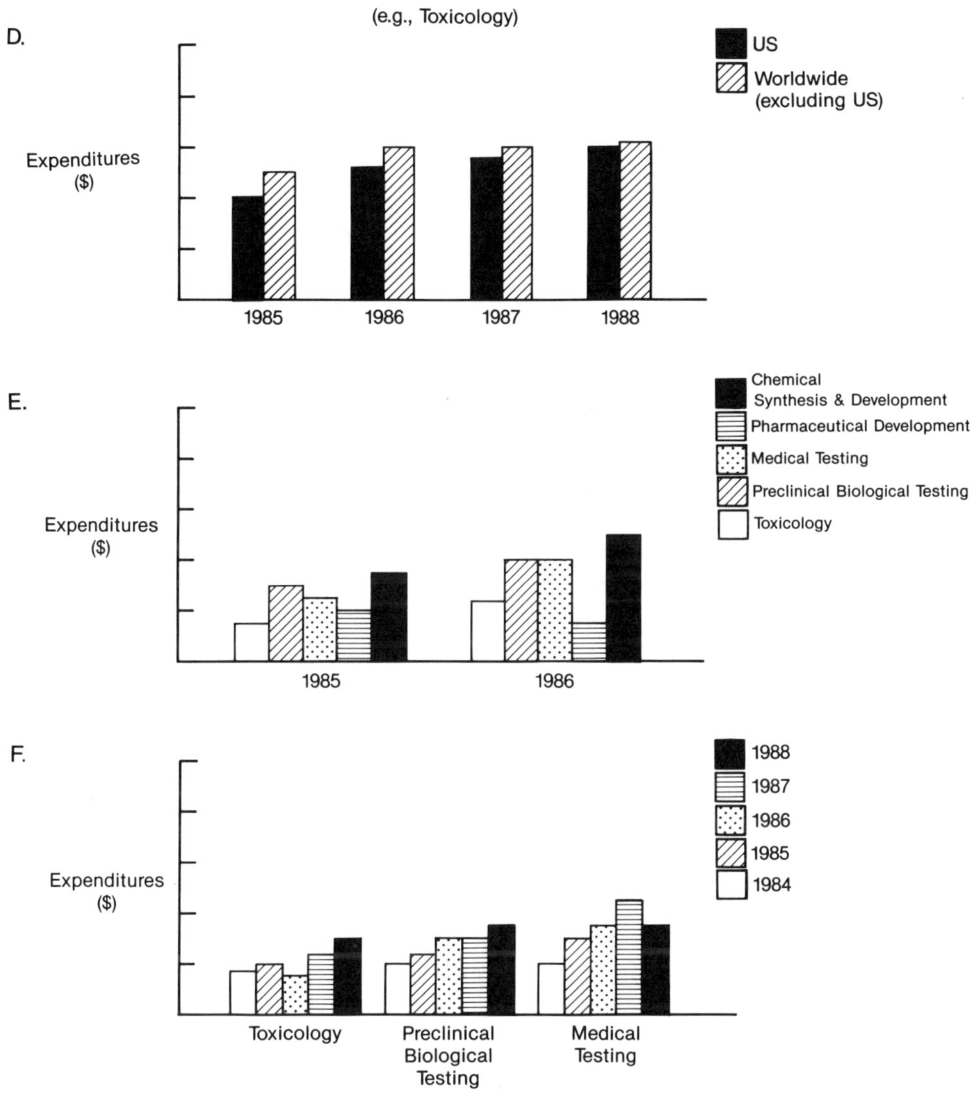

Fig. 23.3. (*continued*)

Forecasting Future Research and Development Expenditures

A simple means of approximating expenditures on research and development activities is to break them down into component parts. These parts are drug discovery projects, development projects, technical support services, and so on. Each of these broad categories may be divided into various components such as internal time and effort, external grants to investigators (e.g., for medical and toxicological contracts), and equipment.

Each of the components may be forecasted separately on a level that can be dealt with comfortably, and necessary components combined. A graph of each compo-

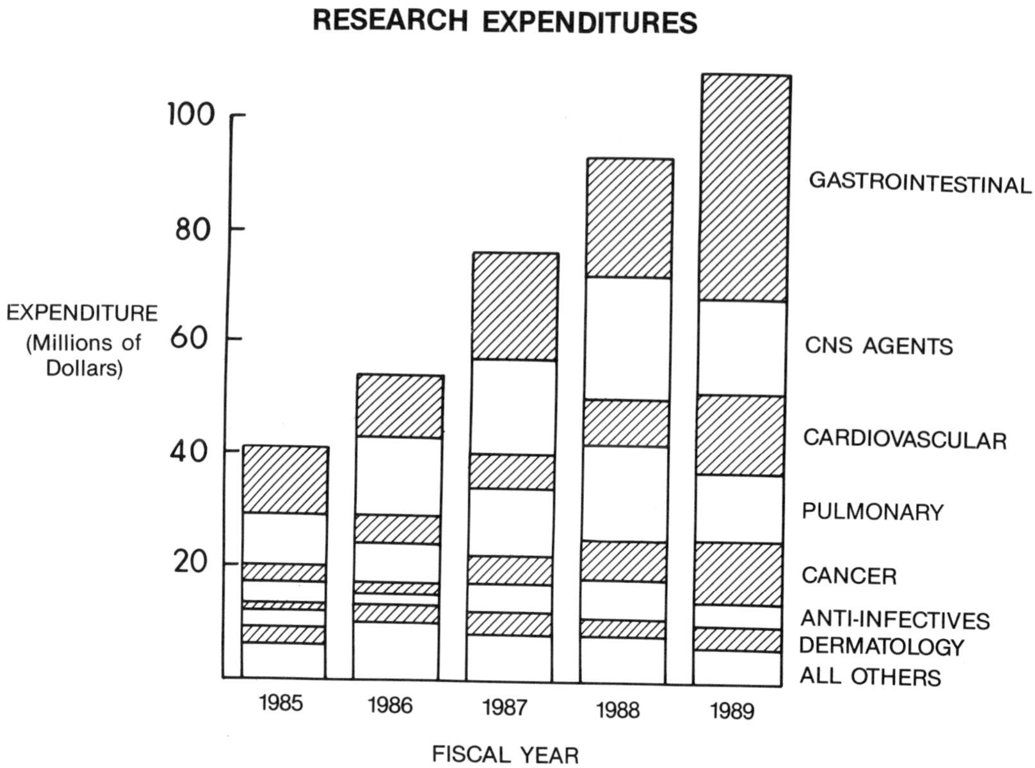

Fig. 23.4. Illustrating expenditures in various therapeutic areas over a period of years. This approach could illustrate development projects, research projects, or both. CNS, central nervous system.

nent's previous levels of spending over a few years will establish trends. Next, one or more people must be enlisted who know to what degree work on each particular project will probably change (increase, decrease, or stay the same) over the next year or two. This enables an extrapolation of the expenditure curve to be made into the future. The better each component is understood, the more accurate is the forecast that will be reached.

Financial Analyses of Projects

Both retrospective and prospective data on projects are collected and used at drug companies. Retrospective data focuses on a tracking of money and time spent on a particular project. This may be done in either a superficial or detailed manner. There is, however, a point of diminishing returns involved in this exercise. The time spent collecting data becomes steadily greater as more data are required, but the quality of the data may not necessarily be more accurate or helpful in interpreting results. Moreover, the staff's resistance usually increases as more data are requested. Most companies require forms with this information be completed every one to three months, although the same company may use shorter (or longer) time intervals as

PROJECTED VERSUS ACTUAL EXPENDITURES

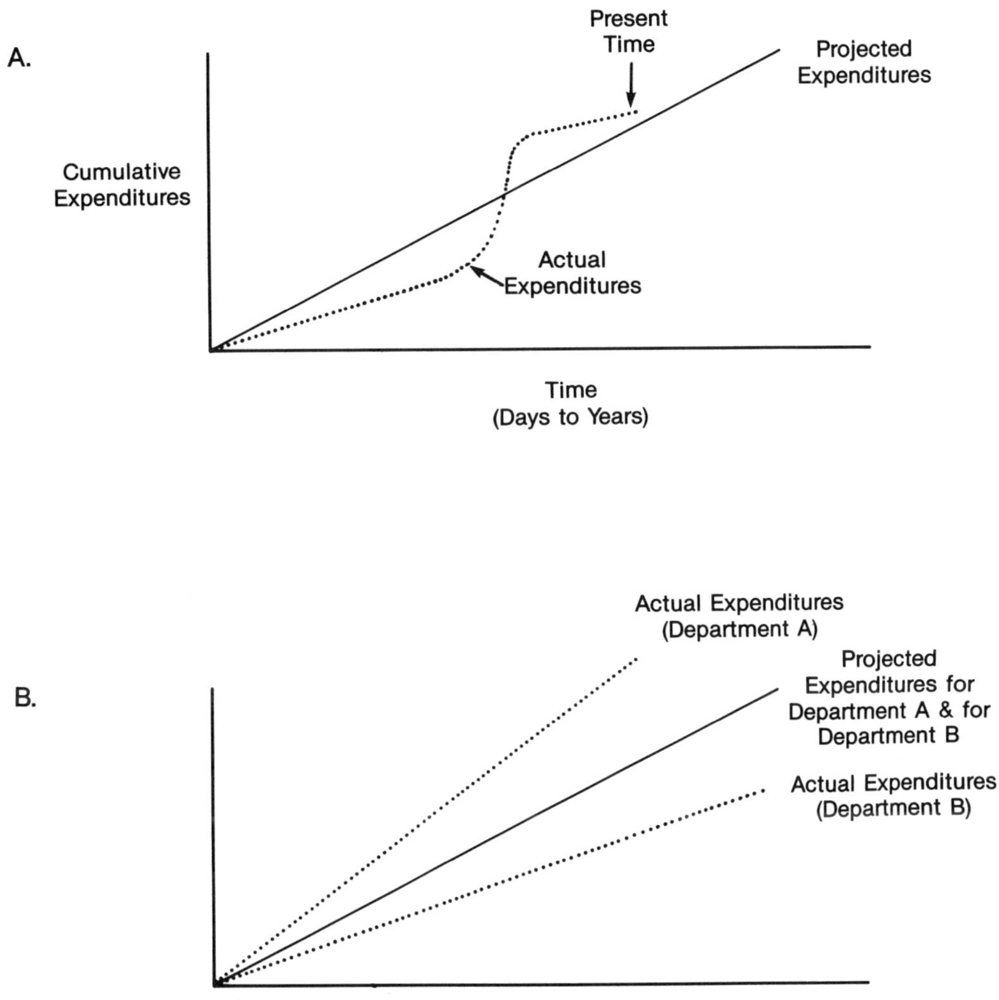

Fig. 23.5. Graphing projected versus actual expenditures over a period of time (e.g., days, weeks, months, years). Panel A illustrates a complex pattern that is presently close to its target. Panel B illustrates under and over spending for two different departments. This type of graph may also be used to track actual sales versus sales forecasts in marketing or actual production versus production forecasts.

well, depending on the function being surveyed and the use that will be made of the resulting data.

Prospective forecasts of expenditures on a project may be made based on retrospective data plus knowledge of future activities that must be conducted. Forecasts may focus on costs to reach any of several time points (i.e., milestones) in a project's life. These include the go-no go decision point, time of NDA submission, or time of initial marketing. Forecasts may be broken down to department, division, or other level, in addition to providing an overall amount. Although many if not most companies make these forecasts, few actually go to the step of creating budgets for individual projects to use in reaching their goals.

Section V

External Interactions and Relationships

24 / *Interactions and Relationships Between Drug Companies and Academic Institutions*

Learning without thought is labor lost; thought without learning is perilous. Confucius, Chinese philosopher. From *Analects* (Book II, Chapter XV).

Shall I tell you the secret of the true scholar? It is this: Every man I meet is my master in some point, and in that I learn of him. Ralph Waldo Emerson, American essayist. From *Letters and Social Aims: Greatness.*

It is demonstrable that many of the obstacles to change which have been attributed to human nature are in fact due to the inertia of institutions and to the voluntary desire of powerful classes to maintain the existing status. John Dewey (1859–1952), American philosopher, educator. From *Monthly Review* (March 1950).

TYPES OF INTERACTIONS

Despite the rather pessimistic comments of John Dewey above, both academic and industrial institutions are recognizing the benefits that can be derived from active collaboration. This is generally viewed as a positive trend with potentially important

Table 24.1. Types of interactions between drug companies and academic institutions

A. Academicians' perspective
   1. Consultants from academia assist drug companies in many different ways
   2. Clinical investigators in academic institutions conduct sponsored studies on investigational and marketed drugs
   3. Academic scientists conduct preclinical studies on compounds furnished by drug companies or evaluate ideas suggested by drug companies
   4. Academic chemists synthesize compounds for testing by drug companies
   5. Academic institutions license ideas or compounds developed at the institution to a drug company for subsequent development
   6. Academic scientists present seminars at drug companies
   7. Students work at drug companies for specific periods, usually ranging from three months to two years on a fellowship or postdoctoral program

B. Drug company perspective
   1. Industry personnel work on a part-time basis at an academic institution either on a fixed (e.g., one half to two days per week or month) or on an ad hoc basis. Their functions would generally involve teaching, conducting research, providing consulting, counseling, and/or treating patients
   2. Industry personnel present seminars or act as visiting professors at academic institutions
   3. Drug companies offer philanthropic grants to academicians for research, travel, and/or other purposes
   4. Drug companies support academic conferences, symposia, or other meetings
   5. Drug companies conduct clinical studies at academic institutions
   6. Drug companies offer fellowships, postdoctoral grants, and other professional opportunities for academicians

benefits to both. The industrial-academic relationship may be viewed from several perspectives, including that of the government and public sector, in addition to the more obvious perspectives of drug companies and academic institutions.

There is no doubt that industrial-academic relationships in the United States are increasing both in extent and importance (e.g., Atkinson et al., 1984). One of the major reasons for this change relates to the decrease in unsponsored research funds available per academic scientist. This has led many scientists, departments, and even entire medical schools to pursue opportunities and relationships with the drug industry. Drug companies benefit from university expertise, and universities are paid for their time and effort. University scientists and clinicans also benefit scientifically, career wise, and in other ways by working on important projects.

There are many types of interactions between drug companies and academic institutions. As indicated in Table 24.1 these interactions may be viewed from either the academic or drug company's perspective. Few companies utilize all of these approaches, and the nature and degree of interactions vary greatly. Relationships are established between a drug company and an academic institution (Table 24.2), between a drug company and an individual academic scientists, or both. Figure 24.1 illustrates the numerous levels within companies and academic institutions at which interactions occur. An important point of this figure is that interactions may occur across different levels as well as across the same level. Some areas where indirect interactions occur are shown in Fig. 24.2. A number of the possible relationships and interactions are described in the sections below.

Ideas for New Drugs

Companies solicit and/or accept ideas from people and groups in academia. A company that establishes products in a new therapeutic area is usually approached

Table 24.2. Selected biomedical relationships between universities and drug companies

Academic institution (city)	Drug company	Length of agreement[a] (years)	Area(s) of agreement
Duke University (Durham)	Du Pont Pharmaceuticals	5	Virology and immunology
Harvard University, Massachusetts General Hospital (Boston)	Hoescht-Roussel Pharmaceuticals Inc.	10	Molecular biology
Washington University (St. Louis)	Monsanto Co.	5	Biomedical areas
University of North Carolina (Chapel Hill)	Glaxo Inc.	5	Numerous

[a] Various options for extensions are included in some agreements.

by academicians and others with novel ideas. For example, after Burroughs Wellcome Co. introduced some antiviral drugs, a number of individuals and groups began to approach the company with novel ideas relating to antiviral products. Even when a newly marketed product does not generate large sales revenue it may establish a company's reputation in a therapeutic area that will attract new ideas with greater commercial potential.

Conducting Research in Academic Institutions

The ability of most companies to conduct all relevant research activities "in-house" is often limited by space and resources (both skilled manpower and specialized equipment) rather than financial resources. Collaboration offers the potential for a company to expand its capabilities on a temporary basis to answer specific questions or to probe specific targets. Collaboration with academicians also allows a company to pursue research in areas where (1) it may supplement its strengths, (2) it is weak, or (3) it is not currently active.

Companies sometimes invest or donate large sums of money to help finance an institution, medical department, or scientific group. Benefits desired by the company are usually defined in terms of services and outputs (e.g., compounds, licensing rights) resulting from the institution's scientists. Numerous opportunities exist for valuable collaboration between companies and outside scientists, institutes, and other groups.

Several different types of relationships exist for research activities conducted in academic institutions.

1. Contract research performed by academicians for a drug company.
2. Research where a company has the right of first refusal for licensing any outputs with commercial value.
3. Research sponsored by a company without the academicians having any special obligations.
4. Research conducted by academicians with a drug supplied by a company.
5. Research conducted by drug company personnel who also have an academic appointment.
6. Research conducted jointly by academicians and drug company personnel.

LEVELS WITHIN DRUG INDUSTRY AND ACADEMIA THAT MAY DIRECTLY INTERACT

Drug Company	Academia
Multi-Company Level	**Non-University Level**
•Trade Associations •Foundations •Professional Societies •Other Groups	•Associations •Foundations •Professional Societies
Corporate Level	**University Level**
•Philanthropic Group	•Entire University •Medical School •Research Institute •Pharmacy School •School of Public Health
R&D Level	**Department Level**
•R&D as a Whole •R&D Department •R&D Section •R&D Project	•Entire Department •Division of a Department •Section of a Department
Scientist Level	**Scientist Level**
•Single Scientist •Single Laboratory •Group of Scientists •Single Project	•Single Scientist •Single Laboratory •Group of Scientists •Single Project

Fig. 24.1. Levels within the drug industry and academia that may directly interact.

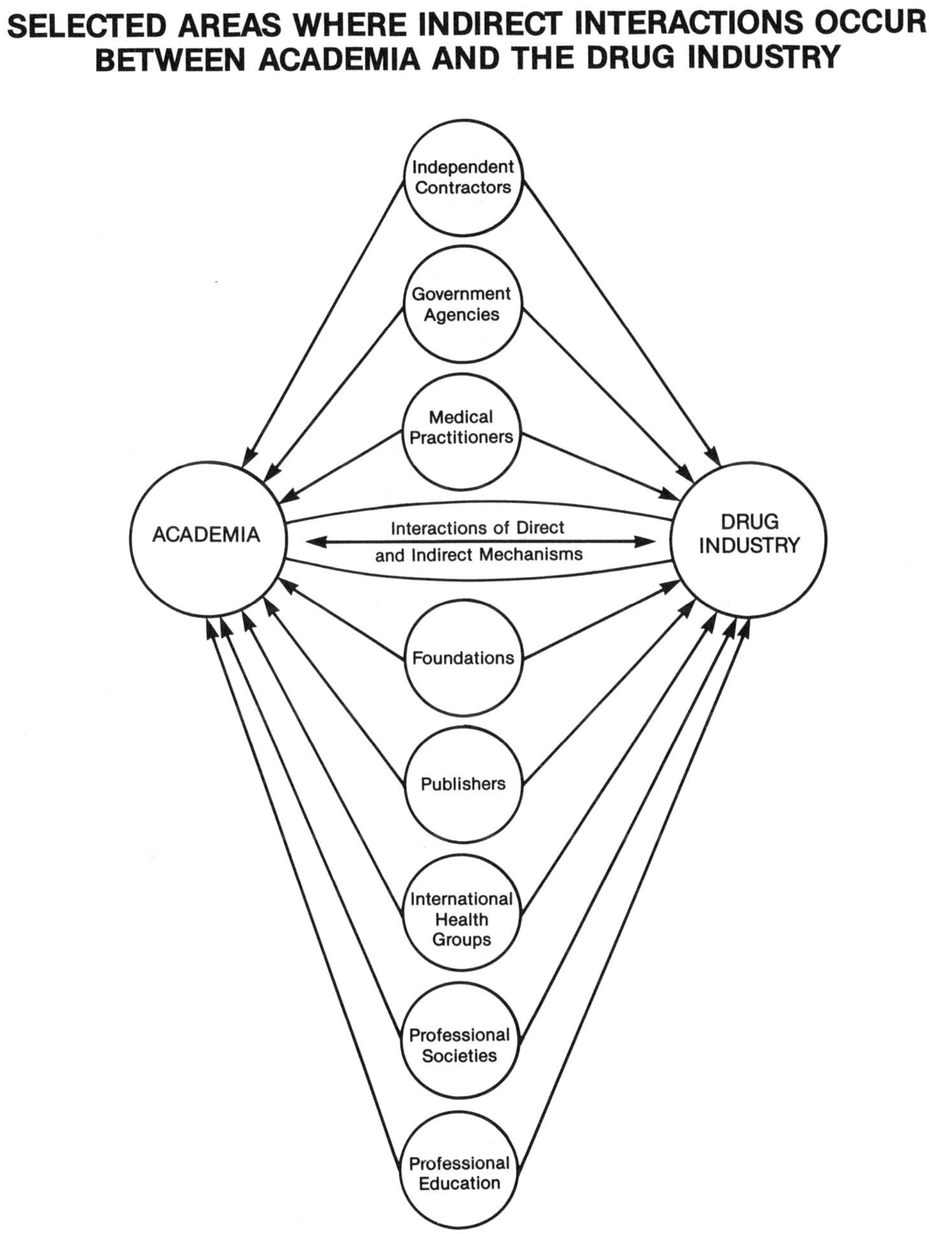

Fig. 24.2. Selected areas where indirect interactions occur between academia and the drug industry. R&D, research and development.

These relationships, as others in this chapter, may be initiated either by the academic or pharmaceutical institution. If the academic group seeks to contact a drug company, they may contact individual scientists, research and development executives, a licensing group, or a new products group in marketing. Industry people may contact comparable people in an academic institution to initiate one of the above relationships.

Conducting Research in a Drug Company

Drug companies can biologically test compounds synthesized by outside (i.e., academic) scientists, who are given funds to support their work. Companies also conduct research jointly with academicians. This is often the result of an academician approaching the company with a novel idea.

Interactions That Maintain and Enhance Professional Status

Industry scientists are sometimes encouraged to participate *directly* in the activities of academia: in teaching, research, advisory committees, and/or patient care. *Indirectly*, they may participate through various types of collaborations, memberships in medical and scientific organizations, and/or attendance at professional meetings. These activities help keep industry scientists informed about advances in their field, maintain their prestige and credibility within academia, open doors that otherwise might remain closed, and provide valuable stimulation to the individuals who participate. Some of these individuals are recognized for their participation through academic faculty appointments.

Clinical Evaluation of Investigational and Marketed Drugs

Most of the clinical studies that companies sponsor to evaluate drug safety and efficacy are conducted in academic institutions or at centers associated with an academic institution. Close relationships with investigators, potential investigators, and other academicians are important for the most effective and efficient conduct of these studies.

Sabbatical Periods

The exchange of sabbatical and postdoctoral personnel, plus fellowship programs, represents a mechanism used by some drug companies whereby new techniques and skills may be obtained from academic sources. These methods are believed to be a cost-effective means to obtain and provide stimulation to the individuals and laboratories involved. Industry provides these academicians with opportunities to participate in drug discovery or development in ways that would otherwise be unavailable.

Consultations

Academicians who are recognized experts in a given area are often asked to provide advice to drug companies on either a specific or general issue. Some consultants are hired with an annual retainer, whereas others are paid on a per day (or per hour) basis. The exact nature of these relationships are highly variable, even within a single company. Various issues relating to consultants are discussed in Chapter 4.

Philanthropic Activities

Many drug companies (e.g., Burroughs Wellcome Co., Glaxo Inc., Merck & Co., Inc.) provide unrestricted money to carefully selected academic investigators to pursue their own research in various fields. Moneys are also given to support (1) travel for professional purposes, (2) attendance at meetings, (3) visiting professorships, and (4) other professional activities. A number of philanthropic foundations within the drug industry are listed in Chapter 29.

Industry-Sponsored Symposia

Symposia sponsored by drug companies are often held in conjunction with medical schools. These may either be part of established clinical or scientific meetings or may be presented as separate stand-alone symposia. The theme is usually centered on a single drug or disease if one company sponsors the symposium. Many symposia are sponsored by multiple drug companies. The information may be published in the medical literature, or printed as a promotional brochure by the company.

Industry Establishment of a Clinical Unit in an Academic Environment

There are several cases in which this has been done. For example, Merck & Co., Inc. established a unit in Thomas Jefferson Hospital in Philadelphia. In some situations the company provides staff to the drug evaluation unit and expects that unit to evaluate primarily the company's drugs. This was done by The Upjohn Company at their own site. In other cases the only obligation of the unit is to submit a bid on certain protocols and offer the company a specified discount if the company decides to conduct the study there. This was the original basis of the relationship between Pfizer Inc. and the University of Miami Medical School.

Industry Use of Hospital Data Bases

This occurs primarily in certain Health Maintenance Organizations (HMOs) and other groups such as the Boston Collaborative Drug Surveillance Program. The data base has the ability for making certain linkages of records. For example, records may be linked between patients, medical history of diseases, drugs prescribed, and adverse reactions. It may be used to investigate drug use and adverse reactions in Phase IV postmarketing surveillance studies.

GUIDELINES FOR INTERACTIONS

More and more individuals and organizations in academia, government, and industry are calling for increased interactions and cooperative efforts between universities and industry (Cuatrecasas, 1984; Bloch 1986). Successful collaborations usually involve the freedom for academicians to publish the results of their activities. The company must insure that they have either patented the results of the collaboration or have the right to license any patents obtained. Depending on the specific circumstances, the patent may be shared or assigned to the academicians with licensing rights given to the drug company.

Conditions and terms of the relationship should be clearly specified. This includes a detailed account of the amount and nature of inputs to be applied by each partner and the nature and timing of agreed-on outputs. Potential problems should be anticipated and discussed thoroughly. A series of ten guidelines for successful university-industry ties was published relating to industry-sponsored research conducted at universities (Varrin and Kukich, 1985). Interested readers are referred to this article for details on these guidelines, which were prepared from an academic perspective:

1. Publication rights should be retained by university scientists.
2. Ownership of all patents should be retained by university scientists.
3. Copyright policies should be established for software developed.
4. The use of proprietary information in research should be minimized. Do not require graduate students to sign confidentiality agreements.
5. Research units with faculty and students should be created. Hire full-time researchers to staff such units if necessary.
6. Faculty should not be permitted to consult with sponsors in the sponsored research area. This guideline is intended to prevent conflicts of interest that may arise if a faculty member provides information to a drug company as a consultant and is then asked to develop the program through the company's agreement with the university. Patent rights are one example where a major issue could result from this type of situation.
7. An academic faculty member who is an entrepreneur and owns a company should not be permitted to sponsor his or her company's research on campus.
8. International agreements must be viewed with caution.
9. Personnel and equipment should be shared with industry in a mutually agreed-on manner.
10. A model research agreement for potential industrial sponsors should be prepared by each university.

Other types of guidelines relate to the attitudes, expectations, and atmosphere in which an agreement is reached. In general, these are the same guidelines that pertain to any major agreement.

1. The agreement must (or should) represent a true partnership. Each partner must respect the other and not harbor suspicions. Each should be desirous and willing to work to build the relationship in a positive and mutually rewarding manner.
2. The needs and expectations of each partner must be clearly expressed at the outset.

3. A scientific review and appeals committee should be established to confirm that the contract is being met. This group may arbitrate conflicts or other problems. It should be composed of members of each institution involved, plus some independent scientists who are well respected and are well known.
4. Each partner must identify the key contacts and representatives. These contacts must insure that active and full communications occur between relevant people and groups.

A few more guidelines that may be considered include (1) all manuscripts relating to the project must be sent to the sponsor 30 days before submission for publication, while the company reviews them to insure that patent protection is not compromised, (2) a guarantee may be given that patent rights will be held within the academic institution, but the company will have exclusive rights to license any patents emanating from the sponsored research, and (3) involvement of younger as well as established scientists will be guaranteed.

Some of the experiences of both academic and industry groups have been published. Lessons learned by the Wisconsin Alumni Research Foundation (WARF) regarding the commercialization of university research were recently presented (Blumenthal et al., 1986). WARF is an independent foundation started in 1925 that administers patents and discoveries of University of Wisconsin faculty. Experiences with academic collaborations from a specific company's perspective (Pfizer Inc.) are described by Price (1985).

ISSUES AND APPROACHES

Large-Scale Relationships

There have been several well-publicized large-scale relationships between major drug companies and well-respected universities. These include the specific relationships shown in Table 24.2. Some issues that are discussed about these relationships include the following:

1. Is academic freedom compromised in an unacceptable manner when scientists can not discuss their research as freely as before?
2. Are the topics being evaluated worthy of research by academic scientists?
3. Are there graduate students who are unable to publish their research findings? If so, how is this issue being addressed?

There are several reasons to challenge the implication that an academic group must make significant compromises in either professional standards or ethics through collaboration with a drug company. Each situation must be evaluated on its own, because the goals established and agreements reached will differ. A number of issues specifically oriented to relationships in the field of biotechnology are described by Blumenthal et al. (1986).

Other Issues

A few other aspects and issues of the academic-industrial relationship are briefly described.

Educating Graduate Students about Career Opportunities Outside Academia

Scientific and clinical departments in academic institutions often do not sufficiently educate the students they train about nonacademic careers. This aspect appears to have been overlooked in the education of most graduate students. A more complete education of graduate students would be provided if major types of possible career opportunities were presented. It would also be valuable if opportunities for visits or even extended rotations of two to four months were made available for students to explore their interest in nonacademic areas. These areas include the drug industry, government laboratories, government regulatory agencies, publishing activities, professional consulting companies, professional societies, foundations, and private businesses.

Contract Services

Relationships between industry and academia vary widely in the amount of collaboration and interaction required. For example, a company may purchase a service from an academic group. In this situation academicians are hired to conduct work without providing any input into its design or specifications. There are numerous occasions when this strictly contractual relationship may be beneficial to both parties. For example, academic chemists may be asked to synthesize certain molecules or pharmacologists may be asked to test certain compounds for money that the scientists use to pay salaries or otherwise support their research.

Patent Issues

Patent issues between companies and academic groups range from the extremely complex to the straightforward. Most academic scientists work under institutional patent policies that require them to turn any patents over to the university. The university in turn negotiates with drug companies to license patent rights.

Duration of Industry-Academic Relationships

The duration of industry-academic relationships vary. Many do not last beyond the time it takes for the work specified in the contract to be completed. In other situations, long-term collaborative relationships seem to offer benefits to both parties (see Table 24.2).

Providing Drug Samples to Academicians

Companies must determine at what point during a drug's development it is appropriate to provide small samples of a new investigational drug to academicians who request them for animal research. If samples are supplied too early in a drug's development then the company's overall program may be vulnerable to premature publication of unreproduced results, and the company's own scientists may have insufficient opportunity to publish their own results on similar research investigations. If the company waits too long before making drug samples available, then academic scientists may become annoyed or angry, synthesize the drug themselves, or lose interest in the company's drug. There is often a gradual loosening of company policy in supplying outside scientists with drug samples during Phases II and III. It is in the company's interests to stimulate scientific publications during the late premarketing period. Companies must exercise caution that investigators who are given samples will not attempt to obtain use patents in potentially important areas the company has not yet researched. This should be handled through the agreement between company and academician that is completed prior to supplying the drug sample.

25 / *Interactions and Relationships Between Drug Companies and Government Agencies*

> *There must be a point beyond which, for example, pre-clinical toxicity or clinical trial requirements become stifling and excessively inhibitory, with a resultant lag in new drug development. If the only sure way to avoid criticism for having allowed on the market a drug that later turns out to be unpleasantly toxic is to reject all new drug applications, it is also the way to insure that no new effective drugs are delivered to the public.* Dr. Louis Lasagna, clinical pharmacologist. From *Psychopharmacology Bull.* (8: 43, 1972).

GOVERNMENT AGENCIES THAT INTERACT WITH THE DRUG INDUSTRY

Interactions between drug companies and the government occur on multiple levels. The major levels discussed are where either the company as a whole or the research and development part of the company interacts with a government agency. This discussion will be almost entirely limited to interactions within the United States. Some fundamental differences exist between the types of interactions that occur in other countries. Governments influence drug companies through laws and regulations regarding drug development, marketing, production, plus drug approval. In addition, regulations influence the physical environment inside the company's facilities. Employees of the company plus patients using the company's drugs are also influenced by many government regulations.

Drug companies interact with many federal, state, and local government agencies and offices. The general influence of government on drug research is described by Stuyt (1983). Some of the most pertinent federal agencies in the United States that affect drug companies and a few types of interactions are listed.

Food and Drug Administration

The Food and Drug Administration (FDA) is undoubtedly the single most important government agency interacting with drug companies. The FDA not only must approve all new drugs before marketing, but it also approves all supplemental applications for changes in New Drug Applications (NDAs), monitors prescription drug advertisements and promotions, and has the authority to remove drugs from the market. It also has broad authority over food substances, cosmetics, medical devices, radiological health materials, and veterinary products.

United States Patent and Trademark Office

The Patent and Trademark Office reviews and approves three types of patents. They are (in decreasing order of commercial value) (1) compound patent (i.e., overall patent), (2) use of a compound for a specific purpose (i.e., "use" patent), and (3) procedural methods of manufacture (i.e., process patent).

Department of Agriculture

The Department of Agriculture (DOA) must approve the importation of biological products into the United States. Products from countries with certain diseases (e.g., hoof and mouth disease) may be quarantined for a period of time.

Federal Trade Commission

The Federal Trade Commission (FTC) monitors and reviews advertisements for over-the-counter drugs and reviews the advertising and promotion practices of a wide variety of consumer products.

Environmental Protection Agency

The Environmental Protection Agency (EPA) monitors materials and the environment involved in manufacturing processes and the waste products produced. These must meet certain rigid standards to protect the health and welfare of employees and the public.

Occupational Safety and Health Administration

The Occupational Safety and Health Administration (OSHA) monitors workplace practices for their impact on the safety and health of employees. There is some overlap with the authority of the EPA.

National Institutes of Health

The National Institutes of Health (NIH) frequently interacts with research and development-based companies to collaborate in joint development of drugs (e.g., epilepsy drugs in conjunction with the National Institute of Neurological and Communicable Diseases and Stroke [White, 1985], anticancer drugs in conjunction with the National Cancer Institute [Schepartz, 1985]). The NIH is primarily concerned in their collaborations with drug companies with conducting large (or small) clinical studies. They are not generally concerned with the development of a new drug.

Drug Enforcement Agency

The Drug Enforcement Agency (DEA) monitors the use of scheduled drugs in production and in research. Scheduled drugs include drugs of potential or actual abuse. DEA tracks all scheduled substances that come into the company (as raw products or drugs to be made into combination products) and also all scheduled drugs that leave the company as finished goods. The DEA occasionally audits the company's records of scheduled drugs and inspects their facilities.

United States Post Office

The United States Post Office (USPO) interacts with drug companies on mail-related issues (e.g., may certain drugs be shipped via the mail service). It also interacts with the FDA and numerous other government agencies on drug issues. The USPO monitors and reviews fraudulent practices that use the mail system for promoting drugs, devices, or substances that impact on the public's health and welfare.

Other agencies that interact with drug companies include: United States Customs, Department of Treasury, Nuclear Regulatory Commission, Consumer Products Safety Council, and the Equal Employment Opportunity (EEO) in the Department of Labor. Nongovernment organizations whose findings and recommendations are accepted by the government include the United States Adopted Names Council (see

Chapter 21) and the *United States Pharmacopeia* which is discussed in several chapters.

REGULATORY ISSUES

Decision Making on Regulatory Issues by Drug Company Personnel

In some companies the regulatory personnel are able to make professional scientific and medical judgments on issues that arise at regulatory agencies. At others, almost all issues must be referred back to appropriate personnel at the home office for input and decision making except for the most mundane topics. The type of training and regulatory experience of personnel in a company's regulatory group varies widely throughout the drug industry. Some heads of regulatory departments are physicians and others are scientists, with or without advanced degrees. A few heads are nonscientists with business, legal, or marketing backgrounds.

There is an enormous level of frustration that is usually experienced by most drug companies in trying to have their regulatory applications reviewed promptly. The single most important method to expedite review is to prepare a well-organized application that interprets data fairly, does not attempt to hide any problems, and leads the reviewer in a logical sequence through the application. It is not only useful, but almost mandatory to have qualified individuals at a company (who are *not* closely involved with the drug) read the application for clarity and logic before it is submitted.

Regulatory Gossip

Virtually all companies have groups and individuals who carefully consider and scrutinize every third- or fourth-hand comment from even junior personnel at a regulatory agency and comments made at meetings, in the press, or at advisory committee reviews. The company's managers look for grains of ideas that may help speed regulatory submissions. Comments made in hallways at federal facilities are sometimes raised to the rank of a Delphic Oracle and can influence decisions about company strategies to help move an application along the regulatory path toward approval. It is often difficult for companies to evaluate the validity of "signals" the FDA is sending or whether in fact any signals are being sent. This process is reminiscent of the rites of slaughtering chickens and examining their entrails as a means of predicting the future.

Regulatory Strategies: Comments and Selected Examples

Overall Regulatory Strategies

In the era before 1962 (i.e., the year of passage of the Kefauver-Harris amendments) the FDA responded rapidly to NDAs. It was usually unnecessary during that period for drug companies to develop a detailed regulatory strategy. A number of studies were conducted and all materials were written up in a short time and submitted as an NDA. In recent decades, however, it has become increasingly important for companies to develop various strategies to expedite (hopefully) progress of their NDA through the agency system and to minimize delays.

Numerous strategies must be developed. The overall strategy is whether or not to have a close or distant relationship during the investigational period. Some companies try to make the FDA a partner in the drug's development (e.g., Merck & Co., Inc. with Mevacor, Burroughs Wellcome Co. with Retrovir). Other companies try to keep a distant relationship with the FDA throughout their negotiations. In addition to this overall strategy, companies develop many other regulatory strategies related to the specific drug being developed.

Specific Regulatory Strategies on a New Drug

When actively developing several indications, dosage forms, and routes of administration for a specific drug, a company must make a number of careful decisions regarding its regulatory strategy. For example, an important decision could be whether to submit a single package of regulatory submissions for related or semi-related indications or to submit a series of individual applications. If the latter approach is adopted, is it better to wait for the initial application to be approved before the second one is submitted or to submit two or more at the same time? The appropriate response to these questions involves the company second-guessing the regulatory agency, often never knowing if they made the best decision.

The regulatory agency may react in many ways to any of these approaches, but the major issue is whether multiple applications on a single drug will be reviewed simultaneously or sequentially. If it can be determined that the review will be simultaneous (or sequential) then this will affect the company's decision of how to submit the applications.

Early discussions with FDA reviewers may help a company develop the most appropriate strategy, although these discussions may not necessarily lead to the fastest approval of their application. With limited resources and huge backlogs of applications, the FDA develops its response based on work load, complexity of the application, and other departmental priorities. A recent publication (Spivey et al., 1987) has documented what many companies have known for many years: It usually takes the FDA as long or longer to approve a supplemental NDA for a new indication than it does the original NDA.

There are sometimes different mechanisms that may be used to file a regulatory application (e.g., either an NDA or Abbreviated New Drug Application [ANDA] may be filed, the NDA may be filed with Division A or B at the regulatory agency, the format may follow guidelines A or B). Many issues arise and the company's response in a particular situation must be governed by anticipated problems to be encountered with each route, and the work load of the different regulatory groups who could receive the application.

Companies desire to minimize their work in preparing detailed and voluminous regulatory dossiers. A typical flow of dossiers between different subsidiaries of the same company is shown in Fig. 25.1.

Responding to FDA Questions

When a letter comes from regulatory authorities, the level of a company's response (e.g., letter, reanalysis, new study) must be determined. A team is often assigned

FLOW OF REGULATORY DOSSIERS BETWEEN COUNTRIES

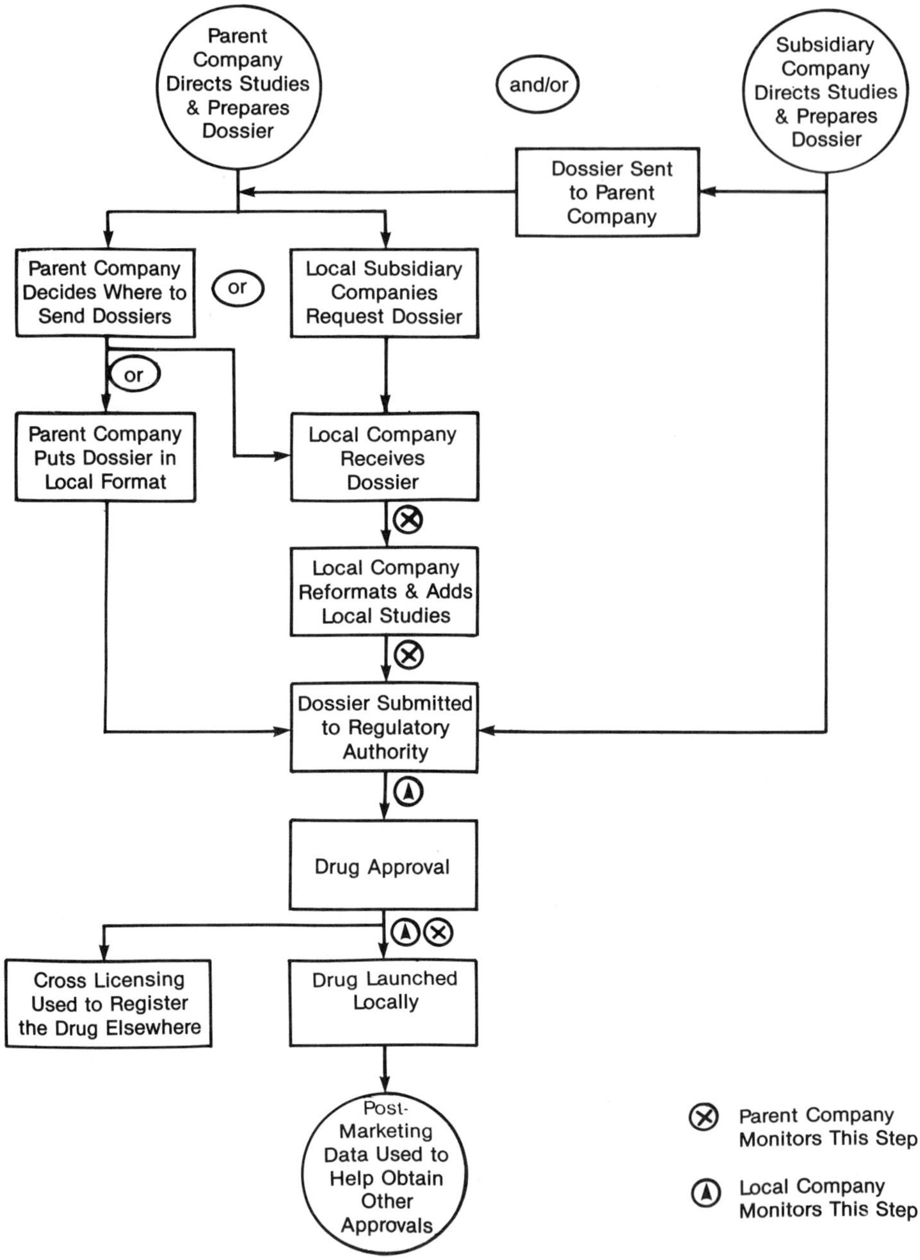

Fig. 25.1. Flow of regulatory dossiers between countries.

the task of completing the company's response. It is possible to respond to a complex or multipart regulatory letter in pieces and not wait until the entire answer is prepared. For example, if a letter contains both chemical and clinical questions, all chemical questions may be answered at one time and all clinical questions may be addressed later. The key point for a company is to be responsive to the FDA's inquiry and prompt in answering.

Electronic Drug Submissions

Some regulatory authorities believe that their reviewing function would be easier if they could tap the company's data base. Companies could allow this to occur if they desire by submitting an electronic or computer-generated NDA submission. Although an electronic submission superficially sounds appealing to many people, it is widely believed both in industry and at the FDA that it would not generally speed up the approval process of new drugs. Also, many reviewers are currently not adequately computer literate. From a company's perspective, this practice would provide complete data on a drug to the agency in an easy to use form and would allow the agency almost unlimited access to reprocess the data and analyze it in any way they desired. This could easily place the company in a highly defensive and untenable position of having to react to regulatory statements regarding analyses the agency performs. Although many, if not most, of these analyses are theoretically possible for an agency to conduct with the hard copy data they currently receive, it is not commonly done by the FDA today. Rather, they send requests to a company for additional analyses. If the company believes a request for additional analyses is unreasonable or inappropriate, they may challenge it. It is far easier for a company to do this prospectively than to attempt to respond to an analysis already completed by a regulatory agency.

Another issue regarding electronic submissions is that a regulatory agency only has one computer system and drug companies have many varieties. Thus, the electronic data of most, if not all, drug companies must be converted to a new format so that they may be compatible with the computers at the regulatory authority. This often takes a great deal of time and effort. Moreover, if electronic data from one company for a single drug were to be sent to multiple agencies, it is likely that multiple conversions of the data would have to be made.

Finally, there are many technical issues that must be addressed. These include such questions as how will it be confirmed that what the company sends the regulatory authority is the identical information package the regulatory authority receives. These brief comments are intended to illustrate that the electronic submission of data is not a panacea or a rapid route to quick regulatory approval of new drugs. Rather, it raises many complex and vital questions for a company to consider in addition to technical issues.

Although a few applications have been submitted by electronic means (and at least one approved), the FDA has made no definitive statement on the process to date. It continues to look for opportunities to evaluate the system more thoroughly and has requested companies to submit applications in this way only after consultation with them.

Are Clinical Trials and Regulatory Applications Receiving Due Process?

This book uses the term clinical study rather than clinical trial because of the operational definitions presented in *Guide to Clinical Studies and Developing Protocols* (Spilker, 1984). Clinical trials were defined as a subtype of clinical studies that deal with evaluations of investigational drugs or are performed with the purpose of being included in a regulatory submission. Clinical studies include all evaluations and research, whether on an investigational or marketed drug (or device).

The term clinical trial raises the question of whether there is an analogy with a legal trial. In a clinical trial it is usually a drug that is being tried rather than an individual or company. Drugs evaluated in clinical trials that use an inadequate study design are not receiving a fair trial.

When applications for a new drug at any government regulatory agency are not evaluated according to current scientific and medical standards, but are influenced by various political considerations, then the drug is not receiving due process. When a government's regulatory agency freely modifies its standards of acceptability for a new drug application, not in an open forum, but according to the whim of individuals within that agency, then the drug is again not receiving due process. Even when an agreement on any issue is reached with the FDA during a drug's development, it is not a binding agreement and may be modified by the agency at any time. The practice is sometimes referred to as the company's ''trying to hit a moving target''.

Many United States drug executives yearn for at least certain aspects of the British System for drug approval. In some situations The Committee on Safety of Medicines (CSM) informs a company by a Section 21 letter that the CSM is thinking of recommending to the licensing authority to grant a license under certain conditions. This letter outlines the deficiencies of the submission and indicates what additional studies, data, analyses, and other work must be done and submitted before the CSM is able to recommend regulatory approval. The company may then direct its activities toward gathering the necessary data. It should be noted that Section 21 letters may also indicate to a company that the CSM is not going to recommend approval of the drug for reasons that are enumerated.

INCREASING THE SPEED OF REGULATORY APPROVAL

The major regulatory issue within the drug industry today is how may a company speed up the regulatory evaluation of their applications? A drug that has an anticipated annual market of 100 million dollars loses by some estimates over a million dollars in potential sales for every four days of its reviewing period. Even small delays become matters of great concern and result in large losses of potential revenue. Under the present system the FDA can always find reasons to delay an application for years at a time.

On the other hand, too few drug company executives put themselves in the position of FDA reviewers and try to critique their NDA prior to submission as outside reviewers would view it. Some companies also take extraordinary amounts of time to answer FDA inquiries. This adds to the total review time and is sometimes blamed on the FDA. Merck & Co., Inc. reportedly practiced their presentation on lovastatin for hundreds of hours before going to the FDA's advisory committee for the presentation (Byrne, 1987). That was wise and appropriate. The primary principle that should govern the regulatory submission, review, and approval process is for both a drug company and the FDA to use medical and scientific reasonableness.

Preparing for Meetings with the FDA

Asking to meet with the FDA or other regulatory agencies to discuss drug development issues without a clear understanding of one's position invites problems. The agency may make almost any request, even based on casual spur of the moment comments or considerations. These offhand or even carefully considered comments may impact directly on the company's development program for many years. If the company has no previous experience in a specific therapeutic area or with a specific disease, then it is worthwhile and important for them to contact leading academic experts and also potential investigators to create a drug development plan prior to meeting the FDA. This plan should be tailored both to the specific drug and to the particular company's requirements.

Thus, an inexperienced company doing research in a specific therapeutic area could rapidly learn the pros and cons of different regulatory approaches from outside consultants and experts prior to requesting meetings with government authorities. The company could invite relevant consultants to these regulatory meetings to provide expertise not available within the company or at the agency. These consultants could help educate the regulators (if necessary) and explain the rationale for the company's suggested development plan. These consultants would also assist the company in responding to questions, criticisms, and other comments from the regulatory authorities. The stature of important and well-respected consultants could be invaluable in helping a company convince regulatory authorities about particular aspects of the proposed or ongoing development plan submitted for a particular drug.

It is essential that company scientists not embarrass the FDA and especially not draw attention of the United States Congress. It is said by some government "insiders" that the greatest mistake a company could make is to get the FDA and a Congressional subcommittee involved in an individual company's problems. A recent example involved Viratek Inc. and its studies submitted for a drug used for treatment of Acquired Immune Deficiency Syndrome (AIDS).

Major Reasons for Delays in Drug Approval Relating to Factors under a Company's Control or Influence

Some of the reasons for delays in drug approval relate to those primarily under control of the regulatory authority (see next section) and others are under the control (to a greater or lesser degree) of a drug company. A few of the reasons for delays in drug approval that can be influenced or controlled by a drug company are given below. Appropriate attention to each point enhances the probability that the application will be reviewed rapidly.

1. *The submission is a poorly organized document that is not clear to the reviewers* If the scientific and medical rationale for clinical or other studies are not clear to FDA reviewers, or if the material is not presented in a logical order, some

reviewers will cease reviewing the submission (and thereby delay the application) rather than immediately asking the sponsor for clarifications. Sponsors must keep in touch with the FDA to follow the status of their applications and to develop an appropriate rapport with the reviewers assigned.

2. *The clinical studies conducted were poorly designed* Not only should individual clinical studies be well designed, but the overall clinical program should also create a clear picture of what was done and why each study was conducted.

3. *One or more important clinical studies were not conducted* If a drug is eliminated from the body by the kidneys, it is important to evaluate how patients with poor kidney function will handle the drug. If a drug will be given in conjunction with another drug in clinical practice, it is important to determine the extent and nature of any interactions.

4. *Clinical studies were conducted poorly* This point is self-explanatory.

5. *Data were poorly or inappropriately analyzed* This point is self-explanatory.

6. *The submission appears to bury or inadequately discuss problems* Reviewers who detect major deficiencies or problems that they believe are purposely buried in an application may become frustrated and angry and delay progress of the application. Actual or potential problems should be dealt with openly and honestly by the sponsor and the company's perspective presented. Major problems with the drug should be discussed in pre-NDA meetings so that the FDA's perspective is obtained. This information should help the company present the problem in the most appropriate manner possible.

When drug-related issues are raised by preclinical, clinical, or technical development scientists, it is important that all three groups should comment on the implications, if any, for the drug. This also provides the regulatory authority with some assurance that the NDA or Product License Application (PLA) document is a whole and not three separate documents written by people who do not communicate with each other.

7. *Developing a "me-too" product with little clinical benefit above presently available therapy* The FDA takes a long time (i.e., many years) to review an application for a drug that they consider of little therapeutic importance.

8. *Submitting additional data to a regulatory authority after an NDA or PLA application is submitted* Some companies submit additional (unsolicited) data several times to the FDA. This is naturally annoying to any regulatory agency, which is attempting to review the specific set of data that were originally submitted.

9. *Submitting a large amount of "dirty or noisy" data in an application* The more that these kinds of data are included in the application, the slower will be the review. If the pivotal studies (i.e., generally the most well-controlled clinical studies) are not "clean," then the delays are almost certain to be long ones. One exception would be if only case studies were submitted for certain orphan drugs or drugs for previously untreatable conditions. There is no guarantee, however, that case studies are acceptable on their own, without a controlled study, to have such a drug approved. For example, ganciclovir was rejected by the FDA's advisory committee because of a lack of controlled studies. Nonetheless, many case reports demonstrated that ganciclovir saved the eyes of many patients with cytomegalovirus infections who could not be treated effectively before this drug.

10. *Submitting an NDA or PLA prematurely so that the drug may join the queue for review at the agency* Regulatory authorities strongly dislike obviously inade-

quate submissions that are prematurely submitted. A company that utilizes this technique usually does so in the hope of obtaining a shopping list of inadequacies to address. When they receive this list they will presumably have completed the studies in the meantime and can therefore obtain a rapid approval of their drug. This practice holds up the review, however, of more complete applications. There is no method at present to deal with this issue in an expeditious manner.

11. *Requesting approval for too many indications* This approach will delay the entire submission in most instances, because the data supporting each indication are judged on their own.

12. *Using inexperienced regulatory personnel* Company staff who do not follow written and unwritten procedures of dealing with FDA personnel may readily delay the company's applications. For example, labeling conferences vary from "rug-dealing" give-and take negotiations to situations where fixed class labels are required to situations where the FDA adopts inflexible positions. The relevant pattern for a particular situation depends on the specific drug (e.g., are 10 other similar drugs available, how strong are the data, how safe is the drug) and the personalities of the negotiators. People who are not aware of, and sensitive to, various situations and subtle personality signs may not achieve the best results possible for their submission.

Some companies believe so strongly in their drugs that they forget that the data must be able to convince others, who review the data with a critical perspective. If the media has praised the drug prior to submitting an NDA, it often substantiates the opinion of many people in the company about the drug's value. There is a potential danger that the company may not present the data as well or as convincingly as possible. In assembling each NDA, a company should think of the FDA's "motto" as "In God we trust, from all others we need data."

Major Reasons for Delays in Drug Approval Relating to a Regulatory Agency

Additional Levels of Sign-Off

The major reason for regulatory delays in the United States probably relates to the two additional levels of sign-off for an NDA after it has been fully evaluated and approved by the medical, chemical, pharmacological, statistical, and pharmacokinetic reviewers at the FDA. The first additional level is the director of the division (e.g., Cardio-Renal, Oncology, Surgical Dental, Infectious Disease) in which the NDA was reviewed. This individual must review and approve all applications that have been reviewed and approved by his or her staff. The second level is by the person who supervises all division directors or is delegated by this person to conduct the review. All of these people are under intense public scrutiny and potentially strong political pressures, whether they approve or disapprove a specific drug. They understand that they may be asked by members of Congress to justify thoroughly their decision in formal meetings. As a result, these regulatory executives appear to demand almost every study or datum that may potentially be required for their defense before they are willing to approve a new drug.

Another reason why the two additional levels of sign-off is inefficient relates to the work load of reviewers at the agency. Reviewers have a heavy work load. Each division head must review all of the applications in his or her division. This often represents more applications than is reasonable for a single individual to deal with. The person at the next most senior level, who is head of all divisions, is like a final funnel that new chemical entity (NCE) applications from all divisions must pass through. His or her work load is *a priori* unreasonable, because of the large number of applications and other responsibilities of their position.

Congressional Review of the Food and Drug Administration

There are certain periods when Congress examines the FDA in intense detail. These times usually relate to examinations of the FDA's effectiveness. Observers of this phenomenon comment that delays on approving new drugs become much longer during these periods. This occurs for several reasons. FDA executives are taken away from their work and have less time to review NDAs. These executives ask FDA reviewers to prepare documents and analyses for their testimony and to help them respond to questions. Thus, the reviewers too have less time to review NDAs. In addition, the FDA executives are less willing to approve (or disapprove) NDAs at a time when the FDA itself, its policies, and actions are being carefully scrutinized by Congress.

Specific Reasons for Regulatory Delay

There are many other reasons for regulatory delays that relate to the regulatory agency. These include the following.

1. Imprecise regulations that may be interpreted and thus acted on in many different ways.
2. High turnover rate of personnel who are reviewing applications. This problem relates in part to problems of pay, benefits, working conditions, and political maneuvering.
3. Problems in storage of applications. This relates to limitations in the facilities and also to regulations requiring storage of documents. NDAs have been reportedly stacked on the floor in reviewer's offices, sometimes in the path to the reviewer's desk.
4. Lack of qualified staff to handle the great (and growing) work load. The FDA's budget for increased resources is insufficient to conduct its assignment appropriately.
5. Bureaucratic "red tape" and regulations. This is self-explanatory.
6. Conservative approach favored by most reviewers. Financial rewards are few for reviewers who approve NDAs. Many fear government action if they appear to have been too lenient in their review, especially if the drug, once approved, causes a serious adverse reaction to patients.
7. Basic lack of trust in drug companies by some regulatory authorities. The adversarial relationship is unfortunate, but few people at the FDA appear to desire any change.
8. Low priority given NDA applications by most reviewers. They are required to assign a higher priority to assignments from or for Congress. Requests by other

government offices or agencies, Investigational New Drug Applications (INDs), and their supervisor's requests also often take precedence. They also must help write new guidelines and deal with postmarketing surveillance issues on approved drugs. It has been stated at public forums that reviewers spend an average of about 30 percent of their time reviewing NDAs.

Questions raised by the FDA on any NDA are primarily a function of the reviewers' personalities. Some questions will always be raised, so that the FDA may document its diligence if it is ever questioned on the subject. Many NDAs (usually approximately 300) are going through the agency at one time.

Priority of Applications at the FDA

The FDA rates the therapeutic value of new chemical entities. Those with a lower rating may be reviewed with a lower priority. There is little that a sponsor can do to increase this rating, apart from a direct appeal to the agency. The ratings are described in Chapter 21 of *Guide to Planning and Managing Multiple Clinical Studies* (Spilker, 1987c).

When an application has a low priority at the FDA (e.g., Class C NDA, supplemental NDA) it may sit untouched for up to four years before the review process starts. Then, as problems or questions arise, the company must *begin* to address them. If the company knew what the major deficiencies were ahead of time they could begin to address them at an earlier time. But, the FDA is unable to do this because of their shortage of reviewers. This is a difficult problem to solve except through using outside reviewers under contract or by hiring more reviewers at the FDA. Some areas of the FDA have more difficulty than others in hiring competent reviewers. Reviewers include pharmacologists, chemists, statisticians, pharmacokineticists, and clinicians.

Techniques for Drug Companies to Speed Approval of Their Regulatory Submissions

A few ideas are presented that are generally known and used (when relevant) by drug companies. Each situation must clearly be evaluated individually.

Experts from outside the company may review a summary of the regulatory application and write an opinion letter. Their letter should be a critical analysis of the data and not a summary. This might be especially useful for regulatory applications that are weak. For example, if the application primarily uses historical data as controls or utilizes data from compassionate plea studies, experts may express the degree to which the application contains substantial data and evidence that will convince physicians working in the same therapeutic area. The concept of what constitutes substantial evidence has been widely debated over the past few decades (Wardell and Lasagna, 1975). The experts would clearly only comment on the part of the application that they were most familiar with (e.g., clinical interpretation and importance, technical issues, social need).

It is wise to provide a desk copy of the relevant part(s) of the drug application for the reviewer's personal use. This will also allow the reviewer to mark it up freely.

This is advantageous because reviewers are not allowed to mark up the official NDA copy. Some reviewers at the FDA like to have personal interactions with company representatives to discuss the NDA, but others discourage such interactions. In situations where interactions are either acceptable or desired by the regulatory agency, it is critical to determine whether there should be a single person at the company who will act as the contact person. It is often desirable for one person to be appointed to fill this role. The person chosen should have a good rapport with the reviewer and be at the appropriate decision-making level within the company. Some companies prefer to deal with the FDA through legal and marketing representatives, whereas others prefer to have clinicians and scientists primarily involved.

Submitting clinical data on a new drug given at different doses is extremely important. If dose-response data are not submitted in an NDA there should be a good reason. There should also be an adequate number of patients who have received a drug prior to NDA submission. This aspect may be phrased in numerous ways. Some companies have reported that there are data on 3,000 patients in their NDA. But when the data are reviewed it may be shown that 1,000 patients received placebo, 500 received an active drug used as a control, and only 1,500 patients received the study drug. Of this latter number, a certain number were normal volunteers and a larger number received subtherapeutic doses and yet others did not receive a full course of therapy. Therefore, it is essential that an adequate number of patients receive adequate doses of a new drug before the regulatory dossier is submitted.

A few other recommendations that may help to speed approval of a regulatory submission are (1) hire ex-FDA employees as consultants, (2) do not go to Advisory Committee meetings with an arrogant attitude, (3) discuss the company's regulatory approach with the FDA at the earliest practical opportunity, (4) discuss issues with all relevant areas of the FDA (e.g., if the drug is a biological product then discuss issues with both the offices of drug research and biologics research), (5) do not change the formulation used in a major way during a later stage of clinical studies (if possible), (6) use only one name (generic) for a drug throughout the application, and (7) prepare reviewer-friendly types of documents that lead the reviewer step by step through the logic and the data in the application. When responding to questions from regulatory authorities, insure that you know what the reviewer is actually looking for in response to their question.

A principle believed by some companies is that taking an extra 6 to 12 months to assemble a first-class NDA will save regulatory review time and yield a more rapid approval overall. The counterargument is that submitting a less than ideal dossier to a regulatory agency allows a company to get into a queue for having its application reviewed and its deficiencies outlined.

Proposal to Speed Approval of New Drug Applications

One possible answer to the overall problem of expeditiously reviewing NDAs is to change the current system. A reasonable system would be for the FDA to appoint an independent group of experts in the therapeutic field where the drug is intended to work. This group would review the preclincial and clinical data of one (or multiple) NDA and in conjunction with other reviews of manufacturing data, arrive at a binding decision on the drug's approval. If the drug is not approved, then each of the reasons should be stated. A list of additional studies and/or data required for approval should also be given. Once that additional work is completed by the company (or other sponsor) the regulatory application (e.g., NDA) should be approved, unless of course the data suggested that the application should be turned down or significant new problems were uncovered. A similar system is operating, apparently well, in Canada, France, and Japan.

This system would avoid most of the major problems that exist with the current system. These problems are well known and will not be enumerated again. Many details of this type of system would have to be worked out prior to proposing any change through legislation. Whether this or another basic model is used to improve the review and approval of new drugs, it is hoped that a more efficient and rapid system will be implemented that will benefit patients, the public, and the pharmaceutical industry.

LEGISLATURES, LEGISLATION, AND LOBBYING ACTIVITIES

State Governments

There has been an increasing involvement between individual drug companies, as well as the Pharmaceutical Manufacturers Association (PMA), with state governments during the last decade. Many people attribute this to greater decentralization of government, promoted by the Reagan Administration. There has been a great deal of cooperation between individual companies in this area with almost none of the competition noted between the marketing groups of many companies. Selected issues are briefly described to illustrate some of the major types of issues faced.

Therapeutic Substitution Laws

A recent issue that is perceived as a threat by research-based drug companies and the medical profession, are the proposed therapeutic substitution laws. These laws would allow pharmacists to fill a patient's prescription with a different drug than the one prescribed, but one which the pharmacist judged to be therapeutically equivalent. Pharmacists claim that they are in a good position to make these decisions.

This practice has greater potential to affect drug company sales than even the generic substitution laws, which allow pharmacists to substitute a generic version of the *same* drug. If therapeutic substitution bills become law, physicians who want a patient to take a specific drug will not know whether the patient was given the prescribed drug or another that was judged by the pharmacist (i.e., a non-MD) to be therapeutically equivalent. The medical implications of this potential change are far-reaching for several reasons. First, are the obvious implications for patient care. In addition, doctors will be losing part of their decision making to pharmacists or committees that decide on acceptable drugs. On the other hand, many physicians want the right to dispense the drugs they prescribe. Pharmacists see this issue not only as an infringement of their turf and a threat to their livelihood, but also a conflict of interest for physicians. Both issues are highly complex and raise many questions.

Several states are considering legislation on therapeutic substitution, which is more recently being called therapeutic alternatives or therapeutic interchange. The drug companies have been swift to respond. The PMA has formed a task force in all states that can be rapidly mobilized to develop an organized approach when proposals are dealt with by legislative committees. This task force includes members of a number of research-based drug companies and uses the PMA as an umbrella organization. The task force plans their approach to include both direct and indirect lobbying efforts as described below.

Lobbying Activities at the State Level

In terms of direct lobbying, PMA assigns their members to visit different key legislators and their aides. In some situations the legislative aides are more important to lobby than are the legislators they support, because the aide is often responsible for developing policy. Direct lobbying is also conducted at various social events. This allows the lobbyist and legislator to meet in a more informal setting than in the state capital and also provides an occasion to develop a better understanding of each other's position and character. The relationship that develops usually improves the quality of subsequent interactions when the lobbyist meets the legislator at the capital building in a more formal environment. Spouses and aides of the legislators may also be invited to this type of social event. This aspect of lobbying is conducted to a different degree by various companies, depending on their budgets for this type of activity and their interest in direct lobbying activities.

In a few states it is often necessary for a drug company to hire specific people to manage their efforts in influencing a bill. This person may be a friend of a powerful legislator who is "suggested" for the role. In other situations it is necessary to "juice the machine" (e.g., contribute to a legislator's Political Action Committee [PAC]) to gain access to a key political leader and/or their aides. This practice is becoming more widespread on the federal level, where certain key Congressmen hold breakfast meetings for their major contributors (i.e., lobbyists) who wish to have an "audience" for discussions and to advise the Congressmen about their views.

Indirect lobbying efforts are conducted by company lobbyists going to consumer pressure groups (e.g., Medicaid recipients, American Association of Retired People), medical societies (e.g., state medical associations, American Medical Association), and disease-oriented groups (e.g., American Cancer Society, Arthritis Foundation) and encouraging them to become involved in lobbying efforts. Activities that these groups are encouraged to conduct include (1) organizing a letter-writing campaign, (2) actively supporting or criticizing certain legislation, (3) visiting the legislators, (possibly by the busload), (4) holding public demonstrations, and (5) testifying in front of legislative committees.

Initiating a grass roots campaign is often the most effective means for a drug company to influence legislation. Companies usually want the public to limit their activities to writing letters or participating in other carefully controlled activities. Companies do not want the public to initiate many different activities on their own initiative. Such activities are often disruptive and counterproductive to the specific goals of a company, which is usually either passage or blockage of specific legislation.

Organizing a Company's Lobbying Activities at the State Level

Companies organize their state lobbying efforts by either centralizing or decentralizing their group of lobbyists and support personnel. The advantages of centralizing this function include a greater ease of discussing issues as a group and also having access to all corporate amenities and staff support. Advantages of decentralization include being closer to the action at the state capitol. But, if the company's staff are based in only a few large cities, then they often have to take time-consuming airplane rides or long automobile trips to reach the appropriate state capitol. The size of a company's total staff working at the state level usually ranges from one to 15 people and is therefore insufficient to be based in each capital. Decentralization only makes sense when there is a large staff, or there is a certain person who the company wants to hire, but who insists on remaining in a specific locale.

Most states do not have any research-based drug companies and therefore do not view drug companies as important contributors to the tax base. Lobbyists who do not live in the state where they are lobbying on behalf of a drug company may have a carpetbagger image that they must dispel. To do this they must build a rapport with the legislators, which is primarily accomplished by serving as a reliable source of information. This is also done by attending fund raisers, inviting the legislator to speak to a health-oriented group or to a company sales meeting, contributing to the legislator's PAC, and inviting legislators to tour the company's manufacturing or research facilities. This latter activity will provide most legislators with a different perspective of the drug industry than the one popularly portrayed by the media. Other activities are to invite legislators to receptions or to a dinner where they may meet people of particular interest to them. Finally, the company may form an umbrella group within a state that acts as a conglomerate of health interest groups to coordinate activities of mutual interest and also to facilitate better access to legislators.

Most companies who have state legislative lobbyists have established some type of early warning system to pick up information to which the company must respond. This may be done through a network of contacts in each state who monitor what is going on within the state government. These monitors may or may not be asked to help with lobbying activities. The monitors learn about relevant information by (1) reading local newspapers, (2) listening to many people, (3) joining various associations (e.g., medical, pharmacy, health), and (4) becoming active in the legislative groups within these organizations. Information on early signs of legislation is especially important, because it is easier to block or modify legislation before it leaves a committee. Once legislation has been reported to the legislature floor, it is much more difficult to modify or influence.

Organizing a Company's Lobbying Activities at the Federal Level

Almost all companies draw a line between state and federal legislative activities. Some companies (e.g., Pfizer Inc., Glaxo Inc.) have their own full-time federal lobbyist who lives in Washington, DC. Other companies have someone based at their corporate headquarters who visits Washington as needed. One difference between state and federal activities is that fund raisers for federal legislators are usually held back at their state rather than at their political office (i.e., in Washington).

The types of bills and activities at the federal level usually differ from those at the state level. Federal activities such as patents, imports, and exports of drugs usually do not affect individual state legislators or lobbyists. In many situations, however, issues are dealt with at both the state and federal levels. When the federal government passes a law there is usually no need for state action. In some situations, however, a state may want to go further in their legislation than the federal law. Drug companies may then have to respond to additional legislation at the state level.

Drug Tampering

A specific example of the different levels of legislation arose a few years ago when capsules of some drugs were tampered with and a number of people were poisoned. Some counties in the United States decided to pass ordinances to help control this problem. Many states also had bills introduced to react to this problem. The federal government became involved and eventually passed a bill. This federal bill removed the need for 50 separate states to each have their own bill. Individual state bills had the potential to require drug manufacturers to produce and/or package their drugs in 50 (or more) different ways to insure their safety. The burden for the companies and confusion this would have created is enormous.

Lobbying efforts of drug companies on this issue were focused in two directions. First, companies told the states that the federal government was trying to pass a bill and suggested waiting for the federal government to act. Second, the companies worked cooperatively at the federal level to obtain the type of bill that they believed would be in the best interests of the general public and the industry.

26 / *Interactions and Relationships Between Drug Companies: Competition and Collaboration*

Successful collaborative negotiation lies in finding out what the other side really wants and showing them a way to get it, while you get what you want.
Herb Cohen, American writer. From *You Can Negotiate Anything*.

COMPETITION BETWEEN DRUG COMPANIES

Competition is a highly complex concept. Few issues concerning drug development invoke as much emotional reaction as the thought of competition. But competition is not an all-or-none issue. Competition usually does not exist on the basis of company A versus companies B, C, and D. Competition may be conceptualized on the basis that each product or investigational drug has its own spectrum of competitors. This spectrum ranges from no competition to fierce and intense competition. It is generally desirable, although usually impossible, for a company to have most of its products and investigational drugs in disease or therapeutic areas where there is little or no competition. This allows them to have most or all of the market share. On the other hand, controlling 100 percent of a small market is generally less attractive to marketing managers than having a small share of a very large market. This is the primary reason why companies are sometimes willing to develop a drug that they know will be a ''me-too'' drug in a major market.

Companies that compete in the marketplace with some of their drugs also collaborate with the same or different drug companies in (1) comarketing other drugs, (2) developing investigational drugs, and (3) conducting research. These are fairly common practices and illustrate why a company's competitors are usually considered either on a drug by drug basis or on a therapeutic area by therapeutic area basis.

Types of Competition Between Companies

Various types of competition exist between companies. One categorization is based on the three areas of drug discovery, drug development, and drug marketing.

Drug Discovery

If it is believed that a specific receptor or enzyme should be stimulated or inhibited to develop a useful drug, many companies will develop biological tests using the specific receptor or enzyme as the target. Each company will then search its catalogue of previously prepared compounds, as well as synthesize new chemicals to accomplish hopefully their goal. If a company is lucky, it will be the only one looking for active compounds against a specific target or receptor. But, the chances of this happening are not great. Scientists and information specialists at all major drug companies continually scour the scientific literature seeking to identify relevant biological receptors, enzymes, or other markers to use as targets for testing compounds. Of course, there will be companies who are alone in looking at certain targets, but these targets will often be ones that are purposely bypassed by other companies.

A company that develops a new animal model to use as a test to evaluate biological activity of compounds has a potentially important competitive edge. The value of this edge depends on both the value of the test and the quality of compounds evaluated in it.

If a drug company wanted to weaken deliberately a competitor, one of the most effective ways is to offer the competitor's most creative scientists or group of scientists better positions at the other company. There are usually a small number of highly creative scientists in any company who supply most of the important conceptual breakthroughs. These people may generally be easily identified.

Drug Development

It has become apparent in recent decades that there is a great difference among companies with respect to the efficiency in how well they develop drugs. Having large sums of money to spend on drug development is no guarantee of having and utilizing efficient methods. In fact, many people claim that the largest companies require an additional year or more to develop a drug compared with the time required by smaller, more efficient companies. The large size per se restricts the ability of large companies to mobilize people effectively. The degree to which this belief is true is unknown and certainly would be difficult to test in a quantitative manner.

Current clinical and nonclinical drug development standards and state-of-the-art methods are described in the *Guide to Clinical Studies* trilogy (Spilker, 1984, 1986b, 1987c), but are not yet adhered to by many companies, particularly in Europe where regulatory standards in most countries are not as rigorous as at the Food and Drug Administration (FDA). It is usually possible for an efficient company to develop a specific drug more rapidly than another company if they utilize good science, and logic, and have excellent employees.

Drug Marketing

Marketing is the area that most people initially think of when competition is discussed. It is the aspect of competition that is most exposed to the public and to all drug companies. The first drug of a new class to reach the market usually retains the largest market share after competitors with an equivalent drug reach the market. This emphasizes the importance of efficient drug development and of reaching the market as rapidly as possible. If only a few months elapse after the market launch of a new drug before the second drug of the same type is marketed; however, it may be possible for the second company to overcome the market lead of the first drug. The second company accomplishes this by looking for a positive attribute or angle that differentiates their drug from the first one on the market. This attribute should be important to physicians and/or patients. Marketing groups are hoping to be winners in terms of gaining the largest market share and do not want to be close. It is generally claimed that being close is only desirable in dancing and pitching horseshoes.

There is a great instability in market share for many therapeutic areas. The therapeutic markets that are most stable have the potential to be disrupted when better drugs are introduced. There are extremely few areas where the "perfect" drug has been discovered. Of 20 major industries, the drug industry was found to have the second highest index of market share instability (Schnee and Caglarcan, 1978; the petroleum industry was ranked first).

Analyzing the Competition

It is usually relevant to identify and analyze the competition on a product by product basis. On the other hand, it is sometimes important to evaluate all of the actual (and/or potential) competitors in a therapeutic area or in a specific market segment. Finally, it may be relevant to analyze a particular company. A drug company may wish to examine another drug company for various reasons (e.g., possible acquisition or merger, cross-licensing agreements, joint ventures).

In looking at a single company, many analyses may be performed. The specific analyses to perform are dictated by the questions posed. A few typical questions are:

1. What drugs are in the company's product portfolio? Is it aging? What is the medical and commercial quality of their investigational drugs? Does the company look at primarily high- or low-risk therapeutic areas? When will the most important new drugs be marketed? What is the forecasted sales picture?
2. What is the financial status of a company and its individual components?
3. What is the quality of the staff, their turnover, their morale, their level of pay and benefits?

4. What is the status of the facilities and equipment in terms of age, value, and state of the art?

5. What are the major corporate strengths and weaknesses? What are the major strengths and weaknesses of the production, marketing, and research and development groups?

Sources of Information on Competitors

Published material in journals, newspapers, professional newsletters, gossip sheets, government reports, annual reports, and other sources sometimes provide useful information on competitors. Many data bases in *Dialog* or other families of data bases are other sources of information that may be searched. Data obtained are often not analyzed or presented in the format of interest. Also, much of these data are out-of-date, difficult to verify, and often inaccurate. Think of the data and information presented on new drugs being developed by your own company. How accurate are the data published in the press and various other published sources?

When a company desires highly specific information on a competitor's drug, it may be possible to contact individuals who have the desired knowledge. These individuals may be current employees at the competitor or ex-employees. Multiple sources are used whenever possible. All methods must be carefully considered for their acceptability from an ethical perspective before contacts are initiated.

A reliability factor must be assigned to all information obtained. Even if an information source is "usually reliable" and a systematic approach is used to obtain information, it is essential not to make rapid or important decisions based on hearsay or conjecture. The assumptions of the source and their perspective must be carefully assessed in evaluating the value of their information. If five pieces of information on a specific question are obtained and have to be integrated, it is important to weigh the information based on its potential impact (i.e., does it relate to the key issue or a tangential question) and also on the likelihood that it is true. This process may be done intuitively, through discussion, or even as a result of carefully assigning a probability assessment or score to the data's legitimacy.

Competition in the drug world does not only exist between major research-based companies, but increasingly involves generic drug companies, small biotechnology companies, and chemical companies that are entering the drug development arena in a major way (Eastman Kodak, E.I. Du Pont de Nemours & Co., Monsanto Co.).

Types of Information often Obtained on the Competitor's Drug Development Program

It is generally surprising how much useful information may be obtained about a competitor's investigational drugs through legitimate means. Such information may be legitimately obtained from a variety of sources, both published and unpublished. Some companies spend much more money and effort than others to obtain this type of competitive information. The usual motivation is not to steal secrets, but to learn as precisely as possible (1) in which area(s) the competitors or potential competitors are working, (2) which drugs are being developed, (3) what advantages and disadvantages the competitors' drugs have, (4) how the competitors' drugs will be perceived, (5) what is the current stage of development of the competitors' drugs, (6) who are the investigators working on the other companies' drugs, (7) what are the competitors' protocols like, (8) how rapidly are the competitors' studies progressing, (9) what are the likely indications the competitors will seek approval for, and (10) other relevant questions. Not all of these questions would apply in any one situation. Companies also hope to learn of mistakes, problems, or positive effects found by their competition, so they may hopefully benefit from that knowledge. Although most of this information does not affect decisions or activities at the company that gathers it, there are cases where the information is extremely helpful in determining how much resource to put on a specific drug project, in determining the development strategy to adopt, or in making another decision.

All companies protect their chemical ideas as tightly as possible before patent applications are filed. After that point it is usually less critical to protect them as tightly. Chemical ideas are rarely stolen prior to being patented. But, once published or available through patent applications, the information may provide another company with interesting or useful prototypes to follow, develop, and exploit. One difficulty for companies that carefully examine published patents and the chemical literature for ideas to exploit is knowing how to separate the 99 percent of areas that would not be fruitful from the 1 percent or less that would be. One problem is that many or most of the best areas to explore for future drugs may already be protected by the company through other patents or may have been researched and found to be of little value. In addition, many promising chemical compounds will turn out on further animal (or human) testing to be more toxic or less effective than originally thought. It is therefore difficult, at best, to know which newly reported compounds are worth exploring.

Interactions between Companies at Professional Meetings

In areas of basic research, scientific methodology, reports on new drugs, and other technical areas, there is often frequent communication between drug company personnel at scientific meetings. There are clear limits that scientists and managers generally follow at such meetings. Areas that should not generally be discussed include information not yet made public on: (1) nonpatented compounds, (2) novel uses of known drugs that have not yet been published, (3) strategies of how drugs are being developed, (4) contents of clinical protocols, (5) names of investigators and consultants, (6) specific areas of research, and (7) areas where a potentially important drug has been discovered. Avoid making the classic error that the public was warned about in World War II England: "Loose lips sink ships."

There is no doubt that some junior-level employees of a company have given away valuable information or even secrets. Chief executive officers have also been accused of giving away important information. The message is that everyone at professional meetings personally knows information that should not be discussed. Remember, the person told may not use the information, but could pass it on (even innocently) to another who might. Many people rationalize their openness by telling themselves "well, I only told one person." But, if that process continued, there would soon be no one left who did not know the information.

What Separates Successful Research-Based Drug Companies from Unsuccessful Ones?

Several factors often play a major role in differentiating successful and unsuccessful companies. In a short time span, good fortune or luck is often extremely important. More controllable aspects that relate to success are having a highly motivated, experienced, intelligent staff who are able to judge the most appropriate compounds to develop as drugs, the most efficient means to develop a drug, the best time to reallocate resources from a dying drug, and the most appropriate means of marketing drugs. This is not to overlook the importance of production and many other areas that contribute to a drug's development and success, but they are rarely responsible for the overall success or failure of a company. Having a highly motivated staff depends on many other factors including those previously mentioned, such as work environment, compensation, responsibilities assigned, and ability to conduct and publish company-related research of personal interest.

The incentive is almost gone for drug companies to introduce more potent drugs that have no clear therapeutic advantages. This "battle of the milligrams" (e.g., where drug A is claimed to be 10 times as potent as drug B) was sometimes a worthwhile area to "wage combat" in the 1950s, but drug companies have moved to new fields of competition.

Increasing competition among drugs frequently means that only the most cost-effective ones in each class will be widely prescribed. "Me-too" drugs may be able to achieve commercial success if they can demonstrate cost savings and equal effectiveness to currently marketed drugs. Cost containment pressures will probably continue and even increase in importance in the future. Although it is possible that the number of marketed drugs which repay their investment will decrease below the one-fourth to one-third that are believed to do so now (Virts and Weston, 1980; Grabowski and Vernon, 1982; Drews, 1985; Joglekar and Paterson, 1986) this is unlikely. It is more likely that drug companies will become more selective about the compounds they choose to develop as drugs, so that a higher proportion of investigational drugs will be marketed to repay their investment.

Pressures on the United States-based drug industry will also come from increased foreign competition within the United States. Additional foreign-based drug companies have entered the United States since 1960, and the general trend of a weaker dollar favors this movement. Foreign-based companies have been obtaining a steadily larger share of worldwide drug sales over the last two decades. The influence that foreign-owned drug companies have on American-owned drug companies may become a more important issue in the future.

Drug companies that are weak because of large legal liabilities, a drought of new products, or another reason are subject to acquisition by another company. This has been a relatively common phenomenon in the drug industry over the last century. A merger of equal partners is usually unworkable. It is generally necessary to have one company dominant. The dominant company usually exerts its view on the subsidiary company and often hopes to be able to improve the efficiency of overall drug development as well as to make a profit.

COLLABORATIONS BETWEEN DRUG COMPANIES

Types of Collaborations between Drug Companies

There are numerous situations when two or more drug companies form a true partnership or alliance. The nature of some of these relationships (e.g., licensing, joint ventures) are described and briefly discussed. Other types of collaborations that are not discussed further include providing a clinical study drug and matching placebo to other companies. Some companies are more cooperative than others in this regard, although most companies want to review the clinical protocol before they are willing to give any of their drug to another company. Finally, trade associations provide a useful forum for various other types of collaborative activities. These are discussed in the following chapter.

Licensing

Independent drug companies often collaborate with each other on projects of mutual interest. This may involve licensing activities whereby one company obtains the rights to develop and eventually market one or more drugs of another company. In some situations, companies will exchange the right to license drugs. This is referred to as cross-licensing. Companies may also license technologies (e.g., drug delivery systems, patented formulations) from another company.

Companies initially sign a confidentiality statement in which they promise not to disclose any confidential information given to them. Under such an agreement companies explore their investigational projects and marketed products that they would be willing (or might be willing) to trade with the other company. Some drug companies attempt to acquire most or all of their drugs through licensing. Some of them have the motto "Search and Development" instead of "Research and Development."

Licensing Groups

Drug companies have developed a large variety of internal staff groups to deal with licensing. Different individuals may be in charge of licensing opportunites in different business areas (e.g., animal products, over-the-counter drugs (OTCs), diagnostics, ethical human drugs, contract manufacturing) of a company. Alternatively, two or even all of these areas may be assigned to a single person. Regardless of the number of licensing groups, a central coordinator is needed if licensing activities are being conducted in multiple businesses. If a coordinator is not used then separate licensing people from one company may independently visit another company and unwittingly create confusion and even negative reactions. Each independent business or research and development (R and D) site in a company may develop its own strategy that may not work well together, unless coordinated.

The size of a group working on licensing opportunities varies from one or a few full-time people up to large organizations of over 100 people. In the latter case, there are people to analyze (1) the research and technical development aspects of what has been accomplished and what remains to be accomplished, (2) marketing aspects and commercial potential, (3) production issues, (4) legal aspects, and (5) financial aspects of the agreement. It is the author's opinion that when these analyses are conducted by the regular staff that a stronger commitment to the licensed drug results, although it undoubtedly takes more time for the regular staff to complete necessary evaluations than for a staff dedicated to these activities.

Developing a Licensing Strategy

The most simple licensing strategy is to license drugs or technologies that are going to earn the greatest profit for the company. Some companies utilize this strategy by reacting to all proposals that are presented to it from outside sources (e.g., other companies, academic investigators, institutions). Although this general strategy has been effective and successful for some companies, in this increasingly competitive world, this approach is too simple to be an effective *modus operandi* and a more systematic and proactive approach is usually preferred by large drug companies.

A more specific strategy may be developed by utilizing portfolio analysis methods to identify various types of gaps in the portfolio that could be closed with a licensed drug or product. Chapter 15 describes numerous types of gaps and types of portfolio analyses that may be used to identify them. In addition to (or instead of) gaps, a company may focus their strategy on creating a strong defensive position around their therapeutic areas or drugs of greatest commercial value. Once the characteristics of desired products or types of opportunities are completed in terms of therapeutic area, stage of development, and potential market size, it enables the person or persons seeking licensing opportunities to have a general "feel" as to what types of products would be most desirable and have the best fit with the company. It is undesirable, however, to develop a highly specific strategy that is too restrictive and becomes almost impossible to achieve. An example of this would be to seek to license an antihypertensive drug currently in Phase II that acts via a specific mechanism and has a specific commercial potential in its third year of marketing.

Elements of a licensing strategy include the following:

1. *Stage of development* The earlier in development the compound is, the less expensive it will generally be to acquire, but the more uncertain its future will be. Licensing compounds at a later stage of development is more expensive, but there is greater assurance that the drug works as hoped.
2. *Commercial potential* Marketing groups must examine the projected market for the new product at the time that it is estimated to be introduced. A certain amount of profit may be required as a minimum incentive to proceed with licensing negotiations.
3. *Research and development staff to develop the drug* Appropriate expertise and resources must be available to place on the drug's development. In some situations some or all of these activities may be contracted to others.
4. *Corporate comfort zone* The product must fall within the company's desires and abilities to have the drug produced and marketed. Parts of these and related activities may be contracted out, but the product should be one that fits the portfolio

of marketed products or is a product that is desired to be marketed. Abilities of sales representatives to handle the product must be considered.

5. *Production capabilities* The company must be able to make the drug themselves or to contract it to another company.

6. *Therapeutic category of the licensed drug or product* This parameter varies in importance from little to critical depending on the precise situation.

7. *Business terms and arrangements* The company may be required to utilize a cross-licensing agreement to acquire the product. Various aspects of the agreement may be determined at an early stage of negotiation (e.g., will up-front money be required, will the license be worldwide, does the other company wish to comarket the drug, is the patent life acceptable). Cross-licensing agreements are becoming increasingly popular and even demanded by some companies with valuable drugs to license.

8. *Risk* This term includes aspects of several of the other elements, plus additional ones. The risks to a company in licensing a drug may be determined in terms of the drug's (1) potential to create liability suits, (2) probability that it will not work as hoped, (3) probability that the drug will not possess adequate safety, (4) projected cost to take the drug to the go-no go Phase II decision point, or to New Drug Application (NDA) submission, (5) probability that it will not be marketed in time to obtain a minimally accepted profit, (6) potential for a complex or unclear patent situation, or (7) having formulation or other problems of technical development or manufacture that may not be able to be completely solved.

The most highly developed licensing strategy is only one element in obtaining valuable opportunities. Some of the crucial factors responsible for one company licensing a specific drug of great value instead of another company include timing, personal contacts and relationships, reputation of being a (the) major company in that area, and serendipity.

Selected Types of Licensing Agreements

Almost any arrangement that can be conceived may be proposed between two or more groups. A few of the more common types of agreements are briefly presented.

1. One company licenses a drug to another for worldwide development and marketing.

2. One company licenses a drug to another for development and marketing in only one country or in selected countries. The original company may participate in the drug's development or may only retain marketing rights in selected countries after the other company has developed the drug.

3. One company initiates drug development and the second may begin their participation at any of several stages (e.g., Phase I, Phase II, marketing). Royalty fees for the license become progressively higher if the second company waits for a later stage before beginning their participation.

4. There may be money paid as part of the original agreement or money may be paid according to any agreed-on schedule (e.g., at end of Phase II, on NDA submission, at time of marketing).

5. A company may develop a drug but license it to another for comarketing in

one or more specific countries. The advantage for the developer is to achieve a better depth and breadth of market penetration.

Factors that are covered in an agreement include (1) identification of what is being transferred (e.g., patents, dosage forms, manufacturing process, marketing services, technical knowledge), (2) the payments that are to be made, (3) the countries involved, (4) the nature of the licensee's participation, (5) how the property transferred is to be used, (6) time requirements (e.g., for completing various stages of drug development), (7) duration of the agreement, (8) any penalties, and (9) conditions under which the contract may be renegotiated or voided.

Reasons for a Company to Consider Licensing a New Drug to Another Company

Companies that are not actively selling their drugs in a country can explore the potential for having a successful subsidiary there through licensing a drug. A company usually incurs less risk if it licenses a drug to another company than if it establishes or acquires a subsidiary in that country. Without the licensing mechanism many companies would have had great difficulty initially entering a new market. Licensing one drug in exchange for another (i.e., cross-licensing) often has several advantages and is often preferred. Additional income made by the original company through licensing has sometimes been extremely valuable (e.g., Boots' licensing of ibuprofen to The Upjohn Company in the United States).

A few potential pitfalls of licensing include limited profits, tax issues, and obtaining royalties in a place and form (e.g., cash versus goods) that is most desirable. Complex bartering arrangements are sometimes created among several countries. Other potential problems are assuring that the licensor adheres to quality assurance and to development schedules. Provisions should be made in the contract to allow the original owner to enter a market eventually, if this may be desired. Otherwise, a company may be precluded from doing so.

Joint Ventures

Two or more companies may enter into a formal relationship where they agree to work together in a specified way. The goal may be to discover a drug, but it is most often to expedite a drug's development or to enhance drug sales and profits. The partners may or may not be equal in the relationship they forge. They will probably have different roles in the venture. For example, one may provide capital, another research (or drug development) expertise, or a marketing sales force. Many variations exist, and a single company may be involved in numerous types of joint ventures.

The primary motivation for embarking on a joint venture is usually to enhance profits or the potential for profits. Nonetheless there are various other reasons that cause drug companies to enter joint ventures. These include (1) sharing risk on an expensive and high-risk project, (2) sharing costs on an expensive project, (3) achieving a better entry to a desired market, (4) satisfying a foreign government that requires participation of a local company, and (5) achieving a larger or more knowledgable group of experts who would have a greater chance of success on a specific project.

Many developing countries insist that a foreign company which wishes to manufacture drugs in the developing country must form a joint venture with a local company. The foreign drug company may only be allowed to be a minority partner in the joint venture that is formed.

Another type of joint venture is for two companies to serve as backup manufacturing facilities to make specific drugs for the other company in case of marketing need or disaster at a manufacturing plant.

Writing and Facilitating Agreements between Companies

Written agreements between companies must be clear to prevent the myriad of questions that would otherwise result. There may, however, be a few instances when this is not desired. For example, it is not always necessary to provide another company with all of the thoughts of company A relating to the agreement, because some information could be used by company B with third parties for other agreements or issues that could hurt company A. A common principle is to provide information in good faith that meets the terms of the agreement, but not to supply more information than necessary.

"What if" exercises can be conducted internally to insure that most important issues have been considered in the agreement. These exercises are designed to find answers to questions such as (1) who has responsibility for what? (2) who has to approve publications and how will this be handled? and (3) how will changes in the agreement be implemented and problems resolved? Roger Fisher and William Ury stated in *Getting to Yes* (1983) "The basic problem in a negotiation lies not in conflicting positions, but in the conflict between each side's needs, desires, concerns, and fears."

A key person should be identified in each company to act as a single channel to unify most or all of each company's communications with the other. Depending on the nature of the agreement, multiple communications channels may be established (e.g., via board members, project coordinators).

27 / Interactions and Relationships Between Drug Companies and Trade Associations

It is interesting to reflect on the defecatory habits of the hippopotamus. The male indicates to other hippopotami the extent of his own territory by defecating all around its perimeter. Outside that ring they can go where they please, but if they come inside it he will fight them to the death. So, too, nations make a ring around their territory: To Elizabeth I, the wars in Holland were beyond the ring but the Armada came inside it. No doubt the United States government wishes it had left Vietnam on the outside of its defecatory ring. And so, too, industrial corporations, consciously or unwittingly, make the same sort of ring around products and sales territories and sections of the market. Antony Jay. From *Management and Machiavelli.*

ACTIVITIES OF TRADE ASSOCIATIONS

Trade associations discussed in this chapter are industry-wide associations. There are approximately six to ten such groups in the United States, whereas there are an extremely large number of other associations that represent a specific segment of the industry. Industry-wide associations have companies and not individuals as members. Specific associations and their primary objectives are briefly described at the end of this chapter.

Advantages of Trade Associations Representing the Drug Industry

Trade associations are involved in many types of activities, including those listed in Table 27.1. Companies are often not in a position to conduct or act on issues that

Table 27.1. Selected activities conducted by trade associations in the United States

1.	Conduct and/or assist in lobbying efforts
2.	Discuss legal issues
3.	Conduct educational courses, seminars, and meetings for health professionals, member companies, and the general public
4.	Hold discussion forums on a wide range of pertinent topics of interest to the industry
5.	Convene problem solving groups on a wide range of issues
6.	Convene advisory groups to assist companies, association committees, and outside groups
7.	Provide scholarships, grants, and awards
8.	Maintain data bases on relevant information
9.	Disseminate information and provide technical assistance
10.	Maintain a speakers' program
11.	Publish journals, special documents, and/or other periodicals, prepare position papers
12.	Establish ongoing relationships with government bodies, health associations, other trade associations, organizations representing health-related groups, academic community, scientific community, consumer groups, news media, trade media, and numerous other groups

an association is able to act on. This is sometimes a result of the size of the effort required, and in other situations it is the lack of credibility that might be associated with having specific companies sponsor reports or events.

A major trade association activity involves lobbying. It often makes more sense for companies to unite and lobby via their associations than to lobby as independent companies. Many issues that companies want to lobby for (or against) are not drug specific, but are germane to the entire industry. For example, at the federal legislative level, drug issues are usually industry specific (e.g., patent issues, product tampering, drug sampling, animal rights) and not company specific. At the state level, the same principle generally holds, although company specific issues are more likely to emerge.

Another major function of most industry-wide trade associations relates to education. As with lobbying, many education issues relate to the entire industry. Some of the specific activities on both lobbying and education are discussed in this chapter. Other aspects of lobbying are discussed in Chapter 25.

Roles of Pharmaceutical Trade Associations and Their Relationships with Companies

1. Important trade associations of the drug industry should be able to collect and present information to politicians that will help them in deliberations on current issues. This information may be in the form of background data, white papers on positions of the industry, or ad hoc information assembled at a politician's request.

2. Associations should endeavor to preempt issues that are developing, but have not yet reached a crisis state. Numerous issues such as the use of animals in pharmaceutical research are in this category. This information should be collected and presented to politicians as a preventive measure to help ward off future problems.

3. There are many industry-wide questions that trade associations can address through collecting and statistically evaluating data. The associations are in a good position to do this because they can gather data from multiple companies in the same format. Data of individual companies are kept private and only averaged or merged data is published or made available to members for their use. These data provide

industry trends and a benchmark against which (with appropriate caveats) a company may compare its own data. The *PMA* (Pharmaceutical Manufacturers Association) *Statistical Fact Book* is an example of this type of data.

4. Scientific and nonscientific (e.g., marketing, production, public affairs) activities of trade associations are highly variable in nature and value. Associations hold many meetings of various types for their members. These are important because they provide a forum for discussing issues of mutual interest. These meetings also help to educate many people. Associations also play an important role in disseminating information on relevant issues to their members.

5. Educational activities include seminars, courses (e.g., for managers and for clinical monitors) and special meetings, in addition to publications and regularly scheduled meetings.

6. Associations have numerous committees to conduct their business and some are composed of professionals who work for their member companies. Some associations request more assistance than others in this regard.

Insofar as lobbying is concerned, associations have a generally successful record of obtaining the type of regulations they support. This is especially true when the association is able to determine and then present a common front of their members who are concerned about a specific issue. There are some occasions when individual companies have widely divergent views. Associations are then unable to present a unified industry view or to lobby effectively.

Criticisms of Trade Associations By Some Industry Personnel

Trade associations are often held accountable for problems they have no control over. An important issue relates to the difficulty of finding a common denominator between their members on many important issues. Because of this restraint, the actions they are able to take become "watered down." In addition, companies are only willing to share information that will not provide any advantage to their competitors, and sometimes an issue is discussed without all of the necessary (and available) information being presented. Discussions may be lacking in substance. All of these limitations relegate many meetings and activities to those of a debating society and may compromise the effectiveness of the association.

MAJOR TRADE ASSOCIATIONS IN THE UNITED STATES

Five major trade associations in the United States are listed. Many other trade associations deal with specific issues of significant importance to the drug industry, (e.g., marketing, chemistry). They are not listed because they do not deal with all or most aspects of the industry.

Pharmaceutical Manufacturers Association

The Pharmaceutical Manufacturers Association (PMA) has 130 member companies, 87 associate member companies, and a staff of 90 (as of 1987). Its headquarters are at 1100 15th Street, NW, Washington, DC 20005. They have their own lobbyists at the national level and help to coordinate activities of individual companies. At the state level, company representatives work under the coordination of PMA staff to pursue industry objectives. This includes monitoring activities at the state level.

National Pharmaceutical Council

The National Pharmaceutical Council (NPC) has 30 member companies and a staff of 12 (as of 1987). Its headquarters are at 1894 Preston White Drive, Reston, VA 22091. It is primarily an information source that does not conduct lobbying activities. Their educational activities are often directed to public awareness and keeping their members informed about various issues.

Proprietary Association

The Proprietary Association (PA) has 83 active member companies, 155 associate member companies, and a staff of 38 (as of 1987). Its headquarters are at 1700 Pennsylvania Avenue, Washington, DC 20006. The PA focuses on over-the-counter drug (OTC) issues. They are active in lobbying at the federal level and also try to coordinate lobbying activities at the state level. They do not have their own lobbyists at the state level but look for allies (as do all associations) to help with lobbying activities. These allies would include consumer groups, other trade associations, professional organizations, representatives of member companies, and various societies and groups.

Drug, Chemical, and Allied Trades Association

The Drug, Chemical, and Allied Trades Association (DCAT) has 500 member companies and a staff of four (as of 1987). Its headquarters are at 42-40 Bell Boulevard, Bayside, NY 11361. It provides several types of forums for members of the various companies and industries to meet and discuss issues of mutual interest. They have a broader base than does the PMA because they include the chemical industry and allied industries (e.g., fragrances, packaging). DCAT also provides college scholarships and publishes a digest and newsletter. DCAT does not get involved in lobbying activities.

Generic Pharmaceutical Industry Association

The Generic Pharmaceutical Industry Association (GPIA) has 26 member companies and a staff of five (as of 1987). Its headquarters are at 200 Madison Avenue, New York, NY 10016. The group represents the interests of companies that make generic pharmaceuticals.

28 / Interactions and Relationships Between Drug Companies and Health Professionals

A bad doctor treats symptoms. A good doctor treats ailments. A rare doctor treats patients. Sidney Harris.

But nothing is more estimable than a physician, who having studied nature from his end, knows the properties of the human body, the diseases which assail it, the remedies which will benefit it, exercises his art with caution, and pays equal attention to the rich and the poor. Voltaire. From *A Philosophical Dictionary*.

IDENTIFYING HEALTH PROFESSIONALS

Groups of Health Professionals

There is little doubt that relationships between health professionals and companies represent the lifeblood of the ethical drug industry. These professionals are the people who cause the company's drugs to be used. Health professionals are described in a broad context and include the following groups.

Practicing (i.e., patient-treating) health professionals

1. Physicians in an outpatient-based practice.
2. Physicians in an inpatient-based practice.
3. Practicing pharmacists in a hospital environment.
4. Nurses in various settings.
5. Specialized groups (e.g., podiatrists, optometrists, osteopaths).

Nonpatient-treating health professionals

1. Dispensing pharmacists in retail establishments, hospitals, clinics, or other locations. Many of these pharmacists provide drug and other medical information to patients.
2. Health Maintenance Organization (HMO), Preferred Provider Organization (PPO), or other health organization formulary committees.
3. Drug information specialists.

TYPES OF RELATIONSHIPS

Relationships With Physicians

The most well-known relationship involves the sales representative. Physicians usually judge companies by their sales representatives and advertisements, the two most visible parts of a company to practicing physicians. Other less frequent interactions include contacts at professional meetings, symposia, educational courses, and exhibits. Companies attempt to educate physicians about their drugs, and physicians often seek information about drugs from their manufacturers.

Other relationships include those of sponsor (company) and investigator (physician). This relationship is exceedingly complex with numerous responsibilities on both parts and is briefly described in Chapter 19.

Types of Correspondence Received from Health Professionals

Companies receive various types of correspondence from physicians and other health professionals. Most fit one of the following four types:

1. Adverse drug reaction report
2. Product complaint
3. Professional inquiry for information
4. Lack of efficacy report

Many companies currently are dealing with this correspondence more systematically than they have in the past. A great deal of the communications is assisted by computers. For example, responses to many frequently requested inquiries may be filed in computers. Also, each complaint may be given a number and the type of complaint noted. Details are obtained for drug name, lot number, reporter's name, clinician's name, hospital's name, and National Drug Code (NDC) number. Trends may be analyzed in terms of the frequency of complaints, types of complaints, and products involved.

Problems Reported by Health Professionals

Most problems reported to drug companies by health professionals fall into one of two categories: patients or drugs. In some cases the problems reported relate to both. Examples of drug-related problems include reports of discolored or crushed tablets. Once the drug has been ingested by a patient the problem is usually considered patient-related. The distinction between patient- and drug-related reports is important because many companies have two separate groups that interact with health professionals on this basis.

Serious adverse reactions reported to a company are investigated when deemed appropriate. This is usually done by telephone unless the importance is so great that on-site evaluation is necessary. Many physician reports directed to a company are not statements that a drug caused a specific adverse reaction, but are specific questions or inquiries. For example, physicians often seek the company's help to rule in or rule out (1) a diagnosis, or (2) a cause of an adverse reaction. Numerous services are often provided by drug companies to physicians and other health professionals to help understand a drug's effect or lack of effect. For example, blood level determinations of an active drug and/or its metabolites are measured when relevant. Tissue levels or direct analysis of the drug itself may be conducted by the company.

SELECTED ISSUES

Problems Created for Marketed Drugs by Health Professionals

The major problem for drug companies that is created by health professionals usually relates to improper prescribing or use of a company's products. It is generally irrelevant to a regulatory agency and the public reading a news story about an adverse event whether a drug was improperly used. The important point to them is the problem for the patient(s) who was affected and the issue it raises for the company.

Problems Created for Investigational Drugs by Health Professionals

Many problems occur for a company in terms of broken promises made by physicians in regard to investigational drugs. These broken promises may relate to any part of initiating or conducting a clinical study. Many of these issues are described in Chapter 20 of *Guide to Planning and Managing Multiple Clinical Studies* (Spilker, 1987c) under the heading "Games Investigators Play."

Other investigator-related problems include publishing data on the same patient(s) in multiple journals. This may be done to assist their career or for other reasons. It is often extremely difficult to determine whether several articles by one author or one group of authors refer to the same or different patients, unless a formal audit of the data is undertaken. The ability to request an audit is in the province of a limited number of groups (e.g., regulatory authorities, Investigational Review Board), which rarely includes a drug company, unless it has sponsored all of the research. Even if multiple publications of the same patients is proven to have occurred, it is not illegal. If the publications point out multiple adverse reactions that overestimate the true incidence, it may cause serious repercussions for the company. This may be in terms of having the Food and Drug Administration (FDA) suspend clinical studies or take other actions (e.g., request studies to investigate the high incidence of the problem). There are few alternatives for a company except to investigate the situation as thoroughly as possible and to discuss the problem with the appropriate regulatory authority. Damage to a drug's reputation by multiple reports on the same patient(s) may be severe and a reputation can be extremely difficult to rebuild.

IMPROVING RELATIONSHIPS BETWEEN HEALTH PROFESSIONALS AND DRUG COMPANIES

The establishment and maintenance of high standards is the key for research-based drug companies to develop successful relationships with health professionals. These standards are of ethical behavior and professional behavior. Respect for a company and its products is important because in many situations a professional must choose one drug from many similar ones to use or prescribe.

A company chooses health professionals to act as consultants, to conduct clinical studies, to conduct scientific studies, or to perform other services. It is important for the company to choose individuals who will provide the best overall service to the company. Conflicts of interest may arise when people are evaluated who are personal friends or relatives of those in important positions at the company.

Drug companies often have professional groups that give presentations on their own drugs or on drug development in general. These presentations may be given to local or state medical organizations, community groups that are health oriented, or to students in health-related fields.

Approaching Health Professionals

It is beneficial to understand why physicians prescribe specific drugs when they have numerous options. This knowledge can help a company target its message to the various groups who are and will prescribe and use its drugs. Some of the more common reasons as to why a specific drug is prescribed are as follows:

1. This is the way I was trained.
2. I am most familiar with this drug.
3. This is the drug that the pharmacy stocks.
4. This is the drug that is best for the patient in my experience.
5. This is the drug that is cheapest for the patient.
6. This is what my friends and colleagues are recommending.
7. This is what the specialists use to whom I usually refer patients.
8. This is the drug that a sales representative left, and I thought I would try it.

Marketing research groups spend a great deal of time and money attempting to better understand these reasons and to develop ways in which drug promotion may be most effective in presenting a drug to physicians.

29 / *Interactions and Relationships Between Drug Companies, Patients, and the Public*

The proverbial wisdom of the populace in the streets, on the roads, and in the markets, instructs the ear of him who studies man more fully than a thousand rules ostentatiously arranged. From *Proverbs, or the Manual of Wisdom*, London 1804.

The public is a bad guesser. De Quincey. From *Essays-Protestantism*.

The views of the multitude are neither bad nor good. Tacitus. From *Annales* (Book VII).

DESCRIBING THE PUBLIC

As the quotes above illustrate, there are many different views about the public. One of the reasons for this is that the public is not a simple straightforward concept.

What Is the Public?

There are many "publics" from a drug company's perspective, and each has its own specific needs and orientations. Each public also has its own perspective and viewpoint about the drug industry. Publics include all lay people, all patients who use the company's products, the local community, lay organizations related to medicine or health, and consumer pressure groups. Various other publics could also be described (e.g., company employees, company retirees). Drug companies deal with publics on local, state, and national levels.

INDUSTRY'S RELATIONSHIP WITH ITS PUBLICS

Types of Relationships

There are four major types of relationships of a company with its publics: (1) philanthropic, (2) product-related, (3) symbiotic, and (4) employer. The last category will not be discussed in detail. Philanthropic activities tend to be strongest at the local level and product-related activities strongest at the national level. Symbiotic or *quid pro quo* types of activities may be strong or weak at any level.

Publics at the Local Community Level

Drug companies hire people who live in the local communities. The company pays taxes and interacts in many ways on a daily basis with the community. It is therefore in a company's interests to do whatever is reasonable to maintain good relationships with their community. One aspect of company involvement encompasses philanthropic gifts of money or personal services.

Financial Support for Local Groups

Contributions from the company are most effective when they fit into well-conceived pattern or plan. Drug companies receive many more requests for funds than they are able to honor. Their choices are much easier to make and are more consistent when decisions are made in the context of an overall plan.

The plan may be to divide their contributions according to a formula, allocating a certain percent of the total to local, state, and federal activities. It could also be based on allocating a certain percent of the total to specific areas (e.g., drug related, nondrug health related, nondrug and nonhealth related). A third means of allocation could be according to various topics of special interest to the company. Other methods or combinations of these are possible. Cutbacks in federal support for various health-related or nonhealth-related activities sometimes place additional pressures on a company to increase its contributions.

Drug companies are often asked to donate money to local organizations, institutions, schools, and other groups. These groups often have nothing to do with health care or health issues, but appeal to the company on the basis of being located in the same neighborhood. Companies often feel quite strongly about being a good community citizen and supporting local charities, numerous nonprofit organizations, and many other types of local groups.

Nonfinancial Support for Local Groups

In addition to outright financial contributions, companies may:

1. Loan their facilities so that other groups can have a meeting or party.
2. Print brochures at cost or underwrite the cost of printing materials.
3. Allow company staff with expertise to assist organizations that desire advice and consultation.
4. Make video programs. These may be unrelated to drugs or medicine.
5. Allow or even encourage employees to serve on local boards.
6. Donate used equipment to schools or offices that range from typewriters to scientific equipment.
7. Provide speakers to local organizations.
8. Provide various services requested.

In providing these or other nonfinancial gifts, the company may not desire recognition or it may restrict its identity to use of its logo or name. This may be at the end of a presentation or on the back of printed material. Services are often provided because it helps to promote the company's name.

Support for Employees and Their Families

Another public that the company interacts with at the community level is the company's own employees. Many companies provide matching grants for employees' contributions to help support schools, hospitals, foundations, public television and radio stations, plus other organizations that meet defined criteria. Scholarships for children of employees are another area of activity.

Other Activities at a Local Level

Product-related activities involve providing information about a company's products to the public and also promoting products. This occurs to a limited degree at the local level.

Publics at the State Level

The state level often overlaps with both the local and national levels in terms of how it is perceived by drug companies. One reason is that many local organizations are also active at the state level, and many state organizations are also active at the national level.

Companies generally have both philanthropic activities and company interests that are pursued at the state level. Philanthropic activities include support to many cultural, educational, and other organizations located in different parts of the state, as well as some organizations that are statewide. Company interests are also served by providing product-related information to the public.

Symbiotic relationships include providing assistance to legislators and other groups of people (e.g., businessmen). Assistance for legislators could range from support through a company-sponsored Political Action Committee (PAC) to help in drafting new legislation.

Legislative activities at the state level are described in Chapter 25. Companies strongly support establishing personal contacts with legislators and building positive relationships, even without having any specific lobbying purpose. Therefore, company executives other than just lobbyists often develop professional relationships with legislators. One type of such contact is for the company to host groups of legislators at a reception with company managers on a periodic basis. Contacts are usually also pursued with individual legislators.

Publics at the National Level

At the national level, drug companies usually provide much less money to humanitarian or philanthropic organizations than they do at local and state levels. Companies tend to tie their contributions more directly to their products at the national level. This is primarily because individual drug companies are not large enough financially to reach effectively the general public at the national level. A significant amount of company contributions are made to support scientific and medical societies, businesses, and meetings or symposia.

Companies donate more than just money. For example, most companies donate drugs to charitable agencies that send them to lesser developed countries, with the assurance that these drugs will not be recycled illegally into normal trade routes.

When proposed activities are associated with a company's products it is more likely that the company will become involved as a sponsor. For example, a company may pay for having a brochure printed on a disease that one of its drugs treats. These brochures would then be distributed in various ways (e.g., public health agencies). A company may help underwrite the cost of a television show dealing with a disease the company's products treat, even though none of the company's products are mentioned by name. Various types of educational materials are produced or purchased that are targeted to professional groups. A few companies produce popular-style publications that they send out to physicians or lay people (such as video tapes), while others concentrate on "throw-away" medical journals. One of the best known (and least often thrown away) of this type is *Ciba Symposia*.

Philanthropic Groups Sponsored by Drug Companies

In some situations corporate philanthropy is made via the company and in others via a separate independent foundation. Many companies have established a philanthropic group, either independent of the company's control or under it. These groups may give money in a highly targeted way that enhances the company's product profile. On the other hand, donations may be made to the most qualified people with few stipulations. Two of the best-known groups that provide such money are the Wellcome Trust in the United Kingdom and the Burroughs Wellcome Fund in the United States. Other philanthropic programs within the drug industry include: Abbott Laboratories Fund, Bristol-Myers Fund, Merck Co. Fund, Schering-Plough Foundation, Hoffmann-La Roche Foundation, Pfizer Foundation, Sandoz Foundation, and the Lilly Endowment.

Company Interactions with the Public: Product-Related Services and Information

Companies generally attempt to avoid providing information about prescription drugs directly to the public. Companies refer patients to their physicians for advice and information when patients call or write letters to the company. A company may, however, provide patients with a general pamphlet about a specific disease. Companies do not usually send a photocopy of a drug's labeling to consumers. Instead the company may refer patients to the *Physicians' Desk Reference*, which is in local libraries and contains the drug's labeling. This is the most checked-out book at the New York Public Library, which attests to its popularity as a source of drug information. McMahon et al. (1987) describes the type and source information actually presented to patients by health professionals.

Companies have an entirely different attitude about sending information about over-the-counter drugs to patients. Many companies provide information on request, relating both to the disease and to the drug.

Information on risks associated with taking drugs is presented to the public by government, academic, and drug industry groups. The government and drug industry usually evaluate a drug's risk in terms of society or on a broad macrolevel of how all patients with a disease, or those of a particular population, are affected. The public usually desires the opposite information, i.e., how are they, their families, and friends as individuals affected. Their interest and reaction is usually on this microlevel. This type of information is usually more difficult to determine because it concerns a specific patient who may react in many ways. On the other hand, population data refers to averages of many people and can provide overall probability estimates of various types of outcomes.

Public Opinion

Public opinion must be recognized and respected by the drug industry as an important force. This statement is based on the influence the public has on (1) shaping new regulations, (2) affecting drug-pricing policies, (3) influencing their physician who is thinking about giving them a prescription drug, and (4) deciding whether to fill the prescription at the pharmacy and to take the drug as directed. Companies want the public to view the drug industry in a highly positive way. The public held a generally positive view of the industry during the 1950s, when miraculous new drugs seemed to appear with great regularity, almost like magic.

Companies also desire to have the public understand something about the complexities, high risks, and high costs of drug research and development. This understanding would better enable the public to appreciate the efforts that go into discovering and developing a new drug and the reasons why its price may appear to be expensive. Another concept that is important to communicate to the public is the risk associated with drugs. All drugs involve some degree of risk to the patient, and potential benefits must be compared with potential risks whenever a drug is to be taken.

Drug companies educate the public via several mechanisms. The major means are to work through their trade associations (e.g., public service announcements, symposia), physicians who treat patients (e.g., brochures and other educational materials, symposia), and directly to patients themselves (e.g., magazine and other advertisements, brochures, patient package inserts). The method of working via their trade associations is discussed in Chapter 27. Companies may encourage physicians to inform patients about the drugs that they are prescribing. This includes information on potential risks as well as benefits from taking the drug. The patient's perceived risks are usually more important than the actual risks, because the former are usually what motivates people's behavior.

Spokespeople are needed who represent the drug industry and can speak to the public about issues in drug development. These people must use language that the public can understand. Using jargon or technical terms often serves to alienate people and is counterproductive.

Why Should the Drug Industry Present Its Story More Clearly to the Public?

A public that is better informed about the complexity and issues of drug development should be more sympathetic to the drug industry. This could have important results. For example:

1. More patients would be attentive to their physician's instructions and would be more likely to comply with their drug regimen.
2. The public would exert a more positive influence on political leaders at all levels of government. This would have both a direct and indirect impact on legislation.
3. Patients who have deleterious medical outcomes that are possibly (or probably) drug related would be less likely to sue drug companies.
4. Information on positive aspects of industry would help counter the few negative stories that tend to dominate news reports about drugs and the drug industry.

The industry has discovered and marketed many drugs that have revolutionized the practice of medicine. Costs of these drugs have markedly fallen relative to the consumer price index and total cost of the nation's health bill over the last 25 years. Profits have also been relatively high for many drug companies compared with other industries, but a large percentage of these profits has been reinvested in research and development to discover and market improved drugs for the future. National and state legislatures and regulations have enormous potential to affect both the incentive and the ability of drug companies to invest huge sums in research. The ramifications of all government activities that impact on drug companies should be carefully considered by the public and by the Congress, to prevent a drought of new drug discoveries in the United States and to avoid killing the goose that lays golden eggs.

Increased public awareness and knowledge of the drug industry can help both the public and the industry. The public will be helped by understanding the difficulties involved in discovering, developing, and marketing drugs in a highly uncertain and tightly regulated market. The pressures on companies to discover or develop new drugs is great, because without new drugs, companies will fail to thrive and may be forced into a merger or may be taken over. Thus, public pressure to promote positive changes in regulations will help the industry, as well as indirectly helping the public through the development of new drugs. One specific example concerns the drug lag and the effect it has had on health. When important drugs are available outside a country, but not inside, many patients may be indirectly hurt. The Food and Drug Administration (FDA) claims that the additional time they take to approve drugs and the additional data they require helps to protect the American public from poorly tested drugs. This is certainly true, but the important question is how much delay results from high standards of science and how much delay results from bureaucracy and other nonscientific issues at the FDA that could be reduced.

The increasing "protection" afforded the American public, however, has come at a price. That price is not just the skyrocketing cost of drug discovery and development, which has reached up to $125 million or more per new drug, but the decreased freedom of practicing physicians to choose the drugs they wish to use to treat their patients. This primarily occurs because numerous drugs available in other countries are unavailable in the United States and physicians are therefore denied use of these drugs.

It is unclear whether patients have fared better because of the FDA's reluctance and slow rate of approving drugs over the last 10 to 20 years. This is an especially important issue because some people believe that individual physicians are in a better position to make medical judgments about their specific patients than is a government regulatory agency, which makes decisions based on usually large groups of patients. The paternalistic perspective within government agencies usually stresses the FDA's role in protecting the American public.

Reactions and Responses of Drug Companies to Consumer Groups

The most important principle for companies to adhere to in relations with consumer groups is to follow high ethical and scientific standards in all aspects of research, drug development, production, and marketing. Although this might appear to put companies and consumer groups on the same side, that is not always true. First, consumer groups sometimes espouse viewpoints that are not scientifically or medically sound. Second, consumer groups have generally identified drug companies as villains and have positioned themselves as adversaries. Nonetheless, it is often useful for companies or trade associations to initiate and participate in open and honest discussions with consumer groups. Telling consumer groups that drug companies want to cooperate may lead to numerous advantages for the companies. If the consumer group is more interested in a confrontation than in achieving a positive result, this fact will become obvious and may possibly be used by the companies to their advantage.

Consumer groups are often effective lobbyists. In some situations they are on the same side as a particular company, and the consumer group may be directly or indirectly enlisted as a ally. One particular situation when a company may seek out a consumer group is when the company desires assistance with an new drug near approval that is more effective and/or safer than existing therapy. This relationship will be particularly fruitful if the company's drug has advantages over a drug(s) that a consumer group is protesting. The consumer group may create media pressure focused on the FDA and Congress to approve the new drug or to remove the old drug from the market.

THE PUBLIC'S RELATIONSHIP WITH INDUSTRY

The public has a general lack of awareness about the drug industry. People use the products of the industry and many groups receive philanthropic help from the industry, but the processes of drug development and the nature of the regulatory environment in which drugs are developed and marketed are almost totally unknown.

Patient Participation in Medical Treatment

For many years little or no interest was paid to patients' views about the drugs they took. With increasing standards of developing drugs, especially after the 1962 Kefauver-Harris Amendments, patients' views have been solicited to a greater degree. Patients' views were originally assessed through the filter of physicians' opinions, i.e., physicians were asked to interpret how patients felt about the drugs they were taking and to describe the beneficial effects of those drugs. During the last decade there has been a gradual change in approach, and now patients are asked directly how they feel about their treatment and how it has affected their disease. Patients are therefore in a better position to have an influence on the type(s) of medical treatment they receive.

One example of patients affecting medical practice concerns the type of surgery used for breast cancer. The views of female patients about their therapy has had a marked influence on the types of surgery performed. The proportion of women who undergo radical mastectomy has fallen and those undergoing simple mastectomy has increased over the last 15 years. This has not occurred because the simpler operation yields better results. It has occurred because the results are not worse for many types of breast cancer and also because more women are now requesting or insisting on the simple mastectomy.

Groups of Patients Versus Groups of Consumers

There is a clear difference between patient associations and consumer groups. Patient associations are usually oriented around a single disease (e.g., cystic fibrosis, muscular dystrophy) or a single therapeutic area (e.g., cardiovascular disease, pulmonary disease). Membership is often composed of patients, family members, friends, and others who are attempting to raise funds that may be used for research, lobbying efforts, education, and sometimes direct help for patients.

Consumer groups tend to be composed of action-oriented individuals who believe that they should improve what they view as a general medical problem. Examples of problems include (1) adverse drug reactions, (2) drugs that they believe should be removed from the market, or (3) alleged improprieties or ethical misconduct of specific companies. Consumer groups tend to use black-and-white terms in their denunciations of drug companies (or the industry) and in their recommendations for corrective action.

Problems or Issues Created by Patients

Companies are often forced to respond to medical pressures brought about by inappropriate uses of their drugs. When drugs are used inappropriately by patients (or by physicians) major problems may be created for the drug company. New adverse reactions may be elicited that cause the drug to be withdrawn from the market, despite the fact that the drug had been used inappropriately. One classic example of this concerns the use of the analgesic drug phenacetin. Phenacetin was often combined with aspirin and caffeine in a combination tablet called APC (i.e., the initials of the three drugs, aspirin, phenacetin, and caffeine). This drug was used to relieve mild pain and only for relatively short periods. Many patients abused this product and took it in larger quantities than recommended by manufacturers or physicians. The drug was often taken every day, sometimes for many years. This is how the problem of analgesic nephropathy was created. The problem was traced to the presence of phenacetin, often used in combination with aspirin and caffeine. Although cases of analgesic nephropathy were not documented in patients who took the drug as directed, the drug was subsequently withdrawn from the market. This was unfortunate for the many patients who used the drug as directed.

30 / *Interactions and Relationships Between Drug Companies and the Media*

> *The great advantage of a strong and clear signal from the top is that even quiet junior managers, when they are tuned into it, can make good independent decisions without worrying. They can answer telephone queries, even press queries, sensibly and decisively rather than timidly and evasively, because they know what the business is about.* Antony Jay. From *Management and Machiavelli.*

INDUSTRY'S RELATIONSHIPS WITH THE MEDIA

Medical news is one of the fastest growing areas in lay media coverage. The news media are more likely to write about a health or high-tech medical problem than ever before. Reporters often visit government agencies (e.g., Food and Drug Administration (FDA), Public Health Service) and the Congress in search of stories. They also read medical publications, attend medical meetings, monitor activities of local drug and health-care industries, plus monitor hospitals and other medically oriented institutions.

Company Policies

Each company has its own policy for dealing with the media. There are, however, a few basic principles to which many adhere.

1. Provide information that is guided by the product's labeling.
2. Restrict comments on other company's drugs.
3. Encourage employee spokespeople not to talk to reporters "off the record," because nothing is really "off the record."
4. Do not comment on questions that are not proper for a company response.
5. Refer detailed medical or marketing questions to the appropriate people.

Although companies do not like to be on the defensive, that is exactly what happens in many cases. Interestingly, the FDA also often finds itself in the same position (as drug companies) with the media. For example, if a new drug is claimed by academic scientists to be great, the media often criticize the FDA and the drug company by asking why the drug is not already on the market. The FDA is often accused of delays and the company of dragging its feet. When a marketed drug, however, has serious adverse reactions uncovered, the media often asks why the drug was allowed on the market and states that it should be removed. The FDA is often accused of slackness and the company painted in even a more unfavorable way.

Interactions between Drug Companies and the Media

Types of Media

The approach a drug company takes with the media is generally the same for radio, television, and printed forms, although some modifications are usually made for each. Working with television is much more time consuming than working with the other media because of the setup time (in a studio or on-site) and frequent run-throughs that are necessary to get a segment to be correct. Radio interviews can be technically much simpler, especially if they are conducted by telephone. In some situations they are conducted at a studio or at a company. On the other hand, radio tends to be stressful because interviews are often live. In deciding whether or not to accept an invitation to participate on a television or radio interview, a company considers the quality of the show, the likely consequences of participating, and the availability of suitable spokespeople.

Deciding to Interact

A company often asks itself the question—is it worth our time to respond to the media? Who else will be there? How will the company appear if it does or does not participate? The forum must be considered appropriate for the company to be able to present a rational approach and adequate time must be allotted to the company.

When the Media Contacts a Drug Company

When the media calls a company with a reasonable question about one of their drugs, most companies attempt to find and provide an accurate answer that lies within the limits of their proprietary information. Companies may not be willing to talk to the media about issues that lie outside a drug's labeling. Labeling is considered the bible from which companies do not stray. Only when a company discusses information presented at a scientific meeting may they be willing to discuss other-than-labeled indications. This is because company scientists are communicating on a scientific level with other scientists and the medical media. Companies often do not even provide reprints of published articles if they relate to indications that are outside a drug's labeling.

The amount and nature of information presented by company representatives often depends on the question posed by the reporter. If reporters ask "What is your company doing in the field of biotechnology" (or disease X), they will usually get an equally general reply. This type of question usually represents a fishing expedition by a reporter who has not done much homework. A better question is for a reporter to ask "What is the status of your compound number AB3456?" But, even more specific questions are better for reporters to pose, such as "We understand that your compound number AB3456 is causing the following side effect. Can you comment?"

Reasons for Confrontations between Companies and the Media

Many news services, newspapers, and reporters read the medical literature on a continual basis and attend scientific conferences. They are quick to pick up stories that they consider newsworthy. Not only do reporters scan well-known periodicals the moment they are available, but they often proactively seek news stories of potential interest. These activities are neither good nor bad per se for drug companies, because a story may be positive, negative, or neutral. Most stories are rarely neutral, even when they are straight news. Therein lies the issue. Even though the media are charged with the devil's advocate role, many reporters prematurely glorify or condemn a new drug, or an old one. This is often a result of two reasons. First, they are in a rush to print the latest medical news about drugs, and second they do not adequately understand the processes of drug development or drug approval. Companies often respond with a more balanced perspective, but their response is often viewed by the public as a defensive gesture, promulgated solely to protect their product. As a result, many people give the company's side little credibility.

The media often react with skepticism about many verbal reports or press releases from drug companies. Many media people do not call companies, because they do not expect to be told the truth. Judging from newspaper and magazine articles, the industry's credibility is often low. This usually occurs because the company is expected to present only its perspective, which is assumed to be unbalanced. The media's perception is strongly reinforced if different company people tell reporters different stories.

Some stories about drugs seem to acquire a life of their own and no matter how many denials and evidence to the contrary, if the story has public appeal—it lives on and on. One minor example concerns the chemical source of thymidine, which is used to make Retrovir. Herring sperm are a natural source of thymidine, and were originally used for making Retrovir. But, Burroughs Wellcome Co. began using synthetic thymidine almost from the start of the Retrovir project and not thymidine derived from herring sperm. Even after the company informed the media that herring sperm were no longer the source used for thymidine, the number of articles describing herring sperm as the starting material for Retrovir have been numerous.

Comments on the Validity of Sensational News on Drugs and Medicine

It almost always seems that the more sensational a news story, the more likely it is that the story is wrong. Reemtsma and Maloney (1974) developed a theory that "the unreliability of instant medical news is so reliable that large profits may be made by betting against the value of medical breakthroughs reported in the lay press." They applied this principle to short sales on the major stock exchanges, advocating Poor's Law (as in Standard and Poor): "Buy on bad news and sell on good." The reasoning behind this is that the insiders have already bought the stock on the good news and forced the price up. As other investors begin to buy stock it will start to fall because the insiders will be selling their stock. These authors present numerous examples of how their principle has worked, plus one occasion when it did not. To prevent mistakes, they recommend attending the press conferences given in association with major announcements so that the value of the breakthrough may be assessed. Most news stories about drugs, however, do not influence the company's stock prices. Moreover, numerous drug companies are not publicly owned (i.e., do not have publicly owned stock).

PUBLIC RELATIONS FOR DRUGS

Public relations to support the marketing of specific drug products is designed to educate and help the audience think about a product or an issue that may have received little prior thought. Public relations is service oriented, and it is successful because it serves the interests of the listener, reader, or viewer. The information is generally useful because it affects the health of the audience.

Role of Public Relations in a Drug Company

The greatest advantage of public relations is the educational orientation. Drug companies may work entirely through outside public relations agencies and not have anyone in a company doing this type of work. This approach is rapidly disappearing, at least among medium and large companies, although each company still maintains contacts with some outside firms.

Many companies have their own public relations group or department that works with marketing departments to structure public relations' programs and activities to insure product awareness. Marketing groups are a major customer of public relations groups and usually work closely with them. Public relations provides an important avenue in the marketing communications effort.

When an important new drug undergoing investigation is of interest to the public and the media, public relations may work closely with medical and research departments to help manage the flow of information reaching the press.

Public Relations of Drug Products

This relatively new field has grown rapidly in recent years and has become widely used in the drug industry. Public relations techniques are communication tools that complement or supplement traditional methods of marketing communications to physicians for educating an audience about prescription drugs.

Public relations is not advertising per se. It involves providing information to reporters and others in the hope and expectation that it will help shape media coverage. A company decides on the advertisements, detailing plan, and educational tools that make up their marketing plan. Marketing managers must then determine what role public relations can play to better reach the public, physicians, nurses, and other health professionals.

Traditional methods of marketing communications to physicians are primarily (1) detailing to physicians by sales representatives, (2) placing advertisements in medical journals, and (3) developing educational tools through meetings, lectures, and exhibits.

The marketing group in a drug company must identify (1) the audience targeted for public relations, (2) the message that they wish to deliver to this audience, (3) alternative means of delivering the message, and (4) what the problems are with currently used methods. Techniques used in a drug's public relation effort might include:

1. Press releases and press conferences.
2. Media events targeted to the public.
3. Special events and public service or education programs.
4. Media tours.
5. Media events targeted to health professionals.

Each of these topics is discussed below.

Press Releases and Conferences

Companies often elect to hold press conferences at the time of a drug's launch, particularly when the drug represents a major medical advance. The press conference helps simplify the information and enables the news to be efficiently disseminated. Some companies also react to important news stories about their drugs with a press release. Press releases are also used on a routine basis to provide news angles for ongoing coverage of a company's products.

Press Conferences

A press conference is in essence a mechanism that permits the company to hold many interviews simultaneously. Most press conferences held by the drug companies in the United States are held either in New York or Washington, DC because the major networks and media are based there. A smaller number are held in Washington. These cities are chosen because smaller media sources are not always able to attend a press conference held in other cities or a relatively out-of-the-way place. Drug companies not located near New York or Washington often send their representatives there for the conference. Press conferences must have effective speakers who are able to communicate technical information clearly and in language that is understandable. They must also be able to field questions effectively.

Press Materials

In preparing for a press conference a company prepares press materials. These materials usually include some or all of the following types of information in a packet that is handed out to reporters. The objective of the packet of information is to provide complete and balanced information on a given topic to assist reporters in preparing their articles or reports. This material is not intended to be promotional. In addition, advertisements are not usually included.

1. *Basic news release* This may contain (1) the name of the drug, (2) how it is to be taken, (3) when it is to be marketed, (4) what the common side effects are, and (5) a summary of the clinical data.
2. *Background on the disease that the drug treats* This material may be prepared by a company, government, academic, or other group.
3. *Fact sheet* This is a list of questions and answers that relate to the major items in the news release and about the drug.
4. *Glossary* Key terms, phrases, and words are defined simply.
5. *Product photograph* A black-and-white glossy photograph of the drug or bottle and other photographs of interest are provided.
6. *Chemical structure* A diagram of the drug's chemical structure may be enclosed.
7. *Package insert* This is usually enclosed.
8. *Important reprints* Published information about the drug that is covered by the approved labeling is usually included.
9. *Synopsis of the reprints* This might be helpful, especially if the reprints are difficult for the lay reader to understand.
10. *Information about the company* This would provide an appropriate means to identify the company's approach, mission, tradition, values, or other factors.
11. *Unique aspects about the product* Many new drugs have unique characteristics that could be featured. Examples would include a large postmarketing surveillance program or an elaborate drug distribution system.
12. *Information about experts* Noncompany speakers at a press conference are identified as to their name, affiliation, training, field of specialty, and any other useful information.

Other Uses of Press Kits and Its Materials

Sometimes one or more pieces of this packet are used for other purposes. For example, the fact sheet may be adapted for use with various groups or individuals. Also, the company may hand out some of the same materials at major scientific meetings. Consumers who contact a company may request disease education booklets or corporate background information. Direct-to-consumer provision of information on specific prescription drugs is of course usually inappropriate for a company to provide. Patient education materials of this nature are usually better directed from manufacturers to physicians.

Media Events

Media events intended to help reporters update the public are of various types, and the following are discussed:

1. Editorial briefings or press conferences.
2. Video news releases.
3. Satellite interviews.
4. Audio conferences.
5. Special events and programs.

Editorial Briefings

These are conducted for magazines and newspapers to provide updates on important topics. The most up-to-date information available is presented by a panel of experts so that an audience of specific reporters can utilize the data. The panel typically consists of both company and independent researchers. Each of the typically three to five panelists speaks from slides for about five to ten minutes each. This is usually followed by questions and answers. The session is often held in association with a medical conference or can stand alone.

Video News Releases

Just as news releases are developed in written form for reporters, a video format can be used to meet the special needs of television. Television stations often accept a video tape from a company, providing it offers solid newsworthy information in an acceptable format and has high production quality. This video is often appreciated by reporters because it provides footage that may otherwise be difficult or costly for a television station to obtain. It can include interviews with prominent national authorities. It may be used at a station's discretion, in part or in its entirety. Stations may choose to insert part of the piece or to hold it for use at a later date.

Satellite Interviews

Satellite interviewing is a relatively new technique that makes nationally known experts available to television news stations around the country to speak on subjects of considerable news value in a cost and time efficient manner. Each station reserves a slot of time on a specified day during which they interview the expert for approximately 10 to 15 minutes on a topic of great interest. In the space of a few hours, successive interviews can be scheduled to several stations who have the requisite technical capabilities. Companies do not charge television stations for this professional service. This method takes significant time to arrange and is usually able to only accomodate a limited number of stations since scheduling more than 10 to 20 stations would make most experts unduly fatigued. One variation of this approach would be for a satellite meeting to be beamed directly into newsrooms around the country and for them to use some of the material presented.

Audio Conferences

Many important newspapers cannot arrange to attend all relevant news conferences held in New York or Washington. The newspaper may be strongly interested, however, in getting its own story. A drug company may provide a panel of experts by telephone conference call. This method can be tied to a video or other type of conference or media event, if it is not tied to a press conference. Or, it can stand alone. Audio conferences, like press conferences, are held because the company has a major story and is trying to manage the information so that everyone who desires access to it can get the news at the same time.

Special Events and Public Service or Education Programs

There is almost no limit to other events or programs that may be produced to provide public service or public education benefits. One example would be a film that could be shown to high schools. Media activity could be built around some of these programs to gain appropriate interest, participation, or visibility. Other events could include health fairs, charity benefits, seminars, symposia, school education programs, and film premiers. Appearances of various experts or celebrities at special events could be arranged to help insure the event's success.

Media Tours

Specific local markets or areas of the country may sometimes be targeted for communications activity because of their risk for a given disease or for other reasons. To provide consumer information, companies may identify a local medical expert or help make a national expert available locally to talk with television, radio, and newspaper reporters in that city. This activity is often called a media tour because more than one interview is conducted.

Media tours are designed to provide consumer education on a health topic. Companies usually build a schedule of interviews with the media around a specific theme or news topic. For example, experts on Acquired Immune Deficiency Syndrome (AIDS) or other sexually transmitted diseases are currently in demand because the topic is in the news. Some topics come up periodically because of the seasonality of the problem (e.g., head lice), and so any promotional efforts of new drugs to treat lice must be tied to the appropriate time of year. The same principle applies to seasonal allergies, colds, and other medical problems that occur periodically with a higher incidence.

Experts who are on a media tour usually want to communicate a specific point to their audience. This educational effort is designed to enlighten the consumer about a health problem or issue. An example could be where the expert discusses a disease and the information that people should understand about it. People are told that if they have the disease, they may wish to visit their physician for a checkup or to discuss whether drug therapy would be appropriate. An address may be given for consumers to write for a free brochure about the disease.

Media Events Targeted to Health Professionals

Media events targeted to health professionals include:

1. Press releases to medical journals and newspapers.
2. Programs targeted via health channels on television or radio stations.
3. Lecture tours of noted national experts.
4. Coverage of important symposia or other meetings.

These events are self-explanatory or they have already been described.

Public Relations for Over-the-Counter and Prescription Drugs

Companies have more flexibility in communicating about over-the-counter (OTC) drugs than they do with prescription drugs. Programs may be sponsored by a consumer product company and the connection of the brand to the program is usually obvious. Sports programs are a good example. A connection of a product to the Olympics or another major sporting event may be desired. This type of advertising and exclusive sponsoring rights may often be purchased. For OTC consumer products such as pain relievers, cold remedies or first-aid treatments, consumer education events and other techniques may also be used to help provide brand-specific information.

For prescription drugs there is educational value associated with public relations' programs. The program may initially discuss the disease and include some discussion of treatment options. But, the company is constrained by the labeling in how much they can say about a drug. In fact, drug names are often not mentioned in a video or other presentation.

PUBLIC RELATIONS FOR THE DRUG INDUSTRY

Improving the Industry's Image with the Public

The media has done an outstanding job of medical reporting in certain areas such as the tampering of Tylenol and other capsules and the ways in which McNeil Pharmaceutical and other drug companies responded. Earlier, the media brought information on hypertension issues of diagnosis and treatment to the public in a responsible manner. One area, however, that usually is poorly presented to the public relates to news stories about new drug development. Drug companies or the FDA are often portrayed as either dragging their feet on an important new drug or of rushing it to the market with disregard for patients' welfare.

The primary reason for this situation appears to be a lack of understanding of how drug discovery, development, and approval actually take place. This may be noted in the superficial approach and distortions present in many news stories. Another reason for the lack of balance and understanding in many news reports relates to the fact that drug companies are restricted in what they can tell the press. This restriction is based on protecting proprietary information, and because certain aspects of a drug's labeling may not yet be approved. As a result, some reporters may feel that the company is suppressing information. When an individual or a group makes charges against a company or the entire drug industry, any response is made from a defensive position. Some people, including reporters, may be unwilling or unable to eliminate their bias against an accused party when judging the company's response.

There is a vitally important need for the story of drug discovery and drug development to be presented to the public. Because drug companies are both too small individually and also have different points they would want to emphasize, it is probably best for companies to work together via a trade association or to cooperate with a government agency to tell their story to the public.

There are many paths that may be followed to achieve this goal. These paths include television, radio, publications, and public speakers. Television programs of a documentary nature could be made on drug development. Wouldn't it be exciting to have a situation drama (comedy?) each week illustrating the trials and tribulations of a research and development director trying to steer a drug through the maze of activities needed to bring it to market? It is easy to imagine many exciting episodes in this type of program.

Publications could be prepared by individual scientists, companies, or by professional associations. These articles might be designed to fit in with each other and with the television and other stories. They could be directed to the public via various magazines as well as through columns inserted in newspapers, newsletters, and other printed matter. Speakers' bureaus could be organized on a state, community, or national level through professional associations as well as individual companies. A trade association or an outside group hired by a trade association could organize these speaking engagements. The speakers could talk about one of a short list of topics of relevance to the public. These talks could be held at professional society meetings, civic group meetings, schools, universities, and at many other locations.

* * * * * * * * * * * * * * * *

The various chapters in this book have attempted to provide an overview of the major issues faced in drug discovery and development. The incredible complexity of this process virtually insures that all investigational drugs will face some or many issues not discussed in this book. It is the uncertainty and primarily the challenge of uncovering these issues and solving them successfully that makes new drug discovery and development such an exciting and rewarding career.

Selected Books about Drug Development or of Particular Interest to the Drug Industry (Many books could fit multiple categories)

See *Principles of Pharmaceutical Marketing* by M. C. Smith (p. 514 and 515) for a list of additional references from the 1960s and 1970s.

General

Decision Making in Drug Research, edited by F. Gross. Raven Press, New York. 1983.

Drug Development, edited by C. E. Hamner. CRC Press Inc., Boca Raton, FL. 1982.

Tragedies from Drug Therapy: For Health Professionals. R. B. Stewart. Charles C Thomas Publisher, Springfield, IL. 1985.

The Pharmaceutical Industry: Economics, Performance, and Government Regulation. E. Caglarcan, et al. John Wiley & Sons Inc., New York. 1978.

The Pharmaceutical Industry. S. N. Wiggins. Center for Education and Research in Free Enterprise, Texas A&M University, College Station, TX. 1985.

Drug Development: From Laboratory to Clinic. W. Sneader. John Wiley & Sons, Chichester, UK. 1986.

The Development of a Medicine. R. B. Smith. Stockton Press, New York. 1985.

Future

Pharmaceuticals in the Year 2000: The Changing Context for Drug R&D, edited by C. Bezold. Institute for Alternative Futures, Alexandria, VA. 1983.

The Future of the Multinational Pharmaceutical Industry to 1990. B. G. James. Associated Business Programmes, London. 1977.

The Second Pharmacological Revolution, edited by N. Wells. Office of Health Economics, London. 1983.

The Bristol-Myers Report: Medicine in the Next Century. H. Taylor and G. Voivodas. Louis Harris and Associates Study 861018, New York. 1987.

The World Health Market: The Future of the Pharmaceutical Industry. D. Tucker. Facts On File Inc., New York. 1984.

Drug Discovery and Innovation

Drug Discovery: The Evolution of Modern Medicines. W. Sneader. John Wiley & Sons Inc., New York. 1985.

Innovation in the Pharmaceutical Industry. D. Schwartzman. Johns Hopkins University Press, Baltimore, MD. 1976.

Retrospectroscope: Insights Into Medical Discovery. J. H. Comroe Jr., Von Gehr Press, Menlo Park, CA. 1977.

Priorities in Research: Proceedings of the Fourth Boehringer Ingelheim Symposium held at Kronberg, Taunus, May 1982, edited by Sir J. Kendrew and J. H. Shelley. Excerpta Medica, Amsterdam. 1983.

Clinical Study Planning, Design, Management, Conduct, Analysis, and Evaluation
(Several books are heavily oriented toward statistics)

Guide to Clinical Studies and Developing Protocols. B. Spilker. Raven Press, New York. 1984.

Guide to Clinical Interpretation of Data. B. Spilker. Raven Press, New York. 1986.

Guide to Planning and Managing Multiple Clinical Studies. B. Spilker. Raven Press, New York. 1987.

The Clinical Research Process in the Pharmaceutical Industry, edited by G. M. Matoren. Marcel Dekker Inc., New York. 1984.

Clinical Trials: A Practical Approach. S. J. Pocock. John Wiley & Sons Inc., New York. 1983.

Methodology of Clinical Drug Trials. A. Spriet and P. Simon. Karger, Basel. 1985.

Issues in Research With Human Subjects: A Symposium, March 20-21, 1978. National Institutes of Health, Bethesda, MD. NIH Pub. No. 80-1858, Bethesda, MD. 1980.

Clinical Trials, edited by F. N. Johnson and S. Johnson. Blackwell Scientific Publishers. Oxford, UK. 1977.

Clinical Trials. D. Schwartz, R. Flamant, and J. Lellouch. Academic Press Inc., New York. 1980.

Concepts and Strategies in New Drug Development, edited by P. U. Nwangwu. Praeger Publishers, New York. 1983.

Fundamentals of Clinical Trials. L. M. Friedman, C. D. Furburg, D. L. De Mets, and J. Wright. PSG Publishing Co., Boston. 1981.

Principles and Practice of Clinical Trials: Based on symposium organized by the Associated Medical Advisers in the Pharmaceutical Industry, edited by E. L. Harris and J. D. Fitzgerald. Livingstone, Edinburgh. 1970.

Clinical Trials: Design, Conduct, and Analysis. C. L. Meinert. Oxford University Press Inc., New York. 1986.

Orphan drugs

Orphan Drugs: Medical Versus Market Value. C. H. Asbury. Lexington Books, Lexington, MA. 1985.

Drug Development, Regulatory Assessment, and Postmarketing Surveillance, edited by W. M. Wardell and G. Velo. Plenum Publishing Corp., New York. 1981.

Orphan Diseases and Orphan Drugs, edited by I. H. Scheinberg and J. M. Walshe. Manchester University Press, Manchester, UK. 1986.

Orphan Drugs, edited by F. E. Karch. Marcel Dekker Inc., New York. 1982.

Regulations

Regulation and Drug Development. W.M. Wardell and L. Lasagna. American Enterprise Institute for Public Policy Research. Washington. 1975.

Drug Development, Regulatory Assessment, and Postmarketing Surveillance, edited by W. M. Wardell and G. Velo. Plenum Publishing Corp., New York. 1981.

Federal Register. Source of specific United States regulations. Supt. of Documents, Washington.

Taking Your Medicine: Drug Regulation in the United States. P. Temin. Harvard University Press, Cambridge, MA. 1980.

New Drug Approval Process: Clinical and Regulatory Management, edited by R. A. Guarino. Marcel Dekker Inc., New York. 1987.

Ethics

Ethics and Regulation of Clinical Research (2nd ed.). R. J. Levine. Urban & Schwarzenberg Inc., Baltimore, MD. 1986.

Case Studies in Medical Ethics. R. M. Veatch. Harvard University Press, Cambridge, MA. 1977.

The Handbook of Medical Ethics. British Medical Association, London. 1984.

Ethical Principles in the Conduct of Research With Human Participants. American Psychological Association, Washington. 1982.

Marketing, Economics, and Politics

Drug Development and Marketing: A Conference, edited by R. B. Helms. American Enterprise Institute for Public Policy Research, Washington. 1975.

Profits, Politics, and Drugs. W. D. Reekie and M. H. Weber. Holmes & Meier Publishers Inc., New York. 1979.

International Pharmaceutical Marketing. S. B. Pradhan. Quorum Books, Westport, CT. 1983.

Principles of Pharmaceutical Marketing. M. C. Smith. Lea & Febiger, Philadelphia. 1983.

A Competitive Assessment of the U.S. Pharmaceutical Industry. Industry Analysis Division, United States Department of Commerce, International Trade Administration, Washington. 1985.

Economics of the Pharmaceutical Industry. P. L. Kahn, E. J. Yang, J. W. Egan, H. N. Higinbotham, and J. F. Weston. Praeger Publishers, New York. 1982.

Drugs and Health: Economic Issues and Policy Objectives, edited by R. B. Helms. American Enterprise Institute for Public Policy Research, Washington. 1981.

Pharmaceuticals Among the Sunrise Industries, edited by N. Wells. St. Martin's Press Inc., New York. 1985.

History

American Self-Dosage Medicines: An Historical Perspective. J. H. Young. Coronado Press Inc., Lawrence, KA. 1974.

Herbs to Hormones: The Evolution of Drugs and Chemicals That Revolutionized Medicine. C. L. Huisking. The Pequot Press, Essex, CT. 1968.

The Medical Messiahs: A Social History of Health Quackery in Twentieth Century America. J.H. Young. Princeton University Press, Princeton, NJ. 1967.

History of Pharmacy and Pharmaceutical Industry. P. Boussel, H. Bonnemain, and F. J. Bové. Asklepios Press, Paris. 1983.

Pharmaceutical Company Histories, vol.I, edited by G. L. Nelson. Woodbine Publishers., Bismark, ND. 1983.

Chronicles of Drug Discovery, vols. 1 and 2, edited by J. S. Bindra and D. Lednicer. John Wiley & Sons Inc., New York. 1981 and 1982.

Business, Competition, and Strategies

(Some references are not specific to the drug industry)

Competition in the Pharmaceutical Industry: The Declining Profitability of Drug Innovation. M. Statman. American Enterprise Institute for Public Policy Research, Washington. 1983.

Competitive Strategy: Techniques for Analyzing Industries and Competitors. M. E. Porter. Free Press, New York. 1980.

Competitive Advantage: Creating and Sustaining Superior Performance. M. E. Porter. Free Press, New York. 1985.

Strategy Traps: And How to Avoid Them. R. A. Stringer, Jr. with J. Uchenick. Lexington Books, Lexington, MA. 1986.

Competition and Marketing Strategies in the Pharmaceutical Industry. Slatter, S. St. P. Croom Helm, London. 1977.

Handbook of Business Strategy, edited by W. D. Guth. Warren, Gorham & Lamont Inc., New York. 1985.

Combination Drugs

Combination Drugs: Their Use and Regulation, edited by L. Lasagna. Stratton International Medical Book Co., New York. 1975.

Fixed Drug Combinations—Rationale and Limitations, edited by K. C. Mezey. Royal Society of Medicine, London, and Grune & Stratton Inc., Orlando, FL. 1980.

Adverse Reactions

The Detection of New Adverse Drug Reactions. M. D. B. Stephens. Stockton Press, New York. 1985.

Monitoring for Drug Safety, 2nd ed., edited by W. H. W. Inman. MTP Press, Lancaster, UK. 1985.

Detection and Prevention of Adverse Drug Reactions: Symposium, Oct. 1983, edited by H. Boström and N. Ljungstedt. Almqvist and Wiksell International, Stockholm. 1984.

Benefits and Risks

The Life/Death Ratio: Benefits and Risks in Modern Medicines. W. S. Ross. Reader's Digest General Books, New York. 1977.

Risk-Benefit Analysis in Drug Research, edited by J. F. Cavalla. MTP Press Ltd, Lancaster, UK. 1981.

Personnel Issues Relating to Scientists

Scientists in Organizations: Productive Climates for Research and Development, revised ed. D. C. Pelz and F. M. Andrews. Institute for Social Research, University of Michigan, Ann Arbor, MI. 1976.

Toxicology

Safety Evaluation of Drugs and Chemicals, edited by W. E. Lloyd. Hemisphere Publishing Corp., New York. 1986.

Long-Term Animal Studies: Their Predictive Value for Man, edited by S. R. Walker and A. D. Dayan. MTP Press, Lancaster, UK. 1986.

The Safety of Medicines: Evaluation and Prediction. P. I. Folb. Springer-Verlag New York Inc., New York. 1980.

Safety Testing of New Drugs: Laboratory Predictions and Clinical Performance, edited by D. R. Laurence, A. E. M. McLean, and M. Weatherall. Academic Press, London. 1984.

Project Management

Project Management Handbook, edited by D. I. Cleland and W. R. King. Van Nostrand Reinhold Co. Inc., New York. 1983.

Project Management: Combining Technical and Behavioral Approaches for Effective Implementation. R. J. Graham. Van Nostrand Reinhold Co. Inc., New York. 1985.

References

Anonymous (1987a): Information for patients about medicines. *Lancet*, II:1077–1078.

Anonymous (1987b): US center for study of drug development 10th anniversary. *Marketletter of IMS International*, 14(11):26–27.

Arkes, H. R., and Blumer, C. (1985): The psychology of sunk cost. *Organ. Behav. Human Decis. Proc.*, 35:124–140.

Atkinson, A. J., Jr., Becker, R. E., Galletti, P. M., Jefferis, J. E., and Wroblewski, R. (1984): University and pharmaceutical industry cooperation: the need to plan for the future. *Clin. Pharmacol. Ther.*, 35:431–437.

Balandrin, M. F., Klocke, J. A., Wurtele, E. S., and Bollinger, W. H. (1985): Natural plant chemicals: sources of industrial and medicinal materials. *Science*, 228:1154–1160.

Balthasar, H. U., Boschi, R. A. A., and Menke, M. M. (1978): Calling the shots in R & D. *Harvard Bus. Rev.*, 56(3):151–160.

Barr, W. H. (1972): The use of physical and animal models to assess bioavailability. *Pharmacology*, 8:55–101.

Bartholini, G. (1983): Organization of industrial drug research. In: *Decision Making in Drug Research.* edited by F. Gross. Raven Press, New York. pp. 123–146.

Bennis, W., and Nanus, B. (1985): *Leaders: The Strategies for Taking Charge.* Harper & Row Publishers Inc., New York.

Berry, C. L. (1986): Unprovable verities. [Editorial] *Hum. Toxicol.*, 5:159–160.

Bezold, C. (editor) (1983): *Pharmaceuticals in the Year 2000: The Changing Context for Drug R & D.* Institute for Alternative Futures, Alexandria, VA.

Blair, D. C. (1984): The management of information: basic distinctions. *Sloan Management Review*, 26(1):13–23.

Bloch, E. (1986): Basic research and economic health: the coming challenge. *Science*, 232:595–599.

Blumenthal, D., Epstein, S., and Maxwell, J. (1986): Commercializing university research: lessons from the experience of the Wisconsin Alumni Research Foundation. *N. Engl. J. Med.*, 314:1621–1626.

Blumenthal, D., Gluck, M., Louis, K. S., Stoto, M. A., and Wise, D. (1986): University-industry research relationships in biotechnology: implications for the university. *Science*, 232:1361–1366.

Bohl, D. L. (editor) (1987): *Close to the Customer: An American Management Association Research Report on Consumer Affairs*. American Management Association, New York.

Bolton, R., and Bolton, D. G. (1984): *Social Style/Management Style: Developing Productive Work Relationships*. American Management Association, New York.

Byrne, J. A. (1987): The miracle company: excellence in the lab and executive suite makes Merck a powerhouse. *Business Week*, October 19:84–90.

Cleland, D. I. (1984): Pyramiding project management productivity. *Proj. Manag. J.*, 15(June):88–95.

Clive, D. (1987): Genetic toxicology: From theory to practice. *J. Clin. Res. Drug Dev.*, 1:11–41.

Cloutier, G., Spilker, B., Lai, A., and Cato, A. (1983): Methods for the assessment of drugs in partial epilepsy. International Epilepsy Meeting, Washington.

Computer Systems Validation Committee of the Pharmaceutical Manufacturers Association (1986): Validation concepts for computer systems used in the manufacture of drug products. *Pharm. Technol.*, 10:24, 26–27 , 30, 32, 34.

Comroe, J. H. Jr., and Dripps, R. D. (1976): Scientific basis for the support of biomedical science. *Science*. 192:105–111.

Cuatrecasas, P. (1984): Contemporary Drug Development—Dilemmas. *Regul. Toxicol. Pharmacol.*, 4:1–12.

de Bono, E. (1967): *The Use of Lateral Thinking*. Pelican Books, Harmondsworth, England.

Deming, W. E. (1982): *Quality, Productivity, and Competitive Position*. Center for Advanced Engineering Study, MIT, Cambridge, MA.

Drews, J. (1985): Judging pharmaceutical research and development from a financial point of view. *Swiss Pharma.*, 7:21–23.

Duncan, W. A., and Parsons, M. E. (1980): Reminiscences of the development of cimetidine. *Gastroenterology*, 78:620–625.

Faust, R. E. (1984a): Envisioning the future of R & D, Part I. *Pharm. Exec.*, 4(9):68–70, 72, 74.

Faust, R. E. (1984b): Envisioning the future of R & D, Part II. *Pharm. Exec.*, 4(10):52–53, 56, 58, 61.

Fisher, R., and Ury, W. (1983): *Getting to Yes: Negotiating Agreement Without Giving In*. Penguin Books, New York.

Futterman, D. H. (1985): What organizational issues determine corporate success? In: *Handbook of Business Strategy. 1985/1986 Yearbook*, edited by W. D. Guth. Warren, Gorham & Lamont Inc., New York. pp. 28-1 to 28-14.

Geneen, H. (1984): Leadership. *Managing*. Doubleday Publishing Co., New York. pp. 125–146.

Goldsmith, J. C. (1986): The U.S. health care system in the year 2000. *JAMA*, 256:3371–3375.

Gottfried, R. S. (1983): *The Black Death: Natural and Human Disaster in Medieval Europe*. Macmillan, London. pp. 158–159.

Grabowski, H., and Vernon, J. (1982): A sensitivity analysis of expected profitability of pharmaceutical research and development. *Managerial and Decision Economics*, 3:36–40.

Grahame-Smith, D. G. (1987): Scores on analog scale for understanding typical new drug at registration (Fig. 1). In: *Innovation and Acceleration in Clinical Drug Development*, edited by L. Lasagna, and A. G. Bearn. Raven Press, New York. p. 152.

Grahame-Smith, D. G., and Aronson, J. K. (1984): *The Oxford Textbook of Clinical Pharmacology and Drug Therapy*. Oxford University Press, Oxford.

Gray, D. H. (1986): Uses and misuses of strategic planning. *Harvard Bus. Rev.*, 64(1):89–97.

Griffin, J. P. (1986): Predictive value of animal toxicity studies. In: *Long-Term Animal Studies: Their Predictive Value for Man*, edited by S. R. Walker and A. D. Dayan. MTP Press, Lancaster, UK. pp. 107–117.

Griggs, W. H, and Manring, S. L. (1986): Increasing the effectiveness of technical professionals. *Management Rev.*, 75(5):62–64.

Guth, W. D. (editor) (1985): *Handbook of Business Strategy. 1985/1986 Yearbook*. Warren, Gorham & Lamont Inc., New York.

Hayes, R. H. (1985): Strategic planning—forward in reverse? *Harvard Bus. Rev.*, 63(6):111–119.

Herzberg, F. (1987): One more time: How do you motivate employees? *Harvard Bus. Rev.*, 65(5):109–120.

Hofer, C. W., and Schendel, D. (1978): *Strategy Formulation: Analytical Concepts.* West Publishing Co., St. Paul, MN.

Humble, J. (1980): Time management: separating the myths and the realities. *Management Rev.*, 69(10):25–28, 49–53.

Hurst, D. K. (1984): Of boxes, bubbles, and effective management. *Harvard Bus. Rev.*, 62(3):78–88.

Inman, W. H. W. (editor) (1986): *Monitoring for Drug Safety.* MTP Press, Lancaster, UK.

Jick, H., Feld, A. D., and Perera, D. R. (1985): Certain nonsteroidal antiinflammatory drugs and hospitalization for upper gastrointestinal bleeding. *Pharmacotherapy* 5:280–284.

Joglekar, P., and Paterson, M. L. (1986): A closer look at the returns and risks of pharmaceutical R & D. *J. Health Econ.*, 5:153–177.

Kahn, P. L., Yang, E. J., Egan, J. W., Higinbotham, H. N., and Weston, J. F. (1982): *Economics of the Pharmaceutical Industry.* Praeger Publishers, New York.

Keidel, R. W., and Umen, M. J. (1984): Winning plays in the R&D game. *Pharm. Exec.*, 4(2):42–44.

Korda, M. (1975): *Power! How to Get It, How to Use It.* Random House Inc., New York.

Lefton, R. E., Buzzotta, V. R., and Sherberg, M. (1980): *Improving Productivity Through People Skills: Dimensional Management Strategies.* Ballinger Publishing Co., Cambridge, MA.

Martin, W. B. (March 4, 1985): Are you a manager or a leader? *Industry Week*, 224(5):93–97.

McMahon, T., Clark, C. M., and Bailie, G. R. (1987): Who provides patients with drug information? *Br. Med. J.*, 294:355–356.

Meyer, N. D., and Boone, M. E. (1987): *The Information Edge.* McGraw-Hill Inc., New York.

Michael, M., III, Boyce, W. T., and Wilcox, A. J. (1984): *Biomedical Bestiary: An Epidemiologic Guide to Flaws and Fallacies in the Medical Literature.* Little, Brown & Co. Inc., Boston.

Millstein, L. G. (1987): Drug product labeling. In: *New Drug Approval Process: Clinical and Regulatory Management*. Edited by R. A. Guarino. Marcel Dekker Inc., New York. pp. 327–361.

Pelz, D. C., and Andrews, F. M. (1976): *Scientists In Organizations: Productive Climates for Research and Development*. Institute for Social Research, University of Michigan, Ann Arbor, MI.

Peters, T. J. (1983a): The mythology of innovation, or a skunkworks tale. Part I. *Stanford Mag.*, Summer:12–21.

Peters, T. J. (1983b): The mythology of innovation, or a skunkworks tale. Part II. *Stanford Mag.*, Fall:10–19.

Pletscher, A. (1983): Drug therapy: Progress and risk. In: *Decision Making in Drug Research*, edited by F. Gross. Raven Press, New York. pp. 25–31.

Porter, M. E. (1980): *Competitive Strategy. Techniques for Analyzing Industries and Competitors*. Free Press, New York.

Porter, M. E. (1985): *Competitive Advantage*: *Creating and Sustaining Superior Performance*. Free Press, New York.

Pradhan, S. B. (1983): *International Pharmaceutical Marketing*. Quorum Books, Westport, CT.

Prentis, R. A., and Walker, S. R. (1985): Pharmaceutical research and development expenditure in the UK. *Pharm. J.*, 235:676–678.

Prentis, R. A., and Walker, S. R. (1986): Trends in the development of new medicines by UK-owned pharmaceutical companies (1964–1980). *Br. J. Clin. Pharmacol.*, 21:437–443.

Price, F. D. (1985): Industry and academia in collaboration: the Pfizer experience. *Circulation*, 72(suppl. 112):I13–I17.

Reemtsma, K., and Maloney, J. V., Jr. (1974): The economics of instant medical news. *N. Engl. J. Med.*, 290:439–442.

Saltzman, E. C. (1985): The no-frills alternative in market research. *Pharm. Exec.*, 5(1):58–61.

Schepartz, S. A. (1985): The national cancer institute's drug development program. In: *Cooperative Approaches to Research and Development of Orphan Drugs*, edited by M. H. van Woert and E. Chung. Alan R. Liss Inc., New York. pp. 73–82.

Scherer, F. M. (1970): *Industrial Market Structure and Economic Performance.* Rand McNally & Co., Chicago.

Schnee, J. E., and Caglarcan, E. (1978): Economic structure and performance of the ethical pharmaceutical industry. In: *The Pharmaceutical Industry: Economics, Performance, and Government Regulation*, edited by E. Caglarcan, W. J. Campbell, G. D. Harrell,, J. E. Schnee, D. A. Siskind, and R. F. Smith. John Wiley & Sons Inc., New York. pp. 23–40.

Schwartzman, D. (1976): *Innovation in the Pharmaceutical Industry.* The Johns Hopkins University Press, Baltimore, MD.

Seidl, G. (1983): Cost of drug research. In: *Decision Making in Drug Research*, edited by F. Gross. Raven Press, New York. pp. 189–194.

Shays, E. M., and de Chambeau, F. (1984): Harnessing entrepreneurial energy within the corporation. *Management Rev.*, 73(9):17–20.

Sheffield, L. J., and Batagol, R. (1985): The creation of therapeutic orphans–or, what have we learnt from the Debendox fiasco? *Med. J. Aust.*, 143:143–147.

Shrivastava, P., and Guth, W. D. (1985): The culture-strategy grid. In: *Handbook of Business Strategy. 1985/1986 Yearbook*, edited by S. D. Guth. Warren, Gorham & Lamont Inc., Boston. pp. 2-1 to 2-19.

Smith, M. C. (1975): *Principles of Pharmaceutical Marketing.* (2nd ed.) Lea & Febiger, Philadelphia.

Spilker, B. (1984): *Guide to Clinical Studies and Developing Protocols.* Raven Press, New York.

Spilker, B. (1985): Development of orphan drugs. *Trends Pharmacol. Sci.*, 6:185–188.

Spilker, B. (1986a): The development of orphan drugs: An industry perspective. In: *Orphan Diseases and Orphan Drugs*, edited by I. H. Scheinberg, and J. M. Walshe. Manchester University Press, Manchester, UK. pp. 119–134.

Spilker, B. (1986b): *Guide to Clinical Interpretation of Data.* Raven Press, New York.

Spilker, B. (1987a): Clinical development of drugs that affect the CNS. In: *Psychopharmacology, The Third Generation of Progress: The Emergence of Molecular Biology and Biological Psychiatry*, edited by H. Y. Meltzer. Raven Press, New York.

Spilker, B. (1987b): Clinical evaluation of topical antipruritics and antihistamines. *Models Dermatol.*, 3:55–61.

Spilker, B. (1987c): *Guide to Planning and Managing Multiple Clinical Studies.* Raven Press, New York.

Spivey, R. N., Lasagna, L., and Trimble, A. G. (1987): New indications for already-approved drugs: time trends for the new drug application review phase. *Clin. Pharmacol. Ther.*, 41:368–370.

Steiner, R. P. (editor) (1986): *Folk Medicine. The Art and the Science.* American Chemical Society, Washington.

Stevenson, H. H., and Gumpert, D. E. (1985): The heart of entrepreneurship. *Harvard Bus. Rev.*, 63(2):85–94.

Stringer, R. A., Jr., and Uchenick, J. (1986): *Strategy Traps And How to Avoid Them.* Lexington Books, Lexington, MA.

Stuyt, L. B. J. (1983): Political and governmental influences on decision making in drug research. In: *Decision Making in Drug Research*, edited by F. Gross. Raven Press, New York. pp. 99–107.

Taylor, H., and Voivodas, G. (1987): *The Bristol-Myers Report: Medicine in the Next Century.* Louis Harris and Associates, Inc. [Study 861018], New York.

Tsurumi, Y. (1982): American management has missed the point: The point is management itself. In: *Quality, Productivity, and Competitive Position.* Deming, W.E. Center for Advanced Engineering Study, MIT, Cambridge, MA. pp. 84–86.

Tucker, D. (1984): *The World Health Market: The Future of the Pharmaceutical Industry.* Facts On File Publications, New York.

Unger, S. H. (1987): Computer-aided drug design in the year 2000. *Drug. Info. J.*, 21:267–275.

Vane, J. R. (1964): A plan for evaluating potential drugs. In: *Evaluation of Drug Activities: Pharmacometrics*, edited by D. R. Laurence and A. L. Bacharach. Academic Press, New York. pp. 23–45.

Varrin, R. D., and Kukich, D. S. (1985): Guidelines for industry- sponsored research at universities. *Science*, 227:385–388.

Vickery, D. M. (1985): A medical perspective. *Drug Info. J.*, 19:155–158.

Virts, J. R., and Weston, J. F. (1980): Returns to research and development in the US pharmaceutical industry. *Managerial and Decision Economics*, 1:103–111.

Waddell, W. C. (1986): *The Outline of Strategy.* The Planning Forum, Oxford, Ohio.

Walker, S. R., and Dayan, A. D. (editors) (1986): *Long-Term Animal Studies: Their Predictive Value for Man*. MTP Press, Lancaster, UK.

Wardell, W. M., and Lasagna, L. (1975): *Regulation and Drug Development*. American Enterprise Institute for Public Policy Research, Washington.

Watson, T. J., Jr. (1987): The greatest capitalist in history. *Fortune*, 116(Aug. 31):24–35.

Weintraub, M., and Northington, F. K. (1986): Drugs that wouldn't die. *JAMA*, 255:2327–2328.

Weisblat, D. I., and Stucki, J. C. (1974): Goal-oriented organization at Upjohn. *Res. Manag.*, January:34–37.

Wells, N. (editor) (1983): *The Second Pharmacological Revolution*. Office of Health Economics, London.

White, B. G. (1985): The antiepileptic drug development program: An example of government–industry collaboration. In: *Cooperative Approaches to Research and Development of Orphan Drugs*, edited by M. H. van Woert and E. Chung. Alan R. Liss Inc., New York. pp. 83–93.

Zinder, N. D., and Winn, J. (1984): A partial summary of university–industry relationships in the United States. *Recomb. DNA Tech. Bull.*, 7:8–19.

Subject Index

N